In the spirit of the Red Banteng

ANTONIE C.A. DAKE

In the spirit of the Red Banteng

Indonesian communists between Moscow and Peking 1959-1965

MOUTON · THE HAGUE · PARIS

Jacket design by H. Salden

D 188
Library of Congress Catalog Card Number: 73-75520

Printed in the Netherlands

to

Vera,
Alexander
and Andrej

for their
patience,
understanding
and love

'As a Party which is constantly surrounded by the non-proletarian classes and which should integrate itself completely with the mass of the people, and especially the farmers, and which now is engaged in a violent struggle against modern revisionism and modern dogmatism on a world scale, our Party should courageously, *in the spirit of the red banteng,* fight all opportunism in ideology, politics and organizations'.

Dipa Nusantara Aidit,
Chairman of the P.K.I.
at the 1st National
Conference of the Party
on July 3, 1964.

Preface

by Richard Lowenthal

For many years, the Communist Party of Indonesia (P.K.I.) was not only known as the largest non-ruling communist party but was widely regarded as that with the best prospects of conquering power. Its art of mobilising and leading the masses by a network of affiliated organisations in town and country was the admiration and envy of communists in all continents. The mixture of militancy and finesse, of firmness of aim and flexibility of tactics shown by D. N. Aidit and the leaders around him was matched only by the leadership of the Italian Communist Party – but while the Italians, for all their skilful manouvering, were still kept outside one governmental coalition after another, their Indonesian comrades had won the confidence of President Sukarno and gradually acquired an influence on government policy that was balanced by that of no other party and held in check only by the countervailing power of the armed forces. In fact, their strategy of cooperating in a 'Nasakom' coalition with nationalist and religious forces but gradually gaining ascendancy over them by pushing a programme of anti-imperialist struggle and radical domestic reform had been the original model for the Soviet concept of the 'National Democratic Front', presented at the communist world conference of November-December 1960 as a directive for communists in all the ex-colonial and semi-colonial countries; and they had continued to follow this 'legal' and 'peaceful' road to power at home even after they had, a few years later, decisively adopted the Chinese view on the need for a more militant offensive against the imperialists abroad than was considered wise by the 'revisionist' Soviet leaders – a view by then shared also by President Sukarno himself. Strong and apparently secure in their influence on the foreign policy of a key nation of a hundred million people, the Indonesian communists could evidently afford to shape their strategy in independence from both Moscow and Peking – and yet be wooed by both.

Then, suddenly, the power of this mighty party was broken almost overnight, and its very organisation destroyed in the frightful massacres of the following months, as a result of the involvement of its leaders in what appeared as a dilettantic military coup attempted by a group of junior officers. So marginal was the actual participation of communist organisations in this coup against the 'anti-communist' army leaders, so totally absent any political and organisational preparation of the party as a whole for a decisive battle, so incredible the approval of this irrational adventure by able and experienced communist leaders close to the seats of power that some of the leading Western students of Indonesian communism concluded at first that those leaders must have been 'entangled' in the coup without advance knowledge and more or less against their will. Yet during the months and years that followed, evidence of their conscious and willing involvement kept accumulating – not only from the trial records of the military regime established by the victorious countercoup, but – more irrefutably – from the conflicting criticism of their policy published by exiled communist survivors under Moscow and Peking auspices respectively: The former blamed communist participation in planning the coup on 'Maoist adventurism', the latter on the 'revisionist' strategy of putting the anti-imperialist alliance with Sukarno ahead of the domestic class struggle, above all of the agrarian revolution - but neither denied that it had taken place.

To the student of communist movements, however, admission of the fact only made the riddle of motivation more mysterious. 'One must not play at insurrection; once one has begun it, one must go through with it to the end.' Thus runs one of the classical maxims of Lenin on which two generations of communist cadres the world over have been brought up. Yet the well-trained and experienced leaders of P.K.I. had done precisely what Lenin had warned against – they had 'played' with armed insurrection without preparing and mobilising their entire party for a life-and-death struggle. As a result, the most powerful non-ruling communist party got involved in an absurd military adventure as if in a dream – and was massacred as if in its sleep.

How could communist leaders of proven ability have chosen a

course at once so unorthodox and so disastrous? It is in the answer to this riddle of motivation that I find the most remarkable contribution of the present book. It presents documentary evidence that President Sukarno himself had encouraged Colonel Untung of his Palace Guard, who later organised the coup, 'to take action against the disloyal generals', and makes it plausible that Aidit and Njoto, the top communist leaders, were informed of this within a few days of the decisive conversation, said to have taken place on August 4, 1965. If that is so, the communist leaders must have felt certain that they were not taking the risk of engaging in a bid for power against Sukarno – which they had no reason to do and no intention of doing – but that they were seizing an opportunity for getting rid, with a minimum of risk, of their main domestic enemies who had at last been recognised by Sukarno as being his enemies as well. Though the enterprise was not legal – least of all the killing of the generals, of which Sukarno had not spoken – it would become legitimate by serving the aims of the leader of the Indonesian national revolution, and nobody would oppose the accomplished fact; but once it was accomplished, Sukarno would no longer have any anti-communist army leaders to balance communist pressure and would become wholly dependent on the P.K.I. By joining in the plot, the communist leaders had thus not turned, in their own view, toward revolutionary insurrection but were merely continuing by different means their strategy of increasing their influence within Sukarno's regime with his own help.

The explanation seems eminently plausible, but it rests in the main on a single document: The record of the interrogation by the military security department of Colonel Widjanarko, personal aide-de-camp to President Sukarno at the time, and of three other witnesses of the crucial conversation between Sukarno and Colonel Untung. The interrogation took place in October-November 1970, four months after the death of Sukarno, and the record came into Mr. Dake's hands in the course of the following year. In his appendix on sources, Mr. Dake discusses in some detail his arguments for believing in the authenticity of this 'Widjanarko report' despite the obvious reasons for doubt, such as the late date of the interrogation (five years after the events in question), the possibility of pressure or direct forgery by the security officials concerned, and the failure of General Suharto's government to publish the document. He points out that the new rulers made no attempt to discredit Sukarno by implicating him in the plot while he was a living rival and could have no interest in doing so after he was dead; and he hints that the record of the interrogation was passed to him by people who, while loyally serving the new regime, may have more lasting and personal motives than its leaders to discover and disclose the full story behind the 'Untung coup' and the murders committed in its course.

Without either knowing these people or indeed claiming for myself any special knowledge of the Indonesian scene, I should like to give here my own analytical reasons for regarding the 'Widjanarko report' as a serious source. The first is, as already stated, that its contents offer, to my mind, the only way to make sense of the otherwise inexplicable behaviour of the communist leaders. This is so true that even the 'Cornell Report', written at a time when the communist leaders' knowledge of the coup plans was not proven, examined at length the hypothesis of Sukarno's having planned the coup, admitted that he might have had serious motives for getting rid of the generals, and rejected his responsibility chiefly on the ground that he would not have planned the coup in this particular way; but the 'Widjanarko report' plausibly states that he did not plan it at all beyond vaguely giving the nod to Untung. The second point I should like to stress is that while General Suharto and his government had a serious interest in whittling down the legendary prestige built up around Sukarno as founder of the state and leader of the Indonesian revolution, they could have no interest in revealing him as having become the deadly enemy of the army leadership – for this would have undermined their own legitimacy as his successors. So they may have suppressed rather than provoked evidence of his complicity in the coup which they must have suspected from the start; and when his closest aide spoke out at last after his chief was dead, they were satisfied to know the truth but on balance saw no reason to publish it.

That leaves the fundamental question of why Sukarno, shrewd politician that he was, should have embarked on a course which was likely to destroy – in case of success no less than in case of failure – the balance of forces on which he had long relied for retaining his leadership. It is here that the coup must be related to the developments of the preceding years, as Mr. Dake has undertaken in the main body of this book – not only with regard to the role of the Indonesian communists 'between Moscow and Peking', as the subtitle claims, but also with regard to the increasingly pro-Chinese turn of the President's foreign policy since about 1963. It was Sukarno's growing reliance on spectacular anti-Western confrontations as an 'alibi' for economic failures at home that made him incline more and more to the Chinese brand of 'anti-imperialism'; and as this policy was opposed for compelling reasons by most of the military leaders but backed to the hilt by the communists, the President, ailing and frequently absent from his country, became steadily more suspicious of the former and more dependent on the latter – until the crushing of the generals' opposition must have appeared more urgent in his eyes than the further preservation of the balance. This general development of the Indonesian crisis has, of course, been described and analysed by other authors before Mr. Dake; his merit, in my view, is to have linked it up in a logical and plausible way with an interpretation of the dramatic climax of coup and countercoup.

Finally, if this interpretation is taken together with the later self-criticism of the surviving pro-Chinese communists quoted in this book, it may also shed new light on the international policy of the Chinese communists between their break with Moscow and the Cultural Revolution. In opposing the application of 'peaceful coexistence' to the conflicts between the underdeveloped countries and the imperialist powers, Peking was then prepared to support any nationalist regime of the former countries that engaged in militant resistance against the latter – regardless of its political and class character: traditional monarchies like Cambodia and military dictatorships like Pakistan were no less welcome allies than national-revolutionary regimes. This policy found its supreme diplomatic expression in the attempt to turn the projected 'second Bandung' – the Algiers conference of Afro-Asian governments – into a demonstration directed against both the United States and Russia. It found its theoretical formula in the transposition of Mao's partisan strategy to the world scale by the slogan of encircling the 'world cities' with the help of the 'world villages' – a slogan originally coined by Aidit in 1964 before being adopted first by Peng Chen during a visit to Indonesia and finally by Lin Pia in his famous speech on 'People's War'. But it amounted in practice to something very different from Mao's own road to power, namely a willingness to subordinate communist party interests to the support of popular, anti-imperialist leaders such as Sukarno – and it was criticised precisely on these grounds by the pro-Chinese group of surviving Indonesian communists after the start of the Cultural Revolution. It appears, in fact, that some of the most active Chinese exponents of this 'classless militancy' in the Third World (such as Peng Chen) belonged to the domestic opponents of Mao, just as did the presumed advocates of more active intervention in Vietnam (such as Lo Jui-ching); and the total failure of this policy, not only in Indonesia but with regard to the Algiers conference and to the attempt to support Pakistan in its 1965 conflict with India (that ended in Tashkent), may well have helped, along with the controversy over Vietnam, to precipitate that decisive phase in the Chinese leadership struggle known as the Cultural Revolution.

When I first met Mr. Dake several years ago, he was an internationally experienced journalist with a keen scholarly interest in the impact of the Sino-Soviet conflict on major non-ruling communist parties. The present study, written as a doctoral dissertation in Political Science for the Free University of Berlin, is based, beyond the published materials available in the West in general and in his Dutch homeland in particular, on the research conducted and the contacts established by him during two visits to Indonesia, in 1968 and 1972. When he embarked on his quest, the 'Widjanarko report' did not exist as yet, and he had no idea of what he would find. I am conscious that the personal history of the author is reflected in the resulting work – in the liveliness of the narrative and the ingenuity shown in unearthing new sources, but also in occasional statements on side-issues which the scholarly caution of a writer trained in a more regular academic career would probably have avoided. If I, as a non-specialist on Indonesia, recommend this book to the readers' attention, I do so in the conviction that it makes a substantial contribution to our understanding of a major problem of contemporary history.

Oxford, Feb. 28, 1973

Acknowledgements

This book was prepared over a number of years following its inception in 1964 as a case history of the impact of the Sino-Soviet quarrel upon a non-ruling communist party.

It has been written on the basis of material which, to the author's dismay, had been gathering dust in his archives. There were times when its completion seemed impossible. That the author finally managed to win through is due to the assistance of people, institutions and circumstances. The favourable factors were chiefly time and luck. Time – the historical process itself – brought to an end the organized existence of the object of the study. It was luck – the discovery of new sources – that brought cohesion and insight where otherwise gaps would have remained.

Of the institutions to which thanks are due, mention must be made first and foremost to the Dutch Organization for Pure Scientific Research (Z.W.O.) in The Hague. Without its aid this book would never have seen the light of day. Mention should also be made of the Free University of West Berlin for its willingness, by way of exception, to allow a manuscript which was not written in the German language to be considered for a doctoral thesis. Then, of course, there are the numerous libraries and research institutions so essential in a field where original sources are like nuggets of gold. The Monitoring service of the B.B.C. deserves special praise in this connection for its valuable Summary of World Broadcasts.

Finally, there are the people who helped. Many of them cannot be mentioned individually because they are too numerous, especially the Indonesians who imparted their knowledge to the author. I would nevertheless like to mention Professor Dr R. Löwenthal of West Berlin, who gave steady support to this venture over the years, although he must have felt at time that his interest was a waste of time. Then, as interpreters – in every sense – guiding the author along the tortuous paths of the relevant Indonesian literature, mention should be made, with grateful thanks, of Mrs. A. Dahar of Utrecht and of Leiden University. Acknowledgements are also due to Dr. Guy Pauker of the Rand Corporation, California, as a scholar and friend, who was most helpful in offering criticism and suggestions for improvement.

This book became available to a larger public than it would otherwise have had owing to that incomparable and vital means of communication: the English language. In this respect my thanks are due to Mr. Humphrey van Loo, Reuters' Correspondent in the Netherlands, for his skillful correction of the text.

Any flaws the book may possess are, of course, entirely the responsibility of the author.

The Hague, March 1973

Contents

CHAPTER 1

Introduction

In the course of October 1, 1965, conflicting reports on some sort of military coup d'état which supposedly had taken place in Djakarta, the capital of Indonesia, reached the outside world. The confusion that took hold of the observers, witnesses and even participants was by no means easy to clear up. But soon the need for some intelligible explanation of the factors that had been at work took the upper hand. Locally, it meant that in the aftermath of what became known as the '30 September movement', the killing of six members of the Army general staff by a mixed group of soldiers and armed youth was defined as a communist plot. Misguided officers of President Sukarno's palace guard had lent their support, but basically the powerful Partai Kommunis Indonesia had been the backbone of the abortive rebellion against the lawful government of Sukarno. Outside opinion was not that easily convinced of the truth of this interpretation, and skeptics from both left and right began to look beyond the simple appeal to the communist bogey. There were tales of anti-Sukarno generals who in their turn had been planning a military putsch; there was the Indonesian President himself who had spent the greater part of the crucial first of October right near the center of the rebellion on the airbase of Halim; there had been evidences of inter-service rivalry and of a 'war of succession' for the throne of Sukarno whose health was said to be fatally impaired. But, above all, there was the incredible sight of a crumbling, weak, and powerless communist party, whose leaders had fled or were groping for salvation and whose cadres were in utter disarray after the Army had turned their wrath and that of the man in the street against them. This was the proud and cocky P.K.I. that could boast of being the strongest communist party outside the communist bloc, with a membership of over three million and affiliated mass organizations of farmers, workers, women, and students that claimed over 20 million followers.

The P.K.I. by many accounts, and also in the eyes of knowledgeable experts in the field, was on a certain road to take over Indonesia in the years to come by the time thc coup of October 1 was mounted, at least as long as Sukarno was not disposed of by the military and barring some other unexpected adverse event. The formal position of the P.K.I. was still that of a vociferous, be it often critical, outside supporter of the President's personal rule, but its factual influence went far beyond the visible aspects of power. The party had come to dominate the Indonesian information media either directly or by way of intimidation. Anti-communist organizations hardly functioned anymore, and the two major political parties left, the muslim Nahdatul Ulama and the nationalist P.N.I., had eliminated themselves as effective opponents because of ineptitude or the subversion of their leaders. The P.K.I., on the other hand, displayed a front of discipline, purpose, and organizational talent that contrasted strongly with the rest of the domestic scene, with the exception of the armed forces. Its leaders, with Dipa Nusantara 'Fortress Indonesia' Aidit the first among his equals, had a reputation for hard work, talent, and incorruptibility. The party formed – with its manifold front organizations and widely ramified grass-roots structure – as it were a state-within-the-state. Its representatives held high administrative posts, especially at a local or provincial level, while at the center of power in Djakarta members of the party's Politburo were wielding considerable influence through both party and state functions. Chairman Aidit was a man normally to be informed or consulted even by foreign diplomats – and not only communist ones – who wanted his opinion more than that of many a cabinet minister. Within the communist world movement the P.K.I. had earned itself a name for independent behaviour, not always shared by the main protagonists of that 'club' – Moscow and Peking – but increasingly taken into account by them. It seemed hardly credible that this party, which had been operating so successfully in Sukarno's Indonesia, had suddenly thrown its chances to the winds; that its leaders – known for their patience and tactical skill – had lost caution and embarked upon what looked like a rather stupid and clumsy adventure. Those with a certain, large or small, dose of sympathy for the P.K.I. began to suspect a 'provocation' whose perpetrators should be looked for in army circles, if not also abroad. But when reasonably trustworthy evidence was put forward that high-ranking P.K.I. leaders, first and foremost Aidit, had been involved one way or another; that armed communist youths had been training surreptitiously for months prior to the 'coup'; that the party paper *Harian Rakjat* had given its blessing in print; that the Chinese comrades also looked compromised, then the problem began to shift. It was no longer of supreme interest *how* things had happened before the avalanche of October 1, 1965, set out to shake the country to its core, but *why*. What made the Indonesian communists do what they did, or leave undone what they were supposed to do? After all, they were trained revolutionaries, possibly tamed somewhat by years of exposure to semi-officialdom, but still – and certainly in the hectic period leading up to the 'coup' – sufficiently conscious of their ultimate calling to bring 'communism' to Indonesia, that is first of all to achieve power to do so, and not to play games. Was Aidit, to take the principal leader, notwithstanding his long and carefully planned way to success, at some stage overtaken by the wrong type of ideas, by the whisperings of extremist opinion on the left, be it Chinese or local? Or were the P.K.I. leaders indeed softened by the opposite fallacy, the thought that numbers and friends in high circles would do the trick?

To try answer these and other related questions is the purpose of the account that follows. However, if this attempt is to make sense, the Partai Kommunis Indonesia should be described and analyzed over a longer period than just the months preceding the climactic denouement at the end of 1965 and the beginning of 1966. At home the P.K.I. was part of the political configuration commonly indicated as the era of Indonesia's 'Guided Democracy', and more commonly described as Sukarno's heyday. This was the period between 1959 when the Indonesian President established his personal rule and rid the country of the last vestiges of western-style parliamentary democracy and 1965 when his decline set in after his authority appeared incurably tainted by his behavior in the aftermath of the '30 September movement'. Within the international context the P.K.I. was in that period operating in a climate not less decisive than the domestic scene. It was in 1959 that the first policy disagreements between Moscow and Peking drew the attention of the outside world, and, while the basic differences that were to come out in due course – colliding national interests – were at first couched mainly in ideological terms, the conflict soon began to dominate state-relations between the two major communist powers. With hindsight we can say that this rift within the world communist movement had to come about sooner or later, that it was given with the first split that broke the seemingly monolithic cohesion of the bloc of communist-rules countries: Tito's break with Stalin in 1948. If a country like Yugoslavia could establish its independence vis-à-vis, and even against, the Moscow-led majority of communist states, China would *a fortiori* be a candidate for this new league of communist 'outsiders', and a much more dangerous and consequential one at that. But when this inevitable development began to take shape, it found both the communist and the non-communist world rather unprepared for its effects. Outside the direct orbit of ruling communist parties, the P.K.I. was one of the most important parties to watch in its evolving posture. It had traits of Chinese origin in having become, with the advent of Aidit in 1951, a mass-based party, while at the same time its domestic orientation turned out to be more Soviet-style in its accomodation with the powers that be.

The issues that sprang up in the Sino-Soviet contest concerned both international affairs and national ones. Was peaceful co-existence feasible, as Moscow under Khrushov maintained, or was it an illusion which for tactical reasons should be kept up, as Peking maintained? What was the character of 'imperialism'; had it changed, was it at least pressured by communist might into reasonable behavior or had the balance of forces in the world not yet shifted in favor of the communist forces? What place should the national liberation movement in colonial and semi-colonial countries be accorded; was it secondary to the major East-West conflict of the two super-powers or should it receive precedence? And from these wider questions the more direct problems sprang up: What road would lead to power; would parliamentary methods suffice or should communist parties outside the bloc prepare more immediately for the day of reckoning, if necessary with arms? Intimately linked to this point was the question of who should lead the national revolution that was going on in many Third-World countries; could one trust to some extent the nationalist forces that by doctrinal definition would always 'waver', or were they beyond redemption? Who were the forces that one should rely on most in the pursuit of power, the proletariat – often virtually absent in developing countries – or the peasants – who were not less often little capitalists? These and related points, expounded more or less esoterically by the scribes of the faith, were of course much more than exercises in being right. They were rationalizations of the past and guidelines for the future. But above all they were the tools of dominant communist minorities where they held power or where they hoped once to possess it. The P.K.I., as one of the most promising of this last category, was a special case, an example it seemed of a new type in the midst of the communist ventures this century had witnessed. With the P.K.I. the nationalist revolution in developing countries seemed almost 'naturally' to change into a communist one without the usual concomitant murderous violence. It appeared to have found a new formula of merited success made up of mixed ingredients, thriving upon the quality of its leaders and the enthusiasm of its followers. So what went wrong, the formula or the facts? To that we shall now turn.

CHAPTER 2

Aidit takes over (1945-1951)

After having been banned for many years, both by the Dutch colonial authorities and by the Japanese occupation forces, the Partai Kommunis Indonesia again emerged officially in October 1945. The party re-established itself under the provisional leadership of Muhammed Yusuf, an Indonesian lawyer by profession and a man with a somewhat mercurial past.[1]

During the war Yusuf had collaborated with the Japanese and he seems to have had ties with a rival of the P.K.I., the national-communist Murba group, led then by a well-known Indonesian revolutionary named Tan Malaka. Yusuf set off to apply a radical 'leftist' strategy that brought him into opposition with the prevailing tendency within the international communist movement which still favored continuation of the wartime policy of cooperation with anti-fascists within a broad political front. It was on these lines that the new P.K.I. leader organized a minor 'putsch' at Cheribon in February 1946, but it failed utterly.

A month later Yusuf was denounced at a Party Congress in the Central Javanese town of Djokjakarta by elements of the P.K.I. who seem to have felt their position strengthened by the arrival of veteran and more moderate communist leaders such as Sardjono.[2] At the end of April Sardjono assumed control of the P.K.I. and established headquarters in Djokjakarta where since the beginning of 1946 the fledgling Republic had its temporary capital.

Another eminent pre-war P.K.I. leader, Alimin Prawirodirdjo, returned to Indonesia in August of that year after a long stay abroad and began to give his support to the more moderate policy adopted by Sardjono.[3]

He formulated what was, in essence, the popular front line that, on the advice of Moscow, had been followed by the international communist movement since the mid-thirties:[4] 'With the dissolution of the Comintern the P.K.I. will pursue an independent course . . . We communists advocate democracy and economic development, with emphasis on the modernization of agriculture.'[5] It also meant that, after the confused leadership of Yusuf, the P.K.I. was willing to cooperate with other parties in the government of the Republic and supported negotiations with the returning colonial power, sanctioning the Lingadjati and Renville agreements with the Dutch. The Renville ceasefire agreement was endorsed on January 17, 1948, by the Indonesian government at a time when it was headed by a left-wing socialist Amir Sjariffudin who was to die that same year before a firing squad as a self-confessed veteran communist.[6]

The fact that Sjariffudin at that time was unknown as a member of the P.K.I. was connected with another prewar tendency, re-established by Sardjono and Alimin, i.e., to conceal the extent of the membership of the P.K.I. and to infiltrate other parties. Many leading communists therefore joined the ranks of the Socialist Party or the Labor Party.[7] Together with the official P.K.I., these two parties formed the so-called Sajap Kiri or Left Wing, one of the main supports of early Indonesian governments.

But a shift towards a less compromising approach was in the offing, and there the Indonesian communists were to follow the lead of Moscow.

It should be recalled that the Soviet Union had begun to advocate a new radical line in international affairs at the founding session of the Cominform in Warsaw in September 1947. According to the Conference Declaration 'during the war two diametrically opposed policies had already began to take shape: on the one hand the policy of the U.S.S.R. and the other democratic countries, aimed at undermining imperialism and at consolidating democracy; and, on the other hand the policy of the United States and Britain, aimed at strengthening imperialism and stifling democracy'.[8] Communist parties all over the world were encouraged at that occasion 'to take up the banner of defence of national independence and the sovereignty of their countries [and] if they are able to head all the forces ready to fight for honour and national independence, no plan for the enslavement of the countries of Europe and Asia can be carried out'.[9] It was important that the communist parties were told to take 'the lead', that is, no longer to put up with a secondary position while working for a national front.[10] At this Cominform conference Zhdanov, the Soviet representative, further outlined what became known as the 'two camp' doctrine, the thesis that had to underpin ideologically Stalin's rejection of the prevailing popular front tactics. No particular attention had then been paid to the problems communists would encounter in colonial and semi-colonial countries, but he made up for that when he addressed himself at the end of 1947 to this issue in the theoretical journal of the C.P.S.U., *Bolshevik*. Here Zhdanov stated that 'in a number of colonial countries a people's anti-imperialist front had been formed, consisting of a coalition of parties having the struggle for liberation as their platform, under the leadership of the communist party'.[11]

With this Zhdanov no doubt had first and foremost in mind Indonesia, a country dubbed in the Soviet press of the time as a 'people's democratic republic', while the P.K.I was described as 'the leader and organizer of the Indonesian revolution'. This exaggerated notion reflected the belief among Soviet leaders that Indonesia could be held up as an example for others of how communists should succeed in taking over the leadership of the national revolution.

However, when Shariffudin was forced to resign as Prime Minister at the end of January 1948, this must have been viewed in Moscow as a serious setback, the more so as a new government – a center coalition of the nationalist P.N.I. and the mohammedan Masjumi Party with Mohammed Hatta as premier – came about in due parliamentary fashion.[12] It is quite likely that, after this, the Soviet Union began to realize that Indonesia was after all not such an ideal textbook case. At any rate, within a few weeks the Soviet representative at the United Nations began to attack the Renville ceasefire as a betrayal of the Indonesian people, disregarding the fact that it had been concluded by a government that was dominated by open or secret P.K.I. ministers.[13]

The sudden opposition of the Soviet Union to the Renviile ceasefire agreement came at a time when the 'Conference of Youth and Students of South East Asia Fighting for Freedom and Independence' was meeting. This convention of young agitators that took place at the second half of February was sponsored by two communist front organizations, the World Federation of Democratic Youth and the International Union of Students.

It has been said that this conference was at the root of the armed uprisings and revolts that broke out in Asia that year. The idea that Moscow, through the Calcutta meeting, 'ordered' the Asian communist parties to resort to violence is probably too simplistic. However, it may have set the scene for future events.[14] As to Indonesia, the Calcutta conference reflected the new Soviet point of view on the question of negotiations with the Dutch: A conference resolution spoke of the Renville ceasefire as 'imposed' on Indonesia, and the Indonesian youth delegates announced their opposition to that agreement. At the same time the country was not yet considered beyond redemption; it was singled out for praise at the conference for having attained 'the highest form of armed struggle'.[15]

Very soon after Calcutta this new-found aversion to dealings with the Dutch penetrated more generally amongst communists in Indonesia. The Front Demokrasi Rakjat, the People's Democratic Front that had taken the place of the Sajap Kiri, also came out against the Renville and Linggadjati agreements. It may therefore be assumed that the signals passed on at the meeting of Asian communist youth leaders were correctly understood by the P.K.I..[16] Rejecting talks with the Dutch brought the Indonesian communists and their various parties into open conflict with the Hatta government, so that 'the pro-communist left found itself forced by the "two-camp" doctrine and the intensification of the cold war to insist with increasing emphasis on the necessity for the Republic's alignment with the Soviet bloc and on the government's firm resistance to the Western imperialists' as one observer has concluded.[17]

But acceptance of the new line of confrontation and opposition must have been less than universal in the P.K.I. So it came to pass that the veteran communist leader, Alimin, announced in May that the P.K.I. was again willing to participate in a national coalition cabinet that had been in the making in order to confront the Dutch with greater unity. Taking its cue Moscow announced it had ratified a consular agreement concluded earlier in Prague between the Soviet Union and a representative of the Indonesian Republic, the communist Suripno.[18] With this disclosure Moscow greatly embarrassed the Hatta government, since it gave the Dutch an excuse to claim that the Indonesian Republic had violated the status quo as agreed upon in the Renville agreement. More important, this 'Suripno-affair' fundamentally disturbed relations between the F.D.R and the other parties, and, consequently, the intended national coalition government came to naught. If that had been the purpose of the Soviets, their operation could be called a success.

This episode is worth recalling in another respect. In order to defuse the issue Hatta told Suripno, who at that time was still in Europe, to return to Indonesia for 'clarifications'. When he finally arrived, early in August 1948, he was accompanied by a 'secretary', who turned out in reality to be Muso, another Indonesian communist leader who had spent many years in the Soviet Union.[19] Immediately upon arrival Muso called for a plenary meeting of the party's Central Committee and there secured approval for a resolution entitled 'the New Road for the Indonesian Revolution'. It was the latest word from Moscow's fountain of wisdom and laid down the line to be followed.[20]

The role of Sardjono and Alimin was attacked and their policy of concealment and infiltration condemned. The three parties of the Front Demokrasi Rakjat were told to merge into one strong 'new' P.K.I. But Muso at the same time made allowance for the fact that even this new revamped party organization would not do the trick and that 'the party of the working class cannot possibly complete the bourgeois democratic revolution on its own'.[21] A national front, including the urban proletariat, the peasantry, and the middle class was therefore considered by Muso as necessary as before, however with the difference that the party should not only participate in such a front but dominate it right from the start.[22] In this respect Muso's strategy was more consistently leftist than the classical version of the 'united-front-from-below', according to which it could be left to the bourgoisie to lead the initial, nationalist phase of the revolution. The Indonesian revolution, therefore, was termed by Muso 'a bourgois democratic revolution of a new type', an expression that could be traced back to Maoist thinking but should be seen against the background of that period when the Chinese communists were considered (by Moscow, too) legitimate experts in communist strategy in colonial and semi-colonial countries.[23]

In the field of foreign policy Muso's 'New Road' resolution rejected neutralism for Indonesia, and it was urged that the country align itself with the Soviet bloc: 'For the Indonesian revolution there is no other place than in the anti-imperialist camp'.[24] Direct diplomatic relations should therefore be established with the Soviet Union, the 'vanguard of the struggle against the imperialist bloc', while recognition of the Republic by the Soviet Union would be 'an unmixed blessing', because this country, 'as a workers' state can only adopt an anti-imperialist position'. Opposition to negotiations with the Dutch was now given an official and clearcut sanction: It was henceforth to be based not on opportunistic reasoning but on principle, because 'these agreements, if put into practice would create a state which in reality would be under foreign domination'.[25]

A major theoretical treatise on the struggle for Indonesian independence published in that period by a Soviet scholar showed great similarity with the points made in the 'New Road' resolution.[26] In it the 'previous mistakes' of the P.K.I. were said to have begun to be repaired 'not until the late summer of 1948', clearly meaning the moment Muso arrived on the Indonesian scene.

While Muso and Sjariffudin toured the country explaining the new policy of the P.K.I., other communist leaders back in Djokjakarta, like Alimin, Sakirman, and Tan Ling-Djie attempted to get the two major bourgeois parties, the mohammedan Masjumi and the nationalist P.N.I., to join in a national front. By mid-September 1948 it was, however, clear that this had come to nothing since both parties remained loyal to the Hatta government of the day. Whatever hopes the P.K.I. may have had of enlisting the 'national bourgeoisie' in the cause of the New Road resolution, at this juncture its prospects hardly looked promising. It was then that fighting broke out between pro-communist troops and government forces in Java's second largest city of Surakarta. On September 17 the fighting came to a halt. But the next day violence flared up again in nearby Madiun. Army commanders with communist leanings decided to act and proclaimed over the local radio station: 'Madiun has risen, the revolution has begun. Workers and peasants have formed a new government'.[27] Muso, Sjariffudin, and others hurried to Madiun to master the situation. Muso proclaimed himself head of a 'National Front Government' but by all accounts did not give the impression that he had been prepared for it. According to information available to Prime Minister Hatta, Muso and the P.K.I. leadership had been engaged in organizing an armed revolt against the republican government, but for a later date somewhere in November-December of 1948.[28] The communist leader apparently had his hand forced by overzealous P.K.I. cadres and radical officers, and once the premature uprising was on its way there was nothing else for him to do but take command, to try to avoid the worst extremity such as wholesale or piecemeal reduction of the armed forces then loyal to the P.K.I.

The rebellion met a dismal end and brought temporary doom to the P.K.I. The Hatta government, taking stern measures, ordered immediate action and, within ten days, resistance in the Madiun area collapsed. At the end of October, Muso was killed in a skirmish near Sumandang, south of Madiun, and one month later Sjariffudin, the communist military commander Colonel Djokosujono, and a score of other P.K.I. leaders were seized. The regular Indonesian army command had all 52 of them executed rather than set them free or let them fall into the hands of the Dutch who, by that time, had launched their second so-called 'police action' against the heart of Republican territory. More than 35,000 P.K.I. members and other 'suspects' were subsequently arrested, and only a few of the leaders escaped: Alimin, Tan Ling-Djie, Setjiadit, and the youth leader Sumarsono. Of the lesser officials Aidit and Lukman disappeared, leaving the country to turn up later in China where they waited for better times.

In the Soviet press the Madiun rebellion was reported with great caution and mainly through citations of non-Soviet news sources. Editorially it was seen as a 'provocation', incited by the increasingly reactionary circles of the Hatta-Sukarno 'clique'. But this did not prevent the Soviet Union from posing as an active champion of the Indonesian cause when the issue came up at the end of 1948 in the United Nations following the second Dutch 'police action'. However, Moscow remained hostile to negotiations with the Dutch that were to lead, at the end of 1949, to transfer of sovereignty over the Dutch colony to the Indonesian Republic. On the eve of the successful conclusion of the Round Table Conference in The Hague, Prime Minister Hatta was assailed in the Soviet press as a 'Quisling'. It was suggested in all manner of ways that, whatever happened at the conference table, the struggle for independence should go forward with unimpaired vigor.

Aidit and Lukman returned from China and Vietnam half a year after Indonesia had become independent. According to their own account they did not learn much during their self-imposed exile, being considered by the Chinese and Vietnamese comrades 'too young and insignificant' to be of interest.[29] It was in that period that the Chinese communist victory was proclaimed by Liu Shao-chi as the relevant example for other colonial and semi-colonial countries on their way towards national independence.[30] This was not disputed at the time by Stalin, who may have thought it still an acceptable variation on a well-known theme and not a challenge to his authority. If Aidit and Lukman took note of this event at all, they certainly did not see any imminent conflict of loyalty in it. Some suggestions are to be found that Aidit's return to Indonesia could be seen in the light of his relations with Moscow and Peking. Thus Hindley writes that upon his return, Aidit 'may have claimed to have the approval of the Chinese communists'.[31] Brackman on the other hand sees in Aidit 'a youthful, dedicated Stalinist' who would ensure that the P.K.I. keep in step with Moscow and who during a visit to the Soviet capital received his orders directly from Stalin to take over the P.K.I. from Alimin.[32] But it seems hard to locate Aidit at that time either on the one side or on the other, the more so as a basic overall identity of views as to the future course of world communism still prevailed in the two main centers of communist power, the Soviet Union and the People's Republic of China.

As to the Indonesian government that assumed responsibility after independence, both communist countries fulminated on occasion with equal vehemence against what they termed the 'Hatta-Sukarno clique'. But in fact the Chinese government was more forthcoming than the Soviet, no doubt because China had more at stake in Indonesia where, for many years, millions of Chinese had been living.

Communist China recognized Indonesia at the end of February 1950, and its first ambassador Wang Yen-shu, a former teacher and member of the P.K.I. from Medan on Sumatra, presented his credentials to President Sukarno in August of that year.[33] The relations between Djakarta and Peking became somewhat strained, as the Indonesian government in August 1951 refused entrance into the country of an additional 50 Chinese diplomats. But for the rest these early years were unmarred by friction. With the Soviet Union the situation was different; although Moscow had extended recognition to Indonesia as early as January 1950, it was not before 1954 that a Soviet embassy was established in Djakarta. A diplomatic mission headed by the Indonesian delegate to the United Nations, Palar, was hardly received when it visited Moscow in May 1950. It came home empty-handed, and only after Stalin had died and a certain 'thaw' had set in were full diplomatic relations established.

By January 1951 Aidit and Lukman had had themselves elected to the new five-member Politburo of the P.K.I., while Aidit became the First Secretary of the party. Other members of the highest policy-making body of the party were Njoto, Sudisman, and Alimin, making for a rather youthful leadership since all except Alimin were in their early thirties. These 'young Turks' had already made their presence felt in the second half of 1950 by reintroducing the line Muso had outlined in his New Road resolution, but which had been left in abeyance on various points. So under Alimin and Tan Ling-Djie the Socialist Party and the Labor Party had been reconstituted as fronts for the P.K.I. The 'Leninist wing', as the Aidit-group came to call themselves, dissolved these two parties again and dropped what they considered to be undue emphasis on political gains through parliamentary action, of which Tan Ling-Djie especially was supposed to have been the sponsor.

In the radical mood to which the new Aidit leadership had brought the party, more than half a million Sobsi-affiliated workers went on strike in February 1951.[34] The Indonesian government under Masjumi-leader Natsir, after initial hesitation, finally got around to taking counter-measures and proclaimed a ban on strikes in 'vital' enterprises, a clause that in fact included almost all economic activity. But the chaos persisted, and in August Sukiman, the successor to Natsir, fearing another 'Madiun', began to round up many P.K.I. members and sympathisers, so that at the end of that month there were more than 2,000 in jail including (by mistake) supporters of the Sukiman government. A number of P.K.I. leaders, including Aidit, went into hiding as a result of these 'Sukiman-razzia's' as the mass arrests came to be called. This gave them an opportunity to rethink their strategy.[35]

NOTES

1. Donald Hindley, 1964, *The Communist Party of Indonesia 1951-1963*, University of California Press, Berkeley, p. 19; Justus M. van der Kroef, 1965, *The Communist Party of Indonesia, Its History, Programme and Tactics*, University of British Columbia, Vancouver, p. 29.

2. Sardjono, a former P.K.I. leader of the 1926 uprising, had been incarcerated in the Dutch concentration camp of Upper Digul in New Guinea until 1942. At the time he and 600 others were evacuated to Australia and invited to join the fight against the Javanese. Sardjono joined the allied propaganda organization, first working in Brisbane and later in Morotai after New Guinea was recaptured. See Arnold C. Brackman, 1963, *Indonesian Communism*, Frederick A. Praeger, New York, p. 34.
3. Alimin escaped Indonesia in 1926 and reached Moscow by way of China. He left the Soviet capital according to his own account in 1943 and joined the Chinese communist in their base area of Yenan where he remained until 1946. Brackman, 1963, p. 56.
4. Only the Ribbentrop-Molotov interlude interrupted this line between 1939-1941.
5. See Brackman, 1963, p. 56.
6. It has been widely doubted whether Amir Sjariffudin had in fact been a member of the Indonesian Communist Party for years. The last Dutch Lieut. Governor-General Dr. H. J. van Mook wrote that Amir was 'unbalanced and insanely ambitious . . . (and) declared himself to be a communist, which he was not'; Brackman, 1963, p. 307.
7. Tan Ling-Djie, who later was purged by Aidit, became a member of the Socialist Party, and Setiadjit joined the Labor Party. The leadership of the central labor organization Sobsi was taken over by a communist, Njono, and the B.T.I., the Indonesian Peasant Front, soon also succumbed to this practice.
8. As quoted by Ruth T. McVey, 1957, *The Soviet View of the Indonesian Revolution*, Cornell University, Ithaca, N.Y., p. 30.
9. McVey, 1957, p. 31.
10. For the application of this new line in Indonesia see p. 9.
11. *Bolshevik*, organ of the Communist Party of the Soviet Union, December 15, 1947, as quoted by Brackman, 1963, p. 66.
12. In retrospect Party historians recognized Sjariffudin's resignation as the ultimate in weakness because he had 'voluntarily handed over power by dissolving the Cabinet of which he was head. Consideration of the question of this power according to Leninist teaching was neglected by the Indonesian communists at that time'. See: D. N. Aidit, 1960, *Complete Works*, Vol. II, as translated by the Joint Publications Research Service, Washington D.C., p. 28. The important 'New Road' resolution that was adopted later in 1948 by the P.K.I. gave this opinion: 'With the fall of the Amir Sjariffudin cabinet the way was opened for elements of the compradore bourgeoisie to seize control of governmental leadership and thus the leadership of our National Revolution, while the Communists isolated themselves in the opposition. It may be said that from then on our National Revolution has been in great danger'; as quoted by McVey, 1957, p. 62.
13. Brackman, 1963, p. 60. Also Aidit, 1960, p. 28.
14. 'It is claimed that orders from Moscow were passed to the South-East Asian

Communists dictating the rebellions in Indonesia, Malaya and Burma and the increased unrest in the Philippines and Vietnam which occurred later in 1948. The writer is not adept enough at distinguishing fact from fancy to attempt a discussion of the secret liaisons of international Communism in this paper'. McVey, 1957, p. 39.

'At issue is whether it was there [in Calcutta] that the Communists received their orders from Moscow for unleashing the subsequent agitation and insurrections . . . it served as a transmission belt for the aggressive belligerent new line'; Brackman, 1963, p. 67.

15. From the main report at the conference as quoted in McVey, 1957, p. 43.
16. McVey, 1957, p. 45, note 91, says this opinion should be accepted with certain reservations, as the Front Demokrasi Rakjat now being in the opposition could also easily have switched roles and have decided to take an 'irresponsible' stance against negotiations, as the mohamedan Masjumi had previously done when they were in opposition against the Sjariffudin government.
17. McVey, 1957, p. 46.
18. Suripno who had been the Indonesian Republic's official representative in Eastern Europe had been authorized by Sukarno to come to an agreement with the Soviet government for the establishment of consular relations. Pending the Renville discussions in January 1948, Sjariffudin had however decided to shelve the preliminary results of Suripno's talks with the Soviet ambassador in Prague, and subsequently Hatta also refused to bring it back to life again.
19. Suripno came to Djokjakarta on August 10 together with a secretary under the name of Suparto, but it soon transpired that this Suparto was none other than Muso, the leader of the abortive 1926 revolt and, ever since his escape from Indonesia, a Moscow resident.
20. That Muso was the link between the Kremlin and the 'New Road' resolution was later implicitly acknowledged by Aidit in his statement 'Menggugat Peristwa Madiun', made on February 24, 1955. Explaining in brief that the P.K.I. could not have carried out a coup in Madiun in September 1948 because it would be 'contrary to Communist theory', Aidit added another reason, namely that a putsch would also have been 'contrary to the proposal made by comrade Muso after he returned home from abroad'. In an attempt to deny Soviet prodding in the Madiun rebellion Aidit did in fact link Muso's New Road message with his 'returning from abroad'. See Aidit, 1959, p. 266.
21. Brackman, 1963, p. 83.
22. A leading role for the national bourgeoisie in this early, first phase of the revolution was countered by the well-known argument in the resolution that with the bourgeoisie there was always the risk that they would go over to the 'imperialist camp'. They were however welcome as 'junior partner' in the proposed front, just as were the rich peasants, who also 'at the beginning could hold anti-imperialistic sentiments'. See McVey, 1957, p. 66, quoting the

New Road resolution.

23. Mao Tse-Tung, 1954, *On New Democracy*, Foreign Languages Press, Peking, pp. 10-12, 18.
24. Mao Tse-Tung, 1954, p. 69, quoting the New Road resolution.
25. Mao Tse-Tung, 1954, p. 66, quoting the New Road resolution. Aidit was to call this part of the New Road resolution particularly 'a sharp self-criticism in the ranks of the P.K.I.'. See Aidit, 1959, p. 294.
26. Aidit, 1959, p. 81.
27. Brackman, 1963, p. 93.
28. Interview with Dr. Mohammed Hatta, March 1972. One of the main criticisms that Muso had levelled at the P.K.I. on arrival from Moscow had been the failure of the Party 'to grasp the meaning of the balance of strength between the Soviet Union and British-American imperialism, after the Soviet Union speedily occupied Manchuria. At that time [August 1945] it had already become clear that the position of the Soviet Union on the continent of Asia was extremely strong and that it pinned down much of the military strength of American, British and Australian imperialism and thus provided a favourable opportunity for the Indonesian people to commence their revolution', as quoted from Aidit, 1959, p. 293, 294. In other words, the P.K.I. had made a wrong assessment of the balance of forces in the area and could easily have followed a more radical line right from the time that Indonesia's independence was proclaimed on August 17, 1945. This was of course an ex-post-facto conclusion, merely designed to serve the purpose envisaged by the New Road resolution. But it must have at that time conveyed to the Indonesian communists an exaggerated sense of strength and collective power that would justify the planning of an armed rebellion.
29. See Ruth T. McVey, Indonesian Communism and China. In: Tang Tsou, Ed., 1968, *China in Crisis*, vol. 2, University of Chicago Press, Chicago, p. 367.
30. *New China News Agency*, November 23, 1949.
31. Hindley, 1964, p. 26.
32. Brackman, 1963, p. 150.
33. Brackman, 1963, p. 141, and Van der Kroef, 1965, p. 46. Propaganda material and financial aid to the P.K.I. started to flow soon after August 1950. Moreover, through left-wing Chinese members of the Indonesian parliament like Siauw Giok Tian, the overseas Chinese began to contribute to the cause of the P.K.I. It was thus that in July 1951 the publication of the P.K.I. daily newspaper *Harian Rakjat* became possible; Van der Kroef, 1965, p. 46 and p. 311, note 4, and Hindley, 1964, p. 67. Siauw became its editor and remained so until 1954 when he resigned to found the Baperki, an organization of urban Indonesian Chinese. Also, Brackman, 1963, p. 202.
34. In January 1950 the Sobsi under Njono had already organized many strikes which all but paralyzed production on the big estates and work in the harbors. These actions gathered strength after January 1951 when Aidit and his followers had begun to take over the P.K.I. from Alimin and Tan Ling Djie.

It is not improbable that Aidit, not yet sure of his grip on the Party and its affiliated mass organizations, may have entertained some doubts as to the wisdom of these radical actions.

35. Hindley, 1964, pp. 54, 55.

CHAPTER 3

Indonesia moves towards 'Guided Democracy' (1952-1959)

In the first months of Aidit's ascent the New Road concept of a national front, dominated by one, consolidated and overtly communist party, had shown itself to be not very practicable given the existing suspicion of the Madiun-tainted P.K.I. Besides, resumption of hard action by the P.K.I.'s trade-union, Sobsi, had imposed new hardship on party members and had all but halted the party's activities. It was thus not surprising that a shift towards a more promising party line was considered, and it was at the Party's National Conference in January 1952 that a first indication was given of its shape. Short-term, rather make-shift policy was going to be replaced by long-term planning, in which the central theme was to be the organization of the masses to give the party a large, independent grass-root movement. During the rest of the decade the P.K.I., under Aidit, was to pursue a policy first outlined at that National Conference.

First of all, the party was to increase its membership in six months from around 7,000 to 100,000. At the same time, a multitude of mass organizations were to be created or revamped, encompassing not only workers and peasants but also youth, women, poor people, ex-servicemen, and others. Secondly, the attitude towards other parties had to change, and Aidit and his close associates embarked on a program to take the P.K.I. out of its isolation. They were willing to regard large sections of the national bourgeoisie as potential allies, having in mind particularly the nationalist P.N.I., whereas the Masjumi and the social-democratic P.S.I. basically remained the 'enemy'.

In 'theoretical' terms Aidit began to divide the political forces into three groups: The diehard force of 'feudalists and compradores' who 'plot with foreign imperialism', the progressive forces consisting of workers, peasants, urban petty bourgeoisie, and revolutionary intellectuals, and in between the two the middle forces or 'national bourgeoisie and all other patriotic and anti-colonial forces including left – rather progressive – landlords'.[1]

By diehards Aidit meant most, but not all, leaders of the Masjumi and P.S.I., while as progressive forces of course qualified whoever was willing to align himself with the P.K.I. The center forces were of particular interest and had to be won over or at least neutralised as anti-communist elements, and cooperation with them was regarded as desirable and to be pursued.

Initially, it seems, there was opposition among the party cadres to this basically 'rightist' strategy, but Aidit succeeded in carrying the party, and consequently this new readiness to cooperate with as many of the political forces as possible – even some which were rather 'reactionary' – became, as Hindley puts it, 'a major characteristic of the Aidit leadership's concept of the national united front as applied to the non-communist political forces'.[2] The new swerve to the right was completed strikingly a few months later when Alimin, at the 32nd anniversary of the P.K.I. in May 1952 stunned his audience with the slogan 'long live the P.K.I., long live Sukarno'.

Meanwhile, the party had already offered its support, albeit reluctantly, to Wilopo, a Masjumi politican who had succeeded Sukiman in April to head a P.N.I.-Masjumi-P.S.I. coalition.[3] This was the first time since 1948 that the P.K.I. was prepared to support a cabinet that did not contain what the party would call 'progressive' ministers. The basis of Wilopo's cabinet began to erode in the course of the year. In August the conservative wing of the Masjumi split off and reconstituted itself as Nahdatul Ulama, robbing the Masjumi of about half its following. Due to the so-called '17 October affair', when army Chief of Staff General Nasution tried a semi-coup d'etat directed against what he thought was parliamentary interference in army matters, the P.S.I. – always close to the military – was compromised and lost influence.[4] So when in June 1953 a police action in North Sumatra against illegal occupation of a large estate resulted in the killing of five squatters, this was enough to spell the end of the Wilopo government. The next month P.N.I. leader Ali Sastroamidjojo formed a new cabinet together with the Nahdatul Ulama and a small radical muslim party, the P.S.I., excluding both the Masjumi and the P.S.I. Nine ministers of this first

Ali cabinet had what Brackman calls 'controversial backgrounds'. Among them were the new Defence Minister Iwa Kusumasumantri and the Minister of Agriculture Sadjarwo, 'the cabinet's only direct link with the P.K.I.' They were said to belong to the 'irrational, radical nationalist fringe',[5] making it easier for the P.K.I. to hail the coming of this Ali cabinet as 'a glorious victory of democracy over fascism'.[6]

In March 1954 at the Party's 5th Congress the policy initiated at the beginning of 1952 was celebrated as a great triumph, and Aidit's political report that had been published half a year before was called one of the most important documents in the history of the P.K.I.[7] The Congress adopted it unanimously and so replaced Muso's New Road resolution of August 1948, consecrating the shift to the right that in fact had already been established policy for two years. The report stressed the need for a People's Democratic Government that had to be based on a national united front of peasants and workers, but it excluded actually only the most reactionary forces, termed the 'compradore bourgeoisie', who were said to be still linked 'by a thousand threads' to the imperialists.[8] Though the aim was still that this united front should be led by the working class, i.e., the P.K.I., the party would be satisfied for the time being if it could retain its complete freedom of action within the front.[9] Given the actual balance of forces in the country, this new interpretation of Muso's old precept was a sign of Aidit's realistic approach.

Another feature of the new P.K.I. was its strong nationalistic slant which had meanwhile led to a more positive appreciation of Sukarno. In the beginning it had been difficult to forget that at the time of the Madiun rebellion Sukarno had put before the country the choice between him and Muso. But by the end of 1952 the Indonesian President had already come to be considered someone 'who in general can at the most be neutralized, especially in revolutionary times'.[10] But Sukarno had been instrumental in keeping the Masjumi and the P.S.I. out of the Ali cabinet and this was duly noted by the P.K.I. Moreover, the Indonesian President also obliged by fully endorsing Aidit who, in November 1954, had strongly recommended cooperation between the three main political currents in Indonesia: 'The Communist trend, the Nationalist trend and the Islamic trend'.[11] So the party did all in its power to appear a truly nationalist, be it left-radical, party that in Aidit's words would 'always defend the red-and-white flag'.

The P.K.I. practiced its policy of 'support and criticism', as Hindley terms it,[12] by giving the government of Ali Sastroamidjojo its parliamentary support while remaining outside it and thus free to act. After October 1954 Ali even had to rely upon P.K.I. votes to stay in power, a situation that gave the communists additional leverage. In general the P.K.I. did not fare badly during the period of the first Ali cabinet which ended in June 1955 when extra-parliamentary pressure of the armed forces forced him to resign. It was a period 'marked by extensive corruption, inflation, and a general decline in the standards of living presenting a fortunate coincidence for the P.K.I.'.[13] The party had succeeded in enrolling more than one million members, and its various affiliated mass-organizations also showed a rapidly increasing membership, allowing the P.K.I. to achieve as was noted 'a spectacular revival'.[14]

Under the next premier, Burhannudin Harahap, the Masjumi returned to power – together with the Nahdatul Ulama and the P.S.I. but to the exclusion of the P.N.I. Aidit began with the accusation that this new combination had to do 'the bidding of the Dutch imperialists'. But when, contrary to all expectations, Harahap started to organize the long-awaited general elections, the P.K.I. Central Committee declared its support for his government, allegedly because it now was 'basically similar' to the previous one under Ali.[15] When, in September 1955, the elections for a new parliament were held it turned out how right the communists had been in their support for Harahap, because the P.K.I. then emerged as the fourth largest party immediately after the P.N.I., Masjumi, and N.U. and claiming over six million votes.[16]

Aidit immediately proposed a National Coalition Government having in mind a cabinet in which all major parties would participate, including both the P.K.I. and the Masjumi. This was a logical step already foreshadowed prior to the elections when he had proposed a broad-based coalition of this kind, even though it cut across the explicit line adopted at his insistence at the Party's 5th Congress in March 1954.[17] The P.K.I. leader, to the dismay of his more orthodox colleagues, invited the Majumi, the representatives of the officially detested 'compradore bourgeoisie', to cooperate with the communists in the name of an all-out struggle against 'the remnant forces of Dutch colonialism'.[18] This was to no effect since not only did the Masjumi turn the proposal down, but it was equally ill-received by the P.N.I. and the Nahdatul

Ulama who were disquieted by the electoral results of the P.K.I.

Harahap had given himself a breathing period, announcing that his government would remain in office until the new parliament convened in March 1956. Meanwhile, he opened negotiations with the Dutch on a number of outstanding issues, but mainly on the continued presence of the former colonial power in West Irian. Trying to steal the thunder of both Sukarno and the P.K.I., Harahap hoped to find the Dutch agreeable to a settlement with a moderate government like his because, as was widely held in Indonesia at the time, 'till the question of West Irian is settled Indonesian politics will be more irrational than rational'.[19] The attempt failed, however, and the talks were broken off at the beginning of February 1956.[20] Immediately afterwards Indonesia unilaterally abrogated the Round Table Agreements of 1949. When the composition of the newly elected parliament was made known a month later, Harahap resigned, making way for a new cabinet. It was again Ali Sastroamidjojo who was asked to form a cabinet, and he brought the three largest parties – apart from his P.N.I. also the Masjumi and the N.U. – back into a coalition. He did not heed Sukarno's wish that the P.K.I. should be included, as Aidit had requested, but would at most (as before) accept tacit or open support by the communists from the sidelines.[21] During the office of this second Ali-cabinet, which lasted only a year, the collapse of the parliamentary system in Indonesia became more and more apparent, since the tendency was inexorably towards polarization between Sukarno on the one hand and the army on the other.[22] Hatta, the independent vice-president, resigned at the end of 1956 as a protest against the way Sukarno conducted himself as president, and shortly afterwards the Masjumi withdrew from Ali's coalition making his government again dependent upon communist votes for its continued political existence.

More important was the shift Aidit and the P.K.I. began to initiate in this period, away from the P.N.I. and increasingly towards Sukarno who – as the new 'force' – was now to be influenced and used.[23] This option in favor of the Indonesian President, who emerged as a dominating force, was not so improbable because Aidit, sensing the rapid decline of parliament under Ali, hoped to find in Sukarno the best guarantee against the growing preponderance of the strongly anti-communist army leadership.[24] The glowing prospects that the formidable electoral victory in 1955 seemed to hold out for the P.K.I. were decidedly dimmed in the atmosphere of anti-parliamentarianism that came to prevail when Indonesia began to fall apart economically and politically.[25] Sukarno in turn came to view the P.K.I. as a natural pawn to be played off against the army. Moreover, increasingly obsessed with completing the 'August Revolution', i.e. above all with getting the Dutch out of West Irian, Sukarno saw in Aidit's P.K.I. a rabidly nationalistic ally of no mean organizational impact.

It was at this juncture that Sukarno produced his 'konsepsi', his concept of a strong executive power, based on a non-partisan or, better, all-partisan popular acclaim. On February 22, 1957, he proposed a gotong royong or mutual cooperation cabinet, and the creation of a National Council composed of 'functional' groups such as labor, youth, and peasants. It was a modified version of Sukarno's earlier ideas on 'Guided Democracy' with which he had come forward after his extensive tour through a number of communist countries in Europe and Asia in the autumn of 1956. The changes were partly the product of strong opposition from the P.N.I. and P.K.I. as these parties feared nothing more than to be 'buried' with the other parties, as the Indonesian President had originally suggested.[26] It was the first time since the adoption of the 'right' strategy in early 1952 that Aidit had attacked Sukarno, but it paid off because the Indonesian President was made to pledge that he would not dissolve parliament, though he kept to himself what its whittled-down position would be precisely. The P.K.I.'s Politburo changed its tune and began to comment favorably on Sukarno's konsepsi, stating that it was 'a new weapon in the struggle to complete the August 17, 1945, Revolution'. It was further said that Sukarno's proposals would in no way disturb the existing party system. As if to prove this the party went all out to whip up popular support for Sukarno who faced strong resistance from the other parties, from Hatta and from some of the military.

In the midst of the clamor Sukarno had caused, Ali Sastroamidjojo handed in his resignation with the result that Sukarno appointed himself – 'citizen Sukarno' – as formateur of a new so-called 'extra-parliamentary business cabinet'. The Masjumi considered this action completely illegal, while the P.K.I. at the other end of the spectrum fully endorsed Sukarno realizing that the only alternatives would have been a Hatta-led government or some kind of military takeover.[27]

Sukarno, seeing the chances of extending his power grow, made himself premier and appointed a non-partisan economist, Djuanda Kartawidjaja, as his deputy in this hand-picked gotong-royong cainet.[28] Many parties were represented, but none by its leading personalities, while the two ministers with a Masjumi background were promptly expelled from their party. The P.K.I. had no representatives, though some members of the cabinet, like the Minister of Information Sudibjo, the Minister of Agriculture Sadjarwo, and the Minister of Education Prijono could be considered very close friends. Aidit was not satisfied (how could he be?) but he called the Djuanda cabinet a step towards '100% implementation' of Sukarno's ideas'.[29] At the same time, the party made further attempts to identify itself with the Indonesian President and by so doing made it more and more difficult for the other parties to attack the communists. This turned out to be of particular importance after the local elections in mid-1957 when the P.K.I. in Java alone polled two million votes more than in 1955. The party to suffer most from this success was the P.N.I. which normally drew support from similar social strata to the P.K.I., especially in Central and East Java among the abangan or secularly oriented village population. The P.N.I. then even considered a front against the P.K.I., and some nationalist leaders began to remind the public that the P.K.I. 'had half its leaders in Moscow, half in Indonesia'.[30] But in the end the tacit P.N.I.-P.K.I. alliance remained intact so as to exert maximum influence upon the Djuanda government.

Meanwhile, a new dimension was added to the political scene when the action to regain West Irian was stepped up. Premier Djuanda forewarned parliament at the end of May 1957 that Indonesia might resort to 'other' forms of struggle, a suggestion that was soon interpreted by Aidit as a call for a 'direct armed attack on Irian'.[31] The new 'cooperation committees', set up by the army to gain control over youth, worker, and peasant organizations, also turned their attention increasingly towards the West Irian issue.[32] In the newly created National Council military action was contemplated, but opinion settled on measures short of war, especially to be directed against the remaining considerable economic interests of the Dutch.[33] In November West Irian was discussed in the United Nations, but Indonesia failed to obtain a relatively mild resolution asking the Secretary-General 'to assist parties concerned' in resolving the problem. Subandrio reacted by saying that there was now no alternative except outside the U.N.

It was soon to become clear what he meant when moves against Dutch property began in the course of December in the form of strikes and confiscations. The initiative for the first seizures of Dutch interests came from a P.N.I.-affiliated trade-union federation closely in touch with Sukarno, who was manifestly the major force behind the anti-Dutch drive. The P.K.I. and the trade unions it controlled followed suit, but from the beginning the communists had shown awareness of the dangers involved in a too-precipitate action against Dutch interests. Thus in October the party daily, *Harian Rakjat*, had still insisted that Indonesia was not in a position to confiscate all Dutch capital in the country at a stroke.[34] But once the ball was set rolling Sobsi-members also took the initiative and seized a number of Dutch estates, banks, and other properties. The government fearing that matters would get out of hand declared that it would assume control of the enterprizes seized and that it needed the military to implement the decision. The P.K.I. did not dare to defy this measure and found itself forced to show approval and to instruct its followers to comply with the subsequent steps taken by the army. In anticipation, the armed forces had already begun to arrest a number of communist leaders as if to illustrate that the P.K.I. had no other choice but to back down and meekly pursue its strategy of accommodation with the powers that be, the Army and Sukarno.[35]

There was even more reason for the P.K.I. to freewheel because the simmering insurrection of the regional army commanders in Sumatra and Sulawesi was about to break out into the open. When this happened in February 1958, Aidit realized that direct military countermeasures from the center were in the interests of the P.K.I., while procrastination and compromise would only strengthen the strongly anti-communist rebels. The central army command should therefore not be antagonized; neither should the government if it could be avoided.[36] But the country's economy deteriorated rapidly due to the combined disruptive effect of the seizure of Dutch properties and the rebellion outside Java. So in September 1958 Sobsi initiated a mass action against the proposed increase in the price of rice and in order not to loose their grip on party and population the Aidit leadership also had to voice strong disagreement with various other government measures. The P.K.I. also became more openly critical of the growing participation of the armed forces, or rather the senior officers, in non-military matters. The party warned against the rise of 'warlordism' and against the exploitation by the army of the state of war that at the end of 1958 was once again extended by a year, enabling the military to exercise many functions otherwise reserved for the civil authorities.

It all resulted in further reliance on Sukarno for protection and support, and gradually the reverse. Between a liberal democracy that had failed in Indonesia and a military dictatorship, the idea of Guided Democracy as presented by Sukarno was the least evil, in Aidit's somewhat inflated rhetoric even 'the most revolutionary policy'.[37] The Indonesian President, however, was about to resume pressure towards a further increase in his personal power because by late 1958 the rebellion had been more or less quelled and commanded less attention. This threatened to put Aidit again in opposition to Sukarno, who had decided that he did not want elections for the time being. He had Djuanda postpone them again for a year against express promises to the contrary. Differences of opinion also arose between the P.K.I. and the president as to the number of 'functional' representatives to be nominated for a new-style parliament, and the authority to do so.[38] On February 19, 1959, Sukarno moved and made his cabinet decide to prepare restoration of the original 1945 Constitution that would grant important executive power to him as president. The party system had to be 'simplified' in order to control it better, and in parliament each second member was to be recruited from a 'functional' group. The P.K.I. Politburo announced its support, but as one of its members later explained this was not surprising and largely happened because the P.K.I. had little alternative.[39] It would have meant, at least in retrospect, 'agreeing with the reactionaries [the Masjumi] to continue the Constituent Assembly' instead of 'uniting with the democratic groups led by Sukarno'. The muslim parties in the Constituent Assembly, the Masjumi, the N.U., and the smaller ones mustered their strength and succeeded in blocking Sukarno's attempt to get his decision to return to the 1945 Constitution passed with the officially required qualified majority. In three successive votes the government failed to secure enough votes, and when, consequently, their proposal had to be considered rejected, Aidit came up with the suggestion either to have elections for a new Constituent Assembly or to restore the 1945 Constitution by presidential decree. Sukarno had probably had this latter solution in mind all along, but as he was abroad his return had to be awaited before any further move could be expected.[40] On July 5, a few days after he regained Djakarta, the Indonesian President indeed brought about a return to the 1945 Constitution by simple decree, thus achieving his aim by what, in fact, was a bloodless coup.

The army, with General Nasution at its head, had been most forthcoming, having placed a ban on all political activities while Sukarno was abroad and being all in favor of bringing to an end the endless bickerings of ineffective politicians.[41] It heralded what was to be Sukarno's golden era, the period of his Guided Democracy that was to carry him to the zenith of his power, but equally to his ultimate doom.

NOTES

1. See: Unite to complete the demands of the 1945 August Revolution. In: D. N. Aidit, 1960, *Complete Works*, vol. II, p. 27, as translated by the Joint Publications Research Service, Washington D.C.
2. Donald Hindley, 1964, *The Communist Party of Indonesia 1951-1963*, University of California Press, Berkeley, p. 57.
3. The composition of this cabinet officially still fell short of the primary aim of the P.K.I. – to isolate the Masjumi and the P.S.I.
4. Justus M. van der Kroef, 1965, *The Communist Party of Indonesia, Its History, Programme and Tactics*, University of British Columbia, Vancouver, p. 61.
5. Arnold C. Brackman, 1963, *Indonesian Communism*, Frederick A. Praeger, New York, p. 191.
7. Van der Kroef, 1965, p. 72 and Aidit, 1959, p. 416.
8. Translated into plain terms this reference to the 'compradore bourgeoisie' meant the Masjumi, the western-oriented, reform-minded muslim party that had to be excluded from any future coalition in which the P.K.I. might participate. Even this, however, was not a strict tenet of Aidit's as became clear as the 1955 elections approached. See p. 28.
9. Van der Kroef, 1965, p. 60.
10. *Bintang Merah*, monthly of the P.K.I., published by Jajasan Pemburuan, Djakarta, October-November 1952, pp. 121-122.
11. Brackman, 1963, p. 212.
12. Hindley, 1964, p. 246.
13. Hindley, 1964, p. 251.
14. Brackman, 1963, p. 199.
15. For a Lasting Peace, For a People's Democracy, *Kominform Journal*, September 9, 1955.

16. In December 1955 elections for a Constituent Assembly the P.K.I. were even to improve on this figure by 50,000 votes.
17. Aidit, 1959, p. 311.
18. Aidit, 1959, p. 319.
19. Mohammed Hatta, Indonesia between the power blocs, *Foreign Affairs*, April 1958, p. 489.
20. According to Dr. J. M. A. H. Luns, then foreign minister of the Netherlands and head of the Dutch negotiating team, Sukarno made any agreement with the Dutch impossible by having decided in advance that the Geneva talks should fail in any case. This version has been disputed in Indonesian quarters.
21. Brackman, 1963, p. 223.
22. Hindley, 1964, p. 255.
23. See below, p. 60, note 14.
24. Hindley, 1964, p. 255.
25. At the turn of 1956-1957 the first autonomous regional councils were established. Their defiance of the central authority was an augury of the open rebellion of the outer territories still to come.
26. Brackman, 1963, p. 234.
27. Hindley, 1964, p. 261.
28. One of the new faces was Subandrio, ex-ambassador of Indonesia to the Soviet Union and to Britain and previously a member of the P.S.I., who was then promoted to foreign minister. Writing in his confinement in 1969, after having been sentenced to death three years before, Subandrio pondering about this nomination called it 'a first demonstration by Sukarno of political love towards me'. He termed it 'a kiss, an eventful kiss' and related that, when he was listening to the sentence pronounced by the military tribunal on October 26, 1966, he turned his eyes to Sukarno's picture behind the members of the tribunal: 'This image reminded me of the presidential kiss of political love, some nine years ago, which now revealed itself as the kiss of death. I was sentenced to death'. Manuscript put at the disposal of the writer. See below p. 396 ff.
29. Aidit, 1960, p. 123.
30. Brackman, 1963, p. 239. Van der Kroef, 1965, p. 93.
31. Brackman, 1963, p. 241.
33. Hindley, 1964, p. 270.
33. At the time estimated at a value of two billion dollars.
34. *Harian Rakjat*, official P.K.I. daily, Djakarta, October 21, 1957. See also: Uri Ra'anan, 1969, *The U.S.S.R. Arms the Third World: Case studies in Soviet Foreign Policy*, M.I.T.-Press, Cambridge, Massachusetts, p. 204.
35. Hindley, 1964, p. 267, and Brackman, 1963, p. 243.
36. Hindley, 1964, p. 269.
37. Aidit, 1958, p. 357. It is clear from this passage that Aidit at the time was under pressure from left-wing critics within the Party to be less accommodating.
38. Van der Kroef, 1965, p. 107.

39. Politburo-member Sakirman in *Bintang Merah* of July-August 1960. See also Hindley, 1964, p. 273.
40. Hindley, 1964, p. 274.
41. General Nasution, interview, March 1972.

CHAPTER 4

The P.K.I. and world communism (1948-1959)

After the premature Madiun rebellion Soviet interest in Indonesian affairs seems to have waned considerably. Hindley suggests that Moscow had for the time being written off its Indonesian comrades, just as it did in 1927 with the Chinese communsists after Chiang Kai-shek had broken with them and all but annihilated their party.[1]

In the Cominform journal of the period 1948-1954 almost nothing was written on Indonesia. Slowly, however, the picture changed, and relations with the P.K.I. took an upward swing.[2] It helped no doubt that Stalin at the end of his life again shifted away from the hard 'Zhdanov' black-and-white division of the world. A first indication of an 'opening to the right' was an interview the Soviet dictator gave in Pravda in February 1951, when on the question of war and peace he stressed that 'at the present time war cannot be regarded as unavoidable'.[3] More formally this new line of trying to find support among non-communists was launched at the 19th Party Congres of the C.P.S.U., later in October of that same year. On that occasion Stalin encouraged communists all over the world 'to take up the banner of national independence and national sovereignty' that had allegedly been thrown overboard by bourgeois nationalists. But he did not instruct them to assert immediate leadership over such a national coalition, or front.

The line that Aidit introduced early in January 1952 for the P.K.I.[4] closely approached Stalin's new prescription.[5] It is tempting to link the new 'right strategy' enunciated by Stalin to the subsequent revision of the P.K.I. policy by Aidit. It is not improbable that this connection existed. Suffice it here to note that, in neighboring Malaya, communist tactics also started to change. Since 1948 the Malayan Communist Party had been waging a fierce terrorist campaign, but, as was noted later, 'from the later months of 1951 the insurgents seem to have concentrated as much on political work – clandestine subversion and penetration of government organizations – as upon military struggle'.[6]

Brackman sees in the arrival of a Soviet newspaper correspondent in Indonesia in December 1951 a possible sign of Moscow's renewed and growing involvement in Indonesian affairs.[7] When, in May 1952 on the occasion of the party's 32nd anniversary, the 'softer' approach was proclaimed,[8] the idea that this turn had anything to do with outside encouragement was firmly rejected. In countering an opinion said to prevail among 'the enemies of the people' that the P.K.I. was an agent of Moscow or of the People's Republic of China, Aidit gave the assurance that 'every policy of the party is determined in a democratic manner by the P.K.I. itself, and without the slighest intercession from foreigners'.[9] The P.K.I., he said, 'has subjected itself to the interests of the people and the national interest'. This statement, however, did not prevent the Indonesian communist leader from copying some of Stalin's recent pronunciations, especially where it concerned foreign policy. Therefore, in this same anniversary address, Aidit said that 'Communists throughout the world, like Communists in Indonesia, need only peace, for socialism and Communism can be built only when peace prevails'.[10] He then proceeded to quote literally what Stalin had said in his February 1951 interview in Pravda on war and peace and on the need for peaceful coexistence. Aidit also urged the P.K.I. to turn to the Soviet Union in order to weaken imperialism, but this, he maintained, was not to imply that the Soviet system should be copied: 'On the contrary, each nation has to travel its own road to socialism on the basis of the development of its national situation'.

Therefore rather early in his career as a P.K.I. spokesman and leader, Aidit began to weave together the two strands of a design for the party that, at that moment, did not seem to pose a threat of contradiction: An orientation towards Moscow and a pursuit of radical-nationalistic aims. Insofar as the P.K.I. and its sponsors in the Soviet Union did not always share the same opinion, Aidit could assert his views, if they related to *domestic* matters. So when the first Ali-cabinet was about to be formed in July 1953, the Soviet news agency, Tass, noted a growing struggle between 'progressives' and 'reactionaries', probably referring to attempts by the P.K.I. to keep the Masjumi and the P.S.I. out of the next government'.[11] Not long after Radio Moscow, in an obvious reference to the fact that the newly appointed formateur, Ali Sastroamidjojo, had come over from Washington where he had been Indonesia's ambassador, insinuated that 'a foreign power is attempting to violate Indonesia's sovereign rights . . . to form a government, if desired'.[12] This adverse Moscow opinion of Ali and his efforts was clearly not what Aidit thought of the situation. Immediately after the formation of the new cabinet he showed he was elated by its composition.[13]

Other signs of the new nationalistic fervor of the Aidit leadership were to be found in what went on during and after the session of the party's Central Committee in October 1953. From an organizational point of view, the removal of Tan Ling-Djie – with Alimin the only remaining P.K.I.-leader of the pre-Madiun period – from the Central Committee, followed somewhat later by the resignation of a close associate of Tan, Siauw Giok Tjan, as co-editor of the party's daily *Harian Rakjat*, is of interest. The elimination of Tan was no doubt part of a further strengthening of Aidit's grip on the party.[15] As regards the attitude towards the peasants which was also an important issue within the party, Aidit showed he differed from those within the P.K.I. who thought that 'because it is more important to stir up the peasants, so they may join in the struggle, all communists must leave the city and work among the peasants'.[16] Party activity in the countryside was a cherished priority for Chinese communists, but Aidit chided those of his own followers who, after having studied the experiences of Mao's China, harbored these ideas and failed to notice that, even under Chairman Mao, the workers had never been neglected as a political factor. Besides, Aidit stressed, it had to be remembered that 'there are specific differences in geography and political development between Indonesia and China that must be taken account of'.[17]

A third issue, again in the political field, concerned the question of who was Indonesia's main enemy. One view was that the United States fitted the part, but Aidit preferred to single out the former colonial power as a target.[18] This was later endorsed by the Soviet Union or at least referred to without unfavorable comment.[19] On all three issues – on Tan, on the peasants, and on the 'main enemy' – Aidit's line carried the day against anticipated opposition from other leaders of the P.K.I.[20]

It would, however, be wrong to conclude from this that Aidit, and in his wake the P.K.I., was anti-Peking, though in practice all three questions were ostensibly handled by the P.K.I. contrary to Chinese or Chinese-communist interests and views. One can rather see, as common denominator, the increasingly independent Indonesian viewpoint from which Aidit proceeded in determining the party's position on current issues. Also, it need not necessarily be inferred that the P.K.I. in this period could be called pro-Soviet for adopting views that were close to what was official thinking in Moscow.

But it is true that very often the P.K.I., and Aidit in particular, followed more or less automatically the lead given by the Soviet Union, the more so as an issue was further away from the Indonesian scene. Thus, exactly as earlier when Stalin was still alive,[21] Aidit in his political report of October 1953 identified himself with respect to a number of general international problems with the views given by the Soviet leader of the day, Georgyi Malenkov, quoting extensively from a speech Malenkov had made two months before in August when he addressed the Supreme Soviet.[22]

A new dimension was added when, at the 20th Party Congress of the C.P.S.U. in February 1956, the new up-and-coming man of the Party, Nikita Kruschov, made his secret speech on Stalin and, as we now know from the Chinese communists, so opened an era of increasingly serious Sino-Soviet controversies.[23] Judging from what he told delegates at the time, Aidit, who represented the P.K.I. at this Congress, initially had hardly anything of note to contribute.[24]

By the end of June, however, Aidit produced a report that is of interest in more than one respect. It was made (and the Indonesian communist leader showed that he was well aware of the fact) after most of Kruschov's secret speech had become known to the outside world.[25] Of the main issues raised during the 20th Party Congress in Moscow, Aidit selected four: Two had an *international* impact and two related to *domestic* affairs.

In the first category he discussed the inevitable *decline of colonialism*, following in detail what Kruschov had said in his public report at the beginning of the Congress.[26] To the prospects of *war and peace*, Aidit did the same, though here a slight difference in emphasis was traceable: The Indonesian party leader gave greater stress than Kruschov to the chances of a major war breaking out.[72]

Of more immediate, domestic importance to the P.K.I. was the question of *peaceful and non-peaceful roads to power*, and the *attitude towards Stalin*. In his June report Aidit asked whether the P.K.I. should reconsider its position on the parliamentary struggle because of the conclusions of Kruschov's report to the 20th Party Congress.[28] Aidit gave the answer to this question himself with a reference to the 5th National Congress of the P.K.I. of March 1954 where it was stated that 'the P.K.I. has taken part and will continue to take a most active part in the parliamentary struggle'.[29]

But parliamentary work alone was not enough now, Aidit continued, because the P.K.I. also had another very important task, 'especially (to) work among labor, the peasants, the intelligentsia, and the mass of workers as well as among the democratic masses'. This correction of Kruschov's 'conversion' to parliamentary methods was pertinent not only because organizing the Indonesian masses was in fact a hallmark of 'Aiditism', but also because at the same 5th Party Congress Aidit had argued the ousting of Tan Ling-Djie on the grounds that Tan supposedly believed too much in parliament.[30] On the one hand, therefore, Aidit could claim to have been ahead of the Soviet comrades in discovering the merits of using a parliamentary system to achieve influence and eventually power. On the other hand, he was able to sound a warning on the basis of the experience of the P.K.I. within the Indonesian context that one should not expect too much of elections.[31]

In addition to the question of the various roads to power, the other issue vital to the Indonesian communists – as, of course, to all other communists – had become the treatment of Stalin and his contribution to Soviet and world communism. In formulating his own and the party's point of view Aidit may have had the benefit of a stay in China and North Korea where he spent two months on the way back from Moscow to Djakarta. It was in that period that Peking's authoritative daily *Jen-min Jih-pao*, after a conspicuous absence of any reference to the Soviet de-stalinization campaign, gave a long analysis of the Stalin era.[32] In the theoretical void that Kruschov had created by his denunciation of Stalin, especially where it centered around the question of where the fault lay – with the system or with the man – the Chinese communists had stepped in with at least something of an explanation. Peking spoke of 'mistakes' of Stalin that were a result of what it called 'undue emphasis on centralization'. While a strong dose of centralization was necessary to build communism this should have been combined under Stalin with a higher level of democracy.[33] In his June report to the P.K.I., Aidit came very close to this point of view by observing that 'to abandon democracy means to work without basing oneself on the intelligence of the masses of the people, whereas to abandon centralism means to permit the masses of the people to be unguided in their struggle'.[33]

So both Mao and Aidit took a central position between those who (as the Soviet communists then were inclined to do) blamed everything on Stalin, and those who (as somewhat later, the Italian communist leader Togliatti did) regarded the system as being at fault and acutely in need of overhaul.[35] But, while Peking was trying to protect Mao from guilt-by-association and at the same time stress that it was wrong to deny the important role of an individual leader, Aidit flatly stated that 'the highest form of leadership in a Communist Party is collective leadership ... To abandon collective leadership means to violate democratic centralism'.[36] This attitude no doubt reflected the working conditions among the leaders of the P.K.I. who right from the beginning of the Aidit-era in 1951 (as they were to do in the years to come) had observed a collective leadership in the real sense of the word.[37]

In his report Aidit showed that he was able to agree with the denunciation of Stalin as Kruschov had formulated it. However, at the same time, he came up with what was, in effect, a serious criticism of the way the Soviet leader had handled the affair. Too much had been made out of Stalin's 'errors', Aidit complained, while the good the dictator had done had been ignored. At the 20th Party Congress this was still to be excused, but 'after the Congress was over and many of the questions concerning Stalin had been distorted by the bourgeois press which added and omitted at will, an official statement from the C.P.S.U. concerning Stalin's errors and virtues is very much needed. If this is not done by the C.P.S.U. it is the responsibility of each Communist Party and also of the P.K.I. to explain within the limits of the possibilities possessed by the parties'.[38] Aidit ended his report by quoting whole-heartedly from a Chinese communist statement that one should continue to study Stalins' writings seriously.[39]

So Aidit critisized Kruschov on the way he had inaugurated destalinization with his famous secret speech at the February 1956 Party Congress and thus joined at this stage his Chinese comrades. But he did so in his own manner.[40]

At the end of 1956 a new factor was added to the equation when in November President Sukarno for the first time visited the Soviet Union, and the diplomatic relations that had finally been established between the two countries in 1954 were given more content. Kruschov offered Sukarno a 100 million dollar loan, ostensibly for a number of mining projects,[41] but partly secretly used for financing the purchase of Soviet or Soviet-bloc military equipment.[42]

Aidit hailed the joint Indonesian-Soviet statement issued at the end of Sukarno's visit as 'an historic event, a contribution to Indonesian-Soviet friendship and to world peace'.[43] But he did so only in June 1957, a considerable delay that possibly indicated that the P.K.I. had meanwhile not been quite sure what to think of the budding relations between Moscow and Djakarta.

Then, in November 1957, with the meeting of 81 communist parties in Moscow on the occasion of the 40th anniversary of the October Revolution, a long and fateful Sino-Soviet dialogue was to begin that initially touched mainly foreign policy issues. In the months preceding the conference, the Chinese Communist Party had switched (after the failure of the 100-flowers episode) from a moderate domestic line to a radical 'left' strategy. This was also to result in a much sterner attitude towards right-wing 'deviations' in other communist countries and parties. It meant that Peking wanted to put Moscow forward again as a center and leading light of world communism, as it would imply the greater responsibility of the Soviet Communist Party for comrades abroad. The final Moscow Declaration, issued at the end of the meeting, reflected Chinese pressure on this point, and particularly the anti-Yugoslav implications it contained were of Chinese origin.[44]

It seems that the P.K.I. had not anticipated this development. For example, Aidit in a commemoration article written before the November meeting had pleaded particularly for a national form of Marxism-Leninism and consequently had paid tribute to the Chinese Revolution.[45] After the conference was over Aidit endorsed its two main documents, the Moscow Declaration and the Peace Manifesto, but in rather general terms.[46] This he continued to do before the P.K.I. Central Committee meeting in March 1958,[47] and one is inclined to believe that this was partly due to the fact that it was difficult to sort out the precise implications of the Moscow documents and partly because the party must have been acutely preoccupied with domestic problems such as the rebellion in the outer territories. Moreover, Aidit was apparently not too worried because the practical policy decisions concerning Indonesia which both Moscow and Peking continued to take, probably independent of each other,[48] were almost identical. So the two communist countries – though China at a somewhat earlier stage[49] – displayed warm support and understanding for the Indonesian government when because of West-Irian it began to radicalize its policy towards the Dutch.[50] A few months later both gave warning that they fully backed the Indonesian government in its charges that the U.S.A. was interfering in its domestic affairs by aiding the rebel forces. There were some signs that China tried to compete with the Soviet Union in offering arms to Sukarno,[51] but, in all, no spillover of any serious rivalry or antagonism between the two major communist powers was noticeable in Indonesia.

By the middle of 1958, when the rebellion had passed the stage of acute danger, Aidit went on a tour to Europe and had a chance to get a first-hand look at the state of affairs within the communist world movement. His first stop – at the end of June – was Prague, where he was briefed especially on relations with Yugoslavia. He addressed the 11th Party Congress of the Czechoslovak Communist Party and a mass meeting of party activists,[52] and on the latter occasion toed the new Soviet-Chinese line of renewed open polemics against Tito who with his policy of non-alignment, he said, was 'equating the foreign policy of the socialist camp with that of the capitalist states'.[53] Aidit however remained quite moderate, avoiding the sharp invective even Kruschov had begun to use earlier that same month.[54] The P.K.I. leader was also a bit on the defensive, denying 'imperialist falsehoods' that the P.K.I. had sent a delegation to the Yugoslav Party Congress of April of that year and explaining that their representative, his second deputy Njoto, had only been an 'observer'.[55] In reacting to the new anti-Yugoslav campaign with certain reservations, Aidit must no doubt have been guided by the excellent relations Djakarta then had with Belgrade, where the Indonesian government had obtained (sometime earlier in 1958) an important credit for the purchase of arms.[56]

Although there had been signs of growing differences between the views of Moscow and Peking, Aidit preferred to stress, upon his return from his trip to Eastern Europe in mid-August 1958, that there was no such thing as a crisis in the communist world.[57] In his report to the Central Committee of the party in November, looking back upon world communist developments in the past half year, the P.K.I. leader steered clear of controversy.[58] He praised the Chinese 'leap forward' that had begun to be drawn into the Sino-Soviet quarrel, and the May conference of Warsaw Pact countries, where the Chinese observer had inserted a note radically different from the more moderate Kruschov line. This May conference, was 'of historic significance'. The meeting between Mao Tse-tung and Kruschov early in August, which was marred by similar differences and ended in the crisis around Quemoy, had been a friendly gathering where, according to Aidit, the Soviet Union had been 'at one' with China.[59] On Yugoslavia Aidit remained silent in his November report, the easiest way to deal with Marshal Tito as honored guest of Sukarno due to arrive in Djakarta in a few weeks' time. But, when the Yugoslav President arrived, the unofficial P.K.I. daily *Bintang Tumur* – always some shades more extreme than the official *Harian Rakjat* – described him as a representative of U.S. interests in South East Asia in line with Chinese charges.[60]

An as yet undisputed point on which Aidit could easily accomodate Moscow was the matter of the 'Asiatic' character of the Soviet Union. In view of later developments[61] it is of interest to see how the P.K.I. leader at that time championed as self-evident the claim that the Soviet Union belonged to Asia and chided those in Djakarta who did not agree with him.[62] But Aidit was less forthcoming towards Moscow when it came to its policy regarding the domestic situation and the position of the P.K.I. Thus it took him until September 1959, at the 6th Party Congress, before he saw fit to even mention the military build-up in Indonesia to which the Soviet Union had begun to contribute heavily since the autumn of 1956.

Reviewing the interaction between the P.K.I., external communist influences, and the domestic Indonesian scene from 1945-1959, as outlined in these first chapters, a few conclusions can be drawn. The early postwar period, apart from the somewhat erratic Yusuf-intermezzo, showed the P.K.I. as pursuing a 'right strategy' under such leaders as Sardjono and Alimin. The party was willing to cooperate with other, non-communist parties for nationalist aims and did so with some success. It did not hesitate to support negotiations with the Dutch colonial power. The true extent of its membership was concealed through the use of fronts, cooperating in the Sajap Kiri, the left wing, while basically the party's aim was to be an elite, vanguard group rather than a party for the masses. This policy enabled the Indonesian communists, partly by chance, to occupy a prominent position and, from June 1947 to January 1948, even to head the Republic's government.

Initially, this line coincided with the policy the Soviet Union had advocated since the mid-thirties and especially during the Second World War. When a new, more radical, 'left strategy' began to be outlined with the Stalin-inspired 'two-camp' doctrine in September 1947, Indonesia was at first still on the side of the angels (even perhaps having served as an example) with communists and crypto-communists in the eyes of Moscow 'leading' the revolution. This ended, however, when Premier Amir Sjarifuddin gave way to a government that was without communists, let alone led by them. The new Stalin line was from then on brought to bear upon Indonesia with full pressure, resulting in Soviet rejection of agreements with the Dutch, even those concluded by fellow-communists and previously endorsed. When the left swing that Moscow came to favor and tried to transmit for Asia through the Calcutta Youth Conference was not adequately implemented and a national coalition, including the P.K.I., was again being seriously considered by Alimin, the Suripno-affair was used by the Soviet Union to compromise the P.K.I. and its chances to participate in the Indonesian government. At the same time a trusted lieutenant was sent to see that no further misunderstanding of the course Moscow wanted to be followed would be possible in the P.K.I. So Muso turned up in August 1948 quickly imposing, with the adoption of his 'New Road' resolution, the practical consequences of the 'two-camp' doctrine. Outwardly this was open renunciation of cooperation with other parties, unless they were willing to accept communist leadership (manifestly an unrealistic proposal), while beneath the surface preparations were made to take the initiative, if necessary by force. The Madiun rebellion may have been a premature affair as far as Muso was concerned, but there seems little doubt that, had it occurred at a somewhat later stage as probably planned, the uprising would have met a similar end.

The consequences of the new, radical strategy imposed from outside were pretty disastrous and caused, apart from massive bloodletting, utter confusion and disarray in what was left of the party. Older leaders such as Alimin and Tan tried to return to their previous tactics, while younger ones such as the trade union boss Njono continued to pursue, whenever possible, the Muso-line by means of tough campaigns even after independence was granted.

A third group, including Aidit, left the country to wait for better times. The Soviet Union, seeing that its policy in Indonesia was a complete failure, withdrew its hand and froze its relations with communists and non-communists alike until, after Stalin's death, it began to break out of its state of cold war isolation. China, still playing only a marginal role in the area and intent on establishing contact with the many millions of overseas Chinese in Indonesia, extended full diplomatic recognition at an early stage and kept its relations with Djakarta on an even keel.

A new phase opened up with Aidit and his close collaborators taking over the leadership of the party in January 1951. At first his policy was announced as a return to what Muso had preached in the 'New Road' resolution, i.e., a left-radical line of isolation and opposition. This was no doubt partly inspired by the wish to display continuity and to present his new 'Leninist wing' as the executors of what the Party had decided in mid-August 1948 before disaster befell them. But the obvious disadvantages of Muso's policy as such must have been clear to Aidit at a very early stage of his tenure. Besides, whatever doubts about the need for a new approach he may have had, they certainly dissipated when the Sukiman cabinet began to retaliate against the continuing Sobsi-actions and threatened to do another 'Madiun' on the P.K.I.

A year after Aidit and his men took over the Politburo, at the National Conference of January 1952, he inaugurated what was in fact to be the policy to guide him and the Party until the '30 September movement', in October 1965, unhinged the whole framework within which the P.K.I. built its spectacularly successful rise to power and prominence. This policy was basically a 'right strategy' of accommodation and cooperation with a wide spectrum of political forces, trying to isolate, neutralize, and continously obliterate the most extreme opponents – whoever they were – while cooperating with all other forces. This policy took shape, in essence, in the period between 1952 and 1954 when the P.K.I., at its 5th Party Congress, formally adopted the Aidit line and dumped Muso's 'New Road' resolution. Officially, the party retained some enemies with whom no truck was to be had, such as the 'bourgeois compradores'. However, Aidit in fact showed he was prepared, as after the electoral success of 1955, to join with even these forces (in point of fact the muslim reformists of the Masjumi Party) a national coalition. Though claiming, certainly at an early stage, that the Party should 'lead the revolution', Aidit in practice settled for much less: Keeping the P.K.I. as much as possible free of outside interference.

Two other features of Aidit's emerging new line were: The Party would become a conglomerate of interlocking mass-scale organizations with the widest popular appeal, and, giving the organizational framework its emotional motivation, the Party would 'pick up the banner of national independence and national sovereignty', i.e. it would for both tactical reasons and out of genuine sentiment become fiercely nationalistic.

At an early stage Aidit would stress that 'each nation will travel its own road to socialism' and in this no doubt the traumatic experience of outside, Soviet communist interference leading to the Madiun affair played a prominent role. *At no time in the period under review – nor later as will be shown – would Aidit or his deputies allow anything remotely similar to what was done with the party through Muso: Imposition upon the P.K.I. by outside communist forces of a policy that would originate elsewhere and run counter to what they as national communist leaders perceived as the party's road to power in Indonesia.*

Seen in this perspective it is open to some speculation what Aidit would have done if by January 1952 Stalin had not slowly began to switch again to a more accommodating policy line but had remained adamant in his 'two camp' doctrine. Probably sooner or later his successors would have made the opening to the right, so at most Aidit and his colleagues – if they had been willing to pay heed to Moscow – might have begun their successful climb back to political relevance at a later date. But as it was, the P.K.I. leaders were spared this dilemma with the swing of the pendulum of international communism that had been set in motion in the course of 1951, at a time when, for domestic reasons, the Indonesian communists were in dire need of such a change.

Concrete issues came to be viewed by the party leadership, particularly by Aidit in the light of this (in communist terms) rather moderate, nationalistic, 'right' strategy, evolved since early 1952. In this way did the rapprochement with Sukarno begin, expressed in May 1952 by Alimin, who for internal party political reasons was never allowed to make a come-back but then must have felt vindicated in his pre-Muso views. Aidit's report of October 1953 to the Central Committee presented more points – such as the position of the P.K.I. members of Chinese descent and the question of who was Indonesia's enemy number one – reflecting preoccupation with nationalist sentiment.

More often than not these policies at the same time put Aidit in line with current thinking in Moscow, although corrections sometimes had to be made, as in the case of Kruschov's unqualified enthusiasm for the parliamentary road to power which emerged at the Soviet Party's 20th Party Congress in 1956. In a matter of great importance such as the destalinization that was injected into the debate within world communism by Kruschov's secret speech, outright criticism of the Soviet leadership was voiced. It may, in this instance, have helped Aidit that the Chinese comrades had already given vent to an opinion that diverged from the Moscow-led majority of communist parties, but what the P.K.I. leader had to say at this point on Stalin was all his own.

In issues removed from the P.K.I.'s direct interest (i.e., in the remaining 'foreign affairs' of the world communist movement – in fact, of the Soviet Union, until the rift with China was to break organizational unity) the Soviet lead was followed as a matter of course, even to the extent that relevant statements by Soviet leaders of the day were repeated literally. This 'free zone' was with time to shift and become increasingly restricted since the P.K.I. was to get more and more enmeshed in Indonesian politics and acquire a wider range of interests. A case in point was the new anti-Yugoslav campaign, following the 1957 Moscow Conference, with which Aidit fell in step but with a wary eye on booming Djakarta-Belgrade relations. Essentially, however, it was a situation still manageable within reason: A kind of 'triangular' tightrope dance, with Moscow and Djakarta providing the other pillars. The advent of Peking as a center of communist power in its own right was seen, however, as making it a conjuring trick for the P.K.I. to keep its balance while at the same time advancing towards final victory.

NOTES

1. Donald Hindley, 1964, *The Communist Party of Indonesia 1951-1963*, University of California Press, Berkeley, p. 31.
2. It has been noted that, for example, in the period 1950-1956 only two P.K.I. delegations went to Soviet bloc countries, while between 1956 and 1960 the number rose to 13. See Hindley 1964, p. 314, note 5.
3. *Pravda*, February 16, 1951; see also Arnold C. Brackman, 1963, *Indonesian Communism*, Frederick A. Praeger, New York, p. 167. The question of war and peace was among communists a good indicator of a right – or left – inclination, as the Sino-Soviet dispute was to show.
4. See above p. 19.
5. Brackman, 1963, p. 167.
6. Richard Allen, 1968, *Malaysia: Prospect and Retrospect*, Oxford University Press, New York-Kuala Lumpur, p. 98. Allen, however, sees as a cause of this change in tactics mainly the fact that the Malayan communists began to realize that a military victory was not on the cards.
7. It was Vassilev Outchav, a correspondent of the Soviet news agency Tass who 'rarely attended news conferences', as Brackman noted; Brackman, 1963, p. 172.
8. See above p. 20.
9. D. N. Aidit, 1959, *Complete Works*. Vol. I, p. 42, as translated by the Joint Publications Research Service, Washington D.C.
10. Aidit, 1959, p. 46.
11. *Tass*, July 22, 1953, and also Brackman, 1963, p. 188. See also above p. 11.
12. *Radio Moscow in English*, July 24, 1953.
13. See above p. 21.
14. Brackman, 1963, p. 202. Siauw Giok Tjan appeared on the scene a year later as leader of what was to become a powerful pro-P.K.I. pressure group for the interests of Indonesians of Chinese descent, the Baperki. This organization catered particularly to the urban, intellectual Chinese Indonesians and formed a link between the P.K.I., the overseas Chinese fund-raising bureau under Chou En-lai in Peking, and its members in Indonesia. It is not unlikely that it also served as fund-raising center for the P.K.I. Its political stance within the Indonesian context was not necessarily to be defined as leftist, although it found itself more often than not in league with the P.K.I. Also: Ruth T. McVey, Indonesian Communism and China. In Tang Tsou, Ed., 1968, *China in Crisis*, vol. 2, University of Chicago Press, 362, 363.
15. When Tan lost his seat in the Central Committee, Alimin was eliminated from the Politburo, indicating that this demise of Tan was, possibly, mainly part of a purge of pre-Aidit P.K.I. leaders. As to the arguments used, Tan was said to have relied too much upon the idea of an elite party, also using parliamentary means to gain influence. This accusation could hardly be called valid in view of the persistent pursuit of parliamentary power by Aidit himself until the road was blocked by the combined action of Sukarno and the

military, see above p. 27. Tan and his associates were also accused of having shown too little appreciation of the historic role the P.K.I. in the national awaking. McVey, 1968, p. 361, concludes therefore that 'a leadership of this temperament [Aidit's] might, even though it did not itself entertain anti-Sinic feelings, find it embarassing to have Indonesians of Chinese extraction occupying leading positions in the Party'.

16. Aidit, 1959, p. 146. Political report to the 4th Party Congress entitled The Road to a People's Democracy for Indonesia, as translated by the Joint Publications Research Service, Washington.
17. Aidit, 1959, p. 146 ff. and also Brackman, 1963, p. 204. See also: Aidit, 1959, p. 291, Birth and growth of the P.K.I., and Aidit, 1960, p. 162, Indonesian society and the Indonesian Revolution.
18. Aidit, 1960, p. 165: 'The main enemy of the Indonesian people from the viewpoint of the extent of its domination in various spheres, particularly in the economic sphere, is Dutch imperialism. In the first place the aim of this (united national) front must be the expulsion of the Dutch imperialists and their armed forces from Indonesia . . . But in the event of American and other imperialists giving armed support to the Dutch colonizers and their Indonesian hirelings, *then* the struggle must be directed against all imperialism in Indonesia' [emphasis added].
19. *Pravda*, November 14, 1953. See also McVey, 1968, p. 369. It seems incorrect to see this P.K.I. standpoint as a deviation from the line Moscow preferred then, as Brackman, 1963, p. 210, thinks. It is equally open to doubt that, as McVey points out, it should be seen as establishing an early claim to an independent line by the Aidit leadership, as other similar signs had been given prior to this.
20. Brackman, 1963, p. 203, suggests that there existed at the time a 'Moscow' faction headed by Aidit and a 'Peking' faction including Lukman and Sudisman. This is possible, although it seems that Lukman, in general, faithfully following Aidit, is rather to be included in the 'Moscow' faction. This would also tie in with the fact that only the question of priority for the peasants – always dear to Sudisman – was treated by Aidit in a way that would suggest that he had met with some real resistance from other P.K.I. leaders.
21. See above, p. 32.
22. Aidit, 1959, p. 149 and Brackman, 1939, p. 210. See also G. D. Embree, 1959, *The Soviet Union between the 19th and 20th Party Congresses 1952-1956*, Martinus Nijhoff, The Hague, p. 77. According to Embree Malenkov's speech 'was not belligerent and did not contain the clichés that had been typical of the worst phases of the cold war'.
23. Donald S. Zagoria, 1962, *The Sino-Soviet Conflict 1956-1961*, Princeton University Press, Princeton, pp. 39, 42, referring to a secret Chinese letter to the Soviet Communist Party dated September 10, 1960.
24. Aidit, 1960, p. 6.
25. Aidit, 1960, p. 14. On June 4, 1956 the American State Department gave a version as it supposedly had been prepared for one foreign communist party;

see Bertram D. Wolfe, 1959, *Khruschov and Stalin's Ghost*, Atlantic Press, London, p. 81. In his June report Aidit said in passing: 'the bourgeois press was very active in mentioning only the errors of Comrade Stalin'.

26. *Pravda*, February 11, 1956.
27. Aidit, 1960, p. 11.
28. Aidit, 1960, p. 13. In his report to the 20th Party Congress Kruschov had shown a new enthusiasm for the parliamentary road to power for communists the world over and is said to have been inspired in this in particular by the spectacular successes of the P.K.I. at two elections in the previous year, 1955. See above p. 22.
29. Aidit, 1960, p. 12.
30. See above p. 44, note 15. Also Aidit, 1959, p. 187: 'The attention and energy of the Party's central leadership were [under Tan], devoted excessively to parliamentary struggle' the charge runs.
31. It should be noted that what Kruschov introduced was not novel in Soviet history; see Wolfe, 1957, p. 55: Zagoria, 1962, p. 231, describes Kruschov's view on the use of parliament for Communists thus: 'He (Kruschov) did not exclude the possibility of violence, but his emphasis was on new elements in the international balance of power'.
32. *Jen-min Jih-pao*, April 5, 1956. See also Zagoria, 1962, p. 43.
33. Zagoria, 1962, p. 48.
34. Aidit, 1960, p. 14.
35. Palmiro Togliatti, 9 Demande sulle Stalinismo, *Nuevo Argomenti*, 20, June 16, 1956.
36. Aidit, 1960, p. 13.
37. On January 7, 1951, it was announced that the new Politburo consisted of Aidit, Lukman, Njoto, Sudisman and Alimin. In October 1953 Alimin was removed from the Politburo and replaced by Sakirman. From then on the core of the P.K.I. leadership consisted of Aidit, who had become Secretary-General and later Chairman, and his two deputies Lukman and Njoto, with Sudisman and Sakirman on the sidelines.
38. Aidit, 1960, p. 14.
39. Justus van der Kroef, 1965, *The Communist Party of Indonesia, Its History, Programme and Tactics*, University of British Columbia, Vancouver, p. 85, is of the opinion that 'destalinisation was to be only very mildly echoed by the P.K.I. leadership'. Brackman, 1963, p. 229, writes that 'on destalinisation Aidit interestingly assumed the position later adopted by Peking: Stalin committed excesses, but the man and not the system of democratic centralism was at fault'. As is shown it was Aidit who followed the Chinese but only partly and with his own emphasis and – what is more – criticism.
40. McVey, 1968, p. 370, says: '... when the Chinese declared their criticism of the Soviet handling of the matter [i.e. Stalin] following the congress, the P.K.I. endorsed their stand'. This is a somewhat simplified rendering, as Aidit did more than endorse the Chinese. The question of prior discussion of matters that affected the international communist movement, contrary to

McVey's account, was not brought up by the P.K.I. in 1956 but later in the ensuing Sino-Soviet debate on who could speak for the movement.

41. According to P.K.I. sources at the end of 1956 the Soviet Union granted 100 million dollar credits to Indonesia, to be repaid in 12 years at 2.5% interest and designed to pay for five mining projects; see Aidit, 1960, p. 400, note 3.
42. See Uri Ra'anan, 1969, *The U.S.S.R. arms the Third World*, M.I.T. Press, Cambridge, Massachusetts, p. 187 ff. Ra'anan describes the text of the loan agreement as 'unusually vague' and notes that two and a half years passed before a more detailed protocol for the use of the loan was signed. On the basis of evidence found, Ra'anan concludes that Indonesia's military relationship with the Soviet Union dates from the autumn of 1956 rather than the spring of 1958, as is generally assumed. Domestic political opposition in Indonesia may have necessitated prolonged secrecy.
43. Aidit, 1960, p. 127, Change the balance of power in order to implement President Sukarno's concept completely. Also Ra'anan, 1969, p. 214.
44. Zagoria, 1962, p. 148.
45. Aidit, 1960, p. 226, The October Revolution and the peoples of the East.
46. Brackman, 1963, p. 261.
47. Aidit, 1960, p. 366, The new phase and the adaptation of the organization to the situation.
48. Ra'anan, 1969, pp. 214, 215.
49. This was in early October 1957, on the occasion of former Vice-President Hatta's visit to China; *New China News Agency*, October 2, 1957.
50. See above p. 25 and also Ra'anan, 1969, p. 194.
51. In the middle of March 1958, ten Soviet ships arrived to replace the Dutch-owned K.P.M. vessels used until the end of 1957 but put out of commission by actions against Dutch interests. These Soviet ships were, contrary to the original loan agreement, financed through the 100 million dollar credit extended in November 1956; see above p. 37 and Ra'anan, 1969, p. 195. They must have carried weapons at the same time, since shortly after the arrival of the ships, arms originating from communist bloc countries appeared in Indonesia. Early in May the first Mig-16 Czechoslovak-made jet trainers arrived, a fact which, together with the other arms deliveries from Eastern Europe, induced the Americans to drop their ambiguous attitude in the civil war and to ease the arms embargo against Indonesia.

    China had offered some weapons early in 1957, probably reacting to similar moves made earlier in the Soviet Union. An Indonesian military mission which went to negotiate on this had to leave China in June 1957 emptyhanded, possibly because at that time Peking had changed its mind and did not want it to look as if it were undercutting Soviet efforts in South East Asia; see Zagoria, 1962, p. 70. Rumors about new Chinese offers of weapons began to circulate in the autumn of 1957, when this kind of inhibition may have counted for less because of the more radical mood left-swing of the pendulum in China; see above p. 26.

52. Aidit, 1960, p. 335.
53. On April 19 the Soviet Union voiced its criticsm of the new draft of the Yugoslav Party Program that was to be adopted at the coming Party Congress in Belgrade. On May 5 the Chinese went into this much further than the Russians and even hinted that the Yugoslavs were in the pay of the imperialists, reviving the old anti-Tito charges of the Cominform resolutions of 1949; see Zagoria, 1962, p. 180.
54. The Indonesian Communist Party daily, *Harian Rakjat*, writing on June 23, three days before Aidit spoke in Prague, followed Kruschov and was much more violent in its criticism of the Yugoslavs than the P.K.I. leader.
55. This must have been considered a 'gaffe' by the other communist parties, as none of them including the Soviet C.P. had sent a representative to Belgrade. And it may have been decided by Moscow at so late an hour that it did not reach Njoto in time for him to change his itinerary. Aidit explained that the P.K.I. had first accepted the invitation to send a representative, had then received the draft program and subsequently changed the status of Njoto to that of an 'observer'. See Aidit, 1960, p. 336, Ra'anan, 1969, p. 220 and Zagoria, 1962, p. 179.
56. See Ra'anan, 1969, p. 219.
57. Brackman, 1963, p. 254.
58. Aidit, 1960, p. 36, Join in taking the path of Guided Democracy.
59. After Kruschov had left, the Chinese communists at the end of August 1958 started to shell offshore Quemoy island that was still held by the Nationalists. This suited the new radical policy of Peking and was as much a challenge to Moscow as to Washington.
60. Peking at that time whipped up anti-Yugoslav sentiment, blaming 'Yugoslav revisionists' for their stand in the Quemoy affair, while in fact it was Kruschov who was aimed at but could not be attacked directly for what the Chinese communists thought his weak support for their claim on Quemoy. See also Ra'anan, 1969, p. 220.
61. See below p. 268.
62. The Indonesian government had failed to send a delegation to the Afro-Asian Youth Conference in Cairo, and Aidit blamed this on those circles in Djakarta which disapproved of Soviet participation in the conference on the grounds that the Soviet Union was not an Asiatic nation.

CHAPTER 5

Peking and the overseas Chinese (1959-1960)

In the course of 1959 Indonesia and China became involved in a serious diplomatic conflict. It was about the millions of overseas Chinese, mostly small traders and craftsmen, who for the greater part had been born in Indonesia but generally retained sufficient foreign characteristics to set them apart from the rest of the population. Anti-Chinese sentiment, never far from the surface of Indonesian life, had been activated by the government's deliberate attack upon the very vital position the overseas Chinese occupied in Indonesian economic life.[1] This dispute was a problem to the P.K.I. since the Indonesian communists could not ignore the nationalist appeal in the anti-Chinese campaign, while on the other hand they did not want to rebuff their friends in Peking.

The main thrust of the action began in May 1959, when the Minister of Trade, Muljomiseno, himself a merchant, ordered cancellation, as of January 1, 1960, of all retail licenses for rural areas in Indonesia. As 90% of these were held by Indonesians of Chinese descent the point made was clear to all.

At the beginning of June a set of regulations on dual nationality were promulgated, as if the Sino-Indonesian treaty on this subject were already valid.[2] Sukarno contributed to the growing antagonism in his speech of August 17, 1959, in which he launched his famous 'Manipol', the political manifesto that was to become a kind of ten commandments of the Indonesian revolution. According to the Indonesian President, all forces and funds that were provenly 'progressive' were to be used for the development of the country. To the extent that these were 'non-national' in origin, they were given the 'opportunity' to be channeled into medium-scale industry, supposedly because they would be more productive.[3] A few days later rupiah notes of 500 and over were reduced to 10% of their value. This again victimised the Chinese-Indonesians, who were in the habit of keeping these notes rather than putting them in the bank. Finally, on August 28, the Army, which since the early days of the struggle for independence had been anti-Chinese,[4] filled in the picture by imposing a ban on the residence of foreigners in West Java.

For the Chinese government all this was a reason for further postponing the exchange of the instruments of ratification of the Treaty of Dual Nationality that Chou En-Lai had concluded in 1955 with the Indonesian government. Ironically enough the discrimination against the rural overseas Chinese was partly due to the activities of over-zealous men in Peking. In 1958 the first attacks on Chinese in Indonesia were directed especially against those who were oriented towards the Chiang Kai-shek régime on Taiwan and were therefore suspected of aiding rebel forces in Sumatra and Sulawesi.[5] They had to register prior to deportation in the event of their acting against the central government in Djakarta. Other measures against these Kwo-Min-Tang Chinese followed, and, by October 1958, the organized part of the K.M.T. group among the Indonesian Chinese were for all practical purposes, eliminated.[6] An important factor in this respect was the Chinese ambassador in Djakarta, Huang Cheng-nan who upon return from Peking at the beginning of 1958 became one of the main forces behind the campaign against Taiwan Chinese.[7] He did so as a result of the shift in Chinese foreign policy that had been inaugurated in the autumn of 1957,[8] designed to achieve a more radical posture.[9] It was the Nationalist Chinese régime and its American sponsors that became the butt of attacks from Peking, and any support was welcome. To seek these supporters in Indonesia, however, was a risky affair because many of the military authorities engaged in breaking up the K.M.T. organizations saw it simply as a prelude to a general action against all other Chinese in the country. In the course of 1959 this began to dawn upon the officials of the Chinese embassy, as was reported at the time.[10] The Chinese tradesmen in the countryside who would be hit by the measures of Muljomiseno and others were mostly inclined to turn to Peking for support if they were unable to remain neutral, while the urban, educated and well-to-do Chinese in the towns were accustomed to sympathize with the Taiwan régime. The measures initiated in 1959, therefore, looked like hitting the People's Republic of China and its image among millions of its nationals in Indonesia.

Meanwhile the P.K.I. cautiously watched developments. Aidit, speaking before Radio Peking in March 1959, uttered only generalities on Indonesian-Chinese relations.[11] He refrained from mentioning even the Taiwan Chinese in Indonesia while all along, during the previous year, the communist-controlled press in the country had harped upon the need to take action against 'K.M.T.-subversion'.[12] The strong measures taken or announced against all Chinese Indonesians then brought to light the dilemma in which the P.K.I. with growing embarrassment found itself. Aidit and his followers were aware of substantial popular support for the anti-Chinese measures, and they were in no position to antagonize the political forces behind them, the Army[13] and to a lesser degree President Sukarno.[14] On the other hand Peking was outraged at the attitude of the Indonesian government and, amongst comrades, had to be spared. At the same time the local Chinese were an important source of funds to the P.K.I. treasury and showed signs of hedging.[15] In a declaration on Sino-Indonesian friendship, on the occasion of the 10th anniversary of the Chinese People's Republic in October 1959, the P.K.I. formulated its compromise position. It spoke of 'misguided and dangerous chauvinism and radicalism against foreigners of Chinese origin'. To nobody's surprise it was alleged that this was inspired by the U.S.A. and by a group of jealous Indonesian businessmen surrounding a Mr. Assaad who, moreover, had meanwhile gone over to the rebels. The blame was further cast on 'a small circle of the upper strata of the Indonesian bourgeoisie who, whether because of bribery or because of naivety and stupidity, can apparently still become prey to these instigations of the United States imperialists'.[16] Distinguishing Sukarno from 'certain Indonesians' who were trying to disturb friendly relations with the People's Republic of China, the P.K.I. avoided being specific about the impending ban on Chinese retail traders and other official measures.

It was at that moment, when the conflict was 'at its hottest',[17] that the Indonesian Foreign Minister, Dr. Subandrio, visited Peking to 'clarify' the position taken up by his government.

This has been described as a 'last-minute attempt' to prevent a further aggravation of the situation, but the Chinese leaders in Peking remained determined to show that overseas Chinese could count on 'protection' from the motherland.[18] The communiqué issued at the end of the visit reflected the strains in the relations between the two countries. It lamely stated that 'both the foreign ministers take cognizance of the fact that, in the process of economic development and stability in Indonesia, the economic position of the Chinese nationals residing there may be affected in some ways'.[19] A solution acceptable to both Indonesian and the Chinese nationals should be sought, it said further. According to reports in the Indonesian press, Subandrio had been subjected by his Chinese hosts to discourteous treatment. He was roused from his bed at two o'clock at night to see Chou En-lai and met with 'a most arrogant attitude'.[20] The visit marked Sino-Indonesian relations at their lowest ebb.

The communist daily, *Harian Rakjat*, however saw enough in the communiqué to comment that it was 'sufficiently satisfactory to both sides' and expressed the hope that it would open the way to a negotiated settlement of the 'unnecessary' tensions between China and Indonesia.[21]

Sometimes later, early in November, things came to a head when President Sukarno stepped in and formulated Governmental Decree no. 10 on the retail traders ban. The day before, on November 2, *Harian Rakjat*, sensing what was to come, sharpened its criticism of 'reactionary circles' who were 'spreading incitements against Chinese residents in Indonesia and against the Chinese People's Republic'.[22] It gave a warning that the anti-Chinese measures might result in economic disorders and were therefore to be condemned as 'anti-Indonesian'. It pointed out that anti-Chinese sentiment could easily degenerate into anti-capitalist action, a development, which could be accelerated without difficulty, the editorial stated, considering the real strength of the 'progressive forces' – i.e. the P.K.I. and its allied organizations. Aidit, at this stage in the debate, introduced the notion that the Indonesian government was fighting 'cats' (the Chinse retail traders) because it was afraid to fight 'tigers' meaning the Western oil companies.

The army under the territorial commander Major-General Kosasih had meanwhile begun to put into rather drastic effect the residence ban on foreigners in West Java ordered at the end of August. It meant in practice the forced displacement of many Chinese who for years had been living in the area, and it led the Chinese embassy to encourage its nationals to put up resistance. Several incidents occurred, some entailing bloodshed, and this in turn led to a diplomatic altercation when the Indonesian Foreign Minister met the Chinese ambassador Huang Cheng-nan on November 17 to discuss the situation. There was name-calling in subsequent lengthy press releases culminating in the Indonesian accusation that things would not have gotten out of hand if only the Chinese embassy had refrained from telling the overseas Chinese to disobey the Indonesian government.[23]

After the text of Sukarno's Decree no. 10 had been published *Harian Rakjat* gave an initial reaction. It made the best of a bad case and noted with approval that foreigners affected by the ban would not have to leave their homes, also noting in passing, however, that the Army could easily circumvent this clause since the Decree allowed for removal if the military regarded this as necessary 'in the interests of security'.[24] In addition, the paper concluded, the ban for good reasons was not to be implemented until provision had been made for the transfer of business activities to industrial enterprises. But this would clearly be a dead letter.

Two days later an official P.K.I. statement confirmed this *Harian Rakjat* article, but this time criticized Sukarno by implication. It said that Decree no. 10 'is in the main not altogether in line with the spirit of the political manifesto of Sukarno and of the Subandrio-Chen Yi joint communiqué'.[25] This statement was reprinted in full by *Jenmin Jih-pao* a few days later, which showed that it had the complete approval of the Chinese communist authorities.[26] The day after the P.K.I. statement was published, Njoto, the hard-line second deputy-chairman of the Party, again warned against the economic disruption that would be the result of the ban, and, as a clear sign that the P.K.I. was displeased with Sukarno's rule, Njoto even tried to reinforce his point by quoting a Sukarno antagonist, the anti-communist former President of the Republic Hatta, who had made the same point.[27]

At roughly this juncture, however, there must have been a change, resulting in the Chinese government concluding that it was preferable to ease tense relations with Indonesia. While still loudly proclaiming that 'it was a grave error to make it appear that the overseas Chinese cannot count on the support of the government of the People's Republic of China', Peking in fact began to move towards a negotiated solution.[28] The first sign of this was a letter written by the Chinese

Foreign Minister, Chen Yi, to his Indonesian colleague Minister Subandrio, on December 9, 1959. It restated the principle of the Sino-Indonesian Dual Nationality Treaty of 1955 to the effect that the Chinese in Indonesia should not have two nationalities but should opt for Indonesian citizenship.[29] Even more important, it gave notice of willingness to finalize this treaty and to exchange instruments of ratification at short notice. It further said that the Chinese who wanted to return to China would be assisted while, for those who preferred to stay, proper protection was demanded of the Indonesian government. The whole tone of the letter, as well as its conciliatory proposals, marked an inclination to accommodate Indonesia.[30] When on January 20, 1960, the Dual Nationality Treaty was completed, Chen Yi seized the occasion to observe laconically that 'the Chinese government has always believed that the holding of dual nationality by overseas Chinese is irrational'.[31]

When one inquires into the reasons for the change of attitude of the Chinese government, it must first of all be noted that there was an official endorsement of the Indonesian measures, be it in a somewhat diluted form, by President Sukarno.

This must have opened Peking's eyes to the realities of Indonesia's political life and made Chinese leaders realize that anti-Chinese actions were not the relatively harmless antics of local military commanders but nationwide government policy.[32] This may have prompted the search for a way out of the rut into which Sino-Indonesian relations had sunk,[33] but there was more to it than that. Smouldering Sino-Soviet differences on strategy and tactics for the international communist movement had, at least according to Chinese interpretations afterwards, moved into the open in September 1959.[34] Moscow then took the unprecedented step of remaining neutral in a conflict between a communist country, China, and a non-communist country, India, over its mountainous border area. This fitted in with Kruschov's foreign policy reorientation which in 1959 had come to be dominated by two tendencies: A direct rapprochement with the United States and closer relations with India and Indonesia.[35] China realized that it was running a growing risk of becoming isolated from Moscow and the communist countries in Eastern Europe, as well as from its Asian neighbors. In their turn the Chinese leaders therefore began 'to mend some of their national quarrels with the neutral Asian states, notably

Birma, Nepal and Indonesia, and to lower the temperature of their conflict with India'.[36] In this respect differences in China's attitude to India, as compared to Indonesia, have been noted elsewhere. The criticism levelled by the Chinese government at Indonesia had always been specific and remained so, while India was clearly condemned regularly in general terms as 'reactionary' etc.[37] The nature of the disputes may also have contributed to difference in treatment, once Peking had decided to go easy on its Asian neighbors. The border dispute with India was to the Chinese no doubt of a more vital character than the problems around overseas Chinese in Indonesia, or at least it was easier to give that impression. Certainly, Peking may also have felt more vulnerable in the ensuing conflict with the Soviet leadership in defending 'the interests of small private enterprise which in China it was doing its utmost to destroy'.[38] It was generally recognized that China was 'sticking to something uncommunistic',[39] and, in a somewhat circumlocutory way, Subandrio made the allusion to Peking that it should 'prevent the Indonesian people from receiving the incorrect impression, that the Chinese people were giving protection to a group of capitalists and monopolists'.[40] Finally, China may have come to the conclusion that, in comparison with the situation on the Indian border, it had very little to make its arguments stick in the case of the overseas Chinese in Indonesia.

The extent to which the Chinese leaders had their eyes on the evolving differences with Moscow while mending their fences in South East Asia was also reflected in the speech made by the Chinese observer at the Warsaw Pact meeting in early February.[41] Kang Sheng, an alternate member of the Chinese Politburo, referred to 'small patches of dark clouds' that temporarily overshadowed China's relations with some nationalist Asian countries. He quoted the exchange of instruments of ratification of the 1955 Sino-Indonesian Treaty after which talks had started on the return of overseas Chinese. But he foresaw – rightly, as it turned out – that 'overall settlement of the overseas Chinese question still needs a certain period of time and may still go through some ups and downs'. In the final analysis he was confident, however, that everything would be solved 'justly and reasonably'. Also the Sino-Birmese border arrangement of the previous month was presented in this light, leading Kang Sheng to conclude that 'these facts give the lie to the slanders of the imperialists and all reactionaries about

China's aggression'.[42] It is not too far-fetched to conceive that to Peking these 'reactionaries' were also to be found in Moscow.

Indeed, as Kang Sheng had predicted, some 'ups and downs' had to be overcome, and the situation regarding the overseas Chinese in Indonesia was to get worse before getting better, although a mixed Sino-Indonesian committee had started to negotiate details of the implementation of the Dual Nationality Treaty. Chinese businessmen were arrested, Chinese newspapers were deprived of newsprint, and there were numerous incidents.[43] Early in April the deputy-leader of the overseas Chinese commission in China, Fang-Fang gave a speech in which he explained the anti-Chinese attitude in Indonesia – as the P.K.I. had done before – as a return to the cold war, inspired by the United States.[44] The Indonesian government lodged an official complaint, and a few days later the rightist newspaper *Times of Indonesia* openly stated that, after the Fang-Fang speech, it was no longer necessary to behave politely to China or maintain diplomatic relations.[45]

In this atmosphere of racial antagonism and ultra-nationalist sentiment, two further incidents took place on April 27, one involving the departure of a ship with overseas Chinese going back to China from the Riao archipelago, the other concerning the house arrest given the Chinese Consul in East Kalimantan.[46] These developments led the official Chinese press agency to charge that 'it is obvious that certain people have been purposely engineering incidents, poisoning the atmosphere . . .'.[47]

Small wonder the P.K.I. felt constrained to produce a clarification of its position in the midst of this turmoil. In a statement May 4 the Politburo 'in view of the continuing slander campaign against the P.K.I.' explained its views.[48] In contrast to its previous policy statement of November 22, 1959, it no longer stuck up for the rights of the People's Republic of China 'to ask for protection of the proper rights of its citizens in Indonesia'.[49] It concentrated instead on the citizenship question stressing that all Indonesian citizens should be equal before the law. The fate of those who wanted to remain Chinese but preferred to stay in Indonesia was therefore ignored. Basically, the P.K.I. supported the new position of the Chinese government which, through negotiation, tried to squeeze as many overseas Chinese automatically into Indonesian nationality as it could.[50] The Politburo, however, avoided polemics or a formulation that could be interpreted as pro-

Chinese. Coming out strongly in favor of democratic rights and against discriminatory measures – in itself a safe and just procedure – it even apportioned some criticism to the overseas Chinese and indirectly to the Chinese government. It spoke of 'the lack of conscious reaction to these discriminatory measures both from the group concerned [the overseas Chinese] and from society in general'.[51] One of these reactions had been the desire of some Chinese to give up and return to mainland China, 'together with persons who had been forced to take this course, because they lost their means of livelihood as a result of the Government Decree no. 10'.

It can hardly have escaped Politburo members that most of this category of Chinese who returned voluntarily – like many workers in the Banka tin mines – had done so on the advice of Chinese diplomats who were bent on disrupting the Indonesian economy as a retaliation against anti-Chinese measures.[52]

In this second phase of the conflict with China the P.K.I. supported Peking's case less wholeheartedly than before.[53] A reflection of this was to be found in the way the P.K.I. reported an exchange of letters between Chen Yi and Subandrio in mid-March. In the official P.K.I. *Review of Indonesia* a summarized version was given of the letter of the Chinese Foreign Minister of March 15.[54] What the Indonesian editors omitted was, as usual, at least as interesting as what was printed. Absent, for example, was the phrase about the positive role the overseas Chinese had played in the economic development of Indonesia, as well as the reference to a request to permit the dismissed Chinese 'workers' to take back all their wages. The first passage was probably considered unpalatable to Indonesian readership, while the second point was most likely considered as meant clearly for Chinese home consumption only.[55] The *Review* also quoted Subandrio's reply of March 26, especially that part of it which stressed that 'both sides should suppress unfavorable reactions in their respective communities'.[56] This remark of Subandrio's had been a reference to the radio war raging between the two countries, but especially of course – seen from Djakarta – to the Peking side of it. The editors of the *Review* must of course have been aware of this aspect, as other colleagues in Indonesia were.[57]

Another sign that Aidit and his Chinese friends did not quite see eye to eye in this period came with the fifth anniversary of the Bandung conference of April 1955. A P.K.I. statement accused the 'American imperialists' of trying to destroy the unity between the Afro-Asian and the communist countries forged by the Bandung meeting. In this wrecking operation, the argumentation ran, they had been aided by the 'modern revisionists'. At the time that meant mainly the Yugoslavs 'who by spreading the tale that the Soviet Union is just as imperialist as the U.S.A. are trying to drag the Asian-African states, in particular India, Egypt and Indonesia into a third bloc'.[58] This was a view similar to that given by Aidit in response to the renewed anti-Belgrade campaign after the 1957 Moscow Conference.[59]

Although the publication at that point of time contained a note of irony, because just then Sukarno was celebrating his continuing special friendship with Yugoslavia's Tito, the observation bore basically a routine pro-Soviet connotation. To the Chinese the Bandung memory had quite a different ring, as Chinese Politburo member Kuo Mo-jo made clear when he complained on the occasion about the 'disruption of friendship between *China* and some Asian and African countries'. Behind this policy Kuo Mo-jo saw the Americans who, 'mustering a handful of reactionary forces . . . have repeatedly stirred up waves of anti-Chinese sentiment and done their utmost to sabotage the spirit of Bandung'.[60] This was manifestly a reference to the prevailing sorry state of Sino-Indonesian relations, so blatantly glossed over in the P.K.I. statement.

This relatively cool period in relations between the P.K.I. and Peking early in 1960 may have been inspired by a growing awareness that Chinese reaction to the overseas Chinese question remained inadequate and without sufficient regard for Indonesian nationalist feeling. On the other hand the Chinese government, since the end of 1959, had gone some way to accommodate Djakarta. It is therefore possible that other influences were at work. One might not be far wrong in assuming that the visit Soviet premier Nikita Kruschov paid to Indonesia at the end of February 1960 had something to do with it.[61] It was thought at the time that Kruschov might use his prestige to mediate in the Sino-Indonesian conflict,[62] or even that Aidit had met the Soviet leader secretly in Hungary in December 1959 to ask him to do so.[63] But as things were, both sides in the affair would have been antagonized if Kruschov had produced something of his own. Officially, therefore, he kept silent on the subject during his stay. However, he was reported in private to have been with the Indonesian government, saying that Peking had no Soviet backing for its militant attitude and that Indonesia had the right to treat its overseas Chinese in any way it chose. The Indonesian President 'should not be worried by Chinese blustering', he counseled.[64] So in the wake of the Kruschov visit the P.K.I., trimming its sails to an opinion shared by both the Soviet Prime Minister and the Indonesian President, must have felt less inclined than before to lean over backwards to the Chinese side in its quarrel with the Djakarta government. It was anyhow a temporary matter. In the course of 1960, for various reasons, the Indonesians decided to patch up their quarrel with Peking so that, to the relief of the P.K.I., the overseas Chinese as a stumbling block in their relations with the Chinese comrades was relegated to the background.[65]

NOTES

1. Approximately 75% of the national distribution system was in their hands, while in some spheres, such as gold, money-lending, dried fish, etc., they virtually possessed a monopoly. See *Far Eastern Economic Review*, Hongkong, April 19, 1962, p. 27.
2. During the first Bandung conference of Afro-Asian countries in 1955, the Chinese and Indonesian governments concluded a Treaty on Dual Nationality in order to resolve the problem of the millions of Chinese in Indonesia, born there or immigrated, whose status was uncertain, and who therefore were subject to political pressure.
3. Wolfgang Bartke, *China Dokumentation*, p. 3.
4. See D. P. Mozingo, 1965, *Sino-Indonesian Relations: A Survey, 1955-1965*, Rand Corporation, Santa Monica, p. 22, note 19.
5. *Kung-sheung Jih-pao*, Hongkong, April 7, 1958. On May 18, 1958 the American pilot Allan Pope was shot down over Ambon. His papers showed that he used to operate out of Taiwan; see Arnold C. Brackman, 1963, *Indonesian Communism*, Frederick A. Praeger, New York, p. 250. There were also accusations on other grounds that Taiwan was helping the rebels and loyalty towards Chiang Kai-shek was therefore becoming a serious liability.
6. Mozingo, 1965, pp. 19, 20.
7. *Kung-sheung Jih-pao*, Hongkong, November 25, 1958: 'Earlier in this year, after Communist Chinese Ambassador Huang Cheng returned from the mainland to Indonesia, he cooperated increasingly with the Indonesian government in suppressing anti-Communist Chinese'.
8. See above p. 37.
9. Donald S. Zagoria, 1962, *The Sino-Soviet Conflict 1956-1961*, Princeton Uni-

versity Press, Princeton, p. 150: 'This new foreign policy called for maximum political and military pressure on the West all over the globe, but particularly in Asia, in the underdeveloped areas in general and wherever the bloc had just grievances as in Taiwan'.

10. *Far Eastern Economic Review*, September 10, 1959, p. 390: One of the officials of the Chinese People's Republic in Djakarta was quoted as remarking to an Indonesian: 'All right, hit the Kuo-Min-Tang institutions, but let us determine where Kuo-Min-Tang starts and ends'.
11. *Review of Indonesia*, May 4, 1959, p. 8. Also: R. S. Karni, manuscript on P.K.I. brochures, p. 14.
12. *Bintang Timur*, March 25, 1958; *Harian Rakjat*, May 5, 1958.
13. On August 13, 1959, for example, the Army ordered that the P.K.I.'s 6th Congress be cancelled, and it was only thanks to Sukarno's personal intervention that it was finally convened on September 7. A condition was, however, that army stenographers would record the proceedings. See Brackman, 1963, p. 265.
14. Since early in July, when Sukarno introduced the 1945 Constitution by decree, the P.K.I. had become an outside partner to Sukarno's 'Guided Democracy' and increasingly began to consider the President as a 'middle force' to be coaxed, influenced and taken into consideration; see above pp. 25, 27.
15. Harold C. Hinton, 1966, *Communist China in World Politics*, Houghton Mifflin Company, Boston, p. 407. Hinton writes that in 1959 the remittances of overseas Chinese in South East Asia to China drastically dropped from an average of 30 million dollars a year to 17 million dollars and explains this partly as a reaction to the harsh treatment meted out to overseas Chinese, who had returned and who were frequently sent to live in people's communes. This reaction no doubt also adversely affected P.K.I. revenue from Chinese Indonesians, generally assumed to have contributed heavily to the otherwise rather meagre funds of the Party. See also: Donald Hindley, 1964, *The Communist Party of Indonesia*, University of California, Berkeley, p. 117.
16. *Review of Indonesia*, political quarterly of the P.K.I., October 1959, p. 5.
17. Interview with Mr. Suwito Kusumowidagdo, ex-deputy foreign minister of Indonesia, March 1972.
18. Mozingo, 1965, p. 24.
19. *Jen-min Jih-pao*, October 12, 1959.
20. *Times of Indonesia*, November 18, 1959 and interview with the former spokesman of the Indonesian foreign ministry, Ganis Harsono, March 1972. This undiplomatic behavior seemed to have been one way of impressing upon Subandrio the might of the Chinese People's Republic.
21. *Harian Rakjat*, October 13, 1959.
22. *Harian Rakjat*, November 2, 1959.
23. *Radio Djakarta Home Service*, November 18, 1959. The same day Sukarno was called upon by Huang Cheng-nan to intervene, on which occasion the Chinese diplomat was informed that Government Regulation no. 10 had come

into force two days earlier.

24. *Harian Rakjat,* November 20, 1959.
25. *Harian Rakjat,* November 22, 1959.
26. *Jen-min Jih-pao,* November 1959. See also p. 50, note 4.
27. *Far Eastern Economic Review,* December 24, 1959, p. 197. Njoto who was to develop into an advocate of Chinese policies within the P.K.I. had gone to China at the head of a P.K.I. delegation for the celebration of the tenth anniversary of the Chinese People's Republic on October 1, 1959, and stayed in Peking for five weeks. No doubt this was useful for coordinating the various points of view in the ensuing November phase of the Sino-Indonesian crisis. See also *Far Eastern Economic Review,* December 24, 1959, p. 1018.
28. The quote is actually from an editorial in *Jen-min Jih-pao* of December 12, 1959, the day after the publication of the letter of Chen Yi to Subandrio of December 9, 1959, that constituted an initial reversal of the Chinese stand and was, no doubt, an occasion for being vociferous.
29. This had been a major concession by the Chinese in 1955 as it constituted a digression from their time-honored principle that a born Chinese would always retain his Chinese nationality.
30. Bartke, p. 6.
31. *New China News Agency,* January 1, 1960; *Peking Review,* February 2, 1960.
32. Interview Ganis Harsono, March 1972.
33. L. E. Williams, Sino-Indonesian Diplomacy, *China Quarterly,* July-September 1962, p. 197.
34. On February 27, 1963 Peking's *Jen-min Jih-pao* carried an editorial entitled Whence the differences? in which it blamed the Soviet Union for being the first country to bring out 'the internal differences among the fraternal parties'. The occasion had been a Tass statement on the Sino-Indian border dispute, issued on September 9, 1959, which the Chinese complained made 'no distinction between right and wrong (as) the statement expressed "regret" at the border clash and in reality condemned China's correct stand', *New China News Agency,* February 27, 1963.
35. G. F. Hudson, Ed., 1961, The Sino-Soviet dispute, *China Quarterly,* London, p. 5.
36. Hudson, 1961, p. 9, note 1. Also Harish Kapur, China and the Third World, *Mizan Newsletter,* November-December 1969, p. 304. Peking also offered Indonesia several thousand tons of rice, but Djakarta declined to accept since the gift was offered 'in a period of tension'. See *Antara News Agency,* December 31, 1959.
37. Mozingo, 1965, p. 31 writes: 'The sharp contrast between Peking's subsequent handling of the Indonesian and the Indian disputes can be linked, in the writer's opinion, to the Chinese estimate that Indonesia was still a reliable force in the "anti-imperialist" movement and therefore had to be reconciled, whereas India by 1959 was an enemy to be discredited and defeated'.
38. Hudson, 1961, p. 5.

39. Interview with the former Minister of Foreign Affairs, Ruslan Abdulgani, March 1972.
40. Subandrio in reply to a letter of Chen Yi of December 9, 1959. See also *Far Eastern Economic Review*, December 12, 1959, p. 1019.
41. This speech, at variance with points made by the East European delegates present, was not published in any of the European countries of the communist bloc.
42. *New China News Agency*, February 4, 1960.
43. *Peking Review*, May 31, 1960; *Berita Indonesia*, March 25, 1960; *New China News Agency*, April 21, 1960 e.a.
44. *Antara News Agency*, April 4, 1960.
45. *Times of Indonesia*, March 15, 1960.
46. *New China News Agency*, May 5, 1960.
47. *New China News Agency*, May 13, 1960.
48. *Review of Indonesia*, no. 6, 1960, p. 7.
49. *Jen-min Jih-pao*, November 25, 1959. See also above p. 53.
50. Indonesian officials wanted the opposite. They insisted on a deliberate choice and, for the time being, rejected claims to Indonesian nationality on the mere grounds that a person had *not renounced* being an Indonesian or had *exercised voting rights* over a number of years without challenge. These two points were endorsed by the P.K.I. statement.
51. *Review of Indonesia*, no. 6, 1960, p. 7.
52. Signalling such a movement, the newspaper *Duta Masjarakat* wrote on May 5, 1960: 'This gives the impression that China is trying to wreck the Indonesian economy'.
53. Mozingo, 1965, p. 40.
54. *Review of Indonesia*, no. 4, 1960, p. 19.
55. *Review of Indonesia*, p. 19; *Peking Review*, March 22, 1960, p. 14; *Far Eastern Economic Review*, February 2, 1960, p. 366. China had always maintained that the 'overwhelming majority' of the overseas Chinese in Indonesia were working people, with only a small number of them not behaving well.
56. *Review of Indonesia*, no. 4, 1960, p. 20.
57. See for example criticism in this respect in the nationalist newspaper *Suluh Indonesia*, March 24, 1960.
58. *Review of Indonesia*, no. 5, 1960, p. 4.
59. See above p. 38.
60. *Peking Review*, April 4, 1960, p. 11.
61. It is interesting to note that, from early in March until the middle of May 1960, the official Chinese news agency departing from its normal procedure, did not find anything of interest to quote from the editorials of the Indonesian communist daily *Harian Rakjat*. This remains a point to consider, even given the fact that *Harian Rakjat* in this period was suspended for some weeks by the military authorities. It was on March 1 that Kruschov left Indonesia after his twelve day-visit.

62. *New York Times*, January 7, 1960.
63. *Suluh Indonesia*, December 12, 1959, *Indonesian Observer*, December 14, See also: Brackman, 1963, p. 270.
64. L. E. Williams 'Sino-Indonesian Diplomacy', *The China Quarterly*, July-September 1962, p. 198. Also Hinton, 1966, p. 433.
65. See below p. 91.

CHAPTER 6

The Kruschov visit (1960)

Early in January 1960 it was announced that Soviet Premier Kruschov intended to visit Indonesia. Leading newspapers at the time called it a 'sudden and unexpected decision' and regarded it as a political move of the greatest significance: A slap in the face of Peking.[1] In Indonesia reference was made to the fact that Kruschov's visit was brought forward[2] and that P.K.I. Chairman Aidit had had something to do with it.[3] Brackman is of the opinion that Aidit had some use for Kruschov 'to ease the pressure on both China and the P.K.I. and demonstrate international proletarian solidarity'.[4] It does not seem likely that Aidit at that moment had sufficient leverage on Kruschov to make the Soviet leader do what he wanted. Kruschov came for reasons of his own. He wanted to build up the image of the Soviet Union in Asia[5] in his ascent to the summit conference with President Eisenhower, scheduled for later that year.

One ostensible purpose of Kruschov's trip to Djakarta was the formal signature of a loan of 250 million dollars negotiated between the two countries in the preceding period. But more important was the fact that during his stay in Indonesia Kruschov came to an agreement with President Sukarno on the sale of arms worth 600 million dollars.[6] The groundwork for this had also been laid in 1959.

When Kruschov set out for his visit to South East Asia, no decision had yet been reached on the total amount of this huge deal, which would naturally have to be paid for with money borrowed from Moscow. Sukarno kept pressing Kruschov during his trip for even more than the Soviet leader was ultimately willing to consent to. The Indonesian President was dead-set on getting the military tools to start his campaign to oust the Dutch from West Irian.[7] But, in objective terms,

Kruschov was helpful enough and forthcoming with his military aid because he saw in Indonesia an ideal opportunity for penetration and influence-building.[8] The Soviet Union and particularly Kruschov had for years been suspicious of Sukarno who for a long time had been considered a national-bourgeois leader in the negative sense in which the Soviet communists looked upon men of such background. The paramount position Sukarno had achieved for himself within the Indonesian political set-up, especially after his semi-coup of July 1959,[9] and the fact that the P.K.I. had entered into some kind of reluctant cooperation with the Indonesian President accounted for the reappraisal Kruschov had made in the second half of 1959. In addition to these considerations, competition with China and the realization that the two main communist powers might sooner or later pursue different and conflicting interests certainly also played a part in Kruschov's venture into an area which Peking basically regarded as its natural preserve.[10]

The Kruschov visit to Indonesia and India was not viewed with much satisfaction in Peking.[11] It came at a time when China was seriously at odds with both countries and – this notwithstanding – Kruschov in both instances handed out substantial financial aid. In Indonesia this gesture of 'largesse' must have been particularly galling to Peking, since the Chinese leaders just were trying to put some pressure on Djakarta in the question of the overseas Chinese by exacerbating the economic difficulties of the Sukarno régime.[12]

Seen in a more general context, the visit for the Chinese must have epitomized what they found was wrong with Soviet aid to underdeveloped nations. This issue had already become a point of friction in relations between Moscow and Peking. The Soviet viewpoint had been expounded by chief-ideologist Michael Suslov in September 1959 while he was accompanying Kruschov on his trip to Peking where he told the Chinese comrades that uncommitted nations 'should be seduced by trade, aid and example'.[13] Indicating what was to come Suslov then continued: 'We are extending aid, and as our opportunities grow, we will extend even more aid to all countries in Asia and Africa'. Somewhat later the old guard bolshevik Otto Kuusinen, in his Lenin Anniversary commemoration speech of April 1960 answering the first open all-round Chinese attacks on Soviet policy, was to describe development aid as an international duty of a communist country: 'We understand that duty to include extending aid to any liberated people, even if they are not a member of the world socialist system'.[14] To the Chinese who could not hope to match the Soviet Union in the foreseeable future in development aid, this Soviet approach especially looked like unfair competition. The Chinese tried to counter it by the argument of 'self-reliance'. Referring to their own recent history Peking began to stress the fact that China had developed quickly without much outside aid and that other developing nations could and should emulate its example rather than become dependent on others.[15]

So on at least two counts Peking had reason not to be very happy about Kruschov's performance in Indonesia: In the overseas Chinese question he failed to support the Chinese case,[16] and, secondly, he engaged in a piece of Soviet salesmanship radiating economic might, exactly a field where China was weak.[17] The coverage in the Chinese news media of Kruschov's trip right from the beginning reflected Peking's misgivings. No mention of his arrival in Djakarta was made by Radio Peking or the Chinese press, and during the visit the New China News Agency only quoted now and then their Soviet colleagues of Tass on Kruschov's whereabouts.[18]

When, at the conclusion of the visit, a joint Sino-Indonesian communiqué was issued, the Chinese quoted Tass more extensively, but it is striking that they omitted four points. One related to Sukarno,[19] but the other three omissions fit the picture we have now of the Sino-Soviet dispute that was then emerging. Against the background of the differences that began to come into the open around Lenin's 90th anniversary celebration later in April, it is not surprising to see what the Chinese did not agree with in the communiqué. First of all, no mention was made of the statement that another world war would be the greatest disaster for mankind. Also left out was the assertion that, thanks to disarmament, the differences between rich and poor countries would be liquidated all the more rapidly. Finally, the Chinese had not bothered to refer to the Eisenhower-Kruschov meeting in Camp David that had been described in the joint statement as 'a tremendous contribution to the cause of easing international tensions'.[20] These three points on which Sukarno had sided with Kruschov without apparent difficulty were unpalatable to the Chinese. They were fond, however, of taking up the Soviet leader on the support he had promised to the national liberation movement in Asia and Africa during his trip to Indonesia. Reflecting editorially on Kruschov's recent tour the People's Daily pinned him down on what it called 'these solemn statements of the Soviet Union against colonialist and imperialist aggression' and (no doubt tongue-in-cheek) predicted that they would be 'a source of inspiration for the peoples of the third world'.[21]

From the start, the P.K.I. displayed more enthusiasm for Kruschov than the Chinese and, reacting to the news of his trip to Indonesia, the party's daily newspaper *Harian Rakjat* called it 'a very important international event', describing the Soviet leader as 'an energetic and militant peace fighter, whose work has made no small contribution to the easing of the international situation'.[22]

For the rest it quoted extensively what Sukarno had told a *Pravda* correspondent, including the remark that Eisenhower would have been equally welcome had he come to Indonesia. Aidit, still travelling in Europe when the news broke, mainly confined himself to quotations from Sukarno,[23] probably finding it better to keep on the safe side and not to play up the event.

When Kruschov had left, Aidit was more jubilant and hailed the visit as 'the most important event for the Indonesian people in 1960'.[24] He singled out the new credit agreement of 250 million dollars with the Soviet Union claiming that the road to the overall reconstruction of the country was now open. Replying to critics who found the longterm loan a burden for posterity Aidit said the opposite was true, provided the money was not used for consumption, as Kruschov also pointed out in his address to the Indonesian parliament. Aidit had spoken in the same vein a few days earlier, on Radio Moscow, adding for the benefit of his Soviet audience, however, that Kruschov while visiting Indonesia must have realized from the people 'how great is the desire of the country for a change in politics and in living conditions', hinting that accommodating Sukarno was not necessarily an ideal.[25]

As could be expected Aidit had had his own calculations as to the effect of Kruschov's visit on the standing of the P.K.I., and he may have hoped for an improved and reinforced relationship with Sukarno as a reward for the financial aid his fellow-communist from abroad had brought. But Aidit must have felt afterwards that his party had not gained much political mileage out of the visit, apart from some propaganda fall-out.[26] He should have known beforehand, however, that it was Kruschov's main aim to court Sukarno who was in fact now regarded in Moscow as the main force to be reckoned with. In a way, Aidit acknowledged this in his statement on March 1, the day of Kruschov's departure, noting that 'one thing cannot be denied: a stronger friendship between the peoples of Indonesia and the Soviet Union, and between Kruschov and Sukarno personally'.[27] The next most important aim Kruschov had in mind in connection with his tour of Indonesia could not have given Aidit and the P.K.I. as much pleasure as they would like to have made it appear. This aim was to impress the world with his show of generosity in extending a multi-million dollar loan for the development of a non-aligned, non-communist country. A sign of criticism within the party as to the true meaning of the many millions promised by Kruschov was the question, put to the Soviet leader at a press conference at the end of his trip in Indonesia, whether the Soviet Union had 'turned over a new leaf' as far as economic aid to underdeveloped countries was concerned.[28] Kruschov of course quickly replied that Soviet aid was 'completely different' from capitalist aid, etc., but he could not have overlooked the doubt implied in the question.[29]

The economic impact so loudly claimed for the promised Soviet credit seems in practice to have been almost nil, if not negative. As pointed out by Ra'anan the credit came when, officially at least, only one third of the previous credit of 117,5 million dollars was used up.[30] Besides, of the new credit 110 million dollars were earmarked for a giant steel mill with a capacity of 250,000 ton to be built in the jungle of Kalimantan, at a time when nothing had yet come of the smaller project that had been planned, or rather talked about, since 1956.[31] This together with other evidence makes Ra'anan conclude that the 1960 credit was actually a financial reserve from which Indonesia might have to draw funds to cover the fact that portions of the previous 1956 loan had been used for military purposes.[32] It may not even have been that because, according to normal Soviet procedure, each project to be financed within the framework of an overall loan-agreement as signed by Kruschov during his stay in Indonesia had to be agreed upon again in detailed negotiations that often never even got off the ground. Only approximately 90 million dollars of the approved loan of 250 millions reached Indonesia in the form of equipment, etc.[33] However, even these capital goods never contributed anything to the Indonesian economy since the projects for which they were intended were either stopped for political reasons in 1965 – such as the Tjilegon steel factory – or had to be abandoned because of utter impracticability – as in the case of the gigantic network of roads planned to cross the jungle in Kalimantan.

The overt loan-agreement of February 1960 included the financing of military training.[34] In this respect it was a forerunner of the secret arms deal General Nasution was to sign in January 1961.[35] One may also assume that the direct procurement of Soviet arms was eased to a certain extent after Kruschov had in principle agreed to help Indonesia with arms on a massive scale, irrespective of the formal heading under which it was to come. In retrospect, therefore, Kruschov's gesture aimed at spreading the Soviet gospel in underprivileged countries hardly amounted to anything in economic terms.

As to its political motivation, it has been observed that even at this stage the Soviet Union was afraid of a Peking-oriented P.K.I.: 'Continuing military commitments to Indonesia in the early '60's may have been designed to forestall this (orientation), by enhancing the authority of the army at the P.K.I.'s expenses'.[36] This conclusion does not seem to be borne out by the facts, but it was true that the P.K.I., up till then, had not been too sanguine about military aid as given by the Soviet Union and the other European communist countries. It had taken the Party three years from the moment that the first arms deal with the Soviet bloc had been initiated in 1956, until the P.K.I. leaders began to make sporadic mention of this at all.[37] If, as seems likely, the Soviet Union in its friendly attitude towards Sukarno in early 1960 was not or not primarily motivated by pre-emptive anti-P.K.I. manoeuvring, the party may nevertheless have had a more clear and sober view than Moscow of the disadvantages for its domestic position of large-scale Soviet aid, especially military aid. Willing or not, the Soviet Union would provide the military leadership under General Nasution with an opportunity to modernize the Indonesian armed forces and so could not but help them to counter the growing political influence the P.K.I. was acquiring through its mass organizations and through its association with Sukarno.

It was also in this period that the P.K.I. for the first time began to be confronted with serious Sino-Soviet differences that could no longer be ignored. The Indonesian communist leadership, judged from available evidence, was beginning to see the looming problem of an international communist movement that would no longer provide an easy orientation or source of support. On the other hand the cohesion of its top leadership and the domestic power base the P.K.I. had built up, guaranteed the Party a reasonable degree of independence of judgment.[38] Some of the points in the debate that emerged between Moscow and Peking must also have sounded rather esoteric for a bunch of hard-nosed party organizers and politicians, not primarily interested in theoretical hairsplitting in western communist tradition.

In the three main issues which in the spring of 1960 began to juxtapose communist China to the Soviet Union – continuation of the cold war or peaceful co-existence, the question of whether war was no longer inevitable, and the chances of a non-violent communist take-over – a general inclination became discernible among P.K.I. leaders to side with the Chinese. A clear example in this respect is Politburo member Sudisman, who wrote a long article in *Harian Rakjat* at the end of May 1960 on the occasion of the 40th anniversary of the Party.[39]

Contrary to Kruschov's main line upheld even following the failure of the Paris summit earlier that month, Sudisman saw an intensification of the cold war, though he specifically confined himself to conflicts between 'imperialism and the peoples of the suppressed nations'. He closely followed the reasoning of the Chinese theoretical paper *Hung Qui* and especially what was written in that journal on the eve of the meeting between the 'Big Four' in the French capital.[40] On the question of war he quoted Lenin in Chinese fashion saying that 'imperialism has within it the sources of warfare and conflagration'. Though opposed to war, the P.K.I. was not afraid of it if others were to unleash it, Sudisman wrote, and ended with the well-known dictum of Mao Tse-Tung about the 'hundreds of millions who would turn to socialism' because of a third, nuclear world war.[41]

The Second Deputy Chairman of the P.K.I., Njoto, had spoken in similar vein earlier in the year in an attempt to cure his audience of some 'superstitions' supposedly prevailing in the Indonesian peace movement.[42] One of these, according to Njoto, had been the idea that humanity would meet its end in a third world war. This he had said was a fallacy, as the only real victim would be 'imperialism'. On the same occasion Njoto had pointed up the notion that world peace could be separated from the national liberation movement[43] and had disagreed with it. It was only logical that, in this context, Njoto brought up West Irian as this unsolved problem ranged Indonesia on the side of China in the category of countries with irrendentist claims, making world peace a rather abstract notion to their leaders, compared with the urgency, or apparent urgency, of full 'national liberation'. The P.K.I. leader even went so far as to say that, so long as colonialism existed, there would be no peace.[44]

Of more practical consequence was the third main issue that began to separate Moscow and Peking: The issue of peaceful or non-peaceful accession to power. As related earlier[45] Kruschov had spoken highly of the possibility of securing power in non-communist countries by parliamentary means on the occasion of his address to the Congress of his party in February 1956. He then said he saw good opportunities both in 'capitalist and former colonial countries'. He was supposed, in introducing this innovation, to have been particularly inspired by the spectacular election results of the P.K.I. the year previously. It has been concluded elsewhere that it was most probably due to pressure from Mao that, in the Moscow Declaration of 1957, the former colonies were excluded as countries where the transition to communism could be peaceful.[46]

This view was again taken up by Hutapea, the Rector of the Aliarcham Academy, the P.K.I. training center of cadres, in an article in *Bintang Merah* published in the spring of 1960.[47] Hutapea charged the revisionists of the second International in 1903 – as if nothing had happened since – with having broached the idea of a non-revolutionary road to power. His rejection of the whole notion of a peaceful method of achieving the communist millenium was so complete that he had no use for the 1957 Moscow Declaration or for the subtleties the Chinese, for all their opposition to the idea, still thought it useful to employ.[48]

It is not surprising to find Aidit in this case of a somewhat more moderate opinion. For example, in his major address to the party on its 40th anniversary, when he also dwelt upon the aspect of violence.[49] In a manner typical of Aidit, the necessary tribute was paid to revolutionary methods with the statement that 'armed struggle is the most important form of struggle for the revolution'. But he qualified this by indicating the three forms of struggle that would be particularly suitable for Indonesia: Guerilla warfare in the villages, revolutionary action by the workers, and a campaign amongst the soldiers.[50]

Combination of these three types of struggle was very important, and, he went on, 'this is part of the theory of the Indonesian revolution, the theory of gaining victory in guerilla war in a country of islands such as Indonesia'.[51] But he made clear that, to him, this was a thing of the past, not to be applied to the situation prevailing in Indonesia after independence. In the period between 1948 and 1951 (that is, while the Muso 'left' strategy was being pursued, the Madiun rebellion broke out, and the party groped for a new line)[52] the P.K.I. had been a chaos, Aidit said, and the theory of armed struggle had therefore proved unworkable. Subsequently, all sorts of 'right' and 'left' errors had been committed, until the party had reached 'maturity' at the March 1954 Congress, when it began to base itself on the maxim 'combine the universal truths of Marxism-Leninism with the concrete practice of the Indonesian revolution'.[53] In short, the theory of the 'three forms of struggle' was to Aidit, to all practical purposes, a dead letter. He had probably no regrets. Later, after the demise of the P.K.I. in the wake of the 30 September movement, this actual neglect of armed struggle, while paying some lip-service to the use of force, was held strongly against him, that is posthumously. 'Facts have shown that "the theory of the Method of Combining the Three Forms of Struggle" was not the result of treating the experience of another country critically and linking it with actual practice in Indonesia, so as to create a revolutionary theory typical to Indonesia . . . The "three forms of struggle" that should be combined, instead of having been guided along the road of revolution, were each guided along the "peaceful road" . . . In practice, the party leadership did not prepare the whole ranks of the party, the working class and the masses to face the possibility of a non-peaceful road. The most striking proof of it was the grave tragedy which happened after the outbreak and the failure of the September 30th Movement'.[54]

While Aidit did not in fact have any use for violent ideas of his leftist fellow-members of the Politburo, at the same time he could not point convincingly to great prospects for the non-violent or parliamatary road to power for the P.K.I. In September 1959 the Djuanda government postponed the holding of general elections for another year. After this followed pressure, especially from the military, to do away with the party system in Indonesia as unfit for the country. Meanwhile Sukarno was playing his own game, seeking ways and means of getting rid of parliamentary control. In a last effort to resist the unfavorable trend the four main parties, the nationalist P.N.I., the muslim Masjumi, the Nahdatul Ulama, and the P.K.I., put up united opposition and rejected the draft budget First Minister Djuanda had submitted to parliament. This was too much for the Indonesian President who – as soon as Soviet Premier Kruschov had left the country – dissolved parliament, thus paving the way for an appointed replacement.[55]

Aidit protested publicly and, in a telegram to Sukarno, termed this arbitrary act 'a regrettable affair for every patriot who upholds the principle of democracy'.[56] The left-wing communist paper, *Bintang Timur*, echoed this protest in its issue of March 10, 1960, but on the same day it was announced that Sukarno had invited the leaders of three of the four big parties (the Masjumi was excluded from this privilege) to discuss the dissolution of parliament in his palace on distant Bali.[57] As a result of these talks *Bintang Timur* reversed its opinion and called Sukarno's idea to appoint parliament suddenly 'a revolutionary act of the President'.[58]

Aidit, who as it turned out later received assurances from Sukarno that the P.K.I. members of Parliament would all be included in the new House of Representatives, followed up with a statement that 'a temporary [appointed] parliament is better than no parliament at all'.[59] He added however, rather timidly, that 'if possible' this year the general elections should actually be held, as promised. Given the trend in favor of the Indonesian communists, Aidit could be sure that the P.K.I. stood to gain from these elections.

It was this heavy dependence on the parliamentary process on the one hand, and on Sukarno on the other that in these months provided fuel for fierce debate withing the P.K.I., as Hutapea, with his sharp and basic attack on non-violent roads to power, had shown.[60] The Chinese too were then trying to show how much they doubted that anything good could come of this reliance on parliamentary machinery. In the *Hung Qui* article celebrating Lenin's 90th anniversary under the slogan 'Long live Leninism' it was stated that 'the bourgeoisie is fully able, at any time, in accordance with the needs of its own interests, to dissolve parliament when necessary'.[61] It added that experience in various European and Asian countries after the Second World War provided additional proof of this opinion and summarized the point to be made with a Lenin quotation that 'to limit or condition (the victory over the majority of the population) to the gathering of a majority of votes at elections, while the bourgeoisie remains dominant, is utter stupidity, or simply swindling the workers'. Though probably not aimed particularly at the Aidit-line within the P.K.I., the Chairman of the Indonesian Communist Party was in a position to take this advise to heart if he wanted to. This attack on what the Chinese communists thought was the fallacy of hoping for a bloodless, parliamentary takeover by local, communist parties was no doubt a sign that Peking, being at odds with neutralist nationalist leaders such as Nehru and Sukarno, thought it would benefit from a more militant posture on the part of their comrades in these countries.[62]

On no occasion did Aidit react to the *Hung Qui* article, and he must have found it better to pass over in silence this Chinese dig at his 'rightist' strategy.

There was another issue apart from the three directly related to the Sino-Soviet dispute[63] that was being heatedly debated within the P.K.I. and on which Aidit found himself attacked from the left. It was the question of who was to lead the revolution in the various stages it supposedly had to pass through.[64]

Sakirman, one of the members of the P.K.I. Politburo, writing in March 1960 considered that the revolution, both in its first or bourgeois-democratic phase and in its second or socialist phase, should be under the guidance of the party.[65] This was the orthodox view (officially also the P.K.I.'s) but, in fact, Aidit over the years had shown that in practice he would settle for less and be glad if the P.K.I. at least could retain its organizational freedom while cooperating with other political parties.[66] Moreover, Sakirman in his article claimed that the Chinese and the Soviet experience on the leadership of the revolution in all its phases had been similar and had shown no differences.[67] Both points made by Sakirman reflected also opinions expressed at the time on the Chinese side.[68] But the whole issue of course also had a lot to do with practical P.K.I. politics, because many leaders of the party felt that more action against opposition to Sukarno was called for[69] and that Aidit was holding back too much. In his address to the party on May 23 Aidit illustrated this cautious attitude stressing that the first part of the revolution – the elimination of foreign capitalists and big landowners that was allegedly going on at the time – should be completed first. Placating the more impatient of his followers with the assurance that a socialist society would be guided 'automatically' by the proletariat, for example the P.K.I., he implicitly accepted that in the earlier, current phase of the revolution the leadership would rest with the non-communists, the nationalists of various shades, but in practice Sukarno and his group, and the military.[70]

Aidit struck the same careful note as in the leadership issue when giving his opinion on the various 'deviations' that were then discussed within the party. In Indonesian communist parlance these aberrations from the right path had long since been dubbed 'capitulasi-isme' and 'avonturisme',[71] which meant the tendency to give in to the powers-that-be too easily on the one hand, and breakneck extremism on the other. In his address to the party on May 23, 1960, Aidit told his followers on this score to avoid both the 'rightist' mistake of exaggerating the importance of cooperation with the national bourgeoisie and the 'leftist' fault of not stressing such cooperation enough.[72] Hutapea, in a second article in *Bintang Merah*,[73] had also given his opinion on the subject saying, in line with official doctrine, that both 'capitulasi-isme' and 'avonturisme' should be avoided: 'In the Party there has to be a simultaneous attack on these two kinds of opportunism' he wrote. But then he proceeded to single out amongst what he called the 'false Marxists' small shopkeepers and farmers with their 'petit bourgeois ideology' as the source of peril in the party, clearly seeing the danger lurking from the right. Politburo-member Sakirman had earlier also warned that both leftist and rightist deviations should be countered in the party, but he had then taken on particularly what he called 'petit bourgeois revolutionarism', a danger that was normally supposed to be found on the left of communist party's scale of political opinion.[74]

On the related issue of 'modern revisionism' Aidit finally kept silent in his P.K.I. anniversary address of May 23. This was at a time when even the Soviets were critical of the Yugoslav communists, considering them the most obvious embodiment of the damnable right-deviation, and were aiming growing criticism at Belgrade as being too neutral between 'the imperialist aggressor and the peaceful country of socialism'.[75] Sudisman in his *Harian Rakjat* article a few days after Aidit's speech[76] went far beyond what Moscow had found proper to attack in the Yugoslavs, and, denouncing 'Tito-inspired' modern revisionists, he followed in detail on this point too the latest Chinese version as expounded by the theoretical journal *Hung Qui* at the time of the Lenin anniversary exchange.[77] However, an official P.K.I. declaration commemorating the 1955 Bandung conference at the end of April 1960, no doubt under influence of Aidit, was kept in a relatively moderate tone as far as its anti-Yugoslav passages were concerned. It blamed the 'modern revisionists' for their attempts to draw India, the United Arab Republic, and Indonesia into a 'third bloc'. This was an old charge against Belgrade, picked up those days by the Chinese too with the difference that the Indonesians did not (while the Chinese did) specifically mention the Yugoslavs by name as the culprits.[78] It should be borne in mind that this official pronouncement of the P.K.I. was issued at a time when President Sukarno was travelling in Yugoslavia as a guest of Tito and also that severe military censorship existed. It is only too likely that these two points contributed to the relatively rather mild reproof the party gave to the Yugoslavs.[79]

In the early, open stage of the debate that the Moscow-Peking differences had initiated within the communist world movement some further[80] points can therefore be made as to the position the P.K.I. was adopting. The Indonesian Communist Party was still very much dominated by its chairman, Aidit, who pursued his 'rightist' strategy which had produced until then considerable success for him and his party. But both inside the party and within the communist 'commonwealth' shifts were noticeable that tended to make this policy of accommodation more difficult to sustain than previously. On *foreign* issues,[81] therefore, Aidit compared with an earlier period probably held the same, rather pro-Soviet, opinions. But the difference was twofold: The P.K.I. leader no longer came out in favor of them publicly if it could be avoided. The more extreme wing of the party, with Njoto and Sudisman in the lead, did exactly the opposite and became increasingly vociferous. On questions having an immediate bearing on *domestic* policies, the left wing was equally ascendent, while Aidit stuck basically to his previous views and tactics. But here the party chairman could not afford to remain silent. Therefore as in his address on the occasion of the party's 40th anniversary in May 1960, he opposed various detractors from the left in the cautious but persistent manner that had made him the undisputed first man of the party. In defending his views Aidit should clearly be ranked as a right-wing communist leader, who wanted to take over the country in a non-violent, organizational way and who did not wish to rush the party into a premature position of leadership that would coalesce the other political forces into an anti-communist front.

In fact he saw the main danger to the party and to himself as coming from the left-extremists amongst his comrades. But, to his chagrin, he must have seen that this wing had powerful arguments and had, moreover, acquired a still-distant, but potentially very powerful supporter, China, which by radicalizing its stand vis-à-vis the Soviet comrades, was beginning to radiate its ideas and tactics far beyond its borders.

NOTES

1. *New York Times*, January 7, 1960.
2. Radio Djakarta, in English, January 2, 1960; *Suluh Indonesia*, December 12, 1959; *Indonesian Observer*, December 14, 1959. Also Arnold C. Brackman, 1963, *Indonesian Communism*, Frederick A. Praeger, New York, p. 270.
3. See above p. 58.
4. Brackman, 1963, p. 270.
5. On his way to Indonesia Kruschov made a stopover of a few days in India which had received a promise at the end of 1959 of a credit of $378 million.
6. Interview in March 1972 with Adam Malik, from early 1960 until late 1963 Indonesian Ambassador in Moscow; at present – late 1972 – Minister of Foreign Affairs. See also below p. 99 and 106, note 26.
7. So Sukarno insisted on acquiring for prestige reasons a second-hand Soviet cruiser, even against the advice of Kruschov who told him that it was an inordinately expensive toy for which even in peace-time thousands of men were needed to keep it operative. Interview Adam Malik, March 1972.
8. See below p. 99.
9. As early as March 1957 Sukarno in the eyes of the Soviet leaders was most probably the eventual victor in Indonesia in the foreseeable future; see, for example, the Soviet periodical *International Affairs*, no. 3, 1958. It was in March 1957 that Sukarno, as 'citizen' Sukarno, formed his own cabinet and Aidit also began to bet on the Indonesian President; see above p. .
10. See above pp. 58, 59.
11. Chinese diplomats in Moscow at the time were extremely suspicious of Kruschov's plans on his Indonesia visit; interview with Adam Malik, March 1972.
12. See above p. 62, note 52.
13. Donald S. Zagoria, 1962, *The Sino-Soviet Conflict 1956-1961*, Princeton University Press, Princeton, p. 279.
14. *Pravda*, April 23, 1960. Kuusinen gave as one of the concrete examples of Soviet aid – besides the Aswan dam naturally – 'a steel mill in Indonesia'. For the vicisitudes of this project see below p. 79, note 31, p. 271.

15. See, e.g., the speech by the Chinese delegate to the Afro-Asian economic conference in Cairo, *New China News Agency*, May 3, 1969: 'We advocate that Asian and African countries be economically independent and rely on their own efforts'.
16. See above p. 59.
17. From all accounts Kruschov seems personally to have been less of a success. On many Indonesians he left, in the words of one witness, 'an unpleasant impression'. He wanted to make as much political capital out of his trip as possible; for example in Bandung where he wanted to address a youth leaders' conference, he sulked when instead the program required him to play the anklung, a simple indigenous instrument, in a neighboring hotel. The beauty of Indonesian batik handicraft escaped him entirely, and the Soviet leader on visiting one of the most famous ateliers suggested to Sukarno it would be better to begin producing textiles in a 'modern way'. Hurt by this insensitivity the Indonesian President retaliated by introducing Kruschov at a mass rally afterwards – in Javanese, which was beyond the grasp of the Soviet Prime Minister – as 'this unseemly little fat man'. He did not come up to the expectations the Indonesians had of a true bolshevik revolutionary, on more counts. They found him 'sweating like a Dutchman', a ghastly judgment indeed. These details were given in an interview in March 1972 by Dr. O. W. Röder, longtime correspondent in Indonesia for the *Süddeutsche Zeitung* and other West German papers.
18. *BBC Summary of World Broadcasts*, editorial report, February 20, 1960.
19. Not mentioned was the praise bestowed in the communiqué on President Sukarno personally for his 'outstanding role' in the realization of Indonesia's foreign policy. This tied in with the state of Sino-Indonesian relations, where Sukarno's role, as far as the Chinese were concerned, might have been 'outstanding' but was hardly deserving of praise.
20. *Tass*, February 28, 1960 and *New China News Agency*, February 29, 1960.
21. *Jen-min Jih-pao*, March 6, 1960.
22. *Harian Rakjat*, January 18, 1960.
23. Aidit in an address to cadres of the Italian Communist Party; *Review of Indonesia*, February 1960.
24. *Review of Indonesia*, March 1960.
25. *Review of Indonesia*, March 1960.
26. The nationalist newspaper *Merdeka* wrote, e.g., 'Kruschov is the best goodwill ambassador of Communism', February 29, 1960. The same day *Antara News Agency* quoted the Soviet leader as saying that he had been called 'a clever Communist who adored Communism'. He was indeed a communist, he said, but not bent on converting everybody to communism.
27. *Review of Indonesia*, March 1960. Though other leaders of the P.K.I. might have felt critical of the close political relationship that had developed between Sukarno and Kruschov, Aidit, basically and steadfastly throughout the years more pro-Soviet than pro-Chinese, may at that juncture have genuinely believed in the beneficial effects of it on the P.K.I.

28. *Pravda*, March 1, 1960.
29. See Zagoria, 1962, p. 263 for a similar exchange between a Chinese journalist and the Soviet Deputy Premier, Anastas Mikoyan, in Iraq a month later.
30. Uri Ra'anan, 1969, *The U.S.S.R. Arms the Third World: Case Studies in Soviet Foreign Policy*, The M.I.T. Press, Cambridge, Massachusetts, p. 188.
31. This was a steel factory at Tjilegon, West Java, on which a start was finally made, but it was abandoned after the September 30 affair in 1965 and left unfinished. At the time of writing (April 1972) talks have been held with Soviet authorities on completion of the project.
32. Ra'anan, 1969, p. 189.
33. Interview March 1972 with Ganis Harsono, former spokesman for Foreign Minister Subandrio between 1959-1966.
34. Interview with Adam Malik, March 1972.
35. See below p. 99.
36. Ch. B. McLane, Foreign aid in Soviet third world policies, *Mizan Newsletter*, November-December 1968, p. 250.
37. See above p. 39 and also *Material for the 6th National Congress of the Communist Party of Indonesia*, 1959, Agitprop department of the C.P.I., Djakarta, p. 100.
38. As to the leadership of the P.K.I. this could be found in the Politburo constituted in September 1959: Aidit, Lukman, Njoto, Sudisman and Sakirman. The latter was appointed in the place of the demoted Alimin in October 1953; the first four had already been member of the Politburo in January 1951 and formed the core of the Aidit leadership that then took over the P.K.I. 'Control over the party of these four is complete' writes Donald Hindley, 1964, *The Communist Party of Indonesia 1951-1963*, University of California, Berkeley, p. 67.
39. *Harian Rakjat*, May 30, 1960.
40. *Hung Qui*, April 1, 1960, and May 16, 1960. This last issue accuses imperialism of employing two tactics, force and deceit; Sudisman literally does the same. Moreover, the examples which underscore the thesis of growing conflict in the third world are identical.
41. Both points are found in the April 1 number of *Hung Qui*.
42. The occasion was a meeting of the Indonesian National Council for Peace in Bandung; *Harian Rakjat*, January 1, 1960, extensively quoted by *New China News Agency*, January 31, 1960.
43. At the height of the Lenin anniversary exchange *Jen-min Jih-pao*, in an editorial dated April 22, 1960, accused the United States of introducing this distinction in order to make the oppressed nations give up their resistance to aggression.
44. *Jen-min Jih-pao* wrote on the occasion of the meeting of the Afro-Asian Solidarity Committee in Conakry that 'to defend peace and peaceful coexistence, the most barbarous rule must be ended'; see *Jen-min Jih-pao*, April 17, 1960. An interesting detail here is that the United States as 'biggest enemy of peace' is blamed for occupying Taiwan and South Korea and for many

other colonialist practices in Asia, while no mention is made of West Irian. Perhaps this was because there were no Americans in sight in that area or because Dutch rule was not yet 'most barbarous'. Most probably this omission had something to do with strained Sino-Indonesian relations.

45. See above p. 35 and 46, note 28.
46. G. F. Hudson Ed., 1961, The Sino-Soviet Dispute, *The China Quarterly*, London, p. 41.
47. *Bintang Merah*, March-April issue, 1960.
48. *Hung Qui*, April 1, 1960: 'Peaceful means are not ruled out'; *Hung Qui*, April 19, 1960, as a Lenin quotation to show that peaceful transition was 'an extraordinarily rare opportunity'.
49. *Harian Rakja*t, May 24, 1960, *New China News Agency*, May 24, 1960, and May 26, 1960.
50. When Aidit formulated this tryptich for the first time it was in a speech to the Party in May 1955 in a passage on the best way the fight against the Dutch was to be conducted: 'Three forms of struggle should have been combined: guerilla warfare in the rural districts (mainly consisting of peasants), revolutionary action by the workers in the towns occupied by the Dutch and intensive work in the ranks of the Dutch armed forces', D. N. Aidit, 1959, *Complete Works*, vol. I, p. 292. Translated by the Joint Publications Research Service, Washington D.C. This method Aidit then contrasted with the Chinese experience, then apparently still emulated by some 'bright boy' in the P.K.I., saying that Indonesia was not China: 'the most advantageous conditions for guerilla warfare are extensive regions, mountainous areas and forest lands which are both wide in extent and far from the towns and the highways. The conditions in Indonesia meet only some of these requirements'. Aidit spoke in the past tense, but it can be assumed that the issue of force to be used as a political method in Indonesia was at that time still alive. Apparently this also remained the case in 1960 when the 'three forms of struggle' were not being related to fighting an outside enemy but an interior one.
51. *Harian Rakjat*, May 24, 1960.
52. See above pp. 12, 14.
53. *Harian Rakjat*, May 24, 1960. The wording has a Maoist tinge. See for example Lu Ting-yi in his Lenin Anniversary report where he says that the Chinese Communist Party and Mao 'integrated the universal truths of Marxism-Leninism with the concrete practices of the Chinese Revolution'. Also see: *Jen-min Jih-pao*, April 22, 1960. In fact, this formula was the legitimation of revisionism, both the Chinese and the Indonesian versions.
54. Build the P.K.I. along the Marxist-Leninist line to lead the People's Democratic Revolution in Indonesia, Self-criticism of the Political Bureau of the CC P.K.I., *Indonesian Tribune*, vol. I, no. 3, January 1967, p. 12. This was written under the guidance of Sudisman in the period after the 30 September movement had failed and Sudisman was the only member of the old Politburo alive and in Indonesia.
55. *Antara News Agency*, March 5, 1960.

56. *Antara News Agency*, March 17, 1960.
57. *Djakarta Radio Home Service*, March 10, 1960. The reformist Masjumi Party was kept out of the Bali conclave ostensibly because they had been involved in the armed rebellion of the outer islands but not less for opposing Sukarno politically with moderate success.
58. *Antara News Agency*, March 30, 1960.
59. *New China News Agency*, April 1, 1960.
60. See above p. 71.
61. *Hung Qui*, August 1960; *Peking Review*, 1960.
62. See Hudson, 1961, p. 81.
63. See above p. 70.
64. See above p. 21.
65. *Bintang Merah*, March-April 1960.
66. See above p. 21.
67. This was of course historically incorrect. After the 1927 disaster at the hands of Chiang Kai-shek the Chinese communists under Mao wanted at all costs to retain the leadership of the revolution, even if the Party still had to cooperate with other groups. In the comparable period in Russia, between the March Revolution and the October Revolution, it was not the Bolshevik party, but first Prince Lvov and later the socialist Kerenski who headed the Provisional Government.
68. See the editorial in *Jen-min Jih-pao*, April 22, 1960, and also the Lu Ting-yi report.
69. In a few weeks it would become clear that, meanwhile, something had been brewing in the Party. See below p. 84.
70. Both words are derived from the Dutch for 'capitulation' and 'adventurism'.
71. *Harian Rakjat*, May 24, 1960.
72. *Bintang Merah*, May-June 1960.
73. *Bintang Merah*, March-April 1960. See above p. 80, note 47. Aidit probably himself more in league with Sakirman than with Hutapea but for the sake of remaining the 'arbiter' between the various factions may have preferred to pose as 'centrist' between the left and the right. In the February 1960 issue of the *World Marxist Review*, writing on national unity, he had assured his readers that 'the Tito brand of revisionism has not found the slightest response in the Communist Party of Indonesia', thus indicating that he saw no danger from the right.
74. *Harian Rakjat*, May 24, 1960.
75. Ponomarev in *Kommunist*, no. 8, 1960. Reference is made to the fact that the Yugoslavs had blamed both the U.S.A. and the Soviet Union equally for the failure of the summit conference, following the U-2 incident.
76. See above p. 79, note 39.
77. *Harian Rakjat*, May 30, 1960. Sudisman charged that the modern revisionists believed the belligerent nature of imperialism had changed and that therefore they did not feel the need to fight this evil. Moreover, he thought that the modern revisionists blurred the lines between capitalist and socialist

countries. These charges all could be found in the *Hung Qui* article of April 19, 1960 and in the Lu Ting-yi report of April 22, 1960.

78. *New China News Agency*, April 24, 1960, *Jen-min Jih-pao*, April 18, 1960 and *New China News Agency*, April 18, 1960.
79. In January 1960 Aidit in a joint communiqué with Albanian party leader Enver Hodzha signed in Tirana had agreed that modern revisionists was the main danger – as the Moscow Declaration of 1957 had also maintained – and that the Yugoslavs were its 'most dangerous representatives'; see: *Review of Indonesia*, no. 2, 1960. There is no reason to assume that Aidit had changed his opinion since that time or had been insincere while in Albania. No doubt he must have felt that time and place – Djakarta, April-May – was now not auspicious for a statement in the same vein.
80. See above p. 39 ff.
81. See above p. 43.

CHAPTER 7

West Irian policy revised (1960)

In the middle of 1960 Indonesian politics took a turn that was to be of decisive impact for the years to come. The focal point around which a new alignment of political forces came to be ranged was West Irian, the last remaining fragment of the former Netherlands East Indies still under Dutch authority.[1] It was Sukarno who, more often than not, was the prime mover here and who, with the prospect of large-scale Soviet deliveries of arms and military equipment[2] was looking for ways to press Indonesia's claim to the jungle island. The Dutch came to his aid by providing a fresh issue when they announced, in the middle of May, that they would send reinforcements to the area. Even moderate, basically pro-Western opinion among Indonesians was struck by the move and especially by the publicity that surrounded it.[3] The conservative *Times of Indonesia* wrote that the Dutch action was incomprehensible as Djakarta had no intention of using force in the West Irian dispute.[4] Foreign Minister Subandrio who hurried back from a visit to the U.S.A. made the same point upon his return in early June.[5] General Nasution, Defence Minister and Chief of Staff of the army, as well as the military leadership more generally, had been reluctant, until then, to commit the country to more than verbal insistance on the Indonesian claims to West Irian. Subandrio had been in close touch with Nasution, taking his cue rather from him than from other political forces around Sukarno.[6] On the other side of the political spectrum the P.K.I. had been equally aloof and had given low priority to the West Irian issue, surprisingly so as at that time it had become to President Sukarno what a close observer of the period called 'an emotional obsession'.[7] Thus the return of the territory to Indonesia featured as number 23 on the list of the 24 May Day slogans for the P.K.I.[8] Even the newspaper *Bintang Timur* which often reflected the more extremist left opinion in the party, wrote early in May that the first requirement for the recovery of West Irian was increased production.[9]

At the beginning of June, Sukarno must have made up his mind that more should be done to regain West Irian and that the 'soft-sell' diplomacy of the Nasution-Subandrio team had to be replaced. The communists were not slow to discover that a wind of change was blowing and began themselves to use the opening for which they, no doubt, had been waiting. *Harian Rakjat* therefore launched the attack by charging that the United States, far from being neutral in the dispute as it claimed, were in fact favoring the Dutch by not allowing Indonesia the use of American weapons against the Dutch, whereas they had not restricted the Dutch similarly.[10] But there was more brewing within the party, as was shown when a few days later the communist-led trade union Sobsi with hard-liner Njono as its chairman extended the attack upon the Indonesian government by shooting down its economic policies. In a statement the Sobsi leadership attacked 'certain ministers' who did not act in the spirit of Manipol, the political charter Sukarno had outlined the year before. This had by now become a tested P.K.I. device for leveling criticism against the Sukarno régime: Basing itself upon some high-sounding speech or document the President had produced, it would charge that in the 'implementation' of it, one or other of Sukarno's assistants – as his ministers were aptly called – had failed miserably. In this case the ministers singled out were Arifin Harahap, who was in charge of trade, for not keeping down prices and Ahem Erningpradja who as Minister of Labor was trying to curb the trade unions. Sukarno was advised to get rid of these two forthwith.[11] Another sign of criticism of the domestic policies of the Sukarno-Djuanda government within the ranks of the P.K.I. were two lengthy articles written by the economic specialist of the party, Politburo-member Sakirman.[12]

In the first place it was an explanation, rather belated, of why the P.K.I. had given its support to the reintroduction of the 1945 Constitution by Sukarno the year previously,[13] judged by many leading Indonesian politicians to be a manifestly unconstitutional act.[14] But, though going along with the high-handed decision of July 1959, Sakirman made no bones about the unsatisfactory position of the party since: Severe curbs on freedom of action and speech; a parliament that, for all practical purposes, was clipped or 'frozen', and a cabinet 'that was not desired by the workers' – as he put it ironically.[15] Even the President was served a warning with the double-edged assurance that 'relations between Sukarno and the masses [read: the P.K.I.] are still firm'. Most illuminating for the mood among the more critical elements within the P.K.I., of whom Sakirman no doubt was an important representative,[16] was this passage:

> Anxiety arises among the comrades now that deteriorating economic conditions create difficulties for the Party in maintaining and tightening relations with groups in power, for it can become possible that the people will consider the groups that support them [the P.K.I.] as being on the side that has to bear responsibility for the unsteadiness of these economic conditions.[17]

China watched these developments within the P.K.I. with great attention, no doubt pleased at any sign that their Indonesian comrades were adopting a more critical attitude towards the Sukarno government which they held responsible for the simmering Sino-Indonesian overseas Chinese crisis. Both the *Harian Rakjat* article, which attacked U.S. policy on West Irian (and indirectly Subandrio) and the Sobsi statement on the poor performance of the country's economy under the Sukarno-Djuanda régime were extensively and prominently reported in the Chinese press.[18] In the Soviet Union developments around West Irian were the only ones that aroused interest. Moscow even produced a protest note against the Dutch government because of the dispatch of an aircraft carrier and profited from the occasion to show its flag as an active supporter of Afro-Asian countries, in particular as 'Indonesia's most faithful friend'.[19]

Then, early in July, Indonesian-Chinese relations entered a new phase of crisis when, in the West Java town of Tjimahi, two Chinese women were killed by soldiers who were enforcing the evacuation of overseas Chinese from the countryside to the major towns.[20] The initial reaction from the Chinese side (two days later, on July 5) still spoke only of 'forces hostile to Chinese-Indonesian friendship [having] begun their bloody persecution',[21] a global reference directed probably at the responsible military commanders known for their anti-Chinese sentiments. However, the official note of protest, dated July 11, implicated Subandrio personally by references to a letter the Indonesian Foreign Minister had sent his Chinese opposite number at the end of

March, promising him an end to the compulsory evacuation of overseas Chinese.[22] The note also recalled that, more recently, at a meeting with the Chinese ambassador Huang Cheng-nan on June 29 that had been expressly arranged to discuss the new, second wave of anti-Chinese actions by army units in West Java, Subandrio again gave his word that the Indonesian government would put a stop to this. An editorial in *Jen-min Jih-pao* on Sino-Indonesian relations on July 14 recalled that 'a handful of Indonesian elements with ulterior motives have always deliberately worked to create incidents . . . with a view to achieving their dirty aims of pandering to United States imperialism abroad and hitting the patriotic democratic forces and all opposition forces at home'.[23] Having brought in the United States, the Chinese paper suggested that these allegedly pro-American elements were working against the national interest of Indonesia, as it was the United States in particular which was sending arms 'in a steady stream' to West Irian, thus preventing its rightful return to Indonesian rule.

This was a direct attack on both the military and Subandrio who had said in May (in Washington) that in Indonesian-American relations 'everything is smooth' – a pronouncement that at the time was immediately picked up by the *New China News Agency* and became left-wing ammunition against the Indonesian minister.

Parallel to the escalation in attacks from the Chinese side, touched off by the Tjimahi incident, the left-wing of the P.K.I. also opened fire on the Indonesian government coordinating their action with that of Peking. On July 4, when the impact of the Tjimahi killings of the day before could not yet have been assessed, the unofficial party paper *Bintang Timur* – as indicated often the mouthpiece of the P.K.I.'s left wing – attacked rather vaguely 'some circles' for defending United States imperialism, while being hostile towards China, the country that had a 'correct attitude' towards the overseas Chinese as well as towards the West Irian affair.[24] In the issue of *Bintang Timur* of July 8 (i.e., well after the anti-Chinese incidents had had a chance to sink in and after Peking had given its first reaction in a *Jen-min Jih-pao* editorial of July 5) the attack was stepped up. It was now directed at some 'ministers concerned' who had been unable to appraise the Chinese People's Republic properly as a foreign political factor. Again linking the overseas Chinese issue with West Irian, *Bintang Timur* also demanded more purpose behind Indonesia's struggle for West Irian.[25]

Then, on that same day, the P.K.I. Politburo published what came to be called the 'July evaluation': A comprehensive indictment of one year of Sukarno-Djuanda government that had failed to provide the promised economic, political, and military stability.[26] It was a strongly worded document that basically resumed, in the field of economics, what had been said earlier in the Sobsi statement.[27] Here again, the Ministers Harahap and Erningpradja were taken to task personally. But an interesting new element was introduced. This was quite apart from a dig at Nasution (not mentioned by name, no doubt because of the military censors) for being too nice – meaning probably too effective – in dealing with the rebels in Sumatra and Sulawesi.[28]

The new element was in fact the full-scale attack on Subandrio for the way Indonesia's foreign policy was being conducted under his supervision.[29] The statement first of all introduced the question of the overseas Chinese by declaring that the foreign policy of 'this minister' had in the past year seriously undermined Indonesia's friendly relations with the Chinese People's Republic 'which is the strongest anti-imperialist country in Asia'. It also criticized him for a recent Australian-Indonesian agreement allegedly restraining Indonesia from recovering West Irian by force, while at the same time making Djakarta respect Australia's recognition of Dutch sovereignty over West Irian. Indonesia was thus further away than ever from realizing its claim over that territory. Finally these two issues, West Irian and the overseas Chinese, were linked by the statement that a battle on two fronts against the Netherlands on the one hand and against 'communism' on the other would mean that attempts to recover West Irian would fail completely.

With the Tjimahi incidents as an accelerating factor, both the P.K.I. and the Chinese government closed in on the Indonesian government, each partner singling out its specific targets. Peking aimed at the military, who were behind the anti-Chinese actions in West Java. The P.K.I. wanted to find scapegoats for the deteriorating economic climate and were after Harahap and Erningpradja. Both joined forces against Foreign Minister Subandrio. The connecting strand common to this escalation from two sides was the link between the overseas Chinese dispute and the West Irian issue, to the effect that both parties tried to convince the Indonesian government (primarily Sukarno) that to conduct an anti-Dutch and an anti-Chinese campaign simultaneously was contradictory and that a choice should therefore be made. It is not unlikely that Sukarno had all along come to a similar conclusion and was willing to take this 'advice' to heart.

Meanwhile, however, the military were not taking lightly the 'July evaluation', or at least the boldness of the communist leadership implied in it. A few days after the publication of the P.K.I. document, Sukarno ordered all political parties to be put under state control.[30] In view of further developments, it can be assumed that this happened as much as anything upon the insistence of the military, who then (on July 16) moved to arrest Politburo member Sakirman, singled out as the main instigator of the 'evaluation'. Three days later, when it was still uncertain what exactly had happened to Sakirman, the Djakarta military commander announced that he had summoned other P.K.I. Politburo members for interrogation in connection with the 'July evaluation'.[31]

But since July 14, Aidit and a number of other top-level communists had been virtually under house arrest and could not leave Djakarta.[32] According to Brigadier-General Ahmad Sukendro, at the time one of Nasution's aides in charge of military intelligence, the action against the Party's leadership was not altogether on account of the publication of the 'July evaluation'. This had rather been adopted by the military as a useful pretext to put the P.K.I. under pressure and to find out what they were after because sometime earlier Sukendro's agents had recovered documents in Semarang that were said to show detailed plans on how the P.K.I. would try to infiltrate the government of Central Java.[33]

Sukarno tried to take the initiative and re-establish the necessary balance. On the one hand he served notice on Aidit and the rest of the Politburo members that he would not hesitate to use his newly acquired powers over the political parties against the P.K.I. if they did not fall into line with him.[34] On the other hand, he cleverly tried to chip away at the armed forces by announcing that the leaders of the socialist P.S.I. and the muslim Masjumi were asked to issue, on penalty of being banned, a declaration of loyalty towards his régime. He thus threatened the continued existence of these two parties, hitting indirectly at the military as both parties had strong ties among the central and local officer corps.[35]

Then, on July 21, he convened the Supreme Advisory Council. At the meeting it was decided, under heavy prodding by Sukarno, that it was time to revise the country's lenient policy towards the Dutch and consider the use of force as a final way of achieving the goal of re-incorporation of West Irian.[36] Sukarno's close collaborator Ruslan Abdulgani, then Deputy Chairman of the S.A.C., announced in an off-hand manner after the session that 'President Sukarno would produce a revised West Irian policy in his forthcoming 17th of August speech'.[37] This 'decision' by the Supreme Advisory Council gave Sukarno leverage over the military, as the 'July evaluation' had given him over the P.K.I.

Sukarno now proceeded to establish himself further as the sole arbiter between competing powers. At the P.N.I. Congress at the end of July, he lashed out against those who suffered from what he called 'communist-phobia' and from related unnecessary anxieties and heartened the hard-pressed P.K.I. by confessing to be in agreement with the communists on a number of important matters such as the destruction of imperialism, the return of West Irian to the Republic.[38]

His Independence Day address on August 17, usually anticipated with some suspense, was not disappointing since it included the announcement of the rupture of diplomatic relations with the Netherlands over the West Irian issue. After years of trying to talk the Dutch into the transfer of their control over that part of Indonesia, Sukarno said 'other methods' were now necessary. As the Supreme Advisory Council had recently suggested, these methods should be 'revolutionary'.[39] Replying to the critics of his government, not lastly, one may assume, the P.K.I., the President admitted that his three-point program – food and clothing, security, and anti-imperialism – had not yet been 'implemented' smoothly enough.

The P.K.I. had more reason to be grateful to Sukarno when a short time later local army commanders in South-Sulawesi and South-Kalimantan decided to ban the regional branches of the P.K.I.[40] After calling in Aidit for consultation, Sukarno arranged for a joint meeting with the General Staff and the army commanders of the areas concerned.[41] It ended in a victory for the President, who established himself as Central Wartime Administrator with authority henceforth to decide these matters. This included outlying districts in which the President's authority, until then, had scarcely been recognized.

In order to help the local commanders to save face and, at the same time, to be sure that things would not get out of hand while he was away at the United Nations session, Sukarno imposed a total ban on political activities until the end of November.[42]

The P.K.I. had meanwhile tried to adjust itself to the critical situation which had arisen after the 'July-evaluation'. It looked at first as if the P.K.I. had become scared of its own boldness. More likely is it that the publication of the 'evaluation' had been a controversial issue within the leadership of the party, where opinions on the policy to be pursued within the country differed widely.[43] Reactions to the arrest of Sakirman had been very timid and consisted mainly of running to Sukarno for protection.[44] Later on Aidit, in a statement on the interrogation of the Politburo members, hardly had a word in Sakirman's favor, mainly stressing that the other leaders of the party, though not detained like Sakirman, had also been restricted in their movements for some time.[45] No mention he made then, or for that matter afterwards, of the party documents found in Semarang, but Aidit seems to have succeeded in convincing Sukarno that they were only prepared for 'training purposes'.[46] The military, he said in the report, had been 'tough, but correct and polite', and Aidit felt confident that their case in coming out with the 'July evaluation' was strong. With this opinion, the socialist opposition paper *Pedoman* in an editorial wrote ironically, it easily could agree, provided the P.K.I. leader would admit that the strength of the party that Aidit was always boasting about was derived mainly from the President's protecting hand.[47]

In the first issue of *Harian Rakjat* after its suspension by the military censors had been lifted it was made clear that the party was going to play it cool, pleading innocuously for 'serving the people best in implementing Manipol'.[48] A few days later Aidit issued a statement in advance of the 17th of August celebrations in low key, saying that 'the people were *somewhat* disappointed over the problem of livelihood and the question of democracy and freedom' [emphasis added].[49]

As to the 'July evaluation' as a method of action, *Harian Rakjat* dug up an interesting quotation from Aidit, dating back to 1956, to the effect that 'Communists must be able to moderate themselves in criticizing the statements and actions of members of democratic parties. Statements and actions which may hurt feelings, but are not important in themselves do not have to be criticized'.[50] The party paper did not dissociate itself from the 'July evaluation' – alluded to as a concrete example of how to adopt the position of upholding 'the freedom of movement of the Party in the united front'[51] – but it stressed that criticism made should be given 'consciously, wisely and responsibly'.[52]

It can be assumed that in this way Aidit had been busy restoring the balance and steering the party back to a safer middle course of steady 'permeation' of the Sukarno régime, combined with building the organizational strength that was the hallmark of Aidit's road to power. The excursion into a more radical approach, leading to the 'July evaluation', probably had Aidit's approval, but the initiative as to what was said and when it was said came rather from the more impatient leaders of the party, people like Sakirman, Sobsi-chairman Njono and chairman of the Farmer's Front Asmu.[53] The subsequent, lukewarm show of solidarity with Sakirman tied in with Aidit's natural reluctance to go out on a limb and back a loser.

The reason why Aidit, despite his usual caution, had given in to pressure from his left wing can only be guessed at, but in all likelihood it had something to do with the more radical course Sukarno wanted to inaugurate at the end of May, after the Dutch announced the dispatch of reinforcements to West Irian.[54] Aidit, then already in close contact with the President, must have sensed that Sukarno, for the sake of a more intensive campaign to regain West Irian, was willing to come to terms with Peking, one way or the other, and to settle the question of the overseas Chinese, foreseeing the need to muster all possible political and diplomatic support including that of China. This made Subandrio in particular vulnerable, and, when the bloody Tjimahi incidents took place in early July, Aidit must have seized on this as an ideal opportunity to apply a wedge. As related earlier,[55] what the 'July evaluation' and the barrage of notes of the outraged Chinese diplomats had in common was the open attack on Subandrio – and the military – for the poor state of Sino-Indonesian relations. This linking up of interests between the P.K.I. and the Chinese, with Sukarno in the background, probably indicated what the President had in mind: More action against the Dutch and improved relations with China. It must have tipped the scales for Aidit in deciding to let his radicals try out their 'July evaluation'.

It is interesting to see, in the light of this possible reconstruction of the events of mid-1960, that it was Subandrio especially who, as a result of the joint action by the P.K.I. and the Chinese, was trimming his sails to new winds.[56] Not having any political backing since he left the P.S.I., Subandrio as Foreign Minister had been operating in the political spectrum between Sukarno and the military. In the question of the overseas Chinese he had zealously defended the policy of the day, earning for himself the reputation of being markedly anti-Chinese.[57] In his mind West Irian had accordingly been relegated to the background. Subandrio now enthusiastically followed suit, especially since Sukarno, with the backing of the Supreme Advisory Council, had moved into a higher gear on the recovery of the jungle territory. The day after the S.A.C. meeting of July 21 Subandrio announced that any military reinforcement of West Irian by the Dutch would be met in kind.[58] While touring East-Indonesia sometime later he said that in the struggle for West Irian 'Indonesia is now pursuing a different method, realizing that her aims cannot be achieved by asking for negotiations with the Dutch. The present method is identical to the method used when the Indonesians won independence: that is fight first. In other words: engage in a physical contest with the Dutch and negotiate afterwards'.[59]

NOTES

1. West Irian, or Western New Guinea as the Dutch called it at the time, was a disputed territory. Its fate should have been settled by negotiations within a year after the transfer of sovereignty by the Dutch over the rest of the former Netherlands East Indies to the government of the Federal Republic of Indonesia at the end of 1949. There had been various reasons, mainly of a domestic Dutch political nature, for treating Western New Guinea differently from the rest of the former Dutch colony. But neither during 1950 nor afterwards was agreement reached between the two countries. To Indonesia it was Indonesian territory occupied by Dutch troops, while the Netherlands rested its case upon legal arguments, reinforced by the conviction that the Indonesian government would be incapable of administering such a vast country inhabited by a few hundred thousands primitive Papuans.
2. See above p. 64.
3. Dr. Sumitro, then one of the leading rebel leaders, described the dispatch of the aircraft carrier Karel Doorman 'as unwise as it was unwarranted'; *Far Eastern Economic Review*, July 18, 1960.
4. *Times of Indonesia*, May 25, 1960.
5. *Review of Indonesia*, July 1960.
6. Close collaboration between the military and Subandrio in the question of the overseas Chinese was another case in point; see above pp. 51, 52.

7. Interview March 1972 with former Foreign Minister Ruslan Abdulgani.
8. *Review of Indonesia*, May 1960.
9. *Antara News Agency*, May 9, 1960.
10. *Harian Rakjat*, June 8, 1960. It was a reference to the talks Subandrio had held in the U.S. with the American Secretary of State Herter in May and indirectly an attack on Subandrio's policy.
11. *Review of Indonesia*, August 1960. The Sobsi statement is dated June 14, 1960.
12. *Bintang Merah*, May-June and July-August 1960.
13. See above p. 27.
14. See for example Dr. M. Hatta, 1960, *Demokrasi Kita*, Pandji Masjarakat, Djakarta.
15. The Djuanda cabinet, which took charge of the running of the country after Sukarno, had introduced presidential rule in July 1959. It had no P.K.I. ministers, due partly to pressure from Nasution and the military. Aidit consequently sought to gain more status for the new Supreme Advisory Council, the highest state body in which national unity or 'Nasakom' was embodied and that comprised both him and his 'opposite number' Nasution. The S.A.C. was in the absence of the President chaired by Sukarno's ally and P.N.I. leader, Ruslan Abdulgani.
16. See above p. 74.
17. See also: Donald Hindley, The Indonesian Communists and the C.P.S.U. 22nd Congress, *Asian Survey*, March 1962, p. 27, note 19.
18. See for example, *New China News Agency*, June 8, 1960 and June 19, 1960.
19. *Radio Moscow in Indonesian*, June 4, 1960.
20. *New China News Agency*, July 5, 1960, *Jen-min Jih-pao*, July 5, 1960.
21. *Jen-min Jih-pao*, July 5, 1960.
22. *Jen-min Jih-pao*, July 14, 1960.
23. *Jen-min Jih-pao*, July 14, 1960.
24. *Bintang Timur*, July 4, 1960, *New China News Agency*, July 4, 1960.
25. *Bintang Timur*, July 8, 1960, *New China News Agency*, July 8, 1960.
26. *Antara News Agency*, July 9, 1960 and July 14, 1960, *New China News Agency*, July 10, 1960.
27. See above p. 84.
28. The 'July evaluation' spoke of double dealing with the rebels, who were too easily pardoned and taken back into the fold by the Central Army Command.
29. That this attack on Subandrio was the main 'news' in the P.K.I. statement was also reflected in the way *Antara* covered it on July 9 giving it the headline 'Communist appraisal of Subandrio's policy'. This first report barely touched upon the other points raised – this was done in its second news report on the P.K.I. document on July 14 – but mentioned three points of criticism against Subandrio's conduct of Indonesia's foreign relations: The Australian-Indonesian communiqué, the 'concessions' to the U.S. (accepting restrictions on the use of American weapons), and the attempts to form a 'third force' with other non-aligned nations like Yugoslavia. Interestingly

the *Antara* news bulletin on both occations made no reference to the P.K.I. statement on Subandrio's 'contribution' to the strained state of Sino-Indonesian relations.

30. *Antara News Agency*, July 12, 1960.
31. See: *Antara News Agency*, July 14, 1960 and July 18, 1960 *New China News Agency*, July 17, 20 and 26, 1960, *Djakarta Radio Home Service*, July 30, 1960 and *Review of Indonesia*, August 1960.
32. This situation lasted until the end of July, while the interrogations of Aidit, Njoto, Lukman and Sudisman took place from July 20 until 30, 1960. At the issue of the Supreme Advisory Council meeting in Merdeka Palace on July 1 and 2, military surrounded the palace and waited for the S.A.C. members to leave. The non-communists were left alone; the communists among them were 'conducted' to a command post to be 'registered'. Aidit did not dare to go out of the palace and asked the President for protection; he got an Air Force officer assigned for this purpose. (Interview March 1972 with the former Deputy Chairman of the S.A.C., Ruslan Abdulgani).
33. Interview, March 1972, with Ahmad Sukendro.
34. *Indonesian Herald*, October 20, 1965.
35. *Antara News Agency*, July 20, 1960. The two parties were indeed banned in August and subsequently went into voluntary liquidation.
36. See also: Arnold C. Brackman, 1966, *South East Asia's Second Front: The Power Struggle in the Malay Archipelago*, Frederick A. Praeger, New York, p. 97.
37. *Antara News Agency*, July 21, 1960.
38. *Djakarta Radio Home Service*, July 25, 1960.
39. *Antara News Agency*, August 17, 1960; *Review of Indonesia*, August 1960.
40. *Antara News Agency*, September 29, 1960; *Harian Rakjat*, September 28, 1960.
41. *Antara News Agency*, September 2 and 4, 1960.
42. *Antara News Agency*, September 13, 1960, *New China News Agency*, September 14, 1960. The whole affair cost Brigadier-General Ahmad Sukendro his job; he was sent abroad on a mission until allowed to return again at the end of 1963.
43. See above p. 71.
44. *New China News Agency*, July 19, 1960. See this page, note 32.
45. *Review of Indonesia*, August 1960. The statement made by Aidit was dated August 2, 1960.
46. Interview, March 1973 with Ahmad Sukendro.
47. *Pedoman*, August 3, 1960.
48. *Harian Rakjat*, August 2, 1960. The official party paper had been suspended temporarily by the military authorities as from July 16.
49. *New China News Agency*, August 9, 1960.
50. *Harian Rakjat*, August 10, 1960.
51. See above p. 74.
52. *Harian Rakjat*, August 10, 1960.

53. It was Njono, for example, who had started the ball rolling with his Sobsi statement in the middle of June; see above p. 84. Van der Kroef in Sino-Indonesian Friendship, *Orbis*, Summer 1964, writes: 'Early in 1961 a serious rift in the party leadership appeared, in part over the Moscow-Peking dispute, but primarily over domestic policy. The P.K.I. economic experts Sakirman and Asmu, along with Njono, who leads the Communist labor front Sobsi, favored a militant denunciation of the weakness of the government's economic policy and of army incompetence and corruption in order to capitalize on widespread discontent'. One can agree with this except for the period in which this rift is said to have occurred. As pointed out here, mid-1960 would be nearer the mark.
54. See above p. 83.
55. See above pp. 85, 87.
56. Labor Minister Erningpradja also gave in and had to put water in his wine as far as his plans for outflanking Sobsi with a new state-controlled trade union was concerned; see *Harian Rakjat*, August 12, 1960.
57. Uri Ra'anan, 1969, *The U.S.S.R. Arms the Third World: Case studies in Soviet Foreign Policy*, The M.I.T. Press, Cambridge, Massachusetts, p. 201.
58. *Antara News Agency*, July 22, 1960.
59. Subandrio speech, as reported by the *Menado Radio Regional Service*, August 11, 1960.

CHAPTER 8

Chinese friends and Soviet arms (1960-1961)

Subandrio's new position on the question of the overseas Chinese provided an even more striking example of his 'conversion' than his newfound belligerent tone on West Irian.[1] On July 26 Subandrio received Chinese Ambassador Huang Cheng-nan for two hours. He commented afterwards that they had reached 'fundamental agreement' on the overseas Chinese, leaving the two parties only a few technical points to be 'ironed out'.[2] The note to the Chinese government that the two discussed could hardly have been satisfactory to Peking since it blamed one of the Chinese diplomats for the Tjimahi incident and said some disagreeable things about Chinese radio and press incidents against Indonesia.[3] Moreover, it did not go into the demands for redress contained in the Chinese note of protest of July 11, saying only that those found guilty – 'if any' – would be punished. Nevertheless, Chinese Foreign Minister Chen Yi in an interview with *Harian Rakjat* in early August, expressed his satisfaction at the Indonesian note and even promised to look into the question of anti-Indonesian broadcasts by Peking Radio.[4] Premier Chou En-Lai appeared at the 17th August reception in Peking and sounded equally benign. He said the problem of the overseas Chinese was only 'temporary'. His deputy, Li Hsien-mei foresaw 'a reasonable overall settlement'.[5] After all the acrimonious wrangling, the *New China News Agency* sounded almost happy to report Sukarno's dictum at the swearing in of the new Indonesian Ambassador to China, Sukarni, that 'we have a little difficulty with China . . . but it is only a scratch on the skin'.[6] In record time the executive agreement needed to put the Dual Nationality Treaty of 1955 into effect was now agreed upon.[7] It provided for far greater numbers of overseas Chinese automatically or easily to acquire Indonesian nationality than Djakarta had initially wanted to concede. More guarantees were also built in for an equitable and speedy settlement of the administrative procedures involved. These concessions by Indonesia, though by no means going all the way the Chinese had hoped, finally paved the way to an accommodation between the two sides. It was Sukarno who, intervening personally, brought about a milder Indonesian standpoint.

Given the time sequence outlined above,[8] it is not difficult to see that it was the priority Sukarno decided to accord to the West Irian issue that provided the motivation for restoring good relations with Peking at short notice, even at the cost of some concessions.[9] By the middle of December the documents were signed, with Huang Cheng-nan still slightly reserved as he observed, rather coolly, that the two governments 'have made initial advances in efforts to achieve an overall settlement of the overseas Chinese question'.[10] Subandrio was more ebullient, looking back upon the whole affair, 'not as a quarrel, but as a difference of view between two friendly countries'.[11] It should provide a foundation for establishing the closest cooperation, he said. 'We need friendship and a common struggle, because most of the Asian and African countries have won independence. We are aware that, after leaving by the front door, imperialism and colonialism often attempt to enter through the back door in the form of neo-colonialism. On this matter our two countries and peoples can establish close cooperation'.[12] For the P.K.I. the prospect of an improvement in relations with China was encouraging because it removed an embarrassing obstacle in their drive for wide public acclaim as a radical but soundly national party. *Harian Rakjat* was jubilant, seeing 'eternal friendship between Indonesia and China' written on the wall.[13] The newspaper felt vindicated, claiming that 'we have always held that differences of opinion between Asian and African countries including those between Indonesia and China are not good for Asian and African countries, particularly these two countries'.

The Chinese were not yet prepared to accept the Indonesian volte-face for what it was, and a *Jen-min Jih-pao* editorial at the end of December, devoted to Sino-Indonesian relations, repeated the reservations of Huang Cheng-nan earlier that month.[14] Chinese Foreign Minister Chen Yi, at the end of January 1961, in reply to a question by the *Antara* correspondent in Peking, said he could not yet accept Subandrio's invitation to visit Indonesia, adding rather cryptically that he wanted to wait until the implementation of the Dual Nationality treaty.[15] Nevertheless, it was two months later that Chen Yi came to Djakarta, sealing with his presence the normalization of relations between the two countries that was to form the basis of a growing involvement ending in the dramatic climax of the 30th September movement four years later.

Looking at this episode from the Chinese side the observation has been made that 'Peking essentially abandoned the objective of attempting to maintain an important political foothold in Indonesia through its ties with the overseas Chinese'.[16] Given that ethnic Chinese, irrespective of their nationality, tend to maintain a strong China-oriented identity, the concessions obtained by Peking seem, however, to have outweighed the concessions made. This argument is reinforced by the possibility that was left open to overseas Chinese choosing Indonesian citizenship to regain their original nationality by returning to China. The accommodation reached with the Indonesian government may therefore not have meant such a big sacrifice to Peking.

In the midst of the evolving Sukarno-led 'rapprochement' with Communist China, the Indonesian armed forces kept playing their own game for a while. Early in October an anti-Peking Chinese newspaper was started, and, by the time it had obtained a license to appear regularly, a pro-Peking competitor was ordered to cease publication.[17] A few weeks later, the office of the Military Administrator in Djakarta ordered all papers and periodicals to stop using Chinese letterpress as from the first of June 1961.[18] By that time, however, the military leadership was getting more and more entangled in the West Irian affair and was increasingly confronted with the consequences of their support for a more militant campaign against the Dutch. Defence Minister Nasution who as a devout muslim was fiercely anti-communist had of course been aware of the danger to Indonesia's internal and external posture involved in such a policy. While fully convinced that the country had a just cause, his utterances remained pitched in low key, though not without the current tributes to nationalist phrasing.[19] To retain the greatest possible freedom to maneuver was one of his foremost concerns, and here the dependence of the armed forces on foreign weaponry was a disturbing factor. It was therefore understandable that Nasution, being part of Sukarno's 'Nasakom' delegation to the

United Nations session, decided to use an otherwise rather pointless stay abroad to sound out the American Defense Department on chances of the United States providing the necessary hardware for the West Irian campaign.[20] This turned out basically to be a failure, as the Americans did not want to do more than take on the equipment of 40 infantry battalions, probably assuming that lack of transportation would make them unfit for use against the Dutch.[21]

On the way home, during the stopover in Kuala Lumpur, Nasution stressed that Indonesia should do its utmost to establish its sovereignty over West Irian by peaceful means within the context of the United Nations.[22] Back in Djakarta, commenting on his trip to the U.S.A., he confined himself to the observation that the Pentagon now had a better insight into the West Irian problem.[23] But while Nasution still made some attempts to get the U.S.A. interested in supplying arms to Indonesia, secret negotiations were going on in Moscow and Djakarta to work out detailed arrangements for the delivery of Soviet arms on the basis of the Kruschov-Sukarno deal earlier that year.[24] Thus when Nasution again left Djakarta in January 1961 on a shopping expedition, this time to the Soviet Union, he was already sure of the outcome. It is not entirely clear whether the Soviet loan for military purposes was initially welcomed by Nasution and the army command.[25] But at any rate at the time the deal with Moscow was to be finalized the Indonesian military were going along with it. On January 3, 1961, the Indonesian delegation officially started talks with their Soviet counterparts, led by Deputy Premier Anastas Mikoyan, and only three days later the previously prepared agreement for the delivery of arms and military equipment at the cost of roughly half a billion dollars was signed.[26] It entailed the purchase of bombers, fighters, submarines, destroyers, etc., to be delivered without delay.[27] No doubt, with the previous Soviet standing offer as a basis, the arms deal must have been clinched earlier.[28] The Soviet leaders gave the most fulsome approval of Indonesian policies towards West Irian, towards which they were 'profoundly sympathetic'.[29] They must have been aware of Sukarno's resolve to use these weapons, not only to exert political pressure but, if necessary, directly, and they must have approved of it.[30] Furthermore, only a few days after the deal, partly as a reminder to the home front that helping to arm underdeveloped countries was a worthwhile pastime for a communist country, they sent a strong protest to the Netherlands government against the stationing of American tactical atomic weapons on Dutch soil, strongly underscoring the evil collusion between the two brands of imperialism in Europe and overseas.[31] Nasution was in something of a dilemma. Clearly satisfied with the results of his visit, he was quoted as having left the Soviet Union saying: 'We have met real friends'.[32] On the other hand, immediately after his arrival in Djakarta, he took pains to assure the Indonesians that the country had by no means given up its 'independent, active foreign policy' but only secured arms where others had refused either to supply them or had been too parsimonious.[33] He explained the bargain with a reference to the Dutch wanting to settle the West Irian affair by force and tried to sound as non-belligerent as possible. Fears that he had all but ceased to oppose participation of the communists in the Indonesian government expressed at the time turned out to be unfounded.[34] If Nasution had helped the communist cause he helped its international, or better still its Soviet version rather than the local variety, for the tangible support extended to the Sukarno regime gave the Soviet Union a perfect opportunity to pose as the champion of anti-colonialism *par excellence*. Mikoyan's speech was full of it: 'By our principles we are the enemies of colonialism. The great Lenin advised us to support in every way the struggle of the people of colonial countries for their freedom and independence and we fulfill this sacred command of Lenin's etc.'[35] *Harian Rakjat* reacted as if to a cue.

In its first comment on the arms deal it stressed the fact that the Soviet Union had, in aiding Indonesia, clearly shown itself to be on the side of the Asian, African, and Latin-American nations in their fight against colonialism and imperialism.[36] And the impression in concerned quarters must have been: most effectively so, offering not only words, but the material that would do the job of dealing with the Western powers.

It is therefore not surprising that China did not show any great enthusiasm for the whole affair. Its central news agency said curtly that 'a Soviet-Indonesian agreement was concluded in Moscow, according to Tass', without giving any details except that it was signed by Mikoyan and Nasution and that the Indonesian delegation had meanwhile left the Soviet capital.[37] In the state of comradely discussion between Moscow and Peking, this cool reaction was perfectly fitting because the attitude to adopt towards the national liberation movement had meanwhile become a hotly debated issue. The new opening Kruschov was creating for his Soviet brand of world communism gained even more in significance by the fact that a few hours before he attended the ceremony of the Indonesian arms deal the Soviet Prime Minister had delivered his first authoritative comment on the Moscow Conference of 81 communist parties of the previous November.[38] In it figured prominently his thoughts on various types of war, specifically sanctioning as 'just' all fights against colonizers, new and old: 'The Communists fully support such just wars and march in the front rank with the peoples waging liberation struggles'.[39] The idea that the lengthy theoretical deliberations of the past months could be put to the test instantly and in a concrete way must have pleased the Soviet leader.

We will see now what had gone on in the public Sino-Soviet exchanges and where the P.K.I. tried to fit in. Early in June 1960 the General Council of the world Federation of Trade Union had a meeting in Peking with Indonesia represented by a Sobsi official, Achadijat. The positions he defended in his address to the Council meeting reflected somewhat radical 'Chinese' views.[40] But as we have seen, the Indonesian trade union leaders were, in general, more leftist than the official P.K.I. line represented by Aidit.[41] One of the main points of dispute was the inevitability of war, and the Chinese representative, W.F.T.U. Vice-President Liu Chang-sheng, introduced something Mao Tse-tung had apparently slipped up on in 1957 during the conference of the 81 communist parties in the Soviet capital. The Moscow Declaration that had resulted from this conference stated that the forces of peace were now so strong that they could prevent 'war'.[42] As this, taken literally, could mean all kinds of war, Liu Chang-sheng now made a distinction, saying that the elimination of world war might be a possibility, but local wars of all kinds remained inevitable. As this applied particularly to colonial and semi-colonial areas, it was only natural that this refinement, introduced by the Chinese trade union leader, received support from various Asian and African delegates. Achadijat may have supported the new interpretation, but in his published speech this was not evident, probably because he was only informed about it while attending the conference.[43] Then, at the end of that same month, an informal meeting of communist party chiefs took place in Bucharest, where they had assembled to attend a Rumanian

Party Congress. It was here that Kruschov mounted the Soviet counter-attack against the Chinese positions as they had been published for the first time at the end of April 1960 as part of the Lenin Anniversary commemoration.[44] Of the impact of this new round in the emerging Sino-Soviet dispute upon the P.K.I. there is very little trace, although some current issues in the continuing debate were noticeable. *Harian Rakjat* therefore found occasion (in an article on 'Nato weapons for West Irian') to ridicule the notion that the nature of imperialism had changed, as their 'hench-men' claimed.[45] The strongest position taken by the P.K.I. was related to Yugoslavia's revisionism, and *Harian Rakjat* charged that Belgrade had never taken a stand against 'imperialism' and had 'prostituted' its foreign policy to the imperialists.[46] This attack was a further elaboration of the anti-Subandrio theme of the 'July evaluation', and it was designed to remove the impression that Yugoslavia and Indonesia were pursuing the same foreign policy. Subandrio, with his mistaken support for a 'small summit' of non-aligned countries was seen as a new sort of 'Hatta'.[47] The relatively harsh and direct condemnation of Yugoslav policies came in the wake of the 'July evaluation', some days before it had become clear that the P.K.I. had stuck out its neck too far. When that moment came a lot of what had been said against Yugoslavia was retracted, no doubt because the military with their excellent relations with Belgrade were already casting their shadow.[48] From then on, until after the end of the Moscow conference in the autumn of 1960, the few pronunciations with a 'theoretical' slant emanating from P.K.I. sources were, as far as can be traced, entirely of domestic inspiration.[49] At the Third Congress of the North Vietnamese Lao Dong Party in September 1960 the Indonesian delegate, Party Secretary Anwar Kadir, is said to have been less 'Chinese' than, for instance, the Albanian delegate on that occasion.[50] His published speech revealed nothing but harmless generalities.[51] There does not seem to have been a steady exchange in the ideological field with the centers of communist opinion-making. The impression therefore prevails that the P.K.I., whatever their numerical strength at the time was, were operating in provincial backwaters.[52] Aidit, who had stayed in Indonesia and sent his alter-ego First Deputy Chairman Lukman to represent the P.K.I., was the first to react to the results of the Moscow conference of November 1960. He apologized for its preliminary character and explained it, saying that 'Bung [Brother] Lukman has not yet returned'.[53] The remarks he then made could have been made irrespective of the Moscow meeting since they reflected general concern lest the P.K.I. might appear foreign dominated or subversive.[54] The report Lukman delivered to the second plenum of the P.K.I. Central Committee on his return at the end of December and the resolution adopted subsequently give at least some indication of the P.K.I. position at the time.[55] On the *organization issue*, that is, the validity for others of conclusions supported by a majority of communist parties, the P.K.I. had no problems – why should it have – and came out squarely in favor of far-reaching autonomy, that is unanimity.[56] Lukman stressed that the Moscow documents were agreed upon in all freedom and equality and not based on 'one party (being) superior to another'. The P.K.I. resolution stated in this respect that 'all Marxist-Leninist Parties are free and have corresponding rights; they base their policies on actual conditions within each country, guided by Marxist-Leninist principles, and they mutually support each other'. On the *substantive issues*, the 'nature of the era' played a prominent role during the conference.[57] Lukman followed more or less the text of the Moscow statement that the communist camp was 'decisively' influencing world events, while the P.K.I. resolution was more neutral and only stated that the world socialist system had become a 'settled' factor in human development. On the question of war and peace, the wording and emphasis of the resolution ranged the P.K.I. rather on the side of the Chinese.[58] But special references in it to the chances of preventing a world war and to the 'historical significance' of the Soviet disarmament proposals point to a more moderate approach.[59] No mention is made of the consequences of a third world war, a point alluded to by Lukman where he spoke of the need to avoid such a conflagration 'so that the collapse of imperialism does not create a catastrophe for humanity'. Revisionism according to the resolution posed the greatest danger. But no mention was made of 'dogmatism and sectarianism' as in the Moscow statement, which said these deviations 'also [could] become the principal danger'.[60] Instead of this, a long diatribe followed against Yugoslav modern revisionist excesses as exemplified by Kardelj's recent publication on 'Socialism and War', ending in an abjuration to 'continue exposing the Yugoslav revisionist leaders', a formula inserted in the Moscow statement on Chinese insistence.[61] The foregoing shows that on the now emerging 'organizational' issue – the independence of a communist party to take positions – the P.K.I. was of one mind. Both left, right, and center factions agreed that the P.K.I. was a free agent within the international communist movement and that they could be so all the easier because the party owed its strength within Indonesia to no one outside the country. It brought the whole party automatically on the side of the Chinese on this count, as Peking then also began to champion this fiercely for itself and for others. As to the substantive issues, the P.K.I. after the Moscow conferences of November 1960, took up a center or rather compromise position between Moscow and Peking on the question of 'war and peace': While some of the wording favored the 'Chinese' bent for picturing the chances of war rather in somber colors, the more moderate side, under Aidit, got in some positive words on disarmament. This middle-of-the-road attitude, exemplified in the P.K.I. resolution on the Moscow conference, may have been typical for the balance of power and opinion within the P.K.I. at that moment, but it had two interesting exceptions. On the one hand there were violent diatribes against revisionism, particularly of the Yugoslav variety which was attacked by name, an escalation compared with April of the same year.[62] On the other hand it contained a full-fledged endorsement of the 'national democratic state' concept that was basically nothing but a more-or-less eloquent plea for a gradualist, 'right' domestic strategy intended to be applied to the Indonesian scene. It could here be tentatively suggested that this was an Aidit ploy to keep things in hand; no truck as far as it concerned his rightist tactics of accommodation and infiltration at *home*, in exchange for a concession to the radicals where it might hurt least, both in terms of domestic considerations and of international-communist orientation, preferably a *foreign* issue such as Yugoslav revisionism. That Aidit was still in essence a moderate was shown by the fact that Lukman, his trusted aide, on the whole range of issues brought up at the Moscow meeting had clearly taken up a position to the right of the final P.K.I. resolution.

NOTES

1. At the end of November 1960, Subandrio was to escalate further and announce that Indonesia could no longer guarantee that no armed conflict would break out between Dutch and Indonesian forces in the West Irian area; see *Antara News Agency*, November 30, 1960. In so doing, he dropped

earlier assurances to the contrary: see above p. 83.

2. *Antara News Agency*, July 26, 1960.
3. *Antara News Agency*, July 27, 1960.
4. *Harian Rakjat*, August 5, 1960, *Antara News Agency*, August 5, 1960.
5. *New China News Agency*, August 17, 1960.
6. *New China News Agency*, August 23, 1960, *Antara News Agency*, August 22, 1960.
7. It took the joint commission, set up in January 1960, 18 sessions and six months to achieve a breakthrough which came with the Subandrio-Huang Cheng talks of July 26. On September 8 the Indonesian delegate Tirtoprodjo, after another six sessions cnly, announced 'complete agreement'.
8. See above p. 84 ff.
9. Harold C. Hinton, 1966, *Communist China in World Politics*, Houghton Mifflin Company, Boston, p. 433, writes: 'Sukarno probably felt that compromise was needed in the interest of more important matters, such as his confrontation with the Netherlands over West Irian which was beginning to come to a head and in which Chinese support might be useful'.
10. *New China News Agency*, December 15, 1960.
11. *Djakarta Radio Home Service*, December 15, 1960.
12. *New China News Agency*, December 15, 1960.
13. *Harian Rakjat*, December 16, 1960.
14. *Jen-min Jih-pao*, December 24, 1960, *New China News Agency*, December 24, 1960.
15. *Antara News Agency*, January 28, 1961. The executive agreement signed on December 15th, 1960, came into force 10 days later. It fixed January 20, 1962, as the date before which those concerned should opt either for Indonesian or Chinese nationality.
16. D. P. Mozingo, 1965, *Sino-Indonesian relations: An Overview, 1955-1965*, Rand Corporation, Santa Monica, p. 28.
17. *New China News Agency*, November 2, 1960.
18. *Antara News Agency*, November 18, 1960. It was not until the end of 1963 that this ban was lifted again; Justus M. van der Kroef, Sino-Indonesian partnership, *Orbis*, summer 1964.
19. See for example *Antara News Agency*, August 13, 1960.
20. *Antara News Agency*, September 20, 1960. As part of the cooling-off period which Sukarno considered desirable after the 'hot summer' of 1960, the Indonesian President had included in his United Nations delegation the chairman of the three main parties, Ali Sastroamidjojo for the P.N.I., Idham Chalid for the Nahdatul Ulama, Aidit for the P.K.I., as well as Nasution; *Antara News Agency*, September 15, 1960.
21. Also Arnold C. Brackman, 1966, *Southeast Asia's Second Front*, New York, Frederik A. Praeger, p. 98.
22. *Djakarta Radio Home Service*, October 13, 1960.
23. *Antara News Agency*, October 20, 1960.
24. See above p. 64.

25. At the time of the Kruschov visit early in 1960, it was rumored that the Soviets had again offered arms but that the Armed Forces had opposed the transaction; Dr. Guy Pauker, General Nasutions mission to Moscow, *Asian Survey*, March 1961.
26. *Tass*, January 3, 1960, *Antara News Agency*, January 6, 1960. An Indonesian diplomat in Bonn, which the mission passed through on its way to the Soviet capital, claimed that the deal involved 400 million dollars. This was denied by Nasution upon his return; *Antara News Agency*, January 17, 1960. *Far Eastern Economic Review*, April 27, 1961 puts it at £140 million, also 400 million dollars thus; ex-Ambassador Adam Melik, now Indonesia's Foreign Minister, put it at 600 million dollars; see above pp. 64 and 77, note 6.
27. *Djakarta Radio Home Service*, January 16, 1960. See for a first-hand account of huge military aid given to Sukarno by the Soviet government the illuminating reports by Hans Martinot in the Dutch daily *De Gelderlander*, March 14, 15 and 19, 1963.
28. Kruschov, during the signing ceremony, saw that Mikoyan was finished much faster than Nasution and joked: 'Clearly Mikoyan underwrote everything a long time ago'; *Antara News Agency*, January 6, 1960.
29. *Pravda*, January 8, 1961, text of the Soviet-Indonesian communiqué.
30. Kruschov interrupted Mikoyan during a formal reception, stressing that the Dutch would be evicted from West Irian soon. This remark was duly published so as to underline Soviet approval of Indonesia's intentions; *Pravda*, January, 1961.
31. *Antara News Agency*, January 8, 1961.
32. *Antara News Agency*, January 6, 1960.
33. *Djakarta Radio Home Service*, January 16, 1961.
34. See, e.g., Pauker, *Asian Survey*, March 1961.
35. *Pravda*, January 7, 1961.
36. *Harian Rakjat*, January 10, 1961, *Antara News Agency*, January 10, 1961.
37. *New China News Agency*, January 7, 1961. When Sukarno earlier had praised the communist countries for their support in the West-Irian affair, *New China News Agency* studiously ignored the comment, while Moscow radio picked it up. *New China News Agency*, November 3, 1960; *Moscow Radio in Indonesia*, November 4, 1960.
38. *Kommunist* (Moscow), January 1961; *Pravda*, January 25, 1961.
39. *Pravda*, January 25, 1961, *Kommunist* (Moscow), January 1960.
40. Donald S. Zagoria, 1962, *The Sino-Soviet Conflict 1956-1961*, Princeton University Press, Princeton, p. 323.
41. Also: Zagoria, 1962, p. 323, note 15.
42. G. F. Hudson Ed., 1961, The Sino-Soviet Dispute, *The China Quarterly*, London.
43. *New China News Agency*, June 8, 1960.
44. See above p. 70 ff.
45. *Harian Rakjat*, June 28, 1960.
46. *Harian Rakjat*, July 12, 1960.

47. The former Vice-President of the Republic was employed on various occasions as a bogey (see also p. 53).
48. *Harian Rakjat*, July 15, 1960. The day after this article appeared, on July 16, *Harian Rakjat* was temporarily banned.
49. In an article commemorating the 1945 Constitution, the editorial department of *Harian Rakjat* was at pains to explain that the 'socialist' or 'second' phase of the Indonesian Revolution had not yet arrived as some thought. Against the background of the problems facing the central P.K.I. leadership, or rather Aidit, in smoothing the ruffled feelings, it is evident that this 'second' stage was not called for, as it would have meant, according to all handbooks, that the P.K.I. should follow its more radical wing and start 'leading' the revolution. See *Harian Rakjat*, August 20, 1960.
50. William E. Griffith, 1963, *Albania and the Sino-Soviet Rift*, The M.I.T. Press, Cambridge, Massachusetts, p. 50.
51. *Vietnam News Agency*, September 13, 1960.
52. So no echo is found of the 'war and peace' articles in *Pravda* by Frantsev and Ponomarev (*Pravda*, August 7 and 12, 1960), the Zhukov article on colonialism (*Pravda*, August 26, 1960), or the discussion of Kardelj's 'Socialism and War' (*Pravda*, September 1, 1960); *Kommunist* (Moscow), 1960.
53. *Harian Rakjat*, December 19, 1960. Lukman had stayed on after the October celebrations for behind-the-scene discussions in Moscow all through November.
54. Aidit explained that a gathering of the Moscow type did not constitute an international communist organization but only a clearing house of ideas and experiences. He stressed that communism was purely Indonesian, since it existed in the country 'before feudalism'. Thirdly, he turned against both the 'import' and 'export' of revolution.
55. *Harian Rakjat*, December 24, 1960 and January 3, 1961; *New China News Agency*, January 5, 1961.
56. The Russians, seeing that the unanimity rule would give China a leverage which in their eyes was unwarranted and undesirable, had tried to establish a sort of majority mechanism during the conference. The outcome, however, was undecided.
57. Zagoria, 1962, p. 350. The point hinges on the degree to which the 'world socialist system', i.e. the combined force of the communist countries, decisively called the tune in world affairs. The Chinese had their doubts here.
58. 'It is emphasised that, as long as imperialism exists, there will be fertile ground for aggressive warfare, and that the aggressive nature of imperialism will not change... However, say the two documents, forces capable of defeating aggressive imperialism plans have been developed.' This paragraph was also quoted literally by *New China News Agency* in its résumé on January 5, 1961.
59. Significantly these two passages were left out in the Chinese news report on the discussion; *New China News Agency*, January 5, 1961.
60. *Pravda*, December 2, 1960.

61. This 'continuous exposure' was not taken up by Kruschov in his interpretative commentary on January 6, 1961, when he merely said that Yugoslav revisionism was unanimously condemned by the communist parties.
62. On revisionism and dogmatism – in Indonesian terms then still called 'capitulasi-ism' and 'avonturisme' – it was hardliner Hutapea who had stressed the danger from the right, Sakirman that from the left, and Aidit had taken a center position. On the 'foreign' version of this issue, 'modern revisionism', Sudisman had attacked the Yugoslav by name then, but the P.K.I. statement had not gone that far. See above pp. 75, 76 and 77.

CHAPTER 9

Growing Sino-Soviet rift (1961)

For Indonesia the year 1961 was dominated by the West Irian problem with Sukarno starting what amounted to a personal crusade to convince the world that, amidst affairs like the Congo, Algeria, and Berlin, the Papuan jungle territory administered by the colonial Dutch was at least as dangerous an issue. Therefore, after having been host to the Chinese Foreign Minister Chen Yi at the beginning of April, when improved Sino-Indonesian relations were consecrated by a formal treaty of friendship, Sukarno embarked upon an extended tour which took him to the centers of world power. Adroitly, he had engineered an invitation by the newly elected American President, John F. Kennedy, whom Sukarno had rightly understood to be anxious not to let him travel exclusively within the communist orbit. The nationalist paper *Merdeka* described the trip, with an exaggerated sense of drama, as a 'last attempt at a peaceful solution'.[1] At that time Kennedy did not seem to be impressed and must have dismissed Sukarno's opening move upon arrival in the United States – 'we shall meet force with force' – as so much bluster.[2] But wherever he could Sukarno did not fail to 'plug' the need for a return of West Irian.[3] The main emphasis was clearly meant to come with the week-long stay in Moscow where Sukarno – on purpose as he claimed – even celebrated his 60th anniversary.[4] In a way, Sukarno could not have wished for more than he got, as Kruschov thought the moment had arrived to make the Indonesian President, at a lavish reception, member of the select club of non-communist leaders of third world countries who 'belonged', by calling him 'Comrade Bung Sukarno'.[5] But on the subject of West Irian, nothing much new could be added, making Kruschov observe that it was 'naturally understood' that the Soviet Union supported Djakarta's case.[6]

The Soviet leaders wanted to avoid too much stress on the military side of the affair as was shown by the paucity of detail which surrounded further arms arrangements concluded.[7] A certain weariness that Indonesia might some day take the military hardware that it was getting from the Soviet Union for more than expensive toys cropped up when Brezhnev – then in his capacity of State President – told his audience at a friendship rally what it was that Indonesia wanted, i.e., should want: No local wars, no world war, but peace for economic and political development.[8]

In this sense Nasution, who also spoke on that occasion, was a better partner for the Soviet leaders than the bombastic Sukarno. Twice during his ten-minute speech – Sukarno took five times longer – the Indonesian general stressed that it would take a long time before the West Irian problem could be solved. While Sukarno was in Moscow, it unexpectedly became known that he would also go to Peking.[9] He left for China on June 13 and, in all, spent not more than 48 hours there, as his previous engagements clearly did not allow for a longer digression.[10] It may very well be that Aidit, who had been Sukarno's precursor in each Communist capital the President visited, had been instrumental in arranging this short excursion.[11] If so, Sukarno must have been grateful for this help because, in terms of his West-Irian mission, the visit, short though it was, turned out to be much more of a success than the Moscow part. For an extremely vain character like the Indonesian statesman's, it must have been gratifying to be welcomed at such a short notice in a fully dressed-up and illuminated Chinese capital replete with his own effigy – including a gigantic oilpainted one – while, for a mass rally in his honor, no less than half a million participants were drummed up.[12] What was more, Sukarno's militant approach was answered in kind by his Chinese hosts, who felt less constrained to praise both the man and his policy now that the dispute of the last few years that had kept the two countries at odds was approaching a solution. For his share in this development the official daily *Jen-min Jih-pao*, on the eve of his arrival, paid a particularly warm tribute to Sukarno personally.[13] The paper also lauded Indonesia for its 'successes' against colonialism, saying that China was closely watching its fight for the recovery of West Irian.

Taking Sukarno up on his own utterances, it quoted him to the effect that this fight 'would never cease', a theme that, from the Chinese side, was to be played up time and again that year. In the joint communiqué Sukarno received the most far-reaching Chinese endorsement to date for his attempts to force the Dutch out of West Irian. This time it was China's government that committed itself and 'unequivocally' expressed once again its all-out support.[14] It was therefore not surprising that Aidit, in his report on his latest peripatetic experiences, almost purring with satisfaction, concluded that Sukarno's visit to China had pushed the Sino-Indonesian friendship 'to an advanced new stage'.[15] Another weapon in Sukarno's arsenal was the Belgrade meeting of non-aligned nations set for the beginning of September.[16]

The Chinese, and the P.K.I., had misgivings as to the usefulness of this forum. To Peking it was going to be a Bandung conference from which it was excluded, while at the same time the main animator – next to Sukarno – was its revisionist archenemy Tito playing host. At an earlier period the P.K.I. had strongly opposed what it then called a 'little summit' that would inaugurate a third, neutralist bloc between East and West.[17] So the party had questioned the use of a conference of 'states pursing an independent foreign policy' and considered it wrong to come up with what it called an ideological concept – a Tito-Nehru-Sukarno concertation – instead of a geographical one that was purely an Afro-Asian one. Many people did not like Tito's Yugoslavia and its revisionism, it was further argued.[18] Both China and the Indonesian communists had softened somewhat but remained apprehensive lest 'Belgrade' would permanently overshadow 'Bandung'. On the day Sukarno left for the conference *Harian Rakjat* warned that no neutral stand towards 'imperialism' was possible and that it would be wrong for the Indonesian delegation to take up a position 'equidistant from either bloc'.[19] On the eve of the meeting the communist party paper stressed that it considered the gathering in Belgrade a step towards another Bandung conference.[20] For his part, Sukarno had taken pains to reassure critics in the same vein as, for instance, in his August 17 speech, when he said that the two conferences would not compete with each other but would be 'complementary'.[21] Chen Yi, in a comment on the same day, expressed the hope that Sukarno was right. However, he added the warning that it was necessary 'to guard the imperialist scheme of sabotaging the conference by diverting its struggle to other objectives'.[22] Now this was a prelude to a basic difference that showed up the Belgrade conference over priorities.

Was the struggle against colonialism to take precedence as Indonesia, or rather Sukarno, advocated or should the conference turn its attention, first and foremost, to the tensions between the two world blocs exemplified by the tension around Berlin, as Nehru was to maintain. As Sukarno had come to Belgrade with the clear intention of enlisting the greatest possible support for his West Irian case, 'anti-colonialism' was at the top of his list, and he made himself the eloquent champion of this view. Personal rivalry with the Indian Prime Minister, who expressed the opposite point of view and thought that colonialism was of secondary importance compared with the world war that was to break out, made it even easier for Sukarno to pose as the champion of Afro-Asian radicalism.

Ruslan Abdulgani, who together with Ali Sastroamidjojo of the P.N.I. and Aidit, was a member of Sukarno's delegation, aptly formulated the difference between the two Asian statesmen. Commenting upon Nehru's point that, before all, an atomic disaster (on Berlin and related matters) should be prevented, Abdulgani said: 'Obviously, we cannot wait until a settlement is reached on a nuclear war that has not yet come, while we are actually under the threat of a conflagration ourselves'.[23] On this issue Sukarno found the P.K.I. wholeheartedly on his side since the Indonesian communists thought it was most 'strange' that a call was made at the conference by Nehru to 'forgive and forget colonialism'.[24] The Chinese coincided completely here, and *Jen-min Jih-pao* wrote in its first editorial on the conference, referring to Nehru: '*Somebody* [emphasis added] at the conference also advanced this argument: the era of classical colonialism is dead and gone'. The paper said that such an opinion was totally contrary to the facts, and it should not be forgotten that peace would be impossible so long as colonialism existed.[25] Here the Soviet Union was on the opposite side, because its leaders thought it was heresy not to give priority to the East-West confrontation in Euope. In a pre-conference commentary *Pravda* stated: 'If [this meeting] is to have meaning, it must look into the tension in Germany'.[26] In its selective coverage the Soviet press stressed especially Nehru's thesis that it was east-west negotiations or world-war.[27] This rather panicky attitude had no doubt been facilitated by the decision of the Kremlin leaders to explode an atomic bomb on the eve of the Belgrade conference, creating an atmosphere of tension conducive to Nehru-type reactions.

Sukarno did not change his prepared text and did not make any mention of the nuclear event. It was left to Abdulgani to express regrets at the resumption of testing by Moscow.[28] Aidit in Belgrade began by being non-committal, pointing out that the danger of a nuclear war was acute.[29] *Harian Rakjat* went further, saying that the Soviet Union had had no alternative.[30] After the conference, so long as Aidit had not yet returned, the paper continued this somewhat cautious line, supporting the Soviet Union on Germany and criticizing Tito and Nehru only indirectly – for having opposed a condemnation of American imperialism.[31] Speaking to the party faithful on the evening of his return, Aidit came out more clearly on the Soviet side – which was also the Chinese – and called the resumption of testing 'entirely correct and timely'.[32]

For Tito he had a particularly keen barb in his aside to the effect that 'perhaps I was the only communist at the whole conference'.[33] For Aidit, as well as for the Chinese, Sukarno was the hero of the conference.[34] The Indonesian communist leader even suggested that not the Belgrade Declaration would in future be the guideline but rather Sukarno's address. The point was that apart from being some kind of tribute to the President it also laid bare the weak spot in Sukarno's performance. Despite all his efforts, the Indonesian President had failed to get a direct reference to West Irian included in the final conference resolution. While Algeria, Angola, Congo, South Africa, Palestine, and Cuba were all mentioned by name in connection with their various plights, Sukarno had to make do with a general clause against all colonial occupation as far as his dispute with the Dutch was concerned.[35] Subandrio, feeling responsible, tried to gloss this over but Ali Sastroamidjojo, being as usual more straight-forward than most of Sukarno's courtiers, admitted that Indonesia could not be content with the results because West Irian had been left out.[36] Indonesian delegates were particularly sore at Tito, whom in private they charged with having sold them down the river to 'pacifists' like Nehru and U Nu.[37] Nehru was also blamed for having obstructed Sukarno's proposal to insert a definite time limit of two years in the paragraph demanding the termination of all colonialism.[38] But the Indonesian government had nevertheless made some headway with respect to West Irian. It got more publicity: China sometime afterwards even organized a West Irian week – and the Americans had thought it better to stay away from the inauguration of the New-Guinea Council set up by the Dutch to give the Papuans a taste of self-government. The weapons bought on credit in the Soviet Union began to show up in Indonesia, such as the TU-16 long distance bombers and did not fail to give some sense of urgency to the Indonesian claims.[39]

At the same time Nasution continued to put himself in a position that made the need for really drastic action less urgent. In London he told a press conference that Indonesia, militarily, had to be stronger than the Dutch 'in all spheres'.[40] Back in Indonesia he elucidated the point by saying 'We must take into account the Dutch power in *Europe*' [emphasis added], thus indicating that, as far as he was concerned, the armed forces were not yet ready for full-scale action against the West Irian territory.[41]

In the Netherlands, however, it had meanwhile begun to be realized increasingly that good intentions with regard to the health and happiness of the Papuans were not in themselves enough to save the situation. In 1961, the then Netherlands Foreign Minister, Dr. Joseph Luns, under general pressure revised his policy with a view to getting him and his government off the hook. The plan was to put the territory under United Nations trusteeship for a period, leaving the decision as to the ultimate solution in the hands of the international organization. This was obviously not what the Indonesians wanted. Djakarta, therefore, mounted a strong opposition, changing its tactics slightly. At the Belgrade conference Sukarno had produced an amendment to the usual Indonesian demand for the immediate transfer of West Irian by saying that, for the time being, transfer of the 'administration' would do, leaving the question of sovereignty in abeyance.[42] *Tass* described the Luns plan as 'collective colonization' and *Radio Moscow* had one of its periodic outbursts of fear of a conflagration in the area.[43] The P.K.I. produced a Politburo statement fully supporting the Sukarno approach and rejecting any form of internationalization.[44] After the first round of the United Nations debate during which Subandrio and Luns crossed swords, full approval was granted also from the Chinese side as appeared from an editorial in the leading South Chinese *Ta Kung Pao.*[45] With its inevitable anti-American slant – referring to U.S. 'penetrations and plunder' in West Irian – the paper pinned Indonesia down to its 'unshakeable determination' to gain the jungle area, citing a bold pronouncement by Subandrio that 'the struggle to recover West Irian will never end'.[46] The climate in the United Nations was not all that favorable to Indonesia, as a number of African nations, partly on vague grounds of racial affinity to the negroid Papuans, began to get interested in the affair. Sukarno, absent with kidney trouble in a hospital in Vienna, was under increasing pressure to do something. After having whipped up nationalist fervor to a steady pitch, he could do not much less than move forward. Moreover, India was preparing to set an example with Goa and other Portugese enclaves, intending to overrun them with a lot of chauvinistic flourishes. In Indonesia this was duly noticed, as in the nationalist paper *Merdeka*, which reminded its readers of Nehru's dictum that he would solve the Goa problem by force: 'Indonesia also has its "Goa-problem" in the shape of the West Irian problem'.[47] At the United Nations, to which Subandrio had returned at the beginning of November, the Indonesian delegation was in close touch with Krishna Menon, the man behind the Goa victories before he was shuttled into oblivion for his failure to prepare against the Chinese attack from the North.[48] The vote taken at the end of that month was inconclusive for all parties concerned, with the Dutch withdrawing their draft resolution after a similar but watered-down version sponsored by the so-called Brazzaville states had failed to get the required two-thirds majority. Subandrio looked at this optimistically, saying that at least the Netherlands had missed their qualified majority. However, Ali Sastroamidjojo, the Indonesian's chief U.N. representative, expressed regret that amongst Afro-Asian countries a clear split had occurred.[49]

Meanwhile, the United States delegation had busied itself with acting as informal mediator, paving the way for the solution that was to be found later: An interim period of United Nations administration, followed by conditional transfer of the territory to Indonesia. At this stage the United States role was resented, however, particularly (though in slightly varying degrees) by the P.K.I., the Chinese, and the Soviet Union.[50] But official Indonesian circles were no less negative towards the American suggestions, especially when on the Dutch side they were celebrated more or less as a victory of the diplomacy of Luns.[51] There had slowly evolved during the year quite a harmonious consensus on West Irian between Sukarno and his entourage, the P.K.I. and both communist superpowers. Of course, there remained differences in interest, emphasis, and tactics amongst these various 'agents', but, though differently motivated, they had to a remarkable degree arrived at a common denominator. The Soviets had in Indonesia a pure (almost laboratory) case for their newly invented 'national democratic state' that they were going to usher into communism with wallet, weapons, and words. Peking was in for any militant cause that had an anti-American tinge, particularly when it could so make up for lost prestige as towards Indonesia. The P.K.I., having gone through the valley after its premature leftist outburst in the middle of 1960, again saw a more rosy future ahead in a close symbiosis with a Sukarno increasingly obsessed by national and personal status symbols. In forging and cultivating a precious link with Moscow and Peking, Aidit and his P.K.I. could play a useful role to Sukarno; at least this was the way the Indonesian communist leader saw it, and he acted accordingly. Thus when Sukarno was finally hoisted onto the next platform of propaganda warfare by a queer mixture of volition and circumstance and issued his long-expected 'triple-command' to free West Irian from the Dutch, it was of the greatest importance to Aidit that he could not only offer a well-organized, multi-million claque at home, but also the steady support of influential friends and comrades abroad.[52]

The quarrel that broke out openly during the 22nd Party Congress of the C.P.S.U. in November 1961 between the political leaders of the two main 'reigning' communist parties, focussed temporarily on Albania. But to Aidit it threatened to disturb the balance that, he sensed, would enable him to restore the Party domestically to good fortunes and to extend its influence within the country further. To the P.K.I. Chairman, trouble could not have come at a worse moment, as is often the case with disagreeable things. Before the consequences of these events are described we should look at what went on in the Party earlier in 1961.

When Aidit went to Moscow to attend the 1961 Party Congress, it was his second trip to the Soviet Union that year. On May Day he had been honored by Kruschov who let him stand on the mausoleum together with the members of the Soviet Party Presidium to view the annual Red Square parade. On that occasion his trip to the Soviet Union had taken him via Prague, while he had been accompanied by Politburo-member Sakirman, one of the main instigators of last year's attempted left course.[53] He had then left the Party in the hands of his first deputy, Lukman, who for the duration of the P.K.I. delegation's tour through the communist world – about 10 weeks in all – had to be vigilant to see that no harm was meanwhile done. A few days before the P.K.I. delegation had taken off in the middle of April 1961 – probably they had been waiting for it – Sukarno had decided the case of the 'July evaluation' of the year before that the armed forces had submitted to Sukarno for judgment. Until then the P.K.I. had run a real chance that it would have been prohibited, but Sukarno gave the Indonesian communists 'another chance': He pronounced his verdict and shelved the issue until, and unless, they relapsed into a similar 'criminal act' as Sukarno phrased it,[54] putting the P.K.I., as it were, on probation. This relatively favorable outcome for the party paved the way for its becoming 'licensed' as a political party, something that had been up in the air until then.[55] After the immediate danger for the party had been warded off, Aidit had apparently thought it wise to take the most exposed of his Politburo colleagues with him on his trip to Moscow and Peking so as to show that the party was one while at the same time keeping an eye on him.

It is suggested that the restoration of the unity in the P.K.I. in that period was brought about by the Malaysia question.[56] It seems, however, that by mid-1961 the most embarrassing and acute consequences of last year's leftward deviation from the cautious Aidit line had been countered and that the formation of Malaysia, only announced as a serious plan at the end of August 1961, could have had little effect on this.[57]

When the P.K.I., temporarily under Lukman's sway, had to be ranged somewhere, it could be positioned squarely on the Soviet side as to its foreign orientation and to the right side – in communist terms – as to its internal policy. Lukman therefore stressed in his speech during the party's anniversary celebration at the end of May 1961 that the first aim of the party was a broad front of national unity to attain freedom and democracy. Only after that phase was concluded, but only then, would any talk of 'socialism' make sense.[58] Looking back on the Moscow Conference of November 1960, Lukman as he had done in his report at the end of December 1960 again gave the world communist movement its pound of flesh, calling it 'the most important political influence of our time'.[59]

His stand was easier now, as the full impact of Kruschov's distinction of wars that could and should be avoided – the global and local ones – and wars that were unavoidable and even just – the liberation wars – could meanwhile have made itself felt amongst the Indonesian communists.[60] This applied both to its theoretical implications, invalidating somewhat the Chinese tendency to look upon Kruschov as soft, *and* to its practical meaning of providing arms and credit for the West Irian claim. Lukman acknowledged this more sophisticated Soviet view, noting that 'Communists recognize the revolutionary and progressive meaning of a war of national liberation, and therefore definitely give it their full assistance'. The Chinese news agency which normally covered P.K.I. events extensively now only briefly mentioned Lukman's talk, disposing of his remarks at the 81st Party Conference in one line.[61]

While defending the party's official middle course[62] against detractors from the left, Lukman did not forget also to turn occasionally against the right. Thus answering unidentified critics who found that *Harian Rakjat* was paying more attention to (for Indonesia rather abstract) 'United States imperialism', than to the more immediate threat from the Dutch variety, Lukman recalled in the party paper that, according to the official position confirmed at the 6th National Congress in 1959, Dutch imperialism was the 'primary' enemy, but American imperialism the 'most dangerous' because 'when it enters it is difficult to detect'.[63] He added reassuringly: 'The announcement in *Harian Rakjat* regarding a number of *wicked actions of the United States imperialists* [emphasis added; the phrase was copied from the Chinese] does not detract from the *Harian Rakjat* view of the wickedness of the Dutch imperialists'. Meanwhile on their foreign trip, Aidit and Sakirman left Moscow on June 1, a few days before Sukarno was to drop in and on their departure gave the impression of being entirely in harmony with their hosts.[64] In Peking Aidit was being shown the sights, some of them as he avowed for the second or third time, like the 'Evergreen' commune.[65] The delegation was arround when Sukarno arrived for his short stay and resumed sight-seeing afterwards, being received a day after Sukarno left by Mao Tse-tung himself.[66] On June 19, Aidit gave an address on Radio Peking giving a mildly favorable view of his experiences with the commune system. In a rather condescending way he excused the Chinese for the apparent mistakes and shortcomings of the communes, which were 'a matter of course, because the Chinese communists still lack experience in building socialism'.[67]

At the same time, however, he said that, without people's communes China would not have been in a position to overcome natural calamities – floods, drought, etc. – that had ravaged the countryside. He also saw in the commune system 'a movement unprecedented in Asia which will have a far-reaching influence in countering Asia's backwardness' thereby endorsing a similar system for non-Chinese areas as well.[68] *Harian Rakjat*, in its rendering of Aidit's speech, referred only to his words on the Chinese communes in passing, while stressing improved Sino-Indonesian relations and the struggle against imperialist ventures in South East Asia.[69] Upon return and before leaving with Sukarno in early September to attend the Belgrade conference, Aidit gave a major speech to the Aliarcham Academy, the higher party school, in which he came out very consistently as the defender of his policy of accommodation with Sukarno and a 'go-slow' view of P.K.I. prospects in Indonesia.[70] In dealing with the vague notion of 'Indonesian Socialism', to which almost all parties in the country subscribed, he called it a fanciful idea if it was to mean something to be realized 'at this time, a period in which imperialism and the remnants of feudalism still exist'. Feeling the need to describe more positively what the P.K.I. was after, if 'socialism' was far-off, he produced this definition: 'The hard core of Marxism-Leninism, which the P.K.I. has always firmly adhered to and which has been proven in practice throughout the history of its struggle, is as follows: a loyalty to and a struggle for the interests of the working class and working people of Indonesia, a struggle which correctly recognizes and appraises the situation and conditions which exist in Indonesian society and their relation to the international situation'.[71] This was hardly a striking formula, except perhaps for the explicit reference to 'the international situation' as one of the factors to be taken into account in operating as a party. But it served once again as a justification for Aidit's basically unprincipled, and therefore probably successful, domestic 'right' policy which had made the P.K.I. even endorse belief in God as one of the foundations of the Indonesian state.

Without accepting the state philosophy that incorporated this belief, the Pantjasilah or Five Principles, the P.K.I. would not have secured legal status as a party. It was just prior to Aidit's lecture that at least some rumblings of opposition to this elasticity of mind, remarkable even for communists, came to the surface. A knowledgeable newspaper correspondent in Djakarta reported in mid-August that one of the grand old men of the P.K.I., Alimin, circulated a document in which he charged Aidit with 'revisionism', not in the least because of his acceptance of belief in God as part and parcel of the P.K.I. by laws.[72]

As related, the conference of non-aligned nations in Belgrade united Sukarno and the P.K.I. (with China in the background) in their opinion that colonialism was still very virulent and in need of final elimination.[73] They also agreed that fear of a third world war should not paralyse the anti-colonialist crusade. However, this in itself did not imply an anti-Soviet stance. It did not prevent Sukarno from endorsing the Moscow line on Germany and Berlin and on disarmament, though he rejected – but not in person – the resumption of nuclear testing. For Aidit this last point presented no problem, as was shown above.[74] On West-Irian – to Indonesians of all shades a crucial test case – the different weighing of priorities between the Soviet Union on the one hand and Sukarno, Aidit, and Peking on the other was in practice negligible.[75] But Aidit especially was aware of the tightrope walk he had to perform to save the situation.

It was the West Irian question particularly that had preoccupied Aidit during his stay in Eastern Europe and China in the autumn of 1961.[76] The Indonesian communist leader had intended to enlist the widest possible support among the other delegations to the Soviet capital for the Sukarno policy of recovering West Irian at any cost.[77] With this in mind the 22nd Party Congress turned out, for Aidit, to represent a severe threat. On the one hand he had been very successful in his self-appointed mission, for which later the party Politburo paid him a particularly warm tribute when it 'enthusiastically' welcomed the results of these talks and especially the two joint statements with communist parties that were of most immediate importance: The Dutch C.P.N. and the Australian Communist Party.[78] On the other hand, the support the P.K.I. required from the international communist movement was to be less valuable when it turned out to be divided against itself.

From Aidit's point of view, therefore, unity was needed more than ever and nothing could distract more from the immediate purposes which the Indonesian communist leader had in mind than open disagreement between the two main communist powers. It was only natural, therefore, that the P.K.I. chairman made a strong appeal for a closing of the ranks when he spoke to the Congress in Moscow, two days after Chou En-lai openly rebutted Kruschov. Back in Djakarta he elaborated on this theme,[79] while the Politburo resolution that was subsequently adopted contained a similar admonition that the unity of the socialist camp was 'an essential condition for developing the struggle of the people against imperialism'.[80] This plea for a restoration of the cohesion of the communist world movement was a recurring theme two weeks later in the resolution of the party's Central Committee regarding the 'difficulties' that had arisen during the 22nd Party Congress in Moscow.[81] It was all the more understandable that the Indonesian communists wanted to have united backing for their ambitions (maximum influence on the Indonesian political scene) because for the first time for a long period, 1961 had brought Indonesian state relations with both the Soviet Union and China to a promising positive level.

Moreover, Aidit himself must have realized that a Chinese Communist Party not restrained within a world framework of broadly-shared opinion would necessarily tend to proselytize among other parties, with a good chance – as in the case of the P.K.I. – of upsetting the inner-party balance of forces.

NOTES

1. *Antara News Agency*, April 27, 1961.
2. Sukarno lectured in California and before reaching the American capital. *Antara News Agency*, April 25, 1961.
3. As in Prague where President Novotny was host; *Antara News Agency*, May 29, 1961.
4. *Moscow Radio Home Service*, June 5, 1971.
5. *Moscow Radio Home Service*, June 11, 1961. Even the Chinese thought it a good show, commenting upon the atmosphere on that occasion that it was of 'exceptional cordiality'; *New China News Agency*, June 6, 1961.
6. *Moscow Radio Home Service*, June 6, 1961.
7. Indonesian Defense Minister Nasution also turned up during Sukarno's stay in Moscow and signed a number of agreements. *Tass* merely reported that they were 'Soviet-Indonesian documents', while less circumspect Indonesian sources indicated that they were related to 'Indonesian arms procurement from the Soviet Union'. *Tass*, June 10, 1961; *Djakarta Radio Home Service*, June 10, 1961.

8. *Moscow Radio Home Service*, June 10, 1961.
9. *New China News Agency*, June 10, 1961.
10. Sukarno flew back to Moscow to reach his original destination of Belgrade.
11. Aidit arrived with Sakirman and Wikana in the middle of April in Prague, spending May in Moscow and June in Peking.
12. *New China News Agency*, June 13, 1961. The equivalent Soviet machinery had turned out only 2000 listeners.
13. *Jen-min Jih-pao*, June 13, 1961. Another token of great honor bestowed on Sukarno was no doubt the fact that Mao Tse-tung came to the Indonesian President to have breakfast, before Sukarno left again around noon, June 15.
14. *New China News Agency*, June 15, 1961. The wording 'once again', given history, context and emphasis, was less than truthful as all-out government support was a new feature.
15. *Harian Rakjat*, June 15, 1961, also quoted by *New China News Agency* of the same day.
16. See *Djakarta Radio Home Service*, June 13, 1961, and *Mimbar Indonesia*, July 3, 1961. The first announcement on holding the conference was made by Subandrio on his return in Djakarta from a preparatory conference in Cairo that took place between 5 and 13 June. Subandrio therefore had to skip Sukarno's Moscow visit, but he also stayed clear of the Peking one, probably not to marr the budding relationship with associations of a troubled past.
17. See above p. 58.
18. *Review of Indonesia*, July 1960.
19. *Harian Rakjat*, August 29, 1961; *New China News Agency*, August 29, 1961.
20. *Harian Rakjat*, August 31, 1961; *Antara News Agency*, August 31, 1961.
21. 'Indonesia is not indifferent towards Afro-Asian solidarity'; *New China News Agency*, August 17, 1961.
22. *New China News Agency*, August 17, 1961.
23. *New China News Agency*, September 5, 1961.
24. *Harian Rakjat*, September 5, 1961.
25. *Jen-min Jih-pao*, September 9, 1961; *New China News Agency*, September 9, 1961.
26. *Pravda*, August 29, 1961.
27. See for example *Pravda*, September 2, 1961.
28. *Djakarta Radio Home Service*, September 4, 1961.
29. *Antara News Agency*, September 3, 1961.
30. *Harian Rakjat*, September 5, 1961; *New China News Agency*, September 5, 1961.
31. *Harian Rakjat*, September 15, 1961, quoting an A.P. report as published in the *Indonesian Observer*.
43. This at least is the version given by *New China News Agency*, September 22, 1961. *Harian Rakjat* of the same day reports that Aidit had described the tests 'justifiable'.
33. *Harian Rakjat*, September 22, 1961; The Belgrade paper *Politika* complained

about Aidit's behavior during the conference. It complained that Aidit had not shown any interest in social conditions in Yugoslavia, but nevertheless had critisized them sharply. *Politika*, December 31, 1961.

34. *Jen-min Jih-pao*, especially was quoted by *New China News Agency* in English, and wrote that 'the important speech made at the conference by President Sukarno carried great weight among the public of all countries'. *New China News Agency*, September 9, 1961. The *Far Eastern Economic Review* found that China had played up Sukarno hoping to make him the spokesman for Asia and Africa instead of Nehru. – *Far Eastern Economic Review*, September 14, 1961.
35. Text of the final resolution in *New China News Agency*, September 7, 1961.
36. *Antara News Agency*, September 6, 1961 and *New China News Agency*, September 6, 1961.
37. *Radio Free Europe*, May 15, 1962. *Harian Rakjat* was diplomatic in writing that the results were 'less than was called for in Sukarno's speech'. *Harian Rakjat*, September 15, 1961.
38. *Bintang Timur*, September 15, 1961.
39. August 9, 1961, *Antara News Agency* reported that a long-distance squadron of TU-16 bombers had been commissioned. A month previously this prospect had drawn critical questions from the London *Times* during a visit Nasution paid to Britain. *Antara News Argency*, July 5, 1961.
40. *Antara News Agency*, July 8, 1961.
41. *Antara News Agency*, July 31, 1961.
42. *Antara News Agency*, September 1st, 1961. Sukarno reiterated this proposal again in Tokyo a few weeks later; *New China News Agency*, September 9, 1961.
43. *Tass* in English, October 4, 1961. *Radio Moscow in English for South East Asia*, October 2, 1961: 'a military conflict can occur any time because Holland encroached in every possible way upon the right of the West Irian population to free existence'.
44. *New China News Agency*, September 30, 1961.
45. *New China News Agency*, October 28, 1961.
46. The Chinese began in general to display an interest in publishing the most violent and hair-raising statements by Indonesian politicians, conveying a picture of a radicalism that frequently was nothing but verbosity.
47. *Antara News Agency*, October 23, 1961.
48. *Antara News Agency*, November 14, 1961.
49. *Antara News Agency*, November 29, 1961.
50. The P.K.I. Politbureau led the way with a statement that the U.S. compromise was 'at best a revised Dutch proposal'; *New China News Agency*, November 26, 1961. This was followed up by an editorial in *Jen-min Jih-pao* of November 28, demanding that the U.S. 'immediately stop its interventionist activities', while the next day *Radio Moscow* charged the U.S. with not being neutral as pretended but clearly after West Irian 'treasures'.
51. *Antara News Agency*, November 24, 1961, citing the Amsterdam paper *De*

Volkskrant. See also Ruslan Abdulgani for Peking Radio on November 26, 1961.

52. On December 19 Sukarno, at a mass rally in Djokjakarta, gave 'orders' to prevent Papuan state being founded, to raise the red and white flag over West Irian and to 'completely mozilize'. With this 'trikora command' he made as if to close the era of discussion with the Dutch and begin an all-out 'confrontation' with them. He was meanwhile in (partly) secret correspondence with President Kennedy to find a solution in a less clamourous way.
53. See above pp. 85, 88.
54. *Antara News Agency*, April 12, 1961; *Djakarta Radio Home Service*, April 12, 1961.
55. The stamp of approval was given two days after the 'verdict' at the same time as seven other parties were officially admitted. *Antara News Agency*, April 15, 1961. In an editorial on the 41st anniversary of the Party, *Harian Rakjat* pointed out – probably with mixed feelings – that it was the first time that the communist party had been recognized by the Indonesian government; *Harian Rakjat*, May 25, 1961.
56. 'Early in 1961 a serious rift in party leadership appeared, in part over the Moscow-Peking dispute, but primarily over domestic policy. P.K.I. economic experts Sakirman and Asmu, along with Njono who leads the communist labor front Sobsi, favored a militant denunciation of the weaknesses of the government's economic policy . . . Aidit, though leaning towards the militants, seems to have been primarily concerned with preventing an explosion. Under these circumstances the anti-Malaysia campaign supplied the issue needed to restore unity and organizational fervor. By the end of 1962 the Malaysia issue had given the party a notable new "momentum" '; Justus M. van der Kroef, The Sino-Indonesian Partnership, *Orbis*, summer 1964. See above p. 95 note 53.
57. *New China News Agency*, August 26, 1961. See below p. 157 and p. 166 note 27.
58. *Harian Rakjat*, May 29, 1961. An editorial was written in similar vein in *Harian Rakjat* a few days earlier and said the Party was working hard 'to strengthen national unity with a view to preventing a split in the anti-imperialist camp'. *Harian Rakjat*, May 25, 1961.
59. See above p. 103. This point was also repeated at the end of June in *Harian Rakjat* when the paper claimed that the socialist world system was 'an absolute factor in socialist development'; *Harian Rakjat*, June 30, 1961.
60. Kruschov's interpretation of the Moscow statement in his speech before the Party cadres on January 6, 1961, *Pravda*, January 25, 1961. See above p. 101.
61. *New China News Agency*, May 28, 1961.
62. See above p. 75.
63. *Harian Rakjat*, June 23, 1961.
64. They must have been briefed extensively on affairs pertaining to the world movement. Upon arrival they were received for a 'cordial, friendly talk' by

ideologists Suslov and Ponomarev, seconded by presidium member Mukhitdinov, who as Soviet Asiatic normally acted as liaison with Asian parties; *Pravda*, April 30, 1961. When they left a month later they had reached a 'complete identity of view' whatever that meant; *Tass*, May 27, 1961.

65. *New China News Agency*, June 11, 1961.
66. *New China News Agency*, June 16, 1961.
67. *Peking Radio Home Service*, June 19, 1961.
68. In 1959 Aidit was still rejecting the peoples communes as unsuitable for Indonesia. The distribution of land was rather the aim. *Review of Indonesia*, April-May 1959.
69. *Harian Rakjat*, June 21, 1961. Aidit had probably wanted to be nice to his hosts on the communes.
70. *Harian Rakjat*, August 28, 1961. The speech was later published under the title: 'Indonesian Socialism and the conditions for its implementation', Djakarta, 1962.
71. *Harian Rakjat*, August 28, 1961.
72. Dr O. W. Röder in: *Süddeutsche Zeitung*, August 12, 1961. See on Alimin: above pp. 6, 9, 12, 13, 14.
73. See above p. 112.
74. See above p. 113.
75. See above pp. 113, 114.
76. Aidit had left Belgrade for Prague and Warsaw and spent a few days there before proceeding to Moscow in order to participate in the 22nd Congress of the CPSU. Unlike the other members of the Indonesian delegation Aidit did not stay in Moscow long after the end of the Congress but went together with Ho Chi Minh to China where they arrived on November 12. He reached Djakarta on November 22, and made immediately 'a brief statement to his welcomers in the office of the P.K.I. Central Committee'; *Harian Rakjat*, December 16, 1961.
77. See for example *Radio Free Europe*, January 3, 1962.
78. *Harian Rakjat*, December 16, 1961: Resolution on the Party Congress CPSU.
79. Aidit told his followers: 'At the meeting with Communist leaders, I frankly advanced my ideas and stressed my hope that all sides would participate in strengthening the unity of the Communist movement and the movement of the world progressives so that all forces could be mobilized for dealing the death blow to imperialism, the main enemy of all the people in the world', *Harian Rakjat*, December 15, 1961.
80. *Harian Rakjat*, December 16, 1961.
81. *Harian Rakjat*, January 10, 1962. The Central Committee met on 30 and 31 December 1961.

CHAPTER 10

Stalin right or left (1961)

Aidit's first reaction when the Albanian affair broke into the open in Moscow was to play down the whole thing. He did this by refraining from any mention of Albania in his speech to the Soviet party gathering.[1] This was the nearest Aidit could get to a neutral position, although the Russians in particular must have viewed it as an effectively pro-Chinese gesture.[2] Kruschov's closing speech on October 27 – a week after Aidit's address – already made it more difficult to abstain since the Soviet leader demanded what amounted to the removal of Albanian leaders like Hodzha and Shehu.[3] It meant pure interference in the internal affairs of another party and was unacceptable to the P.K.I. chief in principle and on practical grounds. As Aidit said upon his return: 'Each party can have its own way of solving internal conflict . . . the Communist party concerned has the full right to make its decision on its internal problems . . . The interference of one party in the internal affairs of another party will only create unnecessary difficulties and disruption in the party interfered with'.[4] At the Central Committee's plenary of late December, Aidit again came out for complete independence of decision-making, saying that each communist party had the right to formulate its own policy. It was not enough even to speak here of 'autonomy' for a party because 'we do not live in a "kingdom" or a "republic" of Communist Parties in which there is strong pressure from "the central government" '.[5] The next step after Aidit's initial neutrality was an indirect expression of support for Albania, coming in the form of a message to the Albanian Workers Party on their 20th anniversary.

Lukman, back in Djakarta and replacing the absent Aidit, cabled Tirana early in November that the P.K.I. considered the A.W.P. a loyal

Marxist-Leninist party and Albania still a fully socialist country.[6] On both counts this contradicted the Soviet stand at the time. It is not clear whether this had the complete approval of Aidit who, while still in Moscow, must have been under considerable pressure to keep the P.K.I. as 'neutral' as possible.[7] At any rate, while in the Soviet Union Aidit became convinced that mediation towards a compromise between Moscow and Peking was urgently needed. Here he found himself in league with Ho Chi-minh, the veteran Vietnamese communist leader. The two of them travelled together on the same plane to Peking and began to sound out the Chinese leaders.[8] In his 23 November report on the Party Congress Aidit made reference to these efforts for the first time, telling his Politburo colleagues that 'Indonesian Communists *cannot remain passive* in facing the fact that antagonism exists among the Communist and workers parties in the world' [emphasis added].[9] This must have failed to get a very positive response from the other members of the Party leadership. At least no mention or sign of a similar wish to be active was voiced publicly during or after the P.K.I. December plenary. Ho, however, was more successful within his party, and on January 10 the Central Committee of the North-Vietnamese Lao Dong-Party sent a secret letter to a number of communist parties calling for a conference to settle the differences and for a cease-fire in the propaganda war.[10] The result was that, in the ensuing months, a proposal to that effect was submitted to Moscow and Peking by the Lao Dong party and four other communist parties including the P.K.I.[11] In April the Chinese leadership said they agreed with the idea, but their Soviet colleagues rejected it a few weeks later.[12]

Thus nothing much came of the attempt at mediation. But the main point here is that the P.K.I., though a party to it, does not seem to have played the role Aidit had envisaged for it upon returning from the Soviet-Union and China in November 1961. This ties in with the differences between Aidit's account of the Moscow session and the Politburo resolution that endorsed his stand thereafter, indicating a shift to the left. On war and peace for instance – a subject commented upon by Aidit in general terms – the resolution states that peaceful coexistence is 'very necessary', but that the struggle against imperialism, colonialism, etc., 'be given *priority* since actually the struggle for peace and the struggle for freedom are truly one and indivisible'. [emphasis added].[13] As should be recalled, this relative priority of the struggle for peace and that of national liberation was an issue that was heatedly debated that month in two international communist front organizations: The World Federation of Trade Unions meeting in Moscow and the World Peace Council gathering in Stockholm. At the W.F.T.U. Congress the Chinese, Albanian, and Indonesian delegates, together with a number of others, opposed the Soviet position that absolute priority should be given to peace and general disarmament.[14] Njono, the Indonesian Sobsi chief, said on the occasion that West Irian was going to be liberated 'one way or the other'.[15] In Stockholm the two Chinese speakers both demanded preferential support for the national liberation movement, saying that disarmament was not a priority. The Albanian delegate followed suit.[16] The whole debate finally turned around the agenda for the 1962 World Peace Congress: Should it feature only peace and disarmament, as the majority of the pro-Soviet delegates claimed, or peace, independence, and disarmament, as the pro-Chinese representatives (mostly Asian, African, and Latin-American supporters) in vain insisted?[17]

Another sign that the party leadership as a whole was in a more radical mood than Aidit was the attack by the Politburo on Yugoslav revisionism and the renewed demand that, in line with the 1960 statement, Tito and other Yugoslav leaders should continuously be 'exposed'.[18] Aidit had not mentioned the Yugoslavs, neither in his address to the 22nd Party Congress nor in his account of it. When the Central Committee plenary confirmed the Politburo resolution, the Yugoslavs thought it time to react. In the Belgrade daily *Politika*, complaints were voiced against the 'duplicity' of the P.K.I. On the one hand the Indonesian communists supported both Sukarno's rather un-Marxist road to 'socialism' and his foreign policy of non-alignment, while the P.K.I. continued at the same time its attacks on Yugoslavia, the paper wrote.[19] The Politburo resolution was described as 'aggressive' since it incited against other social forces.[20] *Harian Rakjat* returned the fire with some broadsides at Belgrade, that it was 'currying favor with the imperialists' in order to get some financial aid from them.[21] While in the meantime the Indonesian communist press was publishing two answers of Albanian party chief Enver Hodzha to greetings received from the P.K.I., both containing onesided attacks on 'modern revisionists,' the official Yugoslav party paper, *Borba*, stepped into the 'debate' with the Indonesian comrades.[22] It protested against the P.K.I. deliberately distorting Yugoslav statements, inspired as this was 'by the hostility of a Communist party in a friendly country'. The anti-Yugoslav fire was kept up by Njoto, who charged a few weeks later that the modern revisionists of Yugoslavia were clamoring for a peaceful settlement of the West Irian dispute. This 'settlement', Njoto sneered, would in fact mean 'non-liberation' of the territory. Basing his remarks on a recent statement by Yugoslav foreign minister Kosa Popovic during his stay in the Netherlands, the P.K.I. Deputy Chairman equated Popovic with his Dutch colleague Luns.[23]

It was not surprising that China again had shown a keen interest in the developments within the P.K.I. The altercations with Belgrade were duly reported by its official news agency, the *Harlan Rakjat* article of January 9 even being broadcast in Serbo-Croatian by Radio Peking.[24] But Peking's interest in the P.K.I. was of course wider and had manifested itself more emphatically right after the Moscow Party Congress. A few days after Aidit had arrived in Peking in November, the full text of the two joint statements on West-Irian, one with the Dutch C.P. and the other with the Australian C.P., were published.[25] As related earlier, these two documents represented for Aidit and the P.K.I. an important asset, since they were to illustrate how valuable the Indonesian communists could be in promoting such a national cause as West Irian worldwide.[26] The P.K.I. Politburo statement against the American suggestions of a compromise on West Irian during the United Nations debate was also reprinted, and one day later the official party paper *Jen-min Jih-pao* in an editioral lent its authority by supporting, in a similar radical vein as the P.K.I., the Indonesian case against the Dutch.[27] On December 1 the same paper gave the full text of Aidit's first account of the Moscow Party Congress proceedings, not so much as a sign of complete agreement – though what Aidit had to say went rather far to suit Peking – but as a self-interested gesture of respect for the opinion of one of the foremost non-ruling communist leaders.[28] Moreover, in Moscow at the W.F.T.U. Congress, the Chinese delegation was instrumental in getting a solid reference to West Irian inserted into the action program then adopted.[29] It was also interesting that on the eve of Aidit's arrival in Peking the Chinese Communist Party sent its 'warm greetings' to the P.K.I. on the account of the anniversary of the 1926 rebellion, that 'great and just revolutionary uprising'. The Chinese communists took that opportunity to flatter the

Indonesian visitor by praising his 'unremitting efforts for the recovery of West Irian' and more generally his 'correct leadership'.[30] It was rather curious that the 1926 rebellion was used as a pretext to say something nice to the P.K.I., but it may have been considered a handy coincidence. It was curious because the 1926 rebellion against the Dutch colonial administration had been organized and initiated by the P.K.I., against the advice of Stalin who had accused the Indonesian communist leaders at that time of being 'left deviationists'.[31] And this self-same Stalin was now taken under the wing of Aidit and the P.K.I. against the renewed attacks on him by Kruschov.[32] Before the anti-Stalin revelations in Kruschov's secret speech in February 1956 the P.K.I. position was that Stalin had been correct in his opposition to plans for revolt in the colonial Dutch East Indies[33], – so that Stalin, as a right-winger in the twenties, had been invoked to dispel the danger of the 'disease of leftwing communism' that had been unwelcome to Aidit in the fifties. But once 'the people's revolt' of 1926 had broken out the party had been correct in 'speedily giving it leadership', so the interpretation of the first abortive P.K.I. rebellion ran until 1956.[34] After Stalin in 1956[35] came to be seen in a less favorable light, his judgment, previously appreciated, was left unmentioned and the rebellion was said to have failed simply because the party had been too young.[36] A year later it was again the 'leftwing communist abuse' by left-deviationist P.K.I. leaders that had damaged the party in 1926. But still Stalin was not mentioned.[37]

In 1960 the P.K.I. already had more courage to speak its mind on Stalin, but it was again the right-wing version of him that was acclaimed. *Harian Rakjat* praised him for his contribution to the nationalities questions as exemplified in his book *Marx and the Nationalities Problem.*[38] Now after the 22nd Party Congress this opinion was repeated by Aidit, who said in his November account that the P.K.I. continued to respect Stalin, 'many of whose speeches and writings are still useful, for example those dealing with revolutions in Eastern countries, including the Indonesian revolution'.[93] Having said or written nothing else on Indonesian communism but the negative appraisal in the twenties of the idea of starting a revolution prematurely on Java, one is bound to conclude that to Aidit Stalin's authority still had to be kept intact, mainly to enable him to moderate posthumously his left-leaning Politburo colleagues who wanted to press for more action, as had happened a year earlier in 1960. Again, as in other instances, also on Stalin the Politburo resolution went further to the left than the central position Aidit had tried to take in his account of the Moscow Congress. Agreeing with almost everyone else in the international communist movement that Stalin's 'errors' – made 'particularly during the latter part of his life' as the current phrase went – should be criticized, the Politburo asserted on the other hand: 'It is impossible to ignore the meritorious service rendered by the Soviet communists and people during the period from 1924 to 1953, including that rendered by Stalin during that same period'.[40]

This theme also appeared in a special *Harian Rakjat* article commemorating Stalin's 82nd birthday, where it is said that without Stalin in the years between Lenin's death and the period after the second world war the Soviet Union would have been nowhere.[41] This formula was less of a glorification than the Chinese or Albanian eulogies of the moment, but it was a far cry from the feverish anti-Stalin cult Moscow was whipping up under Kruschov. What is more, it was a rather consistent continuation of the picture the P.K.I. had given of Stalin over the years, interrupted only slightly in the years immediately after the 20th Party Congress in Moscow in February 1956.

Not very novel, too, was the distinction Aidit made after the 22nd Party Congress in November 1961 between Stalin as a national and Stalin as an international figure.[42] In 1959, when the rumblings of Sino-Soviet disagreement were few and far between, Aidit had ruled that 'it is the right of the Soviet leaders to do what they want with their former leader Stalin'.[43] He repeated this at the end of 1961, saying (not without a tinge of sarcasm) that as Stalin had been the principal leader of the C.P.S.U. 'it is the right of the Soviet communists to do whatever they like about their former leader Stalin – criticise him, put his body in the mausoleum and remove it, change the name of Stalingrad to Volgograd and so on'. To this he added that, on the other side, 'every communist and democrat can speak of Stalin as an international figure'. This was then, as it had also been before the 22nd Party Congress in Moscow, a logical consequence of the independence of mind and the nationalistic sentiment that the P.K.I. under Aidit had defended so strongly over the years.[44]

While the P.K.I. could have lived with a further demotion of Stalin by Kruschov – to Aidit it was their own business – the Albanian affair was inevitably endangering the position of the party. Short-term preoccupation with it would diminish the cohesion of the communist bloc and lessen the bargaining power the Indonesian communist could derive from it vis-à-vis their domestic allies-adversaries, Sukarno and the military, especially on the West-Irian issue. In the long run it was interference in national affairs that made the Albanian case a grave peril to the P.K.I. It was unacceptable that a country forming part of the communist 'commonwealth' could be read out of it by attacking it in front of the assembled communist parties of the world. In his November account Aidit said: 'Whether a given country belongs to the socialist camp is not decided through *subjective* evaluation, but by the objective fact that the country is genuinely building socialism, a society where there is no exploitation of man by man. Albania is a country which is building this type of society, Comrade Kruschov himself does not deny this' [emphasis added][45]. The P.K.I. leader must have been referring here to Kruschov's single-handed attempt to bluff Albania into line in 1960 by threatening it with treatment similar to that meted out by Stalin to obstinate Yugoslavia in 1948: Expulsion from the socialist brotherhood.[46] Stress on the membership of the socialist camp as it stood therefore became more explicit. The 20th anniversary greetings to Tirana, sent in mid-November by Lukman on behalf of the P.K.I. had been in general terms.[47] After Aidit's November account on behalf of Albania, Sobsi leader Njono commented before the W.F.T.U. delegates in Moscow that the P.K.I. welcomed 'the progress of socialist construction in the *twelve* socialist countries'.[48] The greetings for New Year 1962 which Aidit sent were also quite ostentatiously addressed to the communist parties of the twelve communist countries.[49]

Viewing the various reactions amongst the Indonesian communists during and after the Soviet Party Congress of November 1961, it stands out that whatever differences in emphasis existed between Aidit and the sum total of P.K.I. opinion the party was unified on the 'organizational issue' – as had already been evident a year before,[50] being adamant as to its independence within the communist movement. Due to the row over Albania – the new element since the Moscow conference of autumn 1960 – this question of party independence had become more acute and again brought together Aidit and the rest of Politburo in opposing the arbitrary, 'subjective' way Kruschov had tried to declare Tirana a non-socialist country. Another offshoot of the organizational principle so dear to the P.K.I. but of lesser impact than Albania was the Stalin question on which the party agreed that each communist party was free to do with him and his memory what it wanted. But while the consensus in the Politburo[51] boiled down to general appreciation of what Stalin had done, Aidit was more inclined to see in the Soviet dictator the man who in an issue relevant to Indonesia (the 1926 rebellion) had been correct in warning against premature action, i.e., a warning no doubt, Aidit still felt was valid for the P.K.I. in the situation prevailing in Indonesia. On the two substantive issues discussed by the P.K.I. – peaceful coexistence versus anti-colonialism and Yugoslav revisionism – the Politburo took a more radical view – 'Chinese' rather than 'Soviet' – while Aidit in his report on the 22nd Congress had limited himself to generalities or had been silent. Finally, Aidit's attempt to get the P.K.I. to offer its services and to mediate between the two main opponents was also typical of his approach.

Both short-term and long-term considerations made Aidit look for a soft but active approach through compromise and mediation. Two of the three reasons he gave afterwards for abstaining from expressing an opinion on Albania at the 22nd Party Congress concerned his preoccupation with solving problems through consultation, not confrontation.[52] This was because he did not see how 'existing conflicts can be settled more easily by criticizing one Communist Party at the congress of another Communist Party'.[53] Besides, both the 1957 Declaration and the 1960 Statement, Aidit said, prescribed holding meetings and discussions between parties that disagreed. Therefore this machinery should have been used, or as far as the future was concerned should now be used. As we saw, the P.K.I. Politburo was not yet in the mood to follow Aidit on this and take a hand in bringing about a meeting of the chief opponents.

NOTES

1. Aidit spoke on October 21, 1961. See *Pravda*, October 23, 1961.
2. As explained above up to the 22nd Party Congress there was little in Aidit's behavior and in that of 'his' P.K.I. that showed a pro-Peking slant except where it suited the party. See pp. 103, 104.
3. Kruschov's speech on Albania and the Stalin cult, *Pravda*, October 29, 1961: 'We are certain the time will come when the Albanian communists and the

Albanian people will have their say, and then the Albanian leaders will have to answer for the harm they have done their country'.

4. *Harian Rakjat*, December 16, 1961. This part, like many others, was left out in the version *Pravda* gave of Aidit's report on January 6, 1962. The North Korean party chief Kim Il-sung, though less outspoken in his criticism of Soviet conduct than Aidit, also stressed abstention from interference with other parties as 'one of the fundamental principles' in his report to the Central Committee of the Korean Workers Party. *Pravda* found less to suppress here but deleted particularly this passage. See *Kulloja* (Pyongyang), November 27, 1961 and *Pravda*, December 4, 1961.
5. *Harian Rakjat*, January 2nd, 1962; *New China News Agency*, November 10, 1961.
6. *New China News Agency*, November 10, 1961. Also below p. 136, note 47.
7. On November 5, a few days before the P.K.I. sent Tirana its greetings, Aidit saw Kruschov. *Moscow Radio Home Service*, November 6, 1961.
8. *New China News Agency*, November 12, 1961. Like Aidit, Ho Chi-minh in his Congress speech had refrained from bringing up Albania but stressed the need for unity on the basis of the 1960 Moscow statement. William E. Griffith, 1964, *The Sino-Soviet Rift*, George Allen and Unwin Ltd., London, p. 103. During his short stay in China Aidit met Mao Tse-tung, as did Ho.
9. *Harian Rakjat*, December 15, 1961. The quoted sentence was in one of the many paragraphs censured in the *Pravda* version of January 6, 1962.
10. E. Kux and J. C. Kun, 1964, *Die Satelliten Pekings: Nordvietnam-Nordkorea*, W. Kohlhammer Verlag, Stuttgart, p. 141.
11. Letter from the C.C. of the Communist Party of China to the C.C. of the C.P.S.U. of March 9, 1961. *New China News Agency*, March 13, 1963. The other parties were Great Britain, Sweden and New Zealand.
12. Kux and Kun, 1964, p. 141.
13. *Harian Rakjat*, December 16, 1961. Donald C. Hindley, The Indonesian Communists and the C.P.S.U. Twenty-second Congress, *Asian Survey*, March 1962, p. 24, gives the same passage of the *Harian Rakjat* rendering of the resolution but quotes that 'it is essential to *combine* the policy of peaceful coexistence and total disarmament together with the anti-imperialist, anti-colonialist and anti-neocolonialist struggle because the struggle for peace and the struggle for independence are an inseparable whole' [emphasis added]. Hindley concludes from this that the P.K.I. Politburo in December 1961 sided with Moscow on this isuue. As a conclusion from the text this was incorrect, as his translation was deficient.
14. W. E. Griffith, 1963, *Albania and the Sino-Soviet Rift*, M.I.T. Press, Cambridge, Massachusetts, pp. 122, 123.
15. *New China News Agency*, December 8, 1961, and *Harian Rakjat*, December 15, 1961. Griffith, 1963. p. 123, note 4, cannot conclude from Njono's statement whether he took a pro-Soviet or a pro-Chinese position.
16. *New China News Agency*, December 20 and 22, 1961.
17. Griffith, 1963, p. 129.

18. This had been a 'Chinese' formulation in 1960. See above p. 103. The text of the Politburo resolution referred to appeared in *Harian Rakjat*, December 16, 1961.
19. *Politika*, December 31, 1961.
20. *Politika*, January, 1st and 2nd, 1962.
21. *Harian Rakjat*, January 1, 1962.
22. *Borba*, January 11, 1962. Hodzha's replies were published in *Harian Rakjat*, January 12, 1962, answering the November anniversary greetings of the P.K.I. New Year's message.
23. *New China News Agency*, February 11, 1962.
24. *Peking Radio in Servo-Croat*, January 10, 1962.
25. *New China News Agency*, November 16 and 18, 1961. *Pravda* only mentioned the one with the Australian C.P., but only in December.
26. See above p. 120.
27. *New China News Agency*, November 26, 1961 and November 27, 1961.
28. As indicated already *Pravda* gave one month later, as part of its coverage of the December plenary of the P.K.I. Central Committee, a doctored version of this account of Aidit's. His opinion on Albania or Stalin were considered unfit for the *Pravda* readers; *Pravda*, January 6, 1962.
29. *New China News Agency*, December 16, 1962. Actually it was a *quid pro quo*, the action program demanding 'an end to the unlawful occupation of Taiwan and West-Irian'.
30. *New China News Agency*, November 11, 1961.
31. In a speech on May 5, 1925, Stalin said in his only reference to Indonesia that 'the Communists of Java who recently erroneously put forward the slogan of a soviet government for their country suffer it seems from this (left) deviation'. He described that deviation as 'overrating the revolutionary possibilities of the liberation movement and underrating the importance of an alliance between the working class and the revolutionary bourgeoisie against imperialism'. See also McVey, 1965, *The rise of Indonesian Communism*, Cornell University Press, Ithaca, New York, p. 282.
32. In his address to the 22nd Party Congress Aidit had not mentioned Stalin. He elaborated his viewpoint in his account of the Congress of November 23. See also below p. 131.
33. In 1925 Stalin was following a 'right strategy', partly in response to opposite views of Trotsky's with whom Stalin was engaged in a fierce power struggle. When the Aidit leadership formulated its opinion on the 1926 rebellion at the fifth P.K.I. national congress in March 1954, quoting with approval from Stalin's 1925 speech, Aidit equally was applying a right strategy. See above p. 21. In his 1955 speech 'The birth and growth of the Communist Party of Indonesia', Aidit reiterated the official line on '1926', saying that Stalin had been correct in his judgment that 'a resolute struggle against this (left) deviation is an important condition for the training of truly revolutionary cadres for colonial and dependent countries in the East'. D. N. Aidit, Unite to complete the demands of the 1945 August revolution, *Complete Works*, 1959,

vol. I, p. 282, as translated by the Joint Publications Research Service, Washington D.C. Stalin's 1925 speech from which Aidit quoted is edited in London in 1936 in a collection under the title 'Marxism and the National and Colonial Question'.

34. Aidit, 1959, p. 283.
35. See above p. 35.
36. Aidit, 1960, pp. 66-70: 12 November and the Anticolonialist National Struggle, November 12, 1956.
37. Aidit, 1960, p. 223.
38. What was probably meant was 'Marxism and the National and Colonial Question'. The article referred to is in *Harian Rakjat*, December 22, 1960.
39. *Harian Rakjat*, December 15, 1961.
40. *Harian Rakjat*, December 16, 1961.
41. *Harian Rakjat*, December 16, 1961.
42. *Harian Rakjat*, December 15, 1961. Donald C. Hindley, The Indonesian Communist Party and the Conflict in the International Communist Movement, *China Quarterly*, July-September 1964, p. 100, sees it as an innovation.
43. *Review of Indonesia*, April-May 1959.
44. See above p. .
45. *Harian Rakjat*, December 15, 1961.
46. *Zeri i Populit*, December 6, 1961: 'In October 1960 Kruschov stated that he would treat Albania the same way as Titost Yugoslavia'.
47. *New China News Agency*, November 10, 1961: 'The achievements of your party and the people of your country have strengthened and will increasingly strengthen the socialist camp and the international communist movement'. See also above pp. 126, 127.
48. *New China News Agency*, December 8, 1961. It was Chou En-lai who in his reply to Kruschov's attack on Albania coined the 'shorthand' phrase of the twelve countries that together formed the socialist camp, *New China News Agency*, October 19, 1961. Ho Chi-minh followed in an interview with Radio Moscow on November 6, but here the sentence was deleted when this program was rebroadcast a few days later. It had apparently become a sensitive expression.
49. *Harian Rakjat*, December 30, 1961.
50. See above p. 103.
51. See above p. 131.
52. *Harian Rakjat*, December 15, 1961. The third reason mentioned at the first place was rather formal. The P.K.I. delegation to Moscow had not been informed about the pending attack on Albania. This was the case with most, if not all, foreign delegations, including the Chinese. Enough must have been known to Aidit, however, of the sorry state of Soviet-Albanian relations for him to have reacted more explicitly if he had wanted to do so. An element of personal pride had probably slipped in here, as he told an interviewer in 1965 that 'he had been particularly irked by the fact that the Soviets had neglected to inform the other parties'; Ruth McVey, Indonesian Communism

in China. In Tang Tsou, ed., 1968, *China in conflict*, vol. II, University of Chicago Press, Chicago, p. 371, note 22.

53. As it had been remarked, 'despite his preference for private settlement of the Albanian dispute, Aidit has been happy to make very public attacks on Yugoslav policy'; *Radio Free Europe*, May 15, 1962. See below for a possible explanation of P.K.I. attitudes towards Yugoslavia p. 207 ff.

CHAPTER 11

United against the Dutch (1962)

While Aidit had no interest in exaggerating the differences that emerged at the 22nd Party Congress, the Soviet leadership too wanted to keep the situation in hand. In general the period after the Congress was marked from the Soviet side at first by depicting opinion within the world communist movement as endorsing its position. In most cases this was not so difficult since most communist parties had in fact approved or condoned Kruschov's open attack on Albania and his line on Stalin. Adverse opinion could be handled by the expert manipulators of texts that communist leaders – and certainly those in the Kremlin – have at their constant disposal. In the case of the P.K.I., for example, we have already seen that the selective editing of Aidit's report to the Central Committee plenary in Pravda made it a harmless piece.[1] But apart from the normal desire to present a united front to the outside world, in the case of Soviet-Indonesian party relations Moscow had more particular reasons to play it cool. After all, the P.K.I. with its two million members had in a relatively short span become the biggest non-ruling communist party in the world.

In the Aidit leadership the Soviet Union had until then found a loyal and effective partner within a country that had top priority in its foreign policy. Finally and, in a very concrete way through the West Irian claim of Sukarno, coupled with the constant stream of Soviet arms, the C.P.S.U. had prospects of extremely valuable influence building in one of the most promising areas of the world. It was therefore not surprising to see in the ensuing period, right through to the successful conclusion of the West-Irian campaign in mid-August 1962 an extremely close harmony or rather interaction between the various actors on both sides: The Soviet political and military leaders, Sukarno, the

Indonesian army command, and the P.K.I., each playing a part which we will try to describe in more detail. The Chinese, preoccupied with the growing contest with Moscow and in respect to Indonesia still suffering from the immediate past experience of mutual distrust, seemed to limit themselves to a supporting role remarkably parallel to the Soviet approach.

The basic aim on the Soviet side was to promote a state of controlled tension around the West-Irian issue that would guarantee maximization of political returns. So Sukarno's 'triple command' of December 19, 1961, that was issued with the usual bombast so as to pretend that now all boats were being burned as far as the Dutch were concerned was, of course, fully supported by Moscow.[2] But Ambassador Malik who at that time went to Djakarta for normal consultation was asked by Kruschov to convey his concern that things might get out of hand internationally and to urge moderation.[3]

On the declaratory side the Soviet Union kept up pressure on behalf of Indonesia. When President Kennedy expressed fear that Sukarno's decision – the Trikora command – meant a greater chance of an armed clash, the Soviet news agency Tass recalled that the recent recovery of Goa – Nehru's miniwar – had not turned into an armageddon either.[4] With equal conviction the Soviet Union reacted a few weeks later, after the Dutch navy had sunk an Indonesian torpedo boat near the Arau Islands 12 miles off West Irian, that 'a military conflict anywhere in the world can give rise to an international conflagration'.[5] This was made official policy when, after a hurriedly organized visit of the brand-new Chief-of-Staff of the Indonesian Air Force, Omar Dhani, to Moscow the Soviet Union issued a sharp protest against the 'aggressive action' of the Dutch.[6]

It seems that the Indonesians including Sukarno – never a hero in the face of real force – were rather stunned by the incident that resulted from this ill-prepared attempt to land some Indonesian marines on the shores of West Irian.[7] The Indonesian President said in reaction that he would try to keep emotions within the country down and assured that the door for negotiations remained open.[8] The theater commander, General Yani, stressed to newsmen Sukarno's cautious reaction and denied the presence of Indonesian forces in West Irian.[9] Anticipating the trip Omar Dhani was about to make to Moscow and its concomitant impression upon public opinion, Yani added that neither the Soviet Union nor China had promised any support in the event of an armed conflict with the Dutch.[10]

Literally taken this was no doubt true, certainly for China, but it is equally clear that the Soviet Union, having provided the expensive tools for the West Irian confrontation, had a lot at stake in the handling of the issue by the Indonesians and was at pains not to get drawn into it and was trying to manage the conflict. A real armed conflict might have made them face the unpleasant choice – later experienced in the Cuban crisis – of getting involved or losing face by backing down. Deep in his heart Kruschov was convinced that such a choice would not occur and that he was playing a rather safe game because in his view the Dutch would not fight if confronted with overwhelming military potential on the Indonesian side.[11]

What stung the Russians and continued to do so all through 1962 was the growing involvement of the United States, which ironically enough they themselves had helped to elicit by encouraging Sukarno to be more radical in his pursuit of the recuperation of West Irian.[12] Right from the moment that at the end of 1961 the veto in the United Nations had shown the diplomatical stalemate the conflict was in and the American delegate Bingham had suggested some compromise solution, the Soviet Union had tried to shoot down American efforts of what it saw as unwarranted 'meddling'.[13] According to the audience addressed there were variations on this theme. Within a few days Moscow told the public in the Netherlands that the U.S. left it to the Dutch to pull the chestnuts out of the fire, assured the folks at home that the problem around West Irian was not going to be resolved by the policies of the imperialists, and put in front of listeners in South East Asia a feather in its own cap as superchampion in the fight against colonialism.[14] But the main tenor was its rejection of the U.S. as not being 'neutral' between the parties while equally adamant in its opposition to any form of United Nations participation in the administration of West Irian at some period.[15]

On the eve of the informal talks between the Indonesian envoy Adam Malik and the Dutch negotiator Van Roijen (with American ambassador Bunker in the background), Moscow again warned that the good offices of the United States were 'not very good' and that a new plot was being hatched.[16] When later Malik, in Djakarta to report on the talks, was prevented from returning by a cleverly maneuvering

Sukarno, immediate support for this decision was forthcoming from Moscow, where it was held that 'all along' they had had doubts about the success of the negotiations.[17] After Indonesia had accepted the Bunker proposals in principle early in April and acceptance by the Dutch was only a matter of time, policymakers in the Kremlin seemed to have been groping for an appropriate reaction.[18] To that end Subandrio was asked to come over, the initiative ostensibly coming from the Indonesians, who allegedly wanted to buy another batch of Soviet arms. In fact he went to inform the Soviet leaders more directly.[19] Their support remained unabated, and the whole visit was neatly fitted into the war of nerves that both governments were helping to keep alive.[20] Ambassador Michailow made his contribution by stating on Radio Djakarta that Indonesia's position at the negotiating table had been reinforced by Subandrio's stay in Moscow.[21] But some misgivings must have been shown on the Soviet side as to the effect of their military aid, when Indonesia was apparently so eager to resolve the West Irian affair that is was prepared to negotiate seriously and accept United States mediation.

Another aspect may have entered that slowly reduced Soviet interest in the West Irian affair. At the time of Subandrio's visit a *modus vivendi* in Laos, issuing into its formally declared neutrality somewhat later, was taking shape and a *quid-pro-quo* with the Americans not to exacerbate each other in the area might have been a consideration.[22] At any rate it must have dawned upon the Russians that a settlement was in the make and that the main thing was now to prevent the U.S.A. from getting too much credit for it, while continuing to support the negotiating points of the Indonesians.[23] So Air Marshal Vershinin was dispatched to tour Indonesia and repeat the usual phrases of Soviet sympathy.

While the Dutch, for their part, had meanwhile also indicated that they accepted the Bunker proposals as a negotiating basis, the Soviet Deputy Defense Minister kept offering Indonesia 'necessary help'.[24]

The informal negotiations in Washington at the time had reached the stage that Sukarno thought it wise to send Foreign Minister Subandrio to the U.S.A. to have a direct hand in it.[25] On the same day in the middle of July 1961, it was also announced that Mikoyan was to visit Djakarta.[26] The precise purpose of this trip was not clear then, but his main aim seems to have been to check on the preparations for armed action against West Irian and particularly the part the Russian advisory group was playing in that respect.[27] While on the one hand Moscow was not against Indonesia making the utmost political use of the aid the Soviet Union was extending, on the other hand as related earlier the Soviet leaders did not want to be caught unaware. The Soviet Deputy Premier was welcomed by First Minister Djuanda who expressed satisfaction with this 'long awaited arrival',[28] though it was known everywhere that it was a surprise visit as a result of the heightened tension around West Irian that according to Sukarno's wishes should 'fall' before August 17 – the magic date – either at the negotiating table in Washington or otherwise by force of arms.[29] There is no evidence that Mikoyan applied pressure then on Sukarno to opt for settling the West Irian affair by force, as suggested.[30] Apart from information to the contrary[31] it is hardly plausible, since the secret negotiations in Washington had dragged on long enough to give Moscow a pretty clear idea of the various standpoints, and pressuring a country into a military confrontation could never have been successful in such a last-minute fashion. It is true that immediately after the departure of Mikoyan Radio Moscow in its broadcast to South East Asia attacked the Washington talks as a 'treacherous move' and warned against 'a so-called peaceful solution' that would turn out to be the opposite.[32] But from all available evidence it seems that the Soviet emissary had rather come to convey the apprehension in leading Moscow circles that the United States would gain then in the field of propaganda and economics. In his speech at the opening of the Senajan Stadium, built with Soviet funds and materials, Mikoyan quoted an 'oriental saying' to the effect that 'if you take money you will spend it, if you take wisdom it will stay with you',[33] indicating some doubts about the way Soviet aid was consumated in Indonesia.[34] He certainly also must have been aware of the lure exerted by the prospects of economic aid from American side that especially in the field of agricultural products and dollar credits had been more effectively disbursed than what the Soviets passed off as 'aid'.[35]

However this may be Soviet policy adjusted to the things to come and was going to picture the settlement reached formally on August 15 as 'of course a great victory for the peaceloving Republic of Indonesia', as Moscow Radio put it.[36] The main thrust was now to ascribe this success to the correct causes, in essence the support of the Afro-

Asian community of nations and the socialist camp, particularly of course then the Soviet Union.[37] And naturally the efforts of the Indonesian people themselves were cited, of which initially also 'the liberation movement' in West Irian got special mention, a temporary lapse no doubt, as this – together with the assumed mineral wealth that the Dutch and American monopolists had been after – too obviously had been of no importance whatsoever.[38] It was Kruschov who raised the level of argument a bit by stating that both the neutralization of Laos and the West Irian agreement had shown how complicated international problems could be solved peacefully.[39]

The way the P.K.I. operated during this period of secret and overt negotiation showed the Indonesian communists and Aidit especially to be in full unison with the Moscow approach. Or rather, it was often the other way round; the Soviet leaders felt very much the same as their Indonesian comrades and in the field of publicity were frequently prompted by them. We have already had occasion to point out instances where reactions from Moscow came after the P.K.I., or more accurately party chairman Aidit, had given its opinion. Moscow followed his pronunciations both in time and tenor.[40] Of course there had been more talk on the part of the P.K.I. of the need for the use of force or about dealing with the recalcitrant Dutch 'by whatever means' than the Soviets found desirable.[41] But immediate and unconditional transfer of sovereignty – or 'administration' as Sukarno had modified it at the 1961 Belgrade conference – had been the aim of communists in both capitals.[42] Aidit and Kruschov were also agreed as to the role of the United States, which the P.K.I. equally resented especially when it took the form of the Bunker meditation.[43] But, as soon as the Indonesian communists ventured beyond the conflict over the jungle island and related West Irian to issues current in the international communists movement, the Soviet Union remained aloof. Thus, when Second-Deputy Chairman of the P.K.I. Njoto rejected a peaceful solution of the crisis because to him such an approach was tantamount to modern revisionism, he found no response from his Soviet comrades.[44] The same applied to the plea for strengthening the unity of world communism which according to the P.K.I. Politburo resolution of December 1961 was 'an essential condition for developing the struggle against imperialism'.[45] The P.K.I. leadership clearly had in mind here Indonesia's conflict with the Dutch and linked this with the need for unity among all communists. The Pravda version of the Politburo resolution, however, deleted this practical warning against the consequences of disunity.[46] To complete the picture it is interesting to note that an analysis of Aidit's attitude towards the West Irian issue was consequently several degrees more moderate, or less extreme, than for example *Harian Rakjat* – under direction of Njoto – or the Politburo as a whole. The party chairman could not be easily persuaded to make a pronouncement on the use of force. When he did so, as for instance in an interview with the Djakarta correspondent of Associated Press, he put the chances that force was going to be used at fifty-fifty: 'I do not see the possibility of adopting peaceful means as any bigger than that of adopting non-peaceful means'.[47] In other words, notwithstanding the verbal commitment to violence around him – as Njoto among others had shown not long before – Aidit remained, as usual, in the middle, i.e., relatively moderate. Aidit also used the method of quoting a martial statement made by Sukarno, so that he had a good alibi just in case.[48] Both tactically and strategically Aidit trimmed his sails as close as possible to Sukarno.

The P.K.I. made remarkably little reference during the period under discussion to Soviet aid in recovering West Irian. In a statement honoring the 17th of August national independence day that year the 'selfless help of the Soviet Union and the other socialist countries', on a par of course with the national efforts under Sukarno's 'triple command', were hailed as forces that had brought the United States and the Netherlands to their knees in the West-Irian affair.[49] On military matters no words were lost, though to the outside world and certainly to the Kennedy administration the threat of Soviet-aided military escalation with the risk of superpower involvement had played a decisive role in putting pressure on the Dutch to give up their tenaciously held position.[50]

It is likely that rivalry with the Indonesian military establishment under General Nasution would explain this reticence, as the armed forces particularly benefited, politically too, from massive Soviet military assistance.[51] As to the reality of the military threat to West Irian there is no doubt that the Indonesian military command was bracing itself for an armed intervention against the Dutch-held territory and were ready to strike at the end of July 1962.[52] Troops had been assembled near Macassar on the island of Sulawesi, and air and naval forces – especially Soviet long-range bombers and submarines – were in state of alert. As to the eventual outcome of Dutch-Indonesian hostilities, it is a matter of speculation what would have been the result. Probably the Dutch would have inflicted heavy casualties on the Indonesian forces,[53] but in the end would have had to bow out anyhow under the pressure of economic and international-political arguments. At the time the Indonesians themselves were not completely convinced they would make a success of it. Subandrio, for example, stated to a closed session of Indonesian parliament sometime after the Arau incident that Indonesia would not be ready to invade the territory before the end of the year.[54] *Antara* had published later in that same month of February 1962 a report by a D.P.A.-correspondent who had visited West Irian and gave as the view of the Dutch military command that it would take another ten months and a lot of then non-existent landing craft before an invasion could seriously be expected.[55] The dropping of individual soldiers was by and large a complete failure and only good for creating the artificial war atmosphere the various chancelleries in Djakarta. Washington. The Hague and Moscow had to work in.

The Chinese impact upon what was happening around Indonesia in this period was limited and of rather a passive nature. Enough attention had been given to West Irian, but it was mainly in well meaning, rather low-key expressions of official support.[56] There was no particular emphasis on the need to use violence in solving Indonesia's irredentist claim, though the reporting – distinct from editorial comment – showed a slight slant to stress elements of force and impatience at various statements on the Indonesian side.[57] Moscow and Peking seemed to take an almost identical position in the conflict, a situation seen to have prevailed as well in the matter of Laos that year.[58] The Chinese media also gave the Soviet Union its full due as to its unequivocal support for the liberation of West Irian, though – as was the case with the P.K.I. – the military aspect was left out completely.[59]

But in the second half of August, a shift was noticeable insofar that, when it came to congratulating Djakarta on its political success – which was done wholeheartedly – the Chinese ascribed it only to what *Jen-min Jih-pao* in an editorial called 'the protracted struggle of the Indonesian people'. No mention was made of a Soviet or generally communist contribution to the Indonesian feat of arm[illegible] insofar as this was not coincidence, it might have had something to do with the simmering

Sino-Soviet relations which since March had gone throught a period of relative outward calm, only to be disturbed at the beginning of August by a fierce attack on Yugoslavia.[61]

NOTES

1. See above pp. 129, 135 note 28.
2. *Pravda*, December 21, 1961, *Radio Moscow Home Service*, December 21, 1961, *Tass* in English, December 21, 1961. Sukarno's Trikora or triple command was issued on the anniversary of the attack of the Dutch on Djokjakarta in 1948 and on the territory of the Sultan of Djokjakarta, to provide all the symbolic trappings so dear to Sukarno for rallying the people behind his cause. It was basically meant to counter the nefarious effects of the internationalization Dutch Foreign Minister Luns had proposed to the great dismay of the Indonesian government; interview March 1972 with Ruslan Abdulgani.
3. Interview March 1972 with Adam Malik. Soviet Premier Kruschov especially said he was afraid that the Soviet military advisers would get involved. According to the then-Minister of Defence Nasution in an interview on March 1972 the largest number of Soviet advisers in Indonesia at any given moment was around 1,000. They were to train Indonesian personnel in handling sophisticated Soviet weapons – Mig 17, 19 and 21, guided missiles, submarines, etc. – and never fulfilled operational tasks.
4. *Tass* in English, December 22, 1961.
5. *Tass* in Dutch, 1962. The incident took place on January 15, when the Dutch forces discovered through radar two foreign vessels approaching full speed the coast of West Irian. They were assumed to be of Indonesian origin – as indeed they turned out to be – and fired upon by the Dutch at the distance of 15 miles. One of the two ships, the torpedo boat Matjan Tutul, with the Deputy Commander of the Indonesian Navy Rear-admiral Sudarso aboard, was hit and exploded, leading to the death of Sudarso a.o. The other Indonesian torpedo boat withdrew hastily. Notwithstanding Indonesian denials it was clear that the landing of infiltrators was intended, as could be deduced from the otherwise inexplicable number of crew aboard each ship. Under pressure from the navy and the army, Sukarno had to accept the replacement of Air Force Chief Suryadarma, a close friend of the President's who was made scape-goat – all in camera of course – for not having provided sufficient aircover.
6. *Moscow Radio Home Service*, February 8, 1962. Soviet ambassador Michailov had talks with Subandrio, Sukarno and Dhani on the day following the incident. On February 7 the new Air Force Chief left for Moscow, and the next day the Soviet government released its stern warning to the Dutch. The purpose of the visit was to have the Soviet government consent the sale of

the then-most modern Soviet fighter plane, the Mig-21, to the Indonesian Air Force. Kruschov, who received Dhani at his winter resort on the Black Sea, at first refused – as he was wary of its political effect – but later changed his mind. On the Arau incident he said that the Indonesians had let themselves be provoked too early; interview March 1972, Adam Malik.

7. According to the former spokesman of the Indonesian Ministry of Foreign Affairs, Ganis Harsono, a general consensus among leading Indonesians had been that Sudarso's action had been 'a stupid thing'; interview March 1972. It is not excluded, however, that it had Sukarno's advance blessing.
8. *Antara News Agency*, January 1, 1962. This might have been a genuine opinion of Sukarno's but then reflected – possibly only temporarily – a change of heart, as the Indonesian President had not long previously scoffed at Kruschov's concern after the Trikora command, remarking to Ambassador Malik that he could not care less for Kruschov's opinion now that he had acquired the Soviet weapons; Interview March 1972, Adam Malik.
9. In January 1962 a beginning had been made with the dropping or bringing ashore of small groups of armed infiltrators. According to Defense Minister Nasution then, they were not official troops but 'Indonesians, mostly born in West Irian, infiltrating back'; television-interview for *Sydney Radio and Television*, January 12, 1962.
10. *Antara News Agency*, January 23, 1962.
11. Interview March 1972, Adam Malik.
12. By early 1962 the U.S. had become convinced that the Indonesians meant 'business' and were prepared in all earnest for a military showdown with the Dutch on West Irian. The U.S. were informed of Indonesian intentions through diplomatic channels, in Washington, Moscow and Djakarta. This resulted in the visit of the American Attorney-General Robert F. Kennedy to Indonesia and to the Netherlands in February 1962. By accommodating Sukarno, the American government was convinced they could keep Indonesia from turning against the West.
13. For example, *Moscow Radio in Indonesian*, November 29, 1961. It was probably also this uneasiness about the American role in the conflict that made Soviet Ambassador Michailov voice displeasure at the beginning of the secret negotiations with the Dutch near Washington in the spring of 1962; see Dr. Guy J. Pauker, Soviet challenge in Indonesia, *Foreign Affairs*, July 1963, p. 613. In condemning U.S. suggestions as tantamount to endorsing the Dutch proposals, it mirrored the P.K.I. Politburo statement of November 25, 1961 – that is a few days before the echo came from Moscow – that what the U.S. proposed was 'at best only a revised edition of the Dutch proposal', *New China News Agency*, November 26, 1961.
14. *Moscow Radio in Dutch*, December 19, 1961, *Pravda*, December 25, 1961, *Moscow Radio in English for Southeast Asia*, December 27, 1961.
15. *Izvestia*, January 7, 1962, *Moscow Radio in English for Southeast Asia*, January 12, 1962, *Krasnaia Zwezda*, January 23, 1962.
16. *Moscow Radio in Indonesian*, March 15, 1962.

17. *Moscow Radio in Indonesian*, March 29, 1962. That Malik would stay – as turned out only for a while – was announced on March 26. Aidit promptly expressed full agreement with this move according to a *New China News Agency* bulletin of March 28 the day before Moscow came with the same opinion.
18. The Bunker proposals foresaw an interim period of two years in which the United Nations would take over the administration of West Irian from the Dutch. After that the Indonesians would come in and organize, at a date to be fixed later, a way for the local population to express its preferences on a government. The Dutch initially wanted this 'act of self-determination' to be concluded under U.N. authority, but had at an early stage to give in on this point. The transitional period of two years was upon the insistence of the Indonesians in the subsequent official negotiations reduced to nine months, with an additional proviso enabling the Indonesians to hoist their flag on January 1, 1963, 'as the cock crows', as Sukarno had promised.
19. *Antara News Agency*, May 2, 1962.
20. See interview with Subandrio in the Dutch daily *Het Parool*, May 8, 1962.
21. *Radio Djakarta Home Service*, May 11, 1962.
22. Speaking of the confrontation with Malaysia that was to begin to cast its shadows later that year, D. P. Mozingo, 1965, *Sino-Indonesian Relations an overwiev, 1955-1965*, Rand Corporation, Santa Monica, p. 42, sees in the Geneva Accords on Laos in July 1962 a limiting factor as to the commitments the Soviet Union was willing to undertake in South Asia. To the writer it seems that the Laos Accords were more of a tactical and short-term restraint upon Soviet foreign policy in the area, the decisive turning point towards a more defensive posture to come later with the Cuban withdrawal.
23. *Moscow Radio in Dutch*, June 2, 1962: 'The Bunker Plan is far from perfect . . . Everyone understands this, particularly in Indonesia . . . But there may be a real possibility for a settlement of the West Irian question'.
24. *Antara News Agency*, June 18, 1962. *Moscow Radio in English*, June 29, 1962.
25. *New China News Agency*, July 17, 1961.
26. *Antara News Agency*, July 17, 1962.
27. Opinion given by Adam Malik, in interview March 1972.
28. *Djakarta Radio Home Service*, July 20, 1962.
29. On the state of preparedness for military action see pp. 144, 145.
30. Arnold C. Brackman, 1963, *Indonesian Communism*, Frederick A. Praeger, New York, p. 298. Arnold C. Brackman, 1966, *Southeast Asia's Second Front: The Power Struggle in the Malay Archipelago*, Frederick A. Praeger, New York, p. 111, who also relates that Mikoyan abruptly broke off his visit.
31. Interview March 1972, Adam Malik.
32. *Radio Moscow in English to S.E. Asia*, July 25, 1962.
33. *Pravda*, July 23, 1962.
34. See below p. 271.

35. *Antara News Agency* reported on August 28, that is within two weeks after the Dutch and Indonesians had officially reached agreement on West Irian, that negotiations with the U.S. would be opened in September on a 325 million dollar credit. These talks had been delayed as the Americans had demanded as a precondition that the country's finances be stabilized, that is reduced to a tolerable degree of inflation. This in turn had hinged upon a settlement of the West Irian affair, making the result of the Bunker mediation of great importance to Indonesian economic development.
36. *Radio Moscow Home Service*, August 16, 1962. A few days earlier Subandrio had informed Ambassador Michailov of the pending settlement, upon which the Soviet diplomat expressed pleasure with it. *Antara News Agency*, August 9, 1962.
37. *Radio Moscow Home Service*, August 16, 1962, *Neues Deutschland*, August 18, 1962.
38. *Pravda* correspondent Shalkin mentioned this contribution of the West Irian 'liberation movement', but only in the immediate aftermath of the agreement; *Pravda*, August 17, 1962. See also: V. Senen, Another blow to the colonialists, *Azia i Afrika segodyia*, no. 10, 1962.
39. *Pravda*, August 18, 1962. Kruschov had of course at that time, as we learned after 'Cuba', a quite different 'complicated international problem' in mind which he was hoping to solve 'peacefully'.
40. See above for example p. 147, note 13 and p. 148, note 17.
41. The official Indonesian communist press presented a wide choice in this respect: *Harian Rakjat*, January 9 and 18, 1962, April 28, 1962, June 2 and 6, 1962; *Bintang Timur*, December 20, 1961, January 3 and 8, 1962. The non-communist media were certainly not saints in this respect, but sinned less frequently; see *Antara News Agency*, January 15, 1962, reacting to the Arau incident and, less unqualified, *Djakarta Radio Home Service*, March 21, 1962, making the use of force conditional upon failure of the secret talks had just begun.
42. This was of course what Sukarno was also after, but the Indonesian President could afford to compromise somewhat on method and timing, a luxury the P.K.I. did not want to, or have to, indulge in.
43. See above p. 140 and also *Harian Rakjat*, March 7, 1962 and April 14, 1962.
44. See above p. 140. Njoto wrote in *Harian Rakjat* on February 11, repeating what the Party daily had written on January 9 editorially.
45. Resolution of the Politburo of the C.C. P.K.I., December 15, 1962. The New Year greeting sent by the P.K.I. contained a similar plea (*New China News Agency*, December 30, 1961), as did *Harian Rakjat*, (January 9, 1962).
46. *Pravda* reprinted its version of the resolution on January 6, 1962.
47. *Harian Rakjat*, March 6, 1962; *New China News Agency*, March 11, 1962.
48. See his closing speech at the 7th Party Congress (*New China News Agency*, April 30, 1962) and his interview with an A.D.N.-correspondent (*New China News Agency*, July 4, 1963).
49. *Antara News Agency*, August 17, 1962 and *New China News Agency*, August

16, 1962. A curious discrepancy in the two texts invites attention. The Chinese version, no doubt the least doctored of the two, quotes the P.K.I. as saying, that 'the utmost effort *should* be made to avoid shameful concession' and that talks with the Dutch '*should* be limited to transferring the administration of West Irian within this year'. *Antara* removed the implied criticism by making the text in both cases affirmative 'the utmost efforts *were* made', and 'the talks *were* limited to transferring' etc. [emphasis added].

50. See p. 147 note 12.
51. Though an indispensable part of Sukarno's masterful ploy to regain the last part of the former Dutch East Indies, the Indonesian military, on their own, left little positive imprint on the situation. They gave full support to the ultranationalist designs spelled out by the President but displayed within the Indonesian context – for what it is worth – a relative sense of rationality, and leaders like Nasution and Yani were at least among those who, now and then, put the brakes on. Nasution played a role in shaping the outlines of the settlement through a temporary U.N. administration that finally came about. See Nasution after Sukarno's triple command (*Antara News Agency*, December 23, 1961) and Yani after the Arau incident (*Antara News Agency*, January 23, 1962). See on Nasution's backstage efforts Justus M. van der Kroef, 1965, *The Communist Party of Indonesia: Its History, Programme and Tactics*, University of British Columbia, Vancouver, p. 261.
52. According to General Nasution, in an interview March 1972, the Indonesian armed forces were ready to strike in West Irian by mid-August 1962. All Dutch surface vessels were under immediate threat of attack by the combined force of six Soviet-made heavy bombers of the TU 16 type with air-to-sea missiles and 12 Soviet built submarines. According to Nasution, 'it would have been tough'. According to Foreign Minister Luns in an interview April 1972, the Government in Djakarta by that time knew that the United States would not come to the aid of the Dutch in case Indonesia resorted to military actions against them.
53. Dutch military circles reported that, even after the Dutch and Indonesian delegations had come to an agreement early in August 1962, Sukarno ordered 3,000 hastily trained paratroopers to be dropped over West Irian so as to make a last minute show of force. The military effect was nil, as the troops landed scattered over a wide area and for the greater part were quickly taken prisoner.
54. Guy J. Pauker, The Soviet challenge in Indonesia, *Foreign Affairs*, July 1962, p. 616.
55. *Antara News Agency*, February 23, 1962.
56. After each major event, a decision or attempt on Sukarno's life an editorial was dedicated to Indonesian's plight in *Jen-min Jih-pao* or the South Chinese daily *Ta Kung Pao* (*Jen-min Jih-pao*, November 27, 1961 and December 21, 1961, April 1st, 1962; *Ta Kung Pao*, December 22, 1961 and March 30, 1962) or President Liu came up with an encouraging word (*New China News Agency*, January 10, 1962 and March 31, 1962).

57. See *New China News Agency* reporting a Subandrio commentary on Dutch-American discussions in Washington, compared with Antara's. *New China News Agency*, March 5, 1962, *Antara News Agency*, March 5, 1962.
58. Harold Hinton, 1966, *Communist China in World Politics*, Houghton Mifflin Company, Boston, p. 348: 'At the 14 nation Geneva conference on Laos, which met intermittently from May 1961 to July 1962, the Communist participants displayed a degree of agreement which indicated careful prior coordination'.
59 See *New China News Agency* coverage of the Subandrio visit to Moscow and Mikoyan's surprise trip to Djakarta, *New China News Agency*, May 9, and July 24, 1962.
60. *Jen-min Jih-pao*, August 19, 1962. Chinese Foreign Chen Yi had given the lead by omitting reference to the Soviets when he spoke at the annual Indonesian Independence Day celebration in Peking. *New China News Agency*, August 17, 1962.
61. *New China News Agency*, August 4, 1962, *Peking Review*, August 17, 1962.

CHAPTER 12

The Cuban crisis (1962)

Autumn 1962 produced a confluence of developments essentially of immediate and long-term impact on the P.K.I. as it operated within the international communist environment. The Sino-Soviet conflict had entered a more acute stage: At the end of August, Moscow informed its Chinese allies secretly that it wanted to go ahead with negotiations on a test-ban treaty with the United States. Peking, rightly fearing isolation, in vain tried by return mail to talk the Russian leaders out of it.[1] Secondly, the Cuban adventure and the Sino-Indian border war at the end of October and the mounting problems that resulted made it difficult for Aidit to stay out of the quarrel by ignoring the issues. And finally, the Soviet-Yugoslav rapprochement, initiated in May with Tito's speech in Split and Kruschov's 'reply' from Varna, was a new twist posing obstacles to the violently anti-Yugoslav P.K.I.[2]

We have seen that during the ideological lull that preceded, the West Irian affair had been of paramount importance to the Indonesian communist leadership.[3] Together with intraparty unity and a growing identification with Sukarno-oriented radical nationalism, it had provided the local background against which Aidit and his colleagues worked. So when Aidit lashed out against American imperialism, describing it as more aggressive under the Kennedy administration than Eisenhower's brand, he used a 'Chinese' phrase which, however, derived its proper meaning from the growing involvement of the U.S.A. in the Dutch-Indonesian conflict rather than from a wish to please Peking.[4] In this context we can also place Aidit's scepticism displayed towards that long-time Soviet front organization, the World Peace Council. He first indicated he was willing only to sponsor the next W.P.C. conference in Moscow when this meeting was to pay full attention to 'fighting against imperialism and for national independence'.[5]

In the same vein his message to the national congress of the Indonesian branch of the Peace Movement stressed that 'as for the Indonesian people, who are now suffering from aggression and oppression by colonialists and imperialists, disarmament should not mean to disarm the armed struggle for national independence'.[6] Immediately prior to the conference itself Aidit returned to this theme, telling an East German journalist that the W.P.C. meeting, apart from discussing disarmament and world peace, should also 'mirror the most pressing demands of the people of the whole world including those in colonies and semi-colonies . . .'.[7] Moscow of course had a willing ear for an appeal of this sort in the Third World on which Peking was capitalizing.[8] When later in July Mikoyan suddenly turned up in Indonesia, he also met this point by reassuring his audience in the new Soviet-built sports stadium that 'until capitalism disarms, it is the duty of every peaceloving people to strengthen the defence of its country so as to better ensure their independence and freedom'.[9] As one of the world's most energetic arms dealers Mikoyan of course would hardly have done a good job if he had treated the subject in Djakarta in the idealistic terms current at propagandistic peace conference. But to Mikoyan it must also have held a more general anti-Chinese implication, directed against the P.K.I.

The Chinese from their side did not let go the chance of ingratiating themselves with this potentially valuable ally. The greetings Peking sent to the 7th Party Congress the P.K.I. held from April 24 to 30 were accordingly cordial, praising Aidit particularly for his 'correct leadership'.[10] This glowing message was drawn up a month in advance, so Peking must then have already assumed that the 7th Party Congress was not going to let them down. Indeed, at this early stage of open differences between the two communist giants, anything coming their way was welcome to the Chinese, and the P.K.I. meeting turned out to be not at all so bad to them. It was convened because the party statutes and program had to be adjusted according to the requirements of Sukarno's recent legislation. Adherence to Manipol, the political philosophy the Indonesian President had enunciated in 1959, and to Pantjasilah, the five principles of the state including belief in God, as integral parts of the P.K.I. had to be sanctioned by the highest party organ. Its result was that the P.K.I., in the words of an observer, 'took up a sort of national-communist position nearer to Maoism than to Kruschovism'.[11]

Above all, the Indonesian communists wanted to avoid giving the slightest ground for being called at home a foreign-dominated party or abroad a revisionist one.

In his general report to the congress Aidit was responsive to this when he said, on account of the developments within the international communist movement:

> We are Indonesian Marxist-Leninists, we are Indonesian Communists . . . we have to shape creatively the policy, tactics, forms of struggle and organization of our Party based on the concrete situation obtaining in our country. Our Marxist-Leninism is Marxism-Leninism applied in Indonesia . . . Our party is independent and has equal rights, it shapes its own policies.[12]

Earlier the party paper, *Harian Rakjat,* had introduced the forthcoming P.K.I.-congress with the words that it 'would discuss the struggle against imperialism and feudalism [i.e. the recovery of West Irian] and would indicate the best way for this struggle *in line with its own belief*' [emphasis added].[13]

As we saw, this insistence upon independence of judgment is a recurring theme when dealing with the P.K.I. It had all along sprung from the peculiar Indonesian nationalist character of the party and its leadership. However with the growing Sino-Soviet rift, it took on a greater vehemence and acuity.[14]

So Aidit's view on the problems which had arisen between Moscow and Peking reflected this attitude to a remarkable degree, as this passage witnesses; it is worth quoting in entirety:

> The difference of opinion in the international Communist movement is a passing phenomenon. All Marxist-Leninist Parties pursue the same final objective: i.e. to put an end by revolutionary means to the exploitation of man; to create a new world, a world of Socialism and Communism, in which all men live in peace and happiness. We must not forget however, that there are now about 90 Marxist-Leninist Parties in the world today and more than 42 million Communists led by thousands of members of Central Committees, not all of whom possess, or fully possess, the characteristics of Marx, Engels and Lenin. This is why we should not be surprised if there still are people among the Communist leaders who like to exaggerate differ-

> ences of opinion rather than stressing the unity of opinion; who do not give a primary place to primary things; who cannot restrain themselves if there is another Communist Party that holds a different view regarding non-basic, or less basic problems, or problems which are basic but the solution of which can be postponed.[15]

This defence of freedom of action and thought of individual communist parties was pretty strongly worded, and one is almost inclined to look for more than a general wish, prevailing among the P.K.I. leadership and cadres, to assert the right to speak its mind freely. As an attack on Kruschov – one of those 'who cannot restrain themselves – it gives the impression of being more personally directed against the Soviet leader than would correspond with the cautious approach Aidit usually displayed. Not known for his gracious manners, certainly not when opposed, it is quite possible that Kruschov had fallen out with Aidit, either in person when they met during and after the 22nd Party Congress, or in the period thereafter when Aidit was one of those who tried to mediate.[16] However this may be, both the need to look respectably nationalistic and the looming West-Irian affair must have exerted pressure on Aidit, moving him away from the essentially neutral stance that would have suited him best at that moment towards positions finding acclaim rather in Peking than in Moscow. As a windfall this leaning towards the generally more radical 'Chinese' side must have brought Aidit at least the advantage of accommodating his more leftist-minded colleagues in the leadership of the party. No sign of intraparty opposition is to be found in that period, and the assurances on the occasion of the P.K.I. anniversary that the party was operating harmoniously had a ring of truth.[17] This shift further away from Moscow, certainly as it was now embodied in Aidit himself, plus the end of the West-Irian dispute during the summer of 1962, must have been regarded at Soviet communist headquarters with apprehension. As stated earlier, Mikoyan may have been the interpreter of the Kremlin's fears when he suddenly arrived in Djakarta at the end of July, but no record of particular attention on his part for the P.K.I. or its leaders is available. The degree of coordination, therefore, that still must have gone on between Moscow and its straying communist ally is a matter of speculation. There are, however, some indications that in mid-year 1962 the Soviet Union regained some of the ground with the P.K.I. that it had lost in the months after the 22nd Party Congress.

The focal point here seems to have been the new 'externalizer' Malaysia, the federation of neighboring Malay states, including Chinese-dominated Singapore.[18] At the third plenary of the P.K.I. Central Committee at the end of 1961, this new construction was already condemned by the Indonesian communists in a resolution. This had attracted little attention at the time, and the P.K.I. too did not do much to publicize or press the matter, preoccupied as they were with more urgent matters.[19] But it was revived again by Aidit, be it still in a rather indirect way, in an address at party headquarters on August 20 when the P.K.I. chairman gave what amounted to a pep talk to his staff.[20] In it he outlined the new tasks the party should set itself now that West Irian was all but liberated from the Dutch.

It amounted chiefly to a call for continuing 'vigilance' in the face of anticipated sabotage by the Netherlands while the territory was being transferred to the United Nations. Sukarno's triple command of December 1961 was therefore still valid, he said, implying that for the time being no relaxation of domestic militancy was called for. Though delivered in a more expansive and above all more confident tone the speech was similar to what Aidit had written in *Harian Rakjat* three days before on Indonesia's Independence day.[21] There was one difference, however, that is worthwhile noting. In the *Harian Rakjat* article Aidit had confined himself – rather defensively and dully – to purely national tasks 'to consolidate the victory already won, to overcome economic difficulties and to oppose colonialism'. In his speech three days later to the party cadres he introduced a wider perspective that had hitherto been lacking: 'The settlement of the West Irian problem does not mean that imperialists have been buried once and for all, nor that the people would be living a prosperous life. *Around Indonesia are countries under the control of imperialism* and imperialism will not look on complacently while the Indonesian people carry out the Political Manifeste [emphasis added]'.[22] In the context of Indonesian politics this meant a new issue (and there was no doubt that is was Malaysia) that would justify new sacrifices of the people and brinkmanship by its leaders. Brackman points out that 'the Irian settlement severed the umbilical cord between communism and nationalism in Indonesia' and that Aidit, in his first post-Irian comment in *Harian Rakjat*, quoted above, 'weakly groped toward a new political line'.[23] He then continued: 'Doubtless the combined interest of Moscow, Peking and the P.K.I. would best be served at this stage by encouraging a new colonial adventure, Timor perhaps, or ideally East Irian'. The 'adventure', the need of which Brackman foresaw at the time of writing – late in 1962 – was already in the making, albeit not where he had looked for it. As developments were to show, Aidit's remark did not fall on deaf ears with President Sukarno, who notwithstanding the considerable political victory he had gained in making the Dutch retreat must have felt almost immediately the need for a substitute-issue.[24] But, contrary to the West-Irian affair that, by all accounts, struck a sympathetic cord in the Indonesian public opinion if one can speak of such a thing, the confrontation with Malaysia from its inception in August 1962 bore the mark of artificiality, and it would take some time to get Sukarno to see it as a useful issue.[25]

The close relationship and basic identity of views between Aidit's P.K.I. and the Soviet leaders as it still prevailed then is illustrated by the speed with which Aidit's hinting at a new issue for Indonesia was picked up by Moscow. Just two days after the P.K.I. Chairman had outlined (for the first time publicly) that the 'imperialist' danger, even with West Irian settled, was still around, Moscow Radio suddenly linked Djakarta's destiny with that of the neighboring federation that was planned to come about a year hence.[26] As a disputed scheme of the British colonialists, in connivance with Malayan Premier Abdul Rahman, Malaysia had already at an earlier stage been singled out for criticism by the Soviet Union and its publicity organs.[27] But this had been done in terms of the territories directly concerned. Now, in addition to the usual arguments against the proposal, it was suggested for the first time that Malaysia was 'a threat not only to those territories it is to include, but *also to neighboring countries in Southeast Asia*' [emphasis added]. Quoting a Malayan paper it was hinted that Indonesia was unlikely to view these developments 'positively', and the possibility that in the federated territories in Northern Borneo 'right on the border with Indonesia' Seato would build military bases was pictured as a dark but real prospect.[28] So from available evidence and informed opinion[29] the beginning of the dispute about, and later with, the Malaysian federation can be traced back to a P.K.I. initiative, that found immediate, but not permanent, endorsement from the Soviets.[30]

Then the Cuban affair, as well as the Indian-Chinese border war, both in their own way (and within the limited context of intra-communist relations examined here) upset this continued alignment between the P.K.I. and Soviet comrades. Though nothing had indicated that the basic contradictions which had set Moscow and Peking apart – the right of each party to decide for itself, the relative importance of Soviet-American relations over the national liberation movement, the road to power, etc. – were easy to resolve, Aidit may really have believed what he said at the 7th Party Congress that the differences were only temporary. He certainly must have hoped they were and, with both China and the Soviet Union supporting him, have looked forward to a next round of power building within Indonesia, thriving on Malaysia as new external threat and the declining economy as an unsettling factor on the inside. But the two new international issues which turned up in the autumn of 1962 were going to be so many additional points of friction for communists all over the world that fence-sitting became one degree more difficult.

On Cuba Aidit began by declaring 'sympathy' with Castro and expressing the hope, as the Chinese had done the day before, that 'with resolute and disinterested aid from all progressive forces' the Cubans could frustrate the evil intentions of the United States.[31] When the seriousness of the situation must have sunk in more fully – and while Sukarno was still 'studying' the situation – the P.K.I. leadership preferred not to stick out its neck too much. So *Harian Rakjat* instead of giving an editorial opinion took the precaution of quoting the Indonesian Peace committee as saying that it was 'illogical' not to allow Cuba to have arms from the Soviet Union, while the United States was arming half Europe, etc.[32] Njoto followed suit the next day with a similar line.[33] When it was clear that the immediate danger of a Soviet-American clash was over, the party paper finally came out with an opinion of its own which amounted to support for Castro's five demands – especially the one on evacuation of the American military base on Cuba, Guantanamo – that the Cuban leader had posed as conditions for accepting the United States' part of the deal, i.e., lifting of the quarantaine and a promise that there would be no invasion.[34] The real crux was to come with Castro's television speech of November 1, 1962, refusing international inspection of the island and so threatening a vital part of the carefully struck deal between Moscow and Washington.[35] It lasted a week before Aidit came with a statement in which he took a critical line towards the Soviet Union.[36] His views were nowhere polemical in tone as, for instance, the Chinese declarations had been. However, without mentioning the Soviet Union by name, he squarely called the withdrawal of the Russian rockets 'a regrettable sacrifice', as Cuba had been forced to accept this against her will. Up till the issue of Aidit's statement, the P.K.I. had continued cautiously to follow the Soviet version of the cricis and so in an article in *Harian Rakjat*, Lukman had portrayed the U.S.A. as the perpetrator of political crises, while the Soviet Union was the 'sprayer of cold water'. No word had yet been said about Cuban sovereignty.[37]

On the occasion of the 45th anniversary of the October Revolution, Aidit made a speech designed to clear the air somewhat after all the events of the previous weeks.[38] It was a masterpiece of balancing the various contradictory tendencies of the day, while at the same time not altogether forgetting the October Revolution. For the first time since long before, Aidit even went out of his way to praise the Soviet Union for its military and economic aid to Indonesia. The main point in this respect was his thesis that 'love for the Soviet Union' would not make Indonesian communists diminish in patriotism. Whatever he said on the score of the Soviet Union was reported by the Djakarta correspondent of Pravda under the heading: 'The Soviet Union is the true friend of Indonesia'.[39] Not given were the other points Aidit made in his speech which on the whole were of more importance. On Cuba he veered back a little to the middle and left out the previous expressions of regret, saying only: 'The Cuban crisis must certainly be eliminated. Acceptance of the five demands of Premier Castro is the way to eliminate the crisis, for these are the minimum demands for national independence'.[40] Here he ranged himself alongside for instance the North Vietnamese Premier, Pham Van Dong, a fellow-'neutralist' in the Sino-Soviet dispute, who at a Soviet embassy reception in Hanoi had equally supported Castro's five points and called for 'a resolute struggle for independence'.[41] Not everyone in the P.K.I. was pleased with Aidit's renewed caution, but nowhere were extreme expressions used such as the Chinese were then employing.[42]

While there was to follow a period of Party Congresses in Europe for which, apparently, the P.K.I. leadership had decided to base itself as strictly as possible on 1957 and 1960 documents, on Cuba the P.K.I. Central Committee had settled for an unpolemical 'independence-first' line, implicitly anti-Soviet in tenor.[43] In a message to the Italian Communist Party, due to hold its tenth Congress early in December 1962, the P.K.I. stated that the socialist countries, together with those in the third world, 'believe that the fate of the Cuban people, the independence of their country, the sovereignty of their motherland and their own future are determined by the Cuban people themselves, not by the United States or *any other party in the world*' [emphasis added].[44] Therefore, however disagreeable Cuba was as a new issue in the Sino-Soviet relation (especially as it was a clash on a point of concrete policy), the P.K.I. faced it in a gainly consistent manner, inspired by its preoccupation with its independence, both as communists and as Indonesians. In the long run, however, the Cuban crisis was not that easy for the P.K.I. (relatively speaking) in its consequences. It was to be a turning point in Soviet-American relations that opened the way to the nuclear test ban treaty of mid-1963. But, at the same time, it was going to mark the beginning of a less provocative Soviet foreign policy of lower risks, not only vis-à-vis America but also in the Third World.[45] This in turn, was to have its effect on the Malaysia affair which had again brought together Soviet and Indonesian communist leaders only a few months before when the end of the West Irian quarrel with the Dutch was in sight.[46]

With the Sino-Indian border fighting, the second issue, it was rather the other way round. The disruptive effect of it on the Indian brother party, when it became known after the initial phase of the war, was a dangerous example to the P.K.I. of the problems that could beset a communist party when it was forced into a position where it had to choose between national and international allegiance. It was to this contradiction, too, that Aidit addressed himself in his major speech on November 12, 1962.[47] But, in the longer run, anti-Indian sentiments could be mustered so well in Indonesia that to depict the Chinese communists as being eligible for support and the Indian side to be blamed was a rather easy thing to do. In this respect the non-communist public (or better, published) opinion in Indonesia was no less slanted against New Dehli than the communist side. A dress rehearsal at the end of August had already shown this when during the Asian Games in Djakarta incidents put Indian-Indonesian relations in a state of minor crisis.[48] As a result *Bintang Timur*, the communist Djakarta newspaper that had increasingly shown a pro-Peking bias, attacked India vehemently for its foreign policy on the eve of the Chinese military advance down the slopes of the Himalaya on October 20, 1962.[49] Again as with the Cuban missile crisis, the initial reaction of the Indonesian communists was cautious. The first semi-official opinion in *Harian Rakjat* came two days after the Chinese government declaration of October 24, offering negotiations after both parties had withdrawn 20 km behind the 'lines of actual control'.[50]

In step with what Pravda in its first comment on the border war had said the day before, *Harian Rakjat* called the Chinese proposals 'constructive'.[51] But whereas the Soviet paper had been only mildly pro-Chinese and also spoke of the need for an international approach with 'no preliminary conditions dictated' (which the Chinese were in actual fact doing), the Indonesian party paper called India 'prejudiced and stubborn' and displayed scepticism about India's response. Aidit escalated a further step when he sent Kruschov a telegram congratulating him on his decision not to help India with MIG fighters.[52] He tried to pin the Soviet leader down by telling him: 'This [Kruschov's] sentiment of severely condemning the aggressive attitude of Mr. Nehru . . . is shared by all Communists and Indonesian progressive people'. But, in actual fact, Aidit himself got caught. Some ten days later Kruschov went back on his decision and told Nehru that he would have his MIG's and even his MIG factory.[53] This was in line with the restatement of the Soviet standpoint, following the safe escape from the Cuban crisis that had clouded the scene in the initial stage. The Soviet Union had now reverted to its previous position of neutrality between 'fraternal China' and 'friendly India' and was insisting upon ceasefire and unconditional talks.[54] When the Chinese taunted Nehru that he was no longer 'nonaligned' because he took military aid from capitalist countries like the United States and Great Britain, *Tass* published Nehru's denial the next day.[55] But this shift in favor of India was not followed by Aidit who, without looking silly, could not now do much else but stress (as the whole Indonesian left wing did) the need for negotiations on the basis of the Chinese proposals of October 24.[56] Besides, his attentions had been caught by what had happened to the Indian Communist Party. The majority of its Central Committee had followed the lead given by its Executive Committee and thrown itself completely behind Nehru. Scores of left-wing communists had been rounded up and arrested, among whom also – though not for long – ex-Premier of Kerala and C.P.I. Chairman Nambodiripad. It was said that this 'purge' by the Indian police had not been at all unwelcome to the leader of the right-wing of the C.P.I., its Secretary-General Dange. At all events, the Indian party was in full disarray, and Aidit thought it was necessary to calm down feelings within his own party. This brought him to the main theme of his November 12 speech, in which he tried to show that communists could very well support nationalists, so long at least as the well-known 'first phase' – the national-democratic one – was not over.[57] The danger was not nationalism but 'chauvinism', he said, and here India was a clear example of what could go wrong: 'The imperialists have to a certain extent now succeeded in stirring up chauvinism in India. We very much deplore that a section of the Indian working class [i.e., majority of the C.P.I.] has been affected by this imperialist poison'. The remedy for the P.K.I. should be 'simultaneously holding high the two banners of patriotism and internationalism'. This was of course a purely verbal medicine, the main escape hatch for Aidit and his fellow Politburo members being to shun as the plague any situation in which they would be forced to make a choice similar to their Indian colleagues. So on this issue, too, the P.K.I. under Aidit landed more on the side of the Chinese than would have been the case without the border crisis in the Himalaya's.

Yugoslavia was the third field where it became difficult to avoid a sliding away from a safe middle position, allegedly based on the 'sacred' collective scriptures of 1957 and 1960. Here it was the Soviet Union that clearly went against the letter if not the spirit of the 1960 Statement when it was still maintained that the modern revisionist tendencies of the Yugoslav leaders had to be 'exposed'. At the same time that Njoto read the P.K.I. message to the Czechoslovak Party Congress and was having a go at the Yugoslavs for daring to regard Marxism as 'old-fashioned', etc., Kruschov was busy welcoming arch-revisionist Tito in Moscow, solemnly declaring that Yugoslavia was a socialist country.[58] The P.K.I. showed its displeasure by printing a violently anti-Yugoslav article in *Harian Rakjat* on December 8, 1962, the day before Yugoslavia's Vice-President Kardelj was due to arrive in Djakarta on an official invitation.[59] On December 11 the same paper printed an anti-revisionist message sent by Albanian party chief, Enver Hodzha, in reply to P.K.I. congratulations of late November and clearly kept in store for the occasion. Then came, also unnecessarily late, Njoto's Prague speech which was not at all attuned to the new honeymoon Kruschov and Tito were celebrating in Moscow.[60]

On balance it looks that the events in the autumn of 1962 brought a further shift in the position of the P.K.I. within the bipolarization that slowly overtook the world communist movement. External factors – the Cuban crisis, the border war, the Soviet-Yugoslav rapprochement – also had consequences for the P.K.I., though the issues were initially 'foreign' in character. After some hesitation and uncertainty, the automatic orientation towards the Soviet Union had to be abandoned in favor of more sophisticated attitudes.[61] On Cuba, respect for national independence that Moscow had treated so cavalierly became the factor that made the party take a neutralist stand implicitly un-Soviet in tenor. The Chinese-Indian frontier war, with its initial danger for the unity of the party once national sentiment clashed with 'internationalist' duties, brought the P.K.I. – and other political opinion in Indonesia for that matter – eventually to the Chinese side because anti-Indian feeling prevailed. On Yugoslavia it was difficult to follow the Soviet Union as it so manifestly flouted the collective communist opinion laid down in the Moscow documents of 1957 and 1960. Thus here too radical elements within the P.K.I. had an easy time of it. In the long run, however, the Cuban crisis probably had the greatest effect on the attitude of the P.K.I. since the Soviet Union in the post-'Cuban' period began to operate in a more sober mood, with less inclination to get involved in foreign adventures. As we will see, this meant that the Soviet Union was less 'game' than before in a campaign which, initiated by the P.K.I., also came to preoccupy Sukarno: The Malaysia confrontation. When Sukarno was beginning to shift his selfish expectations from Moscow to that other source of international support, Peking, it decidedly became possible or necessary for Aidit to rearrange his priorities, whatever 'pro-Soviet' views he may personally have preferred.

NOTES

1. *Jen-min Jih-pao*, August 15, 1963.
2. *Borba*, May 7, 1962; *Pravda*, May 18, 1962; *Radio Moscow in Serbocroat*, May 17, 1962.
3. See above p. 143 ff.
4. 'The U.S. role in the Congo, its intervention in Laos, its subversive activities and aggressive plans against Cuba, its support of Dutch colonialism on the

West Irian question . . . – all those have indicated that there is no difference between the Kennedy administration and that of the Eisenhower government, and even that it is more aggressive'. Aidit in an interview with the Djakarta correspondent of Associated Press, as printed in *Harian Rakjat*, March 6, 1962.

5. *New China News Agency*, April 7, 1962. This reflects the discussion on the agenda between pro-Chinese delegates and opponents at the World Peace Council meeting in December 1961, see above p. 128.
6. *New China News Agency*, May 20, 1962. Aidit was in good company, as that archdeacon of Indonesian nationalism Ruslan Abdulgani cabled W. P. C. chairman John Bernal at that time that he was too busy to help prepare the conference, struggling as he was 'towards the liquidation of the root cause that hinders world peace and security: to the Indonesian people (this) basic cause is the colonial system which is still entrenched in Asia and Africa, including West-Irian'; *New China News Agency*, May 19, 1962.
7. *New China News Agency*, July 4, 1962. Aidit, as a matter of fact, reacted partly to a lecture given a few days before by Njoto who, as Deputy Chairman of the Indonesian Peace Committee, was about to go to Moscow. Njoto had given a more even-handed 'Soviet' appraisal of the coming Congress, stressing the need to counteract the armament race that unnamed other persons held to be 'a futile policy'. *New China News Agency*, July 3, 1962.
8. *Moscow Radio in Kuoyu to China*; 'Peaceful co-existence is the best condition for those struggling for National Liberation', July 6, 1962.
9. *Radio Moscow in English for SE Asia*, July 23, 1962.
10. *New China News Agency*, April 26, 1962.
11. W. A. C. Adie, China, Russia and the Third World, *China Quarterly*, no. 11, 1962, p. 205.
12. *Jen-min Jih-pao*, May 11, 1962. This was the first time a P.K.I. report appeared extensively in the Chinese press, almost completely made up of direct quotations. A short summary was given on April 28 by *New China News Agency*. The *Tass* version, published on April 26, did not contain any other reference to what Aidit had said on world communism than two sentences: 'Touching upon the question of unity of the international communist movement, Aidit said that differences of opinion in the international communist movement were temporary. He assured that the communists of Indonesia would continue to preserve the unity of the communist and Workers Parties as the apple of his eye'.
13. *Harian Rakjat*, April 10, 1962.
14. In his general report to the Party Congress Aidit did not cite the Soviet 22nd Party Congress as one of the sources of wisdom, but only those documents that were agreed upon collectively, such as the Moscow statements of 1957 and 1960. However, he praised the Soviet Union saying that 'the building of communism, now under way in the Soviet Union, is exerting an extremely broad international influence'. This was reported in the *Tass* version but not in any of those *New China News Agency* put out, which is evidence that the

attitude taken towards internal Soviet developments had become a yardstick in the Sino-Soviet dispute. After the P.K.I. had gone into its disastrous decline following the events of September 30, 1965, Aidit was posthumously reproached for having changed his line here: 'The stand taken by the 7th Congress of the P.K.I. on the successes of socialist construction, the acme of which is the constructions of communism in the Soviet Union hailed with applause by the entire gathering, was later abruptly denounced by the C.C. of the P.K.I. without any reason whatsoever'. From: Appeal of the Marxist-Leninist Group of the Communist Party of Indonesia, published in the Moscow-oriented *Information Bulletin*, no. 18, 1967, p. 52. See also below pp. 230, 239 note 70, 430, 431.

15. *Jen-min Jih pao*, May 11, 1962.
16. See above pp. 127, 133.
17. Njoto, on the eve of the P.K.I. anniversary, wrote that 'a split, or at least cracks in the ranks of the P.K.I.' that the 'imperialists' had hoped to see had not occurred; *Harian Rakjat*, May 23, 1962. Anwar Zanusi, Deputy Chairman of the Radical Farmers' Union B.T.I. and therefore a still-better witness claimed in his anniversary report that 'the unity of the party (is) more solid and more scientifically based than ever before'; *New China News Agency*, May 24, 1962.
18. Dr. O. W. Röder has pointed to the author out that the West Irian affair was in fact for Sukarno not an 'externaliser' but a genuinely nationalistic preaccupation; interview March 1972.
19. According to Arnold C. Brackman, 1966, *Southeast Asia's Second Front: The Power Struggle in the Malay Archipelago*, Frederick A. Praeger, New York, p. 252, the P.K.I. took over control of the Singapore Communist Party from the Peking-dominated Malay C.P. This was 'temporary' and supposedly on condition that the P.K.I. follow a Peking line in the international communist movement.
20. *New China News Agency*, August 22, 1962. In May, Aidit had given an interview to the *Straits Times* in which he denounced Malaysia, charging that Great Britain had devised the new federation in order to keep the countries involved in a state of colonial dependence; *Moscow Radio Home Service*, December 15, 1962.
21. *Harian Rakjat*, August 17, 1962, *New China News Agency*, August 18, 1962.
22. *New China News Agency*, August 22, 1962.
23. *Harian Rakjat*, August 17, 1962; *New China News Agency*, August 18, 1962. See: Arnold C. Brackman, 1963, *Indonesian Communism*, Frederick A. Praeger, New York, p. 298.
24. Howard Jones, who at the time was American ambassador in Djakarta, relates a revealing detail in his book: *Indonesia, The Impossible Dream* (Harcourt, Brace, Jovanovich, Inc., New York, 1971, p. 213). Breaking the news to Sukarno that the negotiations on West Irian in Washington had been concluded successfully Jones told the Indonesian President: 'Your revolution is complete'. Sukarno did not at all react as enthusiastically as Jones had

anticipated: 'Sukarno nodded thoughtfully, spoke quietly to those who were with him. It was not an exultant moment. I had an odd feeling, as though I were witnessing a scene in which a beloved member of the family were leaving home. Sukarno would miss West Irian, I thought. He had won a victory, but he had lost an issue'. Adam Malik in an interview March 1972, remembered Sukarno later in 1962 as being rather unhappy and saying: 'Now I have arms, I could not use them in West Irian, what else is there?'

25. Justus M. van der Kroef, The Sino-Indonesian Partnership, *Orbis*, summer 1964, p. 338, introduces the Indonesian President at a very early stage: 'To Sukarno and to those economic groups which particularly look to him for protection and leadership, the Malaysia issue offered itself as the most immediately available means to perpetuate the status quo and justify once again the postponement of hard and unsettling economic decisions'. To this writer it seems that Sukarno came into the Malaysia affair later, and that from August to November 1962 it was rather a Soviet-P.K.I. collaboration that was the prime moving factor. Sukarno's Independence Day speech 'Year of triumph' shows him in a reflective mood, full of good intentions for the well-being of the Indonesian people, etc., while there are also other indications that he *followed* the prompting of Aidit and the P.K.I., and was not the prime mover as with West Irian; see below p. 171.
26. *Radio Moscow in Indonesian*, August 22, 1962.
27. *Radio Moscow in Indonesian*, August 31, 1961, calling Rahman a 'loyal agent of imperialism'. The Malayan Premier had for the first time broached the idea of a Malaysian federation in an address to foreign correspondents in Kuala Lumpur on May 27 of that year. Developments in Singapore in July and August led to a split in the leading socialist party P.A.P. and (on August 13) to the formation of a Chinese-communist dominated party, the Barisan Sosialis, that strongly condemned plans for Malaysia.
28. See below p. 171.
29. Interview March 1972 with Adam Malik.
30. See below p. 173.
31. *Harian Rakjat*, October 25, 1962. The Chinese reaction was contained in an editorial in *Jen-min Jih-pao* 'Stop the new U.S. adventure' on October 24, 1962.
32. *Harian Rakjat*, October 29, 1962.
33. *Harian Rakjat*, October 30, 1962.
34. *Harian Rakjat*, October 31, 1962. *Jen-min Jih-pao* wrote on that day that United States promises were empty so long as Castro's demands were not met. *Izvestia* argued against aggravating the situation.
35. *New China News Agency*, November 1st, 1962. While making some gestures of gratitude towards the Soviet Union – that they had been 'generous' with their aid, etc. – Castro admitted that there were 'certain differences' with the Russian comrades.
36. *Harian Rakjat*, November 8, 1962, *New China News Agency*, November 7, 1962. Aidit had the benefit (when making the statement on November 7) of

various other communist pronouncements among which the Chinese. In an editorial in *Jen-min Jih-pao* of November 5 the 'appeasement' around Cuba had been strongly attacked, indicating that what had happened had been 'an attempt to play the Munich game against the Cuban people'.

37. The article appeared in the *Harian Rakjat* issue of November 7, in itself late enough to know of the independent role Cuba was playing. Another sign of some disarray in the P.K.I. was the printing in the same issue of a speech Njoto had written, and not delivered, in *1961* after the Bay of Pigs landing: 'If Lenin was still among us, we would certainly be very indignant about the Cuban affair now', a reference to an entirely different 'Cuban affair'.
38. The speech was delivered on November 12 and duly reported: *Antara News Agency*, November 12, 1962, *New China News Agency*, November 14, 1962, *Pravda*, November 15, 1962.
39. Branko Lazitch, in *East-West*, December 16-31, 1962, gives this article as one of the indications that during September, October and November 1962 'the P.K.I. leaders desired to maintain cordial relations with Moscow'. It is not a very strong example, as it is the highly selective version of what Aidit said by *Pravda* correspondent Shalkin. It left out all reference to the Chinese-Indian border question, and the disquieting effect this had had on the Indian Communist Party – the most important part of Aidit's speech – and on Cuba it only mentioned that the P.K.I. leader expressed 'sympathy' with that country. The other examples Lazitch gives are an article by Aidit in the September issue of *Problems of Peace and Socialism*, and another article written in *Pravda* of October 13 (Lazitch erroneously gives September 13 as a date). This last one is an explanation of the West Irian affair, not marked by pro-Soviet signs. The evidence adduced may rather point out that the Soviet Union was interested in maintaining cordial relations with the P.K.I. and not the other way round. While not convinced of the arguments used, the writer finds himself in basic agreement with Lazitch's observation that, from roughly mid-1962, the P.K.I. tried to maintain or restore the somewhat ruffled Soviet-P.K.I. relations. See above pp. 154, 155.
40. *Peking Radio Home Service*, November 15, 1962.
41. *New China News Agency*, November 7, 1962.
42. On November 15, 1962, *Jen-min Jih-pao* warned in an editorial that 'if one retreats, bows down or even begs for peace before imperialism at the expence of the revolutionary people one only encourages imperialism to carry out more aggressively its polities of aggression and war'. The communist paper *Harapan* in Medan on November 16 did not go further than to write that it was 'dangerous to make concessions to imperialism, thus weakening the new emerging forces'.
43. At the Bulgarian Party Congress early in November, the P.K.I. delegate was non-committal and left out any reference to Albania; *East-West*, 16, December 31, 1962. The Chinese delegate, Wu Hsiu-chuan, had expressed regret that the Albanese had been attacked again at the Congress and was later supported by the North-Korean speaker. The message Njoto was to read out

to the Czechoslovak Party Congress a month later was dated November 25, 1962. It spoke of 13 countries 'developing socialism', including Albania (and the newcomer to the fold Cuba) and excluded Yugoslavia. Njoto apparently had no instructions to go beyond that and remained silent, whereas Wu again protested against the 'onesided' charges against Tirana: *Harian Rakjat* December 14, 1962 and Griffith, 1967, *Sino-Soviet Relations 1964-1965*, The M.I.T. Press, Cambridge, Massachusetts, p. 67. The written message to the Italian Party Congress contained no reference whatsoever to Albania; *Harian Rakjat*, December 4, 1962.

44. *Harian Rakjat*, December 4, 1962. See also Griffith, 1967, p. 67, who holds that, at the European Party Congresses, the Indonesian communists shifted to 'a more pro-Chinese emphasis'.
45. See also R. A. Yellon, 1963. The winds of change, *Mizan Newsletter*, July-August, pointing out the decline in priority for Third World policies that marked the last years of Kruschov's reign and beyond.
46. See above p. 157 below p. 171.
47. *Antara News Agency*, November 12, 1962, *New China News Agency*, November 14, 1962, *Pravda*, November 15, 1962. See also p. 162.
48. The conflict turned on the presence of participants from Israel and Nationalist China (Taiwan). Combined pressure from the P.K.I. – against the 'clique' of Chiang Kai-shek – and from the extremist Muslim opinion within and without the Nahdatul Ulama Party – against 'zionist' Israel – had resulted in these two countries not being invited to the Asian Games. When Sondhi the Indian Deputy-Chairman of the Games organization protested at the last minute against this irregular procedure suggesting (in itself correctly) that the Games should not be called 'Asian', the cat was out of the bag. The hoisting of the Indian flag was accompanied by hissing and booing, and soon the Indian embassy was invaded by an angry mob.

    Though Nehru initially stressed that Sondhi was a private person and not an Indian government representative, he could not get around reacting and observed that under Sukarno's guided democracy no demonstration in Indonesia could take place without official permission, implying connivance of the Indonesian authorities. The whole affair was jumped upon by extremists in the press, both communist and non-communist, trying to outdo each other in nationalistic anti-Indian zeal. It further made Nehru remark that China had shown great interest in the affair, and had even encouraged it (*New Dehli Radio*, September 4, 1962). Though hard to prove literally, circumstantial evidence – press coverage and the like – showed that the Indian Premier was not very wide of the mark.
49. *Bintang Timur*, October 17, 1962 under the title: The Indian attitude towards the fourth Asian Games and the second Afro-Asian conference is alien to the attitude of an Asian country.
50. *New China News Agency*, October 24, 1962. The declaration contained three proposals to which continuous reference was made in the Indonesian press: 1. Both parties should accept the lines of actual control and withdraw 20 km

from them. 2. If India had complied with that condition China was willing to withdraw in the North East Frontier Area; in the middle and Western part of the border area involved the situation would remain as it was. 3. The two prime ministers would then begin talks in Peking or in New Dehli. As no one could doubt, this clearly favored Peking, as the Chinese troops had advanced far into the North-east frontier area, and the proposals were unacceptable to India.

51. *Harian Rakjat*, January 26, 1962; *Pravda*, October 25, 1962.
52. *Harian Rakjat*, November 2, 1962. Aidit wrote somewhat pathetically: 'I was really overwhelmed to hear the news'. Ra'anan calls the telegram 'ironical', but Aidit may well have been serious, warning the Soviet leader of where he stood or should stand. See U. Ra'anan, The Djakarta Moscow-Peking Triangle and Indonesia's protracted crisis; manuscript put at the disposal of the author.
53. *Far Eastern Economic Review*, February 28, 1963.
54. *Pravda*, November 5, 1962. Kruschov in his speech before the Supreme Soviet on December 12, 1962, referred in this context to the *Tass* statement of September 9, 1959, the first outward sign that the Soviet Union was not backing its communist ally.
55. *Jen-min Jih-pao*, November 11, 1962. *Tass*, November 12, 1962.
56. Aidit speech on November 12, 1962, on the occasion of the 45th anniversary of the October Revolution; *Peking Radio Home Service*, November 15, 1962. As related above, p. 167, note 39, the Rusian version did not make any mention of his stand on the border war nor on its effects on the Indian C.P.
57. *New China News Agency*, November 14, 1962.
58. *Pravda*, December 5, 1962. The Njoto speech was not printed in *Harian Rakjat* before December 14, 1962, though delivered on December 4. The delay no doubt had to do with the wish to increase its effect, as at that time Yugoslav vice-president and until recently bête noir of every communist left of Tito, Edward Kardelj, paid an official visit to Indonesia.
59. *Harian Rakjat*, December 8, 1962.
60. *Harian Rakjat*, December 14, 1962.
61. In *The Rise and Fall of the Communist Party of Indonesia*, 1969, the Rand Corporation, Santa Monica, p. 22, Guy J. Pauker also draws attention to the fact that 'Their [the P.K.I. leaders'] self-confidence seems to have grown inordinately after Sukarno decreed the abolition of martial law on December 19, 1962, effective as of May 1, 1963. This, according to Pauker, contributed to overestimate the 'revolutionary situation' in the country as a whole.

CHAPTER 13

Malaysia, the new alibi (1962-1963)

Within the shifting pattern of P.K.I. policies in the second half of 1962, a new and crucial issue had come to the fore: Malaysia.[1] Though it was basically 'only' a new federal structure destined to facilitate British withdrawal from direct responsibility for its crown colonies in Northern Borneo, its inception had widespread repercussions. In Singapore and Malaya it encountered opposition, especially in communist quarters, as it was rightly seen as an attempt by both governments to stem the tide and contain the southward push of Peking. Local communist prospects, certainly in Singapore, were dimmed. In addition the British were to remain committed in the area as an officially tolerated reserve force. However, all this did not in itself imply that Indonesia had also become involved. After preparations for a federation of the territories had got under way, Indonesian Foreign Minister Subandrio told the United Nations Assembly in the autumn of 1961 that his country had no objections whatsoever and 'wished them success with this merger, so that everyone might live in peace and freedom'.[2] It was a *quid pro quo* between Malaya and Indonesia, with Djakarta (on request of the government in Kuala Lumpur) saying something positive about the future federation in exchange for Malayan support for West Irian in the United Nations Assembly.[3]

At the same time, back in Djakarta, Aidit met two leaders of the Malayan Socialist Front who had been invited to attend a conference of the Partindo, a fellow-travelling offshoot of the P.N.I.[4] The Socialist Front had brought together a number of left nationalist and communist Malayans and Malayan Chinese. Together with the Barisan Sosialis in Singapore they formed a strong and vocal opposition to the plans of Malayan Premier Tunku Abdul Rahman and his Singapore colleague

Lee Kuan Yew.[5] In both the Indonesian Partindo and the Malayan Socialist Front extreme nationalists of a Malay or 'Greater Indonesia' streak were to be found.[6] One of the two Socialist Front leaders to confer with Aidit was Ahmad Bustamam, a typical exponent of this left-wing Malayan nationalism. It was Bustamam who, after the Brunei revolt in December 1962, was arrested for being involved in this rebellion.[7] In March 1963 the Malayan Minister of Internal Security, Ismail, declared that Bustamam 'had met the leader of the P.K.I. and made plans with him to cripple the progress of Malaysia'.[8] Whatever the truth of this link might have been, as related above some weeks after the meeting at the plenary session of the P.K.I. Central Committee late in December 1961 one of the resolutions adopted was a condemnation of Malaysia.[9] So the P.K.I. was the first party in Indonesia to oppose the new federation on its northern borders, at a time when no other Indonesian faction saw any harm or was able to forget its preoccupation with West Irian to bother about Malaysia.[10] But once the resolution was passed it looked as if the P.K.I. had also again lost interest. Outwardly, the issue remained dormant until Aidit, in the wake of the West Irian settlement, thought it useful to unearth it again.[11] Meanwhile preparations for the merger went on. After the Singapore government had won a referendum on the subject early in September 1962, prospects for its success were considerably enhanced.[12] Fulfilling the prophesy of Radio Moscow of four weeks earlier, the Indonesian government now also began to show it was weary of the Malaysian project.[13] It was Foreign Minister Subandrio who, returning from his successful final performance on West Irian in the United Nations Assembly, sounded the first critical note.[14] While stopping off in Kuala Lumpur, Subandrio said Indonesia would pay the closest attention to the development of Malaysia since the two countries were to have common borders.[15] Then, proceeding to Singapore, Subandrio went a step further. He told the influential local paper, the *Straits Times*, that Indonesia could be forced to take countermeasures if a military base were to be established in Serawak, Sabah, or Brunei.[16] 'If, for instance, it is an American base we shall then arrange for a Soviet base in our part of Borneo. If things go wrong, then we shall have to protect our interests'.[17] A Barisan Sosialis spokesman in Singapore suggested, while Subandrio was around, that the Malayan Prime Minister should discuss the 'misgivings' President Sukarno was said to have, an invitation that must no doubt have put Rahman into a minor fit of rage.[18]

The next phase began with the Brunei rebellion that broke out on the eve of December 7. Leadership of the rebels – a few thousand in all – was claimed by Azahari, chairman of the local Partai Ra'ayat. In September Azahari and his followers had succeeded in winning 54 out of the 55 seats in Brunei's Legislative Council on a clear anti-Malaysian platform. Formally it was still the Sultan who had the power of decision on joining the proposed federation, but the election results had been a setback for Rahman and the British.[19] The background of Azahari's armed action was as confused and incoherent as its leader's mind according to close observers.[20] Azahari, who had left Brunei for Manila with most of his lieutenants hours before the revolt broke out, first claimed that the Sultan was backing him. Though this was not so easily accepted after it appeared that the Sultan barely escaped the rebels by fleeing to a police post, Azahari nevertheless did not break with the Sultan, whose property rights (important in view of the rich oil fields) he continued to recognize.[21] After all, what Azahari had aimed at at an earlier stage was reunification of Brunei with neighboring Sarawak and Sabah under the Sultan. His opposition to Malaysia was further inspired by a clearly anti-Chinese bias that made him despise the 'diseased' state of both Malaya and – especially – Singapore. Although in close touch with ultra-left and communist parties in the area, he was, if anything, a Malay nationalist, hoping for support from the Philipines and above all Indonesia, where he had lived from 1942-1952.

As to Djakarta this support was immediately forthcoming.[22] Sukarno expressed his sympathy a few days after the fighting broke out in Brunei and saw in the struggle a success for his 'new emerging forces', which were about to smash their opponents the 'old established forces'. wherever they could in the world.[23] The P.K.I. pressed for further support, asking that government and people 'openly defend the People's struggle in North Kalimantan.'[24] This was the pattern for the months that followed: Aidit and the P.K.I. trying to push Sukarno towards a new confrontation that would go beyond a mere exchange of mutual recriminations with Kuala Lumpur, and the Indonesian President holding back and using the quarrel to further Indonesia's influence in the area.[25]

The revolt in Brunei had meanwhile been suppressed within a week with the help of British troops, and most of the rebels not captured had retreated into the jungle by the middle of December. But the issue was kept alive by Azahari, who set up residence first in Manila and later in Djkarta as 'prime minister of the Revolutionary State of North Kalimantan'. He could reckon on considerable publicity for his cause as his successful Partai Ra'ayat had been banned by the Sultan, and 'colonial' troops had been used against his fighting followers, showing how reactionary the Malaysian 'scheme' was.[26] It was above all, however, the manipulation of others that made Azahari and his Unitary State of North Kalimantan look real and kept the anti-Malaysian fire burning. The P.K.I. was in the forefront here, with Aidit coming up with the notion that Malaysia was out to encircle Indonesia.[27] Azahari's freedom fighters, he said further, should be given help because they were assisting Indonesia to defeat neo-colonialism in the area, i.e. Malaysia.[28] If necessary, British capital in Indonesia would be held responsible, etc.

It was all going to look depressingly like a replica of the West Irian campaign. There was, however, some difference, apart from Sukarno's hesitation. Reaction from Moscow had been rather restrained. Initial reporting on the revolt had been in quotes from western sources or in factual terms.[29] It was not until the end of December that Pravda came out with a word of support for Azahari's liberation movement.[30] The Soviet interest for the Malaysia issue in general seems to have waned as from late September, possibly due to the Cuban crisis and its aftermath, bringing home to Kruschov the truth of his own thesis that small conflicts could lead to major conflagrations and should be avoided. The opinions given in the various Soviet media on Malaysia were generally in low key and more explanatory than polemic. The merger was represented as a 'potential' danger and an indication of territorial ambitions of Malaya, but these charges all remained rather unspecified.[31] Indonesia was defended against complaints that it in turn posed a threat to Malaya or had aggressive designs towards Northern Borneo.[32] But when Soviet Defense Minister, Marshall Malinofski, arrived in Djakarta the chief message seemed to have been that, as *Radio Moscow* put it, 'the peoples of the East can only make progress in conditions of peace'.[33]

There was another issue which demonstrated the growing reluctance of the Soviet leaders to be drawn into new intrigues and complications in Southeast Asia. This was their reaction to a request of the Indonesian government in the autumn of 1962 to provide them with small arms. It was made as a result of an informal consensus between Aidit and Subandrio, with Sukarno in the background, to extend Indonesia's influence in Southeast Asia. In the atmosphere of a mixture of nationalistic sentiment and leftist-radical thinking, developments in the neighboring territories – North Kalimantan, Singapore, and Malaya – became a preoccupation for Djakarta. Aid to guerilla fighters was one of the ways to implement this auxiliary policy taken in hand by Subandrio's B.P.I., the highest intelligence organization of Indonesia.[34] It was therefore that the Soviet Union was approached for aid which, however, Moscow declined, not seeing sufficient reason for supporting Indonesia's undercover activities in the area.[35] Overtures were thereupon made to the other possible source of arms: China. The result was that Foreign Minister Subandrio went to Peking early in January 1963 to meet with the Chinese Prime Minister, Chou En-lai.

In the Chinese capital there had meanwhile been some initial, rather cautious reactions to the new phase in the dispute around the planned Malaysian federation that had begun with the Brunei revolt. It took the Chinese news media four days before they came up with a first report on the rebellion.[36] Given the known 'sinophobic' character of Azahari this was in some ways understandable. On December 15 (the day the revolt was all but quelled) Peking's official *Jen-min Jih-pao* had a commentary in which support was pledged to the people of Brunei in their fight against British imperialism.[37] Then, when the Indonesian Foreign Minister went to China, the Chinese Premier, Chou En-lai, reiterated this support for the Brunei revolt.[38] In both instances, however, only Brunei was spoken of, and no mention was made of the wider context in which Azahari had tried to put the violent uprising: the whole of Northern Borneo. Neither was Malaysia publicly brought up by the Chinese.[39] There is no doubt that the future of the area between Indonesia and China, and particularly the Malaysian peninsula and related territories, was being discussed during Subandrio's visit.[40] As we have seen it was Indonesia that had taken the initiative here to sound out Peking in view of the preoccupation Indonesian officials were having with Malaysia where China, through the large overseas Chinese element, could be assumed to have an overriding interest. Friction between the two countries could easily crop up again, and it was with this in mind that Subandrio, upon arrival, set the tone for his visit by declaring: 'Either in the past or in *the years to come* it may be that *remnants of the colonial powers* will become an issue between us' [emphasis added].[41] It was clearly his purpose to prevent this from happening. China for the moment, however, had not yet shown whether it wanted more than to go through the motions and (could it do less?) declare its adhesion to an anti-imperialist revolt, as in Brunei. It was still trying to sort out its policy line before being more explicit in its commitments.[42]

The meeting between Subandrio and Chou En-lai probably went off better than either had expected. At any rate it can be seen as the beginning of a close cooperation in international affairs, to be disrupted by the weight of its initial success in the aftermath of the '30 September movement', a little over two years later. At the end of the Subandrio visit the two ministers issued a statement outlining the way ahead: 'United against imperialism'.[43] Subandrio seemed to have felt assured of at least the backing of Peking for a harder approach to Malaysia, and possibly the beginning of some sort of 'spheres of influence' arrangement, in exchange for consideration of China as a global power.[44] He also got the promise of the sale and delivery of small arms which Indonesia had tried in vain to solicit from Moscow, while at the same time Chinese guerilla instructors were to be sent to the Indonesian border area with North Kalimantan.[45] Back in Djakarta he immediately advocated a 'firm policy of confrontation' that would 'not necessarily' mean war.[46] To the Malayan Prime Minister, Tenku Abdul Rahman, this was nothing less than a declaration of cold war between his country and Indonesia. This was an allegation Subandrio naturally denied.[47]

A first sign that Djakarta and Peking had found a common field of action came at the Afro-Asian Solidarity Conference at Moshi in Tanganyika, which opened on February 4, 1963. Close collaboration between the two delegations resulted in a boycott of the representatives of Malaya and Singapore who were not given accreditation, while an Indonesian was accepted as a delegate for Brunei.[48] Similarly, a resolution against Malaysia was approved, demanding full support for the struggle of the people of 'North Kalimantan' (the whole area of Northern Borneo) and recognition of the Unitary State of North Kalimantan of Azahari.[49] As an argument the Indonesian delegate, Abbas, put forward that with the advent of Malaysia Seato would be on Indonesia's doorstep. Apparently this carried weight in the atmosphere of the conference where Sino-Soviet rivalry had sprung up, and the relative merits of peaceful coexistence lost out against the cult of the armed struggle.[50]

The improvement in Sino-Indonesian relations that came about as a result of the budding confrontation with the future member-countries of Malaysia and the cold shoulder Djakarta got from Moscow in this respect did not lack having an effect on the attitude of the P.K.I. It may be too strong to suggest that at this juncture (late 1962 and early 1963) it was the P.K.I that took a 'decision to shift more towards Chinese positions'.[51] But, it certainly is true that to the P.K.I. leaders, and notably to the carefully operating Aidit, the disappointing posture of Moscow in the Malaysia dispute then became one of the factors to take account of henceforth. The left-wing of the Party picked up the banner of the anti-Malaysia action upon the return of Subandrio from China and tried to keep up its momentum without rubbing it in too much. It was Njoto particularly, back from his sojourn in Eastern Europe[52] and then in China, who was active and claimed that he had noticed during his trip how people had followed the Brunei revolt 'with great astonishment'.[53]

In his general report to the P.K.I. Central Committee meeting in mid-February 1963 Aidit wanted to make his audience believe that he had been 'overcome with joy' when he had heard the news of the Azahari revolt. But he put a damper on those comrades who might have been too eager for foreign adventures by saying that what he called 'economic subversion' via foreign aid was more dangerous than the whole Malaysian issue.[54] It is also possible that Aidit softpedalled and thought he could leave it for the moment to Sukarno and Subandrio to carry the anti-Malaysia ball,[55] but in this respect he was soon in for a disappointment. In the middle of March Sukarno, having limited tactical aims in his cat-and-mouse game with Rahman, decided to propose a summit conference on Southeast Asia with his opposite numbers of the Philippines and Malaysia.[56] Aidit reacted quickly, and in an address to the Malayan Youth Union in Djakarta he stressed that Indonesia's opposition to Malaysia was 'a matter of principle'.[57] In other words he had no use for the summitry and diplomatics that Sukarno adored. Aidit's reaction became the theme the P.K.I. reiterated each time a lull in the confrontation with Malaysia loomed.[58]

When during the visit of Soviet Defense Minister Malinofski the Soviet Union gave signs that Indonesia ought to softpeddle its confrontation,[59] thus supporting Sukarno in his endeavour to arrange a 'Maphilindo' summit, the P.K.I. began to display its displeasure. For the time being this was not yet done directly but rather by way of a substitute for which Yugoslavia was an excellent object that was to be linked with Malaysia in a very unfavorable way. Replying to the 'soft' gospel the Soviet Union then was preaching, Second-Deputy Chairman Njoto charged early in April that Yugoslavia was 'encouraging' Malaysia. In speeches in Medan and Djakarta Njoto said, according to *Harian Rakjat*, 'so long as the interview in which the Yugoslav ambassador said that this country was ready to establish relations with Malaysia is not revoked, we shall continue to believe that they are encouraging Malaysia'.[60] Bebler, the ambassador in question, reacted strongly with a documented countercharge showing that *Harian Rakjat* had twice misquoted him, as if he had said that Yugoslavia wanted to strengthen relations with Malaysia once it had come about, whereas in fact he had said he hoped that Indonesia would develop good relations. Bebler added that Njoto, in turn, in his recent speeches had made use of the previous misquotes of the party daily.[61] *Harian Rakjat* summed up this acrimonious debate firstly by concluding that Yugoslavia was in favor of Malaysia, anticipating Indonesian relations with the new federation. Secondly, the article accused Yugoslavia of interfering in internal Indonesian affairs since it wished these relations to be good. For good measure, the official P.K.I. daily's editor – Njoto himself – observed on the subject of invented quotations that they could very well be used 'in the struggle to bare modern revisionism'.[62]

Then in April, at the beginning of a period of intermittent talks between the governments of Southeast Asia that were to last until Malaysia was to become a reality six months later, the visit of China's President Liu Shao-Chi to Indonesia provided a new boost to Sino-Indonesian relations. Liu used it to declare expressly 'the resolute support' of Sukarno in his fight against Malaysia, but Sukarno, though apparently pleased with being taken seriously by a world power like China, did not for the moment want to jeopardize the summit to which Tunku Abdul Rahman had just agreed.[63] Pressure from the American and Japanese side was also contributing to Sukarno's cooperative mood, since his government was in dire need of credits from both countries.[64]

Indeed it came to a meeting between the Malayan Prime Minister at the end of May in Tokio. This was an occasion that paved the way to the Manila Accord concluded between the Deputy Foreign Ministers of the Philipines, Malaya, and Indonesia. The Manila Accord was intended to be ratified at a later stage by the three leaders (as in fact it was when they met at the end of July) and was of considerable importance, as the Philipines and Indonesia accepted Malaysia, if only the United Nations Secretary General was satisfied that it was a genuine act of self-determination by the Borneo territories.[65] Indonesian Foreign Minister Subandrio shifted with the wind and talked of economic growth to which Indonesia should give priority and also of Malayan identity, which was being rediscovered.[66] Reactions to the new turn of events varied. In Indonesia criticism was soon to come from Aidit, who said that he missed 'a sense of anti-imperialism' in the Manila communiqué, while at the same time it did not conform with the 'Bandung principles' (a reference designed to convey disagreement without giving a proper reason).[67] A subsequent P.K.I. statement was more specific and maintained that North Kalimantan had already, on December 8, 1962, declared itself independent (Azahari had done this) and that Indonesia in fact had recognized this new Unitary State. If it did nevertheless come to such a superfluous U.N. 'ascertainment', then at least British troops should have been gone first and political prisioners released, the statement further said.[68] This opinion was more or less shared by the extremists in the P.N.I., the Partindo, and the Murba Party. However, the response to the Manila Accord was generally favorable.[69] From China no comment was given except indirectly by publishing a host of critical Indonesian reactions.[70] On the day after agreement had been reached in Manila, the *New China News Agency* reported that the (virtually non-existent) North Kalimantan National Army would continue to fight.[71]

On the other side of the fence authorities in Sabah and Serawak were embarrassed that Malaya had given in to Philippine-Indonesian pressure.[72] In London there were doubts as to the practicability of any United Nations action as desired by the Manila Accord partners. Preparations for the establishment of Malaysia, fixed for August 31, 1963, went under mounting pressure and, on July 8, the four future members of the Malaysian federation concluded an agreement with the British government.[73] Sukarno was furious and felt betrayed by the

Tunku because he thought the London agreement should at least have been made conditional on the approval of the next summit, scheduled for the end of the month. The Indonesian President resorted to a more radical stance: 'We shall fight Malaysia to the end', and let it be known that Indonesia 'would not stand alone'.[74] The hapless Malayan Prime Minister protested his innocence. He said the agreement reached in London was a mere formality of which he had apprised Sukarno in advance in Tokyo. Aidit immediately came out with an 'I-told-you-so' statement, which added that the summit had now become useless too.[75] Sukarno kept up suspense by not declaring himself ready to go to Manila for the summit with Tunku Abdul Rahman and President Macapagal until the last moment.[76] The summit confirmed the previous arrangements of the foreign ministers, including United Nations ascertainment prior to the formation of Malaysia, and endorsed the 'Maphilindo' concept of regular consultations between the three governments. To Sukarno this meant for Indonesia a voice in the destiny of the area, as he explained in his August 17 speech.[77] On Brunei and Azahari's Unitary State the summit was totally silent, which was an omission in the eyes of progressive opinion in Indonesia. The P.N.I. paper Merdeka pointed this out, declaring that before anything could be 'ascertained' Azahari should be allowed to return to North Kalimantan.[78] The line taken by the P.K.I. at this juncture coincided nearly with the one taken in Peking. It was that the confrontation with Malaysia should go on, and that there should be no truck with the 'tool' of the imperialists, the United Nations Organization.[79]

As to Sukarno and his men, the Indonesian President gave the impression that he was prepared to accept the United Nations' verdict. But Subandrio injected some doubts into the situation.[80] There was some petty squabbling concerning the number of observers Indonesia was allowed by the British to send to Northern Borneo. The upshot was that the Indonesian officials that finally attended came after the United Nations mission had already finished half the job, a point that made Subandrio sound a warning that 'Malaysia was far from settled'.[81]

In Moscow the whole affair did not yet seem to have inspired strong opinions, or at most divided opinions. In the customary greetings on the occasion of Indonesia's Independence Day Kruschov and Brezhnev made no mention of Malaysia but simply (with good reason) wished the country greater prosperity.[82] In a broadcast directed at Djakarta,

Radio Moscow spoke a few days later of achievement of the Manila summit as 'a wise compromise', telling its listeners that a peaceful atmosphere would be necessary for its implementation.[83] The next day, however, the Soviet news agency, Tass, in its English-language broadcast said Indonesia had good reason to discern a dangerous plot in Malaysia. This was contained in a news report that Kuala Lumpur had fixed a definite date – September 16, 1963 – for the establishment of the Malaysian Federation.[84] From now on the anti-Malaysian confrontation was destined to get more and more out of hand. Some doubt seems possible as to the wisdom of the summary way in which Rahman announced the new date.[85] But sooner or later Malaysia would have become a reality, and most of what was to follow now in recriminations, military actions, and political waste Indonesia would have experienced anyhow.

So the stage was set for further escalation. The Indonesian government began by lodging a complaint that was quickly rejected by Malaysia.[86] Kuala Lumpur retaliated instantly by breaking off diplomatic relations. On September 16, the fateful birthday of Malaysia, well-organized rioting began against the Malayan, but particularly against the British Embassy in Djakarta. In the wake of it British-owned companies were 'taken over' by P.K.I.-affiliated trade unions, making Sukarno – under pressure of the military – ban such activities.[87] The next step was a rupture with Malaya and Singapore in the economic field.[88] This was a move that Indonesia was to regret deeply since its economy was closely linked with the Malayan peninsula which channeled one third of Indonesian exports.[89] It provoked Foreign Minister Subandrio to the astonishing statement that this boycot (who 'boycotted' whom actually?) was heaven-sent.[90] Irrationality seemingly began to take hold of Indonesia's leaders with Sukarno leading the way, burning his bridges by issuing on September 25 his order to 'devour' Malaysia and to hell with the consequences.[91] A further memorable contribution to this atmosphere of artificial tension was made by the Indonesian President somewhat later by telling one of his drummed-up audiences that he had documents to prove that Malaysia was designed to encircle not only Indonesia, but also China.[92] This paragraph got special treatment in the Chinese press. Meanwhile, however, a first semi-official reaction from Peking (a comment in *Jenmin Jih-pao*) had rapidly endorsed the most extreme version of 'confrontation' as it was propounded by the P.K.I.[93] It had been followed by declarations of full support by individual Chinese diplomats: The Ambassador in Djakarta and the Consul-General in Medan.[94]

Moscow, meanwhile, was treading warily, clearly conscious that it would lose more of its waning influence on the Indonesian government if it did not back up its new-found radical postures. The pronunciations made in the Soviet Union were not very consistent. Pravda's Djakarta correspondent Shalkin turned out a story about what a neo-colonialist creation Malaysia really was, while on the same day Indonesia-specialist Avrin gave a strangely pro-Malaysian broadcast from Moscow in the Indonesian language to the effect that 'the Malaysian people have always supported the Soviet Union'.[95] A few days later, in a similar broadcast, Avrin quoted a Soviet paper to the effect that 'in the end' colonialism could be forced to retreat, as if implying that too much hurry might be unnecessary.[96] At any rate, the Moscow police authorities did not think it was such a good idea to have Indonesian students in the Soviet capital demonstrating against Malaysia and therefore refused them the required permission.[97] The P.K.I.-aligned Federation of Indonesian students in Djakarta on the first occasion passed a resolution against this 'lamentable attitude'.[98]

More important, the Indonesian government also showed signs of irritation with the Soviet Union. Sukarno began openly to complain that 'our friends in the socialist countries' were belittling the factor of nationalism and that they showed scant comprehension of the fact that the anti-imperialist and anti-colonialist war was being mainly fought in the Third World.[99] It was in this changing climate that Defense Minister Nasution set out on a trip to Moscow, Washington, and some European capitals and after having conferred with Prime Minister Kruschov reported that the Soviet leader had 'again' expressed support for the anti-Malaysian campaign mounted by Djakarta. To show good will, the Soviet authorities at Nasution's request earmarked a further 50 million dollars from the 1960 economic loan for military purposes. They were to finance air defense installations and anti-submarine weapons,[100] that is, arms of a more defensive nature. The Air Force was then after large troop transport plans and MI-6 helicopters with a capacity for 100 soldiers because of the evolving confrontation. But it took another six months and some hard bargaining before the sale of six MI-6's was clinched.[101]

The reception Nasution got in Washington must have been rather cool; at any rate the Pentagon refused to be played off again as in the past (against whom indeed?) and no new arms were forthcoming.[102] It was for Radio Moscow an occasion to lambast Indonesia (no arms or aid from Britain or the United States) and to stress that Djakarta had better stay with its trusted allies and arms supplyers in the communist world.[103] Some days later, Nasution actually claimed that the Soviet Union had given a guarantee in the event that Indonesa were no longer to receive arms from London or Washington.[104] All the same, Nasution must have felt that he now had considerably less political leeway within the Indonesian internal situation than with West Irian, and he was no doubt aware that the Indonesian military had themselves to blame for this. The military side of the anti-Malaysia confrontation thrived to an important extent (although not entirely) on their guidance, cooperation, and help.[105] When he returned home at the end of December, therefore, he must have felt that he had more reason, but fewer means, to resist a further deterioration of the political scene. It was exactly then that Subandrio began talking about 'offensive ways' of fighting Malaysia, an expression that – even in the inflated rhetoric of Indonesian political life under Sukarno – did not forebode well for the immediate future.[106]

Because the P.K.I. had decidedly pushed the Malaysia issue right from the beginning as a substitute for the waning West-Irian affair, directly and indirectly a more radical stance resulted. In the new setting, with Nasution and his strongly anti-P.K.I. impact pushed in mid-1962 into the background, a new Sukarno-Subandrio-Yani configuration was more conducive to influence wielding for Aidit and his colleagues. The Brunei revolt (most probably inspired and certainly aided by the Indonesian and Malayan communists) was a good instrument to bring Sukarno and Subandrio around to a more pronounced anti-Malaysian attitude, with the Indonesian President committing himself only to a limited, tactical aim until his vanity was hurt by the rather unwise way Tunku Abdul Rahman launched the Federation in September 1963. Added to this was the growing reluctance of the Soviet Union to follow Indonesia in its invented 'quarrel' with Malaysia, incurring Sukarno's open criticism. On the other hand, the Chinese showed an inclination to increase moral and material support.

It is this change in the political environment, this new equation that Sukarno and his inner cabinet came to operate with, which for Aidit must have been the most potent consideration in stepping up his pressure to become more of a radical himself. Though basically still the cautious 'moderate' (all proportions guarded of course) Aidit in the Malaysia affair showed that he could challenge Sukarno and egg him on. In doing so he moved closer to the party's left wing.[107]

NOTES

1. See above pp. 157 and 166 note 27. The Malaysian Federation resulting from the Malayan Premier's suggestion was a contrived entity of disparate parts. Initially, it was warmly welcomed by Singapore's Prime Minister, Lee Kuan Yew, as a way out of the mounting problems of this harbor state posed by the combined effect of having a Chinese majority and a highly activist communist organization. Singapores independence, once the British had granted it, was thought to be much in danger, both from within and without, unless closer ties with neighboring Malaya were established. This, in turn, was only attractive to the Malayan government in Kuala Lumpur in the wider context Rahman had in mind because within a federation restricted to only Malaya and Singapore the Chinese would have outnumbered the Malayans. Together with the Borneo territories, however, Malayans and other indigenous peoples formed a majority. The British authorities, recognizing that they should no longer maintain colonies in the area, were the driving force behind the Tunku's suggestion. To them it pointed the way to an appropriate form of independence for the unsophisticated population of Northern Borneo, while at the same time it held out a promise of stabilizing the situation in Singapore.
2. See Hamilton Fish Armstrong, The troubled birth of Malaysia, *Foreign Affairs*, July 1963, p. 683.
3. Interview, March 1972, former Deputy Minister for Foreign Affairs of Indonesia, Suwito Kusumowidagdo.
4. Brackman, 1966, *Southeast Asia's Second Front: The Power Struggle in the Malay Archipelago*, Frederick A. Praeger, New York, p. 88.
5. The Barisan Sosialis had, as a matter of fact, split off that summer from Lee's governing People's Action Party on account of the proposed Malaysian federation.
6. Brackman called them the 'transmission belts' between the forbidden Malaysian Communist Party and the P.K.I.
7. See below pp. 172, 173, 174.

8. *Radio Kuala Lumpur*, March 12, 1963. According to this report Bustamam had admitted that although he was Malayan born he 'owed allegiance to Indonesia'. It was also claimed that he said he knew of the Brunei revolt in advance. In view of the fact that Bustamam was under arrest his alleged admissions have only limited value, though circumstantial evidence would tend to confirm this news report.
9. See above p. 156.
10. See Richard Allen, 1968, *Malaysia, Prospect and Retrospect*, Oxford University Press, New York-Kuala Lumpur. Also Justus M. van der Kroef, Sino-Indonesian Partnership, *Orbis*, summer 1964, p. 334, who stresses that 'the opposition of the Indonesian Communist Party to the formation of Malaysia preceded official Indonesian hostility by almost a year'.
11. See above p. 156.
12. It was not a very fair referendum as the three alternatives given concerned various forms of a federation and not the question of whether or not a federation was desirable. Prime Minister Lee Kuan Yew made no bones about the dubious character of the referendum, justifying it with a reference to the lack of scruples of his communist opposition. The opposition party, Barisan Sosialis, had urged that the ballots not be marked, as a rejection of Malaysia. Twenty-five percent of the voters followed this advice, indicating the extent of the hardcore opposition. See Allen, 1968, p. 156 and Brackman, 1966, p. 50.
13. See above p. 157.
14. Ex-Premier Ali Sastroamidjojo, who was P.N.I. chairman at the time, but did not have governmental responsibility, had opened the debate with an interview in the *Straits Times* on September 24, in which he wondered whether Malaysia would be profitable for Indonesia. It earned him a firm rebuke from the Malayan Prime Minister, Abdul Rahman, not to meddle in the internal affairs of neighboring countries.
15. See *Antara News Agency*, September 26, 1962.
16. It is not clear why the British needed the formation of Malaysia to establish military bases in Northern Borneo when they had refrained from doing so while they were the colonial power in two of the three territories.

    It is also unclear why Subandrio had not voiced this kind of concern earlier while the British were the colonizing power in two of the territories and held a protectorate over the third, the Sultanate of Brunei.
17. *Antara News Agency* from Singapore, September 27, 1963. Subandrio also followed the lead in his sudden concern for military bases in nearby North Kalimantan given by Moscow; see above p. 157.
18. *Antara News Agency*, September 26, 1962.
19. Proportions should be kept in mind here: Brunei with its 80,000 people represented seven percent of the population of Northern Borneo and one percent of the total prospective population of Malaysia.
20. See Brackman, 1966, p. 136.
21. *Manila Radio*, December 11, 1962.

22. Djakarta received advance warning from Azahari in Manilla that they were ready to strike and expected Indonesian support; interview March 1972, Suwito Kusumowidagdo.
23. *New China News Agency*, December 11, 1962.
24. *Harian Rakjat*, December 11, 1962.
25. The failure of the Brunei revolt was due to British intervention and in Indonesia is generally considered the beginning of the confrontation with Malaysia; interview March 1972 General Nasution. Subandrio, previously wavering on this issue, became a supporter of it, while the Army, though aware of the problems involved in a military confrontation in a jungle territory, resented continuing British presence on their borders. The need to keep the military occupied and happy also played a role here; interview Ruslan Adbulgani, March 1972.
26. At the time of the revolt Great Britain still had responsibility for maintaining order in Brunei on behalf of the Sultan, but the impression made by the use of British troops was more true to the real relationship than the formal grounds Great Britain could adduce. The fact that the proscribed Partai Ra'ayat earlier had received an overwhelming popular anti-Malaysian vote made it easy to equate Malaysia with anti-democracy.
27. *Harian Rakjat*, December 18, 1962 and December 26, 1962.
28. See p. 178.
29. See, e.g., *Tass*, December 8, 1962; *Moscow Radio Home Service*, December 9, 1962 and *Tass*, December 10, 1962.
30. *Pravda*, December 24, 1962.
31. See *Izvestia*, April 1, 1963.
32. See *Radio Moscow in Indonesian* on February 27, 1963 and on March 28, 1963.
33. See *Radio Moscow in English for Southeast Asia*, March 30, 1963.
34. During 1962 the political spectrum had shifted further in favor of Sukarno, and in his wake, of Subandrio. In June of that year General Nasution was hoodwinked by the President into believing that he would become Chief of Staff of the combined four armed forces and he resigned therefore as Chief of Staff-Commander of the army in favor of Lieutenant-General Ahmad Yani. The planned integration of the armed forces was subsequently blocked by Sukarno, and Nasution was left with the empty shell of his post as Defense Minister, having to rely mainly on his prestige as highest ranking officer for influence. Nasution himself, in an interview in March 1972, said this eposode was the beginning of a phase in which Sukarno could increasingly play off Yani against himself and drive a wedge into the leadership of the armed forces, especially the army. Sukarno also began to have a direct hand in appointments of other high-ranking staff officers, among others of Major-General Pranoto, who later turned out to be a P.K.I. stooge as general staff member responsible for personnel affairs (see below p. 413). This phase was to end early in 1965 when, in the face of the growing influence of the P.K.I. and Sukarno's imminent alliance with China, the

army leadership began to see the need for greater cohesion (see below p. 357). The effect of Sukarno's political maneuvers in 1962 reinforced his position, which had already grown strongly due to his success in solving the West Irian problem more or less on his terms. This in turn made Subandrio abandon what was left of his orientation towards Nasution and more prone to look, like Sukarno, to the new army command and to the P.K.I. for support and power. The B.P.I. became an instrument to Subandrio, and apart from certain help that the Army, according to General Nasution, gave to Azahari, it was the B.P.I. that channeled money and support to the Brunei rebels.

35. Interview, March 1972, Adam Malik.
36. *New China News Agency*, December 12, 1962.
37. *Jen-min Jih-pao*, December 15, 1962
38. *New China New Agency*, January 2, 1963.
39. *New China News Agency*, January 2, 1963; *Peking Review*, January 4, 1963.
40. The official reason for Subandrio's stay in China was to discuss the proposal of the so-called 'Colombo countries' who had tried to mediate between India and China in their border war. In the Chou-Subandrio talks this was not the only topic, the *New China New Agency* stated on January 5.
41. *New China News Agency*, January 2, 1963. Subandrio also spoke of 'this period of development in which it is so easy to have conflicting interests among *ourselves*' [i.e.China and Indonesia; emphasis added].
42. Noteworthy in this respect is that a statement of support for the Brunei revolt, issued mid-December 1962 by the Central Committee of the forbidden Malayan Communist Party, did not find its way into the Chinese press until late March 1963: *Peking Radio in English for Southeast Asia*, March 27, 1963. At the time the Chinese Communist Party, through the strong Chinese element in the M.C.P., was having some influence. On the other hand the P.K.I. was known to have close contacts and being the more immediate and nearby force may also have had some grip on the M.C.P. As to the reasons that may have moved the Chinese communists not to mention the statement for some time, the fact that it spoke of 'the North-Kalimantan people's struggle for national independence' that had entered 'a new stage' with the Brunei revolt may have been of importance, as this implied the wider context Peking was not ready to accept. Another reason could be that Rahman was accused in the statement of trying 'to undermine the traditional friendship between the peoples of Malayan and Indonesia', and to China this friendship need not necessarily have looked like an unmixed blessing. *Harian Rakjat* did not publish the M.P.C. statement before February 6, 1963.
43. *New China News Agency*, January 8, 1963.
44. This referred to the Chung machine guns of which large consignments entered Indonesia legally from then on. From early 1965 on they were also brought into the country secretly; see below pp. 332, 333.
45. Interview March 1972, Adam Malik, who said he opposed this arms deal.

46. *Radio Djakarta Home Service*, January 20, 1963.
47. *Manila Times*, January 22, 1963; *Djakarta Radio Home Service*, January 30, 1963.
48. *Far Eastern Economic Review*, March 14, 1963.
49. Van der Kroef, 1964, p. 349. Sheikh Azahari himself finally decided to stay in Djakarta, considering the Moshi conference too communist – or Chinese – to his liking; *Melbourne Radio*, 1963; *Far Eastern Economic Review, March 14, 1963.*
50. While Moscow stressed that 'peaceful coexistence creates the situation suitable for the success of the national liberation movement', to Peking this was 'prattle about peace' because the only way to reach complete liberation was 'the road of armed struggle'. Compare, for example, *Moscow Radio in Arabic*, February 5, 1963, and the report of the Chinese delegate Liu Ning-yi on the Moshi conference, *New China News Agency* March 7, 1963. See also Lowenthal, China. In Zbigniew Brzezinski, Ed., 1963, *Africa and the Communist World*, Stanford University Press, Stanford, California, p. 198.
51. In his 'Sino-Indonesian relations' Mozingo writes on p. 38: 'The present writer believes that the P.K.I.'s *decision* to shift significantly toward the C.C.P.'s position took place early in 1963 and was heavily influenced by the attitude of the Soviet and Chinese parties toward the Malaysian controversy' [emphasis added].
52. See above p. 162.
53. *Harian Rakjat*, February 8, 1963.
54. The Indonesian government was at that time trying to take measures to overcome the economic mess which had resulted from years of wasteful political ambitions towards the full 'liberation' of Indonesia by incorporating West Irian. Foreign, and particularly American, economic aid seemed to be a *conditio sine qua non* for recovery. But, in the eyes of Aidit this was 'subversive'. In his February report to the Central Committee entitled 'Courage, courage and more courage' he stated: 'Through painless economic aid, and often also false splendour, the independence of Indonesia is being subverted and weakened by the imperialists'. Compared with this he said: 'The Malaysian neocolonialism must of course also be combatted. However, it is not difficult to mobilise the people to meet such threats'; *Harian Rakjat*, February 11, 1963, Joint Publications Research Service, p. 36. See below pp. 193, 194.
55. The Indonesian Foreign Minister had hinted daily of a 'physical conflict' that might break out; *Antara News Agency*, February 11, 1963. The President told an anti-Malaysia rally: 'We openly oppose Malaysia which the Tunku Abdul Rahman has once again pushed because it is a manifestation of neo-colonialism. Indonesia', he continued 'might be forced to "confront" Malaysia not only politically, but also economically'; *New China News Agency*, February 14, 1963, *Antara News Agency*, February 14, 1963.
56. *Antara News Agency*, March 15, 1963.
57. *Harian Rakjat*, March 16, 1963.

58. See, e.g., *Harian Rakjat*, April 2, 1963, June 13, 1963, July 29, 1963.
59. See above p. 173.
60. *Harian Rakjat*, April 2, 1963.
61. *Harian Rakjat*, April 10, 1963. The remarks had been made while Bebler visited Kuala Lumpur in mid-1962. The first misquote dated from that period; cf. *Harian Rakjat*, June 23, 1962, and *Antara News Agency*, June 15, 1962. The second time *Harian Rakjat* distorted Bebler's words in the same way was in its issue of February 19, 1963, when the Indonesian Communist Party daily reacted to a Yugoslav press report to the effect that Indonesia itself had conjured up the Malaysian crisis.
62. *Harian Rakjat*, April 10, 1963.
63. *Kuala Lumpur Radio in English*, April 5, 1963. Answering Liu's banquet speech at Den Pasar, Bali, Sukarno said: 'Indonesia will strive to wage a struggle to prevent the establishment of Malaysia. Indonesia has clearly stated that, on the question of Malaysia, Indonesia first gives importance to the path of negotiation. Indonesia therefore is all for holding consultations between the Philippines, Malaysia and Indonesia to discuss the question of Malaysia'. *New China News Agency*, April 18, 1963.
64. *Far Eastern Economic Review*, October 24, 1963 and below p. 193.
65. 'The Ministers reaffirmed their countries adherence to the principle of self-determination for the peoples of non-selfgoverning territories. In this context Indonesia and the Philippines stated that they would welcome the formation of Malaysia provided the support of the people of the Borneo territories ascertained by an independent and impartial authority, the Secretary-General of the United Nations or his representative'. Text of the Manila Accord of June 11, 1963, *Far Eastern Economic Review*, October 24, 1963.
66. *Antara News Agency*, June 7, 1963 and June 10, 1963.
67. *Antara News Agency*, June 13, 1963.
68. *Harian Rakjat*, June 20, 1963.
69. For example, P.N.I.-Chairman Ali Sastroamidjojo, a Sukarno man, indicated approval; *Antara News Agency*, June 17, 1963.
70. See *New China News Agency*, June 27, 1963.
71. *New China News Agency*, June 12, 1963.
72. In Serawak, general elections were about to be held, and the Malaysian affair was spotlighted. In Sabah the decision on Malaysia depended on a vote in the Legislative Council. In both territories suggestions for a referendum on Malaysia were scuttled by the British, who now feared a reopening of the debate through the Manila Accord. See *Far Eastern Economic Review*, June 20, 1963 and Brackman, 1966, *Southeast Asia's Second Front*, New York, p. 84.
73. The fifth, Brunei, had participated as an observer at the talks in London, but the Sultan decided to stay out, mainly because he disagreed with the financial share his oil kingdom was proposed to contribute.
74. *Djakarta Radio Home Service*, July 10, 1963. Sukarno spoke at a State Palace reception.

75. *Harian Rakjat*, July 11, 1963.
76. *Antara News Agency*, July 27, 1963.
77. 'Whatever may happen shortly in North Kalimantan, two things are clear: a. Indonesia is no longer being treated like the dummy Togog and allowed just to look on alone at changes in the *status quo* in the surrounding region, especially if those changes concern its safety; b. Indonesia is recognized as having the right and *primary responsibility* for guarding security and peace in the region together with its neighboring states, the Philippines and Malaya' [emphasis added]: Sukarno, in his Independence Day address, as quoted by *Far Eastern Economic Review*, October 24, 1963. Maphilindo had some appeal to the Indonesian military, as it could be seen as directed against Peking; see Brackman, 1966, p. 105. Chinese and communist opinion, not surprisingly, was against the idea, which anyhow did not get off the ground.
78. This implicit criticism of Sukarno in what used to be the President's mouthpiece was to cost the editor, Yusuf, a prominent P.K.I. member, his job a few days later. Yusuf was then just visiting Peking, where he was received by Foreign Minister, Chen Yi, and was allowed to give vent to his disagreement with the Manila summit results; *New China News Agency*, August 17, 1963.
79. See *Peking Radio Home Service*, August 18, 1963 and *Harian Rakjat*, August 24, 1963, on the continuation of the confrontation. The editorial in *Harian Rakjat*, August 19, 1963, against the United Nations was extensively quoted by *New China News Agency* the same day.
80. At a Purwokerto rally the Indonesian President said Indonesia would 'bow its head', if the people of Malaysia wanted the proposed federation; *Djakarta Radio Home Service*, August 28, 1963. Ruslan Abdulgani, one of Sukarno's trusted aids, had apparently let the cat out of the bag by telling an audience in Sumatra that the people of Northern Borneo were being put in jail because they wanted – but were not allowed – to federate with Indonesia; *Kuala Lumpur Radio in English*, August 25, 1963. Even such an anti-Malaysian group like the Chinese-dominated Serawak United People's Party protested, and Abdulgani's statement was forthwith denied; *Antara News Agency*, September 3, 1963.
81. *Antara News Agency*, August 19, 1963. Subandrio, who was soon to become the second man of the Sukarno régime after the death of Prime Minister Djuanda, increasingly tried to play a game of his own.
82. The Soviet leaders wished Indonesia success in the 'development of the national economy, social progress and an improvement in the living conditions of the people'; *Komsomolskaya Pravda*, August 17, 1963.
83. *Radio Moscow in Indonesian*, August 28, 1963.
84. *Tass in English*, August 29, 1963.
85. Originally, Malaysia was scheduled to come into being on August 31, 1963. During the Manila summit Rahman had agreed to postpone this date, as the U.N. mission would not be able to reach their conclusion prior to the end of August. Eventually, the U.N. mission submitted its report to U Thant

on September 14, 1963, two days before the new date, and therefore Rahman had remained within the letter of his Manila commitment. But it would have been less provocative, if Rahman – and the British behind him – had waited with the announcement of the new date, until the mission had completed its work.

86. *Antara News Agency*, September 3, 1963 and September 7, 1963.
87. *Antary News Agency*, September 19, 1963.
88. *Djakarta Radio Home Service*, September 21, 1963.
89. 'A dramatic example of a country surely damaging its own economy for uncertain political gain', commented the *Far Eastern Economic Review* on October 3, 1963.
90. *Antara News Agency*, October 21, 1963.
91. *New China News Agency*, September 25, 1963; *Antara News Agency*, Sepberber 25, 1963.
92. *Antara News Agency*, November 11, 1963.
93. *Jen-min Jih-pao*, September 29, 1963.
94. *New China News Agency*, September 30, 1963.
95. *Pravda*, September 15, 1963; *Radio Moscow* in Indonesian, September 15, 1963.
96. *Radio Moscow* in Indonesian, September 25, 1963.
97. *Indonesian Observer*, September 27, 1963 and *New China News Agency*, September 29, 1963.
98. *New China News Agency*, September 30, 1963.
99. 'When we held the Asian African Journalists Conference, there were those who said that we were fostering A-A-ism . . . breaking up international solidarity. Now that we are going to hold the Asian-African Workers' Conference they say again: another AA, that is also breaking up international solidarity. This has happened, because there has been a mistaken assessment of nationalism as a tool in the struggle against imperialism . . . The struggle against imperialism and colonialism . . . is carried out, brothers, mainly in Asia, Africa and Latin America . . . That is why we foster A-A-ism. That is why we are spreading the idea of emerging forces. Because of this, we have been accused of breaking international solidarity'. Sukarno at a Youth Pledge day gathering at the Soviet-built Bung Karno Sports Palace in Djakarta, *Djakarta Radio Home Service*, October 28, 1963.
100. Interview, March 1972, General Nasution.
101. Interview, March 1972, Indonesian Minister of Information Budiardjo who, from 1962-1965, was Deputy Minister of the Air Force in charge of logistics and conducted many negotiations with the Soviet Union.
102. See *Antara News Agency*, December 12, 1963.
103. *Moscow Radio Home Service*, November 29, 1963.
104. *Antara News Agency*, from Paris, December 12, 1963.
105. The excursions into Northern Borneo began sometime in April 1963, and some went on even while talks were being held in Tokyo and Manila. Early in August Nasution admitted that the Indonesian armed forces were train-

ing volunteers from the British-Bornean territories (they must have been mainly Serawak and Sabah Chinese). *Far Eastern Economic Review*, September 5, 1963. A breakdown of Indonesians made prisoner in that area showed that most of them came from the air force and the police.

106. *Antara News Agency*, December 28, 1963.
107. Also on issues like a national front or Nasakom cabinet and foreign aid Aidit began to display a more radical mood, see below p. 229 ff.

CHAPTER 14

Sukarno prefers action (1963)

While playing their role in the continuing Malaysian escalation, the P.K.I. had achieved at the same time a major victory in the economic field: The liberal economic measures, put into effect at the end of May 1963 as a precondition for the necessary stabilization and foreign credits, had all gone down the drain as a result of the new stage in the confrontation policy.

As a report of the Central Committee session of late 1963 shows, this was an important step towards the economic upheaval which the P.K.I. was more and more convinced was the shortest way to power.[1] Right after West Irian was definitely on the way to a solution on the basis of the Bunker proposals in August 1962, Sukarno had pledged that his government from then on would concentrate on the one major task not yet accomplished.[2] This was the 'food-and-clothing problem', or put more generally, the sorry state of the Indonesian economy after years of neglect.[3] It had generated new heated debates over the most appropriate way to proceed in halting runaway inflation combined with the disastrous drop in overall production then rampant. The eight-year plan announced in January 1961 had not by any means been implemented, as the economists' assumptions were fatally thwarted by political decisions. It had led to a national budget in 1962 that exceeded 116 billion rupiah with an estimated deficit of 40 billion rupiah,[4] apart from the expenses connected with the West Irian campaign that alone already made up 70-80% of the total budget as Sukarno had on occasion declared.[5] The money in circulation increased rapidly, more than doubling from the end of 1962 to the end of 1963. Even with West Irian removed from the list of pressing priorities the deficit in 1963 ran up to 33.5 billion rupiah.[6]

It was therefore clear to all and sundry that drastic action had to be taken to deflate the economy and start cutting coats according to the cloth. It was Prime Minister Djuanda especially, a technician and planning expert by profession, who in the early months of 1963 developed a number of measures to put the country back on its feet. Crucial in these plans was the degree to which outside help would be forthcoming. As a first aid and token of good will the United States government had by February 1963 provided a credit of 17 million dollars to cover the most urgent needs for spare parts and raw materials. But an estimated 400 million dollars was needed to cure only in a minor way the ills of the Indonesian economy and to stabilize it.[7] This meant that the Sukarno regime had to count on foreign aid and credits, mainly from the U.S.A. but possibly also from the Soviet Union. This prospect was accepted by the more sober 'technicians' around Sukarno, who seem to have been in the ascendancy at the beginning of 1963.

However, this was strongly resented by the Indonesian extremists, first of all by the most vociferous P.K.I. which was beginning to stress the need for 'self-reliance'. It already had begun at the end of 1962, when Aidit launched a political offensive in favor of a 'Nasakom' government that is, a government composed of representatives of the three main tendencies in the country: nationalism, religion, and communism. He argued that otherwise 'nothing can be carried out properly' By this he especially meant the economy: 'Any meaningful change in the economic area is only possible if preceded by a meaningful change in the political area, and the most pressing political change is the formation of a Gotong-Rojong [Nasakom] cabinet'.[8] This was one of the two themes played up again and again in the course of the year by the P.K.I., and its related mass organizations, while taking care that Sukarno himself was spared.[9] The other theme was introduced by Sobsi boss Njono early in the campaign: Replacement of incompetent or unwilling officials or, in the current jargon, 'retooling the national instruments of government'.[10] At the end of January Aidit tried to zero in on the attempts of Djuanda and company to create conditions acceptable to the United States for the resumption of full-scale aid.[11] He returned to this point in his general report to the P.K.I. Central Committee convened in February.[12] The greater part of it Aidit devoted to economic problems and the mainly political solutions he was proposing.[13] Aidit warned that Indonesia should not beg for foreign loans but develop its domestic economy with the resources at its disposal.[14] He spoke of 'painless economic aid' that was subverting the independence of the country. But he made clear that, though stressing his aversion to American aid, economic assistance from the communist bloc should also be judged in the perspective of economic self-reliance.[15]

As for Sukarno, he was torn between his predisposition to radical nationalist remedies and his feeling for the limits of political power. This resulted in extremist formulations that brought him close to the P.K.I. and cautious action that had the opposite effect. He agreed that Indonesia 'should not overcome its economic difficulties by relying on loans, but by relying on our own strength'.[16] He also let the P.K.I. help him with the formulation of his Deklarasi Ekonomi, a rather general edict that was soon dubbed the economic counterpart of his well-known Political Manifesto.[17] This Sukarno statement came at a time when the Indonesian President had suggested a 'summit' talk with Malaya's Rahman, a move that did not find much favor in the eyes of Aidit as it suggested an inclination to compromise.[18] Sukarno also seems to have told the P.K.I. that he could not, or would not, accept their request for a Nasakom government[19] and may have bought them off by at least letting them have a say in the drafting of the Deklarasi Ekonomi.[20]

At any rate the P.K.I. used it extensively in the, by then well-known, manner of fully subscribing to a rather vaguely worded Sukarno document, interpreting it in their own way and criticizing the practical 'implementation' of it by Sukarno's ministers. As the cabinet was preparing the executive measures that had to reorganize trade and finances, the P.K.I. proceeded with 'interpreting' Dekon. The main tenor was as already outlined above: A Nasakom cabinet, plus 'retooling' under guidance of Sukarno, were proconditions for any successful remedy.[21] For the rest, in this 'pre-socialist' national-democratic phase of the economy, 'imperialist' and 'feudal' vestiges had to be done with, not meaning much more than the pursuit of the existing P.K.I. policy of a rather revisionist tint: Industrialization, more foreign trade with the communist bloc, land distribution, support for the cooperative sector and for 'national' capitalists.[22]

Of more immediate effect was the view on foreign economic relations: Investment of 'foreign monopoly capital' in a classical manner or in a 'neo-colonialist way' was not permissable; drastic monetary measures were equally to be rejected as they would reinforce 'the position of the dollar' in Indonesia, and credits should only be accepted when one's own resources were insufficient.[23] When on May 26 a set of economic regulations were finally enacted and published by the government, they immediately encountered strong resistance from P.K.I. side.[24] Since the measures put the exchange rate of the rupiah on a more realistic footing – without officially devaluating – and provided other export-incentives, imposed import-restrictions, and tried to curb government spending, it was not difficult to find fault with them. This was even more so because the United States gave signs of great diplomatic and commercial activity. A few days before the measures became public, it was reported that Washington was ready to help Indonesia, provided the economic program was sound.[25] A special emissary of President Kennedy, Wilson Wyatt, conferred with Sukarno on the new measures while the Indonesian President was in Tokio attending the Malaysia summit with Rahman.[26] Simultaneously a far-reaching agreement was concluded in the Japanese capital (with Wyatt in the wings) between Indonesia and three major oil companies, solving a long-standing dispute and putting 40 million dollars at the immediate disposal of the government. It was in this atmosphere of respite and cooperation that Sukarno came to terms with Rahman and paved the way for the subsequent Manila accord.[27] The financial reward in terms of dollar loans must no doubt have influenced Sukarno, as both the United States and the International Monetary Fund were considering extensive credits which would not be available (as in the end indeed happened) to a country that 'does not control its internal situation and does not stop its international adventures', as earlier in March General Clay had remarked in an advisory report to President Kennedy.[28]

The problem for Sukarno was that he practically had nowhere else to turn but to the U.S.A. and possibly Japan. The Soviet Union, that in earlier times had provided an interesting alternative, was not in the mood to get further involved. It had to date invested about one billion dollars in military hardware in Indonesia and had earmarked credits up to 375 million dollars.[29] These credits were designed mainly to finance a steel plant with a capacity of 100,000 tons, a superphosphate plant that would produce 100,000 tons, and some 650 km of highway on Borneo. All this did not get much further than the drawing board, whereas the Senajan sports stadium and a hospital, also Soviet-financed, were finished indeed.[30] But although only a small part of Soviet commitments were used up and the greater part still had to be disbursed, what was left were so-called tied-loans for specific projects.[31] Indonesia's need at that moment was hard currency credits to ease the balance of payments disequilibrium and for indispensable spare parts, etc., to get limited productive capacity back in to full use.[32] As for Moscow, the backlog of unfulfilled commitments all over the third world was mounting. The Soviet authorities first of all tried to keep new commitments down, while at the same time allowing controlled, piecemeal disbursements.[33] This framework was not conducive to being of much help to Indonesia.[34] Pravda wrote that Indonesia should 'rely above all on national forces (and) seek support from genuine friends', but in practice nothing was forthcoming.[35] On the contrary, after West Irian was for all practical purposes over as an issue, and certainly in the newfound soberness after the Cuban crisis, the Soviet Union pressed Indonesia to meet its obligations fully in debt servicing and the repayment of the enormous credits received.[35] In fact, therefore, both the United States and the Soviet Union were impressing upon Indonesia that she should face economic realities.[36] But Moscow, having spent the money and not willing to do more, was in a rather unenviable position, and several times in the course of 1963 had to allow Indonesia to default on her commitments.[37]

The state of relations between the two countries was partly reflected in the publicity Indonesia got in the Soviet Union. Gone were the days of glowing tributes to Sukarno and his 'guided democracy'. The mood was more for sober, even critical, analysis of the state of the economy. Relatively sympathetic observers still put the blame on the colonial past or the reactionaries, at home and abroad.[38] But harder analysis showed that there was no escaping the conclusion that 'at the present time the national problem of the utmost importance is the stabilization of the economy and the restoration of sound finances'.[39] A Soviet expert was later to describe the aims of the economic measures of May 1963 and their effects in rather objective terms,[40] saying that the main aim had been to increase income from exports and that the necessary upswing in production had not materialized. After a temporary improvement of the national economy, the situation was said to have begun to decline again in September 1963.[41] It was not denied on the Soviet side that Indonesia needed help from other countries to develop, but the opinion was prevailing even among serious Soviet observers that communist aid (where was it?) would make possible 'the creation in Indonesia of the basis of an independent, many-sided economy', while American aid would do just the opposite.[42] The more crudely propagandistic statements in the Soviet Union on foreign, particularly American, aid to Indonesia were of course even less charitable[43] and the subject seems to have been caught up in the growing Sino-Soviet rivalry. Due to this, the Soviet Union had to defend itself more and more now on the left flank as well. Peking and its more radical Afro-Asian friends tried to ridicule Moscow and its concept of development aid.

As we have seen, in the growing dispute amongst communists, the P.K.I. until the middle of 1963 had not yet given signs of adhering to extreme views.[44] But no abstract theorizing or dogmatic reasoning was necessary to bring the Indonesian communists also on this point of foreign aid closer to Peking because the Soviet Union, for all its superior defence of aid to developing countries, etc., was, as far as concrete help to Indonesia was concerned, a spent force.[45] This must have dawned upon the P.K.I. which in the past had been an uncertain beneficiary of Soviet 'aid', as evidenced by the strong competitive position Moscow had put the Indonesian armed forces in. But Sukarno and his entourage must have felt that way, too. The situation now was radically different from the time that West Irian had to be made part of the Republic, and when Sukarno in September 1963 embarked upon fullscale confrontation with Malaysia there was no half-way house to fall back on, as could have been expected. The United States immediately retaliated by stopping the new aid program, and also other non-communist sources dried up or were not forthcoming.[46] However, the only alternative, the Soviet Union,[47] was not available either. This no doubt contributed to a cooling off in relations between Djakarta and Moscow and must have reinforced in both Sukarno and the P.K.I. the tendency to go it alone, to practice – as the slogan became more current – 'self-reliance'.[48] At any rate it was only a matter of time now until the May 26 regulations were to be abolished as so many dead letters since they had been based on the assumption of large scale foreign credits. It was Subandrio who – after the sudden death of chief minister Djuanda the leading man under Sukarno – came out in favor of a 'reconsideration' of the policies designed by his predecessor.[49] There would be a considerable deficit because of the absence of economic aid from the United States, he told the nation, and the Malaysia confrontation with its immediate negative economic effects in particular required 'prompt short-term measures, even unconventional action'. The rejoicing was understandably great in P.K.I. circles, as they saw their wishful thinking of the danger about Djuanda's right-wing policy coming true.[50] And though Aidit was to observe at the end of the year 'politics are going to the left, stomachs to the right',[51] he did not want to link the deteriorating economic situation with the policy options taken by the government: 'Nobody really believes that the policy of confronting Malaysia and conducting the Games of the Newly Emerging Forces will require great expenditure of money'.[52] There were, however, people who thought otherwise, and not only the 'neo-capitalist' adherents of the May 26 regulations but also some comrades. But it took time and a disastrous putsch attempt to bring that out.[53]

As with the Malaysia issue at the very end of 1962,[54] the problems of economic stabilization and growth in the course of 1963 persuaded Sukarno and his cabinet to turn to outside help. When this was refused by the Soviet Union because of fear of financial and political over-commitment and by the United States because of the new and violent phase of the anti-Malaysia confrontation, the resulting isolation became another factor to drive the Indonesian government to a more radical stance and to look for support elsewhere abroad. This in turn made it possible for Aidit to step up the P.K.I. offensive at home as was to be decided upon soon at the December plenary of the Party.[55] It began to look as if Aidit's cautious 'gradualist' policy towards Sukarno of 'support and criticism', of infiltration and constant pressure, was bearing fruit, showing those interested both at home and abroad that the P.K.I. under Aidit's successful formula was a political power seriously to be reckoned with.

NOTES

1. P.K.I.-document, referred to as: Internal summary of the C.C. session of December 24, 1963. 'The declaration of Subandrio [that the May regulations were outdated] reflects the diminishing force of the hardheaded rightists.

Therefore the declaration of Subandrio must be received with even more severe actions, so that the government must willy nilly accede to our demands, namely the establishment of a Nasakom-cabinet in this coming year.' See pp. 197, 198.

2. On December 19, 1961. Sukarno had issued his 'Trikora' or triple command, two of which had been more or less solved by August 1962: The incorporation of West Irian and the restoration of internal security. See above p. 139.
3. See Sukarno's 'Year of Victory' speech of August 17, 1962, *Antara News Agency*, August 17, 1962. Subandrio put the cost of the West Irian campaign to Indonesia at approximately one billion dollars: *Far Eastern Economic Review*, January 17, 1963.
4. One rupiah nominally.
5. In his August 17, 1962, speech 'Year of Victory'. See also Dr. Guy Pauker, Indonesia: internal development or external expansion, *Asian Survey*, February 1963.
6. *Narody Azii i Afriki*, no. 4, 1964, p. 53.
7. This was a target used in the May 25, 1963, government measures. See *Harian Rakjat*, December 23, 1963. Pauker, 1963, came to an amount of 300 million dollars, apparently based on current American estimates.
8. Aidit spoke in the Javanese town of Tjiandjur, and his speech had wide repercussions. He tried to bring home his point forcefully. He said: 'Rejecting Nasakom is the same as rejecting the peaceful road of socialism, the same as intending fighting among our people, and the acme of fighting is civil war'. *Harian Rakjat*, December 18, 1962. This led the Singapore *Straits Times* to a headline: 'Aidit: Let Reds in cabinet or civil war'; *Straits Times*, January 10, 1963. *Harian Rakjat* tried to tone down the Tjiandjur Speech by quoting a softer version Aidit meanwhile had given on December 24, 1963, when he recalled (as others had done for him, no doubt) that, since 1960, each party had been obliged to follow the peaceful road. 'This is in accordance with the Party's original desire, favoring peaceful and democratic means as the best', he then added. *Harian Rakjat*, January 16, 1963.
9. *Harian Rakjat*, January 4, 1963: 'If . . . the desire of the President to implement his conception by forming a Nasakom Cabinet has not been carried out, it is not his fault. This is because there are still underhanded forces controlled by the imperialists who still have a political role and are forestalling a Nasakom cabinet'.
10. *Harian Rakjat*, January 5 and 7, 1963. Before harm could be done Aidit made sure that he and Lukman escaped being 'retooled' themselves, as they held nominal ministerial ranks in the Sukarno government: 'The two communist ministers are "small fry" without real powers', Aidit countered to Njono: *Harian Rakjat*, January 8, 1963.
11. The United States, Aidit wrote, were scheming to carry out their plan to stabilize the Indonesian economy through aid. He held out the example of Brazil, recently 'threatened' by Robert Kennedy that it would lose American aid if President Goulart did not 'stop worrying the U.S.' *Harian Rakjat*,

January 30, 1963, *New China News Agency*, January 30, 1963.

12. D. N. Aidit, 'Courage, courage and more courage', political report to the First Plenary Session of the Central Committee of the Communist Party of Indonesia: *Harian Rakjat*, February 11, 1963.
13. The other main subject was the international communist movement.
14. *New China News Agency*, February 15, 1963, in its rendering of the report took pains to stress the point Aidit made on not begging for foreign aid.
15. '... We have also received substantial aid from socialist countries, given without any strings attached, which means that it does not encroach upon our freedom and sovereignty. Aid from the socialist countries is given with the hope that, within a short period of time, Indonesia will be able to stand on her own feet and not remain dependent on foreign aid'; D. N. Aidit, *Harian Rakjat*, February 11, 1963. See also below p. 230. The *New China News Agency* version of Aidit's report omitted any reference to Soviet aid to Indonesia.
16. *New China News Agency*, February 13, 1963.
17. It was P.K.I.'s economic expert Sakirman who seems to have been in on Dekon, as the declaration of March 28, 1963, became known. This may also explain why Sakirman, in the preceding period, had come out rather as an Aidit-type middle-of-the-road critic of the economic situation. Thus, for example, in a major speech in Kebajoran he placed himself between those on the 'right wing' who thought that foreign capital should do the trick and those on the 'left wing' who were clamoring for nationalization of medium and small enterprises as a solution: *Harian Rakjat*, March 1, 1963. Sobsi chairman Njono was, as in the case of 'the July 1960 evaluation', one of those who were most critical of the Sukarno government. Lukman, Aidit's first deputy, could again be seen following the P.K.I. Chairman in his 'moderate' posture: No leftist recklessness, and no rightist despair, he told the Central Committee: *Harian Rakjat*, February 7, 1963.

    It is not clear why Lukman was spoken of at the time as the man who with his faction 'advocates the activist revolutionary line favored by Peking' as Pauker did. In: Indonesia, internal development or external expansion, *Asian Survey*, February 1963, p. 71. If there was anyone who would qualify for that description it was Njoto, P.K.I.'s Second Deputy Chairman, who seems to have come back from China at the end of January fully strengthened in his predelection for 'Pekinese' approaches and who became most active in propagating them. Immediately upon arrival he told the Central Committee plenary that Lenin was right when he said 'force should be used to provoke fear in the ranks of the reactionary': *Harian Rakjat*, February 8, 1963. See below p. 206.
18. See above p. 176.
19. 'Sukarno, according to an Asian diplomat, recently called on Mr. Aidit, chairman of the P.K.I., and asked him to call off the demand for a Nasakom cabinet. Sukarno is reported to have told Mr. Aidit: I am Nasakom'. *Far Eastern Economic Review*, April 19, 1963.

20. In his most elaborate comment on Dekon – a lecture to the fellow-travelling Indonesian Scholars Association on May 11, 1963 – Aidit emphasized that 'for the first time our people [the P.K.I.] have directly and actively drawn up government policy in the economic field; that is, in a field which to date had been considered as a field forbidden to the people [the P.K.I.].' *Harian Rakjat*, May 14, 1963.
21. Aidit in his lecture to the Indonesian Scholars Association, *Harian Rakjat*, May 14, 15, 16, 17, 20 and 21, 1963, Joint Publications Research Service.
22. 'There are some people who feel greatly surprised at the P.K.I.'s approval of the existence of the private sector and, moreover, feel suspicious that this may be a cunning hypocritical trick . . . According to the P.K.I., the problem in the Indonesian economy has not been that there have been too many national capitalists or national entrepreneurs, but the contrary, that there are still too few'; *Harian Rakjat*, May 16, 1963.
23. Dekon contained such a restrictive clause on foreign credits, so the P.K.I. was on good grounds, but in practice it could mean anything. It is interesting to find in Aidit's lecture of May, 11, 1963, the first attack on the International Monetary Fund, of which Indonesia was 'still' a member. This foreshadowed what would happen later when Indonesia withdrew from this institution early in 1965.
24. See *Djakarta Radio Home Service*, June 5, 1963 and *Far Eastern Economic Review*, June 13, 1963 for details of the government measures. Aidit attacked them at a rally the same day (May 26) following the lines of his lecture earlier that month: *Harian Rakjat*, May 27, 1963.
25. *Antara News Agency* from Washington D.C., May 23, 1963.
26. *Antara News Agency*, May 29, 1963.
27. See above p. 179.
28. See also *Harian Rakjat*, May 3rd, 1963, concluding from this report that American aid had strings attached.
29. Ch. B. McLane, Foreign aid in Soviet Third World policies, *Mizan News Letter*, May-June 1967.
30. *Pravda*, August 7, 1963. See above p. 79 note 31.
31. Soviet aid did not include the Western type 'turn-key' projects, that is, projects to be handed over ready and running. The Russians only operated in an advisory, not in an executive, capacity, leaving the actual building, etc., to the Indonesians. This partly explains why Soviet aid barely showed results since it began in 1956. Another reason was faulty planning, as with the steel plant, built on a site without coal, iron or port facilities.
32. An economic survey over 1962 in a Soviet journal concluded that 25% of Indonesia's industrial capacity was used: *Mirovaia Ekonomiki*, no. 8, 1963, p. 75. This corresponds with a figure given by Aidit in his May 11, 1963, speech to the Indonesian Scholars Association. See note 21. Sakirman stated that transport facilities on land could also be used for 25%, while on water 50%; *Harian Rakjat*, March 11, 1963.
33. R. A. Yellon, The winds of change, *Mizan Newsletter*, July-August 1967,

p. 156, comes to an accumulated aid commitment backlog in the period 1961-1963 of 2.4 billion dollars which threatened to disrupt the Soviet economy because Moscow might be asked to make available this huge volume of resources within a very short time.

34. Pauker, writing in *Asian Survey*, February 1963, concluded that 'massive additional economic credits from [the communist bloc] are not likely and would at any rate be of little immediate value since only a small fraction of credits already obtained had been actually utilised'.
35. *Pravda*, January 3, 1963.
36. See also *Far Eastern Economic Review*, April 18, 1963.
37. Ruslan Abdulgani announced in July 1963 that the Soviet Union had granted extension of time for repayment, and Nasution stated in December of the same year that the Soviet Union had doubled the periods of repayment. Both had to go to Moscow for it, cap in hand; *U.P.I.*, July 5, 1963 and *Antara News Agency*, December 12, 1963. Also according to Suwito Kusumowidagdo, interview, March 1972, the Russians remained rather lenient.
38. V. Zharov, *Aziya i Afrika Segodnya*, 1963, no. 8.
39. *Narody Azii i Afriki*, 1964, no. 4. In the next issue of the same journal, M. A. Andreyev followed current P.K.I. analysis, saying that the 'bureaucratic capitalists' – the managers of the state enterprises, etc. – with their anti-popular activity had an unhealthy grip on the state sector. Besides, this important sector of the Indonesian economy, according to the 8-year plan, was not expected to contribute much, but 'as practice shows [it] is not fullfilling even these reduced financial obligations to the Indonesian people'.
40. *Narody Azii i Afriki*, 1964, no. 4, p. 53-55.
41. *Narody Azii i Afriki*, 1964, no. 4, p. 53-55. 'The country's financial and economic position continued to deteriorate; the 1963 budget was left with the enormous deficit of 33.5 billion rupiahs. Inflation became worse ... The cost of living rose sharply ... The production situation remained as acute as in previous years ... Food production for 1962 and 1963 went down by 2% per head of the population'.
42. V. Zharov, *Aziya i Afrika Segodnya*, no. 8, p. 7-8.
43. See *Radio Moscow Home Service*, May 17, 1963, stating that the United States used its assistance program to lead Indonesia astray, away from its principles, etc. This was when the May 26 economic measures were prepared and the U.S. tried to influence them backstage.
44. See p. 200, note 15.
45. *Pravda* gave a typical cross-section of official Kremlin opinion in a long article entitled 'Soviet aid to new countries', August 8, 1963.
46. The International Monetary Fund withdrew its July offer of 50 million dollars credit. Japan, to which Sukarno turned in a desparate last-minute bid for no less than 400 million dollars, was equally out; *Radio Japan*, September 27, 1963.
47. Not to speak of People's China. Its first credit – 30 million dollars in all – was granted in October 1961 as a symbolic gesture in the newly restored

relationship between the two countries. The next credit of 16 million dollars was slow in coming – spring 1965 – and for wholly unproductive purpose: Housing the abortive anti-U.N. or 'Conference of New Emerging Forces'.

48. Njoto was not slow in exposing the Soviet notion of aid by telling Djakarta activists early October 1963 that 'certain people have alleged that a young state could obtain complete independence only by getting economic aid. This is a deception'; *New China News Agency*, October 6, 1963.
49. *Antara News Agency*, December 12, 1963.
50. In an editorial *Harian Rakjat* again saw the May 26 regulations as a 'source of serious damage to the economy' and reacted favorably to Subandrio's admission of failure and need for a new approch; *Harian Rakjat*, December 23, 1963.
51. Aidit's political report to the 2nd plenary session of the P.K.I. Central Committee, delivered on December 23, 1963: *Harian Rakjat*, January 1, 1964.
52. *Harian Rakjat*, January 1, 1964.
53. The Appeal of the Marxist-Leninist Group of the P.K.I., a post-1965 evaluation of pro-Soviet P.K.I. members, had this to say on the state of the economy then: 'The progressive revolutionary forces of Indonesia had time and again tried to find a way out of these economic difficulties, but their efforts had proved futile due to the following causes: a) sabotage on the part of internal reactionaries holding key positions in the major branches of Indonesia's economy, assisted by the subversive economic actions of the imperialists; b) *the sky-rocketing state budget within the framework of confrontation with Malaysia* and the squandering of public funds on major uneconomical projects and all kinds of government political activities' [emphasis added]; *Information Bulletin*, 1967, no. 18, Prague, p. 56.
54. See above p. 174.
55. See below p. 229 ff.

CHAPTER 15

Aidit wants to mediate (1963)

The successes scored by Aidit's P.K.I. had the result that while the Sino-Soviet dispute in 1963 grew in intensity international attention became focussed on the attitude of the P.K.I., by then the biggest non-ruling communist party in the world.[1] Aidit was trying to avoid direct involvement in the quarrel with his customary cautious 'ad hoc' approach to the issues that arose.[2] But in fact he found himself increasingly on the 'Chinese' side. Accordingly it was said of the P.K.I. leadership in that phase that they were 'communist neutrals' who as the year 1963 progressed ranged themselves on the side of the 'pro-Chinese moderates'.[3] It is wise, however, to differentiate here and follow more closely P.K.I. chairman Aidit and his second deputy Njoto who was clearly in that period becoming the exponent of the more radical 'Chinese' approach and Aidit's antipode.

At the end of 1962 the P.K.I. chairman gave his opinion on the question as to how to solve or eliminate the differences in the international communist movement.[4] He then took the view that a general conference of all communist parties, in the tradition of the previous Moscow conferences of 1957 and 1960, would not take place without careful preparation of 'say one or two years'. This was also the opinion of Kruschov when he addressed the East German S.E.D. Congress in Berlin in January 1963 and asked for a stop to polemics.[5] However, Peking had shown interest in propagating the idea of a new conference, to be held without delay, as this had given them (because of the unanimity rule) on two previous occasions leverage far beyond the actual response to their theses among the other parties.[6] The party daily *Harian Rakjat* printed in full the text of the *Jen-min Jih-pao* article that had contained the suggestion of an immediate conference.[7]

This could still be seen as an attempt to give a fair report of the various viewpoints in the Sino-Soviet debate, but Aidit in early February in his report to the plenary of the P.K.I. Central Committee gave signs of having shifted more towards the unqualified Chinese view on a communist world conference, saying that he was 'determined to propose a conference of all Marxist-Leninist parties in the world'.[8]

In his report to the Central Committee Aidit on other points also gave evidence of having moved more to the left since the autumn of 1962. He acknowledged openly that the inter-party discussions he now advocated were needed 'in the face of the split within the communist world movement'. He again treated the familiar issues[9] that had made their impact upon the Party in the past autumn – Cuba, the Chinese-Indian border war, Yugoslavia – but sharpened his tone considerably, denouncing particularly the new habit of using party congresses as platforms to attack other parties.[10] This was the well-known 1961-stand of the P.K.I. that in fact favored the Albanians,[11] while it was not applicable to the Yugoslavs who, on the basis of the 1960 Moscow Declaration, had to be 'exposed'. The presence of a delegation from Belgrade at the congresses of the Italian Communist Party and the East German S.E.D. Aidit found particularly a thorn in his side and he qualified the appearances as 'most unfortunate incidents', aimed at splitting world communism. He also indicated that, to the P.K.I., Yugoslavia continued to remain outside the pale of the 'socialist commonwealth', an issue that had been given a new impetus since Moscow and Belgrade had begun to move towards each other again at the end of 1962.[12]

Interesting it was in Aidit's report that he called the United States Indonesia's Enemy Number One, whereas officially it was still the Dutch.[13] In a way this was 'logical', as the West-Irian dispute with the Netherlands was won and all but over, but, at the same time, it symbolized a more radical trend, now endorsed by Aidit as well.[14] Besides it had a concrete political meaning, because, at that time, the pragmatists surrounding First Minister Djuanda were trying to put some order into Indonesia's deteriorating economy, and it was widely accepted that American dollar aid would be indispensable to success.[15] As we have seen[16] Aidit, concerned foremost with domestic politics, called foreign aid 'subversive' and more dangerous than in fact the Malaysia 'threat'. So the report Aidit gave to the Central Committee in February 1963 represented a further slide towards a more radical posture. On the other hand the P.K.I. Chairman was less extreme than, for instance, Njoto.

At the end of 1962 the Second deputy-chairman of the P.K.I. had attended a number of party congresses in Europe and subsequently spent the month of January in China, where his visit had coincided with the talks Subandrio had with the Chinese Prime Minister Chou En-lai early in that month. He returned at the end of January, bringing greetings from 'Mao, Kim, and others',[17] a hint of the not-very-cordial relations he must have had with the Soviet Russian and other East European communist leaders. To further emphasize the more extremist mood he was in after his foreign trip, he also mentioned that Aidit in 1961, after the 22nd Party Congress in Moscow, had observed that 'the Sino-Soviet conflict was difficult to solve', a remark not reported at the time when Aidit made a statement about the Congress.[18] A week afer he had come back from China Njoto mounted a full-blast attack on the U.S.A. and was the first to call that country Enemy Number One. In his political report Aidit followed suit, as we saw. Many other examples are to be found, all through that spring and summer, of Njoto egging on the first man of the party to ever more extreme positions.[19] In all these instances Njoto was given extensive coverage in the Chinese press. It is not too far-fetched to suggest that Aidit's deputy after his latest sojourn there was considered by Peking to be a man to work with.

Judging from the limited but unmistakable escalation of Aidit's opinion[20] after Njoto returned from China late in January 1963 (on Yugoslavia, on the U.S.A., on a world conference, etc.), one may conclude that it was at this particular stage that the prudent Aidit felt justified to do so. Earlier we saw that it was the budding rapprochement between Sukarno and Subandrio on the one hand and the Chinese leaders on the other[21] that was the salient feature in those early weeks of 1963. So the two parts fit: In an atmosphere of growing antagonism between Moscow and Peking, the carefully nurtured and cultivated nationalistic diversion against Malaysia that the P.K.I. was selling to Sukarno brought China in on a state level – arms for Djakarta. In turn this was reinforcing the domestic position of the P.K.I. enabling and possibly forcing Aidit to radicalize and put more pressure on Sukarno.

The more extreme stand taken by Aidit, and through him by the P.K.I., at the February plenary did not pass unnoticed, and it was especially the Yugoslav communists who reacted violently. This was understandable because the position of Belgrade within the communist world had again been subjected to wide and acrimonious debate, and the Indonesian comrades had contributed to it in a way not particularly favorable to the Yugoslavs.[22] Therefore, in the Belgrade theoretical journal *Kommunist*, soon after the Central Committee of the P.K.I. had concluded its session, a sharp rebuke was published.[23] On the one hand the P.K.I. was praised for its willingness to join a national coalition government under Sukarno – the 'Nasakom' cabinet Aidit had again begun to call for at the end of 1962 – but on the other hand the Indonesian communists were charged with being inconsistent and of pursuing an uncompromisingly hard line in foreign affairs. For instance the Party was said to have abandoned peaceful co-existence for favoring solutions based on force and for opposing imperialism in an irresponsible way.[24] This dichotomy in P.K.I. policies was noted and commented upon elsewhere,[25] but in this issue of *Kommunist* it was expounded for the first time very distinctly.[26]

It took some time before the P.K.I. took up this challenge[27] and it was Njoto who, in speeches made in Medan and Djakarta, was the first to react by putting the rhetorical question as to what the imperialists would do if they were not treated 'harshly'.[28] A more complete answer was given in *Harian Rakjat* later in April when it went into the details of the charges that the P.K.I. was taking extremist positions on foreign issues.[29] The article, interestingly enough, did not waste a word on the positive things the Yugoslavs had said on its domestic policy of accommodation, let alone on the contradiction between the P.K.I.'s domestic and foreign policies. It was, no doubt, a touchy question that was to recur more frequently in the near future and must also have been brought up by the Chinese comrades when Aidit, later in 1963, visited Peking,[30] i.e., from the left side: Why was the P.K.I. in fact so revisionist at home?

In looking for an explanation of the particular animadversion with which the Indonesian communists through the years seemed to have looked on Tito and his independent variety of communism, a number of suggestions have been made. The view has been taken that the P.K.I. opposed Yugoslav revisionism and what it stood for 'not because it is moderate domestically, but because it is unaligned internationally'.[31] The P.K.I. in this opinion had argued that the only way for Indonesia to resist 'imperialism' successfully – and for the party to take over the country – would be to align itself with the communist camp. It is true that Sukarno and Tito, although they did not always see completely eye to eye on priorities,[32] had found a common denominator, resulting in the 'third bloc' approach. This, in turn, may have conditioned the P.K.I.'s resistance to Yugoslavia as one of the foremost exponents of non-alignment. Another view is that, because of the cooperation of the P.K.I. with Sukarno and to a lesser extent with the Indonesian army, 'internal political imperatives require [the P.K.I.] to pursue a domestic policy which places it far closer to Moscow than to Peking'.[33] Anatagonism towards the Tito régime is then explained as a reaction to the 'radical national collectivism' that Sukarno and his advisers were said to have shared with the Yugoslavs, making it hard for Aidit and his men to compete within the Indonesian context for left-nationalist support.

Neither of the two sets of arguments completely fit the facts. It seems that, indeed, at the root of the long-standing anti-Yugoslav bias lay the adoption of a domestic 'right' strategy by Aidit and his team a year after they took over the party in 1951.[34] Aidit, in his general report of February 1963, called it 'the glorious tradition [to] combat revisionism . . . which started the day the P.K.I. was born'.[35] This basically moderate approach in internal affairs, coupled with building strength through mass organizations and with a national front policy from above as well as from below, made the P.K.I. a party which was at least as far from Soviet orthodoxy as the Yugoslav 'revisionists' had been accused of being.[36] A second feature of the policy of the Indonesian communists, in addition to its reformist program, and reinforcing it, was its strong appeal to nationalist sentiment resulting in such slogans as 'Indonesianization of Marxist-Leninism'.[37] Both aspects of the P.K.I. were, in the eyes of Aidit, dictated by domestic conditions, by the climate in which the party had to operate. It was this 'forced' national-communist revisionism of the P.K.I. which from an early stage made the Indonesian communists so loudly expose Tito's brand of the same thing. It was as if they wanted to provide themselves with a valid alibi as a genuine Marx-abiding communist party, especially within the international communist movement, but, of course, also against the local competitors around Sukarno such as the Murba Party. It was like shouting 'thief' lest others catch you stealing.[38] Given this basic motivation that sprung from the Indonesian scene itself, the attitude of non-alignment between the two blocs naturally became a part of the Yugoslav policies the P.K.I. was to denounce continuously. At times, and certainly in the early stages of the emerging Sino-Soviet split, when the P.K.I. began to radicalize its international posture, the most conspicuous part of the Yugoslav-P.K.I. equation may have been the Indonesian communists' attacks on Yugoslavia's foreign affairs – its 'non-bloc' ideas, its dependence on American aid, etc. But it was not a primary aspect. It was rather a symptom if not a habit.

The attacks on the Yugoslav revisionists that went on unabated that spring 1963 may have received additional fuel from the fact that they were at the same time intended as a substitute for showing displeasure at Moscow's behavior.[39] At any rate, while Belgrade was about to be brought back officially to the fold of the true communist states by Kruschov,[40] at the end of March Njoto tried to counter this on behalf of the P.K.I. by stating that 'had the Moscow Statement of the 81 Communist and Workers' Parties not laid down [the obligation to criticize Yugoslav revisionism] the Indonesian revolutionaries would still have criticized it'.[41] It did not belong to 'the category of the debate' within the international communist movement to be critical of the Yugoslavs, Njoto said. With this rather extreme opinion Njoto must have intended to foreclose in advance any attempt to have the P.K.I. endorse a factual change in the 1960 condemnation of the Yugoslavs as Togliatti had suggested earlier in 1963.

Unlike Njoto, the P.K.I. chairman seemed in these months still to have been reluctant to let the P.K.I. give up its organizational non-alignment. Although in his February report to the P.K.I. Central Committee Aidit may have given heed to pressure and followed ideas Njoto had come up with, he remained the realistic party chief, intent on keeping his options open. He was thus quick to welcome the bilateral talks between Moscow and Peking, to which the Chinese consented in their letter of March 9,[42] and repeated his warm adhesion in the weeks to come.[43] It had meanwhile earned him the attention of both parties in the dispute, and in early April the P.K.I. received an invitation to send a delegation to Peking as well as to Moscow.[44] Aidit denied rumors that the P.K.I. had any pretence at mediating in the dispute,[45] but Politburo member Sudisman, who was to accompany Aidit on his forthcoming trip to the two communist capitals, was nevertheless to confirm upon his return that Aidit had intended to get the two parties to mend their differences.[46]

With this mission in mind Aidit had reasons to play it cool and especially not to exacerbate the Soviet Union. He gave various signs of this[47] and even went far out of his way to give the Soviet Union its due as far as its role in the 'liberation' of West Irian was concerned. On the first of May the embattled jungle island was to be transferred to full Indonesian authority, and a few days before that 'Day of Victory' the Politburo of the P.K.I. issued a statement in which the successful recovery of West Irian was ascribed to 'the unity of all the people and the very close cooperation between the people and the armed forces'.[48] No word was lost on the role the Soviet Union might have played in the event. On May 1, however, another statement was issued on West Irian, this time emanating from the Central Committee of the party. In this gratitude was expressed, not only to the Indonesian people and to the armed forces, but also to 'all progressive powers in the world, to the socialist countries, and especially to the Soviet Union for their moral and material support in the struggle of the Indonesian people'.[49] No other evidence is available, but it is not stretching the imagination too far to suggest that Aidit had probably been unable to swing a majority of the Politburo in favor of a kind word to Moscow on account of West Irian and consequently had countered this by putting out another statement with the help of the members of the Central Committee, or at least in their name.[50]

Relations with the Soviet comrades were anyhow already becoming strained as a result of the Afro-Asian Journalists Conference that was held between April 24 and 30, 1963. A preparatory meeting in February had decided to leave the decision about Soviet participation to the Conference itself. The extreme left-wing chairman of the Indonesian Press Association, Djawoto (later Djakarta's man in Peking who refused to return home after the 30 September affair) declared well in advance that the Soviet delegation would have the status of observer 'because part of the Soviet Union is considered as belonging to Asia'.[51] It was a reasonably polite way of saying that the Soviet journalists were barely welcome. The Soviet delegation at the Conference demanded full status, but notwithstanding their protests that the Conference was run in a most undemocratic manner (by Djawoto, who also is said to have been confused because he hardly spoke any foreign language), the great majority of the delegates turned down their request.[52] It was the P.K.I. and especially its Peking-oriented wing that was prominent at the Conference and acted as front for the Chinese, helping them to block Soviet participation.

Sukarno, whose wife Hartini accepted a honorary presidency, took the trouble to open the Conference with a keynote speech in which he appealed to the journalists 'to strengthen the common struggle against colonialism and imperialism', etc. This whole performance did not go down well with the Soviets and, as Sukarno at a later stage[53] was to reveal, Moscow complained to the Indonesian government about the exclusion of its journalists and, more generally, about the 'breach of international solidarity' this sort of exclusive Afro-Asian meetings was said to represent.[54] To what extent the Sukarno régime itself was held responsible by the Soviet leaders for what went on at these Afro-Asian conferences is not clear, but relations with the Indonesian comrades must certainly have suffered. Aidit was more and more out-maneuvered by both his left-wing and gradually also by the Indonesian President.

In the view of those Indonesian communists who, after the *coup d'état* of September 1965 chose Moscow's side, it was since that month of April 1963 that in their words 'our relations [with the communist party of the Soviet Union] were of a formal nature and departed from the standards of relations between fraternal parties'.[55] The major event between the two parties involved was the Afro-Asian Journalists Conference, which must have been taken by the Soviet leaders as a slap in the face of socialism's motherland and produced some traumatic reactions.[56]

Aidit continued to try to steer clear of trouble both inside and outside the party. He devoted an extensive article to his support for the life-long presidency Indonesia's would-be parliament bestowed on Sukarno.[57] He twice censored his deputy Njoto for pushing too far to his liking towards a more violent approach abroad and at home,[58] and he tried to be as effusive as the occasion allowed him in expressions of goodwill towards the Soviet Union while speaking at the P.K.I. anniversary rally in the Djakarta Sports Stadium for which Moscow had paid some 13 million dollars in hard cash. For Aidit this monumental piece of concrete was 'one of the symbols of eternal friendship between the two great nations, Indonesia and the Soviet Union'.[59]

In his ideas on how to mend the Sino-Soviet rift, Aidit rejected both what he called the 'social-democratic' and the 'anarchist' methods; that is, he retained theoretically an ideal middle position. This 'neutral' stance was also reflected in the joint statement of the P.K.I. and the Japanese Communist Party which also contained an appeal to the two major communist parties for 'a concrete settlement'.[60] But when one of the pro-Peking P.K.I. leaders while abroad described the P.K.I. as being neutral between Moscow and Peking.[61] Aidit put out an immediate denial, probably afraid that in the eyes of the Kremlin leaders 'neutrality' would make the P.K.I. unfit to contribute to a solution of outstanding Sino-Soviet issues.

By this time, however, it must have dawned upon Aidit – if indeed he ever seriously had hoped to mediate – that his efforts in Moscow and Peking would be fruitless and doomed to failure. He showed this in a way by telling his well-wishers when he was about to embark upon his world tour that 'the imperialists and Yugoslav revisionists' were trying to torpedo the Moscow talks.[62] The Chinese had used this phrase a few days earlier,[63] when the Soviet communists in the midst of the Sino-Soviet talks in Moscow had published a blistering attack on the Chinese position.[64] To all concerned, the publication of this 'open letter' for all practical purposes meant that the Moscow talks were on the verge of a breakdown, as indeed was made known officially on July 20, the day Aidit arrived in Moscow.[65]

To the P.K.I. and especially to its chairman this widening of the Sino-Soviet rift was to assume crucial proportions as the near future would show. But equally important to Aidit's turning away from Moscow was the other point that bothered him when he left Djakarta for the Russian capital, saying that the same 'imperialists and modern revisionists' that wanted to ruin the Moscow talks were also thwarting a Nasakom cabinet that Aidit had pressed for seriously since late 1962. The P.K.I. still lacked a foothold in the executive branch of the government, and lack of support for this demand, or probably even opposition, from the 'modern revisionist' Soviet side made increasingly for sour P.K.I. reactions. Combined with the realization that the Sino-Soviet rift after all was there to stay, this increasingly cool attitude adopted by Moscow towards the P.K.I. must have been another sign for Aidit that he should begin to look less for outside help in the attainment of his objectives. It did not necessarily mean a complete swing towards Peking as we will see, but it deprived him of substantial bargaining ability vis-à-vis the Chinese comrades, and above all towards his more radical colleagues in the P.K.I. Politburo.[66]

NOTES

1. In his general report to the February Central Committee Plenary Aidit claimed 3.5 million members for the P.K.I. and the affiliated Communist Youth League: *Harian Rakjat*, February 13, 1963.
2. See above p. 163.
3. Griffith, 1964, *The Sino-Soviet Rift*, George Allen and Unwin Ltd., p. 24. See also Hindley, 1964, The Indonesian Communist Party and the Conflict in the International Communist Movement, *China Quarterly*, July-September; Mozingo, 1965, *Sino-Indonesian Relations*, Rand Corporation, Santa Monica, p. 38 and Hemen Ray, Die Indonesische Kommunisten zwischen Maskau und Peking, *Ost-Europa*, March 1964.
4. Aidit speech to the Greater Djakarta Party Organization on December 24, 1962, *New China News Agency*, January 1, 1963.
5. *Pravda*, June 17, 1963.
6. *Jen-min Jih-pao*, 'The differences between comrade Togliatti and us", December 31, 1963.
7. This was the article 'The differences between comrade Togliatti and us"; *Harian Rakjat*, January 8, 1963. It was the first time that one of the documents in the Sino-Soviet dispute had been published in full in the Indonesian Communist press. From now on this was to be more often the case, but generally more with Chinese than with Soviet articles.
8. *Harian Rakjat*, February 11, 1963, *New China News Agency*, February 14, 1963. The Chinese rendering differed on two points from the text the Indonesian Party daily had given. A reference by Aidit to the effect that the P.K.I. had earlier urged a conference be held was deleted, probably not to give the P.K.I. too much credit for this. However, whereas Aidit had spoken according to *Harian Rakjat* of the need for a conference without further qualification, the Chinese news agency had him add 'at the proper time', that is, at some unspecified moment in the future. If this was what Aidit in effect had said it would have meant that he still adhered to his earlier, pro-Soviet view on a world conference.
9. See above p. 158 ff.

10. Referring to the recent party congresses in Bulgaria, Hungary, Italy, Czechoslovakia and East Germany Aidit said: 'The communists of Indonesia are not convinced that the airing of disputes and criticism within the family of Marxist-Leninist Parties before a forum of imperialists will make it earlier to find a solution'; *Harian Rakjat*, February 11, 1963.
11. See above p. 126.
12. See above pp. 162, 163.
13. See above pp. 33, 118. In 1959 it was decided that the Dutch were the prime enemy, but the Americans the 'most dangerous'. On January 30, 1963, Aidit attacked American aid because it had 'strings'; see above p. 199, note 11. This was mild compared with the more general condemnation of the U.S.A. as 'Enemy Number One' that followed.
14. Njoto had led the way on February 8, two days before Aidit delivered his general report to the Central Committee; see further on this p. 206.
15. See above p. 193.
16. See above p. 176.
17. *Harian Rakjat*, January 30, 1963.
18. *Harian Rakjat*, December 15, 1961.
19. See for example Njoto's plenary speech (*Harian Rakjat*, March 1, 1963), his addresses to Indonesian scientists (*Harian Rakjat*, March 9, 1963), in Medan and Djakarta (*Harian Rakjat*, April 2, 1963) and on Marx' birthday (*Harian Rakjat*, May 7, 1963). Hindley, in his article on the P.K.I. and the international communist movement, is also aware of the effects that Njoto's visit to Moscow and Peking at the turn of the year had on thinking within the P.K.I. and concludes that 'more open opposition to the Soviet policy also coincided with a lengthy visit by Njoto to bloc countries'. The 'more open opposition' to Moscow still had to come. However, Njoto did, in fact, keep pushing Aidit and the party to the left.
20. Because of this escalation, a comment of R. R. Gill on Aidit's general report said, the P.K.I. was 'solidly aligned with Peking'. In view of what went before and what was to come, this was too unqualified. See Aidit on the split that has appeared, *Radio Free Europe*, February 16, 1963.
21. See above p. 174 ff.
23. Yugoslavia's position in the Sino-Soviet dispute had recently become more controversial. The Italian party boss Togliatti had in January been the first openly to indicate that the paragraph on Yugoslav revisionism in the 1960 Moscow Declaration was incorrect. The Chinese had countered this with a *Jen-min Jih-pao* editorial saying that the main criterion for doctrinal purity was 'the attitude towards Yugoslavia'; *Jen-min Jih-pao*, January 27, 1963. In April Njoto was to say that, even without the 1960 Declaration, the P.K.I. would oppose the policies of Yugoslavia for splitting the Afro-Asian workers unity, etc.' *Harian Rakjat*, April 2nd, 1963 and p. 209.
23. *Kommunist* (Belgrade), February 28, 1963. This was an elaboration of an earlier thesis developed against the P.K.I. by the Belgrade daily Politika in its issue of December 31, 1961; see above p. 128.

24. Aidit in his general report of February 10, 1963 had made approving reference to Castro's dictum not to put any faith in imperialist propaganda and had followed up this lesson of the Cuban crisis with a conclusion of his own: 'Only force must be used to face and defeat the imperialists and the reactionaries, not cooperation or unnecessary compromise', *Harian Rakjat*, February 11, 1963.
25. The Trotskyite journal *Quatrième Internationale*, in its issue of March 1963, gave a similar criticism from a different angle: 'The P.K.I., on the one hand, can scarcely avoid China's influence over its masses and, on the other hand, pursue a policy of firm collaboration with the national-bourgeois Sukarno after the fashion of the best Kruschovism' (vol. 21, no. 18). The Italian Communist Party, too, was to pick up this theme; see p. 208.
26. In the *Politika* article in 1961 the Yugoslavs had only reproached the P.K.I. for supporting Sukarno and at the same time attacking Yugoslavia, Indonesia's fellow non-aligned country. Now, on a whole range of foreign issues, the P.K.I. was said to be taking a 'hard' line, leaving aside what Sukarno thought about it.
27. Probably the *Kommunist* article was not available to the P.K.I. leadership, before it was translated sometime later, and appeared in a press release of the Yugoslav Embassay in Djakarta.
28. 'Reactionaries in general, including the Yugoslav revisionists say: "The P.K.I. has two criteria – in international policy it is harsh, and in domestic policy it is soft". There is not a shade of truth in this accusation. The P.K.I. is harsh towards the imperialists and other reactionaries because what would they do if they were not treated harshly? ... Internal affairs are a different matter. The P.K.I. is friendly (this is perhaps called soft) towards the nationalist religious, democratic and other patriotic groups because they are part of the popular force, the anti-imperialist and anti-feudal force ... The P.K.I. is extremely critical of deviationists – the reformists who are afraid of complete freedom, and the adventurers who want to omit the phase of the national democratic revolution and want "socialism now" '; *Harian Rakjat*, April 2, 1963.
29. *Harian Rakjat*, April 19, 1963. This article was reprinted in full in the *Peking Review*, May 17, 1963. On the use of force *Harian Rakjat* wrote: 'If we avoid force, then it is clear that the August 1945 Revolution and the Cuban Revolution would never have occurred'. It also charged that both Tito and Nehru, as early as the 1961 Belgrade Conference of non-aligned nations, had 'ganged up' against Sukarno in order to defend imperialism, etc.
30. See below p. 222.
31. Ruth McVey, 1963, Indonesian Communism under Guided Democracy. In: A. Doak Barnett, *Communist Strategies in Asia*, Frederick A. Praeger, New York, p. 184. McVey also mentions the contradictory policies of the Indonesian communists: 'If the criticisms of Yugoslav revisionism are considered to be, in fact, attacks on a moderate approach to relations with non-communist forces – as we assume they are in the Chinese case – then this

clearly involves a contradiction with the policies thus far pursued by the P.K.I. in Indonesia"; McVey, 1963, p. 183.

32. See above pp. 112, 113.
33. William E. Griffith, 1967, *Sino-Soviet Relations 1964-1965*, The M.I.T. Press, Cambridge, Massachusetts, p. 195.
34. *Harian Rakjat*, February 11, 1963.
35. See also pp. 19, 20.
36. In a contemporary analysis of P.K.I. policies a right-wing Italian communist observer described Aidit's revisionist domestic line as follows: 'As the fighting wing of the anti-imperialist front the P.K.I. accepts agreements and compromise even when they amount to very little, provided the movement and the organization of the masses will emerge from it stronger than ever'. He then recalled that in mattcrs as agrarian reform or religion as well the P.K.I. pursued a flexible line, holding out the party as a positive example compared to the hurred extremism of the shortlived communist government of the Indian state of Kerala. See Pajetta, Rinascita, June 8, 1963.

    While lecturing in China in the summer of 1963 Aidit was to defend himself and his revisionist domestic policies by calling it a tactical device to be discarded, once in power, while the Yugoslavs, the real modern revisionists, having achieved state power, continued their 'soft-sell' and made accommodation an end in itself. See below p. 222. The P.K.I. leader had to be careful not to stress the tactical nature of his policies: when Aidit, in October 1964, made an unguarded remark about the temporary nature of the P.K.I.'s acceptance of the Indonesian state philosophy (including belief in God: the Pantasiljah), the cat was out of the bag and it took him a lot of effort to straighten things out again: see *Harian Rakjat*, October 29, 1964 and below pp. 301 ff.
37. Reviewing Aidit's policies and alignment with Indonesian nationalism, Alex Josey observed that 'only when it has been able to capture and exploit nationalism has communism succeeded in Asia': *Far Eastern Economic Review*, February 21, 1963.
38. Pajetta, in Rinascita, was also struck by the strong and ancient anti-Yugoslav tendencies in the P.K.I. and saw behind them a basic and original need for a great clarity and simplicity, for 'thundering denunciations' of the West and its agents, including the Yugoslavs, and all-out admiration for China and the Soviet Union. Hutapea, the director of the Aliarcham Academy of the P.K.I. and one of the radical elements in the party, traced the P.K.I.'s opposition to modern revisionism back to the experience Lenin had in 1902 with 'the rightest-oppurtunistic views of Martov', a typical explanation that fits the writer's analysis. See *Harian Rakjat*, April 22, 1963.
39. See above p. 177.
40. After some initial confusion Kruschov had it his way and succeeded in having Yugoslavia included in the official May Day greetings as 'the Socialist Federal Republic who are *building socialism*' [emphasis added]. This was published on the front page of Pravda on April 11, 1963 as a correction, because earlier

the May Day slogans for that year had only mentioned Yugoslavia as a 'Federal People's Republic' as if still not belonging to the select club of socialist states.

41. *Harian Rakjat*, April 2, 1963 and *New China News Agency*, April 4, 1963. The lengthy article *Hung Qui* dedicated on May 20, 1963 to the P.K.I. also referred to this statement of Njoto who was the only P.K.I. leader beside Aidit to be mentioned in that piece.
42. On March 19 Aidit wrote identical letters to the two party headquarters, expressing emphatic approval of these talks which the P.K.I. 'right from the beginning' already had suggested: *Harian Rakjat*, March 21, 1963. Njoto, however, was especially satisfied with 'the exchange of letters' (*Harian Rakjat*, April 10, 1963), no doubt meaning the Chinese part of it, which formally accepted the Soviet proposal for a bilateral meeting, but 'in fact was a highly polemical document, harsh, unyielding and blandly sarcastic'; William E. Griffith, 1964, *The Sino-Soviet Rift*, George Allen and Unwin, London, p. 115.
43. In an interview with the Djakarta correspondent for Associated Press (*Harian Rakjat*, May 9, 1963) and in his P.K.I. address (*Harian Rakjat*, May 26, 1963).
44. *Harian Rakjat*, April 1, 1963. Chinese Ambassador Yao Ching-ming had gone personally to the P.K.I. headquarters to hand Aidit the invitation in a get-together described later as 'cordial'. Moscow seems to have followed a more formal procedure.
45. *Harian Rakjat*, May 9, 1963 and July 18, 1963.
46. *Harian Rakjat*, October 28, 1963.
47. On Lenin's anniversary, for example, Aidit was to state in a general way that 'to belittle the anti-colonial struggle would weaken the new emerging forces'. This was a hotly debated issue in the Sino-Soviet dialogue, but Aidit kept it as unpolemical as possible; *Harian Rakjat*, April 22, 1963. Also, when speaking on Cuba, Aidit equally refrained from giving any particular anti-Soviet criticism. *Harian Rakjat*, April 29, 1963.
48. *Harian Rakjat*, April 27, 1963.
49. *Harian Rakjat*, May 1st, 1963.
50. After the February plenary the Politburo consisted of seven full and voting members: Aidit, Lukman, Njoto, Sudisman, Sakirman and the newly-elected Adjitorop and Njono. Lukman, the faithful shadow of Aidit, had read greetings of the P.K.I. Central Committee to the National Conference of the pro-Chinese New Zealand C.P. on April 13, 1963, and, in connection with the coming transfer of West Irian, made grateful reference to the 'armed assistance, including the most modern weapons received by Indonesia from the Soviet Union and other socialist nations'; *Harian Rakjat*, April 18, 1963. Lukman, Sakirman and Adjitorop possibly may have supported Aidit on this issue, the others could probably be counted among the more radically inclined Politburo members.
51. *Antara News Agency*, April 9, 1963.

52. *Far Eastern Economic Review*, May 23, 1963. *New China News Agency* recorded with a certain malicious glee the second-class status of the Soviet journalists as observers; April 24, 1963.
54. *Djakarta Radio Home Service*, October 28, 1963.
54. In the 'open letter' the Soviet communists published on July 14, 1963, it is specially mentioned that 'at the Journalists' Conference in Djakarta the Chinese representatives took the line of preventing Soviet journalists from participating as full delegates on the plea that the Soviet Union . . . is not an Asian country!'; *Pravda*, July 14, 1963.
55. 'To brothers at home and comrades abroad, fighting against imperialism, etc.,' 1967, Document of the Marxist-Leninist Group of the Communist Party of Indonesia, *Information Bulletin*, Prague, no. 18, p. 52. It may be assumed that the views reflected in this document were at the same time those of the people who were closely towing the line then current in Moscow.
56. See above p. 190 note 99 and below p. 373 note 65.
57. *Harian Rakjat*, May 20, 1963. It was a necessary thing, Aidit wrote, in order to achieve 'the greatest internal and external force'. Lukman seconded him, saying that anyhow Sukarno 'without the people [read: the P.K.I.] would be nothing'; *Harian Rakjat*, May, 21, 1963.
58. On May 7 *Harian Rakjat* deleted from a recent Njoto speech the sentence: 'It sometimes happens that a favorable international situation fails to be utilized by the revolutionary movement of a given country owing either to the balance of forces inside the country not permitting such utilization, or owing to subjective errors'. This indirect criticism of Aidit's cautious balancing act – 'subjective errors' – in a favorable international climate could be found, however, in the Chinese version of what Njoto had said; *New China News Agency*, May 10, 1963. Some days later, in Solo, Njoto denied that 'peaceful coexistence' between colonizers and the colonized was possible, a phrase from the Chinese arsenal that was kept out of the *Harian Rakjat* text (May 18, 1963), but faitfully reported by *New China News Agency*, (May 23, 1963).
59. Aidit on May 26, 1963, at a P.K.I. mass rally; *Harian Rakjat*, May 27, 1963.
60. *Harian Rakjat*, July 3, 1963.
61. Aidit reacted to a news report from A.P. in Australia that quoted a statement by Antara director and previously *Harian Rakjat* editor Supono; *Antara News Agency*, July 18, 1963.
62. *Harian Rakjat*, July 20, 1963. Aidit left on July 19, having been offered the night before a banquet in his honor by the always-considerate Chinese ambassador Yao Ching-ming.
63. *Jen-min Jih-pao*, July 15, 1963.
64. *Pravda*, July 14, 1963.
65. The official communiqué said only that the discussions would be resumed at a later stage, but no date was set, so in fact it meant that they were broken off; *Pravda*, July 20, 1963.
66. Another sign that, even before his departure for Moscow, Aidit had growing

doubts about the use he and the P.K.I. could derive from the Soviet Union was the – still veiled – criticism of support for a well equipped Indonesian Army, and his eulogy of a popular mass army capable of fighting a 'people's war'. This sophisticated arms support could have come from nowhere other than from the Soviet comrades, though at this stage Aidit brought in only the Yugoslavs as alleged perpetrators. See Aidit's address to the Navy Command and Staff School on July 16, 1963; *Harian Rakjat*, July 18 and 19, 1963.

CHAPTER 16

Visit to China (1963)

As Aidit met his Soviet friends in mid-July, the auspices were not very favorable. He was accompanied by hardliner Sudisman who was clearly sent along to form a 'balanced' P.K.I. team. They had two longer meetings with Presidium member Suslov and party secretary Ponomarev.[1] There was a banquet at which Kruschov was also present, but it seems that the First Secretary did not take part in the official talks.[2] The P.K.I. delegation left soon after for a week's visit to Cuba to be present at the commemoration of the Moncada rebellion on July 26, a good occasion to glorify the Cuban revolution as 'the third peak', after the two previous ones in Russia in 1917 and in China in 1949. Aidit lauded Cuba as the 'Yenan' of Latin-America, a reference to the sanctuary Mao used for years before finally setting out to rout Chiang Kai-shek's forces.[3] Until the end of August Aidit spent the time in the Soviet Union with no clearly defined activities. Perhaps he and his delegation took time off for vacationing since in one of the scarce reports of his moves it was reported that he gave a dinner party at the Black Sea at Gagra.[4] The P.K.I. Chairman was also shown what modern war amounted to – during manoevers of the Red Army – perhaps a hint by the Kremlin not to underrate the consequences of a world conflagration that could result from rash armed action in 'solving' third world problems.[5] Upon his return to Moscow, a last 'exchange of opinion' took place, this time with Presidium members Brezhnev and Podgorny.[6] No further comment or report appeared in the Soviet Press, neither did the visit result in any joint statement. It may be safely assumed therefore that on essential issues as well as procedural matters the two parties no longer found much in common worth publishing. According to Sudisman, who must have been present at all the talks,

Aidit told the Soviet leaders that they should 'stop pampering Tito', put less emphasis on 'economic-construction' and more on the importance of the national liberation movement, and take the lead in an anti-United States coalition.[7]

Compared with the rather obscure neglect in the Soviet Union, the reception the delegation got in China was the complete opposite. Arriving in Peking Aidit and his party got the well-known 'rousing welcome' of the Chinese masses so easily available to the régime when required.[8]

Two days later the second volume of Aidit's selected works appeared on bookstalls throughout the country. Then a busy schedule of lectures and mass rallies began, giving the P.K.I. Chairman tremendous exposure. He was received by Mao Tse-tung himself, and as first foreign 'scholar' Aidit was made member of the Academica Sinaica.[9] He made trips through the country accompanied by leading officials like Premier Chou En-lai and Politburo member Chu Teh and Army Chief Lo Jui Ching, getting the red carpet treatment such as no other non-ruling communist leader had ever had. It showed the importance China attached to Aidit and his million-strong home force, which Peking clearly saw in relation to Indonesia as both a bridge and a wedge.

In this light it is interesting to see how Aidit behaved while fêted in an unprecedented manner. If there is anything that stands out in a detailed analysis of the major speeches he made during his stay in China, it is his ability to remain level-headed and not for a moment to lose sight of his position as a major contender for power in Indonesia and an independent agent within the communist world movement.[10] In his first major speech, to the Higher Party School in Peking, Aidit dwelt mainly on the situation within the international communist movement. He stressed again that the P.K.I. was not 'neutral', but independent, with the result that the party had kept 'the friendship of the fraternal parties'.[11] Aidit claimed that the Sino-Soviet rift had not caused any harm to the Indonesian communists, but – as he added at the Peking mass rally two days later – it would of course have been better if no rift existed.[12] Aidit also said, however, that if a problem were not handled properly by one of the major communist parties, the 'anti-imperialist allies' of the communists elsewhere would lose their confidence in them. This had probably to do with the Cuban crisis, and the uneasiness in Indonesia among the nationalists and the armed forces, who saw their precious Soviet weaponry one day disappearing just like the Cuban missiles. Pajetta mentioned in this connection that the P.K.I. had decided after the Cuba crisis to set up a 'clarification' campaign for its cadres.[13]

The question of party unity came up several times and on one occasion – in Pyong Yang – the P.K.I. leader complained that this unity was so much more difficult to retain in a non-socialist country like Indonesia than in a communist one, where the press was not under the influence of 'bourgeois ideas'.[14] The best contribution to the international communist movement, Aidit stated at the end of his stay in Canton, would be for the P.K.I. to lead the Indonesian people to victory in the Indonesian revolution.[15] For that, again, the P.K.I. had to be fully independent and should not take the easy road of the 'modern dogmatics' who were docile followers of this or that party.[16]

Aidit had thrown in some obviously 'Chinese' elements during the various discourses. At the Peking mass rally he repeated what he had said on earlier occasions in Indonesia: That armed struggle was the most important form of struggle, and that only under the leadership of the proletariat, i.e. the communist party, could the first or national-democratic phase of the revolution be fully won. In Canton he elaborated on this question of who should lead this part of the revolution by using Mao's description – a 'bourgeois-democratic revolution of a new type' – saying that the national bourgeoisie was unable to lead it.[17] He also came up with sympathy for the idea that the communist parties should have their roots in the peasantry who in any case should play a more important role.[18] Finally he paid tribute to Lenin, but especially to Liu Shao-chi and Mao for their ideas on how to create a mass party.[19]

The main thrust of his arguments was, however, of a defensive character, an elaborate justification of his accommodating domestic policy towards Sukarno. In his speech to the 10,000 party cadres in Peking especially he explained that the Indonesian President was important because he could help to overcome the 'phobia', as the fear of the P.K.I. was currently phrased in the Sukarno-style jargon. Pantjasilah and its belief in God was 'sincerely' supported by the P.K.I., and not a bad word should be said about basic scriptures like Manipol and Dekon. Answering unnamed, and no doubt Chinese, critics, he denied that these documents were 'bourgeois smokescreens'. The P.K.I. accepted them, he said, because they would reinforce the 'pro-people' aspect of Indonesian politics.[20]

He also brought up the question of 'structural reform', a concept dear to the Italian communists and Togliatti in particular. It had been dealt with by the Chinese ideologists in the *Jen-min Jih-pao* editorial in December 31, 1962: 'The differences between comrade Togliatti and us', where it was concluded that, what the Italian Communist Party was after in Italy was 'social democracy', something far remote from 'Marxism-Leninism'. Aidit argued that what he and the P.K.I. were striving for at the moment (a national front together with the nationalist and religious parties, support for Sukarno and his wordy mishmash sold as 'Indonesian socialism', a gradual approach in agrarian matters, etc.) had nothing to do with this revisionist 'structural reform' of the Italians. The P.K.I. was only in favor of (nice distinction) 'reformative measures', to be judged not by their actual content but by the 'strategic aims' behind them. In surprisingly plain words Aidit told his Chinese audience what the P.K.I. was aiming at: 'The essence of the question is one of seizing the leadership of the state and of the revolution, and not a matter of "structural reform" '.[21] A major step in that direction, he said, had been his proposal, endorsed by the February Central Committee plenary session, to form 'a people's democratic government... the establishment of a Nasakom Cabinet of mutual assistance and cooperation which will courageously change the social system in the country. Accordingly, the current demand for formation of a Nasakom Cabinet is an important event in the struggle aimed at reaching the strategic goal. In this respect the P.K.I. members consider that the formation of a Nasakom Cabinet is a question of *comparative strength* [emphasis added]'.[22] This is plain spoken and it is only surprising when a body of opinion persistently seems to believe and to make others believe that Aidit and his men were basically cooperative nationalists, be it of an extremist variety, who could not plot an ordinary putsch and would unfailingly play the game.[23] To slowly change the balance of forces by all available means, so long as one looked like winning, that was the P.K.I. message Aidit passed on to the Chinese comrades more clearly than he did or could do to the folks at home. But this was not necessarily what the Chinese communists according to their declaratory stand within the Sino-Soviet debate could applaud. Where Aidit really may have been in accord with his Chinese hosts was in his defense against being called a 'nationalist'. The P.K.I. Chairman several times repeated the standard formula that one had to follow Marxist-Leninist principles but apply them to the concrete situation, for instance in Indonesia. This 'Indonesianization' of Marxism-Leninism could only make an even greater success of the Indonesian revolution and, therefore, be helpful to world revolution, Aidit explained in Canton, but it had nothing to do with 'nationalism'.[24] In a rather contradictory fashion he then plunged headlong into a curious accolade of nationalism, especially of the Afro-Asian variety. 'To me', he said, 'the nationalists who oppose imperialism are far better than those dogmatists and revisionists who embrace the imperialists so affectionately'.[25]

This was most illustrative of the common ground with the Chinese that Aidit had now found, or dared to express: A preference for regional interest at the expense of ideological considerations. In his February report to the Party Central Committee he had still asserted that 'the worst people or communist party is still better than a bourgeois individual or party, as long as they [the progressives and the communists] are fighting imperialism'.[26] The accent had now been shifted to a new dividing line which Aidit rationalized further in his speech to the Canton Party School: 'A comparison might well be made between the past and present actions of the nationalists in Asia, Africa and Latin America, who oppose imperialism, while the revisionists help to doll up imperialism and prolong its life'.[27] Aidit did not yet feel free to be more specific and include direct negative references to Moscow, though on another occasion, in Pyong Yang, he did in more detail reproach the Yugoslavs in a way that was equally applicable to the Soviet Union: Objections to exclusive Afro-Asian collaboration, opposition to the Malaysia confrontation, and (as on the eve of Aidit's departure from Djakarta) 'intervention' in Indonesia's internal affairs with regard to the formation of a Nasakom Cabinet.[28]

At the end of his trip Aidit therefore came home one step further away from Moscow and more critical of its leaders. But in his own mind this did not necessarily mean he was implicitly nearer to Peking than before. To be sure, in his gradualist internal policy he had not made concessions, but he must have become acutely aware, as pointed out earlier, that the freedom to maneuver (both domestically and within world communism) had been for the P.K.I. diminished by the course of events.[29] He tried to make the best of this development and outwardly undaunted by his setback as a mediator, asserted upon arrival in Djakarta that the P.K.I. should play a big role in what he called the process of 'crystallization and consolidation' of the international communist movement.[30] Somewhat impressed, perhaps, by his latest experiences in China, he also spoke of the 'momentous choice' the communist parties in the world were facing. This initial reaction did not recur, however, and was ceratinly absent in the more thought-out report Aidit gave on September 30.[31] In fact, if he had created the impression that it was now a matter of being for or against one of the two leading communist parties, he did everything he could to erase it. He told the party that it should not accept any kind of 'baton'.[32] Faith in its own power – the 'Banteng spirit' – should be its main guiding line. Projected onto the international scene this induced Aidit to laud not so much China alone, but also North Korea,[33] which was held out as an example to the P.K.I. It had 'better solutions than anywhere else in the socialist camp' the P.K.I. leader (rather sweepingly) told his audience.

As was already to be gathered from the tenor of his speeches in China, within the concept of 'independence and equality' that Aidit kept claiming for each communist party and, *a fortiori*, for the P.K.I., a great similarity in interest and purpose between Peking and the P.K.I. had been developed. This found expression in the view that Southeast Asia had now become one of the main 'areas of differences' in the world, whereas the Chinese had been referring to it as a 'storm center'.[34] Aidit also took over the distinction between four types of contradictions the Peking ideologists had developed in their 'counter-program', the June 14, 1963, letter to Moscow[35] and the priorities indicated there. The contradictions between the communist countries and the western democracies, as well as between 'the oppressed nations' and their 'oppressors', were both considered 'basic' by Aidit, but still at par.[36] The struggle for power by communist parties within the western democracies – the third difference – was already more or less out of sight as far as the P.K.I. – and Peking for that matter – was concerned, earning them the reproach of neglect for the role of communist parties of the Italian or French variety.[37] Aidit made a contribution of his own by coming up with a subdivision of world communism into four different types.[38] Roughly the four were: Parties like the P.K.I.

that were 'thorough-going' Marxist-Leninist; parties whose leadership deviated towards revisionism but had an internal opposition; parties that were completely controlled by revisionists, resulting in 'Marxist-Leninist circles' outside them; and parties that had split and produced two distinct organizational centers. The attitude of the P.K.I. towards these various parties, Aidit proposed, would in fact give the Indonesian communists full freedom (quite contrary to Lenin's organizational teachings that only one communist party could exist in one country). The P.K.I. could contribute to further factionalism as Aidit strongly suggested in the case of Dange's Indian Communist Party, or they could recognize a new communist party as the only genuine one. But it was not even excluded to have relations with both old and new.[39] This, to Aidit, was the true sign of the P.K.I.'s 'objectivity', which it was necessary to formulate at that time because, he added cryptically, 'tomorrow or in the near future, we may discover the emergence of an old party and a new party, and who can say whether this will occur in some foreign country, or in our very own'.

At the time when Aidit returned to Indonesia, the domestic scene (as we saw earlier) had just shifted further towards radicalization.[40] The formation of Malaysia in mid-September had taken Sukarno's confrontation policy into a new stage of tension and turmoil. The P.K.I. Chairman (after a long silence on the subject) had thrown himself into the fray again before arriving in Djakarta. He told journalists during a stopover in Hongkong that Indonesia would fight against Malaysia 'to the last man'.[41] He was to find signs that, during his absence of more than two months, tendencies already noticeable when he left had become more marked.

Within the P.K.I. this had, for example, induced Lukman, who had been in charge as First Deputy Chairman until he himself left for China early in September, to recognize that the P.K.I. should accept less outside communist support in its struggle for power than previously.[42] Njoto, in the same period, once more very prominent as P.K.I. spokesman, had likewise moved over further to the left and kept on trying to push Sukarno. A few days after Sukarno's usual Independence Day speech, therefore, Njoto gave a very 'Chinese' talk in Bali.[43] In it he also praised the Indonesian President for a few things he had said: His attack on the existence of foreign bases and his denial that peaceful co-existence would do work between colonizers and colonized. It was probably exactly these points that he himself had suggested to Sukarno while he was preparing his 17th of August speech.[44] But Njoto also made a strong plea against 'structural reform' and spoke in favor of 'structural revolution' as a solution for Asian backwardness, dependence, and poverty. Though it was Nehru, in an article in the American quarterly *Foreign Affairs* of April, who was quoted by Njoto as being in favor of reform rather than revolution, the P.K.I. leader implicitly criticized the Indonesian President who (notwithstanding his rhetoric) was of course in the eyes of Njoto just as much a pseudo-revolutionary as the Indian Prime Minister. In the Indonesian Press, communist or otherwise, this passage in Njoto's talk was at any rate deleted, the only medium to mention it being the Chinese news agency.[45]

The Indonesian government had also shown during the summer (partly due to the rapid deterioration of the Malaysia situation) that it had become more inclined to shift away from policy views endorsed by Moscow and the moderate wing of Third World countries. An example here is the nuclear test-ban treaty, agreed upon in Moscow between the Soviet Union, the U.S., and Great Britain on July 20. Indonesian Foreign Minister Subandrio almost immediately commented upon it favorably as a good basis for world peace.[46] Communist opinion in Indonesia was first cautious; no prominent leader said anything about it until the end of August.[47] *Bintang Timur* was the first communist paper to react and followed partly the Chinese official reaction of July 31 but did not take over the 'big fraud' charge, speaking only of U.S. 'atomic blackmail' still being possible under the treaty.[48] *Harian Rakjat* condemned American underground atomic tests, conducted a week after the signing of the ban – although they were not forbidden – but for the rest had no clear line to follow.[49] On August 23 Indonesia acceded to the partial test-ban treaty, but a few days later under pressure of the Chinese government Subandrio and Sukarno – with the Malaysian confrontation about to require all the diplomatic support Indonesia could muster – lined up Djakarta also behind Peking's counter-proposal to convene a world conference on nuclear disarmament.[50]

In this autumn of 1963 the resultant of the forces exerting influence upon the P.K.I. – both within the country, as well as outside of it – was twofold: It tended to increase the cohesion of the party and especially of its leadership, and it brought the P.K.I. to dissociate itself more and more openly from Soviet communism.[51] Aidit and Lukman had become more convinced over the months passed that the party held the key to power in their own hands, while Njoto and Sudisman felt in their hard line vindicated by the disjointed political climate around Sukarno and Subandrio. It brought the P.K.I. Politburo to a new harmony, also shown in its resolution endorsing the results of Aidit's trip. In it the major points Aidit had tried to get across during his tour of communist capitals were restated neatly and without change in emphasis.[52]

The more open attacks on the Soviet Union that slowly could be discerned had to do with too little and too much that Moscow did: Too little aid, too much interference. The absence of Soviet economic aid was discussed, first by Sudisman and somewhat later by Aidit also. Sudisman in his account of the trip the P.K.I. delegation had made that summer indicated that the Soviet Union had the duty to give more economic assistance to Indonesia than it did.[53] Aidit repeated in the middle of November this opinion, also indicating that 'the socialist countries are duty-bound to render such assistance'.[54] It was, however, part of a major speech commemorating the 1926 rebellion and dedicated mainly to the theme of 'self-reliance'. While warning Moscow that it must help, Aidit told his followers that they should rely 'mainly' on their own efforts.[55] This apparent contradiction did not prevent Aidit from being, for him, rather caustic in his comment saying that 'a socialist country cannot be counted as one if it does not come to the aid of the struggle for independence'.[56] Answering skeptical foreign communist friends who asked what they would get in return for their assistance he recalled that those P.K.I. members executed because of their part in the 1926 rebellion had shouted before their death: 'Long live the Soviets, long live Lenin'. He then continued: 'This kind of assistance and moral support can not be measured in terms of monetary value'. And to make himself completely clear Aidit ended with saying: 'It was even on account of their great love and respect for the Soviet Union that communists at that time in 1926 made many mistakes, because at that time they even wanted to make a Soviet out of Surabaja'.

So – and this was the other point brought up against the Soviet Union – Aidit reproached Moscow, albeit in the past, for having had too much influence over the destiny of the P.K.I.[57] It was apparently a new line decided upon after Aidit's return from China because some days before the 1926 commemoration speech Njoto had also touched upon Soviet influence over the P.K.I. in the past. It had been a talk on the October Revolution, and in it Njoto came to speak on that other P.K.I.-inspired revolt, the Madiun affair of 1948. He gave as his opinion that the Soviet Union, although not involved in the rebellion itself, at that time had been directly influential in the party through the P.K.I. leader Muso.[58] This in itself was for those who knew the history of the P.K.I. nothing new, but it was not exactly 'done' in communist circles to divulge this type of information, and the particular occasion was even less appropriate, making it almost a deliberate affront.[59]

A month later, when the Indonesian government had come around to the conclusion that the country was in need of new economic measures to heed off the adverse affects of the Malaysia confrontation,[60] the P.K.I. was preparing for the second plenary session of the Central Committee that year. The main feature became Aidit's political report with the inspiring title 'Fire up the Spirit of the Banteng'.[61] The P.K.I. Central Committee got together at the end of December 1963 under conditions that according to its Chairman had never been so 'decisive' since the August 1945 revolution. This dictum may have sounded rather exaggerated at the time, but for once it may have been more true than realized then, at least if taken to refer to the P.K.I. itself rather than Indonesia as a whole. A number of priorities were reviewed, and, given all evidence, the P.K.I. switched into a higher gear as it were.

What Aidit had to say in his opening speech had to do with the various aspects of political and ideological problems already familiar especially from his 30 September speech upon return from abroad.[62] Two major changes stand out, neither of which came as a complete surprise. One was a decided shift towards the primacy of the struggle of Asian-African countries over the East-West confrontation in Europe. Aidit formulated this change in ideological terms, saying that of the two 'basic contradictions' of the era – between 'socialism' and 'imperialism' and between the 'oppressed nations' and 'imperialism' – the former was 'the most basic'.[63] It meant simply that the problems the Soviet Union had with the U.S. and Western Europe should be considered of less importance than the fight of young nations for political and economic independence in the rest of the world, or in other words: Charity begins at home, particularly then in Southeast

Asia. There, Aidit maintained, the revolution would break out earlier than in the developed world, and it was a 'Europe-centric' obsession to think otherwise.[64] Compared to what the P.K.I. leader had said barely three months before when he had still put the two types of 'revolutions' in the *same* category, this new formulation showed the Indonesian communists moving again closer to Peking's position.[65]

The second change tied in with this new preference for what in Soviet parlance already had been called the Afro-Asian 'specialized solidarity',[66] but it was more of a domestic nature. It was a new concentration upon the internal Indonesian scene where the victory should be fought and won. Aidit made official P.K.I. policy what Lukman already earlier had concluded in *Harian Rakjat*, that the balance of power at home should be the P.K.I.'s foremost concern.[67] In a slogan this was summarized as 'stand bravely upon your own two feet'.[68] The party should no longer be under the spell of the idea that full national independence – that is, power in the hands of the people and its instrument, the communist party – only could be reached through help of communist countries. 'This idea', Aidit said harshly, 'is being deliberately disseminated in order that the communists struggling for national independence would not dare to express opinions different from those of a certain socialist country, because that would lead to the denial of assistance to their own country'.[69]

There were more anti-Soviet implications in Aidit's report. He came back to the point that Moscow and the other communist states should help the 'revolutionary struggle' in the Afro-Asian countries, even 'without limit' he said. He also attacked the notion, dear to Kruschov, that the Soviet Union should be working to realize a 'communist society' because this would detract funds and attention from defeating imperialism 'with maximum force'.[70] Aidit further warned that in *all* socialist countries – thus not only in Yugoslavia, as was generally agreed among the 81 parties in the 1960 Moscow Declaration, but also in the Soviet Union – capitalism could rear its ugly head again. Finally, the world would be better off without a partial test-ban because it had failed to distinguish between nuclear weapons in the hands of communist countries and of capitalist countries, causing so 'a great setback'.[71] Against well-known points of criticism – that the P.K.I. was nationalistic, that it followed a schizophrenic policy, hard outside and soft inside the country, etc. – the P.K.I. leader gave answers similar as before, but more frank or irreverent.[72] There was also an increase in emphasis on the peasant question, leading Aidit now to rediscover that the Indonesian revolution actually was and always had been a peasant revolution, a thing that should be remembered 'a hundred times'. And towards the Indian Communist Party there was some escalation that drew angry reactions from the comrades in New Delhi, at least from those who were not the 'true communists of India' to which the P.K.I. Central Committee paid its respect in one of its 30-odd resolutions.[73] The overall impression was that the P.K.I. had turned a new page, and especially that Aidit whose previous restraint had kept the P.K.I. rather aloof in the Sino-Soviet conflict and gradualist in its domestic approach had swung his weight behind the reappraisal.

Interesting additional light is shed upon the proceedings of the second plenum by a confidential report of it.[74] It forms a logical complement to the published documents but is more direct in its formulation. As to the international position of the P.K.I. it is said that 'the P.K.I. is free to lead the Indonesian revolution on the basis of Marxism-Leninism, adapted to Indonesian circumstances. In the differences between the Communist Party of the Soviet Union and the Communist Party of China, the P.K.I. is on the side of the C.P. of China. The Party obliges its cadres to study therefore the publications both of Moscow and of Peking'.[75]

In internal affairs the question of the formation of a national unity or Nasakom cabinet was discussed extensively. The party cadres were ordered to have on a mass scale petitions sent through the National Front to Sukarno demanding such a cabinet 'immediately'. More actions were foreseen in the near future because – as it said – 'while we corner the right-wing forces, we should speed up attacks upon them and from early 1964 on intensify them further'. On Nasakom as such the opinion was not very flattering – neither was it on its initiator Sukarno: 'Nasakom is only an illusion of an idealist. That we accept, but it does not mean that we have to give up the class struggle, but within the framework of our aims we must remain polite. Nasakom is the place to develop our aims. Without these aims acceptance of the Nasakom idea would be revisionism'.[76] It further was outlined that the establishment of a Nasakom cabinet was not 'a question of benevolence of Sukarno, but a question of upsetting the balance, from the bourgeois groups to the people'.[77]

The fear of a *coup d'état* by 'counterrevolutionary adventurists and soldiers of fortune', as it appeared in Aidit's political report of December 23, was according to the summary of the proceedings reflected more directly in the discussions of the Central Committee the next day. Stating that the P.K.I. was 'ready for the fight' the summary went on: 'The Nasution group hopes that the P.K.I. will begin, but in this question the P.K.I. will not oblige, because we do not want to be provoked as in the case of Madiun. Of course finally only two forces will remain, meeting each other in the arena, to wit: the P.K.I., and Nasution with the non-party intelligentsia who endanger us considerably. The middle group will certainly look for protection with those whom they consider strong'. Then follows a detailed indication of the position of the P.K.I. in various military districts. On the overall situation for the Indonesian communists within the armed forces it says: 'Understanding is increasing and eventually we will harvest a lot of sympathy amongst the "greenshirts" [the armed forces]; 30% of them belong to the P.K.I. already'.[78]

So at the end of 1963 the stage seems to have been set for the next act that would make what had been until then a play of uncertain character into a distinct tragedy. But if Aidit, the cautious 'organization man' of the P.K.I. had by this time given his sanction to let the party step up its offensive in the months to come, he must have decided so on the basis of the *domestic* scenery. It was as we saw the ambitious, irresponsible streak in Sukarno's political make-up that on issues like the Malaysia confrontation and the priority of activism over planning brought the Indonesian President and his immediate entourage on a parallel course with the P.K.I.[79] And in this new official environment of rather reckless escapism Aidit found it most effective to further the aims of the party with an appropriately aggressive policy of his own. This new mood of Aidit at the end of 1963 was reflected in some major 'doctrinal' changes[80] that were decided upon in late autumn of that year, or at least *long after* the party chairman returned from China. They were not arrived at on the spur of the momentary impact of his failure to mediate or to remain neutral between the two main communist protagonists or for purely ideological reasons, but because of domestic opportunity.[81] Or in his own words, the 'qualitative changes in policy' which Aidit saw and foresaw for the party were made possible by the 'internal factor', with the 'external factor', the international communist movement only in 'supplementary' capacity.[82]

NOTES

1. *New China News Agency*, July 20, 1963; *Moscow Radio Home Service*, July 22, 1963.
2. He may have had an excuse in the negotiations on a partial nuclear test ban with the U.S. and Great Britain that went on at the time in Moscow, or have found Aidit not of sufficient stature. On the other hand, while the Sino-Soviet talks had gone on earlier that month, Kruschov had also stayed out and had even gone to Kiev with some ostentation.
3. *Harian Rakjat*, August 5, 1963.
4. *Review of Indonesia*, September-October 1963, mentioning that Aidit had toasted the Soviet aid to Indonesia over the years.
5. *Pravda*, August 25, 1963, again with a favorable reference to Soviet military aid.
6. *Tass*, August 26, 1963.
7. *Harian Rakjat*, October 27, 1963. Speaking at a mass rally on the results of the delegation's trip, Sudisman actually said that Aidit had made these points to Kruschov which may be true, although there is no evidence that he met the Soviet leader except perhaps socially. In the second half of August, at any rate, Kruschov was taking a 'holiday' in Yugoslavia, which gave the reference to 'pampering Tito' added pungency.
8. *New China News Agency*, August 28, 1963.
9. *New China News Agency*, September 3, 1963 and September 5, 1963. Before speaking to the Higher Party School on September 2, Aidit was introduced by the Director, Lin Peng, who encouraged the audience 'to study the works of Aidit as they did Mao's'. This was clearly a bit too much and did not find its way into the rest of the Chinese press.
10. On September 2 Aidit delivered a speech to the Higher Party School in Peking (*New China News Agency*, September 2, 1963 and *Review of Indonesia* September-October 1963). Two days later he addressed 10,000 party cadres at a mass rally, also in the Chinese capital (*Peking Radio Home Service* and *New China News Agency*, September 4, 1963; *Review of Indonesia*, September-October 1963). He gave an acceptance speech before the Academica Sinaica, mainly reported in the Indonesian Communist press (*New China News Agency*, September 5, 1963; *Review of Indonesia*, September-October 1963). Finally he read a political report to the teachers and students of the Canton Party School (*New China News Agency*, September 25, 1963, *Harian Rakjat*, September 30, 1963).

    During his stay in China Aidit made a short excursion to North Korea and gave an address at a mass rally in the capital of Pyong Yang (*New China News Agency/Korean Central News Agency*, September 11, 1963, *Review of Indonesia*, September-October 1963).

11. The Indonesian version speaks here of the P.K.I. 'taking distance from other parties', as a result of its independent stand. Discrepancies between the Chinese and Indonesian versions frequently occurred, leaving the distinct impression that the Chinese were more reliable in their reporting. Of course they would commit the 'sin' of selective editing but not of changing the words themselves, while this could not be said of the Indonesian communist press.
12. In his Pyong Yang speech Aidit went one step further, saying that the P.K.I. had been 'reinforced' by the split.
13. Pajetta, *Rinascita*, June 8, 1963.
14. The interdependence between the development of the Sino-Soviet split and unity within the P.K.I. had emerged on many occasions in the months before Aidit's departure. Aidit had told the party Central Committee in February that 'now' there was no dissension in the Party, and Njoto on the same occasion had 'strongly agreed' with Aidit. At the end of May the Party Chairman ridiculed 'imperialist' rumors that the P.K.I. was torn between pro-Moscow and pro-Peking or pro-Sukarno and anti-Sukarno factions; *Harian Rakjat*, May 29, 1963.
15. *Harian Rakjat* spoke not of 'victory' but of the 'culmination' of the Indonesian Revolution, a word with a softer connotation probably but equally a barely disguised euphemism for a communist takeover.
16. This remark on the 'modern dogmatists' who followed other parties was generally used in an anti-Soviet context. Aidit, however, did not use it in any of his speeches in China, but in North Korea, and it could as well have been directed against Peking.
17. The experience of the Chinese communists with Chang Kai-shek had brought them to the doctrinal conviction that the communists, right from the beginning of the revolution, should take on the leadership because they had to cooperate with non- and potential anti-communist groups. Formally this was also the line of the P.K.I., but in fact they agreed with a secondary role; see above pp. 8, 21, 74.
18. This may have been a point Aidit genuinely became convinced of as a result of his talks with the Chinese; the theme was to recur more often upon his return, also probably because it fitted the changed Indonesian context.
19. This was in Pyong Yang, but was carried only by the Chinese and Korean news reports. *Harian Rakjat* had Aidit say at this point of his speech: 'Indonesian communists are determined to be an independent party'. This may have had more to do with Djakarta censorship than with the aversion of the three gentlemen referred to.
20. In his Peking rally speech Aidit made the distinction, as he had done earlier, between the 'pro-people's aspect' and the 'anti-people's aspect'. At the time it was hailed as a theoretical innovation of the first order, but later – after Aidit had met death at the hands of his opponents – it was held against him by those comrades who were able to save their skins and who suddenly discovered the shallow character of Aidit's analysis. See the P.K.I. statement of August 17, 1966 and below p. 425. It meant nothing more than that, in the

continuous fight for power, the P.K.I. should help its friends and make short shrift of its enemies, wherever possible.

21. *Peking Radio Home Service*, September 4, 1963.
22. According to *Peking Radio* Aidit had repeated this line on Nasakom, Pantjasilah and the distinction between 'structural reform' and 'reformative measures' in his Canton speech at the end of September. A comparison with what Aidit said at the beginning of his visit to China does not point up a marked shift in favor of Chinese positions. He was nice about the economic problems China had to face – and still faced – and, with a dig at the Russians, thought that 'only imperialists, reactionaries and revisionists are elated about the economic difficulties of China', probably bearing in mind sarcastic articles like the one earlier that month in *Pravda* under the heading: 'Lofty ideals, empty stomachs'. He also shed light upon the 1948 Madiun disaster in a way that must have sounded familiar to Chinese ears but rather unfamiliar to serious historians. Madiun had been a failure, Aidit maintained, because there was no united front, no peasants' participation and no exclusive leadership by the P.K.I. For home consumption he even had a warning to his left-wing and probably those in China most in sympathy with them: Giving his view on the first armed rebellion of the P.K.I., the one under the Dutch in 1926, Aidit (historically out of place, but politically quite fittingly) said that it had not been understood 'then' – meaning now – that 'sympathy, fast growth, prestige and spirit of the cadres' was not enough to wage a rebellion. 'Even left-wing slogans were then advanced' he added, as if shocked.
23. See the so-called Cornell report, 'confidential' version, pp. 123, 124.
24. In the Canton speech it was 'they' who accused the P.K.I. of nationalism. In previous speeches in Peking Aidit had mentioned similar charges of 'bourgeois nationalism' and 'chauvinism' leveled at the P.K.I. by revisionists and dogmatists that is, both left and right detractors. It may be assumed, however, that Aidit was in fact turning more against Yugoslav or Soviet than Chinese criticism. One of the indications to be cited for this view is to be found in the Moscow-oriented post-1965 evaluation of P.K.I. policies, where it is stated that 'the party should deepen knowledge of the universal teachings of Marxism-Leninism in conjunction with concrete revolutionary practices in Indonesia; *it should free itself from the wrong concept of the Indonesification of Marxism-Leninism*' [emphasis added]. Appeal of the Marxist-Leninist Group of the Communist Party of Indonesia, 1967, *Information Bulletin*, Prague, no. 18, p. 63.
25. *New China News Agency*, September 25, 1963. The *Harian Rakjat* version on September 30 is phrased more mildly: 'To me it is even better to see the nationalists opposing imperialism and colonialism than to see the dogmatists and revisionists *attempting* to do it and only embracing those *philosophies* instead' [italics added].
26. *Harian Rakjat*, February 11, 1963.
27. *New China News Agency*, September 25, 1963.
28. *New China News Agency*, September 12, 1963, *Harian Rakjat*, September 18,

1963.

29. See above pp. 212, 213.
30. *Harian Rakjat*, September 30, 1963, *New China News Agency*, October 3, 1963. Aidit came back on September 28 and gave an initial, rather impromptu, talk the next day. His major report on the world tour came on September 30 and was reported in the issues of *Harian Rakjat* of October 4 and 5.
31. Ruth McVey, Indonesian Communism and China. In Tang Tsou, Ed., 1968, *China in Crisis*, Vol. 2, University of Chicago Press, Chicago, Illinois, p. 376 writes that Aidit came home from his trip to Moscow and Peking 'in something of a fury', as he was 'thoroughly snubbed by the Soviets'. Apart from his first impromptu comment on arrival in Djakarta Aidit did not give the impression from his public stand after the trip that he had been moved by his experiences to take up more radical positions, than are described above.
32. The Chinese used to employ the term 'baton', big stick, to indicate unacceptable Soviet domination over other parties and countries. Aidit clearly had in mind here that a Moscow 'baton' was not to be exchanged for a Peking one. Put more subtly: Avoiding the impression that his triumphal visit to China implied leaning towards its viewpoints.
33. For another interpretation: see McVey, 1968, p. 376.
34. *Harian Rakjat*, October 4 and 5, 1963.
35. The CCP's proposal concerning the general line of the international communist movement, *Jen-min Jih-pao*, June 17, 1963. The four types of contradictions were between the socialist and the imperialist camp, between the proletariat and the bourgeoisie in the capitalist countries, between the oppressed nations and imperialism, and among imperialist countries and monopoly groups themselves.
36. 'To be sure, the importance and basic feature of the contradictions between socialism and imperialism cannot be denied. Neither can it be denied that this is a fundamental contradiction underlying the ripening and flowering revolutions in Asia, Africa and Latin America as representatives of the critical contradiction between the oppressed nations and the forces of imperialism and colonialism'; *Harian Rakjat*, October 4 and 5, 1963. This coordinate position of the two 'revolutions' was to disappear shortly in favor of priority for the latter; see below pp. 229, 230.
37. See Pajetta, *Rinascita*, June 8, 1963, and more generally *Kommunist*, (Moscow), 1963, no. 11, p. 33.
38. *Harian Rakjat*, October 4 and 5, 1963.
39. 'How does the P.K.I. view the situation in those countries where there are two communist parties, the old one and the new one? Our position is to cut off contact with the old communist party in a country *if* that party is *only* making limited or weak opposition to the imperialists.' [emphasis added]. *Harian Rakjat*, October 4 and 5, 1963.
40. See above pp. 179 ff.
41. *Indonesian Observer*, September 30, 1963.
42. In an article appearing in *Harian Rakjat* on September 11, probably written

after consultation with Aidit in China where he had been head of a parliamentary delegation to Peking since September 5, Lukman stressed that the balance of power *within* Indonesia was to the P.K.I. its primary concern in the struggle for 'victory' in the Indonesian Revolution, 'international solidarity' coming only on the second place. In other words: Let us first concentrate on our own problems and not rely on outsiders (the Soviet Union by tradition) to help us.

43. *Harian Rakjat*, August 23, 1963; *New China News Agency*, August, 25, 1963, *Review of Indonesia*, September-October 1963. Njoto had mentioned coolly that the Sino-Soviet talks were for the time being put off but he had been satisfied that 'less and less people' were talking then about imperialists launching world-destructive wars or about the excommunication of Communist parties, or 'en clair', that Moscow's ideas were losing support.
44. *Indonesian Observer*, August 9, 1963, noting that Njoto had been summoned to Sukarno.
45. See note 43, this page.
46. *Antara News Agency*, July 29, 1963. No mention of Subandrio's statement was found in the Chinese press.
47. The head of the P.K.I. parliamentary group Ngungtjik, not even too prominent, then only complained that it was not an all-comprehensive ban; *Harian Rakjat*, August 26, 1963, *Antara News Agency*, August 25, 1963.
48. *Bintang Timur*, August 3, 1963. *Harian Rakjat* in softer wording than *Bintang Timur* expressed 'doubts' as to the wisdom of the treaty (August 5, 1963), and demanded atomic weapons for the new emerging forces (August 10, 1963).
49. *Harian Rakjat*, August 15, 1963.
50. *Djakarta Radio Home Service*, August 27, 1963, reporting that Subandrio met the Chinese ambassador that day and that he declared afterwards Indonesia's adhesion to the Chinese idea of a nuclear disarmament conference. Sukarno followed the next day, at a mass rally in Central Java, where he said that support for both Moscow and Peking in nuclear matters was a concrete sign of Indonesia's independence; *Indonesian Observer*, August 29, 1963.
51. See also Hindley, Indonesian Communist Party and the conflict in the international communist movement, *China quarterly*, July-September 1964, p. 114.
52. These points were: A new sense for the position of the P.K.I. in Southeast Asia, complete Indonesianization of Marxism-Leninism, unity on the basis of the 1957 and 1960 documents of the international communist movement, conferences and consultations to bring about unity at some time, meanwhile freedom and equality for the party, self-reliance on the road to that 'greatest monument' the P.K.I.'s ultimate victory in Indonesia; *Harian Rakjat*, October 19, 1963.
53. 'The Soviet Union *has* long provided Indonesia with economic assistance. It is necessary that socialist countries provide this assistance to support the struggle of oppressed nations against the imperialists and colonialists. This

duty, the duty of opposing imperialism and colonialism, is also the duty of the international proletariat' [emphasis added]; *Harian Rakjat*, October 29, 1963. This paragraph came after a critical description of the experiences of the delegation in the Soviet Union. Sudisman had found capitalist elements in the socialist Soviet society (an underground clothing factory in Leningrad) and sharp differences between the village and the city (agriculture being unable to fulfil the needs of the city), both of course not new phenomena, but their being written about by an Indonesian communist was a novel feature.

54. *Harian Rakjat*, November 14, 1963, *New China News Agency*, November 24, 1963.
55. It was indeed a rather confused and contradictory issue. The ideological position of the Soviet Union was that full independence could much better be reached through economic assistance, and then of course coming from communist and not western countries. See *Krasnaia Zvezda*, August 18, 1963, for instance, 'selfsufficiency is unscientific'. See also the Soviet 'open letter' in July 14, 1963: 'Now that the liberated peoples have entered a new stage in their struggle, concentrating their efforts on the consolidation of their political gains and economic independence, do they not see that it would be immeasurably more difficult, if not altogether impossible, to carry out these tasks without the assistance of the socialist states?'. Whatever aid, mainly military, the Soviet Union might have given to Indonesia before, economic assistance was virtually absent in 1963.

    At the same time, while the Indonesian communists were hammering more and more on 'self-reliance' as the correct attitude, they began openly to chide the Soviet Union for not helping their country. Of course these are examples of the obfuscation that accompany ideological justifications.
56. This was the *New China News Agency* version. *Harian Rakjat* had Aidit say: 'We would not be deserving of the name of socialist state if we are not willing to give help and support in the struggle against imperialism'; see above p. 234, note 11.
57. Historically Aidit was not right in this case, as exactly it had been Stalin who had warned for a premature rebellion on Java, but was not listened to by the local P.K.I. leaders. See above p. 130.
58. *Harian Rakjat*, November 3, 1963: 'The Madiun provocation was not what the charges made by reactionaries generally would have it be. Brian Crozier (a decidedly non-communist author), for example, in his book *The Rebels – A Study of post-war insurrections* admits that this so-called "revolt" was not the wish of Muso, that Muso was "under coercion" at the time, and therefore that *Soviet influence in the incident* – if we wish to speak of Soviet influence – had nothing to do with its outbreak, but *was confined to the building of an anti-imperialist national united front*' [emphasis added].

    So Njoto was exonerating Muso (to a certain extent in accordance with the facts) in the Madiun affair but implying direct Soviet pressure as to the overall policy to be followed by the P.K.I. For Muso and the Madiun rebellion see above pp. 11, 12.

59. Njoto gave his address at the opening of the Indonesian-Soviet friendship week on November 1.
60. See above pp. 197, 198.
61. *Harian Rakjat*, January 1, 1964. Aidit opened the second plenum on December 23, 1963.
62. See above p. 225.
63. The pro-Soviet 1967 evaluation by the 'Marxist-Leninist group of the P.K.I.' notes that the P.K.I. had been in agreement with the 1960 Moscow Statement that 'the chief contradiction of our epoch is the contradiction between socialism and imperialism'. It then continues: 'However, the 2nd Plenary Meeting of the P.K.I. [of December 1963] had *drastically* changed the Party's stand on this score by declaring that the chief and decisive contradiction of our time is the contradiction between the national liberation movements in Asia, Africa and Latin America, on the one hand, and imperialism on the other' [emphasis added]. Of course this was considered putting the priorities wrongly: see particularly pp. 48, 49 of the *Information Bulletin*, Prague, 1967, no. 18 that carried the text of this 'appeal'.
64. Aidit called this 'a variation of the dogmatic concept [of] the opportunist parties of the 2nd International', so as to show how wrong the European Communists were; *Harian Rakjat*, January 1, 1964.
65. See above p. 225 on Aidit's 30 September speech; *Harian Rakjat*, October 4 and 5, 1963.
66. See G. Mirskiy, Socialism, Imperialism and Afro-Asian Solidarity, *Izvestia*, July 16, 1963.
67. See above p. 236, note 42 and *Harian Rakjat*, September 11, 1963. In his December report to the P.K.I. C.C. Aidit said: 'We should stress the point that it is the *internal* factor which leads to *qualitative changes* in policy, whereas the external factor of the role of the [international communist] movement is only *supplementary*' [emphasis added]; *New China News Agency*, December 31, 1963. See also below p. .
68. This also applied to the deteriorating economic conditions that should be solved without outside help, Soviet, American or otherwise. See final resolution on the 2nd plenum; *Harian Rakjat*, January 15, 1964.
69. This is the text in the *New China News Agency* version of December 31, 1963. The *Harian Rakjat* rendering is not so clearly formulated and probably corrupt; *Harian Rakjat*, January 1, 1964.
70. The pro-Soviet evaluation of the 'Marxist-Leninist Group of the P.K.I.' complained in 1967: 'The stand taken by the 7th Congress of the P.K.I. [in April 1962] on the successes of socialist construction, the acme of which is the construction of communism in the Soviet Union and which was hailed with applause by the entire gathering, was *later abruptly denounced* by the C.C. of the P.K.I. without any reason whatsoever' [emphasis added]. See above p. 164 note 14 and below pp. 430, 431.
71. Aidit also objected 'vehemently' that no discussion of the project had taken place within the international communist movement, overlooking the fact

that China had been told in advance (but of course opposed the idea).

72. In a long reasoning on the question whether giving Marxism-Leninism an Indonesian 'face' was in accordance with Lenin's teachings Aidit finished by saying that this also 'in practice has proved to be the most useful and advantageous situation for us'; *Harian Rakjat*, January 1, 1964.
73. The Plenum according to the resolution 'extends its highest respects to the true communists of India who are imprisoned by Nehru's government with the help of Dange and his group who claim to be the communist leaders of India but are actually the henchmen of Nehru, a bourgeois reactionary'. *Harian Rakjat*, January 17, 1964. Besides, the P.K.I. C.C. had declared that it would establish contacts with 'true Marxist-Leninists who have been compelled to create their own circle or party'. The Indian Communist Party Politburo on January 16, 1964 adopted a violently anti-P.K.I. resolution because of this encouraging of factionalism. The official Yugoslav paper *Borba* chided the P.K.I. that 'never a more shameful call upon communists in another country to create a new C.P. to oppose the existing one had been made'; *Borba*, January 17, 1964.
74. Internal summary of the C.C. session of December 24, 1963.
75. Internal summary of the C.C. session of December 24, 1963.
76. See above p. 223 on the 'strategic aims' of the P.K.I. as outlined by Aidit in Peking.
77. As to the timing of a decisive shift in favor of the P.K.I. and its accession to power the summary relates: 'Comrade Aidit has said that in 1970 Indonesia will be a socialist state'. See below p. 257 and p. 264 note 57.
78. Of course one can have doubts about the authenticity of the text of this summary, but the general picture given ties in with the problems and with the public approach Aidit and his men displayed towards them at the time of the 2nd plenum. As to details, e.g., in this case of the assumed subversion of the Indonesian armed forces, it is of interest to quote a paragraph from the post-1965 evaluation of pro-Soviet P.K.I. members (*Information Bulletin*, Prague, 1967, no. 18) where it says: '*We often said that at least 30 percent of the Armed Forces are the followers of the Hammer and Sickle*. However, we often also mistakenly forgot what measures of the 30% were loyal to the Party *and* to President Sukarno. One can say with certainly that when the Party and Bung Karno were united these 30% of the Armed Forces would pledge their hearts and souls to them. When, however, they had to choose between the Party and President Sukarno it is a good guess that the majority would demonstrate greater devotion to Sukarno; at best they would occupy an unstable position' [emphasis added]. See p. 58, 59 of the Bulletin.
79. See above pp. 174, 198.
80. See pp. 229 ff.
81. For a different view, see the study by Dr. G. J. Pauker: *The Rise and Fall of the C.P. of Indonesia*, 1969, Rand Corporation, Santa Monica, pp. 29 and 35.
82. See above p. 239, note 67 and the Aidit's December report to the P.K.I. plenum; *New China News Agency*, December 31, 1963.

1. Betjak-riders hailing the new era of 'guided democracy' (July 1959, p. 28).

2. Soviet leader Kruschov on Bali: 'Like a Dutchman' (February 1960, p. 78).

3. President Sukarno and friend: 'If you take money you will spend it; if you take wisdom it will stay with you' (February 1960, p. 64).

4. Chinese foreign minister Chen Yi came to patch up the quarrel: 'It was only a scratch on the skin' (March 1961, p. 98).

Redactie en administratie: N.Z. Voorburgwal 225, Amsterdam-C. Postbus 433. Telefoon 221244, voor Koerierstera uitsluitend 221212 (10 lijnen). Gemeente Giro X 5555. Postgiro 260728. Giro voor abonnementsgelden: Gem. Giro X 10.000. Postgiro 660.000. Bankiers: Amsterdamsche Bank N.V., Bijkantoor Damrak.

HET PA[R]

TWEEENTWINTIGSTE JAARGANG No. 5317

VRIJ, ONVERVEERD

Paroolcorrespondent Dake spreekt in Moskou met minister Soebandrio

INDONESIE WACHT OP OPHELDERING VAN NEDERLAND

Amerikaans plan als uitgangspunt

(Van onze correspondent, mr. A. C. A. Dake)

MOSKOU, dinsdag. — Het optimisme ten aanzien van hervat-[tin]g van het overleg tussen Nederland en Indonesië, waaraan [se]cretaris-generaal Oe Thant van de Verenigde Naties vorige week [ui]ting gaf, wordt in Indonesische kring niet gedeeld. Dit verklaarde [on]s de Indonesische minister van buitenlandse zaken, dr. Soeban[dr]io, in een exclusief vraaggesprek dat wij met hem hadden in de [am]btswoning van de Indonesische ambassadeur alhier, Adam Malik.

[I]ndonesië, aldus Soebandrio, stelt zich op het standpunt dat het [pla]n van de Amerikaan Bunker als uitgangspunt voor onderhandelingen met Nederland aanvaardbaar is. De houding van Nederland [is] volgens de Indonesische minister echter niet duidelijk. Nederland [wek]t volgens hem de indruk dat het geen vreedzame oplossing van [de] kwestie wenst.

Waarnemers menen:

MOSKOU VOELT NIETS VOOR CONFLICT

MOSKOU, dinsdag (ANP). — Het heeft de aandacht van waarnemers getrokken dat gisteren op een ontvangst door de Indonesische minister van buitenlandse zaken, Soebandrio, in het geheel niet rechtstreeks is gezinspeeld op de kwestie Nieuw-Guinea.

De Sowjetrussische vice-premier Kosygin maakte in een korte toespraak slechts gewag van de wenselijkheid „de huidige hangende problemen" snel tot een oplossing te brengen. Deze terughoudendheid vormt een duidelijke tegenstelling tot de opmerkingen van Sowjetrussische zijde tijdens vroegere bezoeken aan Moskou van generaal Nasoetion en president Soekarno. Wes-

SOEBANDRIO
...druk op Nederland...

Cyrano tòch op TV

(Van onze kunstredactie)

ROTTERDAM, dinsdag. — De reeds enige malen aangekondigde, maar ook weer afgezegde televisie-uitzending van de voorstelling door Rotterdams Toneel van Edmond Rostands heldenkomedie „Cyrano de Bergerac", mag nu toch in het komende seizoen worden verwacht.

5. During the height of the West Irian crisis Subandrio visited Moscow: 'Neatly fitted in the war of nerves' (May 1962, p. 141).

6. To enforce its claim Djakarta sent its troops to West Irian: 'Indonesians, mostly born in West Irian, infiltrating back' (January 1962, p. 145).

7. President and Mrs. Liu Shao-Chi being welcomed in Djakarta: 'A new boost to Sino-Indonesian relations' (April 1963, p. 177).

8. Anti-Chinese sentiment, condoned by the military, led to new waves of violence in West Java: 'The Chinese government protested only mildly' (April 1963, p. 265).

9. Well-organized rioting against British property marked a new phase in confrontation over Malaysia: 'Recriminations, military actions and political waste' (September 1963, p. 180).

10. Attorney General Robert Kennedy discussing a ceasefire for the Kalimantan 'war theater with President Sukarno. President Sukarno accepted Attorney General Robert Kennedy's proposal for a ceasefire at the Kalimantan 'front': Double talk to 'my very dear friend' (January 1964, p. 250).

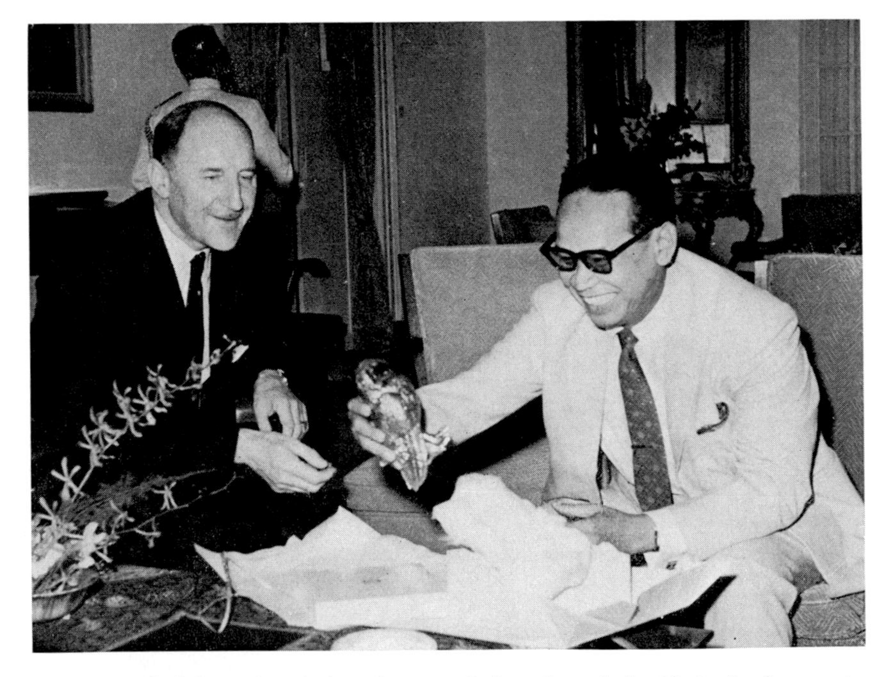

11. Restored diplomatic relations between Indonesia and the Netherlands meant Dutch Foreign Minister Luns was not empty-handed when he visited his colleague: West Irian 'as the cock crows' (July 1964, p. 148).

12. Subandrio went with a 42-man delegation to Peking: 'Secret deals and stimulating ideas' (January 1965, p. 333).

13. Trade Minister Adam Malik had to transfer his duties to Subandrio, with Second Deputy Premier Jo Leimena looking on: A desk to sit at so as 'not to let the P.K.I. get at you' (January 1965, p. 361).

14. Sukarno at the opening of the National Defense Institute, with (left) Nasution and (right) Yani: It was not true that 'the enemy came from the North' (May 1965, p. 364).

15. President Sukarno and P.K.I. Chairman Aidit during the 45th anniversary celebration of the party: 'If the P.K.I. were to die, it would be my loss as a brother' (May 1965, p. 374).

16. The Indonesian communists on the way to power demonstrating in the Soviet-financed Senajan Stadium in Djakarta: 'A remarkable sense of organization and showmanship' (May 1965, p. 319).

15

17. P.K.I. leader Aidit inspecting communist women volunteers on the eve of the Untung coup: 'Vigilance and arms' (September 1965, p. 331).

18. Major General Suharto, Commander of the Strategic Command, taking things in hand on the fateful October 1, 1965: 'Sukarno became very angry' (October 1965, p. 420).

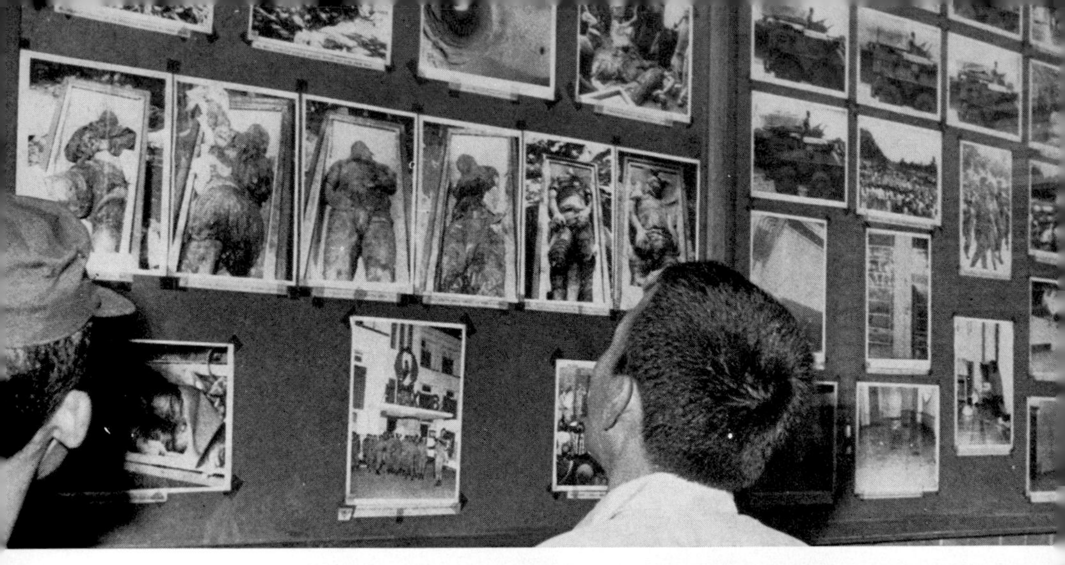

19

20

19. The bodies of the murdered officiers were found in Crocodile Hole: 'Why did Nasution escape' (October 1965, p. 412).
20. President Sukarno had to accept Major General Suharto as new commander of the army: 'Utterly stubborn' (October 1965, p. 414).
21. Changing of the guard. Suharto, the new army commander, with Subandrio, still Sukarno's deputy: Not exactly eye-to-eye (October 1965, p. 413).

22. Lieutenant General Ahmad Yani, commander of the Indonesian army at the time of the Untung coup: To Sukarno at long last it was 'a regrettable affair' (October 1965, p. 420).

23. It took Sukarno a year to come to the grave of Yani: From Crocodile Hole to crocodile flowers, (October 1966, p. 434).

22

21

23

24. The military tribunal that was to sentence exyDeputy Premier Subandrio: 'This image reminded me . . . of the kiss of death' (October 1966, p. 29).

25. Subandrio pleading for life: Leaving out the President's part and 'play the game' (October 1966, p. 443).

26. Lieutenant Colonel Untung of the Presidential Guards on trial as Sukarno's fall guy: 'Prepared to take action against the disloyal generals' (February 1966, p. 384).

27. Testimony by Sukarno's aide-de-camp Colonel Bambang Setjono Widjanarko on the conversion between the President and Lieutenant Colonel Untung: 'After the order a light stroke' (October 1970, p. 383).

----- Pada hari ini, hari RABU tanggal dua puluh delapan OKTOBER tahun tahun 1900 TUDJUH PULUH, kami : --

----- 1. S. SOEGIARJO - pangkat LETKOL CPM - NRP: 12688, ------------

----- 2. AZWIR NAWIE - pangkat ADJUN KOMISARIS BESAR POLISI,---------

djabatan : masing/masing adalah anggauta TEAM PEMERIKSAPUSAT,--------- telah mengadakan pemeriksaan landjutan terhadap seorang laki/laki jang bernama : ---

------------------------ BAMBANG SETIJONO WIDJANARKO ------------
KOLONEL KKO

----- Selandjutnja atas segala pertanjaan-pertanjaan jang diadjukan -- padanja, maka ia - jang diperiksa - memberikan keterangan2/pengakuan2 seperti tertera dibawah ini : ------------------------------------

PERTANJAAN : DJAWABAN :

56. Apakah sdr. mengetahui, kira2 antara tanggal 26 dan 27 september - 1965 UNTUNG adanja laporan kepada Bung KARNO jang mengatakan bahwa gerakan perwira2 madju sudah dapat dilakukan.-------------------------

56. a. Saja tidak tahu ataupun tidak dapat mengingat kembali bahwa bekas Letkol UNTUNG pernah menghadap Bung KARNO sekitar tanggal 26 dan 27 September 1965. Begitu pula saja tidaktahu bahwa UNTUNG telah melaporkan kepada Bung KARNO jang menjatakan bahwa gerakan perwira2 madju sudah dapat dilakukan.--

b. Bahwa saja benar2 tidak mengetahui soal ini tidak berartibahwa saja mengatakan "tidak mungkin". Kemungkinan UNTUNG melaporkan kepada Bung KARNO tersebut dapat sadja terdjadi sewaktu-waktu, baik di Bogor atau di Djakarta, karena sering kali Bung KARNO memanggil orang dengan mendadak, ataupun Bung KARNO mau menerima orang dengan mendadak tanpa -- harus melalui prosedure jang lazim berlaku.---------------

c. Jang tegas saja ketahui, UNTUNG pernah menghadap Bung KARNO pada tanggal 4 Agustus '65 dimana UNTUNG menjatakan kesediaannja untuk mengambil tindakan terhadap Djenderal2 -- AD jang dianggapnja tidak loyal, sesuai dengan keteranganjang pernah saja utarakan.-------------------------------
Djuga saja tahu dan ingat bahwa UNTUNG pernah menjampaikan surat pada Bung KARNO pada tanggal 30 September 1965 malam di Istora, jang djauh dikemudian hari baru saja ketahui -- bahwa isi surat tersebut berisi laporan tentang hari/tanggal permulaan gerakan.----------------------------------
Dari kedua fakta tersebut diatas memanglah wadjar bila sebelum 30 September 1965 itu/mungkin sekitar tgl. 26-27 September 1965, UNTUNG telah melaporkan pada Bung KARNO jangmenjatakan gerakan perwira madju sudah dapat dilakukan.---

57. Pada tanggal 30 September 1965, Djenderal SABUR tidak ada di Djakarta, melainkan ada di Bandung, harap sdr. terangkan:-----------

a. Disamping tentang UNTUNG jang menerima perintah dari Bung KARNO untuk menindak para Pati AD jang membangkang terhadap Bung KARNO, Djenderal SABUR pun diperintah untuk hal jang sama oleh --- Bung KARNO, apakah sebabnja Djenderal SABUR sendiri pada waktuitu tidak berada di Djakarta.-------------------------------

b. Apakah sebabnja UNTUNG jang melakukan gerakan/tindakan terhadap para Pati AD untuk melaksanakan perintah Bung KARNO itu ?------

57.a. Disamping UNTUNG, memang benar bahwa Djenderal SABUR telah diperintahkan oleh Bung KARNO untuk menindak Djenderal2 AD jang dianggap tidak loyal.---------------------

Bahkan dilihat

HARIAN RAKJAT

SABTU, 2 OKTOBER 1965

TAHUN KE XV No. 4

Letkol Untung, Komandan Bataljon „Tjakrabirawa" menjelamatkan Presiden

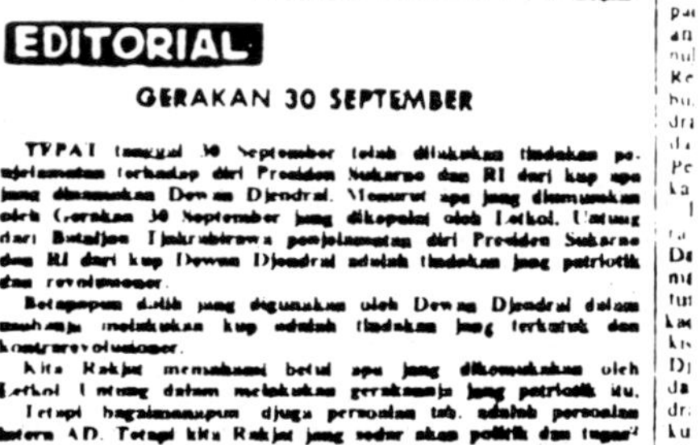

EDITORIAL

GERAKAN 30 SEPTEMBER

TEPAT tanggal 30 September telah dilakukan tindakan penjelamatan terhadap diri Presiden Sukarno dan RI dari kup apa jang dinamakan Dewan Djendral. Menurut apa jang diumumkan oleh Gerakan 30 September jang dikepalai oleh Letkol. Untung dari Bataljon Tjakrabirawa penjelamatan diri Presiden Sukarno dan RI dari kup Dewan Djendral adalah tindakan jang patriotik dan revolusioner.

Betapapun dalih jang digunakan oleh Dewan Djendral dalam usahanja melakukan kup adalah tindakan jang terkutuk dan kontrarevolusioner.

Kita Rakjat memahami betul apa jang dikemukakan oleh Letkol Untung dalam melakukan gerakannja jang patriotik itu.

Tetapi bagaimanapun djuga persoalan tsb. adalah persoalan intern AD. Tetapi kita Rakjat jang sadar akan politik dan tugas² revolusi mejakini akan benarnja tindakan jang dilakukan oleh Gerakan 30 September untuk menjelamatkan revolusi dan Rakjat.

Dukungan dan hati Rakjat sudah pasti dipihak Gerakan 30 September. Kita serukan kepada seluruh Rakjat untuk mempertadjam kewaspadaan dan siap menghadapi segala kemungkinan.

Kongres ke-III CGMI

Letkol. Untung Komandan Batalion „Tjakrabirawa" ... menjelamatkan Presiden dan RI dari kup Dewan Djendral

28. Issue of the P.K.I. daily Harian Rakjat of October 2, 1965: 'The support and the hearts of the people are certainly on the side of the 30 September movement' (October 1965, p. 415).

29. D. N. Aidit

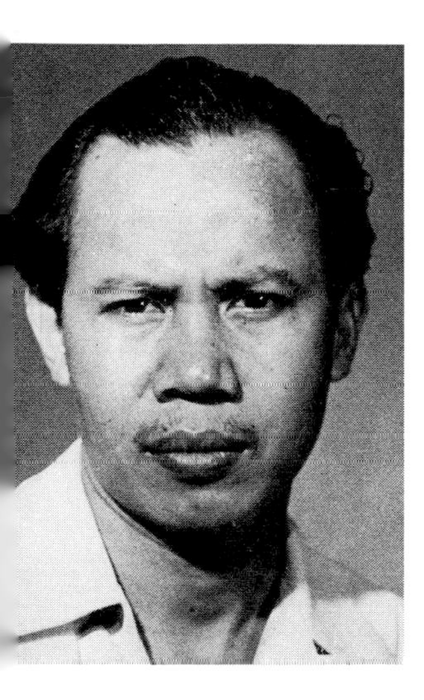

30. Lukman

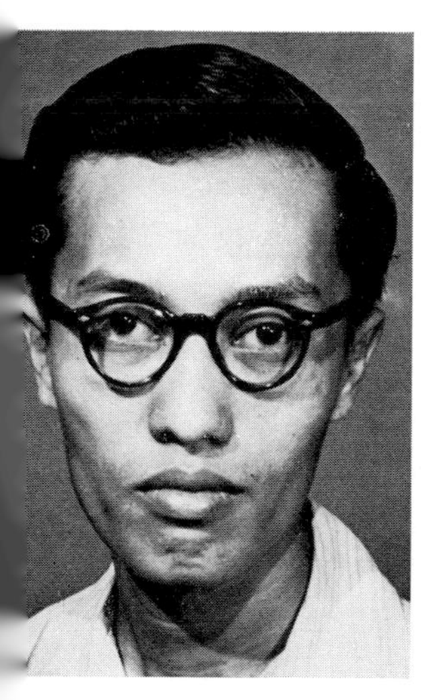

Njoto

32. Sakirman

33. Sudisman

34. General Abdul Haris Nasution with the author (March 1972).

35. Foreign Minister Adam Malik with the author (March 1972).

CHAPTER 17

Agitation among the farmers (1964)

In line with the shift towards more radical views that were endorsed by the December plenary session of the P.K.I. Central Committee, the Politburo set in motion its mass organization early in 1964.[1] The Communist Farmers' Union, the B.T.I., claiming a membership of over six million,[2] had a wide field of action for which Aidit had set the tone when addressing the Central Party School for peasant agitators immediately after the plenary session. He came up, as also before, with the 'Chinese' thesis that the 'villages' of the world – Asia, Africa, and Latin America – should be won over before the 'towns', the rest of the world, could fall. But this time he concluded that it was therefore time to practice these lofty tenets in Indonesia itself and 'win the revolution in the villages'.[3] He referred to difficulties being encountered by the farmers, who were waiting to get surplus land distributed to them on the basis of the Agrarian Law of 1960. The slow pace of execution of this law, designed to alleviate the plight of millions of landless Javanese peasants, had already been used in the course of 1963 to enlist support for P.K.I. policies. Now, however, this B.T.I.-organized needling of village authorities and higher officials had become a full-fledged P.K.I. campaign.

Indeed, there was enough fuel for making trouble in the countryside, as inflation was rampant and peasant conditions were worsening. The land distribution as ordered by the Basic Agrarian Law of 1960 should have been implemented, at least on Java and Madura, before the end of 1963, but it was far from realized. A P.K.I. expert complained during the December plenary that it would take another 30 years, if the prevailing tempo were continued.[4] In itself it was debatable whether the 1960 Agrarian Laws – on the distribution of land and on share cropping – would do much to relieve the pressure on the land and noticeably improve the lot of the peasants, as the government tried to pretend at the time of their enactment.[5] Of a total of about 42 million farmers on Java, statistically reduced to some six million families, more than 60% were landless according to the Minister of Agriculture in 1960.[6] Total surplus land on the basis of the law was estimated at one million hectares so that, at best, the average improvement would be marginal. But, to the P.K.I. leaders, the situation was first and foremost a political asset to be made use of.

In the course of its history the P.K.I. had displayed various attitudes towards the farmers. It began in the twenties, when an urban-oriented leadership, even contrary to Comintern instructions, neglected the peasants as a political force. The 1926 revolt, which anyhow had been a dismal failure, found scant support in the countryside. When the party again emerged after the Second World War, the P.K.I propagated a sharp antithesis between the small farmers on the one hand, and all the other peasant classes.[7] Confiscation of all but the smallest lots was demanded. With Muso's return from the Soviet Union and the adoption of the New Road resolution, a more sophisticated approach was initiated. Apart from the 'poor' peasants, the 'middle' peasants were also considered the victims of imperialism. But 'rich' peasants would not be antagonized, provided that they had not 'opposed the Revolution'.[8] Even for Dutch landowners who were not unsympathetic towards Indonesian independence friendly words could be found. This flexible policy was also adopted by Aidit, when he and his 'Leninist wing' took over in 1951. It became part and parcel of the new party line at the Fifth National Congress in 1954. From then on the appeal to the Indonesian farmers was sloganized as 'land to those who till the land', but in fact the tolerance towards others than the landless and poor farmers remained great. Even then Aidit was of the opinion that 'the essence of the People's Democratic Revolution in Indonesia is the agrarian revolution'.[9]

In the years to come Aidit was careful enough not to take himself too seriously and to overstep the boundary of the official government policy of the day, directed as this was exclusively against Dutch owned lands and plantations. The party also consented to the enactment of the agrarian laws of 1960 which presented a compromise formula between the already watered-down P.K.I. position and the interests of the landed gentry and religious organizations represented in the P.N.I. and the Muslim parties.[10] It has been remarked that 'the party's agrarian policy up to 1963 was in the first place designed to win political power and that a real attempt to ameliorate rural poverty had to await a possible P.K.I. seizure of power'.[11] The new element introduced by the P.K.I. at the beginning of 1964 was a more systematic pressure in the countryside on existing social relations with the ineffectual implementation of the 1960 agrarian laws as a wedge. The B.T.I. cadres began (as they had done more incidentally the year before) to incite the villagers to take the law into their own hands when local or regional authorities, landlords, or muslim priests were uncooperative.[12] The leadership of the P.K.I. provided the ideological coverage for these 'aksi sepihak', unilateral actions, by hook or by crook. Aidit produced the thesis that a proletarian basis for an effective revolution was not very necessary and that 'peasants-plus-Marxism-Leninism' would provide a mighty force.[13] B.T.I.-chairman Asmu 'loudly urged', as it was described, a mass meeting of farmers in Malang in mid-January to step up actions for execution of the agrarian laws, calling these actions 'patriotic and justified'.[14]

Part of the P.K.I. campaign telling the farmers how essential they were to the Indonesian revolution went on in the form of a widely-advertised 'survey' which Aidit conducted with an impressive team of 1,500 collaborators from early March until the end of May.[15] This 'research', as it was called, must indeed have given the party leadership an invaluable insight into the mystic, and less mystic, ways of the Javanese farmer and his village, where the laws of communal living worked out quite differently from what the westernized Djakarta-based communist leaders may have thought.[16]

To the government this purposeful agitation did not augur well, already under constant fire as they were because of widespread food shortages.[17] Even Sukarno, for the first time since long before, was attacked personally by the P.K.I. as being responsible for famine and mismanagement.[18] It was inevitable that some outburst of violence of more than an incidental nature would occur, as in fact happened in May around Klaten, one of the P.K.I. strongholds in Central Java. This local rebellion came in the wake of Aidit's rural survey and was interpreted as a 'pilot'-project for creating more widespread unrest, part of the P.K.I. policy of 'testing strength'.[19] Deputy-Premier Leimena,

Acting President during one of Sukarno's frequent foreign trips, condemned the Klaten rioting but was severely taken to task by the P.K.I. during the First National Conference the P.K.I. held at the beginning of July.[20] The domestic balance of forces had already shifted so far towards the P.K.I. that Sukarno disavowed Leimena not long afterwards in his 17th August speech, in which he explained that it was 'only logical' to side with the peasants as they were everywhere the 'pillars of the revolution'.[21] The Minister of Agriculture got orders to complete land distribution before the end of the year, and special land reform courts demanded by the P.K.I. had to be set up forthwith. In 'ordering' his solutions, Sukarno also declared in passing Indonesia should be self-supporting in food and, as he had forecast sometime earlier he would do, simply forebade any further imports of rice.[22]

The whole performance was of course for Aidit a most welcome sanction, and the P.K.I. leader did not waste time in pressing the advantage home, lauding Sukarno's speech to the sky and telling the party that the best way really to become self-supporting in the food sector was by fully carrying out the agrarian laws[23] or, in other words, continue with unilateral actions, using Sukarno as an alibi. Especially during the two months that Sukarno was again outside the country – attending the Cairo conference of non-aligned nations in early October, getting his health restored in Vienna, and ruining it again with his hectic life in the world's capitals – Aidit and his comrades in the field saw and used their opportunities to weaken the precarious hold of the President's stand-ins, by turns Subandrio, Leimena and Chaerul Saleh.[24] Unrest, riots, terror, and killing in the countryside were prominent in their arsenal, although not only the P.K.I. was at fault here, as religious organizations and P.N.I.-connected landed interests often resisted unilateral actions in kind.[25]

For the B.T.I. it was an atmosphere in which they began to see chances of pressing for more than an allegedly loyal, be it extralegal, implementation of Sukarno's agrarian laws. At the end of September 1964 the B.T.I. leaders declared that even these laws were not good enough and were not conducive to increasing food supplies – as indeed any economist could have told them – drawing from this the less generally shared conclusion that 'this [increase in food] will be accomplished by carrying out a *radical land reform* which will end the monopoly system and feudal exploitation by the landlords as well as carrying out fully the slogan "land for the peasants" ' [emphasis added].[26]

A much-publicized incident, the so-called Indramaju-affair, provided a rather comic note, in that a B.T.I.-led group of peasants disarmed a number of forest policemen – 'rats' in the parlance of the day – and sent them home after having deprived them of their clothes. In itself, however, it was serious enough, involving thousands of demonstrators, often recruited with promises of land and well-organized as a provocation of the authorities.[27] Subandrio had to handle the affair and called B.T.I. Second Chairman Sidik Kertapati to account, without much success.[28] Only a solemn truce forced upon the leaders of the ten political parties by Sukarno and embodied in what came to be called the Bogor Declaration of December 12, 1964, brought some respite. The P.K.I. may very well by that time have discovered that its support by the peasants had suffered from its aggressive actions and that not much was to be gained by unabated continuation.[29] However, a lot of bad blood had already been caused, and continuing tense relations in the villages all through the next year, especially in the Central and East Java countryside, must have contributed in no small way to the bloodbath following the abortive 30th September putsch.[30]

While the B.T.I. began early in 1964 with increased agitation among the peasants, Sobsi had its task among the laborers, especially the plantation workers. Action here was closely geared to the Malaysia issue that in the eyes of the party leadership was handled by the government too gingerly. It began with the take-over of 16 British-owned tea and coffee plantations on January 16. This particular moment was not chosen by accident, as it tied in with Sukarno's confrontation with Malaysia: This policy passed through one of its periodical 'soft' phases, if that is the way to describe a situation in which a country begins to make landings with armed personnel on the shores of another country (as Indonesia started doing that month against Malaysia) and shows at the same time willingness to talk about political solutions.

In any case, Sukarno was in Tokyo having discussions with President Johnson's emissary Robert Kennedy on the very next day, January 17, much to the dissatisfaction of the P.K.I. To show this unmistakably, Aidit released the text of a speech he was going to make on January 18 beforehand, so that *Harian Rakjat* carried it on the day

Sukarno met Kennedy. In that speech the P.K.I. chairman warned Sukarno (of course without mentioning names) that 'it is our duty to prevent all compromise efforts of *certain people* in dealing with Malaysia' [emphasis added].[31] He asked for 'swift and appropriate measures' to deal with the colonial British and had the red flag flown beside the national red-and-white on top of the Shell building in Djakarta.[32] His deputy, Lukman, added in a comment on the situation that the sooner the British firms were taken over the better because then a start could be made with the American ones.[33]

The situation was rather confused, at least in Djakarta, and Sukarno returning on the 20th from Tokyo thought it better not to have his plane land at Kemajoran Airport but on the military airfield of Halim nearby.[34] Under pressure from the military,[35] Sukarno then forbade the unauthorized takeovers and placed the British plantations under government control to ease the situation. These provisional measures, as the communists were hopefully terming them, were of course not to the liking of the P.K.I.[36]

Aidit called the actions against the British interests patriotic and was soon followed in this by the Central Committee of the P.N.I.[37] Subandrio, in a conversation with Sobsi-chief Njono, also felt compelled to pay lip service to the actions of the workers and thought them 'heroic', but warned the communist labor leader not to create contradictions between the government and his Sobsi men.[38] An artificial climate of constant agitation both in the countryside and in the urban areas marked this early phase of the communist offensive.

NOTES

1. See Aidit's speech to the Bachtaruddin Political Science Academy on July 28, *New China News Agency*, January 1, 1964.
2. Djakarta Home Service, September 1, 1964.
3. Aidit on December 29, 1963, before the Central Peasant Cooperative School; *New China News Agency*, January 1, 1964. See also: Lin Piao's famous 'Long live the victory of peoples war!' in *Jen-min Jih-pao*, September 2, 1965.
4. *Harian Rakjat*, January 13, 1964.
5. Van der Kroef, writing in the *Journal of Southeast Asian History*, vol. 4, no. 1 of March 1963, had doubts as to the effects of these laws. In principle the Basic Agrarian Law put minima – two hectare – and minima – varying according to type of land and area from five to 20 hectares per family.

6. See Dr. E. Utrecht, Land Reform in Indonesia, *Bulletin of Indonesian Economic Studies*, November 1969, p. 78.
7. *Bintang Merah*, November 17, 1945.
8. Van der Kroef, 1963, p. 49.
9. The Road to People's Democracy for Indonesia, General Report delivered at the fifth National Congress of the Communist Party of Indonesia, Djakarta, 1965, p. 27.
10. See Utrecht in Land Reform in Indonesia, p. 72. This compromise on agrarian legislation was described by the Minister of Agriculture Sadjarwo as 'a radically revolutionary system ending the landlord system and (entailing) a subsequent distribution of land among the landless peasants, as has been done not only in Russia and the Chinese People's Republic but also in non-communist countries . . . but the plan will be carried out gradually, stage by stage . . . in the first stage we will determine a maximum and a minimum for real property'. (Cited by Utrecht).
11. Van der Kroef, 1963, p. 67.
12. *Harian Rakjat*, January 1, 1964, suggested to its readers that these so-called 'unilateral actions' had begun already in mid-1963.
13. *Harian Rakjat*, January 3rd, 1964. This was to earn him after his death a rebuke from the survivors of the 1965 disaster that befell the P.K.I., who writing in the Indian pro-Soviet journal Mainstream complained: 'In the past the Party had not paid adequate attention to measures aimed at increasing the role of proletarian elements in it or improving its ideological and cultural level. In the recent past the Party tended to ascribe too much significance to the revolutionary spirit of the peasantry.' *Mainstream* (India), March 18, 1967.
14. *Harian Rakjat*, January 25, 1964.
15. *New China News Agency*, June 5, 1964.
16. Aidit in his commemoration speech on the 44th anniversary of the P.K.I. in Surabaya on May 23, 1964 chided 'some comrades' who having become village head were not behaving any better than their despised 'feudal' predecessors; *Review of Indonesia*, May-June 1964.
17. Food export was forbidden from March 10, 1964, on; *Djakarta Radio Home Service*, March 16, 1964. Subandrio told the Indonesian housewives to eat corn instead of rice; *Manilla Radio*, March 9, 1964. President Sukarno had one of his more and more frequent outbursts, this time against foreign photographers looking for hunger pictures; *Indonesian Observer*, March 12, 1964.
18. *Harian Rakjat*, February 2, 1964. See also below pp. 251, 254.
19. Indonesian's peasants and the P.K.I., *Asian Analyst*, August 1965, p. 7.
20. The P.K.I., using one of Sukarno's phrases, called the Klaten incident an example of 'revolutionary gymnastics' and rejected Leimena's charge that this was anarchy as 'shameful propaganda', *Harian Rakjat*, July 16, 1964.
21. This was the speech with the ominous title 'The year of living dangerously' or Tavip for short, a signal monument of the unbalanced rhethoric Sukarno was reverting to under clever prodding of people like P.K.I.-Deputy Chair-

man Njoto. See *Antara News Agency*, August 17, 1964, and Utrecht, 1969, p. 85. Also below pp. 286, 287.

22. *Indonesian Observer*, August 1, 1964. Even without famine the country imported rice at the rate of 120 million dollars a year.
23. Statement by D. N. Aidit welcoming Sukarno's Independence Day speech, *Djakarta Radio Home Service*, August 18, 1964.
24. See also below p. 302 ff.
25. Utrecht, 1969, p. 82.
26. Statement by the B.T.I., *Harian Rakjat*, September 24, 1964. This position was taken at the end of a special farmers' conference ordered by Aidit after the favorable Tavip speech by Sukarno. It followed a report of B.T.I.-Chairman Asmu in which he had extolled the four roles the villages should play: As a source for food; as a recruiting ground for revolutionary soldiers; as a refuge in the event of setbacks; and as bases when the 'cities' could be attacked again.
27. *Indonesian Observer*, November 2, 3, 4 and 5, 1964.
28. *Indonesian Observer*, November 16, 1964.
29. At the same time the concessions Aidit had been able to get in return, for instance the ban on the newly-created anti-P.K.I. 'Body for the Promotion of Sukarno-ism', had been considerable and facilitated the P.K.I.'s temporary toning down of its unilateral actions. See further below pp. 305, 306.
30. Dr. W. F. Wertheim writes in his view on the Untung coup as published in *Pacific Affairs*, June-July 1966, p. 120, 121: 'The P.K.I. evidently did not sufficiently realize that in starting these campaigns against larger landowners, they were abandoning Sukarno's diluted socialism and adopting a clear-cut class-struggle position . . . In December 1964 the P.K.I. leaders were urged by Sukarno, the Nahdatul Ulama and the P.N.I. nationalists to stop the "aski sepihak" movement. It seems that a promise was made, but apparently it was difficult for the P.K.I. leadership to restrain their rural following from going ahead. It appears that in the last few months before the coup, the movement had lost most of its impulse. But the political effects were irreparable'. In view of the highly organized character of the unilateral actions and the measure of control the P.K.I. and its mass-organizations had over their members, at least as long as their leaders looked successful, it is difficult to accept that the P.K.I. leadership 'could not restrain their following'. The year 1965 generally showed less violent actions in the countryside than 1964, as the so-called Cornell report also relates (p. 132, 'confidential' version), but the overall strength of the P.K.I. in the Central and East Java villages had already grown so much that less obnoxious methods than the unilateral actions could be and were used. But the communal tensions generated were already tinder for 'injured' non-communists, egged on by religious leaders, once the shoe was on the other foot in the months following the Untung coup.
31. *Harian Rakjat*, January 17, 1964.
32. *Indonesian Observer*, January 20, 1964.

33. Lukman speaking on January 19; *Harian Rakjat*, January 31, 1964.
34. *Far East Economic Review*, February 20, 1964. Sukarno's deputy Subandrio, spoke earlier that day on *Djakarta Radio* and made a plea 'to follow a single command' – something that clearly had been lacking while Sukarno was away.
35. *Indonesian Observer*, January 24, 1964. The presidential order was signed by Army Chief Yani on behalf of Sukarno.
36. In the course of the year the party kept pressing for a takeover of all British property and made outright confiscation and not only 'control' one of the major themes of the 44th anniversary celebration; *Harian Rakjat*, May 22, 1964.
37. *New China News Agency*, January 24, 1964 and *New China News Agency*, February 10, 1964. A few days afterwards, on February 12, a further six British plantations were taken over, this time near Surabaja where the P.N.I. was in a strong position.
38. *Indonesian Observer*, January 27, 1964.

CHAPTER 18

Moscow begins to worry (1964)

On January 23, 1964, Sukarno ordered a ceasefire in Northern Borneo to be effective two days later. He did so after he had finished his second round of talks with the American Attorney General Robert Kennedy who had come over from Tokyo after consultations in Manila and Kuala Lumpur.[1] The Indonesian President spoke glowingly about the visit and called Kennedy when he left 'my very dear friend'. That same evening at a solidarity conference for Azahari's North Kalimantan fighters, Sukarno gave a fiery speech, mainly meant to cover this 'tactical' retreat, claiming that, his order to stop fighting notwithstanding, 'confrontation' would go on.[2] For the communists this was not enough, as they demanded what they called 'total confrontation'.[3]

At the December plenum Aidit had spelled out what was meant with this policy: On the one hand he had condemned then what he called an 'opportunistic' approach of those who thought still to solve the Malaysia problem by making certain concessions to Rahman, and on the other hand he pointed to an 'adventurous' opinion, intent on inviting 'limited armed action of the British to create panic in the country and use this as an opportunity to end what they call the Sukarno regime'.[4] No doubt the party wanted to steer clear of this Scylla and Charibdis, the 'opportunists' being most of the government leaders, including more often than not Sukarno, and the 'adventurers', the military who for domestic reasons might manipulate the Malaysia confrontation and reimpose the state of emergency under which they would again have the authority to keep the P.K.I. better in check.[5] He also may have meant those of his fellow communists like Njoto who wanted to go further than he judged proper. The third, correct way Aidit had called the 'revolutionary opinion'. This was the current

P.K.I. practise of creating trouble at home and going to verbal extremes, but preventing Nasution and also the more Sukarno-oriented military leaders like Army Chief Yani from improving their domestic position.

Sukarno himself came increasingly under fire of the P.K.I. as he was trying his expert hand at sitting on the fence and having the best of two worlds, playing off the military and the communists. On the day that Kennedy arrived in Djakarta, *Harian Rakjat* warned editorially that any offer of economic help should be repulsed. Aidit apparently was not sure that Sukarno would resist the lure of badly needed dollar help. The party paper quoted in this context the President himself to the effect that confrontations should not be 'just talk'.[6] More directly the P.K.I. chairman turned against Sukarno in the address he held before the North Kalimantan solidarity conference the day after the ceasefire was announced. Aidit called it a 'naive idea' to assume that American mediation in the conflict with Malaysia would not be harmful to the country.[7] Njoto, practising his 'one-up-manship', began chiding 'those leaders who sell themselves to the U.S.'[8]

When Subandrio went to Bangkok for a first discussion of the ceasefire with his Philippine, Malaysian, and Thai colleagues, and when it looked as if he were after some sort of political solution, the P.K.I. began to attack Sukarno personally, though not on his Malaysia policy but where he was weakest at that moment, the sorry state of the Indonesian economy.[9] But by that time the Bangkok conference had been adjourned since Malaysia, as precondition to further negotiations, had insisted upon withdrawal of the Indonesian guerilla's from Sabah and Serawak, a demand not acceptable to Subandrio.[10] It is difficult to judge the precise effect of the hard action the P.K.I. pursued against Sukarno on Malaysia, as the bad start of the first round of Bangkok talks gave the Indonesian government also an excuse to abandon the ceasefire. And this was what in fact happened, though it was not openly acknowledged, as the Indonesian infiltrators resumed action in the jungle immediately after the adjournment of the Bangkok meeting, a moment coinciding with the peak of the P.K.I. attack upon Sukarno.[11]

Subandrio denied any violation of the ceasefire agreement and the theater commander, Brigadier General Suharto – later to become president of Indonesia, but at the time an unknown field officier –

declared that it had been the British who were to blame for the resumption of hostilities.[12] It came to one more foreign ministers conference in Bangkok that floundered, however, even quicker than the previous one and under rather curious circumstances. Indonesia had stressed again a political solution – a new series of popular consultations or something similar – while Malaysia backed by the British first of all wanted to have Indonesia's infiltrators removed. When it began to look, however, as if some agreement could be reached, Subandrio received a telegram from Djakarta about alleged insults British officers had shown towards Indonesian guerilla's that were willing to withdraw from Serawak.[13] Subandrio was summoned by the Indonesian President to return home, in fact breaking off the negotiations that only dragged on then a few days without further results. To Subandrio's deputy, Suwito Kusumowidagdo, who took over after the Indonesian Foreign Minister left, this episode was indicative of the manipulation that went on backstage in Djakarta as to the Malaysian confrontation.[14] Probably Sukarno had been influenced by the strong communist attacks on him personally, and someone had 'planted' the story to him at the right moment; at any rate, while Sukarno kept telling the United States Government that Indonesia did not deviate from the line agreed upon with Kennedy and wanted to talk with Malaysia even at the highest level rather than fight, the Indonesian President prepared his next move that would run quite counter to the impression given.[15] Sukarno must have felt the need to keep moving. The Philippines had indicated that it would soon establish consular relations with Malaysia – denying that this would imply official recognition – and international support for his confrontation policy was slipping further. He let Subandrio first issue the warning that there was a limit to the patience Indonesia could muster and that as Rahman had called for a general mobilization 'the conflict could become a world war'.[16] Then on March 16 the President himself told a conference of military commanders that as a result of Malaysia's decision to mobilize he would ask volunteers to do the job for Indonesia, recalling that with the liberation of West Irian 7 million of them had been registered.[17]

Within days the Minister of Information Ahmadi could announce that already more than 18 million had volunteered to fight Malaysia.[18] Subandrio declared the ceasefire no longer in existence, and it was then only a matter of days to wait for the American response,[19] coming as a declaration by Secretary of State Dean Rusk who announced that no new aid for Indonesia would be forthcoming as long as the Malaysia dispute was not settled.[20] This in turn brought Sukarno to his outburst against the U.S.A. 'to go to hell' with their aid, a suggestion the Indonesian President made at a ground-breaking ceremony for the new State Bank building in the presence of the American ambassador Howard Jones.[21] It was a first class row that left the audience stunned. The Chinese news agency picked up the story with gusto, but within the country the press coverage of the event was rather muted. It was not until five days later that *Antara* came with some sort of explanation of what Sukarno had meant to say in his – unreported – 'recent statement', to wit that no strings should be attached to foreign aid, etc.[22] Nasution had tried to repair the damage a bit by making a moderate speech the next day, blaming the dispute with Malaysia on the continued existence of British military bases and not on some 'vitium originis' that would have been hard to remedy.[23]

Due to the Malaysia issue the President was increasingly driven into a close harmony with the P.K.I., by far the best organized political force in the country. This had at least the advantage of providing him with the mass audiences he loved and needed so dearly.[24] An example was when he delivered his so-called Dwikora-speech of May 3 before a mass audience giving them his 'double command': To strengthen Indonesia and to crush Malaysia.[25]

Sukarno also charged that Rahman even after the elections he had just won did not want to negotiate. The whole performance was a new step further away from a sensible and consistent policy and therefore loudly applauded by the P.K.I.[26]

The U.S. was losing whatever was left of its grip on the Indonesian leader and could only tell once more that really no more aid would be given to Indonesia if it did not mend its ways.[27] But Ambassador Jones could at least some days later report home that Sukarno was willing – as probably all along he had been – to meet with the Malaysian Prime Minister at a Maphilindo summit conference.[28] A new round of prepatory talks were in the offing, and it was no surprise therefore that Aidit did not lose time in showing his opposition. Before Sukarno's decision to attend the Maphilindo meeting had been made public, Aidit dismissed the whole idea of Maphilindo cooperation, calling it 'at first glance not a bad idea', but in fact a thoroughly detestable U.S.-inspired plot.[29] The same situation repeated itself as in February: The P.K.I. stepped up its attacks against the government because of Malaysia and as the culminating point came a strong personal attack against Sukarno himself for his economic policy that provided as easy a target as it had done three months ago.[30] Sukarno reacted by talking with more than one tongue and claimed on the one hand that Malaysia would be crushed by January 1, 1965, and that he had not agreed to any preconditions for the meeting with Rahman.[31] On the other hand he allowed Subandrio to suggest that the day the summit in Tokyo would begin, Indonesia would start withdrawing its troups from Sabah and Serawak.[32] This Subandrio kept saying while in Tokyo to prepare for the summit, having a spokesman announce even that the Indonesian guerillas had already been ordered to begin withdrawal on June 14.[33] Already the day after this announcement was made Subandrio told journalists in Tokyo that some of the Indonesians, while indeed leaving Malaysia territory as told, had been ambushed.[34]

Even Aidit may have been confused, not knowing what Subandrio and the Indonesian military were up to exactly.[35] But he soon would find out, as the summit conference in Tokyo, only meeting one day, ended in failure and did not bring Malaysia and Indonesia much nearer to a solution. President Macapagal of the Philippines had suggested a mediation commission of four Afro-Asian countries to make recommendations. Sukarno had said to agree, even to the point of accepting in advance the findings of the commission, but Rahman kept demanding a full withdrawal of Indonesian guerilla troops first.[36] To Sukarno this reserve made by the Tunku was nothing but 'a nuisance' as he told a mass rally in Djakarta in honor of the visiting Soviet Deputy Premier Anastas Mikoyan.[37] More ominous was that like his main lieutenant and spokesman, Subandrio, had done a few days before, Sukarno also told everybody then that Indonesia should no longer feel bound by any agreements on ceasefire, etc., made previously. For U.N. Secretary General U Thant the Indonesian President reserved at the occasion also a few digs, reminding his audience of the role U Thant had played in 'quickly' sanctioning the findings of the Michelmore mission and so hastening the birth of ill-fated Malaysia. No doubt Sukarno was aware of the possibility that Rahman would turn sooner or later to the United Nations to get redress against the Indonesian armed actions and saw it his interest to slight the world organization and its top executive already in an early stage. Even to cool observers it must have looked as though no outside influence could prevail upon the Indonesian President to moderate his inordinate ambitions and that 'only internal forces could stop Sukarno', as it was concluded at the time in a leading paper in the area.[38] It would take some time, however, before these forces began to move decisively.

In this period Soviet policy quite closely had been following Sukarno in his various attempts to use Malaysia to increase Indonesia's influence in the area. After Robert Kennedy had brought Sukarno in January to announce a ceasefire, Radio Moscow stressed, as if excusing it, that both Indonesia and Malaysia had made concessions, which in fact was not true.[39] Right before the second Bangkok meeting a month later, Sukarno got Soviet support for his probably less than halfhearted intention to continue talking with Kuala Lumpur and for the Indonesian thesis that not only or firstly the guerilla question should be discussed, but the bilateral relationship *in toto*.[40] It brought Moscow in clear contradiction with Aidit who at exactly that moment tried to exert all possible pressure to make Sukarno change his mind and was deadset against talks.[41] Soviet Ambassador Michailov again expressed support for Sukarno in mid-March after the Indonesian President had indicated that notwithstanding the failure of the second Bangkok meeting of foreign ministers, he wanted a summit with Rahman.[42] But when the mercurial Sukarno just after that began calling up volunteers by the millions, Pravda stated rather worriedly that the situation was growing definitely worse.[43] The Malaysian confrontation as such must have looked from Moscow of third, if not lower, priority and barely worth getting excited about were it not for the sake of good relations with Sukarno. His outburst against American foreign aid was passed over in silence by the Soviet media. But when seven secondhand Soviet men of war were transferred to the Indonesian navy, Michailov took the occasion to express, in general terms, Soviet support for Indonesia's 'fight' against Malaysia, mainly meant, however, to bring home to those who were looking more to Peking than to Moscow that 'Soviet aid is not only in words, but also in deeds'.[44]

It was understandable that Michailov thought it fit to remind Indonesia once more that it had more to expect from Moscow than from anywhere else as far as concrete help was concerned. During the preceding days the preparatory committee for the second Afro-Asian Conference, the successor to the 1955 Bandung Conference, had met in Djakarta.[45] At it the Chinese delegation under Foreign Minister Chen Yi succeeded in bringing about a deadlock on the question of whether the Soviet Union should be invited to the full conference or not. It was Subandrio, chosen by the committee as chairman, who played a decisive role in this affair and by manipulating the proceedings helped the Chinese to their 'victory'. Also Aidit had been a member of the Indonesian 'Nasakom' delegation, and he had been actively lobbying in unison with Subandrio and Chen Yi against the Soviet Union's participation.[46] The Soviet Russian relations with both the P.K.I. – already somewhat strained – and with the Sukarno regime became troubled by this event and especially Soviet Prime Minister Kruschov was strongly vexed and kept constantly complaining until his last day in office about the slight the Soviet delegation – and the Soviet Union as such – had suffered during the conference.[47]

The P.K.I. let the situation worsen to such an extent that a few days after the Afro-Asian committee had adjourned its Djakarta session it came to a clash between Aidit and Michailov personally. At the Lenin commemoration, sponsored by the Indonesian-Soviet Friendship Institute, Aidit accused the Soviet Union of colonialism in Uzbekistan and in other Central Asiatic Soviet republics. When Michailov demanded the right to reply, he was treated rudely and, after finally having gotten the chance to answer Aidit's criticism, was told by the audience to get 'retooled', i.e. purged.[48] Then not long after this altercation among comrades, Aidit for the first time brought up the question of anti-P.K.I. splitting activities that he said were afoot in the country. Addressing a Labor Day rally on May 2, the P.K.I. chairman warned that 'the revisionists will make efforts to gather some persons together and form another so-called communist party or so-called Marxist-Leninist Party, coexisting with the P.K.I. But their ugly faces will completely be exposed'.[49] Escalating further Aidit began to be more specific and indicated later that same month of May that it was the Murba Party, the small but influential remnant of Tan Malaka's National Communist Party of the postwar period, that was used by the Soviet Union to split the P.K.I.[50] This party to which Trade Minister Adam Malik belonged and to which third Deputy Premier Chaerul Saleh was near[51] had been reactivated with the return from Peking of Sukarni Kartodiwirjo in March after having served in China as Indonesian ambassador. Sukarni had become Deputy Chairman of Murba and developed great activity. He may for some time have been Moscow's man but was at any rate utterly disliked by the Chinese communists who had done their best to get rid of him.[52]

It was Sukarni who brought back to life the old idea of Sukarno to 'simplify' the political party system in Indonesia. When in mid-May a Murba delegation paid a visit to Sukarno, ostensibly to support his Dwikora-speech, Sukarni afterwards told the press that the President was not opposed to the reduction of the number of parties.[53] The suggestion was made that eventually only one party would be left, probably something like the Arab Socialist Union in Egypt or the F.L.N. in Algeria. In Djakarta at the time the discussion was on establishing what was called a pioneer or vanguard party, a notion that tied in with current thinking in Soviet circles.[54] But accepting a 'vanguard party' in Egypt or Algeria was something entirely different from what it would be in Indonesia. In the two Arab countries the communist parties were prohibited and for Moscow and the local comrades it meant that members of the illegal communist party should and could at least infiltrate the one remaining party. In Indonesia, with a communist party fully legalized and booming, one unitary party would mean a sharp reduction in scope for the communists concerned. It was the last thing Aidit would have accepted, concerned as he had always[55] been to keep his hands untied. On the other hand the idea may have found favor in Moscow as the Soviet leaders increasingly must have been aware that they risked to lose the P.K.I. to Peking's lure. It is quite likely that, with anti-P.K.I. and anti-communist circles in Djakarta like the Murba Party, Nasution's I.P.K.I., and some muslim organizations already behind the idea, some collusion between the Soviet Union, represented by Michailov, and these Indonesian groups to influence Sukarno may have existed. At any rate Aidit intimated as much in his blistering attack at the end of May on the 'revisionists' (i.e. the Soviet Union) who were using the 'trotskyites' (i.e. the Murba Party) to split the P.K.I.[56]

Certainly something must have been going on behind the scenes, and Aidit must have felt it necessary to vent his grievances, justified or not. In the same address late in May 1964 he mentioned that 'highly provocative documents' were being divulged from which it would appear that 'the P.K.I. is going to seize power in 1970.'[57] This was a reference to the confidential account of the December 24, 1963, session of the P.K.I Central Committee. The account later was discussed – and not without vehemence – at a meeting of representatives of the ten political parties with President Sukarno and called a falsification by Aidit.[58] As it was Chaerul Saleh who then was to table the document in an attempt to ward off presidential action against the Murba Party, it is likely that Saleh had gotten hold of the summary account somewhere in April-May and was making covert use of it against the P.K.I. already then. It remains a matter of speculation, but it is likely that Chaerul Saleh who had excellent relations with the Soviet Union – all non-military aid went through his hands – was given the paper by Soviet diplomats. Whether they had acquired the incriminating document rightfully or through some pro-Soviet friend in the Central Committee is a moot question. The latter is quite possible, as for the first time since long before, mention was made, at the same occasion when Aidit blew his stack, of existing opposition within the P.K.I. It was Aidit's First Deputy Lukman who, speaking after Aidit on the 44th anniversary, stressed that 'the struggle against opposition in the P.K.I. since 1951 [when Aidit c.s. took over] had been kept in camera',[59] as if indicating that he wanted to keep it that way but was not sure.

At any rate, the P.K.I. was on bad terms with Moscow, but the reverse could also be noticed. On occasion of the 44th anniversary of the Party, Radio Moscow in Indonesian had hardly anything to say on what still was termed 'that glorious anniversary', but the more on the Aidit-Subandrio-Chen Yi collusion during the Afro-Asian preparatory conference earlier in April[60]: 'Attempts to make Indonesia follow a road of separatism and create closed regional blocs, to oppose international democratic organizations, led by certain groups at home [i.e. Indonesia] and abroad will not have the desired results'.[61] It was also around that time that the Soviet theoretical journal *Party Life* published an article treating for the first time in a more thorough fashion some of Aidit's theses as he had expressed them upon return from China at the end of September 1963.[62]

While the Soviet-P.K.I. relations were clearly cooling off, no immediate sign of a similar development in state relations between Moscow and Djakarta was visible. It attracted some attention, however, that Soviet Ambassador Michailov needed 5 days to come out with an endorsement of Sukarno's Dwikora speech of May 3, meant to mobilize the population against Malaysia,[63] while the Chinese foreign minister Chen Yi gave his blessing forthwith.[64] Soviet Deputy Prime Minister Mikoyan a little while later, on a visit to Tokyo, also gave his backing for Sukarno's Malaysia policy, plugging simultaneously the Soviet way of helping friends by reminding the Indonesians for the umpteenth time that it was Moscow that had provided the weapons thanks to which West Irian was conquered 'without a drop of blood'.[65] It must have been around that time that Kruschov, tiring of Sukarno's double talk, excessive ambitions, and prodigality, decided to have his trouble-shooting deputy make another visit to Djakarta to see what could be done about the Indonesian President as well as about the local comrades because it looked as if with both China was making serious inroads.

NOTES

1. *Antara News Agency*, January 23, 1964.
2. *Antara News Agency*, January 24, 1964.
3. *Harian Rakjat*, January 17, 1964, in a report on the North Kalimantan solidarity conference of January 23-26, 1964.
4. *Harian Rakjat*, January 17, 1964, giving the text of the Central Committee resolution on Malaysia that followed the formulation Aidit had given in his General Report of December 23, 1963.
5. With the end of the interim regime of the United Nations over West Irian on May 1, 1963, the state of emergency – S.O.B., derived of the Dutch expression Staat van Oorlog en Beleg – had been lifted, depriving the military of numerous political advantages. The P.K.I. was constantly afraid that S.O.B. would come back. From their side the military tried to claim in fact they had regained emergency powers, so, e.g., Defence Minister Nasution saying that 'in principle the country is already in a state of special emergency with the commander-in-chief [Sukarno, but under him the military] having the last word'; *Antara News Agency*, March 14, 1964.
6. *Harian Rakjat*, January 22, 1964.
7. *New China News Agency*, January 35, 1964. This was the opinion Sukarno had expressed. Subandrio was taken to task some days later for going one step further and asserting that the U.S.A. would help Sukarno in his anti-imperialist policy; *Harian Rakjat*, January 27, 1964.
8. *Harian Rakjat*, February 3, 1964.
9. Subandrio left on February 10 for the first Bangkok conference and stated in a *Djakarta Radio* broadcast from the Thai capital that the confrontation had now reached the stage of 'politics and diplomacy'; *Djakarta Rodio Home Service*, February 14, 1964. The attack on Sukarno came in an editorial in

Harian Rakjat of February 18. The President was held responsible for famine and mismanagement in the country.

10. *Djakarta Radio Home Service*, February 17, 1964.
11. The well-informed and usually reliable Manila Radio Station reported that the guerilla activities in North Borneo had begun again on February 19. They were for Tunku Abdul Rahman occasion to confirm that he would not negotiate with Djakarta before the Indonesian infiltrators had withdrawn; *Manila Radio*, February 20, 1964. A radio station operating for some time already under the name *Radio Free Indonesia*, probably located in Malaysia, had announced on February 2 that the confrontation policy would be resumed as before the Sukarno-Kennedy talks because of pressure by Aidit. This statement was not further substantiated though. The political and other news the station used to bring, though strongly slanted against Sukarno and the communists, contained factual elements that indicated direct sources in Indonesia itself, especially in Djakarta.
12. *Indonesian Observer*, February 25, 1964 and *New China News Agency*, March 5, 1964.
13. Interview, March 1972 with ex-Deputy Minister of Foreign Affairs Suwito Kusumowidagdo.
14. 'The question "who made this cable" was constantly on my mind. A game was played upon us, I suspect now'; Interview, March 1972 with Suwito Kusumowidagdo.
15. See *Antara News Agency*, March 11, 1964 for a report on a Sukarno-Jones meeting.
16. *Indonesian Observer*, March 14, 1964.
17. *Djakarta Radio Home Service*, March 16, 1964. It was at this junction also that Nasution had come with his remark that in fact a state of emergency existed, giving Sukarno as commander in chief 'the last word'. This meant a signal that Aidit and the P.K.I., having scored some points against and with Sukarno on the domestic scene, should not mistake the situation as far as the armed Forces was concerned. Three days later Aidit, speaking before an air force audience, would charge that 'Yugoslav revisionists (whose) underhand dealings were generally known in Indonesia had even interfered in the internal affairs of the Republic, demanding that the Indonesian government take measures against the Indonesian Communist Party which is firm in exposing modern revisionism'; *Harian Rakjat*, March 23, 1964; *New China News Agency*, April 8, 1964. It is doubtful that in fact Yugoslav diplomats had done anything of the kind, but their cordial relations with the Indonesian military leadership was well known and Aidit's point can therefore be seen also outside its international communist context. Publicly Aidit denied any rivalry between him and Nasution and he had called Nasution in an interview in the *Philippine Herald* early that month even a 'personal friend', a qualification that was to get a sinister twist by subsequent events.
18. *Djakarta Radio Home Service*, March 24, 1964.
19. *Antara News Agency*, March 16, 1964.

20. *Indonesian Observer*, March 21, 1964. According to a report in the New York Times of May 2, 1964, the United States had blocked 200 million dollars in aid and put an end to further food deliveries that could be paid for in local currency.
21. *New China News Agency*, March 26, 1964. Sukarno's behavior on this sort of occasion has been related to his state of health. His immediate entourage, it is reported, had noticed that he could more and more frequently lose his temper in an excessive way. A few days after the incident with Jones, Sukarno was said to be too ill to go to Makassar and let Leimena take his place; *Djakarta Radio Home Service*, April 1, 1964. Jones in his account of the incident gives a rather weak excuse for not having left the ceremony or shown in another way not to have been too pleased with Sukarno's words: 'Sukarno had not pointed his finger at the American Ambassador and said "to hell with your aid". With all his faults Sukarno was not one deliberately to embarrass the representative of another nation'; Howard Jones, 1971, *The Possible Dream*, Harcourt, Brace, Jovanovich, New York, p. 322. Jones wrongly and illogically dates the Rusk statement after Sukarno's outburst, instead of before.
22. *Antara News Agency*, March 31, 1964.
23. *Djakarta Radio Home Service*, March 27, 1964.
24. To celebrate the 21 millionth volunteer against Malaysia Sukarno addressed not less than one million of them on Merdeka Square in Djakarta, at least according to local estimates; *Indonesian Observer*, May 14, 1964. Also his Dwikora speech of May 3 was said to be held before one million people; *Indonesian Observer*, May 4, 1964.
25. *Djakarta Radio Home Service*, May 3, 1964. The name brought back memories of his famous 'triple command' or Trikora speech at the end of 1961, initiating the last phase of the recovery of West Irian. Dwikora seemed to have had less popular response, the million-strong audience notwithstanding.
26. *New China News Agency*, May 4, 1964.
27. *Djakarta Radio Home Service*, May 6, 1964.
28. The initiative ostensibly had come from Manila that had just exchanged consular representatives again with Malaysia, but no doubt the Americans were behind it. See *Indonesian Observer*, May 11, 1964.
29. *Antara News Agency*, May 11, 1964. Aidit just had given vociferous support to Sukarno's Dwikora speech (*Harian Rakjat*, May 4, 1964) and must have felt taken in again by the old fox. The Americans toyed with the idea of using the Maphilindo cooperation, however feeble it was, as a wider framework than Malaysia within which the North Borneo territories could be given some federative status. Aidit spoke scornfully of 'more puppets' as the only result. In private he told Sukarno that Maphilindo was too petty a project for such a great leader as the President was; Interview Nasution, March 1972.
30. For the P.K.I. attack on Sukarno's economic policy see *Harian Rakjat*, May 18, 1964. In Surabaya at the occasion of the 44th anniversary of the

P.K.I. Aidit put the position of the Party in the confrontation with Malaysia succinctly: 'To retreat one single step would mean destruction'; *Review of Indonesia*, May-June 1964.

31. 'We must smash "Malaysia" whether there will be negotiations or not'; *New China News Agency*, May 20, 1964. After a meeting of the Supreme Operational Command Sukarno announced to have consented to the Maphilindo summit 'without conditions'; *New China News Agency*, May 27, 1964.
32. *Indonesian Obsterver,* May 30, 1964; *New China News Agency*, May 30, 1964.
33. *Kyodo* (Japanese News Agency), June 16, 1964.
34. *Djakarta Radio Home Servlce*, June 17, 1964. This looked like a repretition of the Bangkok cable; see above p. 252.
35. Aidit appeared to have been in the dark as to the result of Subandrio's preparatory mission in Tokyo, judging from what he told a National Front Youth League Conference on June 15 according to *Djakarta Radio Home Service*, June 16, 1964. The *New China News Agency* version of this talk mentions also the point Aidit made that it was Indonesia's duty to help North Kalimantan. Its representative in Djakarta, Mangol, meanwhile – probably not even consulted in advance – began to voice protest against the alleged order to the Indonesian infiltrators to withdraw behind the border; *Djakarta Radio Home Service*, June 18, 1964. He reacted too fast as he soon was to find out, or he may have been successful as a lobbyist, an unlikely assumption.
36. The summit conference took place on June 20, preceded by a two-day meeting of the three foreign ministers; *Djakarta Radio Home Service*, June 23, 1964.
37. *Djakarta Radio Home Service*, June 25, 1964. Reacting to news that the British were building (anti-aircraft) rocket sites in Malaysia Sukarno assured his listeners that also Indonesia had its own 'dreadful weapons'. It had been Army sources that had drawn attention to the British plans. The Tass correspondent in Djakarta had picked up the story, right at the time that troubleshooter Mikoyan came to see how the Soviet could retain some influence in Indonesia now that, seen from Moscow, the P.K.I. was probably beyond recovery and Sukarno looked spellbound by Malaysia and in danger of being lost also. In these circumstances having reasons to dangle weapons before Sukarno might have had its advantages, as Mikoyan must have known from previous occasions. See below p. 269 ff.
38. *Far Eastern Economic Review*, July 2, 1964.
39. *Radio Moscow Home Service*, January 24, 1964.
40. E.g., *Radio Moscow Home Service*, February 27, 1964. The Soviet Union may have played a moderating role in the wings during the first Bangkok meeting, not to the liking of those who as the P.K.I. rather saw no meeting at all. Rumors spread from Bangkok and Kuala Lumpur then that the Soviet Union was going to recognize Malaysia. *Antara* had the news that the Soviet Union for the first time since November 1963 had begun buying rub-

ber again at the Singapore market in considerable quantities; *Antara News Agency*, February 18, 1964. It all brought Ambassador Michailov anyhow to assure that no such Soviet recognition was in the affing. More generally he warned 'to watch out that Soviet-Indonesian relations do not deteriorate due to the *adversary*' [emphasis added], *Antara News Agency*, February 22, 1964.

41. See above p. 251. The official party paper called at that time the second Bangkok conference 'poison', as it would mean to surrender first and to talk afterwards; *Harian Rakjat*, February 29, 1964.
42. See above p. 252 and *Djakarta Radio Home Service*, March 15, 1964. Jones met Sukarno on March 11, Michailov made his statement on March 13.
43. *Pravda*, March 21, 1964.
44. *Djakarta Radio Home Service*, April 17, 1964.
45. See below p. .
46. The Indonesian delegation consisted besides Subandrio and Aidit of Ali Sastroamidjojo, Chairman of the P.N.I., Idham Chalid, Chairman of the muslim Nahdatul Ulama, and Major-General Puspojudo for the military; *New China News Agency*, April 9, 1964.
47. Interview, March 1972 General Nasution.
48. See the report of the meeting of April 21 in *Harian Rakjat*, April 24, 1964 and in *New China News Agency*, May 6, 1964. Ruth McVey, 'The strategic triangle: Indonesia,' *Survey*, January 1965, p. 118, called the encounter 'a nadir in Soviet-P.K.I. relations'.
49. *New China News Agency*, June 6, 1964. Aidit added as an indication of the seriousness of the charges he made 'We will never forgive the revisionists'.
50. *Harian Rakjat*, May 11, 1964.
51. Adam Malik, interview March 1972, denied that Chaerul Saleh ever belonged to the Murba Party. Saleh himself would do the same when early in 1965 the Murba Party was temporarily banned by Sukarno under pressure from communist side and both Malik and Saleh were identified with this party and consequently in trouble; see below p. 361.
52. Interview, March 1972, with the Indonesian diplomat Baron Sastradinata who was from 1963 until 1967 posted in Peking, lastly as chargé d'affaires in which capacity he bore the brunt of the combined effect of the deteriorating Sino-Indonesian relations after the 'Untung-coup' and the raging cultural revolution and had to leave China under difficult circumstances.
53. *Antara News Agency*, May 15, 1964; *Berita Indonesia*, May 15, 1964.
54. See: *Yuva Newsletter*, Vol. 3, no. 4, 1964, London, p. 5. Another related current line of Soviet thinking on third world affairs was the point that the proletariat there often was too weak yet to exert influences or lead the country towards socialism. In such cases the idea was that the Soviet Union could replace the local communist party and help the revolution along a transitory 'non-capitalist' path; see, e.g., G. Mirskiy in *New Times*, no. 18, 1964 writing that 'the socialist world system [i.e. especially the Soviet Union] is performing the functions of proletarian vanguard in relation to nations oppressed by imperialists'. The 'short-cut' theory was something Soviet ideologist

Michael Suslov had propounded and, judged by what Kruschov said during his visit to Cairo in May 1964, the Soviet Premier had begun to accept it as an useful approach. See also William E. Griffith, 1967, *Sino-Soviet Relations, 1964-1965*, The M.I.T. Press, Massachusetts, p. 52. Of course the Soviets were making a virtue of necessity and could – as in the case of Indonesia – also apply this 'theory' where the communists were not too weak but just slipping in loyalty.

55. See above p. 21.
56. *Review of Indonesia*, May-June 1964. The occasion was the 44th aniversary of the P.K.I. on May 23.
57. *Review of Indonesia*, May-June 1964. Aidit told his comrades that the opponents of the P.K.I. were living in a dream world, as if the P.K.I. would have 'a time schedule' for the completion of the revolution.
58. See below pp. 306 and 310 note 42.
    Dr. Guy Pauker, in a communication to the author, recalls that the document circulated by Saleh might have been a Murba fabrication. It was at any rate 'a distinct, secret document, not the official account of the P.K.I. C.C. session of December 1963 as stated on your page 258'.
59. *New China News Agency*, May 25, 1964. See also Aidit at the National Congress of the P.K.I. in July 1964 speaking about 'contradictions within the Party'; *New China News Agency*, July 4, 1964 and below p. 283, note 87.
60. *Moscow Radio in Indonesian*, May 23, 1964.
61. The tenor was similar to what was written at the beginning of the Afro-Asian preparatory committee meeting in April in the Soviet government paper *Izvestia*: 'It is generally known that inside the Republic itself as well as outside there are certain circles which oppose the friendship between Indonesia and the Soviet Union', *Izvestia*, April 11, 1964; *Tass*, April 11, 1964. If these 'certain circles' were not found in the P.K.I. and in Peking the paper might have been less circumspect in its description.
62. *Moscow Radio in Russian for abroad*, June 3, 1964 and below p. .
63. *Indonesian Observer*, May 8, 1964. Michailov said that the Soviet Union would help Indonesia in its 'crush Malaysia' campaign, adding again that this aid would be 'concrete'.
64. *Indonesian Observer*, May 5, 1964.
65. *Indonesian Observer*, May 18, 1964.

CHAPTER 19

Is the Soviet Union Asiatic? (1964)

Relations between Peking and Djakarta had been developing all through 1963 with growing intensity. The only real dissonance had been the outburst of anti-Chinese riots in May, not long after the official visit of President Lia Shao-chi to Indonesia.[1] Both sides however had shown restraint: Sukarno had blamed the affair on local 'counter-revolutionary elements', a different approach from what he had to say in 1959-1960[2] and the Chinese government protested only mildly and referred to the explanations the Indonesian President had given. After the Sino-Soviet showdown in July 1963 in Moscow, the Chinese, in their preoccupation with their rivalry with the Soviet Union, had begun to look for partisans even among Western governments, to the exclusion of the U.S.,[3] but their main target was the rest of what was to them the 'friendly world': The Afro-Asian countries.

A major effort to swing the leaders of these nations towards the viewpoints which China propounded in the doctrinal and 'Real'-political quarrel with Moscow was Chou En-lai's tour through Africa and Asia, at the turn of the year.[4] During this trip he particularly tried to speed up a meeting of Afro-Asian leaders at a second Bandung conference and to have it take place before the non-aligned nations got their 'second Belgrade'.[5] The motivation behind this was manifold. First and foremost, of course, the Chinese wanted to prevent both India and Yugoslavia from having a world forum where they could enlist, partly as proxy – Yugoslavia for the Soviet Union – opinion against them. An Afro-Asian conference, however, would have the combined advantage of excluding Yugoslavia – and *a fortiori* as they thought, the Soviet Union – and by their own presence to influence the proceedings. Hence a tug-of-war ensued all through the following period between the two main communist adversaries about the two types of conferences, which to the outside observer at times looked out of all proportion.

When the champions of a second Belgrade meeting (Yugoslavia, India, and the United Arab Republic) fixed a preparatory conference for the end of March, Chou quickly tried to counter with a similar one that, also at short notice, would assemble only Afro-Asian nations.[6] In Indonesia Foreign Minister Subandrio did not show a marked preference one way or the other but warned that a non-aligned meeting should 'not break the Afro-Asian solidarity', i.e. be overshadowed by the Sino-Soviet rift or by the Indian-Chinese border question. At the time Sukarno himself did not see much in the idea of non-alignment as it had been conceived at the height of the cold war. But he did not want to say as openly as his confidant Ruslan Abdulgani did when he stated that Indonesia was in fact no longer a non-aligned nation.[8] China was showing consideration to Indonesia in particular because this country was the most logical ally (together with Pakistan, but there the link with the U.S. was something of a problem) in a new Afro-Asian front. Several gestures were proof of this. At the end of January 1964 a Chinese credit of 30 million dollars for the building of a textile mill, promised earlier, was finalized.[9] Another interesting token of the Chinese wish to accommodate the Indonesian government occurred in March, when the Indonesian branches of the Bank of China voluntarily ceased operation.[10]

On the Malaysia confrontation the picture was not all that clear. Peking was of course behind the general idea of Indonesia's quarrel with her neighboring federation, but also had its own interests to consider.[11] China still saw the United States as the main enemy, while Britain came second, although it belonged to a certain extent even to Mao's 'intermediate zone'. This was a logical classification as the British were in a good position to create trouble for China's profitable Hongkong trade.[12] Moreover too-fierce opposition to the British in Malaysia could easily draw the attention of the world to the fact that China itself was tolerating a full-fledged 'British colony' on its doorstep.[13]

An analysis of the Chinese news coverage of the Malaysia question shows that, in early days of 1964, Peking somewhat passively followed developments with a marked preference for the more extreme, P.K.I.-

inspired sides of Indonesia's position.[14] It reprinted major articles appearing in the Indonesian communist daily press – *Harian Rakjat*, *Bintang Timur* and *Warta Bhakti* – and selected the bits and pieces that suited them best, for example those showing the strong anti-U.S. slant the P.K.I. was then developing.[15] So when Kennedy was about to push Sukarno towards a ceasefire, the Chinese condensed a long *Harian Rakjat* editorial, stressing how intolerable the P.K.I. daily thought American pressure upon Sukarno was.[16]

This method of reprinting P.K.I. opinion without taking any particular position of its own went on until the end of March when, in short succession, *Jen-min Jih-pao* produced two editorials.[17] The first appeared when in Colombo a number of leading non-aligned nations, including Indonesia, were discussing their 'second Belgrade' and its agenda.[18] The official Chinese party paper gave then a very strong endorsement of Azahari's independence movement, for the first time praising the North Kalimantan leader himself. But it further gave an unequivocal boost to the Indonesian side of the affair. 'The Chinese people', the editorial said, 'stand firmly behind the just stand of the Indonesian government and people against "Malaysia". The Chinese people *together* with the people of Indonesia and North Kalimantan are ready to carry through *the common struggle* to uphold the Bandung spirit, defend peace in Southeast Asia and crush any neo-colonial scheme' [emphasis added].

The second opinion was published on the eve of the meeting of the Afro-Asian preparatory committee that was to meet in Djakarta on April 10.[19] While the first editorial came in the wake of Sukarno's martial call for volunteers against Malaysia as a riposte to Tunku's general mobilization, the second was a reaction to Sukarno's 'go-to-hell' outburst against the Americans and their aid.[20] However, its main thrust was to give the Indonesian government a shot in the arm as to its anti-Malaysia position as an opening gambit for the preparatory talks on the next Afro-Asian conference and – not less important – to flatter Sukarno. So the points the Chinese were making were clearly inspired by events in Indonesia, but the timing of publication in both cases showed that they were beginning to see, or better use, the link between Sukarno's Malaysia obsession and their own determination to outflank the Soviet Union and their 'revisionist' agents in the Third World.

It was also at this time, at the end of March 1964, that the Chinese, with the publication of their eighth comment on the main Soviet positions as expounded in the famous July 14, 1963, letter, opened a new phase. They called off the minor ideological truce with Moscow which had in fact been observed for some time.[21] A new offensive was brewing, leading the Russians to publish the text of the speech Presidium member Suslov had made at the February Central Committee plenary and the resolution adopted there both of which had not been made public until then.[22]

As a first field of action, the meeting of the Afro-Asian preparatory committee in Djakarta must have looked convenient enough to the Chinese to step up their support of Indonesia's confrontation policy and find a suitable ally. Due to heightened Sino-Soviet antagonism, this meeting acquired a greater importance to the Chinese, as was vividly illustrated by the sudden appearance of Chen Yi in Djakarta on the eve of the conference, taking over unexpectedly from chief-delegate Huang Cheng-nan who had arrived earlier.[23]

Opening the conference Sukarno brought up the quarrel between the two major communist countries and expressed the hope that the assembled Afro-Asian delegates (representing 22 nations) would promote a rapprochement between them.[24] This was either totally pious or plainly ironical, but anyhow, as the Soviet Union afterwards began to look upon this April meeting as a major affront[25] and the Chinese liked to make it look that way, the complete opposite of what Sukarno wanted was due to happen: A further hardening of positions. It was India which called a spade a spade ('a bombshell' it was termed) by bringing up the participation of the Soviet Union at the full Afro-Asian conference.[26] Chen Yi had to threaten to walk out of the conference in order to convince everybody of the need to find a face-saving device.

The five Arab countries present did not want to take up a position on Soviet membership or on that of Malaysia which was being just as much rejected by Indonesia as was the Soviet Union by China.[27] Most of the other delegations hesitated to take sides. The final outcome, according to the text of the communiqué issued after five days of wrangling, was that 'no consensus had been reached' as to the participation of the Soviet Union, while 'many obstacles still had to be removed' before Malaysia could be admitted.[28] Indonesian deputy Foreign Minister Suwito confused the issue by saying that the admittance of the Soviet Union and of Malaysia to the A.A. club 'had been settled' and that the conference had adopted the negative recommendation of the sub-committee concerned.[29] This committee of five countries had in fact been in session until early in the morning of April 15 and finally had decided to exclude the Russians.[30] Subandrio who was chairman of the plenary meeting had selected the five memmers and used his offices to be present at the discussions. In addition, he also invited Chen Yi as a 'major interested party', so one can assume the meeting was properly rigged.[31]

Contrary to the interpretation by Suwito – and Chen Yi followed him a few days later[32] – the full conference had in fact postponed the matter of the participation of the two countries until the second Afro-Asian conference was to meet. This was to be 'at the Greek calendars', as it turned out next year. For the time being it meant a large stone in the pond. *Pravda* came out with a scathing attack on Chen Yi, whom they accused of promoting racism in Asia while refuting his interpretation of the result of the A.A. preparatory conference.[33] In this article, as well as in a host of other pieces put out by the Soviet media in the weeks thereafter, almost every possible argument was adduced to prove how rightful a place the Soviet Union would occupy at the table reserved for Afro-Asians.[34] For the moment as to the Chinese the question was done with, apart from one lengthy reply.[35] Peking's interpretation was also adopted by the P.K.I., with this difference, that the Indonesian communists even went a step further in distorting the results of the A.A. committee meeting by maintaining that there had been '*unanimity* on agenda, time and place, and also on participation' [emphasis added].[36]

This statement on the April meeting of the preparatory Afro-Asian committee was issued by the party at the end of a special National Conference early in July. Aidit had called this conference right after Soviet Deputy Premier Mikoyan had left the country and probably because of that visit. Moreover, as the P.K.I. leadership must have undergone the presence of Mikoyan as unwelcome meddling with their affairs, the official opinion on what had gone on at the April meeting had been given a further additional anti-Soviet slant.

The ostensible purpose of Mikoyan coming to Djakarta in mid-1964 was a discussion of a new Soviet loan of 400 million dollars for military and non-military purposes.[37] But the main aim was to try to reason with the P.K.I. and to convince Sukarno, if necessary with some heavy arm-twisting, that he should stop blocking Moscow's participation in the second Bandung Conference. In his major opening speech to the Indonesian parliament that had convened especially in his honor, Mikoyan made what he called 'the unity of all anti-imperialist forces' the foremost theme, and as such it was also treated in the Soviet Press.[38] He of course paid tribute to Sukarno, especially as the initiator of the first Bandung conference of Afro-Asian countries in 1955. But he also gave Soviet backing to the second Afro-Asian conference then being prepared, provided it was 'directed at consolidating the forces of the struggle against colonialism and imperialism and not at *disuniting* them' [emphasis added]. This was to be the standard formula with which Moscow conveyed that it would feel impaired if left out. The version *Djakarta Radio* gave made no mention at all of the second conference, or anything Mikoyan had said about it.[39] During his visit the Soviet Deputy Premier did not succeed in getting the Indonesians to endorse his version on Afro-Asian solidarity. The final communiqué spoke of 'complete agreement', but only on 'various issues' of political, economic, and military character, further left unspecified.[40] On Malaysia Mikoyan had not given the impression during his visit that he was too eager to go out of his way to please the Indonesians. References were rather general but of course useful to Sukarno and duly given emphasis by the Indonesian media.[41] The Soviet leader also soft-pedalled the danger for Indonesia involved in the existence of Malaysia,[42] and he reminded the Indonesians that though it was necessary to eradicate colonialism after all only 50 million people in the whole world were at that time in colonial bondage.[43]

All the other tenets of current Soviet doctrine showed up neatly, but contradictions abounded. Peace, Mikoyan said, was the best climate for the developing countries, as their primary task was full independence in the economic field; on the other hand peace had to be fought for, if necessary with arms. Disarmament on a worldwide scale was something the U.S.A. would have to accept sooner or later. However, at the same time young countries of course had to defend themselves, so the Soviet stand was only seemingly inconsistent, etc. Mikoyan was most eloquent when he came to speak about Soviet aid, especially of the military variety.

The economic projects agreed upon between Indonesia and the Soviet Union remained rather in the shade. On the eve of the visit of the

Soviet Deputy Minister for economic foreign relations Sergeev (the official responsible for Soviet aid to Indonesia) spoke once more highly of the various plans: The Tjiligon steel factory, the highways straight through the Bornean jungle, etc.[44] But, in reality, none of them had progressed much since their inception, and Mikoyan must have decided to be blunt as part of his pressure tactics. His line here was that however grave the economic difficulties were for Indonesia the Soviet Union, in its early years, had been worse off.[45] With 'hard work and excellent organization' his fellow countrymen had done a lot, so ran his lesson. He told the Consultative Assembly in Bandung that some further plans were being worked out and that the Asahan dam in Sumatra, for example, would be an outstanding construction, etc. In fact, nothing substantial seems to have come out of the visit in this respect. Mikoyan explained that it was Soviet policy to provide advisers and technicians while leaving it to the Indonesians to do the actual job.[46] This he compared favorably with the West who only 'used people as slaves', meaning that Western experts (unlike the Russian ones) generally had executive responsibilities – and more success. He countered Indonesian complaints that nothing much had been accomplished since the first aid agreements were contracted with a lot of publicity in 1956 by telling his hosts that, in fact, they were to blame. As the projects could be executed only with the help of rupiah counterfunds for payment of local labor and material, and the Indonesian side in most cases had not kept their part of the deal, stagnation had been inevitable. Mikoyan put it relatively mildly when he pointed out in Bandung: 'You have also had other matters of concern which have not allowed large expenditure for these purposes'.[47]

Military aid had been more of a success story – in the narrow meaning of the word – and this may have accounted for making it Mikoyan's favorite topic. He kept reminding the Indonesians that it had been the Soviet Union that had 'greatly' equipped the Indonesian armed forces, with the result that they were now the most modern and strongest in the area, stronger even than the British.[48] He 'disclosed' that Soviet officers, stationed in Surabaya at the time, had been ready in 1961 to join the battle for West Irian, a willingness that had not had been tested because thanks to Soviet arms Indonesia had 'obtained West Irian without firing a shot'.[49]

As a sales talk, this was hardly necessary because all branches of the Indonesian armed forces, with the possible exception of the police, were only too eager in their scramble for more and better military toys. An air force mission under air commodore Budjardjo was at that very moment in Moscow negotiating on the delivery of large transport helicopters, and when Subandrio followed Mikoyan to the Russian capital, he had Army Chief Yani at his side who wanted to get medium range rockets,[50] while the Navy was also promptly promised something by Subandrio.[51]

Not having achieved his aim in Indonesia of getting more support for the Soviet Union as an Asian country in exchange for credit and arms, Mikoyan kept up continuous pressure. Before leaving Djakarta he told a press conference that 'Indonesia can have no doubt about Soviet participation in the Afro-Asian conference'.[52] In Rangoon, during a stopover later that day, he was reported to have said that Indonesia had no objection to Soviet participation. On this statement Subandrio's only comment had been non-committal.[53] But the question was 'far from closed' an editorial in the *Indonesian Observer* concluded, thought at the time to be close to Subandrio and the Indonesian Foreign Ministry.[54] The army newspaper, *Warta Berita*, told the government a few days later that it should react favorably to the Soviet request for participation in exchange for further Soviet aid.[55] Another *quid pro quo* was mentioned by a western news agency: Soviet leniency as to debt repayment and Indonesian acceptance of the Soviet Union as an Afro-Asian country.[56]

Apparently the deal was not yet clinched, notwithstanding declarations from the Indonesian side that another arms agreement had already been concluded and that the Budjardjo mission in Moscow had meanwhile had 'tremendous results'.[57] Mikoyan had consistently refused to give any comment on the military aspects of the current negotiations with the Indonesian government.[58]

Within a week of Mikoyan's departure, Subandrio was on his way to Moscow to continue the discussions.[59] Though not fully satisfied, the Russians got more out of Subandrio's visit in terms of acceptance of their point on the A. A. conference than had resulted from Mikoyan's endeavors in Indonesia. The final communiqué at least retained a joint conference to 'solidarity, no disunity in the anti-imperialist forces'.[60] This was far from an open endorsement of the Soviet thesis but must have reflected a certain moral obligation on the Indonesian side to find some compromise formula amenable to the Russians.[16]

Specifically, also, the Moscow communiqué had linked the need for that anti-imperialist 'solidarity, no disunity' with the opposition against Malaysia that the Soviet Union said it shared with Indonesia.[62] It could but mean that, if Indonesia would not resist Chinese pressure to keep the Soviet Union out of Afro-Asian manifestations, Soviet support for its costly confrontation game – that is weapons and credit on easier terms – would be reconsidered.[63]

What Subandrio had received in return for this rather limited political concession was not negligible. The Indonesian Foreign Minister declared after his final round of negotiations in Moscow that the Soviet Union had '*in general* given us what we wanted' [emphasis added].[64] This meant that not all the wishes of the Indonesians had been fulfilled, for instance as to the medium range missiles he and Yani had come shopping for.[65] But as such wishes were unrealistic anyhow, in practice Djakarta was not so badly off with the deal. The Indonesian Army still had to continue to negotiate, but the Air Force received helicopters and spare parts and the Navy speedboats to make a better show of the unsuccessful landings on the Malayan coast.[66] In all the direct value of the military equipment finally acquired must have been between 50 and 100 million dollars, while the total Soviet military aid program to Indonesia was now claimed 'substantially' to exceed the one billion dollar mark,[67] including that part of the new credit – 300 million dollars – that still had to be earmarked specifically. So understandably in the Indonesian opinion, the complex negotiations had been a success in so far that, as the Subandrio entourage expressed it, 'it was the first time that avowed Soviet support for the Malaysia confrontation had been given'.[68] It is not clear whether this opinion was also shared by Sukarno, who entertained a more provocative concept of confrontation and may have thought that Subandrio had given away too much in political terms. An instance was when the Indonesian Foreign Minister, after the whole deal was over, began to stress that it was actually a neutralization of British bases that was the main aim of the Malaysian confrontation.[69] This was the position which the 'more sober-minded' military leaders, like Nasution, had adopted for a long time.[70] However this may be, to Malaysia and its harrassed Prime Minister Tunku Abdul Rahman, it must all have looked rather discouraging and, to him, the Mikoyan visit had as he said 'changed the picture' and convinced him that, more than ever, he had to look for support from Commonwealth countries, but especially from the U.S.A.[71] His visit to Washington later in July was understandably used by him, therefore, to try to secure military assistance from President Johnson, and in this he was not unsuccessful.[72] This in turn made Subandrio say, after receiving the U.S. chargé d'affaires, that 'good relations with the U.S.A. depend on their attitude towards Malaysia'.[73] Thus was a new spiral set in motion with the aid of the Soviet Union and its concept of 'how to make friends and influence people'.

If one had taken some of Mikoyan's pronouncements during his sojourn in Indonesia literally, then the Soviet Union – e.g., in the dispute with China – was taking a much more virtuous standpoint than its fellow-communist opponents in Peking or elsewhere. In one of his speeches Mikoyan put forward the view that the main difference between Moscow and Peking boiled down to the question of whether 'international communism should be advanced by force of arms or other means'.[74] China, he said, wanted to use armed force; the Soviet Union did not. The irony must not have escaped him that there was a fair chance that the Soviet Union, as far as Indonesia was concerned, was doing just what it accused China of wanting to do, promoting communism by force of arms by creating international tension and thus domestic chaos. But here the question stood out: Who in Indonesia would benefit from Soviet arms? Mikoyan may even have argued, in an imagined mood of frankness, that he was in fact not furthering communism by force of arms but giving the Indonesian armed forces the necessary tools to keep his friendly P.K.I. comrades at bay. Of course this argument has been advanced more generally and, as noted above,[75] all through the period since the Soviet bloc began to be Indonesia's main arms purveyor, the P.K.I. had been aware of this inherent danger and seldom showed real gratitude for Moscow's 'selfless aid', as it was advertised from there. Leaving aside the reality of the danger to the P.K.I. of more, or more sophisticated, equipment for the armed forces, in the prevailing state of Soviet-P.K.I. relations the fact that Mikoyan was playing his own game so ruthlessly must certainly not have contributed to the general atmosphere of comradeship normally to be expected between communist partly leaders.[76]

It seems that as far as the P.K.I. were concerned Mikoyan during his visit was virtually boycotted, that is to say by the leadership around

Aidit, which dominated the party and its media.[77] Mikoyan may have alluded to the frosty treatment he suffered at the hands of the P.K.I. leaders when he remarked at the end of his stay that while he was in Indonesia he had experienced 'both a cold and a warm climate'.[78] In a television speech in Moscow just after the arrival of Subandrio, the Soviet Deputy Premier reporting on his trip mentioned a meeting with 'P.K.I. leaders'.[79] This was probably the Politburo, as he also referred to another session with Central Committee members and members of the Aliarcham Academy of Social Sciences. With the P.K.I. leaders, he said, 'a frank exchange took place among comrades, on all issues of interest'. It had been of a friendly character and 'useful'. The larger meeting Mikoyan described, in contrast, as 'very interesting'. He had given the assembled audience an exposition of the attitudes of the C.P.S.U. within the international communist movement, and, he told his Moscow viewers, he had met with 'great understanding', an expression he did not use to describe his conversation with the P.K.I. leadership.[80] It is not excluded that the larger audience of P.K.I. officials had been more receptive to a number of points Mikoyan made on behalf of Moscow's stand in the Sino-Soviet dispute. It was clear, as indicated earlier, that for the first time in a long period differences of opinion within the party on account of relations with Moscow[81] again existed.

On July 3 at the opening of an enlarged Central Committee meeting, the first National Conference, Aidit was openly speaking of 'contradictions within the party'.[82] It may not even have left untouched the P.K.I. Politburo which over the years had distinguished itself by a great degree of solidarity and cohesion.[83] On the eve of the National Conference, Politburo member Adjitorop was suddenly dispatched to Peking with eight other P.K.I. members, allegedly for 'suggestions'.[84] This in itself might then have failed to arouse any great interest but when early in September 1964 all the other members of the delegation came back and Adjitorop was left behind, attention was drawn. At the beginning of October it was reported that Adjitorop had been arrested in Peking, that he was schizophrenic and was being kept there in isolation.[85] Within days and with some ostentation, the Secretary-General of the Chinese Communist Party, Peng Teh-huai, was said to have had a 'cordial conversation' with Adjitorop in Peking.[86] The situation was rather confused, but the upshot was that Adjitorop remained in China.[87] If this episode was a cold purge, it may have saved him his life because at the time of writing Adjitorop is the only member of the Politburo of that period still alive. All the others have either been killed or executed.[88]

As to the substance of the difference within the party, it can be surmised that its more radical course, adopted at the end of 1963, was at the core of it, as well as the related row over the leaked document[89] that provided, and was to provide, anti-P.K.I. ammunition. Policy on Malaysia must also have been a specific point on which opinion may have been divided within the leadership of the party and here Mikoyan's stay in Indonesia in the second half of June had highlighted the divergent approaches within the P.K.I. That the Soviet leader must have urged his Indonesian comrades to go slow on the Malaysia confrontation can be concluded, for instance, from a sharp attack on 'modern revisionism' printed in the *Malayan Monitor* of June 30, right in the middle of Mikoyan's stay in Indonesia.[90] The article could be seen as a well-informed reaction to what had gone on in Indonesia while Mikoyan was visiting the country. But of course Moscow's tendency to soft-pedal the Malaysia issue must have been known earlier and the reaction was one given by rather unfriendly critics of what the Soviet Union then stood for in that part of the world. It spoke of the many friends the Malaysian liberation movement had been gaining for its anti-Malaysia struggle. But it continued: 'At the same time, many false friends were exposed, chief among them the modern revisionist "comrades" who tried to inject their idea of rapprochement with "Malaysia" or of "toning down" the confrontation policy'.[91] It needs little imagination to see who were these 'modern revisionists' thus taken to task and what the Soviet Union had *in casu* been trying to tell the Indonesians.[92] This reproach in the Malayan communist magazine did not pass unnoticed in Moscow, and in a major *Izvestia* article the attitude of the Chinese comrades towards the Indonesian-Malaysian conflict was exposed as somewhat hypocritical.[91] 'In recent times', the Soviet government paper wrote, 'the disparity between words and deeds has truly become systematic. Thus Chinese propaganda has recently been repeatedly emphasizing China's good relations with, and aid to, Indonesia. At the same time the Chinese's People's Republic has been trading with Malaysia. Moreover, trade between the C.P.R. and Malaysia has been steadily increasing. In 1963 [the year Malaysia was formed] the C.P.R. stepped up its imports from Malaysia by 400%

and exports from Malaysia grew by the same amount. Thus it turns out that the Chinese side is avowing friendship with Indonesia on the one hand while, on the other, it is supporting a country that now serves as a springboard for imperialist provocations aimed against Indonesia'.[91] Publication in China of the *Malayan Monitor*'s anti-revisionist attack on Mikoyan's dealings in Indonesia followed within days.[93] But the P.K.I. did not emulate this example and stayed away from directly taking issue with the Soviet Union. This had partly to do with the fact that Aidit had less use than ever for any internal opposition that might crystallize around a Soviet-inspired faction because he was confronted with a situation he had always tried to avoid: Anti-communists and non-communists making a common front. Slowly such an anti-P.K.I. alliance was taking shape in the summer of 1964, pushed by a number of Murba-oriented newspapers and army officers close to Sukarno, who thought the P.K.I. was trying to take over the leadership of the country.[94] On the other hand official Soviet-Indonesian relations had warmed up a bit again after the Subandrio visit[95] to Moscow and the tacit pledge not to split the anti-imperialist front under Chinese prodding. This made open or veiled disagreements with Moscow for the moment less fitting, at least for Aidit who kept following a course that would maximize returns for minimal risks.

NOTES

1. See above p. 177.
2. See above pp. 48, 52, 53.
3. See Harold C. Hinton, 1966, *Communist China in World Policies*, Houghton Mifflin Company, Boston, p. 46.
4. The trip lasted from mid-December 1963 until the end of February 1964 and included a visit to Albania.
5. For the first 'Belgrade' conference of September 1961, see above p. 111 ff.
6. On February 18, 1964, it was announced that the non-aligned countries would get together on March 23 in Ceylon to prepare the full conference; *Indonesian Observer*, February 18, 1964. Chou En-lai and Pakistan Foreign Minister Bhutto did the same for the A-A side also to meet in March; *Indonesian Observer*, February 24, 1964. Eventually the final date was set for April 10; *Antara News Agency*, March 19, 1964.
7. *Indonesian Observer*, March 23, 1964.
8. Abdulgani made this statement on March 25, at a time when the non-aligned preparatory conference took place in Colombo, Ceylon. See Uri Ra'anan;

1969, *The USSR Arms the Third World, Case Studies in Soviet Foreign Policy*, The M.I.T. Press, Cambridge, p. 2.

9. *Suluh Indonesia*, January 30, 1964.
10. See D. P. Mozingo; 1965, *Sino-Indonesian Relations: An Overview, 1955-1965*, Rand Corporation, Santa Monica, p. 66. It was generally assumed in Southeast Asia that a lot of extra-legal activities were financed through local Bank of China branches. Later in 1964 the Bank's offices in Djakarta, Surabaja, and Medan were handed over to the Indonesian authorities as a gift.
11. See above pp. 174, 175.
12. *Pravda*, September 2, 1964, published Mao Tse-tung's soon famous interview with a number of Japanese socialists in which he developed the idea of this 'intermediate zone', a wide area between the United States and the Soviet Union on the one side and China plus its Asiatic communist neighbors at the other, supposedly not unsympathetic towards Mao's China. See also below p. 309 note 37.
13. In due time the Soviet leaders were to draw attention to this anomaly, which also applied to Macao, the Portugese colony near Hongkong. In September 1964 a Youth Forum in Moscow was to be the scene of a sharp exchange on the position of Hongkong and Macao. The Soviet-sponsored thesis was that both colonies, as well as any other, including Portugese Timor (a hint to the Indonesians) should be liberated. The Chinese retorted that Hongkong and Macao were still Chinese territories; that Peking could decide how and when they would again become full part of the Chinese Republic and that, for the rest, any reference to them was 'interference in the internal affairs of China'. A Soviet commentator, probably noting with delight how sensitive the issue was to the Chinese, noted in pseudo-scorn thereupon that 'the People's Republic of China defended the right to remain a colony'. See *New China News Agency*, September 26, 1964 and *Moscow Radio Home Service*, September 29, 1964. For the use of Portugese Timor as a barometer in the Peking-Moscow-Djakarta triangle see *Moscow Radio in English*, August 17, 1964.
14. See above pp. 245, 246, 251, 254.
15. See *Harian Rakjat*, January 6, 1964 and *New China News Agency*, January 7, 1964, *Harian Rakjat*, January 7, 1964 and *New China News Agency*, January 8, 1964, and *Harian Rakjat*, February 3, 1964 with a violently 'Chinese' Njoto speech that was reported by *New China News Agency*, February 11, 1964.
16. *Harian Rakjat*, January 22, 1964 and *New China News Agency*, January 22, 1964.
17. In fact the first was a regular editorial, the second was signed 'observer', indicating a slightly less official opinion.
18. *New China News Agency*, March 27, 1964.
19. *Jen-min Jih-pao*, April 9, 1964.
20. With a certain relish the Indonesian President was quoted as saying: 'Indonesia will never collapse. To hell with your aid was his stout retort to

United States threats and artifices. This stand reflects the dignity of a nation that has risen to its feet and a severe blow to the vile tricks of the United States imperialists'.

21. See William E. Griffith, 1967, *Sino-Soviet Relations 1964-1965*, The M.I.T. Press, Cambridge, Massachusetts, p. 25.
22. See *Pravda*, April 3, 1964 and *Izvestia*, April 4, 1964.
23. *Far Eastern Economic Review*, May 7, 1964.
24. *Indonesian Observer*, April 10, 1964.
25. See also above pp. 255, 256.
26. *Far Eastern Economic Review*, May 7, 1964.
27. *Indonesian Observer*, May 25, 1964. The Arab countries clearly did not want to antagonize the Soviet Union because of its possible effects on Moscow's attitude towards Israel, and in Malaysia, after all, they saw a fellow muslim country.
28. *Djakarta Radio Home Service*, April 15, 1964; *New China News Agency*, April 15, 1964.
29. *Djakarta Radio Home Service*, April 15, 1964.
30. *Djakarta Radio Home Service*, April 15, 1964. It consisted of delegates from Afghanistan, Marocco, Ghana, Ethiopia, and Cameroon; *Indonesian Observer*, May 25, 1964.
31. Suwito Kusumowidagdo, interview, March 1972, admitted that what went on between Subandrio and Chen Yi at this Afro-Asian committee meeting 'could be defined as a bargain'. See also above pp. 255, 256.
32. On April 18 Chen Yi left on his special plane, characterizing the meeting as 'a brillant achievement', where, among other things, future Soviet participation had been rejected; *Antara News Agency*, April 18, 1964. The full meeting had been set for March 10, 1965; it was postponed twice and in the event never met.
33. *Pravda*, April 25, 1964. The formula, later used by Mikoyan, that the Soviet Union would support a second A.A. conference provided it contributed to solidarity and not disunity was then coined. See below p. 270.
34. One of the points made was that China at a Tashkent conference in 1958 had called the Soviet Union an Asian Nation. The 4,000 kilometer long border in Siberia with China was also used for the purpose. The Chinese had the stronger arguments, among others that Moscow had not taken part in the first conference in Bandung in 1955 and that anti-imperialism alone was not the touchstone but anti-imperialism *and* regionalism.
35. The major Chinese counter points were made in a *Jen-min Jih-pao* editorial on May 31, describing the issue 'closed'.
36. *Harian Rakjat*, July 15, 1964; *New China News Agency*, July 8, 1964.
37. Interview, March 1972, former spokesman of the Indonesian Ministry of Foreign Affairs Ganis Harsono.
38. *Tass*, June 26, 1964; *Pravda*, June 27, 1964. Mikoyan arrived on June 22nd in Djakarta and next day had a first session with Sukarno. It was reported then that the two had 'points of agreement' as to Malaysia and bilateral

economic relations, while Mikoyan had shown 'understanding' for Indonesia's wish to increase rice production; *Indonesian Observer*, June 23, 1964. Mikoyan addressed parliament and the mass rally on June 25.

39. *Djakarta Radio Home Service*, June 25, 1964. Since the beginning of the year a P.K.I. hardliner, Sukirman, had been in charge of Djakarta Radio. His credo had been to make this organization an instrument in the struggle towards 'Indonesian socialism'. See his statement to this effect in a broadcast of March 14, 1964. Apparently he did not consider it his first duty to give news.
40. *Antara News Agency*, July 1, 1964. Strangely enough, the next day the Indonesian news agency had to carry a correction of the text, as it had omitted reference to the Malaysia confrontation – not a minor point! According to the final version of the communiqué the Soviet Union gave support 'as is already known'; *Antara News Agency*, July 2, 1964.
41. See the Indonesian versions of Mikoyan's speech at the Djakarta rally on June 25: *Djakarta Radio Home Service*, June 25, 1964, *Antara News Agency*, June 25, 1971 and *Indonesian Observer*, June 25, 1964.
42. Speaking in Bandung he interpreted the Indonesian dispute with Malaysia as a special concern for the lack of independence of North Kalimantan; *Pravda*, July 3, 1964.
43. *Djakarta Radio Home Service*, report on the Djakarta mass rally, June 25, 1964.
44. *Tass*, June 26, 1964, quoting the Soviet journal *Za Rubezhom*.
45. *Indonesian Observer*, June 25, 1964; *Antara News Agency*, July 1, 1964 and *Pravda*, July 3, 1964.
46. *Djakarta Radio Home Service*, June 26, 1964 in a report of Mikoyan's speech at the Tjilegon building site, where he must have been rather shocked at the lack of progress.
47. *Pravda*, July 3, 1964. On the same occasion Mikoyan acknowledged that some of the plans of the Russians had not been too well thought out beforehand. See also above pp. 68, 69. New plans, allegedly agreed upon, still needed study and therefore time 'to prevent unfavorable speed'.
48. *Moscow Radio* in English, June 28, 1964; *Djakarta Home Service*, June 25, 1964.
49. *Antara News Agency*, July 2, 1964; *Pravda*, July 3, 1964.
50. Interview, March 1972, General Nasution. See below p. 289 and p. 296 note 33.
51. *Djakarta Radio Home Service*, July 9, 1964.
52. *Indonesian Observer*, July 2nd, 1964.
53. *Indonesian Observer*, July 4, 1964.
54. *Indonesian Observer*, July 4, 1964. Though the official communiqué of the Afro-Asian preparatory committee had referred the question of Soviet-participation to the conference itself, the immediate Chinese distortion of this had been that 'the matter was closed' (see above p. 269). The *Indonesian Observer* editorial now said that the view taken during the preparatory meet-

ing in April had been a result of taking sides in the Sino-Soviet dispute and agreed with Moscow that the Soviet Union was an Afro-Asian country. Clearly heavy pressure had been brought to bear upon Subandrio to revise Indonesia's stand.

55. *Warta Berita*, July 11, 1964.
56. *Indonesian Observer*, July 2nd, 1964, quoting A.F.P. from Singapore. On the day after Mikoyan's visit had been announced debt repayment had been linked to it. It was Njoto who, speaking before the party's Aliarcham Academy, warned not to ask for any further debt moratorium because the 'modern revisionists [read the Soviet Union] liked to be paid for their benefactions'; *Harian Rakjat*, June 9, 1964 and Uri Ra'anan, The Djakarta-Moscow-Peking Triangle and Indonesia's protracted struggle; manuscript put at the disposal of the author. The announcement of Mikoyan's visit had been made on June 2, after ambassador Michailov had been received by Sukarno; *Djakarta Radio Home Service*, June 2, 1964. Njoto gave his speech on June 3, 1964.
57. *Indonesian Observer*, July 2, 1964; *Antara News Agency* from Moscow, July 4, 1964. Air Commodore Budjardjo, in charge of logistics for the Indonesian Air Force, had arrived in Moscow on June 3, the day after Mikoyan's trip to Djakarta had been announced; *Djakarta Radio Home Service*, June 29, 1964. According to his own account of March 1972, he had been kept waiting in the Soviet capital until well after Mikoyan had returned from Indonesia. At first, there had been payment problems and other 'petty' arguments. Later this had changed with the result that, of the 12 requested MI-6 giant helicopters necessary for the Malaysia confrontation half were permitted to be sold to Indonesia, as well as some large Antonov-12 transport planes; see below p. 282, note 66.
58. Mikoyan, at a Surabaja press conference, when asked if he had discussed the sale of arms, replied that there were 'other times and means' to do that; *Antara News Agency*, June 30, 1964.
51. *Antara News Agency*, July 7, 1964, saying that Subandrio went 'within the framework of an agreement concluded by the Indonesian government with Soviet Deputy Premier Mikoyan'.
60. *Tass in Russian for abroad*, July 16, 1964.
61. Upon his return to Djakarta Subandrio said Soviet participation had been discussed, and would be looked into, thus confirming that the Moscow talks had made Indonesia reconsider its previous stand, at least outwardly; *Indonesian Observer*, July 23, 1964.
62. *Indonesian Observer*, July 17, 1964.
63. Repeatedly (not only in the final Moscow communiqué), the term was used that the Soviet Union *with Indonesia* opposed neo-colonist plans like Malaysia. This meant a certain Soviet claim to coordination or dialogue certainly in the military sphere between the two countries as far as confrontation was concerned.
64. *Indonesian Observer*, July 17, 1964.

65. The medium range missiles were refused because they could carry atomic warheads; interview, March 1972, General Nasution; see below p. 289.
66. *Antara* added to the Moscow communiqué that 'a further transfer of military weapons for the Indonesian Army to fulfil its task of defending the Republic of Indonesian has been *discussed*' [emphasis added]; *Antara News Agency*, July 18, 1964. A week later it was announced in Djakarta that another military mission would go to Moscow to work this out further; *Indonesian Observer*, July 27, 1964. The Air Force would get 12 large MI-6 helicopters of which 6 would be delivered before August 17, 1964, Indonesia's Independence Day, usually shrouded in dramatic rituals of some kind or other. Also delivered would be a dozen Antonov-12 transport planes to replace the American C 130 Hercules that were for the greater part grounded because of a lack of spare parts which the Americans refused to supply. Both helicopters and transport planes could hold 100 men and were of course thought to be handly in the semi-warfare of the Borneo and Malayan jungle. See *Antara News Agency*, July 4, 1964 and *Indonesian Observer*, Jul- 18, 1964.
67. *Djakarta Radio Home Service*, July 16, 1964.
68. See editorial in *Indonesian Observer*, July 18, 1964.
69. *Djakarta Radio Home Service*, July 21, 1964 and *Antara News Agency*, July 24, *1964*.
70. See above p. 185, note 25.
71. See for a first reaction of Rahman: *Indonesian Observer*, July 8, 1964.
72. *New York Times*, July 23, 1964.
73. *Antara News Agency*, July 25, 1964.
74. *Indonesian Observer*, July 29, 1964. Mikoyan was speaking at a mass rally in Surabaya on June 28, 1964. Earlier, he had characterised the Sino-Soviet quarrel as 'a historical necessity', a phase through which communist states had to pass; *Indonesian Observer*, June 25, 1964.
75. See above pp. 39, 69, 144, 210.
76. The abrupt end of the P.K.I. as an organized political power in the wake of the 'Untung coup' is not in itself proof that in the end the extensive military assistance from the Soviet Union was politically relevant. The destruction of the party after September 1965 did not require sophisticated weapons but a political climate. On the other hand the growing disintegration of Indonesia under Sukarno might very well have given the P.K.I. the same chance to come to power, even if Moscow had not tried to buy influence with large-scale arms deliveries.
77. See also Uri Ra'anan, 1969, p. 3.
78. *Djakarta Radio Home Service*, July 2, 1962
79. *Pravda*, July 12, 1964, *Moscow Radio in French*, July 11, 1964. No other reports about these talks have come to the knowledge of the writer.
80. The *Moscow Radio* version, beamed at France, differed from the Pravda rendering very slightly, as it had deleted Mikoyan's expressed hope 'to have promoted the unity between the two communist parties by holding these talks'.

81. See above p. 258.
82. *New China News Agency*, July 4, 1964.
83. See above pp. 36, 70 and 79 note 38.
84. *International News Service*, October 7, 1964.
85. *Indonesian Observer*, October 1, 1964.
86. *Indonesian Observer*, October 7, 1964.
87. On October 12, 1964 the P.K.I. came with a bulletin that Adjitorop had a liver disease for which he was treated in Peking; *Indonesian Observer*, October 12, 1964. One of the members of the delegation who had returned at the beginning of September said the P.K.I. leader had had a 'nervous collapse'. A news analysis of *Radio Free Europe* suggested at the time that Adjitorop had been pro-Moscow and therefore sent away; *Radio Free Europe*, October 7, 1964. Since the demise of the P.K.I. Adjitorop is the main P.K.I. spokesman abroad and from Peking supports the Chinese point of view on the international communist questions and on the cause of Indonesian communism.
88. See below p. 424.
89. See above pp. 257, 258.
90. The *Malayan Monitor* was a monthly, appearing in London under supervision of the Malayan Communist Party. It had strong ties with the Chinese Communists but also with the P.K.I. and often reflected extreme positions that were not or could not be voiced by the P.K.I. media. The chairman of the M.C.P., Ahmud Mudah, was a close friend of Aidit's; *Radio Free Europe*, August 11, 1964. The article referred to here was reported in China two weeks after its issue; *New China News Agency*, July 16, 1964.
91. To the Soviet Union Malaysia was 'a formally *independent* state' [emphasis added] be it dominated by the British capitalists, as Mikoyan formulated it in his T.V. address after he returned from Djakarta; *Tass*, July 11, 1964. This was not the Indonesian view of course, since it did not recognize the Federation at all. The Soviet veto in the Security Council in September was justified by saying that acceptance of the Norwegian resolution would have meant recognition of Malaysia by Djakarta; *Tass*, September 19, 1964.
92. *Izvestia*, July 12, 1964.
93. *New China News Agency*, July 16, 1964. Another way of indirectly countering possible political gains to the Soviet Union in Indonesia – but probably in the first place in North Vietnam – was the closing of the Hainan Strait for any 'foreign non-military vessel'; *New China News Agency*, July 27 1964. Hinton (1966, *Communist China in World Politics*, p. 48) points out that, officially, the measure had already been taken on June 5 but might have been antedated. The Chinese also did their best to disparage military aid Indonesia would get from the Soviet Union by spreading the word – to a large extent true – that it was second-hand. See for a Soviet denial of this charge, attributed to China, *Moscow Radio in English for Southeast Asia*, July 18, 1964.
94. *Indonesian Observer*, June 29, 1964 on the long drawn-out row between

Harian Rakjat and *Merdeka* in which the P.N.I. paper leveled this kind of charge against the communists and spoke of 'tyranny and terror by the P.K.I.'.

95. *Pravda*, July 30, 1964, speaking of 'imperialist provocations' on the Borneo border; *Moscow Radio in Indonesian*, August 9, 1964, on the same theme and expressing 'deep understanding' for Indonesia's aid to Vietnam and *Pravda*, August 17, 1964, described how nobly outraged the Indonesian people were with the lack of independence of North Kalimantan.

CHAPTER 20

Towards the Cairo non-aligned conference (1964)

While Aidit may for a number of reasons have held back in the period after the Mikoyan-Subandrio arrangement in early July, he was increasingly running the risk of being overtaken from the left side, and this time not only from within the party but also by Sukarno. It was the Indonesian President who was forcing matters to a head and with the prospect of receiving new and appropriate Soviet arms began putting pressure on Army commander Yani now to 'confront' Singapore and Malaya physically as well.[1]

Yani gave in to Sukarno's wish, though rather reluctantly, since large sections of the Army were opposed to it and feared corresponding gains domestically by the P.K.I. with the military engaged at the outer edges of the Indonesian archipelage. So on August 17, 1964, Indonesia's Independence Day, a new series of landings on the coast of Malaya were effected,[2] ringing in a new phase because the Indonesians that were landing were in full dress uniform and were recognizable as belonging to the Indonesian armed forces.[3] In his traditional speech that same day, under the indicative title 'Year of dangerous living', Sukarno, swelling with pride, claimed that 'now men are risking their lives to fight on the front to crush Malaysia'.[4] This was again one of those exercises in strong words like 'There is no compromise in the Malaysia question' and 'Don't try to disturb the Indonesian banteng'. But the Indonesian leader had nevertheless once more managed to force the pace and take people by surprise.

The decision to step up confrontation and now direct it against Malaya proper had been taken somewhere in the beginning of August.[5] Subandrio had given the first indication that action could be expected in a speech addressing anti-Malaysia volunteers in Batudjadjar in

Kalimantan, saying that confrontation would be implemented in 'a revolutionary, offensive way'. Not only in 'our own territory' (the adjoining Malaysian territories?) but 'elsewhere' this offensive notion would show up, he promised.[6] It may have been that the Tonkin Bay incident on August 5, which looked like a threat to North Vietnam, raising the tension in the area, had something to do with the new Indonesian military actions. Djakarta had recently effectuated a rapprochement with both North Vietnam and North Korea, establishing full diplomatic relations with those two communist states.[7] Sukarno may have felt that he now had both the backing of these countries and a suitable climate in which to escalate.[8] The approach of Independence Day with its accompanying need to provide the country with a new boost no doubt told with Sukarno at least as strongly as anything else.

In the whole new 'leftward' slant in Sukarno's foreign policy could be increasingly seen the influence of P.K.I. Second Deputy Chairman Njoto, with whom Sukarno began to develop very close relations. Since late in 1963 Njoto had been informally advising the Indonesian President, especially on foreign issues. But in the course of 1964 this had intensified to the extent that Njoto was in fact operating as a sort of shadow Minister of Foreign Affairs with his own office. In the communist press he was referred to as Foreign Minister Njoto.[9] So when he was appointed as 'aide to the President' at the end of August 1964,[10] becoming a member of Sukarno's powerful inner cabinet, it was not so much a new development as a confirmation of an established situation.

At this time a personal rivalry seemed to have arisen between Aidit and his second deputy which must have complicated relations among the leaders of the P.K.I., already strained by the continued pressure of the more radical elements, of which Njoto was the most outspoken. By exerting influence upon Sukarno directly Njoto threatened to outflank Aidit. However, this 'professional' argument was reinforced by plain jealousy when the time came that Sukarno was due for one of his periodic 'reshuffles' in his cabinet. This was after the President's Tavip Independence Day speech, when word went round that a prominent communist would qualify to be included in the inner circle of Sukarno's counselors. Aidit immediately volunteered eagerly and confessed 'to want to become a better aid' to Sukarno, having as he said 'decided to take part *actively* in the implementation of major Sukarno-policies' [emphasis added].[11] On the same day Radio Free Indonesia[12] reported that 'the P.K.I. was looking for a job for Aidit'.[13] It was, however, announced instead that Njoto had been appointed as 'Minister, aide to the President', a much more influential position than either Aidit or First Deputy Lukman occupied as largely honorific Ministers of State.[14] To Sukarno, apart from motives of playing one off against the other, the choice of Njoto was largely one of personal and ethnic preference, as Njoto – a Javanese with a background of lower nobility and a man with an incisive mind – suited the Indonesian President more than Aidit, the rather plain Sumatran.

Doubtless, however, it had its political impact in that a close Sukarno-Njoto 'congruence' developed, with the P.K.I. leader providing Sukarno increasingly with the ideas and the tactical suggestions the President was always in need of. So the important Tavip speech was largely ghost-written by Njoto, and the hand of the P.K.I. leader was also to be found in Sukarno's address to the Cairo conference of non-aligned countries in October that year.[15] As we have seen Njoto's position within the Sino-Soviet dispute had on a number of counts been decidedly more 'Chinese' than that of Aidit,[16] and his growing weight with the President must have dismayed the P.K.I. Chairman somewhat.[17] To Peking, however, the new configuration around Sukarno boded well,[18] and the Chinese leaders were not slow in stepping up their cultivation of the Indonesian President and building him up as the foremost leader of the 'uncommitted' Third World.

The first occasion that presented itself was the debate in the United Nations on Malaysia. When on September 2 another batch of Indonesian marines had landed on the coast of Malaya Abdul Rahman, Malaysia's Prime Minister, no longer hesitated and, as he had said he would, brought the whole matter up before the Security Council as a case of Indonesian aggression.[19] On the eve of the U.N. debate, the Chinese thought it wise – knowing that the Soviet Union might come to Indonesia's rescue politically[20] – not to be left out of the picture and placed their mightiest verbal battery in position: *Jen-min Jih-pao*. The official Chinese party daily came out with a strong editorial in favor of the Indonesian case, with the customary accusations against the U.S., this time charging that they wanted within the Malaysian federation to set the Chinese against the Malayans. This was probably a reference to the antagonism which a few weeks later was to lead to the secession of Singapore from the Federation.[21] As Antara noted it was 'the first authorized declaration for some time'[22] and what was more contained a rather fierce, no doubt exaggerated but indicative, warning that 'should U.S. imperialism dare to launch aggression against Indonesia, the Chinese people will back the Indonesian people with *all their might* [emphasis added]'.[23] That presumed or feared attack was of course far off, but it meant another step towards a Peking-Djakarta alliance that was in fact to materialize shortly. Aidit got the message but added the more immediate 'enemy' of Indonesia to the formula, saying that 'if *Great Britain* and the U.S. should attack, not only Malaysia but the whole of Southeast Asia would be lost to them' [emphasis added].[24]

At this juncture Sukarno started off for the non-aligned nations conference in Cairo due to open on October 5. The foreign political defeat of Indonesia in the U.N. was still fresh in his mind, and in internal affairs his position became more and more complicated by the growing antagonism between the aggressive P.K.I. and the counterforces they finally evoked. As more often in the past, when things got mixed up it was a good moment for the President to get out of the country, and the occasion this time moreover was quite legitimate.[25] But he left so early and while the country was suffering from such serious incidents that it looked more like an escape.[26] Sukarno stayed away for almost two months during which the instability of the regime was clearly demonstrated and his masterly hand, already however weakening, was badly needed.[27] But he may also have figured that his internal position would actually become stronger when he came home after having chalked up some victories among the non-aligned countries and that his balancing act at home as one of the world's foremost leaders could then again be more successfully pursued. Therefore Cairo could have been worth a thorough preparation to him, making him leave Djakarta long in advance of the Cairo Conference.[28]

But the Cairo Conference of 1964 was for the Indonesian President by far not the same non-aligned get-together he had experienced in 1961 in Belgrade. Things had changed drastically, both in the scale of his own priorities and in the context within which he had to realize them. He had already given a foretaste in his important Tavip speech in which he had announced a solid front between Indonesia, Cambodia, Korea, and Vietnam that 'no evil spirit, no genies, no devil' could prevent.[29] In other foreign policy issues his talk had been thoroughly intransigent and, while scolding the U.S. and endorsing the positions of his Asian communist neighbors, he did not show any consideration for intermediate positions as Moscow might have hoped for. In its domestic policy implications, softness towards the P.K.I. positions prevailed: He extenuated the P.K.I.-inspired unilateral actions in the countryside, praised his ban against independent-minded artists, threatened to 're-tool' again any minister who showed weakness toward 'imperialism', and explained that he had never intended the dissolution of political parties, when he had spoken of 'simplification'.[30] Alarmed by this turn of events Moscow may increasingly have felt the need to see what Sukarno would be up to in Cairo, certainly after he had been helped again in the United Nations by a Soviet veto. The Soviet leaders seem to have been willing to help Sukarno for fear of worse,[31] but at the same time must have had their doubts about the whole tenor of the agitation around Malaysia which was going clearly against Mikoyan's advice to play it cool and against the understanding Subandrio had reached in July.[32] While Sukarno was traveling in Europe, Defense Minister Nasution went to Moscow to continue the negotiations that Yani-Subandrio had left unfinished[33] and no doubt also to provide the Soviet leaders with some direct information on what was going on in Indonesia.[34] Suddenly Sukarno decided to go to Moscow. He had often previously wanted to be 'in' on what Nasution was doing abroad. In Moscow he would allegedly 'witness' some kind of ratification ceremony.[35] Pravda therefore carried the announcement of his visit – and a friendly profile – on the same day that the Indonesian President arrived in the Soviet capital on September 29.[36] Krushov had to interrupt his stay at the Black Sea for the occasion and the day after Sukarno's arrival started official discussions with him.[37] The exchange between the two leaders went on pretty badly, as could be judged from the summary way Sukarno explained later that day that the talks with Kruschov had been marked by 'friendliness and frankness'.[38] The Soviet Prime Minister, together with Mikoyan, had welcomed Sukarno upon arrival 'warmly',[39] but he was conspicuously absent when the Indonesian guest left again the next day, Kruschov having preferred to return to his Black Sea resort instead. Njoto was later to relate that the Soviet Premier and the Indonesian President had had 'a sharp quarrel'.[40] General Nasution was present at the official dinner where Kruschov literally fulminated against Sukarno lining up with Peking, comparing a closer Peking-Djakarta alignment with the Hitler-Mussolini axis of the pre-war period and telling his astonished guests that 'all axes will be destroyed'.[41] Evidence of the atmosphere in which the talks had been conducted was also to be found in the various qualifications in the final communiqué.[42] As to specific issues, on Malaysia the Soviet side repeated the formula already used at the end of the Subandrio visit in July.[43] Again it was said that 'the Soviet people *jointly* with Indonesia' supported the liberation struggle of North Kalimantan, meaning that some coordination should be observed. On the reinforcement of Indonesia's military capabilities, the various translations had textual differences, showing some confusion as to what had been agreed on.[44] Important in view of what Sukarno was going to say in Cairo was the common opinion the two parties expressed that 'peaceful coexistence is the only reasonable basis for international relations'. Also, on general disarmament both agreed that it was of 'decisive importance for peace', while the partial nuclear test ban 'had eased the international tension'. So on these three points, dear to Moscow and disputed in the Sino-Soviet wrangling that went on at the time, Sukarno ostensibly agreed without difficulty.

On the eve of the non-aligned conference this must at least have been a reassuring thought for the Kremlin leaders. But in addition it was even agreed in Moscow that the Indonesian delegation to Cairo would 'make a working paper in conformity with the Indonesian-Soviet communiqué'.[45] While Nasution signed some papers speeding up the transport of war material and then flew back to Djakarta,[46] Sukarno descended in Cairo. On the day of the opening of the non-aligned conference for which 57 countries had gathered, *Pravda* published a sermon stressing that non-alignment was entirely different from neutralism.[47] Rather arrogantly it asserted that 'the majority of countries participating in the Cairo conference gained their sovereignty in the recent past, relying on the support of the Soviet Union and other socialist countries'. The only country singled out here by name was Indonesia which, 'in its struggle to liberate West Irian was able to count on its strong army which was equipped with up-to-date material supplied by the USSR'. This fresh reminder to be grateful may not have reached Sukarno in time because, after having opened the conference on October 5th as first speaker after Nasser, he delivered the next day his main speech[48] and must have shocked even the more skeptical among the Soviet leaders who just had had conversations with him less than a week ago. It was one of the best and most cogently reasoned speeches Sukarno ever made, and there is no doubt that it was Njoto who had had a hand in it.[49] Just as three years ago, Sukarno said, the 'old established forces' were still very strong and 'we are not making much headway'. As in Belgrade he remarked that colonialism was not dead but had appeared in a new cloak, neo-colonialism.[50] But he saw differences: Firstly it was now clearly an era of contradictions, and he cited the fact that 'among the followers of a single ideology there are divisions and diverging trends'.

Secondly, security as a problem between the superpowers no longer existed (they knew the penalty of war would be self-destruction), but the security of the developing nations was therefore all the more at stake. Here Sukarno must have had his self-created Malaysia problem in mind. Thirdly, there was peaceful co-existence, a relationship originally devised, the Indonesian President said, for ideological reasons. However, following Mao the Indonesian President asserted that there were no longer any major ideological conflicts, only those concerning national interests. The major contradiction in the world today – between the 'nefos', the 'newly emerging forces', and the 'oldefos' – was one of the domination of the weak by the strong and not between two potential equals like the U.S. and the Soviet Union. Peaceful co-existence, therefore, had taken on another meaning: It could only be applied once rough *equality* had been established, once the ex-colonial and young nations – mainly in Asia, Africa, and Latin America – had ended the prevailing domination of the old forces. Here he cited Cyprus, Cambodia, Vietnam, and, of course, Malaysia.[51]

In an aside that must have been noted with particular interest in Moscow, Sukarno remarked on the widely cherished concept of peaceful co-existence: 'Our understanding of peaceful co-existence cannot perhaps be entirely taken for granted. Maybe we are not talking about the same thing'. In plain language the peaceful co-existence the Indonesian President was now talking about would only be possible *after* 'imperialism and colonialism' had been eradicated, something Sukarno had already earlier maintained, e.g., when he answered – rather belatedly – to Kruschov's speech of New Year 1964 on the peaceful solution of border questions.[52] More plainly even, Sukarno's concept had nothing to do with the current Soviet notion of peaceful co-existence and fully played into the hands of the Chinese. This was duly noted by the Indians and the Yugoslavs and at first only passively reported by the Chinese media which were slowly awakening to the fact that they had found a real friend in Sukarno.[53] Subandrio called it 'a new definition of peaceful co-existence',[54] but showed he was aware that, somehow or other, the Russians might not be very pleased. He said upon return in Indonesia he hoped that Soviet-Indonesian relations would 'remain the same'.[55] Anyhow, the 'twist' Sukarno had given in Cairo had left nothing much intact of the fine wording of the Soviet-Indonesian communiqué, drafted at the end of Sukarno's flying visit, let alone of the promise to operate in Cairo on the basis of a working paper that would reflect common Soviet-Indonesian viewpoints.[56]

The conference itself, enlivened no doubt by Sukarno's performance (Tito especially seems to have been very angry), quarreled about the priority of various themes. In this the Indonesians scored a point in having 'anti-colonialism', etc., at the top of the list of problems to solve. The Indians, as in 1961, had wanted peace first but had to give in and accepted a compromise formula. It was claimed of course from the Indonesian side that 'the greater part of the Indonesian ideas had been taken over'.[57]

To a certain extent formulas launched by Sukarno had indeed found their way into the final communiqué, like the 'nefos-oldefos' contradiction. But his new concept of peaceful co-existence was not endorsed,[58] and on the Malaysia confrontation the result was even less glorious. Here Indonesia had to make do with the passage against foreign military bases in general, in which nowhere the word Malaysia was to be found. As it was explained from the Indonesian side, the passage finally accepted had been 'intended by Indonesia particularly for the British military forces, bent on surrounding Indonesia'.[59] But it should be added that the final text spoke of bases established 'against the will of the countries concerned', so weakening further the application of this clause to Indonesia's case against Malaysia, at least in the eyes of most of the participants.

In Moscow the result was considered not too unfavourable, and the fight between the champions of peace-first and anti-colonialism-first was soothingly called 'a false contradiction'.[60] In all, considering the final outcome, the Soviet Union had not much to complain of.[61] Moscow therefore, officially at least, dismissed as so much nonsense talk about a 'so-called Peking-line'.[62] But criticism of Sukarno's stand was not slow in coming. A report on the Cairo conference in the government newspaper *Izvestia* lashed out: 'With a view to discrediting socialism in the eyes of the non-aligned countries the erroneous story is being advanced that peaceful co-existence between the Soviet Union and the United States allegedly extends to ideology as well'.[63] This was applicable to Sukarno who – true to his unreliable self – had lost no time in forgetting whatever he had signed in Moscow and without delay had gone out for the opposite 'Chinese' line of confrontation and extremism. But he must have kicked Moscow more in the shins than he might have realized, and no doubt his behavior caused sufficient displeasure for the Soviet leaders to look for ways to retaliate. Rumors soon had it that the Soviet Union had temporarily suspended arms deliveries in order to make the Indonesian government mend its ways.[64] The Indonesian President after having antagonized in succession Moscow, Belgrade, and Cairo[65] had continued unperturbed his world tour. His first stop-over was in Paris. Here, he had a festive luncheon with the Chinese ambassador, Huang Cheng, previously stationed in Djakarta during the most critical years of Sino-Indonesian relations and now a close friend. Sukarno, getting a foretaste of the lauding Premier Chou En-lai was soon to have in store for him, was congratulated on what was called his 'distinguished role in Cairo'.[66]

It was at this moment that Sukarno was informed about things that were afoot behind his back in Djakarta, and supposedly it was the Chinese who conveyed the warning, having as always excellent intelligence working for them in Indonesia. But these reports did not prevent Sukarno from accepting an invitation from Premier Chou En-lai to come to see him, adding one more flying visit to this trip. Between two previously scheduled visits to Tokyo and the North Korean capital of Pyong Yang, Sukarno was going to meet the Chinese Premier in Shanghai for 48 hours, with Chou En-lai coming down from Peking to compliment the Indonesian leader.[67] It was to be a decisive encounter that would direct the course of Indonesia's foreign policy for the next twelve months. Chou's accolade and his expressed admiration for Sukarno's 'major success' in Cairo must have been heartening for the Indonesian President, coming after his one-man performance among the non-aligned countries and in the midst of rumors of his impending resignation because of ill-health that were spreading in Djakarta.[68]

So Chou must have found Sukarno in a receptive mood, with the Indonesian pondering, while being wined and dined by his Chinese host, that things were not too bad after all.[69] It certainly must have made him feel more prepared to face his home base again, where affairs had meanwhile become rather disjointed during his long absence.

NOTES

1. Interview, March 1972, General Nasution.
2. *Kuala Lumpur Radio*, August 17, 1964; *Singapore Radio*, August 17, 1964. In the Soviet Union these landings were said to be malicious inventions; *Moscow Radio in Indonesian*, August 23, 1964; *Moscow Radio Home Service*, August 29, 1964. Kuala Lumpur, after a similar denial by *Djakarta Radio*, quoted a Philippine journal that five Indonesians and one Malayan would be tried because of the landings; *Kuala Lumpur Radio*, August 30, 1964.
3. *Far Eastern Economic Review*, September 10, 1964.
4. *Antara News Agency*, September 10, 1964. This event was probably what Sukarno had meant by his daring title 'Year of dangerous living' or Tavip for short: It was dangerous for others.
5. Dr. O. W. Röder, Djakarta correspondent of the *Süddeutsche Zeitung*, noticed a change in the course of the Malaysia confrontation policy of the Indonesian government somewhere around July-August; *Süddeutsche Zeitung*, November 19, 1964.
6. *Djakarta Radio Home Service*, August 13, 1964.
7. As result the South Vietnamese Consultate-General closed down; *Indonesian Observer*, August 11, 1964.
8. Hanoi of course had been delighted with the closer relationship, as had the P.K.I.; *Indonesian Observer*, August 13, 1964 and *Harian Rakjat*, August 12, 1964. As a kind of instant reward Ho Chi-minh had come out again and now in full-blast in 'total support' for Indonesia's Malaysia policy. It was Aidit, a long-time advocate of these friendship, who immediately coined the term 'Djakarta-Pnom Penh-Hanoi-Peking-Pyong Yang axis' soon to become, as had more often been the case, a part of Sukarno's verbal arsenal'; *Antara News Agency*, August 12, 1964.
9. See, e.g., *Harian Rakjat*, October 30, 1964.
10. *Antara News Agency*, August 26, 1964.
11. *Antara News Agency*, August 25, 1964.
12. See above p. 260 note 10.
13. *Radio Free Indonesia*, August 25, 1964.
14. *Antara News Agency*, August 26, 1964.
15. See below pp. 291, 292.
16. See above p. 206 ff.

17. *Antara News Agency*, August 25, 1964.
18. At the time of the United Nations debate on Malaysia the *Indonesian Observer* accused the P.K.I. of collusion with Peking, writing that 'the hardheaded group wanted to synchronise Indonesia with Chinese policy'; *Indonesian Observer*, September 12, 1964. A similar charge was made a month later by Trade Minister Adam Malik – the only cabinet member to speak out and take action against the foreign policy the country was following. He told a Murba meeting that Indonesia should not follow 'a certain country', as the 'hardheaded group' wanted it, pleading instead for a 'free and active' foreign policy and gratitude towards the Soviet Union; *Antara News Agency*, October 15, 1964. It struck Indonesian observers in China at the time that Njoto, who was often visiting Peking officially and unofficially, was always received with the utmost deference by the Chinese authorities, with a total disregard of protocol requirements; interview, March 1972. Baron Sastradinata, former Indonesian chargé d'affaires in China.
19. *New China News Agency*, September 5, 1964. The Security Council was due to hear the case on September 9.
20. This they did by vetoing a mild resolution that had the approval of all other members of the Security Council except Czechoslovakia. Djakarta duly thanked Moscow; See *Antara News Agency*, September 11 and 19, 1964.
21. *Jen-min Jih-pao*, September 9, 1964.
22. *Antara News Agency*, September 10, 1964; Reuters said 'since long', both probably referring to the editorials of previous March. See above pp. 267, 268.
23. The coordination behind it was shown by editorials in similar vein in the official party papers of North Korea and North Vietnam, using the same reference as quoted from *Jen-min Jih-pao*; see *Indonesian Observer*, September 11, 1964, on the North Korean and *New China News Agency* of the same date on the North Vietnamese declarations.
24. *Antara News Agency*, September 12, 1964. Aidit mentioned Great Britain because that country to most Indonesians was still more plainly an 'enemy' than the USA. Somewhat later, while visiting Indonesian Timor with a parliamentary delegation, Aidit repeated what he had said earlier in Djakarta, but now only mentioned Great Britain; *Antara News Agency*, September 23, 1964. Two days later the Chinese 'pledge' was repeated by Peking's representative at a Sobsi-congress. He said that '650 million Chinese are with you, come what may, if U.S. imperialism . . . etc.; *New China News Agency*, September 25, 1964.
25. Sukarno was due to visit a number of other places besides Cairo. Among them Vienna, where he was accustomed to have his state of health checked (it became a source of speculation and was to have political consequences) and Belgrade where he would meet with fellow non-aligned statesman Tito. While Sukarno was still in Indonesia, no mention was made in this program of Moscow which was squeezed in later as it turned out.
26. Sukarno left on September 17. The day before communist youth groups had ransacked the offices of the *Merdeka* newspaper as a sign of censure of the

paper's anti-P.K.I. opinions; *Indonesian Observer*, September 15, 1964. At the same day the Army had appointed regional Army chiefs, throughout the country with the intention of re-establishing some kind of factual 'state – of – emergency' authority, *Far Eastern Economic Review*, November 12, 1964. In many places anti-American demonstrations were rampant being directed especially against the USIS offices and the Peace Corps.

27. See below p. 300 ff.
28. *Antara News Agency*, September 17, 1964.
29. *New China News Agency*, August 17, 1964. In enumerating this axis there is no reference yet here to Peking, which was nevertheless highly praised as a country that had become master in their own house, etc.
30. See above p. 244. One of the ministers 'retooled', that is purged, was Ahem Erningpradja, Minister of Labor who had been the target of the P.K.I. for his resistance to a Chinese-P.K.I. dominated Afro-Asian Workers Conference and as an ex-P.N.I. labor leader had been inclined to make a more moderate approach.
31. Interview, March 1972, with Ganis Harsono.
32. See above pp. 272, 273.
33. See above p. 272. Nasution succeeded in getting agreement on the delivery of short-range rockets – 30-50 miles – which he thought he needed to close off the Straits between Sumatra and Malaya, although, in the event, nothing came of it because Indonesia first had to train the necessary military technicians; interview, March 1972, General Nasution. As to the medium-range rockets that were refused to Yani earlier, Nasution was told that the Soviet Union was prepared to help them reach any target that they wanted to aim at with these medium-range weapons, as that was completely within Soviet capabilities. Against the background of the growing Sino-Indonesian intimacy Moscow certainly may have been reluctant to provide Djakarta with vehicles that potentially could carry nuclear warheads, for fear of thus letting the Chinese into their secrets.
34. According to *Antara News Agency*, Defense Minister Nasution flew to Moscow 'to assist Sukarno in his talks'; *Antara News Agency*, September 23, 1964. He arrived a few days before the President.
35. Interview, March 1972, General Nasution.
36. Sukarno stayed less than 48 hours and confusion reigned as to the nature of this visit. *Pravda* called it an unofficial one (September 29, 1964). The President himself thought it had been an official one (*Indonesian Observer*, October 2, 1964).
37. *Tass*, September 30, 1964. In the presence of Mikoyan, since the end of July President of the Soviet Union, the three had met, with Nasution also present, on September 29. *Moscow Radio Home Service*, September 29, 1964.
38. *Moscow Radio Home Service*, September 30, 1964.
39. Mikoyan had welcomed Sukarno by saying that 'if you were to stay a bit longer, you would see what progress the Soviet Union has made since your last visit three years ago'. To which Sukarno, not less prickly, replied that

though he admired the Soviet Union, Indonesia had also progressed over the last three years; *Antara News Agency*, September 9, 1964. Before Sukarno left the chartered Pan-American luxury liner he travelled in, a stream of platinum blond stewardesses burst out of the plane, and Kruschov innocently remarked to Nasution on the welcoming pad 'I always thought Indonesian girls were dark'.

40. *Harian Rakjat*, April 23, 1965 and Uri Ra'anan; 1969; *The USSR Arms the Third World: Case Studies in Soviet Policy*, The M.I.T. Press, Cambridge, Massachusetts, p. 4.
41. Interview, March 1972, General Nasution. The pro-Peking orientated C.G.M.I., the Indonesian Communist students organization, and the Pemudah Raja, the communist youth organization, were a thorn in Kruschov's flesh.
42. *Pravda*, October 2, 1964. It spoke of 'sincere cordiality, friendship and mutual understanding', but unity of views was not particularly mentioned.
43. See above p. 273 and p. 281 note 63.
44. Pravda said that agreement on reinforcing Indonesia's defensive capabilities 'was expressed'; *Pravda*, October 2, 1964. The *Indonesian Observer* wrote that agreement 'was reached'; October 2nd, 1964. *Harian Rakjat* had it that an agreement 'has already been reached', October 3, 1964. The Russian version, less committal, is probably the correct one. General Nasution denied that the Soviet Union ever put anything in the way and stressed its government remained forthcoming towards arms requests until after the 'Untung coup', but he admitted that payment difficulties between Moscow and Djakarta existed; interview, March 1972. Air Commodore Budjardjo referred to problems the Indonesian Air Force then had in obtaining spare parts, while the training program for pilots also ran into difficulties; interview, March 1972. See p. 385 note 14. *Harian Rakjat* had a curious sentence at the head of the communiqué, not found anywhere else and, although self-evident, likely to have been invented: 'Soviet-Indonesian relations are certainly based on the principle of mutual rights, benefits and respect for sovereighty'.
45. *Djakarta Radio Home Service*, October 3, 1964.
46. *Indonesian Observer*, October 9, 1964. Nasution lauded the agreement made, the fourth he said since the beginning of the arms trade between the two countries. No details were given.
47. *Pravda*, October 5, 1964; *Radio Moscow Home Service*, October 5, 1965. This was an old theme dear to Moscow, which feared a really organized third bloc as much as it did an Afro-Asian one dominated by the Chinese. The West, so *Pravda* said, was trying to make believe that non-alignment was rather like opposition to both 'imperialism and socialism' and this was of course all wrong. To the Soviet-Union non-alignment had the advantage of limiting 'the sphere of activity of the aggressive blocs, [broadening] the zone of peace . . .'
48. *Antara News Agency*, October 7, 1964.
49. Njoto was one of the members of the Indonesian delegation while Aidit, who had been present in 1961 in Belgrade, had remained in Indonesia. Right

after the conference, Njoto went to Moscow where he addressed Indonesian students and gave a detailed account of what he called the five victories of Cairo. *Harian Rakjat,* reporting on this meeting called Njoto 'Minister of Foreign Affairs'; October 30, 1964. Njoto was also the dominating personality in the three-men 'political team' within the large Indonesian delegation, which decided on the line to be followed; *Antara News Agency,* October 2, 1964. Finally, the whole line of thinking in Sukarno's address reflected a style and pattern that was typically Njoto's.

50. In 1961 this had put Sukarno in opposition to Nehru, who thought the East-West relations between the super-powers the most important issue at the time. See above p. 112.
51. On economic development as a prerequisite for ending the last vestiges of colonialism – a tenet held by people like Tito and outside the non-aligned circles of course Kruschov – Sukarno said this only made sense 'when we have torn up by their roots *all the institutions, all the links* that make us subservient in any way, in any fashion, to the old order of domination' [emphasis added]. This was a clear and clairvoyant picture of what Sukarno had in mind and soon would aim at in practice, e.g. when he walked out of the U.N. at the end of the year.
52. Kruschov made his speech on December 31, 1963, and with it wanted to appeal to many Afro-Asian countries which had border disputes that either did or could involve armed clashes. The reasoning was that collective agreement to solve them only through mediation, etc., would eliminate this important source of tension in the world. At the back of Kruschov's mind was no doubt a major border problem he might himself have on his hands – along the 4,000 km frontier with comradely China. The Soviet Union tried to elicit reactions, preferably favorable. Sukarno gave his in fact negative one in June; *Antara News Agency,* June 19, 1964.
53. In India it was said that Sukarno had given 'a new twist' to peaceful co-existence. In Yugoslavia Sukarno's notion was called 'a distortion of the meaning of a policy for non-aligned countries'. See *New China News Agency,* October 10, 1964.
54. *Antara News Agency,* October 21, 1964.
55. *Indonesian Observer,* October 21, 1964.
56. See above p. 290. Suwito Kusomowidagdo related that the speech he had prepared for Sukarno while waiting for his arrival in Cairo was completely discarded by Sukarno; Interview, March 1972. The Indonesian President preferred Njoto's input apparently.
57. *Antara News Agency,* October 11, 1964.
58. The official text said that peaceful co-existence was the only way to maintain world peace, but this could not 'fully' be achieved so long as imperialism still existed; *New China News Agency,* October 12, 1964. *Antara* twisted the sense by leaving out 'fully', so that it could count this point as one of the many that had been contributed by Indonesia; *Antara News Agency,* October 11, 1964. This news agency kept claiming Sukarno's triumph on this point;

October 13, 1964.

59. *Antara News Agency*, October 13, 1964.
60. *Moscow Radio Home Service*, October 12, 1964.
61. An *Izvestia* article on October 13 summed up the various points where the conference had taken stands close to Moscow's: On the Moscow treaty, in disarmament, on peaceful solution of disputes, and on peaceful co-existence as the only reasonable policy.
62. *Izvestia*, October 13, 1964.
63. *Izvestia*, October 17, 1964. To Moscow it had been a Chinese heresy, now also being peddled by Sukarno.
64. *Kuala Lumpur Radio*, October 29, 1964, quoting P.K.I. sources in Djakarta.
65. Unfavorable reactions and irritation at the Indonesian government showed up in the United Arab Republic, while Cairo began to drag its feet on the Second Afro-Asian Conference and showed signs of hedging on Indonesia's confrontation policy against Malaysia; *Indonesian Observer*, November 14, 1964 and *Djakarta Radio Home Service*, November 14, 1964. Relations with Yugoslavia after the Cairo conference were characterized by Tito's reply to the question of whether his country had bad relations with Indonesia: 'That is a matter of opinion'; *Indonesian Observer*, November 14, 1964.
66. *New China News Agency*, October 22, 1964.
67. *New China News Agency*, November 4, 1964.
68. During the Cairo conference Sukarno had a serious attack of kidney trouble that was at the source of the rumors spread later that autumn in Indonesia, while Sukarno still was travelling abroad. Interview, March 1972, Ruslan Abdulgani. See below pp. 303, 304.
69. Sukarno came home from this visit to Sjanghai very pleased as he had been received, in his own words, better than in Indonesia. He especially was touched by the thousands of children along the road from the airport to the town, singing in Indonesian 'Sukarno, you belong to whom?', a popular love song in which his name had been substituted. Interview, March 1972, General Nasution. It was one more example of the shrewd way Peking was playing upon the Indonesian President and his weaknesses.

CHAPTER 21

The revolution without the great leader (1964)

One of the explosives left undefused after the departure of Sukarno to Cairo was the issue of 'the simplification' of the party system. The growth of P.K.I. influence within the country and its orientation towards Peking abroad had resulted in attempts to reduce the number of parties – that is to emasculate the P.K.I. – or create dissension within the P.K.I. with similar effects.[1] The opposition to Aidit and his men found encouragement from external forces such as the Soviet Union and, possibly, Yugoslavia.[2] Inside the country the forces trying to make a front against the trend staked out by the Sukarno-Subandrio-Njoto alliance were organized in particular by Trade Minister Adam Malik who belonged to the anti-P.K.I. national communist Murba and Mohammed Diah, owner of the nationalist newspaper Merdeka who had a P.N.I. background. Their ploy was to use Sukarno to fight Sukarno: By continually swearing their loyalty to the Indonesian President, they tried to counter those aspects of his current policy that were dangerous in their eyes, laxness towards P.K.I. campaigns such as the 'aksi sepihak', the unilateral actions that brought dissension into the heart of the Indonesian villages, and the growing orientation towards China. The organization set up, the Body for the Promotion of Sukarno-ism or B.P.S., quickly became a center of political activity, especially after Sukarno had temporarily left the scene. The B.P.S. recruited many followers among the non-communist newspapermen who had been watching with increasing exasperation how slowly all the news media had been taken over or infiltrated by P.K.I. members, fellow-travellers, or spineless Subandrio-adepts. Special reporting teams were set up, with mobile facilities, to cover what happened in the countryside far from the Djakarta scene and often remained unreported in the national press because of the selective tactics employed by the communist bureau men at the Antara News Agency.[3] The tactics the B.P.S. used were often similar to what had been experienced from the communist side, and it was Malik, a dyed-in-the-wool, experienced agitator from his youth, who provided the brains behind the B.P.S. Quotations from Sukarno, e.g., his fiercely anti-communist speeches at the time of the Madiun rebellion – 'Muso or Sukarno' – came in handy, as well as loud publicity to expose weaknesses or gaffes of opponents. The basic thing was that at least some sort of organized resistance was put up that was non-military in background, although of course the military provided support and some cover.

Aidit showed great caution, probably more than many of his radical followers thought necessary, and tried to sound the least provocative.[4] He of course remained dead-set against the idea of disbanding parties or creating a pioneer monopoly party, but he must have felt he was not too strong, since the absence of Sukarno had deprived him of a most valuable ally in the somewhat adverse climate of that autumn 1964. The P.K.I. chairman saw a 'vanguard party' only after the leadership of revolution had been taken over by the working class – the usual long-term approach – and made clear on various occasions that, notwithstanding the charges of his opponents, the P.K.I. did not see the features of a revolution in the present situation.[5]

Sobsi-chairman Njono was of a slightly different opinion when, opening the Congress of this communist trade-union in September, he quoted Sukarno to the effect that a leading party should imply that other parties could very well remain, but as 'sergeants' not as 'generals'.[6] Njono drily remarked then: 'It all depends on which is the leading party'.

Notwithstanding the relative caution Aidit observed, he was very active, especially with 'teaching' at the Revolutionary Cadre Training School, and could easily slip up. This did in fact happen when he was speaking on the state ideology, or Pantjasilah, and gave the impression (rightly so) that the P.K.I. once the revolution was in its 'socialist' stage had no use for that philosophy, with its rather embarrassing belief in God. The result was an uproar, started by N.U. member of parliament Chalid Widjaja, who charged that the P.K.I. only saw Pantjasilah as a tactical means of achieving its aims of sole power.

The row was used by the B.P.S. to make a point, and the press as far as it sided with the B.P.S. movement – and that was the greater part – cried murder: The skeptics were not wrong about the communist aims; not Manipol but the Communist Manifesto was the P.K.I. guide book, etc. This and similar charges were all over the place thrown at the P.K.I.[7] Aidit put up a massive defense, for some time not missing a single day in personally defending his stand and correcting the 'slander' heaped upon him and the P.K.I.[8]

The main point Aidit tried to make (if successful, it might have been enough) was to have said just the opposite from what his distractors wanted to put into his mouth: Pantjasilah was not a way 'only' to unify the nation, but 'uniquely' designed to do so, he was supposed to have meant, and therefore the five-fold state philosophy would also be a necessary tool, once 'socialism' had been reached.

P.N.I. Secretary-General and crypto-P.K.I. man Surachman had to come to Aidit's help by volunteering testimony that Aidit had been right.[9] As leader of the Revolutionary Training Cadre School, where Aidit had given his incriminating talk, this carried some weight. Nevertheless, *Harian Rakjat* also published a transcript of what Aidit had said, but this was not of much use as it left various interpretations open.[10] The best way out for a settlement of the dispute, Surachman suggested, was to put the whole affair before Sukarno.[11]

The plight Aidit was temporarily in threw some light upon internal P.K.I. relations, though some caution in judging should be exercised, because the available sources are mainly Murba-oriented newspapers. Reports in that section of the press mentioned a split between Aidit and Njoto.[12] Opponents of Aidit criticized him internally for his handling of the 'Pantjasilah-incident', or rather for creating it,[13] and called him, according to the *Indonesian Observer*, 'bombastic' and 'emotional'. On the other hand they praised Njoto, who was described by his alleged faction as 'intellectual' and 'objective'. In itself it is not improbable that, on occasions like this, existing rivalry came to the fore, and it could be a pointer as to how precarious the balance at the P.K.I. top level could become once the stress was really on, as it was to be one year hence.

The other side, the B.P.S., was looking for support from First Deputy Premier Subandrio, who returned from Cairo and took over from Leimena. The third man of the régime had been in charge of current affairs in Djakarta while Sukarno and Subandrio had been at the Cairo conference, but Leimena's grip on the situation had been slippery and without authority.[14] Subandrio instantly had his hands full, and apart from the Aidit affair there were the twin-events of Kruschov's 'resignation' and the explosion of China's first atom bomb, both occurring on the 16th of October, the day before Subandrio's arrival from Cairo. On Kruschov Sukarno's deputy had, for the moment, no comment. As to the nuclear blast at the Lop Nor site he said it would have been better if it had not happened.[15] Non-communist opinion tended to regret the sudden disappearance of Kruschov from the Soviet scene, but *Harian Rakjat* immediately expressed its 'joy', and Aidit was quoted as having called it a 'good event'.[16]

Just before the news about Kruschov and the Chinese bomb broke, another development, of a more domestic nature, loomed. Rumors began to spread somewhere around October 14, after the Cairo Conference had been closed[17] and delegates returned to Djakarta, that Sukarno's state of health was deteriorating and his extended stay in a Vienna clinic had not resulted in any improvement. It was at this time, too, that Trade Minister Adam Malik openly took a stand against what he called the 'obstinate group' (the P.K.I.) which he said was trying to entangle Indonesia in the Sino-Soviet dispute. The country should not make too many enemies, he said, clearly alluding to the Cairo conference, where Sukarno had not made himself popular with India and Yugoslavia.[18] Malik and his Murba circle tried to enlist Subandrio and shape things up while Sukarno was away and progress could be made in setting up some organization capable of putting the brakes on the P.K.I. The instrument to do this was the Body of Promotion of Sukarnoism which, it was hoped, would receive the official blessing of the Constituent Assembly.[19]

At that particular moment the extremely ambitious Subandrio, sensing, or hoping, that Indonesia was already in the 'pre-post-Sukarno-era', openly brought up the question of what was to happen once Sukarno was gone or incapacitated.[20] Speaking to the Police Academy in Sukabumi, he publicly asked how the revolution would be carried on 'when Sukarno can no longer lead it'.[12] An immediate reaction from Sukarno, then in Tokyo, was put out by the Indonesian embassy in the Japanese capital, saying that 'Sukarno was still the effective leader of the country'.[22] The source of the rumors was conveniently given as

Kuala Lumpur, from where in fact reports on Sukarno's state of health had been published. But this had been done by quoting, among others, Indonesian sources like Subandrio.[23] The Deputy Premier had made a gaffe by laying himself open too soon as an eager contestant in the succession struggle that he thought was around the corner.[24]

It was later denied by Sukarno that this episode brought Subandrio into disrepute, but it was Malik rather than the Acting President who was summoned to Tokyo.[25] Meanwhile, the machinery was put into reverse, and Subandrio let it be known that he had been 'misquoted', etc.[26] He had become apparently more prudent now and was non-committal towards the B.P.S. and warned its members not to let themselves be provoked by attacks from others – i.e., the P.K.I.[27] He was made by the B.P.S. press to look like supporting them but in fact was hedging.[28] But Aidit too kept playing it cool and had similar admonitions, especially for his young followers, who should 'not allow themselves to be provoked by the counter-revolutionaries', i.e., the B.P.S. coalition.[29] He told them 'not to take action and to beware of the authorities'.

This was the point at which Sukarno finally returned home, having completed his various trips and excursions.[30] The situation changed from night to day, or the opposite, depending on the way one looked at things. At first Sukarno himself kept somewhat out of the limelight, but the P.K.I. regained its courage, possibly not only because of the presence of the President but also because of some of the news he brought with him.[31]

A few days after Sukarno's return, the P.K.I. began to take the initiative again and opened its offensive against the B.P.S.[32] *Bintang Timur*, banned for some time, was again allowed to appear,[33] and B.T.I. Chairman Asmu, as first in a row of P.K.I. politicians, suggested the peasants should be armed, giving as a motive the threat of an invasion by the Americans.[34] Munir, the new Sobsi President, spoke of a 'heightened offensive' of Manipolist forces, i.e., the 'true' Sukarnoists, or better, those who would join the Sukarno-P.K.I. bandwagon that the P.K.I. hoped was about to start again.[35]

The B.P.S. meanwhile acted as if nothing had changed, quoting Subandrio's promise of 'help' to support their case and charging that the P.K.I. had again begun their attacks to force President Sukarno to interfere – which was probably true.[36] Most prominent non-communist Sukarno-adherents like Navy Commander Martadinata, Minister of

Religion Zuhri and Siliwangi Commander Adjie continued to express support for the B.P.S. But things were changing.

Sukarno was taking matters in hand again, and Subandrio, as usual one of the first to get the message, must have concluded that it would be better to review his neutral-benevolent attitude towards the Sukarnoists. After some delay caused by the unexpected visit of Chinese Foreign Minister Chen Yi at the end of November,[37] Subandrio turned his attention to the B.P.S. and began distancing himself by charging that 'attempts were again being made to create ideological conflicts among us'.[38] Sukarnoism, the Deputy Premier stressed, should not divide the people and 'measures' should be taken to prevent it. The winds were changing, and Subandrio was arranging his cloak accordingly. Having done that, he conveniently left for New York to attend the session of the General Assembly of the United Nations, leaving to the President the problem of how to cut the knot.

In this respect Sukarno again showed himself to be the past master at dealing and wheeling, and at once executed his plan in quick tempo. On the one hand Sukarno could not but have noticed the disorder the P.K.I. had created with its unilateral actions in the countryside, where now the P.N.I., strongly represented in Central and East Java, had also threatened to revolt against its own leadership, or at least to go it alone. On the other hand he saw a B.P.S.-coalition, in his name but in fact threatening to deprive him of his major countervailing force against the military, the P.K.I., and this was also difficult for him to accept. So the first straw in the wind was the demand of the central leadership of the P.N.I. (Djakarta-based and left-Sukarno oriented) to prohibit B.P.S.[39] But together with five other parties the P.N.I. also demanded an end to the illegal actions in the villages. The B.P.S. press went on until the last moment to claim fullblown continuating of its role 'on behalf of the revolution' and cited important names still behind it.[40] But on December 12 Sukarno called representatives of all ten political parties to his palace in Bogor and had them confer from midday until midnight, hammering out finally the Bogor Declaration, an edict that had to restore the peace between them.

For the P.K.I. Aidit and Lukman were there, and the P.K.I. Chairman was personally able to defend his four-point ethical code, prescribing the parties to be nice to each other and solve disputes amicably through 'musjawarah' talks.[41] This code became part and parcel of the

Bogor Declaration, against which Aidit had to concede that the same method should also be applied to the disputes in the countryside; armed action was out. Intensified confrontation with Malaysia and still unannounced, but likely, prospects of sharp action against the B.P.S. fraction must have made this one concession on the part of the P.K.I. palatable to Aidit, certainly since it appealed to his own cautious policy of infiltration from above and from below. Under a restored Sukarno this again promised in his view the best and most sure way to power.[42]

Aidit did not have to wait long. On December 17, barely five days after the Bogor edict, Sukarno announced his decision to dissolve the B.P.S. and to have its 'function' taken over by Subandrio's Retooling Board.[43] Another week and the B.P.S. was a forbidden organization, and the way was open to purge those who had exposed themselves too much during Sukarno's absence.

Sukarno had with uncanny agility manipulated the situation, using his prestige and his personal power to redress a development that very well might have cost him his job, or at least a great deal of his power. The P.K.I., especially the way Aidit had led it during the crucial immediately past period, did not quite measure up – in a way surprisingly – to the expectations one might have had, considering its organizational impact and pretence, but through Sukarno they had a chance to recover the lost ground. This complex relationship and the limits it showed should have been a warning to the P.K.I. and its leaders that, whatever strength they might have had then, it was still only Sukarno's power that could keep them out of trouble. To the communists' advantage, however, Sukarno was often in need of exactly such a dependent partner as Aidit's leadership provided, so that their mutual weaknesses could cancel each other out and even, paradoxically, form a source of impressive power as the coming year was to show. As such the outcome of the struggle for power underneath Sukarno's umbrella at the end of 1964 could be called 'a resounding victory' for the communists.[44]

NOTES

1. See above p. 257.
2. Apart from what has been recounted, the extent to which both Soviet, and, to a lesser extent, Yugoslav diplomacy may have been in a position to in-

fluence events in Indonesia in an anti-P.K.I. direction is a matter of conjecture. The P.K.I. may have at times felt it worthwhile to exaggerate 'interference' from these sides, just as in an earlier period labeling the P.K.I. as 'pro-Moscow' was used to detract from their standing as a reliable national partly.

3. Interview, March 1972, Zein Effendi, Chief-Editor *Djakarta Times*, in 1964 one of the leading men of the B.P.S. movement, which was to cost him his job at the *Antara News Agency*.
4. See, for example, a speech he made on the island of Timor which he visited as head of a parliamentary delegation between September 12 and 18, 1964. He stressed that no 'confrontation' between parties should take place (as distinct from actions against 'landlords'), and he took care to declare that the P.K.I. was not anti-religious or anti-private property; *Harian Rakjat*, September 21, 1964. See also Aidit at the final session of the Sobsi conference where he launched the idea of 'party ethics': following Manipol (the central Sukarno 'philosophy' or charter), consultations and not confrontation, and mutually refraining from criticism of fundamentals; *Indonesian Observer*, September 28, 1964.
5. *Harian Rakjat*, September 21, 1964, *Harian Rakjat*, October 6, 1964. But as a sop to his own hardliners he now and then made a distinction, for instance when he began a series of talks for the Revolutionary Cadre Training School (a National Front institution that was a good front for P.K.I.-indoctrination of non-communists). He then remarked that the 'first stage' of the revolution had certainly been reached and that 'the revolutionary forces had to be organized more perfectly now'. Probably this did not mean that the first so-called 'national-democratic' stage of the revolution was already over, but may have been meant less dogmatically. In this period also the basis was laid for more organized subversion within the armed forces with the creation of a committee under Sjam Kamaruzzaman, later to be tried for his part in the Untung-coup. See below p. 378.
6. *Harian Rakjat*, September 24, 1964.
7. *Indonesian Observer*, October 18, 1964, October 20, 1964 and October 23, 1964.
8. *Harian Rakjat*, October 22, October 26, October 29, 1964.
9. Surachman who later played an important part in splitting the P.N.I. into a pro- and anti-P.K.I. group went into hiding not long after the Untung-coup and was eventually shot.
10. 'If we were already one and wholly unified', Aidit was supposed to have said literally, 'there would no longer be any need for the Pantjasilah. You must agree that the Pantjasilah is the instrument *par excellence* for unity, do you not? If we were already "one" and fully unified, what more would be felt to be necessary to weld us together'? *Harian Rakjat*, October 30, 1964. This text would seem to confirm that the protests of the non-Communists, especially the muslims, had some foundation. Maybe it was put forward with malicious intent by the Njoto-faction.

11. *Indonesian Observer*, October 30, 1964. This was also a usual ploy in Indonesia.
12. *Berita Indonesia*, October 24, 1964. Njoto was at that time in Moscow, where he gave a speech to the Indonesian students on the Cairo conference on October 27. See above p. 297, note 49. See for other indications of rivalry between the two P.K.I. leaders above pp. 286, 287.
13. *Indonesian Observer*, October 24, 1964.
14. For instance he tried to silence criticism on the desperate rice situation by forbidding the press to write about it. No one obeyed. *Indonesian Observer*, October 15, 1964.
15. *Antara News Agency*, October 18, 1964; *Indonesian Observer*, October 21, 1964.
16. *Suluh Indonesia*, October 17, 1964. *Harian Rakjat*, October 17, 1964 and *Indonesian Observer*, October 17, 1964. See further below pp. 313, 314.
17. See above p. 299 note 68.
18. See above p. 292. These two countries just had been attacked once again by *Harian Rakjat. Indonesian Observer*, October 14 and 15, 1964.
19. A delegation of the anti-P.K.I., military backed Soksi trade-union went to Bandung, the seat of the Assembly, to lobby for the B.P.S.; *Indonesian Observer*, October 28, 1964. Later from Soksi-side the publication of a number of articles written by Sukarnofan Sajutti Melik were promoted; *Indonesian Observer*, November 4, 1964.
20. Sukarno was made president for life in May 1963, but Subandrio may have thought that Sukarno was soon advised by his doctors to resign.
21. *Indonesian Observer*, October 26, 1964. He said at that occasion also that the Indonesian revolution, just like the Russian one, was a 'left' revolution, but that for Indonesian 'left' did not mean 'communist'. He reacted on the Pantjasilah-incident by remarking that the Indonesian state philosophy had precedence over the Communist Manifest.
22. *Tokyo Radio*, October 27, 1964. *Djakarta Radio Home Service* reported from Tokyo that Sukarno's health had much improved since Vienna; October 27, 1964.
23. Of course for propaganda reasons Kuala Lumpur made more out of it than could be based on facts. So on October 29 its radio station happily announced that the fall of Sukarno was only a matter of days. There are no indications that there have been serious reasons for this to have happened.
24. Subandrio had top level consultations with Ali Sastroamidjojo, Djambek of the National front and finally Aidit (on the Pantjasilah-affair also) on the day after his speech to the Policy Academy increasing the rumors that a coup d'état was afoot, but the talks may have been nothing but nervous chatter.
25. *Antara News Agency*, October 31, 1964. Malik was called allegedly to accompany Sukarno on his coming trip to North Korea, but there he never was reported to have arrived. His trip partly had a private character, as he was asked to talk Sukarno's Japanese-born fourth wife out of accompanying the President to Shanghai.

26. *Kuala Lumpur Radio*, October 30, 1964.
27. *Indonesian Observer*, November 14, 1964; *Antara News Agency*, November 11, 1964.
28. According to the *Indonesian Observer* he had promised 'help'.
29. *Harian Rakjat*, November 14, 1964. Aidit was speaking before a Pemudah Rakjat – People's Youth – meeting on November 12. The opening of the attack on him and the P.K.I. he put at October 17 (the moment Chalid Widjaja took him to task on his Pantjasilah statement). Tensions were rife and Aidit may have felt his grip on the communist mass movements slipping. In North Sumatra for instance the day before the local P.K.I. had demanded the closing of 'B.P.S. papers', and after a mass meeting Pemudah Rakjat ransacked a restaurant for trivial reasons; *Indonesian Observer*, November 12, 1964.
30. The President arrived in Djakarta on November 13, 1964.
31. See further below p. 327.
32. *Harian Rakjat*, November 17, 1964.
33. *Antara News Agency*, November 18, 1964.
34. *New China News Agency*, November 21, 1964. It was Chou En-lai who first suggested arming a 'fifth force' in Indonesian so as to 'reinforce' Indonesia's capacity for confrontation and help with the necessary weapons. See below p. 327. This was first broached between Chou and Sukarno when they met in Shanghai. Chen Yi elaborated upon this theme when he turned up suddenly in Djakarta at the end of November. 'Cooperation' in the field of 'atomic science' was also a topic then. See below p. 334. The P.K.I. leaders must have been briefed soon after the Chou-Sukarno talks by the Chinese.
35. At the end of September Politburo member Njono had resigned as Sobsi-chairman and was succeeded by Munir. Njono was known as one of the best organizers within the P.K.I. leadership, and a year later he turned out to have been in charge of the communist armed youth groups that had to supervise, and partly execute, the Untung coup. Being free from the daily management the 3.5 million strong Sobsi organization Njono was now able to take on fresh tasks.
36. See *Indonesian Observer*, November 19, 1964 and *Antara News Agency*, November 23, 1964.
37. Chen Yi arrived on November 27 and left again on December 3. He was preceded by the Indonesian Ambassador to Peking, Djawoto, who arrived as unannounced as Chen Yi on November 25. To what extent Chen Yi's presence also had a bearing on domestic Indonesian affairs is not clear from the evidence available; see below p. 328. But it certainly reinforced the arguments in favor of the Chinese-Indonesian alliance that Sukarno brought back from Shanghai and that would in his mind have served his purposes: unity in the face of external danger and personal aggrandisement.
38. *Indonesian Observer*, December 4, 1964.
39. *Antara News Agency*, December 10, 1964; *New China News Agency*, December 18, 1964.

40. *Indonesian Observer*, December 11, 1964.
41. *Djakarta Radio Home Service* reported that Sukarno had been 'ill', but it turned out that the swollen feet he had, making it difficult for him to walk, were only symptoms of his kidney trouble and not a reason for resigning; *Indonesian Observer*, December 14, 1964; *Djakarta Radio Home Service*, December 13, 1964.
42. To compound Aidit's troubles Chaerul Saleh had brought up the preceding week the 1963 P.K.I. document in the inner cabinet, and it also formed one of the points of discussion at the Bogor meeting. Saleh and Aidit had a sizeable quarrel, but the alleged fisticuffs between the two did not occur according to witnesses. Aidit succeeded in getting his denial of authenticity (the document was not written in P.K.I. style, he claimed) more or less accepted by Sukarno, probably not because his argument was convincing but because a compromise deal with the various political forces represented was a must for the President. See also above p. 264, note 59.
43. *Djakarta Radio Home Service*, December 17, 1964; *Indonesian Observer*, December 18, 1964.
44. *Far Eastern Economic Review*, December 24, 1964.

CHAPTER 22

Peking, the red beacon (1964-1965)

All through 1964 the domestic political scene was by and large opening up for the P.K.I. new vistas of influence building, not in the least thanks to Sukarno and the climate of dissolution he allowed, and consequently the Indonesian communists seem to have lost a good deal of their interest in the details of the Sino-Soviet wrangling. After the Party under Aidit had concluded in the crucial months at the end of 1963 that the balance of power at home was the thing to concentrate on[1] and that they had better not expect too much from outside communist forces, the rift between Moscow and Peking could be looked upon with more equanimity. Added to this was the inclination among the party leadership and cadres at least not to be bothered too much by 'theoretical' questions, partly because the level of training did not encourage this and partly because flexibility or opportunism had been a successful formula for the P.K.I. under Aidit. The Indonesian communists had to operate within the context of a very special political society that did not put a premium on doctrinaire justifications but on skillful maneuvering. When the situation finally seemed to permit or necessitate a more dynamic approach within Indonesia itself, the split within the communist world movement began even to be of some use as a mechanism for playing off one 'spiritual' center of Marxist thought against the other.[2] All in all, the ins and outs of the dispute could be faced in a more detached way.

Aidit himself had done his best especially during and after his trip to China in 1963 to come up with some innovations in communist political thinking in order to underline the independent stand of the P.K.I. as well. For instance he began to term the 'revisionist' parties that tended to side with Moscow 'modern dogmatists' because, as he put it, they were 'dogmatic' in following a leading party, i.e., the Soviet Communist Party. It was Njoto who gave Aidit the honor of this 'invention', though he himself may well have thought it up.[3] At any rate it had found its way into the jargon of the Peking-oriented communist parties,[4] as a convenient way of appearing balanced in denouncing both revisionists and dogmatists as the 1957 and 1960 Moscow documents required while in fact being partisan. Aidit also gave a systematic description of four types of communist parties that he thought had come into existence since the difference in the movement started to spread like a bush fire.[5] Here it was the opposite side that took note of the new formula that Aidit had advanced. The Soviet paper *Party Life* in its issue of June 1964 paid attention to the statement Aidit had made immediately after he returned from China at the end of September 1963.[6] The Soviet article was part of a theoretical refutation of those particularly Chinese but also increasingly Indonesian communists who advocated the notion that splitting of parties was a natural phenomenon.[7]

It was the first time that a more general opinion of an Indonesian communist had been taken seriously, and in this article, besides Chinese opinions, no other except Aidit's was taken into account. For the state of Soviet-P.K.I. relations it was significant that nowhere was it made clear exactly whose opinion was being criticized, not even that it was Indonesian. But, closely following Aidit's original text, it referred to those who said that 'the international communist movement is now allegedly undergoing a process of "selection, crystallization and condensation" and that there are at present four types of Communist and Workers Parties'.[8] Then followed the four types mentioned by Aidit, and his point that a communist party could very well have relations with more than one communist party in one country.[9] Of course, this heresy was rejected by the Soviet party, but it was all done in a rather gentlemanly way, as if the heretics were not yet beyond hope like the Chinese.

An analysis of P.K.I. opinion on major issues of the dispute that was breaking up the cohesion of world communism as reflected in P.K.I. publications after the December 1963 plenary yields a few general conclusions apart from the one mentioned that 'theory' had a low rating in the eyes of leading Indonesian communists, engaged as they were in forging ahead towards their 'socialism'. One is perhaps the conclusion that the tone of their debate with the Russians nowhere resembled the acerbity of the exchanges between Moscow and Peking, though in their stand they were in 1964 drifting at least as far from them as the Chinese. This no doubt had something to do with the distance, both geographically and in interests, between the two. The moment not only opinions but hard action were involved (as for instance in the April-May period when the unity of the party may have been thought to be jeopardized by Soviet meddling) the tone immediately became sharp and personal.[10] National character probably also had something to do with the way the differences were phrased, Indonesians being polite and evasive where others might be straightforward and brutal. The reflection of the Sino-Soviet disagreements in Indonesian communist thinking had another feature in the rather limited range of interests it covered. After all, Indonesia was a major power in terms of population only and was run by a handful of people, the overwhelming majority being totally immersed in their numerous and pressing daily problems and having little access to outside information. So 'revisionism' could hardly mean anything if it was not made visible in something either good or bad. Therefore, one frequently came across an attempt to explain the communist jargon in terms that would make sense to non-believers as well.[11] This must have been a hard job, requiring the use of slogans, simplifications, and tireless effort. But, as pointed out, though the P.K.I. leaders showed a remarkable energy in getting their mass organizations geared to the necessary climate in which they could realize their aims, whatever was not immediately connected with their task tended to drop more or less out of sight.

A case in point here was the fight going on for or against another world conference of communist parties. All through 1964 opposition to such a gathering was made, but it looked as if the topic had lost its interest to the P.K.I. leaders once they had decided that the two great powers had first to get their differences mended (if that was still possible) before a new round of multilateral talks could be thought of. All their various meetings with like-minded communist parties, mostly of the Southeast Asian area, had something to say about it; but the variations were limited: Bilateral talks first, no hurry, proper preparations, etc. A slight interest could be noted again the moment Kruschov had been dropped and Aidit thought – as did the Chinese – that relations between China and the Soviet Union might improve.[12]

Repeating his first reaction and saying that the 'resignation' in itself was a good thing, Aidit saw 'new and closer relations' between Peking and Moscow as a distinct possibility.[13] This was still the case after Aidit had received Soviet Ambassador Michailov on November 11 for a first-hand account of Kruschov's fall.[14] After that visit *Harian Rakjat* reported that according to Aidit, 'Soviet-Indonesian relations will improve'.[15] This may have been a result of indications given by the Soviet representative that the new leaders were more 'open-minded' and less involved than Kruschov with the Murba Party through Malik, ex-ambassador in Moscow and with the army through Nasution.[16] Chou En-lai's announced trip to Moscow to attend the October Revolution celebration was called a good sign by Aidit.

On Kruschov's pet project, the conference of communist parties, Aidit suggested it would be better to postpone it because the proposed date – December 15 – was very close. Aidit's soft-spoken reaction may also have reflected what had been the Chinese viewpoint – 'wait-and-see' – which Ambassador Yao Ching-ming must have conveyed when he called on Aidit on November 5.[17] Meanwhile, however, Brezhnev had made his first major policy declaration, to which Peng Chen gave an initial reaction the next day to the effect that, to the Chinese, Kruschov's fall had not meant much since the Soviet Union apparently stuck to its guns.[18] Then China published a strong Albanian attack on Moscow. This was already an indication that Peking was preparing to reject completely whatever slightly modified approach Brezhnev and Kosygin had in store for them. This came on November 21 with an article in the theoretical journal *Hung Qui*, after which Moscow again began to lobby actively for the preparatory conference of the 26 communist parties, but postponed it for practical reasons until March 1, 1965.[19]

Meanwhile the P.K.I., preoccupied with the domestic scene, had indicated that it was shifting back to a more 'Chinese' stand in the Sino-Soviet dispute.[20] On December 8 *Harian Rakjat* published parts of an address that the Australian pro-Peking communist leader Hill had given to the Aliarcham Academy a week earlier and in which Kruschov was attacked as the 'fifth column' of the West within the socialist fortress.[21] The joint declaration of the P.K.I. and the Australian C.P. was even less generous and concluded that 'the revisionists', i.e. the successors of the ousted Soviet leader, 'would try to continue

Kruschov's disastrous line'.[22]

As to the conference the two parties went one step further than the formula the P.K.I. had adopted on the last occasions, before the fall of Kruschov.[23] In addition to adequate preparations, attendance by all communist parties exercising power (including the Albanians) was a new *sine qua non*. After this it was hardly necessary for the Soviet Ambassador Michailov to get the formal reply of the P.K.I. to the invitation for the March conference. However, he nevertheless took the trouble.[24] The P.K.I. would not attend 'a single conference', he was told, except on the same two conditions already formulated together with the Australians – thorough preparation and the full participation of all reigning communist parties. In addition it was said that it would be better not to convoke the March meeting at all since it would threaten to split the international communist movement and only create problems, rather then solve them.

This was a pretty hard standpoint, very ungraciously brought home to the Soviets.[25] The P.K.I. had overcome its initial hesitation following the disappearance of Kruschov, equally reflecting Chen-Yi's advice and the new-found self-confidence that the Party had been given by recent developments in Djakarta where Sukarno had helped them to a very significant breach in the ramparts of the opponents, the B.P.S., and its affiliated forces within the press, the civil service, and the army.[26]

The hard line towards the Soviet Union on the communist conference found a corresponding issue when Sukarno suddenly decided to quit the United Nations Organization. During a meeting of Koti, the supreme body for fighting Malaysia, on December 30, 1964, Sukarno, who was not always informed on the details of state affairs, discovered that Malaysia, instead of fading away as of January 1, 1965, as he had predicted, would secure a seat in the Security Council of the U.N.[27] This was enough to make him explode in anger while exeryone present was hoping that someone else would tell the President that it was madness to leave the world organization for that. But nobody actually did, and Sukarno's step was endorsed.[28] Subandrio after first having ordered immediate execution of Sukarno's whim had doubts and second thoughts,[29] realizing of course that this step would alienate the Indonesian President still further from the greater part of world opinion, not in the least in the European communist states.[30] But Sukarno could not be persuaded to revoke his decision and announced on January 7, 1965, that Indonesia had definitely quit the U.N.

In Moscow embarrassment was drowned in a lot of publicity on the massing of British troops on the jungle border with Indonesia and on their evil intentions in general.[31] Subandrio tried to reassure the Soviet Union and promised according to Pravda that 'Indonesia would fulfil its duty'.[32] Ambassador Michailov was instructed to visit the Indonesian Foreign Minister and did so twice on January 5, handing him on one of these occasions a personal letter from Soviet Premier Kosygin who urged that 'Indonesia had better continue the struggle within the U.N. [because] otherwise the struggle of the Soviet Union in the U.N. against the imperialists would become more difficult'.[33] Sukarno's January 7 speech was reported in the Soviet Union without comment,[34] while Belgrade was furious and, as Subandrio later related to Chou En-lai, 'Nasser, Tito, Nkrumah, the Congo, Sato, and Bandaranaika urged reversal of the decision'.[35] The Chinese were just as much taken by surprise as anyone else,[36] and it took them some days to sort out this windfall. However, by January 6, a *Jen-min Jih-pao* editorial in a first comment, expressed support for Indonesia's pending withdrawal and told its readers that the seating of Malaysia in the Security Council was a 'provocation', etc.[37] Meanwhile, Yao Ching-ming had already conveyed this message officially to Subandrio[38] in a conversation in which, as we may assume, details of the forthcoming trip by the Indonesian Foreign Minister to Peking were also discussed. This trip was now to take place under favorable auspices for the budding Djakarta-Peking axis.[39]

It was interesting to see how Aidit was increasingly taken into account by foreign communist diplomats, at least as much as Subandrio. On January 8, the day after the U.N. walkout had become definite, the ambassadors of the Soviet Union, Hungary, and Poland went to see the communist party boss.[40] It proved the concern the European communist countries felt for the growing involvement of both the Indonesian government and the P.K.I. with Peking. But it was equally indicative of the status Aidit had achieved as a representative of a semi-official force in the country. Ambassador Michailov seems to have once more tried to get Aidit to pay a visit to Moscow, but was told that the P.K.I. leader had 'no time'.[41]

As to Sukarno's decision to quit the U.N. Aidit had immediately given his blessing, calling it 'a correct and firm stand' that put the Indonesian Republic in the forefront of the anti-imperialist struggle.[42] In the first few days after this unprecedented step, the P.K.I. Chairman also pretended that this move had received the support of the 'new emerging forces and primarily of the socialist countries although not all of them had been asked to take the same view'.[43] Somewhat later, however, Aidit showed a greater sense of realism. He turned ultra-nationalist when he commented on January 31 that the communist states faced a test as to how thorough their opposition to colonialism actually was. He added that 'some of them praised Indonesia's U.N. policy and other socialist countries did not. Indonesia's line is more progressive than that of socialist countries'.[44] As to the alignment of the P.K.I. within the communist world movement, Aidit stuck to the position that the P.K.I. had not sided with Peking and had remained entirely independent: He favored neither a Moscow nor a Peking type of communism, he declared to a western audience.[45]

It was in this climate that thc Soviet Union tried once more to get the P.K.I. to change its attitude on the forthcoming preparatory conference of the 26 communist parties, which had earlier been postponed because of Kruschov's fall and was due to open in Moscow on March 1. Michailov again had talks with Aidit, and though the nature of the March meeting had been readjusted to accommodate the more moderate among the pro-Moscow and pro-Peking parties invited, the result remained negative.[46]

To Aidit it must clearly have been of secondary importance by now what had happened around the Moscow meeting, since the domestic scene was of so much more interest to the P.K.I.[47] He followed rather than kept abreast of developments. Meanwhile, he was increasingly anti-Moscow. After Chinese and North Vietnamese students had staged demonstrations in front of the American Embassy in Moscow (protesting against the U.S. bombings of North Vietnam) timed to embarrass the March preparatory meeting, Aidit voiced his support[49] and expressed sympathy with the injured Chinese and North Vietnamese students.[49] The ultra-left wing *Bintang Timur* was allowed to go one step further and condemned what it called 'the brutal suppression' by the Soviet armed forces and police of a thoroughly democratic demonstration.[50]

As to the results of the March conference itself, Aidit waited until it was over and until he had had occasion to receive the first official Chinese reaction. Only then did he find time to receive Soviet chargé d'affaires Sevostinov to give him the P.K.I. stand.[51] What transpired was a softly-phrased rejection of the whole idea of a meeting such as had taken place earlier that month in Moscow because as Aidit had remarked between 1943 and 1957 the international communist movement had also operated well without wide-scale meetings.[52] The conditions for a future conference were the same as formulated in mid-December 1964.[53]

It seems that until this time Sukarno may have been a restraining influence on direct attacks on the Soviet Union by P.K.I. organs. However, for reasons of his own the Indonesian President slowly began to care less. Strong condemnation of the Moscow meeting by pro-Peking parties asking the new Soviet leaders to recant openly and exercise self-criticism (signs of a further escalation of the Sino-Soviet dispute) were not reprinted in Indonesia.[54] But early in May, while the P.K.I. was preparing to celebrate its 45th anniversary in a grand style, the inhibitions on the Soviet Union were increasingly thrown to the wind. Aidit congratulated his Malayan alter-ego – the strongly anti-Moscow Malayan C.P. – on its 'militant style and contributions to the unity of the international communist movement'.[55] At the same time he had a statement printed in *Harian Rakjat* which was made by the Malayan communists not less than three months previously but probably considered at that time still too obnoxious or provocative to be published.[56] Certainly, if one considers the early date of its composition, it was an extremely violent and open diatribe against the present Soviet communist leaders. It repeated earlier Chinese charges that Kruschov 'highandedly' stole the leadership of the Soviet communist Party, but added, and this was new as far as it concerned a P.K.I. endorsed opinion, that 'the leadership of the Soviet Union is still loyal to Kruschov's revisionist line'. It also repeated the new demand that Moscow had to recant before the Kremlin leaders could again be accepted as Marxists. It was still not a direct attack against the Soviet Union bearing official status for which it could be held responsible, but it did not fall very much short of it and showed the mood the Indonesian communists were in at that time as far as their erstwhile friends were concerned. The official P.K.I. anniversary statement somewhat later called them 'modern revisionists' but also 'volunteers of imperialism', while Kruschov's fall, it was pointed out, had not meant that the fight against these 'modern revisionists' would slacken.[57]

In his political report to the 4th plenary session of the P.K.I. Central Committee that preceded the festive celebrations at the end of May, Aidit spoke of 'great faults' made during the Kruschov era, resulting in the split within the international communist movement.[58] Whoever made the same faults would also fall by the wayside, he warned, adding the charge that the modern revisionists were now 'more subtle and more dangerous'.[59] The Indonesian Communist Party chief also explained why he had not gone to Moscow for the March meeting. It would have meant 'fuel to polemics', he had written to the Soviet comrades, and the P.K.I. preferred to retain 'formal unity' over a further split. This was probably wise.

All this had been a pretty accurate introduction to what the Soviet representatives could expect in Djakarta when they arrived for the 45th P.K.I. anniversary, officially to be commemorated on May 23. The delegation from Moscow, not too high-powered under second-string alternate Presidium member Rashidov, arrived on May 13, just in time to be in Djakarta when the Chinese, with their expertise in fireworks, exploded their second A-bomb.[60] It was a technical achievement whose sophistication even surprised experts in the West. But its propaganda effect as well as its timing was at least as important. In that respect also the P.K.I. showed, within their limitations, a remarkable sense of organization and showmanship during the anniversary festivities.[61] On the political level it showed up in the way the P.K.I. tried outwardly to retain its self-assumed air of independent agent within the communist world, while in fact being as partisan as their actual circumstances had made them to be. The P.K.I. headquarters were adorned with two main portraits, of Aidit and Sukarno. No living foreign communist was given the honor of decorating the building, but the preference was nevertheless not hidden by the smaller paintings of Marx, Lenin, and Stalin.[62]

On May 23 a mass rally was held in the Soviet-built Senajan stadium, where only Sukarno and Aidit spoke, and on May 26 an only slightly less massive reception was held giving foreign dignataries the chance to convey their congratulations publicly. Here both Peng Chen, the leader of the Chinese delegation, and Rashidov were given the floor, and the decorum of communist unity was kept, both giving a low-keyed speech (Peng Chen only relatively).[63]

Meanwhile, however (on May 25) the hardliner Chinese Politburo member and Mayor of Peking had addressed the P.K.I. Aliarcham Academy of Social Sciences, and, to put it mildly, what he had to say could hardly have pleased the Soviet delegation.[64]

No doubt knowing what the P.K.I. was up to while asking Peng Chen to speak at this particular place and time, Aidit introduced his guest speaker with a few words that must have riled the Soviets. Aidit called the Chinese Communist Party a 'red beacon', adding that 'in the past we could not immediately grasp the meaning of the statements on modern revisionists by the C.C.P.: a signal that will become our line and guiding light'.[65]

Apparently restrained in speaking his mind when giving his previously agreed speech on March 26, Rashidov called a press conference immediately afterwards to at least show that the Peng Chen speech had not passed unnoticed.[66] At the same time he must have lodged a complaint with the P.K.I., but this only came out after the Yugoslavs news agency Tanjug (no doubt briefed by the Soviet delegation) reported that on June 9th the P.K.I. had not yet found occasion to answer 'the protest'.[67] In all Rashidov and his party may not have felt too happy afterwards about this extended birthday party.

So while for the P.K.I. then the Sino-Soviet rift had become a fact of life, the independence Aidit and his colleagues had continuously tried to maintain shifted in the course of 1964 and early 1965 from a neutral to a more pro-Chinese version. It was still comparatively moderate in tone. For example direct anti-Soviet references were limited to those instances in which the P.K.I. in its internal existence felt threatened, e.g., during April-May 1964. But the distance taken from Soviet positions became nevertheless increasingly wider. A particular case was the world conference of communist parties Moscow wanted to hold so eagerly. P.K.I. opposition to it while Kruschov was still in power in the Soviet Union seemed suspended for a while after the Soviet leader had been ousted by his colleagues in October 1964. In close parallel development with Peking, but always shades less extreme, Aidit had again, after Brezhnev had shown his color, picked up the issue of the communist summit to reject it more categorically by raising the ante.

When Indonesia quit the United Nations Organization as a result of Sukarno's increasingly unbalanced behavior, it provided an issue that was to bring Aidit almost automatically into line with Peking on the interstate level rather than with Moscow, which looked askance at the Indonesian President's antics. Other questions, such as the beginning of direct American involvement in Vietnam from February 1965 on, tended to forge a bond with the Chinese on the ground of regional-nationalistic interest. But the major factor making even the 'moderate' Aidit turn his eyes to Peking was, again, the *domestic* trend that had set in with the emerging Sino-Indonesian partnership, for which we have to return to the fateful meeting between Sukarno and Chou En-lai in Shanghai in October 1964.

NOTES

1. See above p. 230.
2. See above p. 234, note 14.
3. *Harian Rakjat*, February 10, 1964.
4. The term 'modern dogmatic' was found for instance in the Chinese-Albanese communiqué issued at the end of Chou En-lai's visit to Albania in the beginning of 1964; *New China News Agency*, January 9, 1964.
5. See above page 225.
6. *Party Life*, June 1964, in an article entitled 'Against splitters, for unity of the communist movement'. See above p. 258.
7. The major exposition of this thesis had been given by Chou Yang, one of the foremost Chinese ideologists of the day in a speech given at the end of October 1963 and published two months later. See Griffith, 1967, *Sino-Soviet Relations 1964-1965*, The M.I.T. Press, Massachussets, p. 16.
8. From Aidit's report on his trips abroad in *Harian Rakjat*, September 30, 1963. See above pp. 225, 226.
9. *Harian Rakjat*, October 4 and 5, 1963; See above p. 225.
10. So Aidit's outburst 'we will never forgive the modern revisionists' when amalgamations of parties was thought to be imminent and promoted by the Soviet Union; *Harian Rakjat*, May 2, 1964; See above p. 263, note 49.
11. See Lukman in *Harian Rakjat*, January 19, 1964 and Aidit in *Harian Rakjat*, March 17, 1964.
12. *Harian Rakjat*, October 24, 1964.
13. He added that, of course, one could not immediately expect the new leaders to drop the conclusions of the previous Soviet Party Congresses, the 20th, 21st and 22nd Congress, by now seen as the root of all evil by the Peking-oriented communist parties. For the time being it looked as if Aidit were giving Brezhnev and Kosygin the benefit of the doubt.
14. Michailov had come directly from the Soviet Union; *Antara News Agency*, November 12, 1964.

15. *Harian Rakjat*, November 14, 1964. A discrepancy is noticeable in the *Harian Rakjat* rendering, and the way both *Antara* and *New China News Agency* phrased this part of Aidit's comment on Michailov's report. *Antara* writes that Soviet-Indonesian relations would not undergo any change; *Antara News Agency*, November 12, 1964. *New China News Agency* said that Aidit saw 'no harm' to these relations; *New China News Agency*, November 20, 1964.
16. See Uri Ra'anan, 1969, *The USSR Arms the Third World: Case Studies in Soviet Foreign Policy*, The M.I.T. Press, Cambridge, Massachussets, p. 5.
17. *Antara News Agency*, November 5, 1964. Yao was said to have expressed appreciation for Sukarno's performance in Cairo, and – though this was not reported – to have briefed Aidit on the suprise meeting Chou En-lai had had the day before with the Indonesian President in Shanghai. Aidit in turn, at least according to the official *Antara* account, had complimented the Chinese on their 'technical achievements', meaning the atom bomb.
18. *Pravda*, November 7, 1964 and *New China News Agency*, November 8, 1964.
19. *Peking Review*, no. 48. The letters to the 26 communist parties members of the preparatory commission were sent on November 24; Griffith, 1967, p. 65. A P.K.I. press release of December 14 speaks of a letter of December 1, inviting the preparatory committee to Moscow for March 1.
20. It is likely that the sudden appearance of Chinese Foreign Minister and Politburo member Chen Yi was also related to this new phase in the Sino-Soviet conflict. Chen Yi arrived on November 27 and left Djakarta again on December 3; *Djakarta Radio Home Service*, November 30, 1964 and *Indonesian Observer*, December 3, 1964. During this short stay he saw many Indonesian officials including, naturally, P.K.I. chairman Aidit. See below p. 328.
21. *Harian Rakjat*, December 8, 1964; *New China News Agency*, December 17, 1964.
22. *Harian Rakjat*, December 14, 1964; *New China News Agency*, December 17, 1964.
23. See for the P.K.I. view then prevailing: Communiqué of the Japanese C.P. and the P.K.I.; *New China News Agency*, September 7, 1964 and Communiqué of the Ceylon C.P. and the P.K.I., *Harian Rakjat*, October 2, 1964. Both were demanding 'adequate preparations' and preliminary bilateral consultations.
24. P.K.I. press release, December 14, 1964, *Indonesian Observer*, December 15, 1964 and *New China News Agency*, December 18, 1964.
25. Michailov was also told that the P.K.I. had accepted an invitation to send a delegation to Moscow, but that the date still had to be fixed 'depending on developments within the international communist movement', P.K.I. press release, December 14, 1964.
26. See above pp. 305, 306.
27. Malaysia would take its seat for one year, taking turn with Czechoslovakia

that following a political deal had occupied the seat during 1964.

28. Interview, March 1972, Ruslan Abdulgani, then member of Koti and present at deliberations. The *Indonesian Herald* was to report (January 3, 1965) that the decision had been made 'in a fit', but later the opposite was stressed from Indonesian side, so often and so emphatically – 'no emotion involved', 'well-conceived' etc. – that already then it lacked credibility; see *New China News Agency*, October, 1964.
29. Subandrio, normally an almost thoughtless executor of Sukarno's whims even was worried into sleeplessness; interview, March 1972, Suwito Kusomowidagdo.
30. Subandrio just had returned from a trip to the United Nations and had spent on the way back to Djakarta some days in Moscow. While there Subandrio voiced criticism on the U.N. but not of the nature to predict Indonesia's exit from the world organization. It is of course not excluded that, with or without support from the P.K.I., Subandrio may have put the whole idea to the Indonesian President but it seems unlikely. See for Subandrio in Moscow: *Indonesian Observer*, December 21, 1964.
31. *Moscow Radio in English for Southeast Asia*, January 5, 1965, *Tass* in English, January 7, 1965, *Moscow Radio in Indonesian*, January 8, 1965, etc.
32. *Pravda*, January 5, 1965.
33. An official, internal account of the conversations the Indonesian Foreign Minister had later that month with Chou En-lai in Peking shows that the Soviet Union wanted Indonesia to reconsider its decision before it was made final on January 7, 1965. The account will be referred to as Transcript Subandrio-Chou En-lai talks. Here reference is made to what went on between the the two ministers on January 24, 1965.
34. *Tass*, January 7, 1965 and *Pravda*, January 8, 1965.
35. Transcript Subandrio-Chou En-lai talks, January 24, 1965. The Yugoslav party daily Borba wrote that Indonesia's act would have a negative effect on the whole of Southeast Asia; *Borba*, January 4, 1965.
36. Subandrio said to Chou: 'Outside Indonesia this exit from the U.N. came suddenly, but to Indonesia it had been clear already'; Transcript Subandrio-Chou En-lai talks, January 24, 1965. The context is such that the outsiders meant included Chou.
37. *New China News Agency*, January 7, 1965.
38. *New China News Agency*, January 6, 1965 and *Antara News Agency*, January 8, 1965. As also Yao Ching-ming saw Subandrio twice on one day.
39. See below p. 329 ff.
40. *New China News Agency*, January 9, 1965. He used to keep chatting to other visitors while he kept Michailov waiting.
41. *Kuala Lumpur Radio*, January 12, 1965.
42. *New China News Agency*, January 3rd, 1965.
43. *New China News Agency*, January 9, 1965.
44. *New China News Agency*, February 12, 1965.
45. In an interview on *Australian Radio*, February 12, 1965.

46. The Japanese Communist Party had received word that the March meeting was not to be for the purposes of 'drafting' a new Moscow statement but merely for 'consultations', Griffith, 1967, p. 85, note 260.

    At about the same time (the second half of February) the Soviet theoretical periodical *Kommunist* went to press with a major foreign policy statement notable for the absence of references to collective mobilization against the Chinese, etc.; *Kommunist*, February 1965, no. 3.
47. See below pp. 329 ff.
48. The demonstrations took place on March 4, 1965, and were not too gently dispersed. The event was exploited to the limit by the Chinese.
49. *New China News Agency*, March 12, 1965.
50. *Bintang Timur*, March 18, 1965; *New China News Agency*, March 18, 1965.
51. On March 19 *Jen-min Jih-pao* printed a first full-scale attack on the results of the March Moscow conference which it called a 'schismatic' meeting, attended by 19 'units', meaning communist parties. Listed as absent were the seven 'fraternal' parties of Albania, Vietnam, Indonesia, China, Korea, Rumania, and Japan. In harsh language it condemned the meeting as 'unilaterally and illegally' devised by Kruschov, then forced upon the participants again by his successors. Chou En-lai claimed before Subandrio that Kruschov might not have fallen if China had agreed to come to Moscow on the date first proposed, December 15, 1964; Transcript Subandrio-Chou En-lai talks, January 27, 1965. Sevostinov was received on March 27, as by then Michailov had left as he was about to be replaced by a new ambassador; *Indonesian Herald*, March 30, 1965.
52. This was a reference to the period between the dissolution of the Comintern during the Second World War and the Moscow Conference of 1957 where the first of the two communist 'charters' had been agreed upon. The Cominform of the postwar period was ignored.
53. *New China News Agency*, March 31, 1965. See above p. 315.
54. Statements, for example, by the New Zealand and Malayan C.P., both normally very close to the P.K.I., appeared in the Chinese press only; *New China News Agency*, March 31, 1965 and April 1, 1965 respectively.
55. *New China News Agency*, May 3, 1965.
56. The statement was printed in full and carried the dateline January 31, 1965; *Harian Rakjat*, May 3, 1965.
57. *Harian Rakjat*, May 7, 1965.
58. The political report was delivered on May 11, and appeared in *Harian Rakjat* on May 14, 1965.
59. This was on the same day that the Chinese Communist Party expressed a similar opinion that 'modern revisionism without Kruschov was even more dangerous'. *New China News Agency*, May 11, 1965.
60. *Antara News Agency*, May 16, 1965. The Chinese test took place on May 14.
61. See below p. 365.
62. *Antara News Agency*, May 18, 1965.
63. *New China Newc Agency*, May 26, 1965.

64. Peng Cheng stressed how justified the fight by 'the Chinese C.P., the P.K.I., and other parties' against Kruschov had been as this ex-Soviet leader had been at the head of the 'political detachment of the bourgeoisie'. Of the new leaders he said that their actions 'all went against our hopes'; in tactics they were 'more crafty than Kruschov and the greatest splitters of modern times'. Peng Chen added touchingly that 'for him' he would welcome the day that the Soviet leadership would admit their mistakes; *New China News Agency*, May 28, 1965.
65. *New China News Agency*, May 26, 1965.
66. The Soviet Union, he said according to *Pravda*, could not ignore the provocative slanderous attacks on the policy of the C.P.S.U. and the Soviet state. Peng Chen had abused the hospitality of the P.K.I. for his own disruptive purpose and that was utterly regrettable; *Pravda*, June 7, 1965.
67. *Tanjug* from Djakarta, June 6, 1965.

CHAPTER 23

Sino-Indonesian honeymoon (1964-1965)

A decisive turn in Indonesian-Chinese relations had come about with the short meeting President Sukarno and Premier Chou En-lai had in Shanghai in the autumn of 1964.[1] To Sukarno it must have meant an opening, an escape from the rut his foreign policy had got him into and an escape from the disturbed situation at home that otherwise might have compelled him to cut short his trip and return to Djakarta.[2] To Chou and the Chinese Indonesia was beginning to look more and more like an almost ideal partner, and Sukarno's speech had illustrated what the combined effect of frustrated foreign ambitions and skillfully applied domestic pressure could do to a man like the Indonesian president. China's new standing as a potential atomic power and Indonesia's non-alignment alibi were the two most obvious bargaining points. The meeting of the two must have been too short to have had detailed results, but it was significant enough that the two parties in the discussion registered afterwards 'complete unanimity'.[3]

Apart from the protestations of mutual admiration that marked their public appearance, the outline of a deal must have sketchily been discussed and agreed upon.[4] In at least two fields Chou offered specific support and cooperation. First of all economically, though this must have been done with a certain reticence, as both partners professed 'self-reliance' as their main stock-in-trade and the Chinese Premier probably had to be the more serious in this respect, knowing the voracious capacity of the Indonesian economy and the limits of the Chinese.[5]

The second field was military affairs, where Chou advanced 'cooperation' in nuclear technology and brought up aid of a more conventional nature to bet the bogged-down Malaysia-confrontation back on the tracks again. It was not very clear what sort of cooperation in atomics Chou may seriously have entertained, but Sukarno must certainly have seen propaganda value of it. On Malaysia Chou suggested the formation of a 'fifth force', an armed militia of farmers and workers and a strengthening of the landwar strategy to score up some successes in the jungle 'war' in Kalimantan. Here China could in fact be of practical assistance as it had both experience and weapons to offer. It is interesting to see how considerate, or shrewd, the Chinese were in keeping Aidit posted on the sudden meeting of the two leaders in Shanghai, probably fearing that the P.K.I. might feel bypassed.[6] Traces were very soon to be found in Indonesia of the notion of some sort of 'cooperation' in atomics that had been discussed by the two Asian leaders. Three days after Sukarno had returned from his two-month tour that had also taken him to Shanghai, one of his close confidants, Brigadier-General Hartono, chief of the logistics department of the Army, announced that, in the course of 1965, Indonesia could have its own atomic bomb. In view of later pronouncements in this field, it can be concluded that there was a direct relation between Sukarno's return and Hartono's statement. The Chou-Sukarno talks took place not long after China had exploded its first A-bomb, and this feat had supposedly greatly impressed the Indonesian President. He may have felt the wish to share some of the glory as a fellow Asian, and a vague deal – close Sino-Indonesian political cooperation in exchange for an outward sign of participation in the development of A-weapons – may have come to his mind. Chou En-lai, with his customary skill, probably held out a first, tentative and sketchy promise.[7]

The same day that Hartono made his remark (summarily dismissed at the time in the West on the grounds that Indonesia would of course on its own not be in a position by a long shot to have nuclear capacity), some remarks were made on the Indonesian communist side. It was Hutapea, rector of the P.K.I. Aliarcham Academy and a strong pro-Chinese, who said he saw 'certain prospects within the freedom forces' which are very encouraging. He coupled his remarks with the reminder that there was no need to be afraid of nuclear threats.[8]

As to conventional weapons, there are strong indications that Sukarno at a very early stage, (during the Shanghai meeting) agreed in principle that China would place small arms at Indonesia's disposal. The Deputy Foreign Minister Suwito Kusumawidagdo who was in

Shanghai during the talks later had no clear recollection of this.[9] Another witness, Sukarno's aide-de-camp Bambang Widjanarko, relates however that Suwito told him at the issue of the talks in Shanghai between Sukarno and Chou that the Indonesian President had accepted an offer of arms.[10] At any rate it is certain that Chou during the talks suggested to Sukarno that the peasants and workers of Indonesia should be armed as a so-called 'fifth force' in addition to the army, navy, air force, and police.[11] According to Chou, this suggestion, which was to play a very vital role during the coming months leading up to the 'Untung coup', was by January 1965 an accepted point for the Indonesian President.[12] Sukarno has never admitted this, though evidence that Chou was right is available.[13]

The issue of arming the Indonesian citizenry was injected into the discussion – and was to stay there until the '30 September movement' in 1965 – a week after Sukarno came back from his extended foreign tour and two weeks after his meeting with Chou. It was Asmu, the hardliner Chairman of the communist-dominated multi-million-member strong Farmers' Union, who was the first among the Indonesian communist leaders to propose publicly that the peasants be armed on the grounds that there was a threat of invasion by the Americans.[14] The matter was discussed during the sudden visit Chinese Foreign Minister Chen Yi paid his friends in Djakarta at the end of November. His not very plausible excuse for dropping in was that he had not been in China when Chou and Sukarno met.[15] But he had obviously come to spell out the agreement the leaders of the two countries had reached. He was accompanied by an unspecified 'large delegation' and saw many prominent people in the Djakarta set. During his stay he was reported to have elaborated on the need for a more conventional warfare in Kalimantan against the Malaysian territories there.[16] Such an approach had a number of advantages, especially as it would reduce dependence upon the air force and navy and thus deprive the Soviet Union of considerable leverage over the Indonesian armed forces while giving China some. Chen Yi used his time well. He saw Sukarno at least twice for more than two hours and spent two working days with Subandrio.[17] On the second day, outside Djakarta, the Indonesian army commander General Yani was also present, as well as the Indonesian ambassador in Peking P.K.I.-member Djawoto and his Chinese opposite number in Djakarta Yao Ching-ming.[18] Military matters were therefore no doubt discussed but not mentioned in the final communiqué which referred to exchanges of information and experience on the present stage of common struggle against imperialism.[19] That plans in the field of atomic testing had been dealt with also may be inferred from the fact that upon his return Chen Yi was welcomed in Peking, among others, by Wu Heng, Vice Chairman of the Chinese Scientific and Technological Commission in charge of nuclear affairs.[20]

In any case, at the same time that Sukarno was announcing that Indonesia would withdraw from the United Nations and its agencies and was about to join the Chinese People's Republic as an outsider, Peking published the annual report Chou En-lai had given the Chinese National Assembly in which he spoke glowingly of the emergence of 'one Asiatic bloc of more than 700 million people', including North Vietnam, North Korea and Cambodia and also Indonesia.[21]

As shown earlier, the Chinese were caught unawares when Sukarno suddenly turned his back on the United Nations.[22] It took them some time to adjust and after one initial approving gesture in *Jen-min Jih-pao* they gave a full-blown governmental endorsement of Indonesia's policy which indeed could not have been more favorable to their current approach.[23] Within days Subandrio left with his party of 42,[24] including P.K.I. Deputy Chairman Njoto who seemed to have been assigned to follow Subandrio like a shadow. On his departure the Indonesian Foreign Minister, eager to show off and make the most of his assignment after the doubtful services he had rendered Sukarno in the B.P.S. period, said that he would discuss military aid in Peking.[25] In the event of an attack on Indonesia, he would not hesitate to ask China for aid, he added. He toned down this statement somewhat during his short stay in Rangoon, dropping hints that no military alliance with China was aimed at.[26] Also Sukarno thought it wise to calm down the fears aroused left and right in and outside the country and denied that '*more close* revolutionary ties' [emphasis added] with Peking were in the making.[27]

The new foreign policy developments had meanwhile been followed with increasing concern in various quarters. Moscow had tried to get something of a grip on the emerging situation but not with much success.[28] Of course the United States was also worried, but this had by now been its normal state as far as Sukarno and Indonesia were concerned. The shoe was really pinching inside the country, and more specifically those circles that still had axes to grind: The leadership of the armed forces, or better, of the army. It was at this juncture that the army leadership got together to see if their various factions, in face of Sukarno's drastic reorientation towards Peking, had not more in common than might be thought, judging only by personal rivalries.[29]

It was at this moment too that the threads were spun which, in a most unusual and dramatic way, were to lead first to complications and then to a denouncement of unheard-of implications. Within nine months the country was to be shaken to its foundations, a terrible bloodbath was to follow, and it was to take years to get the picture straight on what precisely had caused it all. But, early in 1965, the main actors in the play were still fully unaware of the part they had been assigned, neither could they know the issue. One of them happily sat chatting in Peking, working with consummate skill as Sukarno's main aide and hopeful successor, Indonesian Foreign Minister Subandrio who, though personally no friend of the Chinese, had been instructed to implement the new alliance and complied as usual hoping to ingratiate himself with the Indonesian President and make himself at the same time acceptable to the P.K.I.[30]

The details of what went on in the Chinese capital while the Indonesian delegation was there can be deduced from the discussions Premier Chou En-lai had with Subandrio on three successive days.[31] In all they spoke with each other for more than 24 hours.[32] One of the main points Sukarno had asked him to raise with the Chinese, Subandrio said, was the problem of 'how to incite the Soviet Union more against neo-colonialism'. Chou was of course very skeptical in this respect; he even interrupted Subandrio who was the first to give an exposé and told him that Indonesia should renege on its debts to the Soviet Union and at the same time ask for more arms.[33] On Malaysia Subandrio complained that there was no seat in the Security Council for an Asiatic country, or, if so, it was always a member of the Commonwealth. At this point Chou concurred, wondering why the Soviet Union did not bother and kept silent on this issue 'while at the same time it considers itself a part of Asia'. Subandrio then told Chou that the Soviet Union was about to try to get Malaysia to withdraw from the Security Council voluntarily.[34] All through the conversations, Chou was trying to egg Subandrio on in respect to Moscow, suggesting at one point to 'have our joint declaration ready exactly in time so that we can give it to the Soviet Union. Then we shall fully discuss it when Kosygin comes to Peking'.[35] But Subandrio countered by saying 'let us not proceed rashly; that would weaken our struggle. We should not drive the Soviet Union into the arms of the imperialist bloc'.[36]

On the other hand Subandrio's comments on the Soviet Union and the other Eastern European countries were full of reproaches about 'revisionism', etc., not unbecoming to an Indonesian communist, and they must certainly have been on a wavelength to which Chou was attuned. With the full approval of Chou Subandrio concluded his analysis: 'Indonesia thinks: will the struggle against imperialism finally be continued without the Soviet Union and Company. We are preparing ourselves for that event'.[37]

It is interesting to see, in the light of subsequent events, the prospects for Indonesia Chou in turn foresaw and thought should be 'prevented' by continuing vigilance. He saw a possible common military demonstration by the neocolonialists, i.e. the United States and Great Britain, provocations around Indonesia to keep a crisis situation alive, the dropping of spies on the Indonesian islands, the bribing of bad elements to commit subversion inside the country, and finally corruption and incitement 'to murder the President, Subandrio and others who visit the Chinese People's Republic, because they are considered pink-reds'.

All these evils were to haunt Indonesia in the coming months in one way or an other, not necessarily as fears that appeared justified but as concerted wishful thinking for ulterior motives. At this stage, however, it was only an occasion for Chou to suggest his remedy: Vigilance and arms. He again elaborated in detail upon the creation of a 'fifth force', armed patriots, and claimed it was a subject the Chinese had great experience with because Chiang Kai-shek had kept dropping spies in coastal areas that could not be hermetically closed off. It was here that Chou suggested that Sukarno had already agreed to arm the Indonesian people. (Aidit had just joined the melee and had asked for the same publicly two weeks before.) Chou said Sukarno should become commander-in-chief of this new people's militia. As to the arming of the militia Chou was more than generous; he told Subandrio that the arms were ready for the taking. Presumably, this had already been discussed at an earlier stage, e.g. in Shanghai and during the Chen Yi visit in November. He said: 'The light arms for the people's army are available. They can be tried out to see if they are adapted to requirements. We shall assist with the setting up of a repair workshop plus spares. This is the first production of the Chinese People's Republic. It is more than fitting that the C.P.R. should give arms to aid in the struggle for freedom. But Mao has said: without payment. Victory is difficult to assess in terms of money'.[38]

The transcript does not register any response from Subandrio. His spokesman Ganis Harsono was to tell the press later that the Chinese had offered to make a gift of the arms, but Indonesia had refused them on those terms.[39] During the Subandrio trial in October 1966 it appeared that a total quantity of 100,000 small arms, machine guns of the Chung variety, had in fact been offered by the Chinese.[40] Deputy Foreign Minister Suwito, a witness during this trial, declared that he had overheard his erstwhile chief tell the then Information Minister Ahmadi that 'the question of small arms that China promised to supply Indonesia had better not pass General Nasution, but they be stored in our own warehouse'.[41] This remark was made during the flight back from Peking to Djakarta after the conclusion of Subandrio-Chou talks,[42] so it can be deduced from this that, at a very early stage, Subandrio was in collusion with the Chinese to smuggle arms into Indonesia. At his trial Subandrio said that he had reported on the arms to President Sukarno, but he had not admitted any arrangement with Peking that might have been concluded, nor implied *a fortiori* that the President had any knowledge of this arms deal, which had to be kept outside normal army channels. But, with the evidence Widjanarko gave (and certainly in the light of what went on in the following months)[43] there is no doubt that Sukarno was fully informed of what went on in Peking. What is more, Subandrio was acting under instructions from the President to acquire Chinese arms. This is all the more interesting because the Minister of Defense General Nasution was kept informed of the offer (not the deal) by Major General Murshid, a member of Subandrio's delegation representing the army upon which Nasution had told Murshid that the army did not need these Chinese arms.[44] General Murshid, a close confidant of Sukarno, was later found involved in the '30 September movement'[45] and jailed.[46] So, from the time of the Subandrio-Chou talks at the end of January 1965, the Indonesian President, behind the backs of the highest military authorities (especially of the army leadership) had begun to have small arms available for some future use. As was later disclosed at the various trials, the chief of the air force, then Air Marshal Omar Dhani, went to China on the orders of Sukarno on September 16 without normal clearance,[47] and this secret flight was connected with the 100,000 Chinese arms of which Dhani allegedly thought he could claim one quarter as the share for the air force. It is not clear how many of these arms had in actual fact arrived in Indonesia prior to or immediately after the '30 September movement' on October 1, 1965 chanced its arm. What is certain is that in the period between January and October Omar Dhani made several more secret trips to China, either in a Hercules transport plane or, when no shipment of arms was involved, in the President's Jetstarliner.[48] Illegal arms transports from China was also channeled through other lanes, such as ships owned by the national shipping company Pelni and handled by reliable P.K.I. employees.[49]

During the Chou-Subandrio talks in Peking, secret deals were being concluded and stimulating ideas were being exchanged (e.g. how to sell various plans to Sukarno).[50] But also publicly the two officials were providing clues for interesting conclusions. So at the official banquet Chou had given his Indonesian counterpart, he coined the phrase that was to guide the destinies of the two countries in the coming months: 'If the British and American imperialists impose war upon Indonesia then the Chinese people will not stand idly by'.[51]

Subandrio had already rapidly picked up the finer shades of Chinese political jargon and got a rousing ovation from thousands of organized Chinese at a rally when he lauded the 'intimate friendship' that prevailed between the two countries that would 'unite us always and in all circumstances against the U.S.-led imperialists everywhere'.[52] For the sake of his hosts he conveniently forgot to mention British imperialists who were not such a specific target of hostility for the Chinese public. But to an Indonesian official like Subandrio they were not an enemy to be forgotten for other reasons than local convenience.[53]

After being received by Mao and President Liu Shao-chi, Subandrio had completed his mission.[54] Before he left for home *Harian Rakjat* had called it 'a brilliant achievement' which would consolidate Sino-Indonesian relations.[55] Close relations with the Chinese embassy may have helped the editors to predict the results of Subandrio's trip so accurately. At any rate Yao Ching-ming was again sent to inform Aidit, and this time also Lukman, on how affairs had gone in Peking. Due appreciation was expressed for the new, largely verbal, Chinese commitment 'not to stand idly by' in the unlikely event of a British-American attack on Indonesia.[56] This formula had also found its way into the joint communiqué and was to be repeated in the coming period.[57] On the economic side the agreements made caused some confusion. Altogether, 80 million dollars had been promised to Indonesia, of which 50 million seemed to have been arranged for during the Chen Yi visit.[58] The additional 30 million dollars Chou had agreed to were earmarked for the construction of textile mills, about the only industrial field in which the Chinese could offer assistance.[59] Subandrio vaguely mentioned 'additional credits' that would be forthcoming, and the talk was about another 100 million dollars.[60] The 50 million dollar deal of November 1964 consisted of a grant of 10 million dollars, 'at the discretion of President Sukarno'.[61] The other 40 million dollars were for project aid, described by one of Indonesia's Deputy Foreign Ministers Omar Yadi as destined for 'basic material for existing industries and other basic materials'.[62] It is not impossible that this referred to the plans to build accommodation for a counter-United Nations Organization, the Conference of New Emerging Forces or Conefo that Sukarno had in mind. China was to assist in the construction which began later in 1965 and was brutally disrupted by the 30 September affair. Building material had been sent from China for the purpose, but it seems that the Chinese had a rather flexible concept of what should come under this heading and included arms in it.[63]

The deal in the atomic field had originated with the first Sukarno-Chou tête-a-tête in Shanghai early in November 1964 after China had exploded her first atomic bomb.[64] Indonesia, it was then given to understand, would have her own atomic device later in the course of 1965. Matters relating to nuclear cooperation must also have been discussed during the Chen Yi visit.[65] Not long after this visit, the same Brigadier-General Hartono who as chief of the logistics department of the army had first dropped word about the Indonesian atomic bomb, said that it all depended on a decision by Sukarno because Indonesia had the qualified physicists to produce an A-bomb.[66] It was not until after the Subandrio-Chou talks at the end of January 1965 that the subject again cropped up in the Indonesian press.[67] *Antara* announced that 200 Indonesians were working on a atomic bomb and that there would be a 'surprise' in store for October 5th of that year.[68] A Chinese delegation under Wu Heng, the deputy chairman of the Chinese Atomic

Commission, left Peking on February 24[69] and was received by Sukarno in the presence of the Ministers Pusponegoro, for scientific education, and Azis Saleh, for people's industries.[70]

The activities of the Chinese delegation caused Yani, the commanding general of the army, to caution that close cooperation with Peking-China did not make Indonesia communist.[71] What he meant was the 'scientific-technical agreement' that was signed on March 16 between Wu Heng and Sudjono, Minister of National Research.[72] Wu Heng called it a 'good thing' in the struggle against colonialism, a blanket phrase Sudjono had also used at the beginning of the negotiations.[73] On the same day that the two government delegations concluded their talks, Aidit received Wu Heng (the story gets monotonous), was given the details, or better perhaps, the background of the deal, and told Wu that he was all for 'cooperation and exchange of experience between Indonesia and China in the scientific and technical fields'. Natural science, he asserted, was of great importance to the Indonesian revolution, and he was convinced that 'we should smash western domination in this field'.[74]

From this time on Indonesia did not display any interest in the prevention of nuclear proliferation, probably one of the reasons why the Chinese may have held out on the agreement that Wu Heng came to hammer out.[75] It was said to have been concluded for a period of five years.[76] Billed as 'a new phase' in Sino-Indonesian collaboration, it seems to have spelled out plans to establish certain experimental laboratories near Bogor.[77] Its main point was, however, to prepare for a testing site in Indonesia for which the island of Mentawei, west of Sumatra, was chosen. It would have given the Chinese additional experience and in addition may also have caused considerable propaganda fall-out for both Peking and Djakarta.[78] After first having mentioned October 5 (Armed Forces Day) as a tentative date for the test, Hartono's office later announced that it would be November 5.[79] This was the newly arranged date on which the ill-fated second Bandung conference was due to open.[80] The fact that both times the date chosen had a symbolic tinge showed the prestige nature of the whole project – at least to the Indonesians.[81]

Of course this aspect was also strongly present on the Chinese side, but here there was at least something substantial to show. The second A-bomb China exploded came on the eve of the 45th anniversary of the P.K.I. which was to symbolize the success formula of the more militant Peking approach in storming the fortresses of world reaction, be it imperialist or revisionist.[82]

Aidit, who was host at that time to many foreign communist dignitaries and was feeling himself increasingly to be Sukarno's self-appointed deputy, had an immediate word of praise ready for the Chinese. He pointed to the fact (as Peking before him had already) that nuclear weapons in the hands of anti-imperialists was entirely different from the imperialists possessing them.[83] This was the anti-revisionist, or rather anti-Soviet, phrase soon to be more current, including among non-communists in Indonesia.[84] In his message to the Peking-sponsored Tokyo Congress in July against A- and H-bombs, Sukarno joined in urging all 'peace-loving' nations to acquire nuclear weapons.[85] The Moscow Treaty, duly signed and ratified by his government barely two years ago, probably no longer had much to recommend it, engrossed as Sukarno was in his pursuit of ultimate power for his country, if not for himself.

NOTES

1. They met on November 4, Sukarno coming from Tokyo and Chou 'by special plane' from Peking. *New China News Agency*, November 4, 1965. Sukarno left again the next day.
2. See above p. 293.
3. *New China News Agency*, November 4, 1964.
4. At the official banquet Chou was most effusive in his public praise of Sukarno, knowing human vanity and particularly Sukarno's. His Indonesian guest, with his customary modesty, replied that the Cairo conference had in fact been a success thanks to him but that he had spoken against imperialism 'on behalf of all the people of the world'. *Indonesian Observer*, November 6, 1964.
5. To Subandrio, Chou was to say at the end of January: 'We are prepared to help according to our capacity. We are not yet in a position to honor everything. Albania with its 1.6 million inhabitants cannot yet be fully supported by the Chinese People's Republic. But we can share our experience on economic self-reliance (April 1965). We must know the precise situation in Indonesia'; Transcript Subandrio-Chou En-lai talks, January 25, 1965. By 'April 1965' is meant the 10th anniversary of the Bandung conference.
6. Yao called on Aidit for 'a friendly chat'; *Antara News Agency*, November 4, 1964.
7. See below p. 335.
8. *Harian Rakjat*, November 16, 1964.

9. Interview, March 1972.
10. Official, internal report on the interrogation of Colonel Bambang Setjono Widjanarko by officers of Kopkamtib, the official military authority in charge of security. Widjanarko put the date of the visit to Shanghai in June 1965, confusing it with another trip to Cairo he made with Sukarno. As aide-de-camp of Sukarno, Widjanarko has been continuously in the presence of the Indonesian President, notably in 1964 and 1965, and therefore is of considerable interest as a witness. His statements have been thoroughly checked and are only used when corroborated by other witnesses or as part of circumstantial evidence. Widjanarko was in jail at the time of his interrogation, October-November 1970. To his testimony, reference will be made as: Widjanarko Report. The reference here is to Part I, p. 9.
11. See p. 331.
12. Transcript Subandrio-Chou En-lai, January 27, 1965.
13. See below p. 332.
14. *New China News Agency*, November 21, 1964.
15. *Antara News Agency*, November 27, 1964.
16. *Radio Free Europe*, January 28, 1965.
17. *Indonesian Observer*, November 30, 1964; *Antara News Agency*, December 1, 1964; *New China News Agency*, December 1, 1964; *Djakarta Radio Home Service*, December 2, 1964.
18. *New China News Agency*, December 2, 1964.
19. *Djakarta Radio Home Service*, December 3, 1964. For the anti-Soviet implication in the communiqué see above p. 309 note 37.
20. *New China News Agency*, December 8, 1964. More of Wu Heng was to be heard in 1965, when he headed a delegation to Indonesia. See pp. 334, 335.
21. *New China News Agency*, December 31, 1964. The report was presented during the last session on December 21, 22, and 23.
22. See above p. 316.
23. The first reaction came on January 6; see above p. 316. The second was an official government declaration issued on January 10, three days after Sukarno had finalized his U.N.-walkout. He had helped, the Chinese told him, 'to liquidate blind faith in the United Nations' which was (well-known-phrase) made out to be 'a paper tiger'; *New China News Agency*, January 10, 1965. The *Far Eastern Economic Review* of that week suggested that China had committed itself in advance to compensate financial losses Indonesia might incur by leaving the U.N.; *Far Eastern Economic Review*, January 14, 1965. This does not seem to be born out by fact, as this supposed a prior and more than vague understanding, of which there is no sign. On the contrary, Subandrio opened his talks with Chou on January 24 as follows: 'After the visit of Chen Yi I wanted to send an Indonesian economic mission to discuss economic cooperation between the two sovereign nations. But now the Republic of Indonesia brings up the anti-colonial struggle and exit from the U.N.'; Transcript Subandrio-Chou En-lai talks, January 24, 1965.
24. *Indonesian Observer*, January 20, 1965.

25. *Antara News Agency*, January 21, 1965.
26. *Reuters* from Rangoon, January 20, 1965.
27. *Antara News Agency*, January 23, 1965.
28. See above p. 323, note 40.
29. See below pp. 357, 358.
30. It is almost pathetic, but certainly indicative of the boundless ambition Subandrio had to become president that the Indonesian Foreign Minister himself went around, upon his return from Peking telling everyone that Sukarno had evaluated his efforts 'highly'; *Antara News Agency*, February 2, 1965.
31. Use is made of the official, internal transcript of these talks on January 24, 25, and 27, 1965, referred to before. See above p. 325, note 33.
32. On January 26 the Chinese news agency reported that the two had spent 24 hours together; *New China News Agency*, January 26, 1965.
33. Subandrio: 'So Indonesia is withdrawing from the United Nations without making trouble for the Soviet Union; on the contrary it gives them an advantage'. Chou, interrupting: 'Don't pay your debt to the Soviet Union, they do not help Indonesia. Do not only not repay your debt of one billion dollars but even ask for more, 90% for arms'; Transcript Subandrio-Chou En-lai, January 24, 1965.
34. This had probably been part of the deal the Soviet Union was trying to strike with Sukarno and may have been discussed when Ambassador Michailov met both the Indonesian President and Subandrio on January 8. After this audience Michailov had been reported as saying only that Indonesia was a sovereign country free to determine her own policy so as to benefit her own interests; *Antara News Agency*, November 14, 1965. But in mid-March the Soviet representative Federenko made noises of protestation in the Security Council, calling Malaysia's presence 'illegal' because the federation was a product of neo-colonialism, etc.; *Antara News Agency*, March 18, 1965. The *Indonesian Herald*, after the demise of the *Indonesian Observer* (because of BPS affilation) the new mouthpiece of the Indonesian foreign minister, commented editorially that this Soviet diplomatic action was late but still welcome; *Indonesian Herald*, March 18, 1965.
35. Soviet Premier Kosygin was to arrive in Peking on February 4, on the way to Hanoi. Chou supposed at the time that it had to do with military deliveries and sneered that Krùschov would not have made a stopover in Peking but rather in New Dehli.
36. Transcript Subandrio-Chou En-lai talks, January 27, 1965.
37. See below p. 350.
38. Transcript Subandrio-Chou En-lai talks, January 27, 1965. The arms refered to were the 100,000 Chinese manufactured Chung light machine guns which were to play a role in the '30 September movement'. See below p. 404. It should be noted that, in the delegation Subandrio took with him, no representatives of the army except general Murshid were included.
39. *Antara News Agency*, January 30, 1965.
40. Proceedings of the Subandrio trial, October 1 and 22, 1966, verbatim tran-

scripts of fifth session.

41. Proceedings of the Subandrio trials, 11th session. Information Minister Ahmadi, a 'Subandrio-man', is still in jail at the time of writing. One of the minor things held against Ahmadi was the fact that a videotape of the speech President Sukarno held in Senajan Stadium on the evening of September 30, 1965, and kept in the archives of *Djakarta Radio and TV* was wiped. The passage in question was one in which Sukarno told his audience that they could go to sleep calmly, but that he still had some affairs to tend to; see above p. 327.
42. Interview, March 1972, Suwito Kusumowidagdo.
43. See below.
44. Interview, March 1972, General Nasution.
45. See below p. 405.
46. At the time of writing, May 1972, he is still in jail.
47. See below pp. 403, 404.
48. Interview, March 1972, with Air Commandore Budjardjo who, from early 1965 onwards, was posted as Indonesian ambassador in Phom Penh, the capital of Cambodia, a place Dhani passed through on one of his trips to China, and with Baron Sastradinata who was stationed as commercial counsetter in Peking and suddenly discovered Dhani, when be was moving about in the Chinese capital unannounced.
49. Widjanarko relates that on October 1, 1965, the Gunung Kerintje, a pilgrim ship, left Shanghai with a load of Chinese guns, arriving at the end of that month in Tandjung Priok harbor near Djakarta where it was unloaded. The cargo was stored in downtown Djakarta in one of the warehouses Subandrio had called their 'own'. Widjanarko Report, II, p. 27.
50. See below p. 351, note 17.
51. The banquet was given on January 24; *Indonesian Observer*, January 26, 1965. Overlooking contemporary history Subandrio was depicted by Chou as 'an old friend of ours'; January 24, 1965.
52. *New China News Agency*, January 26, 1965.
53. Subandrio was asked to solicit action against Hongkong but was told by Chou that Hongkong was only of minor importance compared with the 600 million Chinese at Sukarno's disposal; interview, March 1972, General Nasution.
54. Curiously enough, it was not a purely ceremonial meeting with the two Chinese leaders, but it was suggested by the presence of Deputy Minister for internal security Ling Yun on the one hand and Police Chief Sutjipto Damakusumo on the other that security affairs, probably related to the proposed cooperation in the atomic field, were also discussed and at the highest level; *New China News Agency*, January 27, 1965 and Uri Ra-anan, 1969, *The USSR Arms the Third World: Case Studies Soviet Foreign Policy*, Cambridge, Massachussets, p. 5. It may very well have been contrived by the Chinese to give cooperation in this field an air of gravity which (to them) it in fact lacked.

55. *Harian Rakjat*, January 27, 1965.
56. *New China News Agency*, January 28, 1965. The consideration for Aidit was so great that on the same day, when the joint communiqué was being published in Peking, the Chinese theoretical journal *Hung Qui* printed an article by Aidit on the peasant actions in Indonesia to crush the 'village devils', etc.
57. *New China News Agency*, January 28, 1965.
58. Transcript Subandrio-Chou En-lai, January 25, 1965.
59. A year before another 30 million dollars had been earmarked for the building of textile mills, while still earlier in 1962 credits were also mentioned. Nothing much seems to have come of it all.
60. *Kyodo* (Japanese News Agency), February 15, 1965.
61. It is not clear whether this was a polite form of bribery. See for details of Sukarno's ways of making money on the side p. .
62. *Djakarta Radio Home Service*, February 10, 1965.
63. See below p. 422 note 40.
64. See above pp. 326, 327.
65. See above pp. 328, 329.
66. *Indonesian Observer*, December 23, 1964. A few days before, Minister-Coordinator Sartono, speaking in Bonn, also told his audience that Indonesia could make its own A-bomb, concluding that this would be all to the good as it would promote Indonesia's capacity for peaceful action in the world; *Antara News Agency*, December 21, 1964.
67. The transcripts of the talks only indirectly refer to atomic matters. Non-proliferation, Chou said, was directed against the Chinese nuclear bomb but this was not said openly. Speaking on the July 1963 talks in Moscow, Chou relates: 'The Communist Parties of the C.P.R. and the S.U. met, but it was a fake performance. At the same time a red carpet was laid out for the three western delegations (sic) on nuclear testing. In June the S.U. had said that an agreement on nuclear testing was impossible'.
68. *Antara News Agency*, February 2, 1965.
69. His official title was Deputy-Chairman of the Chinese Scientific and Technological Commission; see *New China News Agency*, February 24, 1965.
70. *Antara News Agency*, February 26, 1965.
71. *Antara News Agency*, March 2, 1965. Wu Heng had just begun his talks with his real counterpart, Sudjono, Minister for National Research; *Indonesian Herald*, March 1, 1965.
72. *New China News Agency*, March 16, 1965.
73. *Indonesian Herald*, March 1, 1965.
74. *New China News Agency*, March 16, 1965.
75. See Uri Ra'anan, 1967, *The USSR Arms the Third World: Case Studies in Soviet Foreign Policy*, The M.I.T. Press, Cambridge, Massachussets, p. 6.
76. *Djakarta Radio Home Service*, March 16, 1965.
77. Information received from Dr. E. de Vries, advisor to various Indonesian governments on agricultural affairs.
78. Professor Djuned Pusponegoro in charge of scientific education, fell out of

favor in 1965. He was by no means a communist and may have opposed the deal the Chinese came to conclude. This could also explain why he disappeared from the scene during Wu Heng's stay in Djakarta and why the actual agreement was signed by Sudjono.

79. *Radio Free Europe*, July 29, 1965. The announcement of the army logistical office was on July 27.
80. At the end of June the fall of Algerian strongman Ben Bella caused so much commotion that the Afro-Asian conference scheduled to open on June 29 was postponed; see below pp. 348, 349.
81. It was nowhere assumed that Indonesia had a nuclear development capability, so the bomb or missile to be used would have been 'made in China', notwithstanding a special Indonesian bureau for atomic and missile affairs that was set up in June 1965. *Radio Free Europe*, July 29, 1965.
82. The day was May 14. See above p. 319.
83. *New China News Agency*, May 15, 1965. *Indonesian Herald*, May 15, 1965.
84. The Indonesian Peace Committee, also taken over by the anti-Soviets, hailed the second Chinese nuclear test as 'a reinforcement of the new emerging forces of peace'; *Indonesian Herald*, May 20, 1965. See also the P.K.I. monthly *Bintang Merah* of June 29, attacking the Soviet proposals for non-proliferations as 'ridiculous and senseless'.
85. *Radio Free Europe*, July 29, 1965.

CHAPTER 24

The Afro-Asian horizon shifts (1965)

In its rivalry with the Soviet Union the Third World had been one of China's obsessions. In the Afro-Asian countries great efforts had been made to win friends. It had resulted in an organizational victory the year before when, in full concert with Indonesia, they had been able to thwart Soviet participation in the second A.A. conference during the meeting of the preparatory committee in April 1964.[1] Whatever the finer points of this 'score' against Moscow had been, it had meant a moral setback to Kruschov and his team at the time. In the following June, in Geneva, another meeting of the same A.A. committee had not improved the Soviet cause, and, together with other reasons, it may have forced on Kruschov the conclusion that he had better show himself less eager to participate and save his honor.[2]

So at the end of July 1964, Kruschov announced that the Soviet Union no longer had any wish [read: interest] to impose itself upon the Afro-Asian countries, thus trying to withdraw gracefully.[3] Brezhnev and Kosygin, after having overthrown Kruschov that autumn, went a step further and, in a conciliatory mood (or whatever between competing Communist bosses might be the equivalent), wrote a letter to their colleagues in Peking on the subject. They offered to make the participation of the Soviet Union in the second Afro-Asian conference no longer 'an object of contention' between the two countries.[4] A further development in bilateral and other relations, however, must have spoiled the initial goodwill of the Kremlin leaders. Particularly after the March meeting in Moscow, which the Chinese and six other Communist parties including the P.K.I. had boycotted, they must have felt less charitable. Another round of wooing of Afro-Asian countries began, and Moscow tried politely to make it clear that it wished not to be forgotten as a candidate for the Second Bandung conference. It is hard to judge to what extent the Soviet leaders themselves by mid-May 1965 (a good four weeks before the conference was finally scheduled to open in Algiers) thought they had succeeded in getting a foot in the door.[5] At any rate they suddenly showed more than a wish and let it be known that they considered it their 'international duty' to participate.[6]

This was a clear signal to all those who understood the esoteric lingo of communism (first and foremost in Peking) that Moscow again meant business. The whole affair was where it had been before Kruschov called it off in July the year before, and it was to be expected that the Soviet Union would again bring its whole weight to bear to force its way into the second Afro-Asian conference or, failing that, to prevent it from taking place altogether. The timing of the renewal of the Soviet 'application' is of some interest. It is suggested that it had something to do with the visit the Indian Prime Minister Shastri paid to Moscow in mid-May of 1965.[7] This is very well possible, and at least Shastri was capable of being a most useful help in this respect to the Soviet leaders. As such he was also pushed to the fore by the Soviet media.[8] But the deeper reason for stepping up their offensive for the Soviet leaders may very well have been the growing Peking-Djakarta alignment of which the P.K.I. celebrations in the second half of May (after all that had gone before) was such a vivid example. It is significant in this respect that the first announcement of Moscow's self-confessed 'international duty' came in a radio broadcast for Southeast Asia, amid the mirth and merriment in Djakarta where Peng Chen two days previously had opened for China a new round of verbal warfare with his blistering denunciation of Brezhnev-Kosygin policies.[9]

The Chinese may have understood this new turn well and this can explain why a mutual Sino-Indonesian decision was taken to send Subandrio to China to take stock of the situation as to the second A.A. meeting. It should be recalled here that Subandrio upon his return talked about 'other adversaries' (than the usual imperialist western brand) who were 'undermining' the A.A. plans, clearly meaning Moscow.

As related earlier, the year before particularly Subandrio had shown hesitation on the issue of Soviet participation as a result of pressure exercised during the Mikoyan visit and that he had consequently tried to dodge the question.[10] The Cairo conference and Sukarno's explicit behavior, in fact rejecting the Soviet-sponsored concept of peaceful co-existence, had made it almost impossible for Indonesia to continue sitting on the fence and pretending to be a 'regular' non-aligned nation. Its further rapprochement with China reinforced this tendency, and, in all, there was even less reason to be considerate towards the Soviet Union on the second A.A. conference than before the Mikoyan tour-de-force of 1964. But, fortunately for Subandrio, Indonesia's point of view had not been put to the test because meanwhile Kruschov had decided to withdraw as gatecrasher. But Moscow must have been in no doubt as to where Indonesia in fact stood if it came to the crunch.

In the joint press release at the end of the Chen Yi-Subandrio talks in November 1964 both parties had pledged to honor the decisions of the April 1964 preparatory committee.[11] In plain language this meant espousing the Chinese view that the Soviet Union had already been refused as participants, and at best (if Indonesia wished to be less brutal), that the main conference should unanimously decide, which in practice would amount to the same thing.

Indonesia's U.N. walkout had added a new dimension to the Afro-Asian tangle and was widely discussed by Chou and Subandrio during their long sessions in January 1965. It was in fact to 'explain' the whole U.N.-affair to the Chinese that Sukarno had told Subandrio to go to Peking.[12] Subandrio was emphatic that Indonesia would not return to the U.N., even if and when Malaysia was no longer a member of the Security Council.[13] He told Chou: 'We are ready to build up a new United Nations on the basis of the present forces. The charter-switch (sic) must be neo-colonialism. Only thus would the United Nations reflect the desires of the world population in its longing for justice. The crisis in the U.N. began in fact with the exclusion of the Chinese People's Republic'.

Buttering up Chou, he had gotten from the Chinese Premier the assurance that China also no longer wanted to become a member of the United Nations.[14] It was some time later that year that China did indeed publicly profess not any more to be interested in becoming a member of that world organization. This was in Djakarta, where Chou En-lai had headed a delegation to celebrate the tenth anniversary of the Bandung conference. Now that Indonesia was no longer a member of the U.N., he said in a touching show of solidarity, China would not be for membership either. A new world body was under consideration, progressive and revolutionary in nature, and that should be the aim, rather than wasting time on the New York 'outfit'.[15]

On the A.A. conference, the 'second Bandung', Chou also had made a number of observations in January 1965 to Subandrio, which gave an insight into his thinking at that time. The Indonesian Foreign Minister had asked him what he should do about the Soviet Union when it came to inviting governments to the Conference of new emerging forces, then planned for early in 1966. Chou warned him not to discuss the matter too soon with Moscow: 'If you do that the Soviet Union will demand that it participates in the second A.A. conference in order to sabotage the Conefo. The preparations should be taken step by step'. And on that participation Chou was adamant. He warned against 'sabotage' in the coming months and stressed 'whatever happens the Soviet Union must not be permitted to participate'. He reasoned that the whole conference would be spoiled, as it would be turned into a Chinese-Russian debate on Marxism-Leninism and degrade the image of the A.A. conference.[16] He had volunteered some useful advise on the invitations and thought that the main theme of the conference should be the abolition of foreign military bases, especially British ones, 'though this of course cannot be achieved quickly'.[17] (In this field Chen Yi must have been active early December 1964, while in Djakarta. It only took a week after he had departed before P.N.I. Secretary General Surachman, later to be shown up as a P.K.I.-stooge and an active participant in the '30 September movement', had set up a 'committee against foreign bases' and began a nationwide campaign or at least announced that he would do so.)[18]

Another point that had been discussed by Chou and Subandrio in Peking was the tenth anniversary of the 1955 Bandung meeting. Upon return in Djakarta the Indonesian foreign minister passed on the idea just as Chou had suggested it: 'Let Sukarno, for the celebration of the tenth anniversary of the A.A. conference invite as many people, as many heads of state as possible'.[19] Chou thought that many countries wanted to learn about Indonesia's ideas on what should happen to the U.N. and were therefore interested in coming to Djakarta, especially if it was on a sufficiently high level.[20] Sukarno was only too pleased and, never reluctant to have a party, quickly obliged. After Ben Bella had asked for another delay, this time from May to the end of June, Sukarno promptly announced at a mass rally that the Bandung anniversary would be celebrated in Djakarta 'in a grand way'.[21] The next day Aidit expressed the hope that the tenth anniversary would be held 'in a grand manner' and a bit later went a step further, saying that 'the success of the Bandung commemoration will decide the success of the second A.A. conference'.[22]

And so the theme rolled on, to end indeed in a number of official festivities around April 18, thus illustrating how Chinese-Indonesian 'cooperation' went on and how things got moving even on a point that was of relatively minor importance.

When, finally, Chou's idea of making the most of the tenth anniversary of 'Bandung 1955' had to be put to the test, the result in terms of pressure in favor of the Sino-Indonesian views of A.A. cooperation was rather meager.[23] Chou and Chen Yi descended from the heavenly city, while also Sihanouk and Hanoi's Pham Van Dong were present.[24] Sukarno gave a welcoming address in which there was a notable barb aimed at Nasser, whose 'Egyptian revolution', contrary to a number of other revolutions not enumerated, had 'not yet been completed'.[25] This riddle was to be solved a few days later when reports from Cairo trickled in suggesting that Malaysian Foreign Minister Tun Abdul Razak had succeeded during this visit to the capital of the U.A.R. in swinging Nasser's opinion more in favor of Malaysia than before.[26]

Pravda had a rather mild article, written by one of its veteran experts on 'Eastern affairs' Yuri Zhukov, reminding the Bandung fans that, after all, it had been the Communist countries which had enabled them to win the liberation battle. He gave a vivid example in mentioning the hardware North Vietnam was about to receive from Moscow.[27] The only one apart from Pakistan Foreign Minister Bhutto who had anything nice to say about the Soviet Union was no one else but North Vietnamese Premier Pham Van Dong, who mumbled something about gratitude towards the Communist commonwealth.[28]

Sukarno showed himself particularly grateful towards the Chinese government, which as the Indonesian President recalled had 'effectively assisted in making this political venue for Conefo'.[29] He speaking at assisted in making this political venue for Conefo'.[29] He was speaking at stadium a day before the official April 18 Bandung commemoration. China, it was stressed on all sides, would help build the new world center and provide the material for it.[30] The Chinese from their side had nothing but praise for the present course of Indonesian policy, as borne out by the now almost obligatory *Jen-min Jih-pao* editorial before the ceremonial occasion. And after the event they professed their full agreement with Sukarno's 'profound analysis'.[31] One part of Sukarno's speech, most of which concerned current problems besetting the outside A.A. world, should have stuck out. As on previous occasions, but with more emphasis, Sukarno brought up the point that apart from the chaos the colonialist Dutch had left behind as a legacy there were now also cases of 'sabotage' within the country.[32] This kind of remark was only much later to acquire its proper significance. All in all, as a design to get the new Unted Nations started, the Bandung commemoration was not much to write home about. The main hurdle now came with the actual and much-talked about A.A. conference, which (thanks to the Russians) again got a lot of publicity. The appropriate machinery for it in the Soviet Union got into high gear following the announcement at the end of May which was in fact a renewed claim to participation.[33] The usual arguments were brought forward, and on accasion it was again Indonesia in particular which was warned to remember past benefactions it had received, arms usually being referred to.[34] To Djakarta the problem with Moscow in this respect was of course secondary compared with the fight to keep Malaysia out of the Algiers meeting.[35] Subandrio, for the purpose of lining up some wavering African countries, left ten days before the foreign ministers were due to meet on June 24. Meanwhile, it was India that had to bear the brunt of the attacks in the Indonesian press.[63] To Sukarno India was willing to cooperate 'with the devil himself' to get Malaysia admitted to the A.A. club.[37] He made no mention of the Soviet Union on this occasion, simply stressing that the conference could better be 'compact' and united than broad and weak. This theme, already current since Sukarno spoke on the 45th anniversary of the P.K.I., was repeated by its probably author, ghostwriter Njoto.[38] But the Deputy P.K.I. Chairman did not mention the Soviet Union either, only reproaching their anonymous proxies, the modern revisionists, of helping the West, etc. Munir, the new radical Sobsi Chairman, pressed the government (as if this were necessary) not to let Malaysia slip in but to be sure to leave the conference if that should unfortunately come about.[39] This was at the same moment that the Chinese, too, publicly went on record as saying that they 'would never give ground' and would resist Soviet participation to the end.[40]

Then on June 19 Ben Bella was arrested and Commander-in-Chief Boumedienne took over and sent the deposed Algerian President to some far-off desert prison. Coming at the very eve of the second A.A. conference the new man in power let it be known that the meeting would normally take place.[41] The Indonesian government immediately recognized Boumedienne's new position, clearly to make sure that in so doing it would increase the chances of the conference actually coming off.[42] It certainly did not do so because there was any more affinity with Boumedienne than with Ben Bella, the general being described as an austere soldier and fanatical muslim. But it is possible that Subandrio was glad with the fall of Ben Bella, as the Algerian leader had been playing the card of the Soviets more than that of the Chinese lately.[43] The Chinese did not react as fast as the Indonesians; it took them two days before they published a factual announcement of Ben Bella's dismissal.[44] But, after an initial hesitation, Peking also recognized Boumedienne, probably with the same motives as Djakarta.

Together with Njoto, Aidit was about to leave for Cairo and then for Algiers as part of the Indonesian delegation. Being most anxious to see the conference succeed, Aidit very quickly produced a full endorsement of Boumedienne. He understood fully, he said, why the Algerian general had seized power from Ben Bella.[45] Boumedienne had brought back the spirit of the 1954 revolution from which Ben Bella had been deviating. Boumedienne in power was described as the 'savior of the A.A. conference'. This curious eulogy, indirectly and directly, of Boumedienne did not actually fit the facts. As *Antara* had written more correctly in a report from Algiers: Boumedienne, if anything, would be more conservative (the Indonesian news agency kindly called it 'liberal-progressive') than Ben Bella.[46] Moreover, he was a very strict follower of Islam, a not particularly endearing feature to a man like Aidit.[47]

Together with remarks Aidit made when he was in Cairo a few days later, some deeper sense to his words may be discerned. In the Egyptian capital Aidit spoke of 'the 19 June affair' and repeated what he had said earlier in Djakarta, that it was a return to the revolution of 1954.[48] He stressed further that it was wrong to call the affair a coup d'état, 'as if it meant an important revolution'; it had in fact involved only three persons in all, who had been dismissed. The same theme was repeated a few days later by *Harian Rakjat* editor, Naibaho, who had been in Algiers when the 'affair' (to use Aidit's phrase) had taken place. He called it a blessing in disguise: Ben Bella had been following Yugoslavia in economic affairs, had invited U Thant to open the A.A. conference, and so on. But Naibaho, too, by the time he wrote the article for *Harian Rakjat* (having joined Aidit in Cairo) emphasized that it was wrong to call it a coup d'état.[49] It was rather 'a reshuffle'.[50] In the light of what was to happen, or rather might have happened, two months hence in Djakarta, it is not too far-fetched to see Aidit projecting himself into the situation that had developed in Algiers. A left-wing nationalist leader Ben Bella (read Sukarno) had been replaced because he had deviated from the revolution of 1954 (read the Indonesian revolution of 1945) and with a slight 'reshuffle' (a few people replaced and added, rather like a Nasakom team) the whole June 19 affair (September 30 affair) had been settled: It could not be called a coup d'état.[51]

But while Aidit may have been day-dreaming in allegories, reality in Algiers was in a full state of flux. The preparatory committee had met but, due to India, could not come to any conclusion on whether or not the conference should be held. The delegate from New Delhi tried, and even almost succeeded, in getting through a decision that the whole conference be recessed. This would have meant that all the carefully made 'recommendations', etc., of the preparatory committee, and especially the ones that had effectively paralyzed decisions on the participation of the Soviet Union and Malaysia for that matter, would have been null and void again. Chen Yi, Subandrio, and Pakistan Foreign Minister Bhutto, seeing that the committee might mess up the whole thing, directly intervened and decided to 'postpone the opening'. They thus avoided the ingenious ploy which the Indians (no doubt with Soviet brainwork behind it) had devised.[52] The Chinese and P.K.I. leaders in Cairo, as well as in Djakarta, put up a front and expressed 'full agreement' with the postponement.[53] Pravda, understandably, called it 'a wise decision', as it would make possible the 'further reinforcement of unity' between the Afro-Asian countries.[54] The only one openly to turn sour was Subandrio. In a first reaction from Algiers, forecasting that the Conefo in 1966 would now certainly be a success, Subandrio complained about some unnamed 'external forces' that had influenced affairs.[55] In Cairo, however, no doubt reflecting the mood Sukarno was in, he came out with what amounted in fact to the first open attack against the Soviet Union. In an interview with the Middle East News Agency in Cairo Subandrio, looking back on the recent events in Algiers, said that 'to overcome the present situation Afro-Asia must unify its forces to oppose colonialism'.[56]

After this rather harmless introduction, however, he then went on to say: 'Ten years ago the Soviet Union was a "protector" for Afro-Asia in dealing with colonialism, but this Soviet "protection" is no longer adequate'.[57]

So for Indonesia Subandrio had inaugurated a new era: Anti-imperialism without – that is probably against – the Soviet Union, a situation, he had already told Chou En-lai in January, Djakarta had been preparing itself for.[58] The preparation was to turn out to be less thorough than was required and, as with so many things Indonesian more verbal than anything else, but this time above all also more dangerous.

NOTES

1. See above pp. 255, 256, 268, 269.
2. See also William E. Griffith, 1967, *Sino-Soviet Relations 1964-1965*, The M.I.T. Press, Cambridge, Massachussets, p. 58, where Kruschov's desire to disengage the Soviet Union from Southeast Asia is further mentioned as a factor.
3. This was July 27, 1964. See also an editorial in *Jen-min Jih-pao* of June 18, 1965, reminding its readers of this fact.
4. *New China News Agency*, June 18, 1965.
5. After the Algerian Prime Minister Ben Bella had secured Algiers as a site for the second Bandung Conference, he had met with a number of difficulties in getting the event organized. The grand ideas on how to receive the guests from the Afro-Asian world in particular played tricks on him and made him ask twice for a delay.
6. *Moscow Radio in English for Southeast Asia*, May 27, 1965. *New Times* (Moscow), June 2, 1965.
7. Shastri arrived in the Russian capital on may 12; *Bulletin of the Institute for the Study of the U.S.S.R.*, July 1965. The Chinese were among those who connected Shastri's sojourn in the Soviet Union with the harder line towards participation in the Second A.A. conference; *New China News Agency*, June 18, 1965.
8. See *Moscow Radio in Persian*, June 16, 1965, reporting that Shastri had said it was 'essential' that the Soviet Union should participate.

9. The first sign from Moscow came on May 27, in a radio broadcast by Moscow for Southeast Asia. See also above p. 325, note 64. Generally it had been situated later, in the beginning of June; See Griffith, 1967, p. 125, note 398. For the Peng Chen Aliarcham speech see above p. 320.
10. See above pp. 272, 273.
11. *New China News Agency*, December 3, 1964. *Indonesian Observer*, December 3, 1964.
12. *Antara News Agency*, February 2, 1965.
13. Transcript Subandrio-Chou En-lai, January 24, 1965.
14. The conditions for a change of views were severe: first the U.N. should stigmatize the U.S.A. as an aggressor, then this country should withdraw from the United Nations and finally the whole organization should be 'retooled', as the Indonesian rendering of the talks said.
15. *Antara News Agency*, April 24, 1965.
16. 'If the Soviet Union participates there are two possibilities: Either we let the Soviet Union force peaceful co-existence down our throat in order to weaken anti-imperialism. That we cannot accept. Or we continue to carry the banner of anti-imperialism, and then the Soviet Union will be isolated. That is not good for the Sovict Union. Better therefore to keep the Soviet Union outside the conference and let them support it as much as possible.'
17. With due regard for the personal susceptibilities involved, Chou had this proposal to make on the invitations: 'Let Sukarno invite the people and Ben Bella be host because Ben Bella is President [of the conference]. That will feed his self-esteem. This should be suggested with the necessary cunning: Sukarno the leader of Asia; Ben Bella the leader of Africa'.
18. *New China News Agency*, December 11, 1964. When the A.A. conference was again postponed in June 1965, a special international meeting against foreign military bases was prepared and was due to take place early in October 1965. The military authorities in charge at that time, under Major General Suharto as responsible officer in the post-September 30 confusion, could not or would not call the conference off, though it was designed to be a total P.K.I.-Chinese front. As a way out the participants were hustled off to Bali and no one ever heard of the results of their meeting.
19. Elaborating on the idea after Subandrio had summed up on who could be invited Chou said: 'Send the invitations to the heads of state. This will be thought discrimination, but our efforts will be concentrated on some countries you mentioned. Give Macapagal [the President of the Philipines] a place of honor. When Mongolia comes it will cut a sorry figure by itself. Also Japan we should plug a bit. If it does not want to come it will alienate itself from the A.A. countries. Sato [Prime Minister of Japan] wants to disengage himself from the U.S. That we should use. We should do our utmost for Ghana, Nasser, Hassan, Kenyatta and Ben Bella'.
20. 'There is therefore a good chance that many countries will want to come to Indonesia for the celebration of the 10th anniversary of the first A.A. conference, possibly to ask Indonesia to re-enter the U.N.' Subandrio replied:

'Once out, always out. But Indonesia will invite other countries to try to convince us, so that we can talk to them'.

21. The new postponement was announced in the first week of February; *Indonesian Observer*, February 10, 1965. Sukarno was making his announcement on February 12; *New China News Agency*, February 12, 1965.
22. *Antara News Agency*, February 13, 1965 and *Djakarta Radio Home Service*, February 22, 1965. While in Cambodia Sukarno also stressed that on April 18 he expected a 'great concourse' of A.A. leaders; *New China News Agency*, March 4, 1965.
23. The *Far Eastern Economic Review*, generally rather fair in its judgments, called it 'a dismal failure'; *Far Eastern Economic Review*, May 13, 1965.
24. *New China News Agency*, April 16, 1965.
25. *New China News Agency*, April 18, 1965. Sukarno also wanted the Soviet Union to return the Kurilles to Japan, a point that made the Kremlin leaders furious with him.
26. *Antara News Agency*, April 22, 1965.
27. *Pravda*, April 18, 1965; *Indonesian Herald*, April 28, 1965.
28. *New China News Agency*, April 18, 1965.
29. *Antara News Agency*, April 19, 1965.
30. *Indonesian Herald*, April 20, 1965.
31. *New China News Agency*, April 24, 1965.
32. *Djakarta Radio Home Service*, April 18, 1965.
33. Fearing to be misunderstood, *Pravda* fulminated against those who, for some reason or other, had got the 'false idea' that the Soviet Union could not care less for its share in the conference. It was well meant, but rather late because it appeared on June 29, the day the conference had once more been postponed.
34. *Moscow Radio in English for Africa*, June 9, 1965.
35. See the so-called Mandala (war theater) speech Sukarno made at this juncture; *Djakarta Radio Home Service*, June 11, 1965.
36. *Bintang Timur*, June 10, 1965; *Indonesian Herald*, June 10, 1965.
37. *New China News Agency*, June 11, 1965; *Antara News Agency*, June 11, 1965.
38. *Harian Rakjat*, June 14, 1965.
39. *Antara News Agency*, June 18, 1965.
40. The Chinese maintained – probably correctly – that this opposition had nothing to do with the ideological conflict between Moscow and Peking. Mongolia [clearly on the Soviet side] would be welcome, the argument ran; *Jen-min Jih pao*, June 18, 1965.
41. *Indonesian Herald*, June 22, 1965. The declaration was made on June 20. It was said at the time that Boumedienne had chosen this rather unsuspicious moment because, if he had waited until after that international gathering was over, Ben Bella might have had so much international stature that an overthrow might have been impossible. Equally it was said that Boumedienne might not have been a free man himself by that time.

42. *Antara News Agency*, June 26, 1965. On June 24 the foreign ministers of the participating countries were to have met, the heads of state not before June 29. The 15-nation strong preparatory committee that had made the notorious April 1964 decisions or non-decisions was meant to get together on the day before the foreign ministers were formally to meet.
43. Ben Bella was said to have instructed his ambassadors in the weeks before his fall 'to smooth things out', *Far Eastern Economic Review*, June 24, 1965. Being more close to Moscow may also have antagonized the Indonesians but there is no evidence to suggest this.
44. *New China News Agency*, June 21, 1965.
45. *Djakarta Radio Home Service*, June 22, 1965. Thinking in terms of Sino-Soviet antagonisms he may first of all have registered the defeat of a Moscow orientated left-nationalist whose departure, moreover, would result in a reshuffle of the cards at the conference table.
46. *Antara News Agency*, June 22, 1965.
47. The reaction on the Soviet side was more true to type. The Kremlin was far from pleased and received the envoys Boumedienne immediately sent to various capitals rather frostily; *Antara News Agency*, June 23, 1965. In the Eastern European press criticism was more open, and for Castro – a personal friend of Ben Bella – the coup d'état was a scandalous affair.
48. *Indonesian Herald*, July 3, 1965. The statement was made in Cairo on June 30.
49. *Harian Rakjat*, July 5-8, 1965.
50. Strangely enough the version *New China News Agency* put out of the statement Aidit made in Cairo differs from the one quoted above from the *Indonesian Herald*. It has Aidit say also that the fall of Ben Bella could not be considered a coup d'état, but then it continues: 'Because it is a revolution of great importance'. If Naibaho had not repeated in *Harian Rakjat* a version close to the one in the *Indonesian Herald* a mistake by this paper could have been assumed. Now clearly the *New China News Agency* version is, either deliberately or not, not what Aidit had said.
51. See below p. 463.
52. See for the Chinese side of the story *New China News Agency*, June 29, 1965. Subandrio's version was to be found in the *Indonesian Herald* of June 30.
53. The new date set was November 5, 1965. See for the Chinese reaction: 'the April 1964 decisions are still valid', the *Jen-min Jih-pao* editorial of June 29. Lukman, back in Djakarta, said that the P.K.I. was not in the least discouraged; *Djakarta Radio Home Service*, June 29, 1965. The *Indonesian Herald* editorialized that dissension between A-A countries had never been greater, and it regretted the decision; June 29, 1965.
54. *Pravda*, June 28, 1965 and *Tass*, June 28, 1965.
55. *Antara News Agency*, June 28, 1965.
56. Interview as reported by the *Djakarta Radio Home Service*, July 1, 1965.
57. In February 1965, briefing parliamentarians on his trip to China, Subandrio

used the same expression, but then it was not intended for publication, although *Antara* put it out as a story against Subandrio's wish. Interview, March 1972, Suwito Kusumowidagdo.

58. See above p. 331.

CHAPTER 25

Plot on Bali (1965)

In the aftermath of the confusion surrounding the Algiers conference Subandrio, on the orders of Sukarno, was more active in getting Indonesia publicity than just by talking to the correspondent of the Middle East New Agency. He also talked to the editor of *Al Ahram* and provided him with what looked like a major scoop.[1] The Indonesian Foreign Minister told the Egyptian paper that the Sukarno government had proofs of an American-British plot against his country. From the draft of a letter the British Ambassador in Djakarta Gilchrist was supposed to have prepared for the London Foreign Office it had become clear that military action against Indonesia was being prepared and was imminent.[2] Later Subandrio, during his trial, was to declare that he had approached *Al Ahram* in order to draw attention to the problem Indonesia had to face with its neighbours.[3] In this he succeeded. Within days 'indignation' was rampant in the Indonesian press.[4]

Somewhat later, the Indonesian chargé d'affaires in London was asked for an explanation by the British Foreign Office.[5] What he told the British officials was not published, but the press afterwards reported his saying in public that 'there are indeed plans for an attack upon Indonesia and the assassination of President Sukarno'.[6]

The accusation against Britain was new to the outside world, but in Indonesia Subandrio had already mentioned the letter earlier. At the end of May, the day before he was to make his flying visit to Canton to meet Chou En-lai, the Indonesian Deputy Premier, speaking on May 26 at the P.K.I. reception on occasion of its 45th anniversary, said for the first time more or less publicly (it did not get into the papers then) that Sukarno had proof of a 'counter-revolutionary movement' within the country.[7] There existed a Council of Generals that was plotting against Sukarno, he said. Besides, the President had a letter written by the British ambassador, Gilchrist, in his possession which showed that those generals were in collusion with the British.

That same day, before Subandrio made this announcement, Sukarno had met top-ranking officers of the armed forces. According to reports at the time the meeting was hastily arranged.[8] Present were Defense Minister Nasution, Army Commander Yani, Navy Commander Martadinata, Police Chief Sutjipto and for the Air Force the Deputy Commander Herlambang.[9] At the time Antara said the meeting had been arranged 'to inform the military leaders about the American and British design to use Malaysia as a base against Indonesia'.[10] The President had told the top brass to do some 'introspection' because 'the imperialists will exploit any split among their forces and the people'.[11]

At the Subandrio trial in October 1966 Herlambang, heard as a witness, told the military court that during this encounter Sukarno had brought up the Gilchrist letter and had asked those present what they had to say about it. He especially questioned Yani, Herlambang said, as there was a phrase in the letter referring to 'our local army friends'.[12] The President asked if there were units that could not be trusted or persons who had contacts with Americans.[13] Yani replied that whatever occurred in this field took place under his supervision. As to the Council of Generals, he did not deny its existence but explained that they met to consider the yearly promotions.[14]

The Gilchrist letter, produced by Subandrio, had already been around for some time before it was discussed by Sukarno and the military commanders. It had reached him early in May, Subandrio was to declare at the trial, and had been sent to him anonymously.[15] It had been written on the original stationary of the British Embassy.[16] For the rest, its authenticity had not been checked, or at least not seriously, as such a document should have been. It was a clumsy forgery that, once passed on by Subandrio, took on the semblance of an official document.[17] At the same time that Subandrio, as chief of the Indonesian intelligence, received the Gilchrist letter, he had also received first word of the existence of the Council of Generals.[18] His Chief of Staff at the B.P.I., general Sutarto, had heard it 'independently' from two P.K.I. members of parliament, Harjowisastro and Wiratmono.[19]

This 'information' was supplemented by indications that some officers wanted to kill Sukarno, Subandrio, and Yani. All through this period, from early 1965 onward, a lot of tension had built up within the country, and it was clear that, with the growing polarization between the P.K.I. and the armed forced, particularly the army, anything could happen. But it was not so clear that the reports on the Council of Generals and assorted affairs had little to do with facts but were inspired rumors.

It is very easy to point here to the P.K.I. as a source because evidence from the trials after the 30 September movement had failed are there to support this view. On the other hand, the situation that had arisen in Indonesia was too complex to be explained solely by the devious machinations of the Indonesian communists.

As related earlier, the end of 1964 had shown to what extent Sukarno had re-established himself at the center of the web of power. The orientation towards Peking, already clearly discernable for some time, had moreover begun to assume more definite shape with the Chen Yi visit that pointed to cooperation also in the military field. Resuming their offensive in all fields the P.K.I – especially after the Bogor meeting of December 12 – were forging ahead to the detriment of those elements within the Indonesian political community which until then had still been in a position to resist the pressure of the communists.[20]

It was under these circumstances that a number of leading generals of the army for one of their regular meetings got together on January 13, 1965.[21] The two main officers present were Nasution and Yani who were each considered 'chef-de-file' of two rival groups within the army. It seems that, in the face of the tensions within Indonesia and especially because of the looming turn towards a more Peking-oriented foreign and military policy, the meeting brought a greater degree of unanimity than either of the two groups had assumed. But attention was focused on the preponderant role the P.K.I. was playing under Sukarno's protection. As far as differences between the two could be formulated here it concerned the Sukarno-P.K.I. relationship. Yani, always having been more close to Sukarno than Nasution, thought that Sukarno would remain the more dominating of the two. The Defense Minister, however, having had long-standing experience with Sukarno and probably also more anti-communist than Yani, had strong doubts on this point. But both men, in line with the tradition of the army and with its practical orientation as to tactics and armament (most of which came from the Soviet Union) were in full agreement in regarding the close Sino-Indonesian cooperation as a potentially dangerous development that had to be slowed down if it could not be prevented.[22]

It was this encounter and its resulting strengthening of the cohesion of the army leadership that began to kindle Sukarno's ire, sensitive as he was to any organized opposition that might upset the applecart and challenge him in his supremacy as an arbiter of national affairs. From this moment on (meetings of this character could hardly be kept secret from the President) Sukarno must have felt threatened, as he feared that his usually successful game of intrigue and cajolery, of playing off one faction against the other, of pitting one individual against the other, might (at last, one could say) have met some compact resistance among the army leadership.

It was here too that the notion originated that within the Army a 'Council of Generals' existed that was aiming at Sukarno and his presidency. It needed only some more or less skillful maneuvering to exploit the suspicion that must have been engendered in Sukarno's mind. This function the P.K.I. now began to perform, and, in a limited sense of the word, with a good deal of success. It would, however, be a misrepresentation to picture the machinations Aidit and his aides were to undertake as the main source of the disaster that befell the country in the course of 1965. Though increasingly dependent on the various services the P.K.I. was rendering the President, Sukarno was to remain an independent agent until the very last and, anticipating here the train of events still to be described, the date of October 1, 1965 will stand out. Pressured from many sides, Sukarno still was guided more by his own boundless ambitions than by the dictates of others, including the Indonesian communists.

It was the day after the generals got together in January 1965 that Aidit for the first time openly asked Sukarno to 'arm the peasants and the workers' as the phrase was – meaning the creation of an additional force, alongside the existing four the army, navy, air force, and police.[23] Though Sukarno by that time may have had information of what had gone on at the Nasution-Yani meeting it remains improbable that the two events were directly related, and that Aidit made use of the situation.[24] At any rate Aidit, when received that day by Sukarno together with the chairman of the two major parties left over (Hardi for the P.N.I. and Chalid for the N.U.), seized the opportunity to put forward his request that the civilian population be armed to counter the dangers posed by Malaysia and Great Britain.[25] It had been suggested by Chou En-lai to Sukarno in October 1964 when they met after the Cairo conference but later was to be claimed by Sukarno as his own idea.[26]

Aidit went on the air straightaway after the talk with Sukarno announcing what he had asked the President and telling the Indonesian radio listeners that Sukarno had thereupon laughed and 'nodded'.[27]

No immediate reaction was forthcoming from Sukarno, but Kuala Lumpur reported the same day that the President had rejected Aidit's point about arming the Indonesian masses because he did not think it was necessary.[28] Rumors then circulated that Subandrio had tried to scuttle Nasution but that the Defence Minister had been resued by the local army commanders who had come over from their various posts.[29]

Sukarno displayed some reaction by telling visitors a week after Aidit's plea that his régime was 'considering the communist proposal to arm civilians'.[30] For some time after that Sukarno did not say publicly anything very definite about it, and from published accounts it is hard to know what his real thoughts on the subject were. As we saw, Chou gave the impression at the end of January 1965 that Sukarno had in fact already agreed to the idea, and we know that he must have sent Subandrio to China to clinch a deal with Peking which Chou had already offered earlier.[31] Having plenty of reason to hide the real state of affairs, as the purpose of the secret arrangements with Chou could hardly be to the liking of the army leadership, the President of course did not want to show his hand.

While the President, in pursuing his own aims, was trying to increase his leverage by dealing with the Chinese in various ways, Aidit and the P.K.I. also went their own way. In January 1965 the P.K.I. chairman several times returned to the theme of arming the peasants and workers, unleashing what he termed the 'red drive', the effectiveness of which he boasted about on several occasions – and with good reason.[32] *Harian Rakjat*, recording that Sukarno had not yet approved the idea of a fifth force, also turned against the President,[33] while Aidit openly charged that 'those who oppose the supply of arms to the farmers and the workers are disloyal to the Nation'.[34] By this time, however, the results of the Chou-Subandrio talks must have come to the knowledge of the P.K.I. leadership (Second Deputy

Chairman Njoto was with Subandrio's delegation in Peking), and Aidit must have realized that the synchronized communist action in Peking and in Djakarta had yielded the beginning of a breakthrough that, given time and some patience, might help the P.K.I. in acquiring some sort of people's militia. At a rally to commemorate the 14th anniversary of *Harian Rakjat* on January 30 Aidit again spoke on the same subject of arming the population.[35] One passage of his speech was censured and did not appear in either the communist press or in what was left of the non-communist one,[36] but was given by the Chinese media.[37] That was the compliment he paid China for its help in the background: 'I am grateful to those states of the socialist world that have extended support to my proposal of arming the farmers and the workers', adding – no doubt for the benefit of the opposing army and navy leadership[38] – that 'only those devoid of patriotism oppose it'.

Having received the report of Subandrio about his visit to Peking, Sukarno once more took up the theme of 'arming the nation' and, knowing that he would soon have the tools, told an audience that he would in fact do so 'if necessary'.[39] Aidit and the communist side had meanwhile toned down their campaign for a people's militia, the P.K.I. chairman telling listeners in Australia in a radio broadcast for example that 'no patriot could be against arming the farmers and the workers', giving this clause a softer touch by adding 'in the event of a British attack on us'.[40]

Meanwhile, other developments had taken place on the home front in the early weeks of 1965. With his customary skill Subandrio forecast events and warned that the process of 'crystallization' the Indonesian society was in at that particular moment of time could force people 'to part with comrades who had turned into counter-revolutionaries'.[41] He repeated this exactly two weeks later, then adding warm praise for the P.K.I and for Aidit personally as being 'utterly progressive', at the same time calling it a 'dirty lie' to go around saying that Sukarno was nearing his end.[42] As related earlier, it was precisely Subandrio who had brought up the subject of Sukarno's health in public for the first time while the Indonesian President was still touring abroad in autumn 1964.[43] Trying to make up for the gaffe that had cost him the wrath of Sukarno, the First Deputy Premier began to deny the role he had played himself while Sukarno was away, while at the same time heaping flattery upon the President by telling the nation that 'only once in a century is a man like that born'.[44] With his reference to comrades-turned-counter-revolutionaries Subandrio excused himself in advance for the other role (besides Sukarno-sycophant) he was going to play, that of a spineless friend-dropper. In those days when Subandrio was sounding his ominous warning, both the third Deputy Premier Chaerul Saleh and Trade Minister Adam Malik were in trouble. Both had Murba affiliations and had survived the first days after that party had been banned 'temporarily' by Sukarno (under pressure from the P.K.I.) on January 6, 1965. Soon that was to change, since Malik had, in due course, to transfer part of his responsibilities to Subandrio[45] and then, thanks to protection from the President, got a nominal promotion to the nondescript function of 'minister-coordinator-for-the-implementation-of-guided-democracy'.[46] Saleh was directly and publicly attacked by the P.K.I. leadership which did not forgive him for his role in exposing the Indonesian Communist Party as a subversive organization.[47] Before the ban on the Murba Party but soon after the Bogor meeting that ended so well for the P.K.I. Aidit had begun to mention the 'false documents' that were in circulation and that were to show allegedly that the communist wanted assume power.[48] Then, when his position was further reinforced by Sukarno's decision to forbid the Murba Party, Aidit had gone one step further and accused unnamed 'political bandits' in that party of having been responsible for the slanderous documents.[49] Escalating further he began naming the culprit, saying that the P.K.I. Central Committee 'repudiated the role played by Saleh' in the case of the false documents.[50] It took until the end of March before Aidit succeeded in getting Chaerul Saleh removed from his crucial job as supervisor of the state's main economic sector, the nationalized and heavy industries. Saleh had to make do with only a part of his previous field of action – the 'commissions' he had received through his job had reputedly made him the richest man in Indonesia. But, for the moment, he was also saved by Sukarno who warned after the 'reshuffle' against Saleh and Malik that 'internal conflicts should not be exacerbated'.[51]

Aidit's 'red drive' got more steam after the United States began bombing North Vietnam early in February. Calls were heard immediately to confiscate all American enterprises in the country.[52] Not long afterwards *Antara* spread the word that the B.P.S. had been supported, if not financed, by the American Central Intelligence Agency and that Sukarno had proofs of it.[53] Sukarno used this point as an excuse to have all 'B.P.S.' newspapers banned, adding however, rather incongruously, that anyway 'no such thing as a free press should exist in any revolution'.[54]

The first U.S.I.S. office was closed down in Medan, the announcement being made by Subandrio during a speech before the conference of the regional P.K.I. branch of North Sumatra. Such institutions poisoned thinking in Indonesia, the Deputy Premier told his cheering audience.[55] Not to make things too one-sided, Subandrio also put forward the notion that communism was no longer Aidit's monopoly but should be shared.[56] As to relations with the United States (termed 'rather tense' by Subandrio), he said he had no intention to strain them further or break them off.[57]

When, thereupon, President Johnson's special envoy Elsworth Bunker arrived, he was treated rudely and achieved nothing in his talks with Subandrio who, among other things, declared that he thought it was perfectly 'natural' that gas and electricity were cut off for American residents in Djakarta.[58] It was untrue, he said, that the P.K.I. was forcing the hand of the government. Nevertheless, the Foreign Minister thought it better suddenly to undertake a pilgrimage to Mecca and disappeared while his American guest was still around, not returning before Bunker left on April 17.[59]

During Bunker's stay, and in his presence, Sukarno had another of his rhetoric bouts further convincing the American diplomat that Sukarno's course was irreversible. It was when Sukarno addressed parliament and coined the phrase 'banting stir', the wheel had to be turned.[60] One of the things it meant was that the confrontation with Malaysia had to be cranked up and (this was for Bunker) that absolutely no foreign aid capital would be relied on to help the country get onto its feet, because it was on its feet already.[61] It was earlier that month in Bandung that the army had opened a seminar to study the requirements of the current phase through which Indonesia was passing.[62] The seminar was a direct consequence of the discussions which had started early in January among leading army officers. On the second day of the seminar Sukarno, only then having heard about it, immediately invited the top brass assembled in Bandung to come to his palace in Bogor. He began with a friendly chat but suddenly turned against the whole idea of the seminar and was especially outraged with Yani whom, at the beginning of the meeting, he had praised to the skies.[63] It must have contributed to his already highly suspicious state of mind towards the army leadership and may in part have explained his 'Banting Stir' to the parliamentarians.[64]

At the end of the month Nasution was once more invited to visit Moscow.[65] It was the time that again, upon the instigation of Bunker, there had been some talk by Indonesia of meeting Tunku Abdul Rahman. For his part the Malaysian Prime Minister had softened his previous views that he would talk only after the Indonesian had completely stopped their guerilla warfare. This may also have been counseled by the Americans. After some preparatory moves had been made, however, the P.K.I. put up so much pressure that the plan to meet in Tokyo had to be dropped.[66] It was, of course, denied that the P.K.I. had anything to do with the decision, as it was agreed by all 'Nasakom' leaders at a closed meeting on April 30, that Sukarno would stay at home.[67] But there is no doubt that the P.K.I. was strongly against the idea, and Sukarno may have used them to reinforce his own reluctance.[68]

The point was rather that Sukarno was showing an increasing disregard for normal political behavior and was losing the wish, or power, to keep up even a semblance of decorum. The meeting in Tokyo had been partly stimulated and (certainly as to its practical details) prepared by the Japanese government. The Japanese ambassador, however, had to learn from Sukarno's speech on May 1 that Sukarno had decided not to go.[69] He had not been given any warning in advance, as the barest courtesy required.[70]

This in itself minor episode opened, with even greater prospects of success, the next phase of Aidit's 'revolutionary offensive' as it came to be called from the moment that the P.K.I. Chairman announced it on May 5.[71] It was followed next day by a P.K.I. statement inaugurating the May festivities for the party's 45th anniversary and particular the plenary session of its Central Committee that preceded it.[72] The tone of the statement was relatively cool, probably intentionally leaving the more interesting points to be made by the communist leaders, both Indonesian and foreign. One paragraph, however, is worth recalling since it showed something of the thinking within the party leadership only some months before the test was to come on relations with the armed forces. It was the duty of the P.K.I., the declaration said, to see that 'under all circumstances the armed forces *or a majority* will stand with the people on the side of the revolution' [emphasis added].[73] This was exactly what Aidit for his part tried to do at the end of September 1965, to get as many supporters as possible (the air force) to neutralize those who wavered (the navy and the police) and to have at least a number of army units to do the trick.[74]

In his general report of May 11 Aidit set the tone for the campaign in the coming months: 'The nation is at boiling point; therefore intensify the revolutionary struggle at all points'.[75] He warned, however, that 'the enemy still has power and we should not trifle with him', a remark no doubt noted in army circles. On the same day Sukarno, opening the new National Defense Institute, also intimated that difficult days lay ahead: 'We are now facing decisive moments', he told the assembled military and civilian authorities.[76] He then explained his vision on the situation in the world, imploring his audience that as Indonesia was 'the principal enemy' of the neo-colonialists and imperialists – even more feared than the communist bloc he added, seriously one must assume – 'necolim' was the principal enemy of Indonesia. It was therefore quite untrue that 'the enemy came from the North'. This was the catch phrase, the core of the philosophy he assumed – not incorrectly – the army leadership was adhering to, and it was a direct reference to the fact that to Nasution and Yani, when the chips were down, it was not Great Britain or the United States that threatened the existence of Indonesia but China, 'the enemy from the North'. It was at this stage of the debate between Sukarno and the Army leaders that Aidit produced a new bone of contention. Two days after Sukarno had given his admonition to look for the right enemies, the P.K.I. Chairman publicly urged that the armed forces should be given a 'Nasakom-team' in order to 'outline policies'.[77] In plain language this would have meant the injection of politics into the armed forces, with a direct voice of the communists in a field where, until now, they had to make do with subversion and propaganda. This idea of having political commissars in Indonesian barracks was, of course, out of the question for the military, and Nasution seized the opportunity to make this clear to all and sundry.[78]

But now it was again Sukarno's turn to try to test the reaction of the military leaders be it on a different field: In his first lecture to the National Defense Institute, the Indonesian President again brought up the idea of a 'fifth force', saying that he had 'not yet' accepted it.[76] This was interpreted as a trial rite to see what Nasution, Yani, and the others would now think of the idea and to prod them, if not even irritate them.[80] Then, having told the country during the P.K.I. celebrations that he, Sukarno, 'embraced the P.K.I.',[81] he first called as we saw the commanders of the armed forces together, and then two days later he also assembled the regional commanders of the various branches of the armed forces and equally gave them a piece of his mind.[82] He told the army that it should get rid of its 'comphobia' (its fear of communism) and fulminated against divisive tendencies among leading officers in the services. He was particularly annoyed by the 'squabbles' within the navy and the police.[83] At both occasions Sukarno warned that there were plans to attack the country (the Gilchrist ploy) and to 'kill a number of leaders'.[84]

As no evidence has ever been produced to substantiate these charges which Sukarno made in front of the military leaders of the country (other than the so-called Gilchrist letter) and as this 'proof' by all accounts was a 'plant' or deliberate fake, it is interesting to recall the threats Chou En-lai had foreseen as being in store for Indonesia[85] and to compare this with the Gilchrist forgery. Sukarno claimed he had proof that the Americans and British were ready to launch an attack on Indonesia[86] and if that failed to kill 'several Indonesian leaders, first of all Sukarno, Yani, and Subandrio'. A third alternative mentioned was a 'limited attack'[87] from the outside combined with a coup d'état from the inside by 'friends' who wanted to get rid of the same three leaders. And finally 'if this also fails, they will attempt to topple Sukarno, Yani, and Subandrio, among other things by exposing all of their secrets, particularly about their personal life, so that people will revolt against Sukarno, Yani, and Subandrio'.[88] But it had been Chou who told Subandrio at the end of January 1965[89] to take care and prevent a military demonstration by the U.S.A. and Great Britain, the assassination of Sukarno, Subandrio, and other Indonesian leaders, provocations to keep a crisis situation alive, and subversion and corruption. All the elements which Sukarno (with no foundation in fact) had sketched as proven plans had been suggested as possible dangers by Chou four months earlier. So, if the Indonesian President had been put up to all this by the P.K.I. members in and outside Subandrio's secret service, the B.P.I., (as it is reasonable to assume after the trials against

Subandrio and others) this was done in collusion with the Chinese who also had every interest to make Sukarno believe the hairraising exploits of the wicked imperialists and their local henchmen.

In this light one should see also the 24-hour surprise visit the Indonesian Foreign Minister paid to China on May 28, 1965, where in Canton he met the Chinese Prime Minister Chou En-lai.[90] The news that Subandrio would go came only a few days before the day of departure,[91] and in Peking, too, no advance notice was given of the meeting.[92] Subandrio went 'at the request of President Sukarno[93] and according to one Indonesian source for discussions on 'an important issue',[94] while Antara reported at the same time that the talks were related to 'projects *carried out* in Indonesia and the forthcoming Afro-Asian conference' [emphasis added].[95]

As to the Afro-Asian conference that was to be held the next month in Algiers, the speech of Peng Chen to the Aliarcham academy on May 25 had been a violent rebuttal of Soviet pretenses in all fields but especially of its claim on a seat at the Afro-Asian table. In theoretical terms, Peng Chen's basic theses had been that 'the contradiction between the oppressed nations of Asia, Africa, and Latin America and the imperialists headed by the U.S.A. is the principle contradiction of the contemporary world', while, moreover, 'the Krushov revisionists' denied this. It had been a strong attack, an escalation in fact, that was the more unpallatable to the Soviet leaders as it had not been delivered at home but in the heart of what Moscow still regarded as 'neutral' territory, Indonesia. Peng Chen's speech set the tone for the forthcoming Algiers conference and was no doubt meant to be such. From the Chinese side this was probably an important reason for accepting or soliciting Subandrio's flying visit.[96]

The reference on the Indonesian side to the fact that 'projects carried out in Indonesia' would also be discussed may have meant the Conefo project, the building (with Chinese aid) of a hall that was to house the counter-U.N. Sukarno and Chou En-lai had been planning.[97] As this Conefo-project later appeared to be intricately linked up with the '30 September movement'[98] and the Sino-Indonesian cooperation that lay behind it, it is very likely that Subandrio had also been instructed by Sukarno to look into the practical aspects of the alliance, the secret arms deliveries and other asserted points.[99] This assumption is the more plausible as the delegation that went to Canton was identical to the leading members of the giant delegation that went to Peking in January 1965: Apart from Subandrio, Njoto was also there, as well as Deputy Commander of the Air Force Herlambang. The fact that not only Afro-Asian politics were discussed (the talks went on until the early hours of May 29)[100] is also clear from the presence of General Lo Jui-ching, then Chief of Staff of the Chinese armed forces.[101] Laying a link here with the Gilchrist letter is not too farfetched, making the alleged American-British plot to attack Indonesia for Djakarta another factor in deciding to send a delegation to China for unscheduled talks. To be sure, it was the day after the trip was announced that Sukarno, in front of the commanders of the four armed forces showed, or pretended to show, his concern[102] and that Subandrio was authorized to make public allusion to 'counter-revolutionary plots'.

If the dangers of the assumed Anglo-American conspiracy and further Sino-Indonesian collaboration to counter it was indeed what was meant by the 'projects' that were to be discussed in Canton, the results of these talks remained uncertain because on his return Subandrio no longer mentioned the 'projects'. It is possible that, in view of the secret character of the points involved (arms shipments outside army channels, military aid to Pakistan, etc.)[103] and the increase in alignment with Peking that they entailed, Subandrio had no use for making any public mention of that part of the conversation. The Indonesian foreign minister commented after his trip only on the Algiers conference. He said that this meeting of Afro-Asian countries was undermined by 'necolim and other adversaries', a reference to both western countries and Eastern European communist countries.[104]

At any rate there is a strong impression that the 24 hour talks in Canton reflected the dramatically growing involvement of China in the plotting that went on in Indonesia.

When Subandrio returned on May 29 also the regional commanders had received the latest information on the Gilchrist letter in the pep talk given by the Indonesian President. It remains hard to gauge the extent to which Sukarno himself was at this stage active in the plot around the fake document. But even if he was more of a victim than a victimizer, the Indonesian President in his paranoic vision of Indonesia and particularly of himself at its head only too eagerly rose to the bait held out for him. It is also not beyond doubt that Subandrio, so much in the center of the ploy, was in on all the combined intrigues around the Gilchrist letter, and his extra-ordinary laxness in verifying this 'document'[105] points to at least some tacit cooperation in it all, aimed at putting Sukarno in the proper mood for certain actions.

It is not quite clear what the reaction of the assembled officers was, but the least one could expect was a slightly embarrassed surprise. But few, if any, among them could have suspected that they were so close to a part of what their Great Leader and commander-in-chief told them he feared: The killing of 'a number of leaders'. Even less likely was it that they would have believed they were in the presence of the man who was about to plan and authorize those killings himself. Nevertheless that was the true state of affairs, as we follow the story a bit further and see how Sukarno, not long after his meeting with the military commanders, celebrated his 64th Birthday.[106] He hid himself from the public that day as he had announced in advance.[107] He did it 'on purpose' as he confined to the nation afterwards.[108] Why he did so was not quite so obvious, but more is now known of what he did while celebrating his birthday on Bali. It was on that day that he and a number of his courtiers, like Subandrio, Leimena, Saleh, Muddah Dalam, and General Sjafiuddin, heard him discuss the recalcitrant attitude of the army leadership.[109] These headstrong generals should not only think of tactics, he complained, but also about world strategy. The Djakarta-Peking axis was a new strategy and 'the danger did not come from the North but from Necolim' and this new strategy should be followed. General Sjafiuddin, then military commander of Bali, now in jail, was to remark that among the army leadership some did not agree with that new strategy. 'Some groups are loyal, other are not', Sjafiuddin told Sukarno, according to the Presidents aide-de-camp Bambang Widjanarko who was present on the occasion. Sukarno thereupon retorted that if what Sjafiuddin said was true then this should be changed and 'an improvement should be made withing the army leadership'. At this point Subandrio suggested hearing Yani directly so as to check the points Sjafiuddin had made. Sukarno dismissed this but told Sjafiuddin himself to start checking up on the 'loyalty' of the army leadership.

It was this crucial meeting that laid the foundation for the plans to eliminate the most 'obstinate' among leading army generals. In the months to come Sjafiuddin (but not alone he) reported regularly to Sukarno.[110] Bambang Widjanarko cites the period from July to September during which Sjafiuddin was in close touch with the Indonesian President on the question of 'loyalty'. The tenor of these reports was that indeed there was a core of 'disloyal' (i.e., anti-Sukarno) generals – and this in turn made Sukarno decide they had to disappear.[111] The intrigues that were finally to lead to the murder of six generals[112] and, in its wake, thousands of innocent victims were successfully foisted on the ill mind of a decadent dictator who could not bear the idea of being opposed. Sukarno indeed had good reason to hide himself from the world on that 6th of June, 1965.

NOTES

1. *Al Ahram*, July 5, 1965.
2. At the time Subandrio held many and varied jobs, not the least of which was Chief of the Indonesian Intelligence Service B.P.I.
3. See proceedings of the Subandrio trial, 2nd session.
4. The Chairman of the Muslim Nahdatul Ulama Party was calling for a holy war, if what Al Ahram had heard from Subandrio was true; *Antara News Agency*, June 8, 1965.
5. *The Times* (London), December 12, 1965.
6. *Antara News Agency*, July 13, 1965.
7. See trial proceedings of the Subandrio trial, 2nd session.
8. *Radio Free Europe*, July 19, 1965.
9. *New China News Agency*, May 26, 1965.
10. *Antara News Agency*, May 26, 1965.
11. *Antara News Agency*, May 26, 1965.
12. Proceedings of the Subandrio trial, 8th session.
13. General Yani himself was known for his generally pro-American thinking, having received his training in the United States. It did not, however, make him adopt a Washington-oriented political line.
14. Proceedings of the Subandrio trial, 8th session, witness by Herlambang.
15. Air Force commander Omar Dhani had been told about the 'Council of Generals' by Brigadier General Supardjo as early as April 1965; Nugroho and Ismal, 1967, Djakarta, *The Coup Attempt*, p. 36. Supardjo was tried, sentenced and shot for his part in the '30 September movement'.
16. Proceedings of the Subandrio trial, 2nd session. At the end of 1964 the British Embassy had been raided by young demonstrators among whom members of the Communist Youth Organization Pemuda Rakjat.
17. According to General Nasution it had been clear from the beginning that the letter was a fake; Interview, March 1972. Apparently, at the time no way of expressing this publicly was employed.

18. Proceedings of the Subandrio trial, 2nd session; statement of Subandrio.
19. After the failure of the '30 September movement' Politburo member Njono was found hiding in Djakarta in the house of Wiratmono.
20. In his general report to the 4th plenary in May Aidit was to call the meeting at Bogor and its resulting Declaration 'the pinnacle of victory', claiming that it was the P.K.I. that had reversed the situation then; *Harian Rakjat*, May 12, 1965.
21. It was the Generals Sudirman, Sarbini, Basuki Rahmat and Sumantri, considered as belonging to the 'Nasution' group, and Parman, Suprapto, Harjono, Sutojo, Sukendro and Muskito of the 'Yani' side. The meeting may also have saved Nasution from losing his position as Defense Minister, as Subandrio with Sukarno's connivance and under P.K.I. prodding early in January 1965 had tried to remove Nasution from his post. Sukarno, adept at intrigues, had begun to spread the rumor that he wanted Yani to become Deputy Prime Minister – like Subandrio, Leimena and Saleh – and to 'groom' him as his successor.
22. According to General Nasution the meeting of the generals as such did not react against the growing official orientation towards Peking, as the army leadership was not united enough for this, having also a 'P.K.I. faction'. Interview, March 1972. Nasution saw three phases: First from 1959 when he and Sukarno agreed on reintroducing the 1945 Constitution until 1962, characterized by growing disagreement between the two and ending with the installation of General Yani as commander of the army and Nasution being kicked upstairs. The second phase showed that Sukarno succeeded in 'separating' Yani from Nasution, with Yani following the President closely and urging others also to 'integrate' themselves with Sukarno, an attitude Nasution says he for various reasons could and would never adopt. The third phase for Nasution came with the January 1965 meeting, when the rift began to be healed and a new basis for unity between the Army leaders was found in 'supporting Nasakom *spiritually*'. This implicitly meant rejection of the P.K.I. interpretation, gradually also endorsed by Sukarno, that national unity should also be implemented *organizationally*, e.g. in the army, by introducing political appointments of which, of course, the P.K.I. was the sole beneficiary.
23. *Indonesian Observer*, January 14, 1965. Aidit spoke of 10 million farmers and five million workers that could be considered eligible for being armed.
24. The opposite may rather be true, as Aidit had prepared the publicity around his demand for a fifth force too well to have been improvised. Immediately after he left the presidential palace, where he had been received by Sukarno, he made a broadcast on Djakarta Radio telling everybody that he had suggested the arming of civilians to Sukarno; *Djakarta Radio Home Service*, January 14, 1965.
25. 'No force on earth would defeat the Indonesian Republic' he told Sukarno to make the idea attractive; *New China News Agency*, January 14, 1965. Present on the occasion also was Asmu, chairman of the powerful Com-

munist farmers organization B.T.I.; *Indonesian Observers*, January 14, 1965. It was Asmu who had been the first to propose arming the peasants; *New China News Agency*, November 21, 1964. See above p. 304.

26. See above p. 318 and below p. 394.
27. *Djakarta Radio Home Service*, January 14, 1965; *New China News Agency*, January 15, 1965.
28. *Kuala Lumpur Radio*, January 14, 1965, supplied interesting information on events in Indonesia, notwithstanding the tension between the two countires. However, it had a decidedly anti-Sukarno, anti-P.K.I. bias and was apparently based on Indonesian army intelligence, which had links with K.L. through military commanders in Sumatra who felt they no longer had publicity channels in Indonesia.
29. *Washington Post*, January 20, 1965. See p. 370, note 21.
30. Sukarno said this on January 20, the day Subandrio left for his trip to Burma and China; *Kuala Lumpur Radio*, January 31, 1965.
31. See above p. 332.
32. For instance, at a rally of the Communist Women's organization on January 19; *Harian Rakjat*, January 21, 1965.
33. *Harian Rakjat* told its readers on January 25 that Sukarno did not agree with Aidit on the subject.
34. *Kuala Lumpur Radio*, January 20, 1965.
35. *Harian Rakjat*, January 31, 1965.
36. In the early weeks of 1965 the Indonesian press was in the process of a purge against all 'B.P.S.' or 'Sukarnoist' elements. The P.K.I.-dominated Indonesian Press Association P.W.I. had demanded a 'retooling' of Antara on January 13 and forthwith got what it wanted; *Kuala Lumpur Radio*, January 14, 1965. At the end of February, at a P.W.I. rally, a ban on all B.P.S. newspapers was demanded, with the result that, next day, this was effectuated; *Antara News Agency*, February 23, 1965; *Indonesian Observer*, February 24, 1965. (For the *Indonesian Observer* it was the last time it would go to press, and only in September 1966 did the paper resume publication). On March 1, 1965, Air Force Chief Omar Dhani congradulated the communist P.W.I. Chairman and *Warta Bhakti* editor, Karim, on the successful elimination of B.P.S. elements, for which gesture Dhani was told in return that the Air Force was the 'favorite' of the P.W.I. Both Karim and Dhani were involved later that year in the 'Untung putsch' and still are, at the time of writing, in jail.
37. *New China News Agency*, February 12, 1965; *Radio Peking Home Service*, February 12, 1965.
38. The army under General Yani as well as the navy under Rear-Admiral Martadinata (a Nasution-man) were against the idea of a fifth force. The police were, too, but were soon to get a new commander, more pliable to Sukarno's wishes. In the navy, attempts were also made to eliminate Martadinata which resulted in a weakening of his position. See below p. 379.

39. *Indonesian Observer*, February 12, 1965; *New China News Agency*, February 12, 1965.
40. *Australian Broadcasting Corporation Home Service*, February 13, 1965.
41. *Djakarta Radio Home Service*, January 4, 1965. Two days later the Murba Party was to be banned temporarily and its President, Sukarni, on orders of Sukarno, was jailed. See also *Indonesian Observer*, January 2, 1965 reporting the first open attack on Sukarni, and *Indonesian Observer*, January 6, 1965 as well as *Radio Free Europe*, March 29, 1965 on the Murba ban. That it was the Indonesian President who had Sukarni put in jail was confirmed in an interview, March 1972, with one of those present at the Palace when the order was given.
42. *New China News Agency*, January 16, 1965; *Indonesian Observer*, January 16, 1965.
43. See above p. 303.
44. *New China News Agency*, January 16, 1965; *Indonesian Observer*, January 16, 1965.
45. *Antara News Agency*, March 13, 1965.
46. *Antara News Agency*, January 31, 1965. Malik got a room in the presidential palace and at least a desk to sit at, but the main purpose of all this in the words of the President himself was 'not to let the P.K.I. get at you'; Interview, March 1972, Adam Malik. The 'minister-coordinator' was to survive the ordeal of those days, both physically and politically, and a year later succeeded Subandrio as Foreign Minister, a post he still holds at the time of writing (June 1972), while at the same time being a candidate for the still vacant vice-presidency of the country.
47. See above p. 310, note 42.
48. *Radio Free Indonesia*, December 22, 1964, reporting on a speech made by Aidit to police officers at the police academy in Sukabumi. The report added that the documents in question had a pro-Chinese tenor; see also above p. 231.
49. *Indonesian Observer*, January 19, 1965.
50. *Harian Rakjat*, January 22, 1965.
51. *Antara News Agency*, March 31, 1965 and *Indonesian Herald*, March 31, 1965. Saleh was put in jail after the 30 September affair, though there were no indications that he had had anything to do with it. As a matter of fact he was in China at the end of September at the head of a parliamentary mission. He died in jail, officially following a heart attack, but some doubts about the truth of this report were expressed. An intelligence report that came to the knowledge of this writer indicated he committed suicide by taking poison.
52. *Indonesian Observer*, February 15, 1965.
53. *Antara News Agency*, February 22, 1965. It would not have been surprising if the C.I.A. had been fully aware at the time, in the second half of 1964, of the use the B.P.S. could have had in keeping both Sukarno and the P.K.I. in check. What measure of 'support' could have been the result of

this sort of consideration is anyone's guess, but one of the leading persanalities behind the B.P.S., Zein Effendi, denied the charges categorically as entirely unfounded and not serious.

54. *New China News Agency*, February 24, 1965.
55. *New China News Agency*, February 27, 1965 and February 28, 1965.
56. *Indonesian Herald*, March 1st, 1965.
57. *Antara News Agency*, March 17, 1965. This statement came after Subandrio had met American Ambassador Jones, who told him that President Johnson wanted to send troubleshooter and old Indonesian hand Elsworth Bunker to Djakarta to take a look at things. The official announcement that Bunker would be coming at the end of March 25; *Indonesian Herald*, March 25, 1965.
58. Information supplied by dr. G. Pauker; *Indonesian Herald*, April 6, 1965.
59. *Izvestia*, March 31, 1965; *Indonesian Herald*, April 9, 1965.
60. Information supplied by dr. G. Pauker; *Antara News Agency*, April 12, 1965.
61. There are no indications that Bunker had come to offer anything in exchange for good behavior. The communists feared something of the kind, writing, upon his arrival, in *Harian Rakjat* that 'the most stupid view' was to expect the Indonesian people to be bribed; *Harian Rakjat*, April 2, 1965. The P.K.I. must have been hopelessly out of date. The only point Bunker and Sukarno agreed on was the withdrawal of the Peace Corps members from Indonesian territory; *Antara News Agency*, April 15, 1965.
62. It was held from of April 1-5, 1965.
63. According to Nasution loyalty to Sukarno was then not in question, the problem only being 'the strong anti-P.K.I. attitude of the army leadership that Sukarno wanted to neutralize'; Interview, March 1972.
64. It was Yani who when things had already taken a more critical turn, remarked that 'banting stir' was necessary but did not mean either going to the left or the right; *Indonesian Herald*, June 30, 1965. The journalist who dared to write, somewhat later, that in fact Yani had meant that things should be carried on as they already were, was given house arrest for this remark, inflicted upon him by the board of the local Surabaja P.W.I., the journalists organization.
65. *Indonesian Herald*, May 30, 1965. He was to leave on May 9. The Kremlin leaders were furious with Sukarno, especially because of the speech the Indonesian leader had made at the Bandung conference commemoration on April 18, 1965; see above p. 346. Kosygin, for example, insisted that Indonesia should recognize the Soviet Union as an Asiatic country and tried to reinforce his arguments by saying: 'Why, we even have an Asian as President!', a reference to the fact that Soviet President Mikoyan was born in Azarbaidjan; Interview, March 1972, Nasution.
66. On April 23 presidential aide, Minister Oei Tjoe Tat said that Indonesia was ready for the talks in Tokyo; *Antara News Agency*, March 24, 1965. The P.K.I. press was flooded with sabre-rattling congratulations to the

Malayan Communist Party for its 35th anniversary and staunch opposition to the modern revisionists and especially for their meritorious 'armed struggle'. Ruslan Abdulgani, alternating with Subandrio as spokesman for Sukarno, foretold that the talks would not be held as Rahman was in Tokyo to see a football-match, a motive making him an unworthy partner at the conference table apparently; *Indonesian Herald*, April 29, 1965.

67. *Antara News Agency*, May 4, 1965.
68. *Kuala Lumpur Radio*, May 2, 1965 put the blame on the P.K.I. only, a charge later denied by Nasution.
69. *Far Eastern Economic Review*, May 13, 1965. In his Labor Day speech Sukarno indeed, as already Abdulgani's earlier remarks had foreshadowed, gave as ground for his refusal that Rahman's only ostensible reason to be in Tokyo was a football match; *New China News Agency*, May 1, 1965.
70. Malik, who had regularly access to Sukarno in that period also described him as increasingly short-tempered and quickly irritable.
71. *Antara News Agency*, May 6, 1965. Aidit was addressing employees of the Ministries of Security and Defense on Bali.
72. *Harian Rakjat*, May 7, 1965.
73. *Harian Rakjat*, May 7, 1965.
74. See for details of the trick Aidit had in mind below p. 392 ff.
75. *Harian Rakjat*, May 12, 1965.
76. *Antara News Agency*, May 11, 1965.
77. *Antara News Agency*, May 14, 1965.
78. *Antara News Agency*, May 24, 1965. Indonesia is not turning communist and there will be no 'Nasakomisation' of the armed forces, he said upon return from his trip to Moscow. Yani said the next day that Nasakom 'in spirit' among the armed forces was sufficient, a softer way of saying the same as Nasution; *Indonesian Herald*, May 25, 1965. Sukarno was to reassure the regional military commanders who met on May 28 that he did not endorse the idea of a 'political' Nasakom set up in the armed forces; *Djakarta Radio Home Service*, May 28, 1965.
79. *Antara News Agency*, May 20, 1965 and *Radio Free Europe*, June 8, 1965.
80. Sukarno also had a nice point for the Russians, saying in his lecture that according to Ho Chi-minh the Chinese had sent their officers abroad [read to the Soviet Union] 'and had learned nothing'.
81. At the P.K.I. rally on May 23, to an audience of 100,000 people Sukarno, carried away by his emotion (or not), told them: 'If the P.K.I. were to die, it would be my loss as a brother'; *Djakarta Radio Home Service*, May 23, 1965.
82. The top commanders met on May 26, the regional commanders on May 28. See above p. 365 and *Djakarta Radio Home Service*, May 28, 1965; *Radio Free Europe*, June 8, 1965; *New China News Agency*, May 29, 1965.
83. At the end of February there had been a mutiny of younger naval officers in Surabaja, calling themselves 'progressive revolutionaries'; it was a bloodless dress rehearsal for what was to be done to the army leadership later that

year, a Subandrio-P.K.I. inspired attempt – probably with Sukarno backing – to achieve a change in the navy command. Rear-Admiral Martadinata managed to stay on top, but his position was weakened and he shifted accordingly from a pro-Nasution to a more Sukarno-centered attitude. In May Sukarno directly interfered in police affairs, having the incumbent police chief replaced by a man more dedicated to his person, Sutjipto. This change was made by the President after the P.K.I. had strongly criticized police actions in the countryside against illegal occupation of land by communist-inspired squatters.

84. *Antara News Agency*, May 28, 1965.
85. See above p. 331.
86. *Antara News Agency*, May 26, 1965 and *Djakarta Radio Home Service*, May 28, 1965.
87. The 'limited attack' had been something the P.K.I. already in a very early stage had feared as a reaction upon army provocations along the North Kalimantan border after which a state of emergence could be engineered against them.
88. *Djakarta Radio Home Service*, May 28, 1965.
89. See above p. 331 and transcript Subandrio-Chou En-lai, January 27, 1965.
90. *New China News Agency*, May 28, 1965.
91. *Antara News Agency*, May 25, 1965, announcing at first that Subandrio would leave on May 27, while in fact he was to leave on May 28.
92. Interview, March 1972, Baron Sastradinata.
93. *Antara News Agency*, May 25, 1965.
94. *Indonesian Herald*, May 28, 1965.
95. *Antara News Agency*, May 28, 1965.
96. For the Soviet Union Peng Chen's attack in Djakarta was an occasion to renew its claim to being admitted to the second Afro-Asian Conference in Algiers; see above p. 351, note 9, where it is indicated that Moscow gave signs of this resumed interest two days after Peng Chen's Aliarcham speech.
97. The rather embryonal cooperation in the field of atomic science may also have been included as a 'project'.
98. See below p. 422, note 40.
99. See above pp. 332, 333.
100. Interview, March 1972, Baron Sastradinata. Mr. Suwito Kusumowidagdo who was also in Canton with Subandrio denied any knowledge of talks on other subjects than the A-A conference, but said that 'many private talks' went on; Interview, March 1972.
101. Interview, March 1972, Baron Sastradinata.
102. See above p. 356.
103. See below p. 403.
104. See above p. 350.
105. Proceedings of the Subandrio trial, 2nd session.
106. This was on June 6; he spent the day at his residential palace in Tampaksiring on Bali.

107. *Indonesian Herald*, June 5, 1965.
108. In a radio broadcast on June 8: 'I purposely hid myself'; *Djakarta Radio Home Service*, June 8, 1965.
109. See Widjanarko report II, p. 8.
110. Police General Sudirgo also reported to Sukarno that allegations of 'disloyalty' of a number of army generals were correct; see Widjanarko report III, pp. 25, 26. Sudirgo is at the moment of writing – June 1972 – in jail.
111. See Widjanarko-report III, p. 24 and below p. 381.
112. Also killed, but not as previously planned by the authors of the 'Untung putsch', was a lieutenant and the young daughter of General Nasution.

CHAPTER 26

Sukarno decides to strike and is struck (1965)

It was in that same month of June when Sukarno's anger at the Army leadership took on more definite shape that the P.K.I. above ground continued its 'red drive' and underground pushed their cause at least as energetically.

The day before the President's memorable birthday party in Tampaksiring, Njoto led a mass P.K.I.-'show' in the Senajan stadium, recapitulating in his address the results of the previous months.[1] He thought that the P.K.I. was not free from 'defects and errors', but on the whole there was not much reason to complain. He thought it was time – once again, one would say – to 'launch a policy of revolutionary offensive'. About the nature of this offensive he had been reassuringly frank, in the negative sense that is, when he told an anxious western interviewer some days earlier that for the P.K.I. 'communism is not on the agenda today'.[2]

What was on the agenda was much more simple, as Aidit was to explain when speaking to a meeting of bank employees, i.e., indoctrination and military training.[3] He also said that not 'socialism' (read communism) was the aim at the moment but bringing the 'national-democratic revoltuion' – the well-known first phrase of the revolution – to a good end. Before achieving that noble aim, there was still a lot to be accomplished. The party had formulated the remaining tasks, before 'communism' was on the agenda, quite clearly and succintly in its draft-resolution, which was later to be adopted by the fourth Central Committee plenary session in mid-May.[4] They were condensed into 'six steps towards our aim', and together formed a good 'shopping-list' of P.K.I. wishes and a guide to what was going to happen – if all turned out to be ideal in this world: 1. Eliminate the bureaucratic capitalists, 2. mobilize the farmers behind the P.K.I., 3. establish a Nasakom cabinet, 4. infiltrate the army, 5. tighten party discipline, and 6. fight imperialism and revisionism. Translation into plain language was hardly necessary and certainly with hindsight the priorities were neatly enough indicated. The first item, in accordance with Aidit's dictum to concentrate on the 'most obstinate enemies', was to take on the leading officers, who were still a factor to be reckoned with very seriously either in a military or in a civilian capacity.[5]

Then came the peasant revolt, the unilateral actions and raids in the countryside that were later to provide tinder for unprecedented bloodshed.[6] A greater direct voice in the affairs of state for the party had been a major point, but now ranked only third, as much having in fact already been accomplished.

The infiltration of the army, taken in hand more systematically at the end of 1964 under Sjam, was something to keep working on, but could hardly be expected to inspire much general enthusiasm.[7] But it still figured before party discipline, the key factor that was later to be dismally lacking after the P.K.I.'s involvement with the '30 September movement' dawned upon its followers and mass defections took place.[8]

It is significant how low was the rating of anti-imperialism and anti-revisionism, i.e., the foreign policy aspects of the P.K.I., its anti-Western and anti-Soviet attitude, still so loudly proclaimed.[9]

Infiltration of the armed forces had met with varying success up to that moment. The air force could probably be considered fair game for the P.K.I., certainly with a man like Omar Dhani at the helm. He was a staunch supporter of Sukarno through thick and thin, as his later demise as an accomplice in the '30 September movement' was abundantly to demonstrate.[10] At the same time, however, he could easily be considered a non-card-carrying P.K.I. man and made no bones about his predilections.[11] In May 1965 'indoctrination courses' in Marxism started in his house and were probably more a social event than an intellectual exercise.[12] He was also the first, and only, service commander openly to endorse the communist demand that the farmers and the workers be armed.[13] It was Dhani too, who at a very early stage already recorded (and experienced no doubt) Soviet resistance to the foreign policies Aidit, Sukarno, and the Chinese together were peddling increasingly in the second half of 1964. Early in March 1965 he suggested making the air force independent of the Russians, forbade his officers to go to the Soviet Union for training, and said he was interested 'only' in getting repair facilities and spare parts from that country.[14] A month later he repeated this, calling for 'self-reliance' in weaponry.[15] Air force officers and men were also to be prominent (more than those of other service branches) in the preparation and execution of the aims of the '30 September movement', but this was to a great extent induced by the behavior of the leadership of Dhani and company.[16] Weak spots also appeared within the navy, as the February mutiny in Surabaja had shown.[17] After Aidit had put in a word on the 'Nasakomisation' of the armed forces, it was non-communist Rear Admiral Eddy Martadinata who felt compelled to go all the way and personally tell Aidit in his P.K.I. headquarters that he could not oblige.[18] This Canossalike step must certainly not have endeared him with less 'considerate' colleagues in the army. But all in all (judging from available evidence) Martadinata was to emerge from the trying period around the September affair as perhaps a weak officer but at least not a voluntary participant.[19]

It was at this time that in connivance with air force officers the training of about 3,700 young members of the Communist Pemudah Rakjat and the Gerwani was beginning at the main airbase near Djakarta, Halim.[20] The army had once again made clear that they were dead set against the whole idea and also did not accept the comparison with China that was set up as an example by the P.K.I.[21]

On another level the Special Bureau Aidit had created to infiltrate the army and navy was especially active. It seems, however, that notwithstanding the revolutionary climate the P.K.I had helped to create and maintain, no definite plans were yet prepared. It seems it was all rather long-term planning, otherwise it was not easy to understand that the two leading men of the party, Aidit and Njoto, left at the end of June together with Sukarno for the A-A conference, that was supposed to take place in Algiers. After that the two P.K.I. leaders were not to return to Djakarta but proceeded instead to Western-Europe as scheduled.[22] Njoto remained in the Netherlands, and Aidit arrived via Paris in Moscow where he was received by Politburomember Michael Suslov.[23] He made a trip to Tashkent – not a place to visit if one has urgent matters of state to attend to – and went from there to Bucharest to be present at the Rumanian Party Congress.[24] On July 17 Aidit and his delegation arrived in the Rumanian capital, and he was back again in Moscow at the end of that month.[25]

He may have had some talks with Soviet party leaders, but nothing was reported in the press except that he had left on July 31.[26] He had probably missed a fellow-countryman who had been in Moscow for a sudden visit (the second in two months) and had left on July 24, his major 'opponent and personal friend', Defense Minister Abdul Nasution.[27] The Indonesian general returned to Djakarta empty-handed, since the Soviet Union appeared to have finally shut off further supplies of arms.[28] It is appropriate here to recall the attitude Indonesia had taken at the Algiers non-conference at the end of June, and especially the sour reaction to, if not attack on, Moscow which Subandrio had been allowed to vent afterwards while still in Cairo.[29] The Kremlin leaders may well have had enough of Sukarno by now and have decided to do some arm twisting on Nasution in order to stiffen his resistance to the President.[30] Sukarno may have expected something of the kind, and it is not at all sure that he was not somewhat pleased that Nasution had suffered a setback in Moscow. Be that as it may, he thought Nasution's return an appropriate occasion to start brandishing his 'secret weapon', so he could tell the Russians that he could easily do without them and that the same would go for Nasution and his army. Therefore, on the day the Defense Minister returned from Moscow, Sukarno made a speech in Bandung saying that 'insh Alah' Indonesia would 'soon' have its own atom bomb.[31]

Then some crucial days came at the end of July and early August 1965. A further polarization was taking place with the P.K.I. on the one hand demanding the complete banning of the Murba Party,[32] the national-communist party that had been banned 'temporarily' in January and among whom Sukarno used to recruit many of his cronies and ministers, and on the other hand a definite hardening of the position of the army as to the arming of the civilian population. Sukarno must have felt caught between two centrifugal forces, himself in the middle, tyring to keep both of them in line and manageable at an increasing cost to himself. Besides, the Indonesian President, under continuous strain and suffering from kidney stones, was far from being in good shape. For his kidney he had been treated over many years, both by western doctors, in Vienna mostly, and also by a team of Chinese doctors which had visited him each half year since 1961. A group of Indonesian doctors held final responsibility for his health and were always represented when other doctors were examining him or giving him treatment. The Chinese team[33] had had a remarkable success in ridding Sukarno of painful kidney grit with a combined treatment of acupuncture and ancient herbs. But the President, in order to maintain a minimum of good health, should have led a more sedate life instead of living it up as he was used to doing.[34] The result was showing, particularly in this period, making Sukarno irritable and explosive as never before. At the same time he was subjected to daily tests by the Chinese doctors who had come over from Peking for the half-yearly medical check-up. They arrived in Djakarta on July 22.[35]

Then, on July 30, 1965, General Yani, the army commander who was basically a Sukarno man,[36] but also strongly anti-P.K.I. called together his general staff and a number of local military commanders at the Senajan sports stadium. Then and there he told this top-level meeting he had finally made up his mind on the two current issues: The 'fifth force' and the injection of politics into the armed forces, both points continually raised by the P.K.I. and (so far as the fifth force was concerned) also backed by the President.[37] For a long time Yani had thought he could better float with the stream (i.e. Sukarno) but he told the assembled army officers he now believed he could no longer do so. This opinion at which he had finally arrived (and he must have known it would bring him up against Sukarno sooner or later) Yani expressed publicly that same day when addressing Indonesian students, although he phrased it a bit more mildly. The army commander said he agreed to the idea of arming the people but added two riders which in fact weakened his apparent endorsement. These were that such a people's militia should only be used 'against necolim', i.e. the outside enemy, and that it was not necessary to have 'separate sections', i.e. organizations outside the reach of the army.[38] As a matter of fact Yani had gone further and said that the existing army-backed civil defense corps, the Hanship, was still sufficient. So he effectively and publicly blocked the 'fifth force' in the form demanded and already prepared for by the P.K.I. and secretly and to a limited degree endorsed by Sukarno.[39] Moreover, by convening the meeting at Senajan stadium, of which Sukarno had of course been immediately informed, Yani had made his decision official army policy and – to Sukarno – identified himself completely with Nasution, thus giving further proof of a dangerous cohesion in the highest army circles.

This final move against him must have made Sukarno hopping mad and have reinforced what he must have had in mind ever since the Tampaksiring meeting early in June when he let himself be talked into believing that a group of generals were conspiring against him[40] to get rid of those 'disloyal' officers who were thwarting his plans for the country.[42] Then, on the next day, July 31, after Yani's defiance had had time to sink in, or possibly after the scheming Subandrio had had occasion to draw Sukarno's attention to the whole affair as was his habit, the next step was taken. Subandrio, who had just returned from a trip through Africa after the Algiers debacle, sent an urgent telegram to both Aidit and Njoto to return forthwith.[41] It could be assumed on the basis of the testimony of Sukarno himself that the President had asked Subandrio to call back only Njoto. For this Sukarno had plausible grounds, since Njoto had been close to the President and was a member of the inner cabinet, while Aidit had only the rank and title of minister, as some other dignitaries around Sukarno had been given, but no governmental function.

However, during his trial Subandrio denied a statement to this effect – given by Sukarno in writing as he was excused from appearing in court – and maintained that the President had told him to recall both communist leaders, Njoto to help prepare the 17th of August speech and Aidit 'because he had been away too long'.[43] There is reason to assume that Subandrio was telling the truth and that Sukarno was lying.[44] The cables being duly sent to The Hague to trace Njoto, and to Moscow and Peking to find Aidit, reached their destination, but it was in Peking, on August 1, that Aidit heard of it from Indonesia's Ambassador Djawoto.[45]

Originally, Aidit was to have left Peking on August 7 to go to Hanoi from where he would have gone to Djakarta on August 12.[46] Even after having received and acknowledged on August 1 the first call by telegram to return to Djakarta, Aidit indicated that he wanted to proceed with his schedule as planned.[47] A special plane was prepared meanwhile to take him home as was reported by the Chinese chargé d'affaires Colonel Mo on August 4 to Subandrio's Ministry.[48] On August 5 Aidit was received by Chairman Mao for a chat, and Aidit indeed left Peking on August 7, but then did not fly to Hanoi but directly to Djakarta where he arrived that same day. Njoto was in Moscow when he received the call to come back on August 1[49] and joined Aidit in

Peking before the two of them left together on August 7 for the Indonesian capital. At first, not knowing what was behind Sukarno's summons, Aidit continued relatively leisurely his stay in Peking, waited for Njoto, and was not in a hurry to heed the President's call immediately. He changed his plans, however, and dropped the idea of visiting Hanoi somewhere on or after August 4.[50] It was on that day around 8.30 in the morning that Sukarno suddenly suffered a cerebral insufficiency or what is commonly called a light stroke.[51] There were symptoms of slight paralysis which were impeding his speech and ability to walk. His Indonesian doctors, however, quickly diagnosed it as not of lasting effect.

The word spread fast, however, that Sukarno had fallen ill, and in the prevailing atmosphere it set off rumors. Aidit must have been informed, either that day or on August 5, and if no details reached him in Peking, he must have judged that the collapse of Sukarno had been serious because the Chinese government, being informed by the team of Chinese doctors in Djakarta,[52] had decided to send two more doctors immediately, this time two neurologists[53] making the total team ten in all. They arrived together with Aidit and Njoto on the special plane made available by the Chinese government, initially only intended to take the two P.K.I. leaders back from Peking. Arriving in Djakarta Aidit and Njoto, one may guess, were mainly if not exclusively concerned with Sukarno's state of health and of course with the effects a possible elimination of the President, be it even of temporary nature, could have on their political fortunes.[54] They had not yet been informed of the reasons why Sukarno had initially recalled them both through Subandrio on July 31. Even now these remain shrouded in mystery. But, on the strength of circumstantial evidence, it may be assumed with reasonable certainty that Sukarno wanted the two communist leaders back because since Yani had so openly defied him on July 30 the President had been in the agonizing process of deciding to have a number of recalcitrant army generals eliminated.[55] He must have foreseen that he would need the wits and organizational talents of the P.K.I. leaders to make sure that the operation would not fail. But a fact is that, having 'lived' for some days with the solution he must have vaguely envisaged, Sukarno had made up his mind definitively on August 4 early in the morning. It was then that he asked one of his trusted Tjakrabirawa guard officers, Colonel

Untung, 'whether he was prepared if ordered to take action against the disloyal generals', as one of those present five years later was to testify.[56] To this Untung, the loyal dupe who was to be the fall guy for what erroneously became known as the 'Untung coup', replied affirmatively: 'If you let us take measures against the generals, I shall execute any order of the Great Leader'.[57]

Not long after this scene that must have moved Sukarno considerably with all his lack of scrupules, the Indonesian President, to the dismay and fright of those present, was struck and fainted. An infinitely short interruption of the bloodstream in the brains had occurred, a phenomenon that medical science closely links with the psychosomatic situation, both long and short-term, Sukarno was then in. However 'dramatic' this collapse may outwardly have been, it was of less political importance than has been concluded on the basis of incomplete evidence.[58] It was the decision immediately preceding – and causing – the stroke that counted and that was to set in motion a chain of events of really dramatic dimensions. It was Sukarno himself who initiated the 'Untung coup' hoping that he could remain its controlling force, the magician who could lay the ghosts he was conjuring up. But it spelled the beginning of his doom, and in his ego-induced mania of arrogance he was struck with a blindness which, in the event, was not only to destroy him but barely failed to plunge the country itself into the abyss as well.

NOTES

1. *Antara News Agency*, June 5, 1965.
2. *Far Eastern Economic Review*, June 3, 1965.
3. *Harian Rakjat*, June 9-10, 1965.
4. *Harian Rakjat*, May 7, 1965.
5. See Aidit's general report on May 11, *Harian Rakjat*, May 12, 1965.
6. This is not to imply that the P.K.I. only was to blame for what happened especially in Central and East Java, in the wake of the '30 September movement', as religious fanaticism had certainly been the sorry counterpart of the slaughter. A description of the why and wherefore of that period, however, falls outside the scope of this book.
7. See above p. 307 and below p. 392.
8. See below p. 433.
9. During his trial Njono was to remark that 'for the P.K.I. foreign policy is not important because it is determined by its domestic policy'; Proceedings of

the Njono trial.

10. During his trial he showed himself loyal to Sukarno, more, probably than would have been necessary even within the political context of that period, with Sukarno still alive and a symbol to handle with a certain undeserved care. See below p. 410 note 17 and p. 442 note 2.
11. One of the nicest touches in this allegiance was the assistance his air force gave in dropping leaflets over the Senajan stadium, when the P.K.I. celebrated its 45th anniversary; *Nieuwe Rotterdamsche Courant*, May 24, 1965.
12. *Indonesian Herald*, May 13, 1965.
13. This was on June 22; *New China News Agency*, June 24, 1965.
14. *Djakarta Radio Home Service*, March 2, 1965. He certainly meant to say that he would be pleased if the Russians wanted to give him that little help. Moscow must have ceased to help him out some time after the Chen-Yi visit in December 1964 because Chou, in front of Subandrio, ridiculed Soviet military aid: 'What is the point of supplying arms without spare parts'; transcript Subandrio-Chou En-lai talks, January 25, 1965.
15. *Djakarta Radio Home Service*, April 8, 1965.
16. See below p. 403 ff.
17. See above pp. 365 and 374 note 83.
18. *Indonesian Herald*, June 26, 1965; *Antara News Agency*, June 26, 1965. Martadinata's posture towards the 'fifth force' idea at that time was roughly similar to the attitude of the army leaders Yani and Nasution. Aidit was told by Martadinata that if such a 'strategic reserve' were created, it should be 'within the armed forces', i.e. under the command of regular officers.
19. Martadinata was with Sukarno at Halim Air Base on October 1 only after being summoned by the President and apparently unprepared for what was afoot, something that could decidedly not be said of Omar Dhani. See below p. 379 note 1. Martadinata died in 1966 in a helicopter-crash under rather strange circumstances, the air force claiming that the accident had been due to 'fog', but no foul play was proven.
20. Nugroho and Saleh, 1966, *The Coup Attempt*, Djakarta, p. 143.
21. The army newspaper *Angkatan Bersendjata* carried a fully documented and elaborate article showing that a people's militia in China only worked when both government and armed forces were under one leadership, the communist party. The reasoning was not completely logical but the purpose was clear. See *Angkatan Bersendjata*, July 1, 1965.
22. Aidit spent a few days in Paris and arrived in Moscow on July 7; *Indonesian Herald*, July 9, 1965. This paper called it 'nothing less than sensational' that Aidit had been to the Soviet capital, taking into consideration the frosty relations with the Russian comrades. *Radio Zagreb* thought that the P.K.I. was the only pro-Chinese communist party that had good relations with Moscow; July 9, 1965. There was even talk, probably P.K.I.-inspired, of Aidit trying to 'mediate' between Moscow and Peking; *Antara News Agency*, July 20, 1965. This could hardly have been an idea Aidit seriously entertained as he had done in 1963. But at any rate, taking his time in Europe did

not indicate that either he or Njoto were in a particular hurry to prepare something drastic in Indonesia.

23. *Tass*, July 7, 1965.
24. Aidit arrived in Tashkent on July 11; *Tass*, July 11, 1965. There he met one of the P.K.I. secretaries in charge of foreign affairs, Karel Supit, who coming from Djakarta may have briefed him on the latest developments in Indonesia. But Supit was clearly meant to become part of the Aidit delegation to Bucharest and after that to Peking. See the proceedings of the Subandrio trial, 9th session.
25. *Indonesian Herald*, July 20, 1965. On July 22 Aidit conveyed greetings to the Rumanian Party Congress, mainly praising the independent position the Rumanian Communist Party was taking up within the communist world and telling them not to forget Southeast Asia which at the time was to Aidit 'a focal point' to watch; *Agerpress*, July 22, 1965. Pravda barely paid attention to his activities in Bucharest.
26. Pravda wrote that Aidit had visited the country 'from July 7 until 31' completely ignoring the Rumanian trip; *Pravda*, August 1, 1965.
27. Nasution had been in Moscow in May, arriving again in Djakarta on May 20; *Antara News Agency*, May 20, 1965. He was invited in the wake of the Bandung commemoration that brought Sukarno and Chou together in the second half of April; *Indonesian Herald*, April 30, 1965. In July his visit must have been even shorter than the one in May, in all a week at most, as he gave a speech on July 17, warning that Soksi – the army-backed trade-union – should give military training to its cadres (*Djakarta Radio Home Service*, July 17, 1965). He was reported 'back from Moscow' on July 24; *Djakarta Radio Home Service*, July 24, 1965.
28. Nasution himself said upon return that he had not gotten the ships he had asked for, and apparently the only deal he had made concerned military workshops that would enhance Indonesia's 'self-reliance'; *Djakarta Radio Home Service*, July 24, 1965. A few days before the army paper *Berita Yudha* had written that 'certain socialist countries' were unwilling to sell Indonesia weapons; July 20, 1965.
29. See above p. 350.
30. Nasution himself now claims to have had only a minor influence, let alone power in that period, being defense minister without any operational command and holding a function that was much more purely administrative than was realized by outsiders. Nasution, though, was in charge of the civilian armed guards, the Hansip, which fell under the control of the army and had been instituted to take some of the heat out of the raging (P.K.I.-inspired) debate on a people's militia.
31. *Indonesian Herald*, July 26, 1965. *Antara's* version was that Indonesia would have its own A-bomb 'within three years'; July 24, 1965. The logistics bureau of the army announced on the day after Sukarno made his speech that there would be an 'atomic test' in November; *Radio Free Europe*, July 29, 1965.

32. *Harian Rakjat*, July 26, 1965. The communist party paper quoted approvingly P.N.I.-Chairman Ali Sastroamidjojo, who had said somewhat earlier that he thought '9 parties enough', i.e. the ten existing ones minus the 'frozen' Murba Party.
33. According to Dr. Rubiono Kertopati, one of Sukarno's private physicians, the normal composition of the team of Chinese doctors was one surgeon-urologist, two internists and two acupuncturists of whom at least one would have had a normal medical training.
34. Sukarno, apart from his normal duties as head of state and chief executive, was leading an extremely hectic life that would have exhausted any man of lesser energy. One of his most absorbing 'hobbies' was entertaining women, for which activity he was given a special stimulant, cantharides or Spanish fly. Its side effect, however, was to poison the one kidney left. He was therefore caught in a vicious circle as far his health was concerned.
35. Police report on the visit of the Chinese medical team, July 22, 1965 through September 1, 1965.
36. Yani was a tough, professional soldier with a strong sense of loyalty to the President who had elevated him to his post as army commander and strongly influenced him in other ways, so much so that Sukarno persuaded him to accept as his second wife a woman who had ceased to interest the President personally.
37. Interview, March 1972, ex-Major-General Otto Bojoh of Sukarno's Kostrad.
38. *BBC*, July 30, 1965.
39. See above pp. 327, 328.
40. See above pp. 368, 369.
41. Apart from mistrusting Nasution and now also Yani, Sukarno had developed a particular antipathy towards Brigadiers-General Parman and Sutojo Soswomihardjo and according to Widjanarko, Sukarno, while received army leaders in Medeka palace sometime before October 1, 1965, had been openly scolding Parman and Sutojo; see Widjanarko report I, p. 5. Parman was in charge of military intelligence and Sujoto was Auditor-General and Law Inspector of the army. Both were among the six generals that met their deaths at the hands of the Untung raiders; see below p. 408.
42. Subandrio had returned to Djakarta on July 25; *New China News Agency*, July 26, 1972. According to several witnesses, including himself, and documented by copies of Foreign Service cablegrams, the urgent summoning of the *two* P.K.I. leaders on July 31, 1965, is an established fact. Not so the point of who in fact gave the order to recall the two, as Sukarno maintained in his written statement submitted during the Subandrio trial that he only asked Njoto, who after all was one of the members of his inner cabinet. See the proceedings of the Subandrio trial, 9th session.
43. See the proceedings of the Subandrio trial, 9th session.
44. Sukarno's written statement is at any rate hardly credible on a number of other counts, for instance that the 30 September movement had come as 'a complete surprise to him'. See below p. 434.

45. Proceedings of the Subandrio trial, written statement by Karel Supit, P.K.I. secretary especially in charge of relations with foreign communist parties and part of Aidit's delegation to Moscow and Peking in the summer of 1965; proceedings of the Subandrio trial, 9th session.
46. Code telegram from the Indonesian Embassy in Peking to Subandrio, no. 164/PEK/VIII/'65 dated August 3, 1965.
74. Code telegram from the Indonesian Embassy in Peking to Subandrio, no. 164/PEK/VIII/'65 dated August 3, 1965.
48. Code telegram of the Indonesian Ministry of Foreign Affairs no. 93186, dated August 6, 1965.
49. Code telegram of the Indonesian Ministry of Foreign Affairs no. 93186, dated August 6, 1965.
50. Code telegram of Aidit in Peking to Lukman in Djakarta, no. 4712/Sal B., sent on August 3, 1965, received in Djakarta on August 4, 1965 at 10:15 hours local time, showing that Aidit had received Sukarno's instructions to come back but was not yet planning to skip the Hanoi visit.
51. A communication to this writer by Dr. Rubiono Kertopati, confirmed by Dr. J. Leimena in Interview, March 1972. Dr. Leimena, a physician by training and in August 1965 Second Deputy Prime Minister of Indonesia, was one of the first to visit Sukarno in the course of the morning of August 4, 1965. The police report on the movements of the team of Chinese doctors shows that they normally gave Sukarno their treatment around noon or at the end of the afternoon. For August 4 the records mention that, at 8 : 30 hours, the team received instruction from Police Commissioner Mangil – one of Sukarno's aide-de-camps – to hold themselves in readiness. At 11.15 four members of the team arrived at Merdeka Palace for the 'treatment'.
52. Police report on the movement of the team of Chinese doctors.
53. Dr. Wang Hsin Te and Dr. Tan Min Hsun were dispatched by the Chinese government and their arrival was discussed by the members of the Chinese medical team already in Djakarta on August 6, 1965 at noon, according to the police report on the movements of the team. The next day at 12 : 00 they landed at Kemajoran Airport on board the special Chinese plane.
54. See below p. 391.
55. They certainly had nothing to do with Sukarno's health, as is suggested by Nugroho and Saleh in *The Coup Attempt*, p. 6, because the President collapsed long after the two P.K.I. leaders were recalled, on August 4 (and not 5, as is written in *The Coup Attempt*, p. 5).
56. Widjanarko report III, p. 1. Apart from the testimony of Bambang Widjanarko, the author is also in the possession of declarations confirming this dialogue between Sukarno and Untung and given by three witnesses, t. w. Suratni, Sukardi and Jacob Amanda who were also present in the palace that same morning. According to these witnesses, the only other person whose presence they recalled was the commander of the Tjakrabirawa Guard, Brigadier General Sabur. See also below pp. 405, 406.
57. Communication by General Nasution, Interview, March 1972. This remark,

according to Nasution, Untung confirmed not long before he was executed at the beginning of 1966, having been sentenced to death for his role in the 30 September movement. It would indicate that some evidence of Sukarno's responsibility for the so-called putsch must have been available to the Indonesian military authorities at an early stage.

58. See an article in the Dutch weekly *Vrij Nederland* of September 10, 1966 under the title 'Plot accelerated by Sukarno's collapse'. There is no doubt that the stroke occurred after Sukarno talked to Untung; also, medically speaking, he could not have conducted any conversation of that nature after he had had a slight stroke.

CHAPTER 27

The Politburo meets (1965)

A lot of what went on after that fateful 4th of August 1965 is known from the trials of a number of Indonesians, communists and non-communists, for their participation in the '30 September movement'.[1] The fact however that Sukarno himself was behind the measures Untung was about to take sheds additional light on and gives cohesion to what would otherwise have been believed (for lack of precise evidence to the contrary) an affair concocted mainly by some cunning Indonesian communists and abetted by the Chinese. At most, in that one-sided version, the President had made faulty decisions the moment he got involved in it by the moves of scheming subordinates who brought him to the center of rebellious action, the Halim Air Force Base near Djakarta.

One should remember in judging the role of Aidit and his Politburo in subsequent events that the P.K.I. Chairman on his return from China on August 7 knew about the President's illness of August 4, but he did not necessarily know more than that.[2] Though the P.K.I. Politburo body met immediately upon the return of Aidit,[3] the party had not yet been put into gear. This meeting of the Politburo was mainly intended to bring Aidit into picture and according to Njono, who was present as a member was 'informative' in character. It was decided that they would meet again some days later. The main concern to the P.K.I. leadership seems at that moment indeed to have been Sukarno's state of health which threatened to revive the same situation that had existed almost a year ago when Subandrio came back from Cairo with stories that Sukarno had been incapacitated during the non-aligned conference. This in turn had then started a series of unsettling rumors and a jockeying for position that the P.K.I., but only thanks to Sukarno, survived fairly well.[4]

The antagonism of mid-1965 between Sukarno and the army leadership centered, as related, on the issue of the 'fifth force' and relations with the Soviet Union and China, and fear of a counter move, a preventive coup d'état by the army, encouraged as it was by the P.K.I., was even more credible than the year before. Certainly in the mood of conspiracy in which the P.K.I. had been operating, if not for years then certainly in those last 12 months, it was easy to think that the generals would have contingency plans similar to the ones the P.K.I. had been working on.[5] There is no proof whatsoever that the P.K.I. was right in this assumption. The leading generals were surprised and, insofar as they were alive after those murderous early hours of October 1, they barely managed by a combination of sheer luck and improvisation to get control of the situation again, and it seems very unlikely that they had any active, organized intentions of their own[6] as Aidit believed or perhaps wanted his Politburo members and other followers to believe.[7]

Aidit was upon return from China not yet informed about what had gone on, about the reasons behind the sudden recall of the President, and the P.K.I. chairman was first of all bent on getting his bearings as quickly as possible because as he observed during that first Politburo meeting 'the problem is actually to be the first to be informed of the President's death since whoever knows about it first will be able to take the initiative'.[8] This curiosity took him the next day, on August 8, to the presidential palace in Bogor to see Sukarno who had gone to rest in his residence in the mountains outside Djakarta. Aidit was seen in the room where Sukarno was staying.[9] He was afterwards seen getting a 30-minute briefing by the Chinese doctors who must have told him what they thought had happened to Sukarno and what the prospects were. There are indeed indications that the Chinese doctors regarded Sukarno's state of health more seriously than their Indonesian colleagues.[10] Whatever the Chinese may have told Aidit and whatever Aidit may have believed himself, at the next Politburo meeting (on August 16)[11] Aidit told its members that Sukarno was seriously ill and had only a small chance of survival. At best he would be permanently paralyzed. He told the Politburo further that the Council of Generals wanted to liquidate the P.K.I. and that some officers wanted to prevent this. Aidit asked for the opinion of those present but started by saying that he personally would not be against letting these officers go ahead with their plans.[12]

This additional information that Aidit gave his comrades showed that he was now more fully posted than upon arrival. It is possible that the President himself told him in Bogor that he was through with the opposition of the army leadership and that, for that reason, he wanted Aidit and Njoto to return. For this, however, Sukarno, whether ill or not, was probably too clever. He surely had other ways of getting the message through to Aidit. Even if the President had hidden from the P.K.I. leader the real reasons behind the urgent summons or had passed off his instructions to Untung as 'information about progressive officers' that he had somehow received, Aidit would soon have found out what Sukarno was really after, as the P.K.I.'s Special Bureau Chief, Sjam, had been in touch earlier with some disaffected officers such as Colonel Latief. This officer, in turn, was a link with Tjakrabirawa guardsman Untung. A fact is that on August 13 Sjam was called to see Aidit and was told that Sukarno was ill, that a Council of Generals was active, and that he, Aidit, wanted more information. At least this was what Politburo-member Sudisman said at his trial.[13]

On the next day Sjam, with Special Bureau members Walujo and Pono, got together to discuss what was then already being termed the 'Aidit-plan'. The next step was a first meeting of Sjam and his associates with officers who sympathized with the P.K.I., probably on August 15. Present were Sjam and Pono for the P.K.I., Colonel Latief, Lieutenant Colonel Untung, Flight Major Sujono (a commander of the defense unit of Halim Air Base), and another air force officer, Captain Wahjudi. For most of them it was the first time they were meeting each other, and, as Untung said during his trial, the purpose was to 'get acquainted'.[14]

Only the existence of some 'counter revolutionaries' who wanted to exploit the illness of the President to stage a coup d'état was talked about. This was the line followed by the P.K.I. or rather by Aidit (who stressed the President's illness), and it was convenient to the military investigators in subsequent trials to continue that strand of the conspiracy rather than the initiative the President himself had taken in the affair. The second meeting of the same group took place some days later, when for the first time Sjam brought up the existence of the Council of Generals. The hardships of lower-ranking officers was also injected into the discussions.[15]

In the weeks to come this mixed company of officers and P.K.I. officials met several times drawing up concrete plans for an operation that had as its aim to eliminate seven generals of the Army staff, among whom Nasution and Yani, to take into custody or 'safeguard' a number of military people and civilians, and to have at its disposal a core of some batallions together with armed and trained youths to make sure that the Djakarta area would be under control. In the period leading up to August 17 (Indonesia's independence day) Subandrio and Njoto both were informed about the preparations of the pretended 'coup' that their two chiefs, Sukarno and Aidit, were cooking up but both were probably in doubt as to who would trick whom. They met frequently at Subandrio's home.[16] The reason Subandrio gave was that the two had to discuss the Independence Day speech of the President, which may very well have been true. However, it was more the version of Aidit and Njoto than the input of the foreign ministry that was finally used by Sukarno in his address to the nation.[17]

At the second Politburo meeting on August 16, after the Untung-Sjam group had become 'acquainted' for the first time, Aidit knew that the link between the communist and presidential conspirators had been laid. He convinced his colleagues that the serious illness of the President was making the army nervous and made its leaders prepared to deliver a blow against the P.K.I. at any time. He secured agreement on proceeding cautiously. Only the other two of the inner leadership of the Party, Njoto and Lukman, knew that there was more between Aidit and his colleagues than what he told them. But the P.K.I. Chairman wanted, above all, to prevent a wider knowledge of Sukarno's involvement and other details of what went on so as to be on the safe side – and, no doubt, follow Sukarno's wishes in this also. It was also for this reason that he blew up the story of the President's failing health ('a small chance to survive', etc.) in order to sound more convincing. In actual fact Sukarno delivered his usual Independence Day address on August 17, and there was very little to show that he was then, or would be in the near future, in such a dire physical condition as Aidit – and later those who pushed the communist side of the plot exclusively to the fore – wished to pretend.

The P.K.I. declaration of August 17 said – with the knowledge of hindsight understandably – that 'the growth of the strength of the people [read P.K.I.] is accelerating'.[18] The goals set could be reached 'fully and radically with speed, if the revolution is *concrete*'. [emphasis added]. Then the phrase came that was to be heard from now until midnight of September 30 that 'the revolution should be brought to its peak'.

More interesting than what the P.K.I had to say – after all, long since its part in the 'Untung-coup' has been known – is Sukarno's August 17 speech called Takari, for short, from its title 'reaching to the stars'. The Djakarta-Peking axis figured prominently in it, but on the home front Sukarno sounded a particularly strong warning against the 'corruptors' of the country, the rich and rotten among his compatriots who were living on the backs of the people. 'Do not be startled' he continued then, 'if struggle between groups flares up and consumes the luxury living of the swindlers'.[19]

He had the same phrases as Subandrio earlier that year when his Murba ex-friends were thrown to the dogs in January: The revolutionaries of to-day are the counter-revolutionaries of to-morrow. It did not even matter if one 'had been a balding general in 1945', because even such a character would not be safe from sliding into the counter-revolution. This was generally taken to be an obvious sneer at Nasution.[20]

On the 'fifth force' (now an idea'I launched') he told the nation that he would 'surely make a decision after further consideration', thus formulating another threat to the army command. On the Revolution, which was after all being celebrated that day, Sukarno spoke of 'the final victory which we can already glimpse', and no doubt this was not what his audience – be it the simple or the initiated – would have thought he had in mind. His 'final victory' was the elimination of the existing army leadership, neither more nor less. The echo of Takari came with a pep-talk Aidit gave the Greater Djakarta P.K.I. organization which, he told, 'always stands in the front line in carrying out the duties of the revolution' and which 'will play the most important role in each *definite* national event [emphasis added]'.[21] Aidit recommended study of Sukarno's Takari speech (the normal recipe each year) but repeated on his own account that 'people should not be surprised if conflicts erupt to destroy the luxurously living corruptors and thieves'. He praised the fact that the President had told the nation that his patience with the stagnating 'revolution' was limited but sounded a warning of his own

– careful as he was to make sure he regained or kept the initiative he was risking losing to the President – adding: 'and what is more important: the patience of the people [read the P.K.I.] is limited'.

On August 25 Aidit had another session late at night with Sjam, this time accompanied by the two aides of the Special Bureau chief, Pono and Walujo.[22] According to Sudisman it was then decided to proceed further with the actions to 'prevent' the coup d'état and make it look like a limited and internal army affair. The next day this was transmitted to the mixed Untung-Sjam group who had agreed on a joint contingency plan. The decision Aidit and Sjam made on August 25 – which Sjam in turn had passed on to the future implementors of the Untung coup – was ratified on August 28 at an extended Politburo meeting, the third within three weeks.[23] Njono, who at a first confession told his military interrogators that at this meeting the decision was made to stage a preventive coup against the army leadership, retracted this declaration again during his trial. He then said that it was decided on that occasion to inform Sukarno of the Council of Generals and to leave it to him to see what was to be done about it.[24] Sudisman, however, confirmed the first version of Njono as the correct one and even gave the division of the various tasks among the members of the Politburo.[25] During that third meeting Aidit according to an eye witness acknowledged that Sukarno also had a hand in the anti-army action, warning his colleagues that Sukarno should not be given operational command, as this would probably mean 'concessions sooner or later'.[26]

On the outside the P.K.I was going all out to reach the 'revolutionary peak'. Besides demands for a total ban on the Murba Party big anti-American demonstrations were staged in front of the U.S. embassy with demands for a rupture in diplomatic relations.[27] Neither were the Russians spared. Aidit gave a tough anti-Soviet speech to a communist writers' convention and told them to beware of the 'remos', his newly-coined word for the modern revisionists, who were 'disarming the anti-imperialists spirit of the people'.[28]

In the next few weeks Indonesia, unbeknown to the outside world – which in fact was all but a handful – witnessed a complex and remarkable rivalry-cum-cooperation between the Sukarno 'faction' and the Aidit 'faction'. Outward signs were visible, but behind the scenes, too, the two 'plots' (the Sukarno version and Aidit's) must have clashed, or at least caused friction. Sukarno was most eloquently represented by Subandrio who, all through September until he left for Sumatra in the early hours of the 28th, was raising the temperature in the country and agitating against those who were to be the victims in the early hours of October 1.[29] On September 2, talking to students in Menado, he urged that 'the people should take over the leadership from the corruptors'.[30] A day or so earlier in Surabaja he had done the same and told his audience that, so long as there were the 'bureaucratic capitalists' and the 'economic dynasty' (codewords for the top military and the civilian-military leaders of the country's economy that is the Nasutions and the Salehs), East Java would never get its economy back in shape.[31] At a Partindo conference he again demanded the abolition of corruption,[32] and some days later, he told the Indonesian Student Council that 'the opposition to the bureaucratic capitalists will now soon be launched'.[33] About the victims of tomorrow he had this to say: 'In any revolution some people are bound to fall, because they were left behind and had perhaps committed treason against the Revolution'.[34] Here he had already escalated into the charge of treason against people who should have known they were referred to, the curiously silent top military of the army. At a Sobsi Council meeting, where Aidit also spoke, Subandrio said that to foresee 'the present stage of the Revolution calls for the *realization* of concepts and ideas initiated by Indonesian minds' [emphasis added].[35] Indonesia, he continued, 'should launch *joint* actions to wipe out the corruptors, the bureaucratic capitalists and the corruptors of the state coffers' [emphasis added]. It was precisely this phrase 'joint actions', etc. (i.e., the P.K.I-Sukarno plot against the generals) that was picked up by the Chinese news agency to send back home.[36] *Antara* did not report, whereas *N.C.N.A.* did, what Subandrio had said about 'some so-called Communist countries which have of late shown no desire to fight imperialism' and who were not treated by the 'imperialists' as adversaries. That Sukarno was very much treated as an adversary by the imperialists, as Subandrio maintained, was also reported in the Chinese press, but not in Indonesia. Why *Antara* left these anti-Soviet and pro-Sukarno phrases out was not clear. Perhaps censorship of the military was behind it.

Parallel with this increase in vitriolics on the part of the Sukarno-liners, the P.K.I. 'kept up the revolutionary offensive'. Lukman demanded, as if it were a small thing 'all state instruments to be purged of all reactionary elements'.[37] *Harian Rakjat* followed this up with a similar call to 'retool' the government apparatus, quoting in this connection Subandrio's Menado speech of a week earlier.[38] Aidit, made 'supreme son of Indonesia second class' by Sukarno (together with General Puspojudo, to keep the balance) told the same student conference Subandrio had talked to that they should 'push the revolution to its peak' and quoted liberally from the Takari speech, especially the well-known passage about the 'corruptors'.[39]

Meanwhile Sukarno, after the definite ban on the Murba Party and having remained in the background a bit, took on the so-called '1945-generation', a sort of influential pressure group of veterans of the 1945 revolution against the Dutch and one of the few remained bulwarks, or potential bulkarks, of 'un-Sukarno behavior'. Sukarno personally drew up a list of 27 members who were to form a closed and coherent group, fully entitled to operate, if only they took care that whatever they did was unanimously agreed upon and moreover had the sanction of the President himself.[40] It was a complicated way of saying that the group had in fact ceased to function or exist, and it was Aidit who took upon himself to say it in those simple words, of course contradicted by prominent 1945-man Chaerul Saleh, against whom the whole move from Aidit's side had been set up and whose voice was becoming each day weaker anyhow.[41]

NOTES

1. See John Hughes, 1967, *Indonesian Upheaval*, David McKay Co, Inc., New York; Basuki Gunawan, 1968, *Kudeta, Staatsgreep in Djakarta*, Boom en Zoon, Meppel, Guy J. Pauker, 1969, *Rise and Fall of the Communist Party of Indonesia*, Rand Corporation, Santa Monica, California, and Arnold O. Brackman, 1969, *The Communist Collapse in Indonesia*, W. W. Norton & Co, Inc., New York.
2. See above p. 383. See for a different view: Pauker, 1969, p. 48.
3. Nugroho and Saleh, 1966, *The Coup Attempt*, Djakarta, p. 119 Politburo member Njono told his judges that the meeting took place from 14 : 00 to 16 : 00 hours that day. According to the police report on the movements of the Chinese doctors the plane from Peking carrying both the P.K.I. leaders and the two neurologists had landed at 12 : 00 hours. So the two statements tie in with each other.
4. See above p. 306.

5. Sjam's Sepial Bureau, under personal supervision of Aidit had been one of the measures taken by Aidit, Lukman and Njoto. The other Politburo members seem to have been kept out of this, including even Sudisman, and Sjam had to deal in person only with Aidit. The Special Bureau must have had both an offensive and a defensive function, that is, to promote subvesion within the armed forces and to get inside information from informers.
6. Not having plans for a preventive coup did not mean that the army command did not discuss the situation which had arisen through Sukarno's sudden illness. According to General Nasution, Yani and his staff met either on the very day Sukarno had a stroke (August 4) or one day later in order to see what the new situation required of them. That plans for action against the P.K.I., let alone against Sukarno, were far from Yani's mind is evident from the fact that, on the eve of the 'Untung putsch' on September 30, 1965, when information that something was afoot in the capital circulated and it was suggested to Yani by his colleagues that he should at least have the guards at his house doubled, the army commander refused such a simple measure. Interview, March 1972, General Nasution.
7. Naivety abounded, it seems, not only on one side. Sudisman in his statements during his trial declared that general information of a confidential nature that Aidit used to pass on to his Politburo colleagues – including Sudisman – was accepted without much questioning. See also an identical remark by Karel Supit during the Sudisman trial, 11th session.
8. Proceedings of the Njono trial; testimony by alternate member of the P.K.I. Politburo Peris Pardede, February 15, 1966. Njono did not object to the statements Peris Pardede made on that occasion, although he withdrew part of the confession he had made himself out of court earlier.
9. Statement by one of Sukarno's personal physicians, Dr. Sukaman, during the Subandrio trial; proceedings of the Subandrio tiral, 9th session.
10. The Indonesian doctors reported that the Chinese team, while briefing Aidit on August 8, had 'a very serious air'. One of them, Sukarno's personal physician Dr. Siwabessy, told General Nasution when the two of them attended the Sukarno funeral in June 1970 that if Aidit had listened to his (Siwabessy's) advice he would have had a more realistic and sober judgment than he had received from the Chinese. It is a moot point whether the Chinese doctors were acting in good faith if and when they gave such a gloomy picture of Sukarno's health after he had a stroke early in August 1965, and to what extent they were bound by political instructions from Peking to do so. Given the generally high caliber of the Chinese team (for the greater part American-trained) one is inclined to assume purposeful deceit.
11. The testimonies refer only to 'some days before August 17' e.g. Peris Pardede; see proceedings of the Njono trial, February 15, 1966. *Harian Rakjat* published a statement of the Politburo in its issue of August 17 that reflected the latest developments, and the party paper must have published it on the earliest occasion after the Politburo had agreed upon it. Besides, Aidit gave the report he had promised at the first meeting on August 7, and from his activities on

August 13 and 14 it can at least be deduced that he had not yet assembled all the necessary 'informations' then; see below p. 393. Military investigators confirmed that the second Politburo meeting took place on August 16, 1965.

12. Proceedings of the Njono trial, testimony of Peris Pardede.
13. Proceedings of the Sudisman trial, July 5-17, 1967. The Sudisman trial is rather remarkable in that it showed this top ranking P.K.I. man – who after the party went underground in the autumn of 1965 was in effect its leader – as a courageous and convinced communist who had been left out of the detailed scheming which Aidit, and to a lesser degree also Njoto and Lukman, had been undertaking without informing their closest associates. Sudisman provided a lot of background information, taking full responsibility – but not blame – for what had been done in the name of the party and made a dignified last confession of faith in his ideals, nowhere giving the impression that he had been brainwashed or forced to talk. See also Pauker, 1969, p. 57.
14. Proceedings of the Untung-trial. See also Nugroho and Saleh, 1966, p. 14.
15. Nugroho and Saleh, 1966, p. 14.
16. Trial proceedings of the Subandrio trial, 3rd session.
17. Subandrio's Deputy Foreign Minister, Suwito, complained during the trial against his former chief that he had been asked to make a draft speech for the occasion, but that to his surprise he did not find anything left of it, when the President spoke on August 17.
18. *Harian Rakjat*, August 17, 1965.
19. *Antara News Agency*, August 17, 1965.
20. The official text to be published in full – *Antara* gave only a summary – spoke of a 'baldheaded general in 1945', but from other sources it appeared that Sukarno had been even more insulting.
21. *Harian Rakjat*, August 21, 1965.
22. Proceedings of the Sudisman trial; testimony of Special Bureau Chief Sjam, 7th session.
23. Proceedings of the Njono trial, first session.
24. Proceedings of the Njono trial, first session.
25. Proceedings of the Sudisman trial, 2nd session.
26. Interview, March 1972, General Nasution.
27. *Antara News Agency*, August 30, 1965.
28. *Harian Rakjat*, August 28, 1965.
29. *Indonesian Herald*, September 28, 1965. Subandrio left with 14 other ministers for a so-called 'turba', a visit to the countryside. One of those who accompanied him was his 'shadow' Njoto. The trip was postponed once, but Sukarno later was to deny that either the postponing or the trip itself had anything to do with what happened at the end of the month. See trial proceedings of the Subandrio trial, 9th session. See also the Widjanarko report II, p. 18.
30. *Indonesian Herald*, September 3, 1965.
31. *Antara News Agency*, September 2, 1965.

32. *Indonesian Herald*, September 7, 1965.
33. *Antara News Agency*, September 13, 1965.
34. *Antara News Agency*, September 13, 1965.
35. *Antara News Agency*, September 14, 1965.
36. *New China News Agency*, September 14, 1965.
37. *Djakarta Radio Home Service*, September 4, 1965.
38. *Harian Rakjat*, September 10, 1965.
39. *Indonesian Herald*, September 14, 1965 and *Harian Rakjat*, September 14, 1965.
40. *Antara News Agency*, September 15, 1965; *Indonesian Herald*, September 15, 1965. Adam Malik, who together with Chaerul Saleh had forced Sukarno at gunpoint more or less to proclaim Indonesia's independence on August 17, 1945, was not among the 27 on the list. Probably he felt by that time honored by this distinction. Aidit and Saleh were still on it, as were a mixture of other 1945 people.
41. *Antara News Agency*, September 21, 1965.

CHAPTER 28

Remove the bodies (1965)

The unison harmony of the Sukarno-Subandrio duet on the one hand and the P.K.I.-chorus on the other was marred during September on account of an issue that at first sight was rather puzzling. The long list of institutions, people, and attitudes the P.K.I. wanted to get rid of included the muslim student organization, H.M.I. It was one of the few organizations capable and willing to put up resistance to the P.K.I. wherever it could without antagonizing Sukarno too much. How could it be otherwise after all the whittling down that had gone on in the past? On the other hand, Sukarno himself must not have been too fond of a militant muslim youth group, well organized and decidedly anti-government in Central and East Java – away from the Djakarta center. Nevertheless, Subandrio in mid-September gave express instructions not to ban the H.M.I., no doubt with full backing of Sukarno.[1]

It became an issue when, the very next day, *Harian Rakjat* published a resolution, adopted by the Central Java P.K.I. Committee, again expressly demanding a ban on the H.M.I.[2] The Communist Student Organization at a conference of their own also expressed their abhorrence of the continued existence of the H.M.I.[3] Sukarno then inververned and gave the 'order' that the H.M.I. was not to be banned but put under the 'supervision' of Kotrar, the so-called retooling body, headed by Subandrio.[4]

It was the same method as adopted with foreign enterprises illegally taken over by P.K.I. and other workers. They were put under government supervision to save face and look revolutionary without going too far. Sukarno warned that his order had to be obeyed. This was intended for the left, the P.K.I., and not for the H.M.I. itself. However, Aidit notwithstanding his far-reaching collusion with Sukarno on the

Untung coup (or perhaps just because of it) did not heed Sukarno's clear warning and told an assembled crowd of plantation workers that the H.M.I. ought to be 'destroyed'.[5] On the same occasion he incited his audience to take over the actual control of the state enterprises from the 'bureaucratic capitalists'. He told the workers not only to entertain 'social-economic demands' but to go beyond them and strike out for political power. It was a choice, he said, between being 'hammer or anvil'.[6] He finished his seditious speech with the words: 'Take over, take over, and again take over'.

At this moment Sukarno must have realized into what dangerous waters he had sailed by allowing Aidit to get together on a plot being devised at that very time by their various subordinates. He gave a few signs of backtracking a bit on the extremist viewpoints he had himself endorsed publicly. Addressing together with the Second Deputy Premier Leimena a meeting of railway workers, Sukarno warned that 'any contrarevolutionary movement among the railway workers will be immediately suppressed'.[7] This was as much against 'counter-revolution' from the right as from the left. But the P.K.I. did not listen and, especially on the H.M.I.-ban, did not know where to stop. On September 29 *Harian Rakjat* urged the Youth Movement 'to clean up the leadership' and again came out against the H.M.I. On the other targets they said: 'Stir up the revolution in every way until the thieves and corruptors are completely cleaned out of the political and economic leadership'.[8]

On the evening of that day it almost came to a clash between Sukarno and Aidit. During a mass rally in the Senejan stadium the first speaker was Leimena who on the orders of Sukarno once again told the students, 'despite shouts from the crowd' as it was reported, that the H.M.I. should further be left untouched.[9] Then, when things were getting out of hand, Sukarno, scheduled to speak next, left the floor first to Aidit. The P.K.I. Chairman then openly defied Sukarno but covered it up, making it look as if he was ridiculing Leinema. He said to the students: 'You should wear a sarong if H.M.I. is not eliminated'.[10] Sukarno was to remember this challenge of Aidit later when, trying to get out of the mess he had got himself into after the 'Untung coup' he was turning against Aidit.[11] But at this time he still needed Aidit, and trying to calm down the mass of students he told them that the H.M.I. would be forbidden to operate 'if it proved to have deviated', a condition of sufficient elasticy to alow the incident to pass. Sukarno did not forget to tell his hosts, the communists student organization C.G.M.L., that however much he 'loved' the C.G.M.L. he would ban them too if they 'deviated'.[12]

This incident with the H.M.I. is remarkable insofar as it has a background that should be seen in a much wider context than the mere Djakarta scene, which kept the leaders of Indonesia preoccupied almost exclusively that second half of September. The protection Sukarno gave to the muslim student organization was not only a policy the President followed because he did not want to be told too much what to do by the communists, it had international ramifications since at that very moment Indonesia was engaged in secretly helping Pakistan in its war against India on Kashmir. It did so at the request of China which had a great interest in enlisting Indonesia and having it line up openly against its archenemy at that time, India.

As Sukarno had reasons, particularly in September, to retain China's aid and support, he consented to send two Mig jet planes to Pakistan and promised naval movements and the dispatch of field artillery and Russian-made tanks.[13] Nothing seems to have come of the naval movements that were to 'threaten' India. Not much is known about the field artillery, but the Migs and the Russian tanks according to Colonel Bambang Widjanarko's testimony were actually dispatched.[14] This support was given to Pakistan which from September 1 had been at war with India.[15] It was kept secret, however, in order to prevent a complete break in relations with New Delhi and avoid trouble with the Soviet Union.[16] On the other hand it would be a strange thing at this point where Indonesia in fact, though maybe not very effectively, was helping Pakistan, to unleash an action against the muslim H.M.L. within the country.[17] For Aidit however, not bothered with state affairs as Sukarno was, the H.M.I. provided a good occasion to show his hand to the President just enough to make him aware that he should not take him, or the aid of the P.K.I., for granted.

The issue was the more sensitive for Sukarno because in that very month – to be precise on September 16 – he had as we have seen[18] sent Air Force Chief of Staff Omar Dhani to Peking to discuss the question of aid to Pakistan.[19] It was on that very day that Subandrio firmly took up a position for the first time against the P.K.I. demand to ban the Muslim Youth Organization. The Sukarno-Subandrio line of that time may have been to avoid at all costs having the Pakistan-China-Indonesia cooperation marred by irrelevant demands against the M.H.I., an organization that could probably be dealt with appropriately anyway sooner or later.

The second if not the main reason was to get arms from the Chinese, that is to say that more of the promised Chung machine guns could be shipped to Indonesia. Dhani must have taken some of these arms with him in his Hercules transport plane; some were also loaded later into an Indonesian vessel, the Gunung Kerintje, arriving only at the end of October 1965 in the harbor of Djakarta, Tandjong Priok.[20] According to the Widjanarko report the arms to reach Indonesia were stored in an air force warehouse in downtown Djakarta and from there for a part distributed, the last time on the evening of October 1 near the Senajan Sports Stadium which together with the nearby construction site of the Conefo building was a center of activities for the 30 September *putsch*.

Sukarno therefore had plenty of reasons to keep the flight of Omar Dhani secret and not to inform the army of its multiple purposes. It would be to no good – certainly not at this stage – to let the army in on this illegal arms transport, intended to provide light side arms for the communist youth groups of the Pemudah Rakjat and of the Gerwani women's organization. There is no doubt that Sukarno was aware of the distribution of these weapons to communist trainees.[21]

But while Sukarno did not want to get into difficulties with allies like China and Pakistan and with an opponent like India, the domestic scene was the field of action which absorbed his fullest attention as we will see.

Subandrio's secret service must at least have done some work because on September 7 Subandrio heard from one of his subordinates, Kartono Kadri, that 'the P.K.I. wanted to stage a coup d'état on September 19'.[22] This information may very well have been true, as Subandrio's departure for Sumatra, finally taking place on September 28, had first been scheduled for September 17, and in both cases was planned two days ahead of the 'putsch' date.[23] As he was participating himself in the 'P.K.I.-coup' he should have given Kartono Kadri a dressing down for not being better informed. On September 17 Subandrio was once again told that the date would be the 19th.[24]

At his trial Subandrio said he passed on the information, not being particularly impressed by the seriousness of the charges.[25] It is quite probable that some last-minute snags had turned up and that the date had to be postponed until September 30. At any rate it was not a lack of conspiratory meetings that could be blamed for it as the Sjam-Untung group met regularly during September.[26]

Having amassed weapons, Njono was also very active and conferred with his 'section' commanders on September 21, 23, and 26 getting ready for 'D-day'.[27] On September 28 he held 'maneuvers' with 2,000 of his men, a dress rehearsal of the actual operation still not yet defined[28] because it involved some discussion in various groups. On September 23 a decisive meeting took place in the Presidential Palace. Present were, according to Colonel Bambang Widjanarko, Subandrio, Leimena, Chaerul Saleh, Dhani, Brigadier General Sabur – the commander of the palace guard and boss of Untung – and General Murshid. It was General Murshid who reported to the President with everybody attending that there did in fact exist a disloyal Council of Generals that did not agree with the President's policy, etc.[29] Sukarno then asked general Sabur how he had proceeded with the preparations, with his 'order'. Sabur said more precise and detailed instructions were still needed. Sukarno then and there gave Sabur the order to 'go into action against the generals as soon as as possible'.[30] Second Deputy Premier Leimena, a representative of the Christian minority among the leaders of the Sukarno era, was interrogated in the course of 1969 by the military investigation team about his role in the period that led up to the 'Untung putsch', as he was also present on various other occasions where the destiny of the 'disloyal' generals was discussed.[31] According to Nasution it is clear from the declaration Leimena gave to the investigators that Sukarno's deputy knew in advance that the Indonesian President wanted to get rid of a number of generals.[32] Of the fateful get-together on September 23, 1965, Leimena himself admitted that he remembered the occasion and that he had then also understood that Sukarno had in mind the Army General Staff.[33] But, he maintained, 'I did not know whether Sukarno wanted to get them out of the way, I was preoccupied with other thoughts during that meeting'.[34]

The 'action' talked about between Sukarno's friends and admirers that 23nd of September had two sides: The military operations involved, led by the commander of Sukarno's guards regiment, Brigadier General Sabur,[35] with Untung as front man, and the political aspects that were to be taken care of by the P.K.I. Meanwhile, the man who was really going to run the show as far as the military side of the 'Untung-coup' was concerned, was Brigadier General Supardjo, normally then stationed in Kalimantan on the 'front' with Malaysia but who turned up surreptitiously in Djakarta at the end of September. On September 28th he was recalled from his post to the capital by Omar Dhani at Sukarno's request.[36] The Indonesian President knew at the time he told Dhani to summon Supardjo back that this general was already in Djakarta, but he liked to deceive as many people as possible to keep all the reins in his own hand. On September 29 Supardjo had a first conference with Sukarno in Merdeka Palace, while he should have been commanding his troops in the jungle fight against Malaysia.[37]

From then on Supardjo was the liaison officer between Sukarno and Aidit. On the day he was first seen in the Palace he told Sukarno that he had come from a meeting with P.K.I. representatives.[38] That must have been the Sjam-Untung group, meeting for the tenth time since they first began back in August.[39] Sjam, the chief of Aidit's Special Bureau, said at his trial that on that occasion General Supardjo was present for the first time. After that the general had gone to see President Sukarno and tell him that 'the progressive officers were on the move'.[40] It was at this stage too that Supardjo, taking over from Sabur, got to know Untung.[41]

At that tenth session D-day was fixed for October 1, 4:00 in the morning. Word spread quickly, along the military lines to the air force units involved at Halim and through Untung and Supardjo to the others. Sjam took care of the P.K.I. and, in the afternoon, Njono, the 'commander' of the armed communist youth was informed by Sukatmo, the chairman of the Communist Youth Organization. On the evening of that day, September 29, when all was set to have the army decapitated in the early morning of October first, the Senajan stadium was packed with thousands of students, who were, as we saw, addressed first by Leimena, then by Aidit, and finally by Sukarno.[42] With the background of the decision taken that day, and at least known to two of them (Aidit and Sukarno), it is now also more understandable that Aidit was in a mood to challenge the President, in order to show him that the deal that held them together did not make the P.K.I. Sukarno's prisoner. Aidit of course even hoped and expected, certainly in the long run, the opposite. Sukarno must have thought similarly and both miscalculated grossly as further events abundantly showed. Aidit was the first victim, and Sukarno did not bat an eye in dropping the P.K.I. Chairman the minute that Aidit became a liability. It is interesting to see that within days of the 30 September debacle, Aidit was already an 'unperson' to Sukarno. As was reported at the time, a 'high government official', – no doubt it was Subandrio who was desperately trying to rescue both Sukarno and himself – gave an insight into Sukarno's post-Untung reasoning.[43] Sukarno it was said, was now thinking of a new communist party, not Peking-oriented but genuinely national.[44] 'The present leadership will be dropped. Aidit is *persona non grata*. He signed his own death warrant when he openly defied Sukarno on the fateful night of the 28th [sic] of September'.[45]

More fateful, of course, was the night of the 30th of September. It came at the end of a day abounding in rumors and evil forebodings. In China hundreds of Indonesians, many of whom had been conveniently shipped out of the way such as Chaerul Saleh, Ali Sastroamidjojo, etc., were preparing to celebrate the Chinese First of October and heard Chuh Teh thank them at an official banquet for the 'great contribution' Indonesia was making to the cause of the Afro-Asian world.[46] And another high Chinese official 'predicted' that the position of the overseas Chinese that had left Indonesia against their wish would 'soon' improve.[47] Chou was to announce that 'Indonesia will bring us a great present on our national day'.[48]

And in Djakarta the final preparations were being made to make it a really 'great present'. Njono had his 2,000 men armed and ready: Sabur was hurrying back to Djakarta for 'urgent matters', and P.K.I. Politburo alternate member Anwar Zanusi was saying that 'the motherland is in an advanced stage of pregnancy'. It would be a 'Nasakom-baby' he predicted, but 'first the midwife has to drive out the devils'.[49]

In the evening Sukarno again had to go to the Senajan stadium, this time to address a congress of technicians, probably a less exitable crowd than the night before.[50] He began in a low key, speaking on Indonesian socialism for which technical science was indispensable. Then he stopped and the rumor spread that he had again fallen ill.[51] What happpened was something quite different, if we can trust the evidence of an eyewitness like his aide Widjanarko. He told his interrogators in October 1970 that halfway through the speech he had arrived to hand over to the President an urgent letter from Lieutenant Colonel

Untung. Sukarno interrupted his speech to withdraw with his aide-de-camp to a quieter place and read the message. What Untung wrote is not known but can be guessed. At any rate Widjanarko saw that Sukarno was visibly pleased with what he had read, went back to the meeting, and continued his speech, 'being excited and gay and even making Leimena sing a song'.[52] At the end of his talk he said: 'Go home quietly everybody. I have to arrange some important matters that may keep me up until deep into the night'.[53]

What went on after that is sufficiently described elsewhere with varying accuracy.[54] Suffice it here to relate some events that complete the picture of the shadow play that had been going on for so many weeks and ended that night in bloodshed and murder of a rather atrocious variety. While at Halim Air Base, Sukarno at first seems to have been fully confident that morning of October 1, 1965, that the affair would come off well. He heard Supardjo's reports that Djakarta was under control and that the generals 'had been taken care of'.[55] But this mood changed, and seeing some writing on the wall – not the least of which was the sudden activity Suharto was deploying from his strategic command vantage point – Sukarno around noon sent one of his aides to get the uniform he had been wearing the night before. When he got it, Sukarno took out Untungs letter which had given him so much pleasure the night before and tore it to pieces.[56]

The President remained at Halim but was finally counseled to leave. Being pressed to do so by Suharto, he went to the Bogor Palace, which was at least 'neutral' territory. He did not after all go to central Java with the special Hercules airplane which was ready and waiting for all eventualities. The President spent the next few days in his Palace at Bogor, meanwhile having ordered Supardjo to stop whatever fighting was still going on. Supardjo hid himself in the Bogor Palace until he went into hiding elsewhere on October 5.[57] Meanwhile, Omar Dhani, another refugee at the President's Palace, had received a radiogram from Halim Air Base.[58] It said that 'traces' of the missing generals had been found nearby Halim. Then Sukarno – it was already in the middle of the night of 3 to 4 October – ordered one of his Tjakrabirawa officers, Colonel Saelan, to go and get what was left of the bodies.[59]

As it was dark, Saelan and his soldiers were given powerful lamps and left for Lubang Buaja. Later Saelan had to report to the President that he had failed to carry out the order 'to remove the bodies of the generals' because just when they had arrived at the place where the murdered and mutilated six generals and Nasution's aide Lieutenant Tendean had been dumped, commando troops of Suharto's strategic command had beaten them to it and where busy digging up the remains of the victims of Sukarno's 'final victory'. Later one witness was to explain that 'by removing the bodies of the generals it was intended to efface all traces'.[60]

NOTES

1. *Djakarta Radio Home Service*, September 16, 1965.
2. The conference in Central Java took place from September 6 to 10; *Harian Rakjat*, September 17, 1965. It resolved that 'it is a noble duty to set the revolutionary situation so that it can move toward maturity'.
3. *Indonesian Herald*, September 21, 1965. Subandrio gave a memorable speech to communist students and, that same day, to Sobsi-plantation workers, see above p. 396.
4. *Antara News Agency*, September 22, 1965.
5. *Harian Rakjat*, September 25, 1965.
6. *Harian Rakjat*, September 27, 1965; *New China News Agency*, September 27, 1965. The speech was made on September 25.
7. *Indonesian Herald*, August 29, 1965.
8. *Harian Rakjat*, September 29, 1965.
9. *Radio Free Europe*, October 13, 1965.
10. *Radio Free Europe*, October 13, 1965. A sarong is a typically female garb, so the implication was clear. Aidit also had a barb for 'leaders with many mistresses', a remark Sukarno must have made note of and remembered. Leimena had been 'surprised' that Aidit was attacking him so violently; interview March 1972.
11. See p. 407.
12. *Indonesian Herald*, September 30, 1965.
13. Widjanarko report II, p. 28.
14. Widjanarko described the complicated way Russian-made tanks were readied for transportation through air force channels to the harbor of Tandjong Priok, where a Pakistan freighter took them aboard.
15. *Indonesian Herald*, September 3, 1965.
16. The Indian Foreign Minister, answering questions in parliament on the violent P.K.I.-inspired anti-Indian campaign in Indonesia, said that no break in relations was being considered at that time. 'Supply of arms to Pakistan, however, would be considered a hostile act' he added; *New Delhi Radio*, September 14, 1965.

17. During his trial Dhani did not give details of the military aid to Pakistan he had discussed in September 1965 in Peking, but he said that, at the time, he foresaw that the Soviet Union would stop sending spare parts for his air force in retaliation; see proceedings of the trial of Omar Dhani, 2nd session.
18. See above p. 333.
19. See proceedings of the trial of Omar Dhani, 2nd session.
20. See above p. 339, note 49.
21. See the Widjanarko report II, p. 26, 27.
22. Subandrio trial, 6th session.
23. Subandrio trial, 6th session. Subandrio and Sukarno of course denied that the departure of Subandrio to Sumatra – and of so many others, especially to China – had anything to do with the Untung-coup. Witnesses other than Widjanarko – he himself could not answer the question – testified that on September 26 Sukarno and Subandrio met in the Presidential Palace, and discussed the various places to go to: Subandrio would go to North Sumatra – as he did –, Leimena, not present, would stay in Djakarta – as he also did, – and the President might go to Central Java, as he eventually did not.
24. According to Dr. Rubiono Kertopati, one of Sukarno's physicians, the President had booked right after Independence Day a trip to Mexico to take him out of the country for two weeks from September 6, 1965 onwards. It would have meant that he would have been outside Indonesia at the date of the putsch as initially planned: September 19. The outbreak of the India-Pakistan war prevented this trip, 'the last of my life' Sukarno pathetically lamented.
25. See proceedings of the Subandrio trial, 3rd session.
26. On September 6 and 12, 26 and 27. See proceedings of the Sjam trial, 2nd session.
27. See proceedings of the Njono trial.
28. See proceedings of the Njono trial.
29. Sukarno was putting on an act in asking Murshid to report on the Council of Generals. (He had at an earlier stage told Murshid he wanted to replace Yani and thought of him, Murshid, as his successor.) After Murshid had reported Sukarno asked him: 'Murshid, is this really true', to which the answer can be guessed. See Widjanarko report III, p. 25.
30. Widjanarko report III, p. 26.
31. For instance at Tampaksiring, Bali, on Sukarno's birthday on June 6, 1965; see above p. 368. According to Leimena's own account he was present on several occasions that summer when Sukarno met the military leaders of the country, and as a measure of his intimacy with Sukarno he saw the President during the month of July each day. Interview, March 1972 Dr. J. Leimena.
32. 'I can say that Sukarno had indeed decided to get us out of the way. There are testimonies by witnesses, one of whom is still alive, Leimena'; interview, March 1972, General Nasution. The Indonesian word used by Sukarno 'bereskan' is ambiguous, meaning to clean or to purge but also to liquidate. At the time of writing, June 1972, it is still bon-ton in leading well-informed circles in Indonesia to leave open the question whether Sukarno knew that

he was signing a death warrant for the 'disloyal' generals, when he let them be 'kidnapped' or 'taken into custody' by the Untung raiders. To outsiders this would seem incredible courtesy, as far as those Indonesians really have access to the facts. General Nasution, himself a near-victim of the 'Untung putsch', whose young dauchter lost her life as a consequence of Sukarno's 'action' put the chance that Sukarno really knew what he was doing at '50-50'

33. Interview, March 1972, Dr. J. Leimena.
34. On the Tampaksiring discussion, when Sukarno 'allowed' General Sjafiudin to investigate the loyalty of Yani, Leimena though present was equally rather vague, using the argument 'I had a rice crisis on my hands then'; interview, March 1972, Dr. J. Leimena. It is said that, by influencing Sukarno at a critical moment on the day of October 1, 1965, and by convincing the President that he had better go to 'neutral' Bogor instead of taking a plane to Central Java as Aidit pressed for, Leimena helped avoid a near-certain civil wan. For this contribution Suharto, so the argument goes, has shown corresponding leniency.
35. Sabur, though fully involved as Tjakrabirawa commander, was released from jail at the end of 1971 after a heart attack and has no sentence.
36. See the proceedings of the Omar Dhani trial, 1st session.
37. Proceedings of the Supardjo trial.
38. Widpanarko report II, p. 16.
39. Proceedings of the Sjam trial.
40. Widjanarko report II, p. 16.
41. Sabur left that day on a 'holiday' taking his family with him to Bandung, where he told Brigadier General Dharsono of the Siliwangi Division that 'for the first time he did not 'agree' on some point with the President. The next day, on September 30, he returned alone to Djakarta for some 'urgent matters' but denied later that it had had anything to do with the Untung-coup.
42. See above p. 402.
43. *Radio Free Europe*, October 13, 1965.
44. It was a good 'text' at that moment, as not a fraction was known of what is known today, but the deliberate distortion against Aidit and the Chinese as exclusive evildoers can no longer be maintained. See below p. 442.
45. The report gives the 28th as date, but from the context it is clear that this must have been the 29th, when the incidents around the H.M.I. occurred and Aidit told Sukarno 'to wear a sarong'; see above p. 402.
46. *Indonesian Herald*, October 1st, 1965, *Antara News Agency*, October 1st, 1965.
47. Interview, March 1972, Nasution.
48. Communication of one of the Indonesians present in China at the time.
49. *Harian Rakjat*, October 2nd, 1965.
50. *Indonesian Herald*, September 30, 1965.
51. See Dennis Warner in *Reporter*, November 18, 1965, writing that Sukarno spoke for one hour and 10 minutes and 'had to be treated by doctors'.
52. Widjanarko report II, pp. 10, 11.

53. See above p. 339 note 41.
54. See above p. 409, note 1.
55. Patting Supardjo on the shoulder after the General had reported his 'mission completed' Sukarno chided him: 'Why did Nasution escape?'; Widjanarko report II, pp. 12,13.

    Earlier that same day the news that Nasution was 'not accounted for' had already had its influence. While driving from his fourth wife Dewi's house along a staked-out route to the Merdeka Palace, Sukarno got word by radio from a police officer at Nasution's house about the escape of the Defence Minister. The President changed his plans, drove to the house of one of his other wives and finally decided not to go to the Palace as planned but to go to Halim Air Base instead; interview, March 1972, General Nasution. See Arnold C. Brackman, 1969, *The Communist collapse in Indonesia*, W. W. Norton and Co, Inc., New York, p. 87, who writes that Sukarno went 'inexplicably' to Halim. Halim had been prepared for such an emergency, as a Hercules transport plane – the Presidential jet plane had gone with Subandrio and his delegation to Sumatra – had been readied for Sukarno in advance. On the evening of September 30, one of the President's aide-de-camps, Colonel Saelan, had gone over to the airbase to inspect the place where Sukarno could be put up the next day. Sukarno must have regretted the premature and rather panicky reaction which took him too early to Halim and in the wrong company, that of the losers. Moreover, it was an additional sign of his complete involvement in the 'Untung putsch'.
56. Widjanarko report I, p. 14.
57. Widjanarko report I, p. 13.
58. Dhani had left Halim for Central Java at the same time as Aidit, on the night of October 1 to 2, but was back again at the airbase on the afternoon of October 2 and went from there to Bogor. Aidit remained in Central Java waiting to see what could be salvaged of the shattered enterprise only to meet death at the hands of the army on November 22, 1965 after an abortive attempt at an armed revolt at the end of October.
59. Widjanarko report I, p. 13. See also John Hughes, 1957; *Indonesian Upheaval*, David McKay, New York, p. 123.
60. Widianarko report II, p. 20.

CHAPTER 29

Aidit becomes expendable (1965)

In the course of Saturday October 2 Sukarno had been forced to take a stand in the '30 September affair'. Early that morning troops under Major General Suharto had seized the airbase of Halim without encountering much resistance.[1] In the afternoon Suharto, having heard that Sukarno was in Bogor, went to the palace there and had his first meeting with the President, which took place in a rather chilly atmosphere. Suharto had assumed command of the army as Chief of the Strategic Command, the Kostrad, but was not in a hierarchical way the first to have filled the vacancy created by the disappearance of Yani, though he was after the army commander the highest officer in the army who had troops under his command and therefore used to replace Yani when he was abroad. Officially, while still at Halim in the early afternoon of October 1, Sukarno had appointed himself commander of the army and Major General Pranoto as 'caretaker' for the actual handling of army matters.[2] Pranoto was the choice of the P.K.I., not being a man of strong character who had been favorably inclined towards the P.K.I. leadership in the past and had done them favors while in commanding positions on Sumatra and Kalimantan.[3] With Sjam and Aidit Pranoto had gone to Halim late in the evening of September 30 but had left again and was in town the next morning, and was prevented from going to Halim by Suharto. So when Suharto met Sukarno the next day, the roles had to be properly assigned. Thus Suharto also formally received the authority to continue the task he had assumed the moment he took things in hand on October 1. It must have been a tense situation, but in the end Sukarno had to give way and agreed to give Suharto responsibility for order and security. This in fact meant sidetracking Pranoto.

It was at Bogor that 2nd of October that Sukarno's first personal broadcast was recorded, to be transmitted by Djakarta Radio at 1:30 hours in the morning of Sunday October 3, after an introductory speech by Suharto.[4] From then on Suharto also had official status and being 'utterly stubborn', as the President used to describe him, turned out to be a tough opponent.[5]

Things were not looking very rosy for the conspirators around Sukarno who only had the advantage of knowing a little bit more than the new army leader. But that could soon change. It was now a matter of '*sauve-qui-peut*', 'every man for himself and the devil take the hindmost'. Subandrio, having heard of the bad turn of events in Djakarta, did not hurry to get back from Sumatra. However, he could not postpone it much longer and arrived 'looking nervous' at Kemajoran airport early on Monday October 4.[6]

Later that same day, 24 hours after the bodies of the victims had been found at Lubang Buaja, Suharto announced their sorry end. For the next day, Armed Forces Day, all ceremonies were cancelled and instead a state funeral was held for the seven officers killed. Nasution, still suffering from shock and his narrow escape, made a short speech in which he rejected the accusation that the victims had been 'traitors'. Reflecting the depth of his agony he said: 'Slander is more criminal than murder' and announced that it would be proven that what had been said about the generals was untrue.[7] Sukarno was not present but had sent Subandrio instead who cannot have felt at ease when in an even shorter address he prayed: 'May their souls find a proper place in the hereafter'.[8]

Sukarno, still in Bogor, declared the generals and Nasution's aide 'national heroes', and after having conferred this title upon them, he had a chance to watch a five-minute film on Indonesia's TV-station about the mutilated state the seven were in when found at Lubang Buaja.[9] The next day he held the first full-fledged cabinet session. Among those present were Lukman and Njoto. The P.K.I. Chairman was not there but, through Njoto, had given Sukarno a message asking him to use the National Front and the police – that is *not* the army – to restore order and to take upon himself the political side of a solution.[10] That same day, in Semarang, the communist newspaper *Djalan Rakjat* printed the text of that message which was dated October 2.

Meanwhile, the central leadership of the P.K.I. was in complete disarray. Njono was arrested on October 3. On October 5 Lukman who had returned from Central Java and Njoto who had come back the day before with Subandrio from Medan in Djakarta put together a statement denying any involvement in the Untung coup.[11] This they handed over, together with Aidit's letter, to Sukarno at the first cabinet session. The credibility of the statement was seriously impaired of course by the clear evidence to be found in the *Harian Rakjat* edition of October 2. It had carried the text of the Untung announcements and an editorial in which it read that 'the support and the hearts of the people are certainly on the side of the 30 September movement'.[12] It had gone to press the day before, at any rate after Sukarno had appointed Pranoto[13] – around 13.30 hours – and probably somewhere towards the end of that afternoon, when things did not look too bad. Initially it was the most embarrassing part of the affair to explain away for those who thought that the P.K.I. could not have been involved.[14] The paper's editor of the day was just not so lucky as his colleague in Semarang who was able to print with the same dateline, October 2, Aidit's first attempt to extricate the P.K.I. from the tangle into which he had got it. With all the later evidence this last issue of *Harian Rakjat* lost much of its interest. But for those who suspected the exclusive P.K.I. responsibility for the affair, it was an equally misleading signpost.

Abroad it was picked up as one of the early clues to what had actually been happening around the first day of October. But as a close observer at the time remarked 'anyone who is not totally confused is just badly informed'.[15] Among the confused was the Soviet press.[16] From the afternoon of October 1 Moscow Radio gave regular reports, but all from western sources, quoting Kuala Lumpur Radio and Associated Press but not Soviet correspondents.[17] On October 2 *Pravda* carried a short resumé of Untung's first announcement about the prevention of the coup of the Council of Generals but also quoted from non-Soviet sources.[18] After that, short news items appeared in the Soviet media, with Sukarno's two short radio talks of October 2 and 3 only being reported after a delay of several days.[19] On October 6 Tass began to report mass arrests of Indonesian communists but noted that Lukman and Njoto had still attended the cabinet session of Sukarno in Bogor.[20] On the same day – but printed the day before – the Soviet army paper *Krasnaia Zvezda* carried an article praising the Indonesian army and its achievements in the past, in terms unrelated to the current situation[21] and printed it next to a news item saying that 'Djakarta had been liberated form the putschists'.[22] As from October 6 it may have begun to dawn upon those who were setting the line for the media in Moscow that there was more afoot than some sort of rebellion of subordinate officers – as had happened often in the past in Indonesia. This time the rebellion might have had the support of leftist elements.

Moscow Radio on October 6 and *Pravda* the next day reported the attacks from the side of the muslim party N.U. and its paper *Duta Musjarakat* upon the P.K.I. It gave the content of the P.K.I. statement of October 5 – the denial of involvement – and added that nowhere in Indonesia had this statement been printed or published.[23] This was the theme for the next few days until on October 11 Brezhnev and Kosygin sent a message to Sukarno wishing him well and congratulating him on his good health and expressing the hope that 'all anti-imperialist forces would work together'.[24] It also spoke of 'actions by reactionary forces [trying] to strike a blow at the most active anti-imperialist forces'.[25]

Notwithstanding the ideological differences with the P.K.I. in the immediate past, Moscow began apparently to see that it could not easily ignore wholesale attacks on a communist party, certainly not on one which, until then, had been the largest outside the communist block. Some sign of criticism of past P.K.I. policies and attitudes could not be suppressed though. So Indonesia expert and onetime Tass correspondent in Djakarta Avrin commented on Moscow Radio that 'more often at the peak of unity incidents occur', having in mind the abortive Madiun rebellion of 1948 which in current Soviet thinking had become a negative example. Avrin reminded his listeners that it had taken 'many sacrifices and a lot of money' (not saying whose) to repair the damage caused by such 'incidents'.[26] But he also insinuated that it was the imperialists – the West – who had tried on September 30 to 'split the national front under cover of a coup by cadre officers'.

The Soviet government paper *Izvestia* started to call the Untung coup a 'rebellion',[27] and it showed doubts as to the truth of his initial announcements by writing: 'Untung said the coup had been divised *supposedly* to prevent a coup planned by a reactionary council of generals' [emphasis added].[28] Only then did it give the first comment on the incriminating *Harian Rakjat* editorial of October 2, suggesting that the Indonesian Communist Party paper had made 'a wrong analysis' by expressing in print 'support of the people for the revolt'. Up to then it looked as if the policy makers in Moscow were still playing it by ear, but slowly a change towards a greater commitment in favor of the P.K.I. began to emerge. Meanwhile, back in Djakarta, further pressure had compelled Sukarno to drop Pranoto completely (he never had any authority anyhow), and Suharto was appointed official successor to the murdered Yani, as full commanding officer of the army.[29]

A few days later the P.K.I was banned 'temporarily' and only in the Djakarta area, but this was an augury of what could happen anytime in the rest of the country.[30] Moscow expressed 'concern' at the situation, especially because of the ban.[31] According to Yugoslav sources in Moscow the Soviets were even 'greatly disturbed by events in Djakarta'.[32] Now it had become clear that the P.K.I. as a communist organization was the target of the new group in power, and not only individuals belonging to it.[33] This was also the theme of the first authorative editorial comment on the situation after the Untung coup, published by *Pravda* on October 26.[34] It recalled the P.K.I. October 5 statement of non-involvement and tried to separate the P.K.I from 'some individuals' who might have taken part in the attempted coup. 'Political adventurism, putschism and sectarianism are alien to Marxistm-Leninism' the Soviet paper wrote. It warned that the attempts now being made to prevent Indonesia from undergoing 'an independent, democratic development' would fail. Moscow was now clearly trying to forget old quarrels and come to the rescue of the P.K.I. as a group of fellow communists, seeing also that Sukarno's authority had become tained and that there could be some merit in his – rather desperate – idea to get what he supposedly now had in mind: A 'really' national communist party.[35] It had been Subandrio who had tried to peddle the idea to those who wanted to listen,[36] and Sukarno, trying to regain some grip on the situation, put in a word also, saying that Indonesia could not be governed without 'a' P.K.I.[37] Therefore, however disgruntled Moscow may have been with Sukarno on the eve of the Untung coup, and certainly with the P.K.I. leadership, it began to see its interest in a certain restoration of P.K.I.-Sukarno power. The new Soviet ambassador Seytenko expressed this orientation in a two-hour talk with Sukarno-confidant Ruslan Abdulgani, after which the Soviet diplomat told the press that 'the Soviet Union was confident that Sukarno would overcome the consequences of the abortive coup'.[38]

In China an embarrassed silence reigned for the first twenty days of the month of October on what happened in Indonesia. On October 1 news of the arrest of seven generals, including Nasution, had been diffused by the Chinese in Peking among some of the many Indonesians then present for the National Day celebrations.[39] This was apparently the 'birthday present' Chou En-lai had spoken about that Indonesia was going to give China, but it got the wishes of the planners of the Untung coup garbled and took them for accomplished reality. They must have quickly realized that the whole plot was turning sour in a way that could be most awkard to them. On October 2 the Chinese 'experts' working on the Conefo building left Djakarta for China.[40] Probably they were on the Indonesian air force plane that went to Canton on October 2, 1965.[41] A hectic long-distance telephone exchange then took place between Chou En-lai and whoever was on the plane from the Indonesian side in Canton.

At a banquet given to one of the Indonesian delegations the Chinese hosts spoke of 'imperialist plots' that should not mar Sino-Indonesian relations.[42] On October 4 President Liu Shao-chi and Premier Chou En-lai sent Sukarno a cable congratulating him on his 'good health'.[43] Then Subandrio began to imply Chinese collusion with Untung, speaking of 'Chinese weapons' that had been furnished. Still seeing more chance of survival in playing the anti-Chinese card that came naturally to the Indonesians, he denied that the P.K.I. supported the rebels.[44] It is not quite clear whether, in plugging this line, he had the backing of Sukarno, who may still have been more inclined to save both his partners than to start antagonizing the Chinese to save his skin domestically. But it must have been difficult because the Chinese, for their part, were not too cooperative. They did not send any representative to the funeral of the generals and, moreover, did not lower their flag at the embassy compound in downtown Djakarta, though this had been requested by the government.[45] Being put in a tight corner Sukarno let it be known a little later that this 'rude' attitude of the Chinese government had been 'an eye-opener' to him'.[46] Refusal to lower the flag, away from the funeral, plus the fact that he had not been congratulated by the Chinese, were given as the reasons for Sukarno's ill-feelings towards them.[47] Again the idea of a P.K.I. 'whose leader were more Indonesian than Chinese' was plugged.[48]

For their part, the Chinese were finally about to react too. On October 16, the day after Suharto had officially been authorized as a successor to Yani, Indonesian soldiers raided the office of the Chinese commercial counsellor and were said to have found incriminating documents of undisclosed nature. Two days later Peking sent an official note of protest against this 'improper' behavior, at the same time complaining about the 'lies and slander' the Chinese People's Republic had been subjected to in Indonesia after October 1.[49]

On October 20 *Jen-min Jih-bao* carried its first editorial on the whole affair and gave a fairly factual account of what had happened since early that month in Indoneisa, naturally slanted in favor of the P.K.I.[50] It recalled the *Harian Rakjat* editorial of October 2 that had endorsed the 30 September movement as a 'patrotic and revolutionary action'. It said that a great agitation had occurred over 'the execution of Yani, former army commander and some army generals'. Aidit was quoted from his *Djalan Rakjat* article of October 2 as saying that the Untung coup had been an 'internal army affair'. The P.K.I. statement to the same effect of the day before and Sukarno's remark that it had all been 'an incident of the Revolution' was also mentioned. As to Sukarno himself it had indirect criticism that he had allowed Suharto to replace Pranoto, while the anti-Chinese sentiment within the country and related incidents in the outlying islands were also reported.

The Indonesian newspaper *Api* demanded the departure of Chinese ambassador Yao Ching-ming and a few days later carried a vague warning against 'Chinese' in general.[51]

At that moment Sukarno thought it necessary to get his lines with the Chinese straightened out again a bit, and he called in Yao, whom he met twice within 24 hours.[52] There was no one present at their meetings except an interpreter. It did not prevent the Central Committee of the Chinese Communist Party from adopting a resolution at that very moment in which 'American imperialists and Kruschov revisionists' were blamed for events in Djakarta.[53] But in the next note of protest to the Indonesian government on November 4, favorable reference was at least made to 'orders' Sukarno had given, be it without much result, to curb anti-Chinese excesses.[54] The next *Jen-min Jih-bao* editorial also treated Sukarno more generously and directed its fire more at the Indonesian army and the Soviet government than at the nominal head of the Indonesian state.[55] One may assume that this opinion, not so unfavorable to the President, was a consequence of his talks with Yao Ching-ming.

On November 9 Yao went to see Foreign Minister Subandrio while Sino-Indonesian relations continued to deteriorate rapidly.[56] Djakarta Radio even had a broadcast stating that the Chinese leaders had 'of course' been informed by the P.K.I.-leaders of what had been organized at the end of September and called the Chinese 'the natural enemies of the Indonesian people'.[57] After the Yao-Subandrio meeting the Indonesian Foreign Minister let it be known that 'relations between China and Indonesia would be good under any circumstances'.[58] It was the same day that Sukarno for the first time commented unfavorably on the Untung coup, calling it 'a regrettable affair'.[59]

The meaning of all this was clear: Aidit had been openly dropped by Sukarno, who preferred an improvement in relations with China to anything else. The Chinese were prepared to do likewise with the P.K.I.-Chairman and gave priority to their interests of state (the protection of the overseas Chinese, for instance) and what was left of Afro-Asian collaboration.

The army went on implicating the P.K.I. more and more directly. The regional secretary of the Djokjakarta P.K.I. committee was reported to have confessed that the P.K.I. 'masterminded' the 30 September movement.[60] Nasution thereupon endorsed this view literally and demanded the 'extermination' of 30 September elements.[16] Amid anti-Chinese rioting all over the country the Chinese again gave a serious warning and sent a note of protest, complaining that the Indonesian government was doing nothing against it.[62] This time, however, there was no mention of the Indonesian President. As far as Peking was concerned, he had been written off as a source of support for them.

NOTES

1. The 'attack' began at 3.00 in the morning and by 6.30 it all was over. See Background material concerning the abortive council d'etat in Indonesia, Indonesian Embassy, Cairo, 1965, p. 3.
2. See the order of the day of Sukarno of 13.30 hours, October 1, 1965, in *Indonesia*, Cornell University, April 1966, p. 151.
3. At the time of writing Pranoto is in jail charged with having been the P.K.I.'s military trump and part of the Sukarno-Aidit plot.
4. See also *Indonesian Herald*, October 11, 1965.
5. When Sukarno heard that Suharto had started action against the '30 Septem-

ber movement', he had become 'very angry'; Widjanarko report I, p. 17.

6. *Radio Medan*, October 4, 1965, and proceedings of the Subandrio trial, 6th session.
7. *Djakarta Radio Home Service*, October 5, 1965. Nasution referred to the accusation by the Untung coup in his initial statement broadcast on October 1, 1965 at 7.15 that a council of generals existed and formed 'a subversive movement sponsored by the C.I.A.'.
8. *Djakarta Radio Home Service*, October 5, 1965
9. *Djakarta Radio Home Service*, October 6, 1965.
10. See proceedings of the Subandrio trial, 7th session.
11. *Indonesia*, Cornell University, April 1966, p. 188. It had become the fashion to deny any connection with the abortive plot. On October 4th the P.N.I. also issued a declaration of innocence. It was later revealed that on the morning of October 1 P.N.I. Secretary-General Surachman had issued a statement of support for the '30 September movement'; *Angkatan Bersendjata*, October 11, 1965.

    P.N.I.-Chairman Ali Sastroamidjojo was in China at that time. Surachman had succeeded in ousting his anti-communist opponents early in August, making the P.N.I., as far as he had a grip on it, more or less a Communist front. Surachman went into hiding and was later found and shot.

    Ali Sastroamidjojo, in an interview March 1972, was still of the opinion that Surachman, though in the wrong by acting on his own on October 1, was basically in good faith. Ali admitted that his going into hiding was 'a bit strange'.
12. *Harian Rakjat*, October 2, 1965. A cartoon, displaying some army generals in a bad light added to the bad impression the issue had made. Warta Bhakti, one of the non-official P.K.I. papers, also supported the Untung-coup editorially in its October 2 issue.
13. Pranoto's appointment as 'caretaker' of the army was in that issue as a 'stop press' item, that is: put in at the last moment possible.
14. Cornell report 1966, p. 178; Wertheim, *Pacific Affairs*, spring-summer, 1966, p. 116.
15. Stanley Karnov in *Washington Post*, October 2, 1965.
16. *Izvestia* writing on October 2 about the 'confused situation' in Indonesia.
17. *Moscow Radio Home Service*, October 1, 1965.
18. *Pravda*, October 2, 1965. Of the Untung announcement it omitted the reference to the C.I.A. involvement. This same omission could be seen in the *Harian Rakjat* rendering of the same declaration of Untung. Given the sources Pravda indicated it does not necessarily mean that Pravda took the *Harian Rakjat* version as more authentic than the one that was broadcast by rebel-held *Djakarta Radio*, early October 1, 1965.
19. *Moscow Radio Home Service*, October 5, 1965, also speaking of a ban on 'the newspaper *Harian Rakjat*', not indicating as it did the next day that it concerned a communist newspaper; *Moscow Radio Home Service*, October 6, 1965.

20. *Tass*, October 6, 1965.
21. *Tass*, October 6, 1965. The Chinese were to get very exercised about this as to them it implied taking sides against the P.K.I.; *New China News Agency*, October 19, 1965.
22. *Krasnaia Zvezda*, October 6, 1965. This article clearly carried a connotation favorable to Nasution's Indonesian army.
23. *Moscow Radio Home Service*, October 6, 1965; *Pravda*, October 7, 1965.
24. *Tass*, October 11, 1965.
25. *Moscow Radio Home Service*, October 11, 1965; *Indonesian Herald*, October 13, 1965.
26. *Moscow Radio Home Service*, October 12, 1965.
27. *Izvestia*, October 12, 1965.
28. *Izvestia*, October 13, 1965.
29. This was on October 15; *Radio Free Europe*, October 16, 1965.
30. The P.K.I. in Djakarta was banned on October 18; *Antara News Agency*, October 20, 1965.
31. *Pravda*, October 20, 1965.
32. *Radio Belgrade*, October 20, 1965.
33. *Pravda*, October 23, 1965. It is possible that, as has been suggested, Moscow did not mind too much about action taken against the P.K.I. as it had been Peking-oriented anyhow; *Philippine Radio*, October 26, 1965. It seems from the total context though that, however, the Soviet leaders may have welcomed a purge of the pro-Peking leadership of the P.K.I., a total demise was not considered in their interests.
34. *Pravda*, October 26, 1965.
35. See above p. 407.
36. That had not been many. None of the papers had carried anything on this 'national-P.K.I.-without Aidit', as they were all army-controlled or anticommunist. The only paper to come out in favor of it had been Mimbar Revolusi, a N.U.-oriented paper, run by Subandrio-friend and N.U. Secretary-General Aminudin Azis, October 10, 1965.
37. *Radio Free Europe*, October 20, 1965. Of course within the terms of what Sukarno meant by 'governing', the President was right.
38. *Antara News Agency*, November 1, 1965.
39. See Arthur D. Dommen, *China Quarterly*, January-March 1966. Ex-Brigadier General Ahmad Sukendro, whom Dommen quoted, denied the truth of it in an interview, March 1972.
40. *Antara News Agency*, October 19, 1965. What sort of 'experts' these were is not certain. It must have been a bit fishy, and they may have been connected with the smuggling of arms from China to Indonesia. Allegations of this kind (weapons in crates supposed to contain 'building material' for the Conefo headquarters) were denied after the 'coup', but the denials came from Koti, the Supreme Operational Command, then still under Subandrio; *Indonesian Herald*, October 22, 1965. On October 15 the newspaper *Api* had a report that the P.K.I. had been involved in arms smuggling. According to other

sources it was General Pandjaitan in charge of logistics who discovered a few days before the 'Untung-coup' that the smuggling was going on, with the result that he was added at the last moment to the list of 'generals to be taken care of'. In first instance he was not on the list; communication by Ex-Brigadier-General Ahmad Sukendro, former chief of army intelligence, who received word on September 16, 1965, of seven generals going to be kidnapped, including himself, but without Pandjaitan; interview March 1972. His statement was corroborated by others.

41. Interview, March 1972, Baron Sastradinata.
42. *New China News Agency*, October 3, 1965.
43. *New China News Agency*, October 4, 1965.
44. *Hilversum Radio*, October 7, 1965.
45. *Kuala Lumpur Radio*, October 6, 1965.
46. On October 11 the Indonesian government lodged a protest against the flag incident with the Chinese Embassy. It was then that Sukarno was critical of Peking, but only indirectly; *Radio Free Europe*, October 13, 1965.
47. Behind this story one senses Subandrio who clearly intended it for home consumption, as Liu and Chou had in fact been kind enough to congratulate Sukarno, but this was conveniently passed over in silence; see above p. 407.
48. *Radio Free Europe*, October 13, 1965.
49. *New China News Agency* already carried it on October 19, 1965. The editorial also noted that, from October 1 until 16, no word had been received from the *New China News Agency* correspondent in Djakarta. It was said later that the *New China News Agency* transmitter in Djakarta had been sealed by the military.
50. *New China News Agency*, October 18, 1965.
51. *Associated Press*, October 24, 1965 and *Associated Press*, October 26, 1965.
52. *United Press International*, October 26, 1965 and *Indonesian Herald*, October 27, 1965.
53. *New China News Agency*, October 27, 1965.
54. *New China News Agency*, November 22, 1965.
55. *New China News Agency*, November 7, 1965. *Izvestia* particularly was chided for its treatment of the 30 September movement in its October 12 edition; see above p. 416.
56. *Djakarta Radio Home Service*, October 31, 1965.
57. *Djakarta Radio Home Service*, November 9, 1965.
58. *Djakarta Radio Home Service*, November 9, 1965.
59. According to *Antara* at least; see *Antara News Agency*, November 9, 1965.
60. *Antara News Agency*, November 24, 1965.
61. *Antara News Agency*, November 27, 1965.
62. The note was handed over on November 19. Mention of its was made by *New China News Agency* on November 22, 1965.

CHAPTER 30

Hindsight

The P.K.I. was decapitated in the course of the next few months, after the bloody purge of the army command for which it was quickly blamed. Chairman Aidit was executed in Central Java on November 22, 1965, and his Second Deputy Njoto soon after on December 4. Lukman, the only one of the triumvirate still at large, was captured on April 29, 1966, and killed 'while trying to escape'. Sakirman, the Party's number four, was captured in November of that year and executed.[1] The fifth member of the P.K.I. Politburo, Sudisman, was arrested on December 7, 1966, tried in July 1967 and, having been given the death sentence, was executed on October 29, 1968.[2] Coupled with the persecution of lesser P.K.I. members, it is understandable that it took the remnants of the party time to organize themselves and produce some assessment of the disaster that had befallen them. An initial, more general, reaction was given in an appeal issued on November 20, 1965,[3] in which it was stated that the party had operated completely in accordance with instructions of the President. It claimed further that no arms had been found among party members and that the P.K.I. still fully adhered to the state philosophy, the Pantjasilah. It was a rather apologetic piece, completely in line with Aidit's initial approach of hiding behind Sukarno, and was consequently denounced in subsequent P.K.I. pronouncements.[4] The next declaration was issued on the occasion of the party's 46th anniversary on May 23, 1966, supposedly in Djokjakarta, and appeared in the Peking-oriented *Indonesian Tribune* in November of that year.[5] It was a preliminary appraisal of the 'most difficult position' in which the P.K.I. found itself after the mass-scale murders and arrests of the previous months. It foreshadowed, however, the trend towards a more radical, if not desperate, view of communist prospects in Indonesia that was to be found in more detail in other P.K.I. documents to be published in the *Indonesian Tribune*. Thus it rejected what was called the 'emergence of modern revisionism' within the party that had been a consequence of the pursuit of power through parliamentary, peaceful means. This was a first open indication that Aidit's 'revisionist' approach to domestic affairs[6] could no longer be accepted, a development which given the disastrous events of the autumn of 1965 was hardly surprising. Aidit himself came in posthumously for a strong rebuke with the conclusion that 'a subjective, onesided and superficial interpretation [of Marxist-Leninism] and petty-bourgeois arrogance will only impede one's efforts to achieve a systematic understanding of Marxist-Leninism'.[7]

Another statement followed, this time with Indonesia's traditional 17th of August Day of Independence as the occasion.[8] It reflected a further step towards a critical analysis of the party's past, going all the way back even to 1945 and to the reasons why the August 1945 revolution had not succeeded. The statement took up the Zhdanov-line that had prevailed during 1947-1948[9] and that had brought Muso back from his exile into the limelight of Indonesian communist affairs for a short and rather unhappy period in the summer of 1948. A guerilla war against the Dutch should then have been used as the only way to defeat the colonial power, it was now concluded 21 years later. The P.K.I had not understood this, however, and when it finally got around to it (after Muso's return) it was too late, as 'even the correct course that was decided upon in the resolution of the Politburo of the Central Committee entitled "A new road for the Republic Indonesia" could not avert the defeat'.[10] After this defeat – the Madiun rebellion – the Indonesian state had remained an instrument of exploitation for the benefit of the dominating national-democratic (read non-communist) classes, and it had been 'an empty illusion' to assume that the democratic, 'pro-people' (read pro-communist) aspect could have won out without the use of force.[11] It had also been a mistake to let the anti-imperialist struggle prevail over the fight against domestic feudal forces, or in other words, to make the P.K.I. policies within the country subordinate to foreign political aims, shared and taken over by the Sukarno government. This preference for internal action had, throughout the years, been a preoccupation of Sudisman[12] and of the August 1966 statement of the P.K.I. of which this communist leader, being the most authoritative member of the Aidit Politburo still at large, was no doubt the author.[13] No interpretation of the events that led up to the 30 September movement was given in the P.K.I. statement, but the near future was depicted as 'in essence' an armed struggle of the peasants for the realization of an agrarian revolution.

Though 'Chinese' in approach with its accent on the peasants, the statement did not make a direct reference to China or Mao. This was left to the next and most important document of the underground P.K.I. which was to appear in that period, the well-known 'self-criticism' of the Politburo of the party's Central Committee under Sudisman.[14] But even so, and though increasing use was made in this 'self-criticism' of doctrinal notions dear to the Chinese (a protracted armed agrarian struggle as the road to power) the document still was striking as reflecting a 'national', Indonesia-based P.K.I opinion.[15]

The 'self-criticism', again probably rightly attributed to Sudisman, was dated September 1966 and published as an interpretation of the events of the year before and as guidance for comrades in the underground. It distinguished three major 'theoretical' errors of the party leadership under Aidit, though his name was not actually mentioned. First of all, the P.K.I was said to have operated too peacefully, too much in the parliamentary style in its quest for power. Secondly, the folly of the 'two-aspect' theory was once more (and this time more elaborately) exposed. Thirdly, the party was said to have lost its independence within the national front, having identified itself too much with Sukarno and having put national interest above class interest. The resulting policies were qualified both as 'rightist opportunism' and as 'leftist adventurism'.

On the one hand, especially in the early years, the party under Aidit had been too keen on getting a share in the powers structure: 'The main consideration for such an [unprincipled] stand [of achieving power through parliamentary means] did not start from the independent interests of the proletariat, but rather from the need to save the alliance with the national bourgeoisie'.[16] Later, the party had begun to criticize the various modern revisionist lines of the Soviet Communist Party, but the P.K.I. 'nevertheless continued to maintain good relations with the leadership of the C.P.S.U. and the influence of modern revisionism in our Party was by no means eradicated'. Here Aidit was quoted in a critical sense as having erred in saying that modern revisionism in the party was 'a latent, not an acute danger'. It was now high time that 'our party should abandon the line of preserving friendship with the modern revisionists'.[17] Aidit was also criticized extensively for having put national interest before class interests, and the second plenary of the 6th congress held at the end of 1960 was particularly cited as the beginning of this.[18] It was this plenary that endorsed Sukarno's demands concerning the conditions under which a political party in Indonesia could operate. Its outcome had represented a victory for Aidit's middle course and provided the necessary basis on which a few months later Sukarno was able to decide the pending case against the party concerning the July 1960 P.K.I. 'evaluation' and was able to license the party officially.[19] The 'self-criticism' sees Aidit's erroneous priority – national over class interests – illustrated in another slogan of that period: 'Overthrowing imperialism is the primary task'. The party Chairman's preoccupation with national anti-imperialist aims is given as a reason for the neglect of the local scene: 'This error rendered it impossible for the Party to build a strong and consolidated alliance of the workers and the peasants, despite the growing influence of the Party in the rural areas, because . . . all contradictions among the classes in the country . . . had to be subordinated to "the main contradiction, . . . the contradiction between the Indonesian people and the imperialists" '.[20] Therefore a peaceful pursuit of power in the shadow of Sukarno and consequently more attention for foreign political ventures than for domestic hard work had led to 'rightist opportunism'.

On the other hand it also produced 'leftist adventurism' the climax of which had been the events of September 30. This left deviation according to the 'self-criticism' showed up particularly in 1964-1965 when, indeed, a number of political victories were achieved: A boycott of American films, banning of the Cultural Manifest, dissolution of the B.P.S. and the Murba party, etc. However, to claim therefore, as was done in the theses for the party's 45th anniversary,[21] that 'an increasingly mounting and ripening revolutionary situation is developing in our country' had been utterly premature.[22] Overcome by wishful thinking 'the Party leadership had attempted to push forward the "ever ripening revolutionary situation" to become "a revolution". This had been stressed in the Statement of the Political Bureau of the Central Committee of the P.K.I. on August 17, 1965. This Statement called on the communists to work harder in order to push the present revolutionary situation forward to its climax, so that the people "can achieve not only ever greater victories, but also fundamental victories". This was the essence of the other mistake; the "Leftist" mistake which dragged the party leadership into adventurism that has brought such a great disaster to the party and the revolutionary movement in general'.[23]

Apart from ideological errors, as indicated, the 1966 'self-criticism' also contained severe criticism in the organizational field, complaining that the mass character of the P.K.I. had in fact been a window-dressing to impress the 'national bourgeoisie' in the national front, an outgrowth of the peaceful road to power that was to deprive the proletariat of a really effective 'vanguard' party. Too great a personal rule was also mentioned (no names), while it was claimed that 'the competent leading body of the Party, the "Political Buro" was prevented from functioning properly, often having nothing more to do than to endorse the steps taken by the leadership'. This was no doubt a reference to the 'inner circle' of Aidit, Lukman, and Njoto who as a so-called Dewan Harian or Executive Board handled most of the party's affairs, including the crucial decisions in the course of August and September 1965. Though no details on the inner-party discussions of that period are given the 'self-criticism' clearly aims at conveying the impression – truthfully or otherwise – that the other party leaders, including the rest of the Politburo, were then left out because 'it was not seldom that . . . the Political Buro had to consider certain problems while having only a fragmentary and superficial knowledge of them'.[24] In the 'self-criticism' the remedy prescribed for the P.K.I. was fairly simple: To study the communist elders from Marx through to Mao, to avoid friendship with modern revisionists, and to organize a peasant revolt through a revolutionary front led directly by the working class.

It would not be long before this approach could be tested in practice when in June 1968, in the Central Javanese region of Blitar, the Indonesian army launched an attack on some base-areas held by armed communists under P.K.I. leader Hutapea, completely routing them within ten days. The 'Chinese' slant of the 'self-criticism' in suggesting that a peasant revolt would be the course for Indonesian communists to freedom has been noted.[25] But a sense of realism still prevailed notwithstanding the high praise of the 'armed revolution of the peasants under the leadership of the proletariat'. This revolution, it was said, 'cannot be enforced from outside [and] will break out on the basis of the high consciousness and the conviction of the peasants themselves, obtained through their own experience in the struggle and through education by the working class'. The 'self-criticism' as related earlier, was written when Sudisman was the leading P.K.I. man in the underground and reflected the predilections of this Politburo member of peasant background for domestic, radical agrarian activism. In this sense Sudisman was, and had been, more 'Chinese' than any of his colleagues in the Politburo. However, it did not mean any particular preference for organizational ties with Peking.[26] This was to change, however, with the further demise of the original P.K.I. leadership later, in the closing months of 1966 when Sakirman was arrested and shot and Sudisman himself was also caught. It seems that then a real radicalization had set in, and Peking was asserting a direct influence upon the remnants of the P.K.I organization in Indonesia itself which were still beyond the reach of army units. It was at this juncture, too, that Politburo member Adjitorop, who since the middle of 1964 had been residing in Peking, in a speech at the Fifth Congress of the Albanian Workers Party in Tirana in November 1966, again took up the themes of the August 1966 Statement and of the 'self-criticism' of the next September.[27] There were clear indications[28] that, before the arrest of Sakirman and Sudisman, the P.K.I. Politburo in Java had been in close touch with Adjitorop and the Peking group of P.K.I. members.[29]

But, before turning to the activities and, above all, views of this China-based emigré group and of the Chinese comrades themselves, mention should be made of another document, officially emanating from a 'Marxist-Leninist Group of the Communist Party of Indonesia'.[30] It was first published in March 1967 in Ceylon,[31] and a summary appeared that same month in the pro-Soviet Indian weekly *Mainstream.*[32] There is reason to doubt that this 'Appeal to the Brothers at Home and Comrades Abroad' had been drafted by representatives of the group in Indonesia itself.[33] At any rate it was an elaborate counter-analysis, designed to refute the arguments, if not the conclusions, of the 'self-criticism' after this had been in wider circulation by its publication in the *Indonesian Tribune* in January 1967. At the same time it must have been considered by those behind it as an instruction to separate from the more radical P.K.I. remnants, first around Sudisman and later around Hutapea and others. The need for a clear break is evident from one of the recommendations of the 'Appeal', where a plea is made for 'a clear line of division between those who still continue to advocate ultra-leftist and sectarian principles, those who in the past unambiguously pushed the Party towards adventurism and opposed cohesion in the international Communist movement'.[34]

Basically the 'Appeal' defended the positions assumed by the Aidit leadership since 1951 and confirmed at the 1954 Fifth ann 1959 Sixth Party Congress, t.w. gradualist, cautious tactics, evading right and left deviations – 'capitulasi-ism' and 'adventurism'[35] – and pursuing a change in the balance of power at home to the advantage of the 'forces of the people'. But, so the argument ran, the party had not escaped this dilemma on a number of points. As to the question of violence or non-violence they should have been considered more clearly as alternative with the peaceful way as a first priority. But this approach had been dropped 'later', when only force of arms was seen as the method open to the P.K.I.[36]

As a matter of fact the P.K.I. had never done this under Aidit, but it served to lead the authors of the Appeal to the conclusion that 'this revisionist leftist point of view was instrumental in paving the theoretical way for the gamble known as the September 30 movement'.[37] At the same time the party leaders had succumbed to 'petty-bourgeois ideology', a right deviation, by putting national interests above class interests – especially since the second plenary of the P.K.I. Central Committee in December 1960[38] – and making it appear as if 'allegedly, class interests contradict national interests. In actual fact this was a deviation from Marxism-Leninism, which teaches that the interests of our class encompass the best interests of the entire nation'.[39] Here too the punishment was not lacking: 'Petty-bourgeois political views and nationalism have resulted in an inability correctly to understand the burning issues of the day, and this crippled the anti-imperialist struggle and the fight for peace on an international scale[40] and hurled Indonesia into the catastrophe of the September 30 movement'. At another level the Appeal approached the preoccupation of the P.K.I. with nationalistic aims from the opposite side (compared to the 'self-criticism') stressing that it had resulted in a 'lopsided point of view' and in 'a weakening and disappearance of friendship between the two major parties [the P.K.I. and the Soviet Communist Party] . . . This is what led us to the 1965 tragedy'. To the '30 September movement' and the causes of its failure the Appeal gives much more detailed attention than the 'self-criticism'. The similarity in approach is striking because the Appeal also concluded that it was nonsense to speak of a 'revolutionary situation' on the eve of the 30th September 1965 and equally adduced Lenin as a crown witness.[41] The thesis of the 45th anniversary of the party that the revolutionary situation was 'ripening' was also exposed as a serious error of judgment. The only difference in the analysis was that the Appeal linked China with the hasty support of the P.K.I. leadership for the 30 September movement: 'Following the return of our leaders from a trip abroad, which also included one of the Asian countries (July-August 1965) it became known that the party leadership had taken a rash decision in beginning preparations for playing the role of a "savior" with or without President Sukarno and other democratic forces. All this took place at a time when there was no revolutionary situation in evidence, no instability was manifested in the position of the ruling quarters and the broad masses were not prepared for armed action. There was only a danger of a counter-revolutionary plot and there were also the diseased kidneys of President Sukarno . . . It truly was a gamble of the first water which had nothing to do with the Marxist theory of armed uprising'.[42]

Finally in organizational matters the Appeal chided the negative side of the P.K.I. as a party of the masses that was conceived as not much more than 'one which has a large membership'[43] and which admitted new members 'without sufficiently rigorous selection'. The personal shortcomings of the party leadership were also mentioned in a brief reference to 'the cult of personality that flourished in the party', but this was apparently considered as only of subordinate interest.

The remedy for the party's ills that the Appeal had to offer was less clearcut than in the 'self-criticism'. A return to the old truths of the Party program as it had been adopted at the Fifth Party Congress in 1954 and amended at the next in 1959 (that is, to Aidit's gradualist policies, including a broad national united front) was one suggestion. Rebuilding the party was another priority, but here the 'workers' were especially to be courted, and not primarily the peasants. Good relations between Indonesia and the 'Socialist-bloc countries' should also be aimed at by the party, while short shrift should be made with ultra-left-wing elements in opposition to unity within the international communist movement.

Comparing this document with the 'self-criticism' we see that both rightly define the Aidit-line as a revisionist approach but differ in their appreciation of this phenomenon. The Appeal considered it basically commendable but criticized the party when it supposedly went off too much to the left as in its concept of armed struggle as the only way to achieve power. It considers the 30 September movement as indicative for this deviation in that it characterizes it as a result of 'suicidial leftist policies'. In this, strangely enough from a theoretical point of view, the Appeal finds itself fully in league with the 'self-criticism' which termed the 30 September movement 'leftist adventurism'. But for the rest Aidit's policies in the eyes of those who exercised 'self-criticism' were to be rejected as too cautious and 'rightist'. As to the party as an organization, the criticism of the two documents runs remarkably parallel, both seeing negative traits in its previously praised mass-character and in Aidit's personal handling of the party affairs. Agreement also existed about the charge that, under Aidit, nationalist aims had precedence over class interest. But to the Appeal, this meant (eventually) the wrong type of 'anti-imperialist', that is, anti-Soviet policy, while according to the 'self-criticism' it had resulted in too great a preoccupation with foreign issues in general to the detriment of the class-war at home. Finally, the 'self-criticism' saw the relations with the Soviet bloc as still too friendly, while the Appeal harked back to the happier relationships of earlier times.

As to the P.K.I.'s future, the two documents presented completely contradictory visions – armed peasant revolt or a broad united front,[44] the only common element being the irrelevancy of this kind of advice given the sorry state of the party, in which it would remain for years to come.

The Appeal is the only one of the two documents to pay attention to the '30 September movement' in some detail, even claiming to base itself on an 'analysis of the facts'. The responsibility of leading members of the P.K.I. is assumed as self-evident, and the affair is defined as 'a movement spearheaded against the coup, a movement that overthrew the General's Council and was *at the same time* a revolutionary movement aimed at the establishment of a state power that would be a harbinger of a people's democracy' [emphasis added].[45]

Subandrio's intelligence reports on the General's Council made the party move (take 'preventive steps') after an expanded meeting of the party leadership.[46] The 'Movement' failed because of the 'recklessness' of some party leaders, of the 'muddleheadedness' in ideology and organization, and because of 'excessive revolutionary zeal, a desire to achieve a quick victory'. The failure to get the masses on their side and to create a people's militia, while after things had gone awry the party rank and file had committed 'shameful mass surrender' and the party leadership had shown 'passivity and panic' were cited as concrete mistakes.

This interpretation of the events around October 1, 1965 seems to indicate that the authors were willing to take evidence presented before the military tribunal in the trials against Njono, Subandrio, and possibly Omar Dhani as valid. No inclination was shown to minimize the involvement of the party, as Sudisman was to do at his trial[47] and had done to a certain extent in the 'self-criticism'; while the P.K.I. leader did his utmost to limit the responsibility for the '30 September movement' to a few leaders, the Appeal implicated a much wider group with reference to the 'expanded meeting' of August 28, 1965.

Apart from representing the view of a number of 'moderate' P.K.I.-emigrés, the Appeal, with its rather unnecessary pro-Soviet slant, can be seen as coming close to the opinion that must have prevailed at the time of writing (winter 1966-1967) in Moscow.[48] From the period immediately after the Untung coup until the time that the appeal was prepared and published, the Soviet media had basically taken the line that the '30 September movement' was an internal affair of the army.[49] But then a more critical note was to be detected in Soviet publications on the events of October 1965 and the role of the P.K.I.,[50] reflecting similar opinions as given in the Appeal published in March 1967 in Ceylon. Thus Pravda, commemorating the P.K.I.'s 47th anniversary, referred to 'documents circulated recently by various groups in Indonesia', from which could be deduced that the party leadership had committed serious errors in the period leading up to October 1965.[51]

This reappraisal from the Soviet side of the responsibility of the P.K.I. coincided with a harsher view of Sukarno. The Indonesian President had been fighting a rearguard battle ever since he had been told by then Major-General Suharto on October 1 that he should leave the airbase of Halim forthwith and detach himself from the putschists.[52] At the end of 1966 this tug-of-war with the 'New Order' that Suharto, Nasution, Malik, and others were trying to establish came to a head with the arrest of Sudisman but especially of Brigadier-General Supardjo, the military leader of the Untung coup and main liaison-officer between Sukarno and the P.K.I. both before and during the purge of the generals of October 1, 1965.

For sime time the whereabouts of Supardjo had been known to the Indonesian military, but his arrest was timed in such a way as to exert maximum pressure on President Sukarno.[53] Evidence had been mounting all through 1966 that Sukarno had played a prominent role in the elimination of the army's general staff.[54] Within the military establishment strong voices were heard saying that the President be tried for the part he had played, and General Suharto was between two fires. Sukarno was pressed hard to give the Indonesian parliament his view of the 1965 coup and finally gave his explanation (on January 10, 1967, in a written statement) asserting that the arrest and murder of the generals had been to him a 'complete surprise'. According to Sukarno those responsible for the coup had been the leadership of the P.K.I., western subversive organizations, and a number of incompetent 'cranks'.

This inadequate account by the President made Suharto – or possibly some more anti-Sukarno military in a position to do so – decide to have Supardjo arrested two days later. With the military brain of the '30 September movement' as a trump card, the screws were now put on Sukarno. The trial of Supardjo was to take place in the second half of February and was postponed for several days, until finally Sukarno gave in under the weight of evidence against him, reinforced as it was with what Supardjo had to say in camera about Sukarno's involvement.[55] An announcement was made in the name of the President that 'realizing that political conflict in the country needs to be ended for the sake of the people, the state and the nation' he would transfer 'authority' to General Suharto. The deal was clinched and Supardjo could now be tried (the trial began February 23, 1967) without the need to have him divulge publicly Sukarno's direct responsibility for the Untung affair and the murder of the generals. General Suharto, to the end reluctant to dispose of Sukarno (both out of considerations of loyalty and of political expediency) addressed the People's Congress, the Indonesian Parliament, on March 7, 1967 with a sober speech. He criticized Sukarno for his protection of the P.K.I. but declared that the life-time President who was about to be stripped of his power did not appear to have master-minded the plot or even played an important role in the Untung coup. Suharto, however, added the proviso that this opinion stood 'unless there are facts we haven't been able to discover until this very day'.[56] On March 12 Sukarno was declared by parliament to have lost all his presidential powers and General Suharto was made Acting President with special authority to decide on a trial of Sukarno, a discretion that was never used.[57]

Soon after the final fall of Sukarno the Soviet press began to react, stepping up its criticism of the former Indonesian President, who had been spared hard words until then. His foreign alignment against the Soviet-Union – in Afro-Asian affairs – and his reckless extremism in the Malaysia confrontation leading to isolation and economic disaster were now openly attacked.[58] No mention was yet made of his – possible – role in the 30 September movement, but it was noted that 'historians still have to tell us how great was the personal responsibility of Dr. Sukarno for what Indonesia had to endure'.[59] It is fair to assume that the impact of both the trials of 1966-1967 and the demise of Sukarno – and its background – had caused the Soviet leaders to reconsider their interpretation of the Untung coup. They arrived at the version transpiring from the Appeal of the 'Marxist-Leninist Group' of the P.K.I. To some extent a different version (the previous Soviet view that the Untung coup had been an 'internal affair' of the Army)[60] was again ventilated but official Soviet opinion tended to settle for the one that was given in the pro-Soviet Appeal.[61] An extensive comparison of the two major documents – the Appeal for the 'Marxist-Leninist Group' and the 'self-criticism' of the Sudisman-P.K.I – in a specialist Soviet magazine[62] illustrated this, as it approvingly followed the explanation of events and attitudes the Appeal had given. More than the 'Marxist-Leninist Group' this Soviet analysis advanced the negative effect of communists participating in the Indonesian government and getting blamed for its actions, while at the same time they were excluded from the 'really decisive organs of power'.[63] But for the rest it was in agreement with the pro-Soviet group and specifically rejected the charge leveled in the 'self-criticism' that it was 'revisionism' that had caused the P.K.I. to fail in its mission. It called the Appeal 'useful for working out a program of action with which to try to raise the Communist Party of Indonesia from the ruins'.[64]

In an article in the leading theoretical journal *Kommunist*[65] in the spring of 1968 the current Soviet views on the P.K.I. and its decline are again found with due emphasis on the issues within international communist movement and the Indonesian communists' attitude towards them. On the Untung coup it is again accepted that the P.K.I. gave its support. However the Central Committee and *a fortiori* the rank and file of the party were discharged from responsibility.[66] In line with the newly found critical tone in respect of Sukarno, one of the main mistakes of the P.K.I. is said to have been its 'total and unconditional' support of the Indonesian President.[67] A change in the overall attitude of the Soviet party was again to be noted in the summer of 1968, probably as a result of the suppression of the last remnants of armed resistance of the Hutapea-group in the Blitar area in East Java[68] and of other army actions eliminating local P.K.I. strongholds. The Soviet press was not slow to blame Peking for inspiring Indonesian communist underground groups to 'go off into the jungle to organize partisan warfare against the 400,000 strong government army... This line led to the death of more hundreds of patriots'.[69] But, at the same time, there was again a reassessment of the P.K.I. as a participant in the Untung-coup. In a commentary on Moscow Radio in September 1968 it was again claimed that 'there are no grounds for accusing the P.K.I. of having been involved in the September 30 movement'.[70] It is not unlikely that this renewed preoccupation with the fate of the Indonesian comrades[71] was intimately linked with the Sino-Soviet rivalry, Moscow seeing a chance of ridiculing Mao's ideas on the need and ultimate success of gun-barrel communism. In November 1968 both Yusuf Adjitorop, the emigré-leader of the China-based P.K.I. group, and the Chinese Communist Party itself were under fire from Moscow because they had failed to condemn the executions of Njono and Sudisman.[72] Other signs that published opinion in the Soviet Union had entered a state of flux was a word of praise for Aidit and his successful efforts to rehabilitate the P.K.I. after the Madiun rebellion of 1948[73] and (in a way implying the opposite) a recommendation to consider armed action against the Suharto regime, providing that it should not become 'a display of revolutionary impatience' as the Maoists would show but a seriously prepared armed struggle.[74] As to the background of the Untung putsch no new visions were advanced from the Soviet side by early 1969, except that a new Soviet-inspired program of the 'Marxist-Leninist

Group' of the P.K.I.[75] even more squarely and unconditionally than before blamed the events leading to October 1, 1965, on the 'Maoist policy of incitement to armed uprising before the situation was ripe'. This program, apparently formulated under a post-Blitar shock, also gave a revised opinion on the use of force by Indonesian communists, compared with the Appeal of the Group of two years earlier. It was recognized that the parliamentary or peaceful road to power was rather improbable and force perhaps the only way. But this view was qualified by demands that first the P.K.I. should be rebuilt and should dispose of armed units. Above all, there should be 'a clearcut revolutionary crisis that would bring about a revolutionary situation'. By then this seemed a rather unnecessary caution for the handful of Indonesian communists willing to think about the future of a new P.K.I. So while, since the dark days of October 1965, the Soviet view of the past and future of the P.K.I. had fluctuated between a certain respect for facts and a distinct need for tactical convenience, the Chinese comrades were developing their own approach.

Given the closeness of the P.K.I. and the Chinese Communist Party prior to the Untung coup, this approach turned out to be surprisingly narrow in scope. As we have seen Aidit and his group were soon dropped as a factor to be reckoned with, once the P.K.I. chairman had sunk his chance and Sukarno appeared unwilling or not in a position to come to his rescue.[76] In the course of 1966 the Adjitorop group was given the chance to operate more publicly[77] and peddled the use of violence as the best way out of the rut the P.K.I. had got into. The Chinese government, at its wit's end over what to do given the drastic setback it had suffered in Indonesia, began to advertise Adjitorop's view,[78] and by the end of the year 1966 the organization of the pro-Peking faction, both in Peking[79] and in Tirana, seems to have been shaped up a bit, establishing direct lines with the underground P.K.I. in Central and East Java.[80] But it took the Chinese leadership a considerable amount of time before they came out with a summary of the views expounded by the Sudisman group in August and September 1966. It was not until July 1967 that both the August 17, 1966, Statement and the 'self-criticism'[81] were published in shortened version by the official Chinese news agency.[82] The Chinese rendering did not add anything new or even mildly interesting that would illuminate the current view of the Chinese C.P. except that the news bulletin opened the story with what it thought was most important: 'To achieve complete victory, the Indonesian revolution must take the road of the Chinese revolution, i.e. adopt as its main form of struggle the armed agrarian revolution of the peasants under the leadership of the proletariat'.[83] To endorse Sudisman's version of events and policies of the P.K.I. it took the Chinese officially another five months,[84] and no doubt it would not be amiss to attribute this odd and uncoordinated pattern of reactions to the fate of the PK.I. to the turmoil China was then in due to the Cultural Revolution.[85] The basic theme, developed in the eighth plenary session of the Central Committee of the Chinese C.P. in August 1966,[86] kept recurring in the following years with no variation: the P.K.I. had learned 'the incontrovertible truth of the great leader Chairman Mao that "political power grows out of the barrel of a gun" ', and the Indonesian Party would act accordingly, it was continuously asserted. That this precept of Mao's worked in practice was claimed in exaggerated terms by the Chinese press, in reports of armed struggle in several areas of Java and Kalimantan.[87] On the substance of the events of October 1, 1965 no original Chinese contribution has appeared so far.

Outside the circle of immediately interested parties, like the P.K.I. itself and the communist leadership in Moscow and Peking, a wide array of opinion has been formed on the Indonesian communists and their downfall in the aftermath of the Untung coup. Scholars, writers, and journalists have contributed since 1965 to a host of literature on the subject and covered extensive ground. A major 'school of thought' has sprung up on the assumption that the Untung coup was what it professed to be: A revolutionary action against a corrupt and wicked clique of generals, an internal affair of the army.[88] Its bible is – or should one say has been – the well-known Cornell-report[89] that circulated since early 1966 among a restricted number of people. An intricately argued reconstruction of the events that had led up to and followed October 1, 1965 ended with the dictum that 'the October 1st group was essentially an internal army affair, stemming from a small clique in the Diponegoro Division in Central Java, which attempted to use both Sukarno and the P.K.I. leadership for its own ends, and succeeded merely in irreparably damaging the moral and political authority of the one, and causing the physical destruction of the other'.[90] Alternative possibilities further were rejected one by one t.w., the P.K.I.

acting on its own, a planned move by Sukarno with or without the P.K.I., Untung acting completely on his own, and an unplanned spontaneous move by Sukarno or by others. Here is not the place to consider the arguments used to dismiss these four cases as lacking in substance,[91] nor for that matter the arguments and evidence adduced for the 'internal army affair' version, except to say that the report was remarkable for its clever reasoning and for an utter lack of facts. Written within three months after the Untung coup took place, this deficiency in documentation should not come as a surprise, but all the more astonishing is the wide and lasting effect the Cornell report had upon what normally passes as informed opinion.

The report left a trail of publications in its wake but being distributed on a 'strictly confidential' basis, authors who clearly had access to it apparently did not want to refer to it.[92] A few notable examples such as that of Dr. Wertheim[93] and Lucien Rey[94] initially set the tone for the conviction, especially in western academic circles, that in fact some obscure army officers rooted deeply in Central and Eastern Javanese soil, had braced themselves in the course of 1965 to do away with a handful of decadent generals.[95] Some of these authors have delved deeper and have come up with the construction that what motivated Untung and his companions in Djakarta was inspired by the unsettled, 'revolutionary' situation prevailing since 1964 in the Eastern and Central Javanese countryside. Wertheim was one of the first to draw attention to this possible aspect of what had happened in the Indonesian capital,[96] and his views were reflected later in the doctoral thesis of one of his students, Dr. Basuki Gunawan.[97] There is no doubt that when the P.K.I., in the course of 1964, stepped up its actions in the countryside – the 'aksi sepihak' or unilateral actions to implement extra-legally the land reform laws of 1960 – it began to generate the atmosphere that later was to explode into scenes of mass murder in the wake of the Untung coup.[98] But neither the more superficial 'young Turks' theory of Rey and company, nor the socio-economic 'restive peasants' explanation of Wertheim had done anything to illuminate the palace intrigues in faraway Djakarta in the period before October 1, 1965.

While the Cornell report rejected P.K.I. involvement in the Untung coup except 'peripherally' by some members of communist mass organizations[99] and Wertheim followed suit,[100] Rey already had more difficulties with the accumulated evidence that by the spring of 1966 tended seriously to implicate the P.K.I.[101] McVey early in 1967 still tended to stick to her earlier anonymous opinion, albeit slightly modified, opting for a passive role of the Indonesian communists: 'The P.K.I. appears to have undertaken the encouragement of 'progressive-revolutionary' officers who wished to prevent a move by the generals, and from the beginning of September [*sic*] it prepared its local cadres to meet an expected situation of emergency in the capital'.[102]

Dahm, writing in 1970, could still not see the role of Aidit as more than that of a reluctant participant in the 30 September plot.[103] Wertheim, too over the years, remained convinced that the leadership of the P.K.I. had nothing to do with the Untung coup.[104]

Collusion between Untung and the P.K.I. is also widely accepted by those who for the rest are reluctant to blame the Indonesian Communist Party too much for what happened. The most common explanation then put forward is that both partners in the '30 September movement' at a given moment decided to stage a preventive coup in order to take over the initiative from a group of army leaders who were supposedly conspiring in the Council of Generals against Sukarno and the P.K.I.[105] It is possible that the P.K.I. leaders (Aidit, Lukman, Njoto) really believed that organized opposition among the army general staff existed and that a coup was imminent, but since no evidence of concrete plans whatsoever of this type have since been adduced,[106] it can be safely assumed that they themselves considered it only part of the 'psy-war' that went on and that it was a useful ploy to keep the P.K.I. cadres motivated.[107] In Soviet circles, too, doubt as to the soundness of the charge was voiced immediately after the Untung coup,[108] although for the sake of expediency Soviet opinion later went along with the P.K.I.'s contention.[109] McVey still gives some credence to the 'army plot' as having had some substance in fact, notwithstanding the total absence of any proof. She is of the opinion that 'the army leadership (in particular the group of seven generals attacked by Untung's "September 30 movement" which constituted what amounted to the army's politburo) had come to debate whether . . . it might not be necessary to act before Sukarno's natural passing from the scene'.[110] Adherents to the 'preventive coup' theory so rationalized the fact that the P.K.I. – and to a lesser degree also Untung and company – had made up its mind to move against the generals, explaining the timing of the whole affair with reference to Sukarno's allegedly imminent death in July-August 1965.[111] A lot of inaccurate reporting and contagious legend has spread around what the pro-Soviet 'Appeal to the brothers at home, etc.' referred to when it ironically stated 'had a revolution occurred [in October 1965] it would have been based not on the revolutionary situation, on the support of the revolutionary masses, but would rather have hinged on Sukarno's lesioned kidneys'.[112] Without knowing all the details now available, writers as Hughes[113] and McVey[114] at an early stage expressed doubt as to the precise relevance of Sukarno's state of health prior to the Untung coup. Others have been less discerning and have gone along.

The crucial element in the fateful destiny of the Indonesian communists, the role played by Sukarno in the '30 September movement', has naturally drawn the attention of those engaged in deciphering the facts. At the end of the spectrum is the Cornell report that proclaimed his innocence although admitting that he got somewhat involved after the coup. Experts on Indonesia like Hindley[115] and Dahm[116] maintained that the Indonesian President was left uninformed in advance of what could happen on the night of October 1, 1965. From McVey's paper on Indonesian communism and China one could conclude implicitly that she too, in essence, exonerates Sukarno as to his actions before the massacre of the generals.[117] At the other end are Hughes,[118] Brackman,[119] and Van der Kroef[120] who asserted that Sukarno was privy to the plot, but they have only reasoning and some circumstantial evidence to support their allegation. Hughes, who comes nearest to the truth, still does not see Sukarno as the man who wrote out an order for the 'generals' removal'.[121]

In describing or analyzing events the authors, fascinated by the subject, have posed many questions they have had to leave unanswered: Why did the P.K.I. act against its previous policy of 'patient practice'?[122] Why were 'the causes of army disaffection not known with certainty'?[123] 'For what reason could the communists give so clearly the impression of having burned their boats behind them'?[124] What made the P.K.I. act 'like a party that had been compelled prematurely to put its plan into action'?[125] Further, could it be true that Aidit and the P.K.I. leadership, in 'contemplating the need for reducing the anti-communist military leadership . . . considered acting without Sukarno, their benefactor, sole effective protector and ally against the military'?[126]

It is clear by now that it was Sukarno's towering personality and suspicious megalomania, using others and being used, who held the key to these mysteries. 'The order of the past is the order that should be followed; do not dimly follow the scriptures; conscientiously keep to the main thread, the essence of what is: keep down passion, unceasingly rising'.[127] For those who searched for the meaning of events in Indonesia in the years described, the warning seems particularly apt but not always heeded.

NOTES

1. The Indonesian Communist Party, *The Interpreter*, The Hague, November 1968, p. 12.
2. Dr. Guy Pauker, in an evaluation of the 30 September movement, put at the disposal of the author draws the attention to these summary executions of the four leaders of the P.K.I. in 1965 and 1966 as 'very regrettable, leaving gaps in our information which will not be filled'. Others including Sudisman, the most important P.K.I. leader left – were not to be put to death, he notes, without due process: 'A reading of the records [of the military tribunals] reveals that once the decision was made – or it happened by accident – that their lives be spared, these individuals were investigated and tried according to procedures which may differ in detail from the principles of Anglo-American evidence but represent a genuine legal process.'

   The decision to shoot without trial, or to try and execute legally, the leaders of the P.K.I. may very well have been contingent upon both the attitude of the persons involved and upon their knowledge of Sukarno's role. Those shot summarily – besides Aidit certainly Lukman and Njoto – as members of the party's unofficial Dewan Harian, or Executive Board, must have had full inside information on Sukarno and his plans for the army generals. It is quite logical to assume that under interrogation they brought this aspect to the fore. Of Aidit Brackman reports, citing an 'unimpeachable source', that the P.K.I. chairman when arrested, declared: 'If you shoot me, you will also have to shoot the President'; Arnold C. Brackman, 1969, *The Communist Collapse in Indonesia,* W. W. Norton and Co., New York, p. 111. This charge against the President must have been rejected by the military at the time, either as not deserving of belief or as too dangerous to be known, and it must have contributed to the immediate execution of the P.K.I. leader. Sukarno, consulted by Suharto the day before the emerging army strong man left suddenly for Central Java at the end of November 1965, probably could or would not oppose the untried end of Aidit. See Hughes, 1967, *Indonesian Upheaval*, David McKay, New

York, p. 166. Sudisman, who initially wanted to be shot also without trial, decided for making a public defense of the party, possibly on the condition that he would not implicate Sukarno. Similarly, Subandrio, Omar Dhani, and Supardjo must have consented 'to play the game' and to leave out the President's part in exchange for a trial and – as far as the ex-Foreign Minister and ex-Air Force Chief was concerned – for a non-execution of the dealth sentence.

3. *Information Bulletin*, 1966, Peace and Socialism Publishers, Prague, no. 5.
4. See p. 427.
5. *Indonesian Tribune*, 1966, vol. 1, no. 1: Hold aloft the good name and honor of the communist. The *Indonesian Tribune* was published in the Albanian capital Tirana from November 1966 onward and was the mouthpiece of the pro-Chinese faction of the P.K.I. rump.
6. On international affairs the statement continued the pre-30 September 1965 P.K.I. tradition of rejecting modern revisionism as 'harming the international proletarian struggle and the national liberation movement'.
7. Hold aloft, etc. *Indonesian Tribune*, 1966, vol. 1, no. 1.
8. Take the Road of Revolution to Realize the Tasks Which Should Have Been Accomplished by the 1945 August Revolution, *Indonesian Tribune*, 1966, vol. 1, no. 1, sometimes erroneously referred to as the 'self-criticism' of the underground P.K.I.
9. See above p. 8 ff.
10. Take the Road etc., *Indonesian Tribune*, 1966, vol. 1, no. 1.
11. The one to entertain that 'empty illusion' was of course none other than Aidit, who had developed his 'two aspects' theory of state-power, the state being at one and the same time in the service of the exploiting and of the exploited classes; see above p. 234 note 20.
12. See also above p. 239 note 67.
13. Sudisman (not for long) headed what has been called the second P.K.I. Central Committee, after the one that was in function at the time of the 30 September movement, and preceding the third C.C. under Hutapea. See Dr. Justus M. van der Kroef, Indonesian Communism Since the 1965 Coup, *Pacific Affairs*, October 1969.
14. Build the P.K.I. along the Marxist-Leninist line to lead the People's Democratic Revolution in Indonesia, *Indonesian Tribune*, 1969, vol. 1, no. 3, January.
15. Ruth McVey writes in this respect that 'it seems likely that the authority of the Chinese example was being used, as it had been by Aidit 15 years previously, to give doctrinal legitimacy to a still uncertain leadership. In any event, the reliance on Maoist authority seemed not to be coupled to hopes of Chinese intervention, for it was stressed that the Indonesian agrarian revolution "cannot be enforced from outside" '; see Ruth McVey, Indonesian Communism and China. In: Tang Tsou, Ed., 1968, *China in Crisis*, vol. 2, University of Chicago Press, Chicago, p. 393.
16. Build the P.K.I., etc., *Indonesian Tribune*, 1967, vol. 1, no. 3, p. 9. Special

mention is made of the unauthorized change by Aidit of the election manifest for the 1955 elections, after the 5th Party Congress of 1954 had laid down the line (see above p. 22) and of the Party's endorsement of the conclusions of the 20th Party Congress of the CPSU as far as a peaceful transition to communism was concerned (see above p. 35).

17. Build the P.K.I. etc., *Indonesian Tribune*, 1967, vol. 1, no. 3, p. 9
18. Build the P.K.I. etc., quotes Aidit as if in his report to that 2nd plenary in December 1960 he had coined the slogan 'placing class interest under national interest'. In fact he had been less extreme in his formulation, saying in his report to the 2nd plenum that 'the tasks of the Indonesian revolution are to establish the political authority not of just one class, one group, or one party, but the political authority of all the People, the authority of gotong-rojong'. See *Harian Rakjat*, January 2, 1961. This was a rendering by Aidit of the relevant decision made by the Indonesian parliament in its session between November 10 and December 7, 1960 to accept Sukarno's dictate for all political parties. It is true that he – together with the other members of the Politburo – suggested to the assembled comrades that they should accept the decision of Indonesian parliament and bring the Party Constitution into accord with it.
19. See above p. 117.
20. Build the P.K.I., etc., *Indonesian Tribune*, 1967, vol. 1, no. 3, p. 19. A practical lesson for the underground comrades in 1966 was drawn from this *ex post facto* interpretation: 'The primary task of the Indonesian revolution at the present moment is the overthrow of the rule of the reactionary classes within the country, who represent the interests of the imperialists, in particular the United States imperialists'; see Build the P.K.I. etc., *Indonesian Tribune*, 1967, vol. 1, no. 3, p. 20. The Moscow-orientated version 'The brothers at home, etc.' also sees the 2nd plenary of the Central Committee of the P.K.I. in December 1960 as the occasion for the Party to make 'a cardinal mistake in the field of theory [with] the thesis of "subordinating class interests to national interests" '. It comes, however, to a different, less practical conclusion; see p. 430.
21. 45 years of the Indonesian Communist Party, *Harian Rakjat*, May 7, 1945. 1945.
22. Build the P.K.I., etc., *Indonesian Tribune*, 1967, vol. 1, no. 3, p. 20.
23. Build the P.K.I., etc., *Indonesian Tribune*, 1967, vol. 1, no. 3, p. 21. See also *Harian Rakjat*, August 17, 1945.
24. An indication that Aidit gave only summary information to the party leadership is given by Sudisman in his lengthy, dignified 'justification' at his trial. According to Sudisman, Aidit had only told the Politburo that 'progressive officers' wanted to prevent a coup by the Council of Generals and issued only an instruction to the regional branches to listen to the announcements of Radio Indonesia: 'Such an important question should have been discussed in the plenary session of the C.C. of the P.K.I. because of its national relevancy'; see proceedings of the trial of Sudisman, June 1967. In

describing this and other factors related to the 30 September movement, Sudisman added: 'It is not my intention to deny that persons of the P.K.I. were directly involved in the 30 September movement. No, as I have explained, the leadership of the P.K.I., including myself, were involved in the 30 September movement, but the P.K.I. as Party was not'. *Indonesian Tribune*, 1967, vol. 1, no. 3. It had clearly been Sudisman's intention by his public stand at the trial to provide a platform for the Indonesian communist movement, from which on a more propitious occasion they could stage a comeback, as happened in 1951, three years after the Madiun rebellion.

25. The 'self-criticism' comments: [To achieve complete victory the Indonesian revolution must also follow the road of the Chinese revolution ... [which] has laid down the general law for the revolution of the peoples in colonial or semi-colonial and semi-feudal countries'; *Indonesian Tribune*, 1967, vol. 1, no. 3, p. 11.
26. On the contrary, one could say, as he had never shown much affinity with the Njoto-type of high-brow foreign-political radicalism that emerged increasingly in the period of 1963-1965 and put the P.K.I. in this sense on Peking's side.
27. For the first time Adjitorop's group had acted independently with a message, sent on March 31, 1966, to the pro-Chinese Communist Party of New Zealand, saying that one day the party would 'resume its responsibilities towords the proletariate', but that this would not be by peaceful means. See also *The Indonesian Communist Party*, Interpreter, The Hague, November 1968, p. 22.
28. In October 1966 the P.K.I. Politburo in Central Java reported the expulsion of *Harian Rakjat's* Moscow correspondent Anwar Dharma, from the Soviet Union a month previously; *New China News Agency*, January 28, 1967. The P.K.I. Politburo then expressed gratitude to Peking for their 'assistance to Indonesian communists now in Peking'. Later Dharma wrote a letter (probably from Tirana where he went after Peking) resembling closely the points made in the P.K.I. August 1966 Statement.
29. This group must have numbered around 500 people, mostly P.K.I. members, who remained in China where they had come to celebrate the anniversary celebrations in Peking on October 1, 1965.
30. 'To brothers at home and comrades abroad fighting against imperialism for independence, peace, democracy and socialism, for a sound Indonesian Revolution', *Information Bulletin*, 1967, Peace and Socialism Publishers, Prague, no. 18, p. 40.
31. Tribune Publications, Colombo, Ceylon, March 1967.
32. Indonesian Tragedy; A Communist Re-appraisal, *Mainstream*, March 11 and 18, 1967.
33. Hanafiah, the Indonesian ambassador to Ceylon at the time of the 30 September movement, had refused to obey an order to return to Djakarta and at first remained in Ceylon. He eventually turned up in Moscow, where

he headed the Moscow-based pro-Soviet P.K.I. wing. It is not excluded that he lent his not-too-impressive authority to the Appeal.

34. *Information Bulletin*, 1967, p. 63.
35. See above p. 75 and the discussion within the party in the spring of 1960.
36. *Information Bulletin*, 1967, p. 53 writes: '... under present historical conditions, especially after the emergence of the world socialist system, *there are chances* of a peaceful victory for the revolution. Whether revolution can develop peacefully or not depends largely on concrete historical conditions in each individual country'.
37. *Information Bulletin*, 1967, p. 54. The conclusion of the 'self-criticism' that a 'dualism' existed as the use or non-use of force is more to the point: 'The Party leadership held that the better the Party prepared itself to face the possibility of a non-peaceful road, the greater would be the possibility of a "peaceful road" '. In practice the Party leadership did not prepare the whole ranks of the Party, the working class and the masses of the people to face the possibility of a non-peaceful road. The most striking proof of it was the tragedy which occurred after the outbreak and the failure of the September 30th movement'; see Build the P.K.I., etc., *Indonesian Tribune*, 1967, vol. 1, no. 3, p. 12.
38. See above pp. 104, 444 note 18.
39. *Information Bulletin*, 1967, p. 46.
40. The international communist issues as they had split the world communist movement and influenced the P.K.I. were given a lot of attention in the Appeal and were fully in accordance with the Soviet point of view. Characteristically, the 'self-criticism' had not wasted a word on it.
41. See above p. 427. The Appeal wrote: 'Lenin taught us that revolutions are not made to order. A revolution must needs be preceded by a revolutionary situation. The objective symptoms of a revolutionary situation are as follows: the inability of the ruling classes to hold power in its old form. Usually, it is not sufficient for a revolution to occur when the lower classes do not want to live as before. What is needed is that the upper classes, too, cannot live as before;...' etc. The self-criticism quotes Lenin from 'Two Tactics of Social Democracy in the Democratic Revolution': 'According to Lenin a revolutionary situation, or a revolutionary period, is a period "when the the old super-structure has cracked from top to bottom; when open political action on the part of the classes and masses who are creating a new superstructure for themselves has become a fact" '.
42. *Information Bulletin*, 1967, p. 57, 58.
43. *Information Bulletin*, 1967, p. 44. This was an early criticism from the Soviet side, vide Kruschov who supposedly warned Aidit that a communist party was not a grocery store where one tried to sell as much rubbish as possible.
44. See for the opinion that both documents accept the revisionist 1954 party program Rex Mortimer, Indonesia: Emigré post mortems on the P.K.I., *Asian Survey*, November 1967.
45. *Information Bulletin*, 1967, p. 54.

46. Reference is here made to the Politburo meeting of August 28, 1965, at which as far as the P.K.I. was concerned the final decision was taken to go ahead with the 'preventive coup'. The members and candidate members of the Buro were present as well as regional representatives and some members of the Central Committee.
47. See below p. 448 note 66.
48. Rex Mortimer, Indonesia; Emigré post-mortems on the P.K.I. *Asian Survey*, November 1967.
49. See above p. 417. An article in the Soviet weekly *Literary Gazette* of April 16, 1966, described the Untung coup as 'a culmination point... a conflict between various forces united by the concept of Nasakom'. It further tried to distinguish between the P.K.I. and 'communist ideology', showing a willingness on the Soviet side to sacrifice the P.K.I. in order to save whatever was possible of a remnant 'communist' cause: 'anti-communism in any form is incompatible with the revolutionary and democratic movement'. See also Peter Howard, The U.S.S.R. and Indonesia, *Mizan Newsletter*, May-June 1967, who notes that in 1966 the Soviet communist view did not deny participation of the P.K.I. leaders in the Untung coup but maintained they were 'misled by outside forces'.
50. Van der Kroef, Indonesia's 'Gestapu': The view from Moscow and Peking, *The Australian Journal of Politics and History*, November 1968, p. 164.
51. *Pravda*, May 28, 1967.
52. See above p. 408.
53. Dr. E. L. C. Schiff, ranking Dutch diplomat. See also John Hughes, 1967, *Indonesian Upheaval*, McKay Company, New York, p. 280. Hughes writes that the arrest of Supardjo, two days after Sukarno's unsatisfactory explanation of the Untung coup, 'might have been pure coincidence'. It was not.
54. Hughes, 1967, p. 270, 277.
55. Dr. E. L. C. Schiff, ranking Dutch diplomat.
56. Hughes, 1967, p. 282. It is accepted now in informed circles in Indonesia that this condition was a built-in caution that might have stretched the truth as then known quite seriously, but with good intentions.
57. Sukarno died in June 1970 in his palace at Bogor, where he had been confined ever since the loss of his presidential powers.
58. See Howard Jones, 1971, *The Impossible Dream*, Harcourt, Brace, Jovanovich, Inc., New York, p. 112.
59. *Komsomolskaya Pravda*, March 19, 1967.
60. Suchahya, The 'New Order' in Indonesia, *World Marxist Review*, October 1967, who says it was 'absurd' to hold the P.K.I. as a whole responsible for the October putsch, while at most 'some individual members' had been to blame.
61. *Pravda* carried a message on the 50th anniversary of the October Revolution from Indonesian Communists said to be operating underground and who realized the errors of the theoretical principles they used to adhere to in the past. *Pravda*, November 9, 1967.

62. A. B. Reznikov, *Narody Azii i Afriki*, 1968, no. 1, pp. 35-50.
63. Here Reznikov seems to endorse without actually saying so, the views of the 'self-criticism' where it vehemently rejected Aidit's theoretical underpining of his revisionist policies, the doctrine of the 'two aspects' of state power. The same theme of the consequences of P.K.I. collaboration with the 'bourgeoisie' had been very soon dealt with after the Untung putsch in the issue of *Izvestia* of March 15, 1966.
64. The disastrous influence of the Chinese Communist Party on the P.K.I. and the resultant anti-Soviet position taken by the Indonesian communists, especially after December 1963 is given extra weight by Reznikov to a greater extent than by the Appeal.
65. Some Lessons of the Events in Indonesia, *Kommunist*, no. 15, 1968, pp. 110-123.
66. The distinction Sudisman had tried to make at his trial between a small inner core of a few Politburo members being responsible for the '30 September movement', and all other P.K.I. members who had remained innocent may also have been understood in Moscow for its useful implications for the future of the P.K.I.
67. Contrary to the Appeal and to Reznikov, *Kommunist* dates the beginning of the P.K.I.'s shift towards the 'Mao Tse-Tung-line' from the end of 1962. At the end of 1962, the P.K.I. on a number of issues like Cuba and Malaysia had shifted to the left, away from Soviet endorsed positions.
68. The major action in East Java began on June 8, 1968 with the 'Operation Trisula', resulting in the capture or death of over 850 communists including Hutapea who was among those who did not survive. See *Angkatan Bersendjata*, August 10, 1968.
69. See *Litteraturnaja Gazeta*, August 14, 1968.
70. *Moscow Radio in Indonesian*, September 21 and 25, 1968.
71. The Soviet government lodged an official protest against the planned execution of P.K.I. leaders Njono and Sudisman.
72. *Mizan Newsletter*, March-April 1969 and Brackman, 1969, *The Communist Collapse in Indonesia*, W. W. Norton and Co., Inc., New York, p. 163, note 8.
73. *Pravda*, July 30, 1968.
74. *Radio Peace and Progress*, April 5, 1969. See also a commentary in similar vein in *Pravda*, September 14, 1968.
75. This program was published in May 1969 in India; see *Asian Analyst*, 1969.
76. One attempt, though of rather macabre character, was made in this respect on the Chinese side by asserting three weeks after Aidit had been shot that reports on his death were 'a complete fabrication'; see *New China News Agency*, December 2, 1965 and *Peking Review*, December 10, 1965.
77. See above p. 429.
78. *Jen-min Jih-pao*, August 12, 1966, giving a report on the plenary of the Chinese C.C. then in session.
79. See Statement of the Government of the Republic of Indonesia, of Septem-

ber 15, 1966, containing a protest again the presence in China and the activities of the Adjitorop-group.

80. See above p. 429.
81. See above p. 426 ff.
82. *New China News Agency*, July 7, 1967.
83. This is a quite literal quote from the middle part of the 'self-criticism', *Indonesian Tribune*, 1967, vol. 1, no. 3, p. 11.
84. *Hung Qui*, November 11, 1967. A preliminary reaction had been given in *Jen-min Jih-pao*, August 18, 1967.
85. See on this point Brackman, 1969, p. 152. Brackman notes that the Cultural Revolution began on November 10, 1965, only a few weeks after the Untung-coup.
86. *Jen-min Jih-pao*, August 12, 1966.
87. *Peking Review*, January 12, 1968 and February 16, 1968.
88. The first statement broadcast on *Djakarta Radio* on October 1, 1965 at 7:15 a.m. said that 'according to a statement obtained from Lieutenant Colonel Untung, the Commandant of the September 30 movement, this movement is solely a movement within the Army directed against the Council of Generals'.
89. Coup of October 1, 1965, mimeographed report, Januari 10, 1966. It circulated anonymously among some western scholars. The report was introduced with the following caution: 'You will understand, however, that because of the provisional character of the analysis, and because of the repercussions which knowledge of this report may arouse in some quarters, we do not wish it to be given further circulation. This copy is therefore for your eyes only. The material in it is common property; feel free to use it as you wish in publication, but *please do not refer in any way to this document*' [emphasis added]. Five years later, in April 1971, this 'provisional' report was finally published officially by Cornell University, divulging what for a long time had been known: That the authors of the report were Ruth McVey and Benedict R. Anderson, both with Cornell University in 1966, with the assistance of Frederick Bunnell. As a justification for the rather curious way of presenting what pretended to be a scholarly exposition designed 'to develop a factual basis for a more informed discussion of the September 30 movement' – as the new introduction by Anderson ran – it was said that 'if it became known that we had presented a hypothesis, friends and acquaintances of ours, who had no knowledge of our analysis, might yet be held accountable'. A preface by the leader of the Indonesia project of the Cornell University, George Mc T. Kahin with the dateline Djakarta, June 2, 1971, announced that McVey and Anderson were engaged in a 'comprehensive in-depth study of the Untung group and its background' that was to be 'the soundest and most comprehensive yet to appear'. Reference will be to: Cornell report 1966.
90. Cornell report 1966, p. 83.
91. The report comes close to the truth, though assuming that Untung was

operating on his own: 'Mass participation was thus not only not forthcoming but was not desired; but how then could the Untung group have hope to succeed? There would only seem to be one possible explanation for this peculiar approach, namely that the President was the essential figure in the manoeuvre, for if military strength was clearly insufficient and massive demonstrations not counted on, then it must have been Presidential authority that was to tip the scales'; p. 140.

92. See above p. 449, note 89.
93. Dr. W. F. Wertheim, Indonesia Before and After the Untung Coup, *Pacific Affairs*, spring-summer 1966.
94. Lucien Rey, Holocaust in Indonesia, *New Left Review*, March-April 1966.
95. Rey, 1966, p. 36: 'But all we can really say is that the P.K.I. was wrecked by the sudden brusque emergency of forces into the political arena which had been brewing silently in the officers' clubs in Semarang and Djokjakarta, forces it was unable to cope with because unable to predict'.

    J. van Tijn, 1966, The Triumph of the Army and the Mass Murder of the Communists, *Vrij Nederland*, September 24. 'Neither the Army nor the P.K.I. who had been spying upon each other for years, had counted on a coup such as Untung's'.

    Ruth McVey, Indonesian Communism and China. In Tang Tsou, Ed., 1968, *China in Crisis*, vol. 2, University of Chicago Press, Chicago, p. 383: 'So far it is impossible to discern whether and how much Sukarno, the P.K.I., the air force and perhaps other parties knew of the cabal, consisting largely of middle-rank Javanese officers to which Untung belonged'.

    Donald Hindley, Alirans and the Fall of the Old Order, *Indonesia*, April 1970, p. 34: 'The (special) Bureau [of the P.K.I.] had discovered within the Air Force strong resentment against the Army's military and political preponderance; within the Army a small number of officers were deeply disgruntled. The causes of this Army disaffection are not known with certainty'.

    Dr. E. Utrecht, 1970, Footnotes to Dewi's letter to General Suharto, *Vrij Nederland*, April 25. 'The standard of living differed increasingly between the corrupt military leaders in Djakarta and the main cities, and the impoverished soldiers . . . At the end of 1964 a small group of officers and subaltern officers of the Brawidjaja-division in East Java began to make plans to remove the Army leadership, etc.'.
96. Wertheim, 1966, p. 130: 'Why did the inevitable clash occur in 1965? The main reason was that the poor peasantry had become restive and could no longer be prevented from voicing claims which did not fit in with Marhaenist [Sukarno's] ideology and the Nasakom political pattern'. In 1970 he repeated this view that the enforced land reform, initiated by the P.K.I. and the violent reactions of the muslim population against it had been the deepest cause of the 'Untung coup'; *De Groene Amsterdammer*, August 7, 1970.
97. Dr. Basuki Gunawan, 1968, *Kudetá, Staatsgreep in Djakarta*, Boom and

Zoon, Meppel, pp. 110, 130.

98. See above p. 245. Wertheim takes a rather naive view of the P.K.I. leaders who initiated the 'aksi sepihak' writing that 'The P.K.I. evidently did not sufficiently realise that, in starting these campaigns against the bigger landowners, they were abandoning Sukarno's diluted socialism and adopting a clear-cut class-struggle position'.
99. Cornell report 1966, p. 124.
100. 'Serious students of Indonesian politics agree that there is little to prove that it was the P.K.I. which started the whole affair – on the contrary, there are many indications disproving such a possibility. But there were a few circumstances which more or less compromised the P.K.I. – for example, the involvement of communist youth groups, receiving military training on Halim airfield near Djakarta, in the murder of the generals though in fact they acted under military orders; and Aidit's presence, not voluntary, on Halim airfield, where the conspirators had established their base (President Sukarno was also taken there)'; Wertheim, 1966, p. 115, 116.
101. Rey, 1966, p. 33, writing that the P.K.I. after the coup 'had already been fatally compromised' further concluded: 'It is difficult to explain these blunders'.
102. Ruth McVey, 1968, p. 383.
103. Bernhard Dahm, 1971, *The History of Indonesia in the Twentieth Century*, Frederick A. Praeger, New York, p. 236: 'It is hard to suppose that he [Aidit], the brilliant P.K.I. theoretician, took a major part in planning the clumsy and abortive coup, but the party was to suffer bitterly for the ineffective support of the "progressive officers"'. Utrecht, 1970, admits that 'some' leaders of the P.K.I. indeed have participated in the 'Untung coup', but not 'The Communists' of Indonesia. He still maintained that the Cornell report is a tenable document.
104. Wertheim, 1966, The Killing of the Communists, *De Groene Amsterdammer*, October 8: 'It is not in the least certain that the leadership of the P.K.I. or some members of the Central Committee played a role of any importance in the preparation and execution of the putsch'.
105. A. B. Reznikov, *Narodi Azii i Afriki*, 1968, no. 1, pp. 35-50; Donald Hindley, *Indonesia*, April 1970; E. Utrecht, *Vrij Nederland*, April 25, 1970; Ruth McVey, 1968, p. 378.
106. See above p. 391.
107. The basic decision whether and when to launch a coup (or rather a purge) was Sukarno's, and was motivated by irritation at being thwarted by the army's staff and not by evidence of their plotting a putsch against him; see above p. .
108. See above pp. 415, 416.
109. Rezkinov, 1968, pp. 35-50.
110. McVey, 1968, p. 378.
111. We have seen that, for other reasons than was the case with the alleged sinister plotting of the Council of Generals, the 'health' issue *followed* the

inception of the '30 September movement' and did not precede or *a fortiori* cause it; see above p. .

112. *Information Bulletin*, 1967, no. 18, p. 58.
113. Hughes, 1967, p. 109.
114. McVey, 1968, p. 379, note 31.
115. Donald Hindley, 1970, p. 35.
116. Dahm, 1971, p. 229.
117. McVey, 1968, p. 388: 'While the New Order's lumping together of Sukarno and the P.K.I. was effective during the period of post-Guided Democracy hangover, it is historically perilous, since it would be easy for a future dissident military or political challenger to claim it was after all the generals and not the founder of the Republic who had betrayed the nation'.
118. Hughes, 1967, pp. 56, 65, 107.
119. Brackman, 1969, p. 11.
120. Van der Kroef, 1969, p. 35.
121. Hughes, 1967, p. 114.
122. Arthur J. Dommen, The attempted coup in Indonesia, *China Quarterly*, January-March 1966, p. 155.
123. Hindley, 1970, p. 34.
124. Gunawan, 1968, p. 189.
125. Hughes, 1967, p. 108.
126. McVey, 1968, pp. 378, 379.
127. From the Nagarakrtagama, a song by the 14th century Javanese poet Prapantja, that served as introduction to the Cornell report.

CHAPTER 31

Conclusion

If we try to pick up the main threads of the picture that the P.KI.. presented in all its wide and colorful ramifications in the twenty years between its re-emergence after the Second World War and its decline at the end of 1965, caution is called for lest the multitude of interacting factors related above are reduced to too simple a pattern. On the other hand a certain risk has to be taken in order to formulate the results of an account that has attempted to let facts speak first and foremost, and to have the conclusions wait.

If we follow the story from the beginning, a first point that can be made is *that the P.K.I., up to the Madiun rebellion of September 1948, could in fact be termed a foreign, i.e. Soviet-dominated, organization.* This is not intended to imply, of course, that all its acts and attitudes were dictated from the outside but means that its policies were influenced decisively by the line prevailing in Moscow where then in spirit and in organization world communism had its command center. Most essential for this relationship of political dependency is, it seems, domestic policy which, as far as the P.K.I. was concerned, and apart from short spells in 1945 and in early 1948, had been in line with first the 'right' and then the 'left' strategy Stalin was pursuing. Soviet influence, bent on frustrating deviations (the Suripno affair) and used to rule by proxy (Muso's mission) was evident. *It was Aidit's merit that he and his team that took over in January 1951 broke through this barrier, which would otherwise have doomed the P.K.I. to continued sectarianism and plain failure.* This basic tenet of independence as a national party was at first buried under the semblance of continuity that covered Aidit's takeover and initially made him fall back on Muso's hard line. Facilitated by Stalin's return to a less rigid, more 'rightist' policy, but more than that forced by Indonesian circumstances (the disintegrating effects of the Sukiman razzia's), Aidit opted for an accommodating posture at home, for a policy of 'support and criticism', of permeation from below and association from above which, given patience and time, would pave the way to power, as it nearly did.

In establishing at an early stage a strong vested interest in independence – and backing this up with mass organizational force – Aidit by no means intended to turn his back on Moscow, let alone break with its leaders. *Rather, he began to substitute as of January 1952, when his new domestic approach took shape, the preponderant dependency upon the Soviet comrades for an affinity, for or an orientation towards their policies.* The underlying preoccupation of Aidit and his closest associates with political and especially organizational independence made them allergic to outside communist interference and was to play a prominent role in the years to come.

In terms of policies to pursue both locally and internationally, no problems were yet in sight, since Stalin's right strategy suited Aidit fine in his attempt to restore the P.K.I. at home to grace and fortune, and because the foreign aspects of international communism did not trouble the P.K.I. leader either. This happy state, however, did not prove a permanent one, and the first inkling that diverging views and interests could crop up came with the 20th Party Congress of the C.P.S.U. in February 1956 and more specifically with the famous secret speech Khruschov then gave. Issues, then brought to light, came close to the core of P.K.I. positions; they were vital to its leaders in their quest for power – e.g., the use of parliamentary methods or the authority of Stalin – and were treated by Aidit and company at that stage of the intra-communist debate in a way that reflected their own interest rather than outside authority. *It would mark the beginning of a dichotomy between what, simply put, could be termed 'domestic' and 'foreign' policy questions, i.e., issues which, depending upon political expediency, were respectively to a larger or to a smaller degree considered essential to the P.K.I. leadership.*

Before turning now to the main episode described and analyzed – the period from 1959 to 1965 which coincided with both Sukarno's heyday and with the growing polarization and even atomization within the communist world – one important dimension should be added to the framework within which the P.K.I. under Aidit was operating. The national communist slant in the P.K.I.'s basic credo tended to make them adopt a stand as free as possible from tutoring by foreign communists. *But at the same time the rightist, accommodating strategy at home that Aidit had opted for brought the party a new dependency, that of Sukarno.* It would turn out to be as fatal as Stalin's preponderance over P.K.I. policies in 1948 that had led to the Madiun disaster.

When, in the course of 1959 – with the Indian border question and nuclear issues as examples – China came to feel itself thwarted and antagonized by its major communist ally, the Soviet Union, this simmering state of disagreement was at first mainly reflected in terms of ideology, of 'theory'. The questions then current in the ensuing debate touched upon the need for peaceful co-existence, the nature of 'imperialism', whether war was inevitable, etc. 'Revisionism', particularly of the Yugoslav variety, as an attempt to remain neutral between 'East' and 'West-orientated ideological blocs was also a point, as was the role of violence in attaining domestic power. In this stage, the early months of 1960, the P.K.I. showed especially that it had a vociferous wing of leaders such as Njoto, Sudisman, Hutapea who in general had a preference for the more radical approach as was propagated by Peking. *Aidit, however, was then – and remained basically until his fall – a communist moderate, an 'organization man' to whom tactics came first and ideology second.* He would not easily commit himself and could afford not to; the more the problems discussed within world-communism were 'foreign', the further they were removed from his immediate interest. But when a matter did touch the heart of his line, as was the case, for example, with the question of who was to lead the revolution in (for the P.K.I.) the current 'first' or national-democratic phase, he was sure to take a stand.

In problems which dominated the Indonesian scene for a longer or shorter time, and in a tangible fashion, Aidit could in general still prevail over his more radical colleagues without too much effort. The question of the overseas Chinese that posed a dilemma to the party in 1959 and 1960 was a case in point. Aided by the fact that the Chinese government for reasons described above toned down their demands, Aidit was able to keep the P.K.I. on the line Sukarno pursued, balancing between extremists of both left and right. The 'July-evaluation' of mid-1960, when Aidit was either overruled or let the radical wing of the party vent their grievances on purpose, was more difficult to master in its adverse effects. But if the P.K.I. leader succeeded in this, it was not in the last instance due to his growing alignment with Sukarno whose towering authority was to Aidit a focal point of first magnitude. West Irian exemplified this because as we saw both in 1957 when Dutch business interests in Indonesia were made to pay for the policy of the government in the Netherlands, and in 1960 when the prospect of Soviet arms brought an escalation in the West Irian policy of the Indonesian government, *it was President Sukarno, and not Aidit and the P.K.I. who initiated action.*

The conference of communist parties held in Moscow in November 1960 and attended for the P.K.I. by Aidit's alter-ego Lukman was a good occasion to take stock of the party's overall position within the communist world. The 'organizational issue' which came increasingly to the fore in the discussions was whether Moscow and a majority of communist parties could lay dawn the line for others?

It brought the P.K.I. from left to right on the side of the Chinese. The generally shared motivation here was the strong sense of independence, of owing nobody outside Indonesia anything. *As to the substantive questions, P.K.I. reaction afterwards showed that on peaceful co-existence, on the likelihood of war, etc, (that is, on 'foreign' issues in general), the sum total of the Indonesian Communist opinion at that moment was mildly pro-Soviet.* Two 'domestic' issues formed an exception here: On the one hand there was the newly-developed concept of the 'national-democratic state' as a halfway house to a people's republic – a Soviet-inspired idea, fully and enthusiastically endorsed by the P.K.I. and especially by Aidit. On the other hand it was 'modern revisionism', which was attacked violently. Though the P.K.I. took a 'Moscow' stand on the first issue and a 'Peking' stand on the second, their motivation in both cases was the same: The P.K.I.'s gradualist, 'revisionist' strategy at home. For this strategy, a national-democratic state was a useful framework, and an anti-Yugoslav campaign was an equally useful alibi.

A year later, at the end of 1961, the effect of the Sino-Soviet quarrel showed up in the isolation in which Aidit to a certain extent found himself vis-à-vis the rest of the P.K.I. Politburo. On the occasion of the 22nd Party Congress of the C.P.S.U., the P.K.I. chairman had opposed Khruschov's interference in the internal affairs of the Albanian comrades and 'divided' Stalin into a national and an international figure, with the clear purpose of safeguarding on both counts the P.K.I.-cherished organizational independence. In this the Politburo was easily able to follow him. But on the substantive questions – priority for the anti-colonial struggle, continued 'exposure' of the Yugoslav revisionists, praise for Stalin 1924-1953 (and not the Stalin 1926 whom Aidit needed to ward of his left-wingers), etc. – the P.K.I.'s leading executive body was more radical, to the left, 'Chinese', than its chairman. His attempt to mediate in the Sino-Soviet conflict was also not taken up by the Politburo.

In 1962 various tendencies continued to exert an influence upon the attitude of the P.K.I. and the members of its leadership. First of all there was the virtual end of the West Irian question, with the successful conclusion of the Van Roijen-Malik negotiations in August of that year. It was to spell the end of a factual identity of views on the West Irian claim that the Sukarno-Aidit-Moscow-Peking quartet had held together in a certain way. Its 'successor issue', Malaysia, at first showed signs of similar cohesive effects, but there were differences. *One was that with the action against the proposed merger of Malaya, Singapore, and the British trust territories in Kalimantan, the initiative this time came from the P.K.I. who wanted to outpace Sukarno, and not from the President.* An other difference was that soon after Malaysia was 'discovered' as a useful tool for power-wielding, the Soviet-American confrontation over Cuba in the autumn of 1962 reversed the expansive mood of the Khruschov-régime. From then on a lower level of risk-taking was decided upon in Moscow – eventually resulting in the Moscow test ban of July 1963 – while all sorts of foreign adventures, the Indonesian anti-Malaysia campaign included, lost whatever priority they might previously have had in the eyes of the Kremlin leaders. *This in turn brought about a slow, but decisive realignment of the Indonesian government under Sukarno towards a closer relationship with China.*

Meanwhile, within the P.K.I., Aidit had endorsed or promoted a more radical domestic approach with the elevation of the Malaysia-issue to the status of Indonesia's chief-bogey. The development inside the communist world and particularly the Sino-Soviet rift which had passed from ideological shadow-boxing to concrete political contradictions went in the same direction. The net result at the end of the year 1962 was that Aidit – through the positions he took on the Cuba crisis, on the Indian border war, and on the Moscow-Belgrade rapprochement – emerged as no longer pro-Soviet but as a neutralist. *While still in essence sticking to his rightist, gradualist 'domestic' policy, Aidit by late 1962 had begun to shed at least outwardly his pro-Soviet stance in 'foreign' communist questions.* This shift came about partly because the behavior of the Soviet leadership was genuinely dubious in Aidit's view. For example in the missile crisis, when Cuba itself appeared to Moscow totally as a *quantité negligeable.* It was partly due to the continuous pressure at home by his more radical colleagues. This pressure got increasingly heavy due to the collaboration on state level between Indonesia and China that took shape with Subandrio's visit to Chou-En-Lai in January 1963. Njoto's stance after a visit to China in that same period to which Aidit subsequently paid heed was an indication of the strength of this leftward push in the field of 'foreign' affairs. The P.K.I. chairman did his best, however, while shifting to more radical positions not to allow the Party to slide into an anti-Soviet attitude, as his manipulations of a Politburo pronouncement around May 1963 on Soviet aid showed. Moreover, Aidit had still not yet given up his ambition to attempt mediation between Moscow and Peking and wanted to keep all his options open. The turning point for Aidit must have come in the course of 1963, when he became a real neutralist in the Sino-Soviet quarrel, while at the same time allowing the party to escalate at home into more radical ventures than had yet been tried. *It was not the appeal of 'Chinese' ideas or effective pressure brought to bear upon him during his visit to China that caused him to act as he did, but on the one hand the realization that the P.K.I. in his climb to the top could expect no help from Moscow, to the contrary, and on the other hand the favorable shifts in the balance of power inside the country in the autumn of that year.*

The gist of the argument Aidit had tried to get across while traveling in China in the summer of 1963 was the soundness of his subversive accommodation with the powers that be in Indonesia, primarily of course with Sukarno. There are no signs whatsoever that he came back with more appreciation for what the Chinese leaders then stood for than when he left Indonesia, though it is true that the cold shoulder he got while in the Soviet Union cooled his personal attachment to the communist motherland. A resolve to go it alone – 'self-reliance' in the political sense – and more concentration on internal affairs, took firm shape in November-December 1963. To be free from both Moscow and Peking in their quarrel and beyond became an asset to Aidit in a period when the opportunities at home expanded: Sukarno had gone overboard in the Malaysian confrontation mainly as a result of personal rancor, the economy went to seed in a most hopeful way, and with the death of moderate First Minister Djuanda the P.K.I. had found in his successor Subandrio a man whose boundless ambition would make him a good object for manipulation. *So a new line towards more radical actions at home among peasants and workers and towards neutrality that tended to be pro-Chinese in the Sino-Soviet dispute came to be ratified by the December plenary of the P.K.I. Central Committee, opening the final act of the play.* In this sense one could speak of a victory of the Sudisman-Njoto wing – Sudisman the man who wanted radicalization inside the country, and Njoto the man who wanted it towards the outside world. But it remained Aidit who kept the party in a firm grip, choosing his new tactical moves with consummate skill and mindful to push towards new boundaries with prudence.

Turning more towards shifting the balance of power at home in favor of the party also had its effect upon the way the growing antagonism between the Soviet Union and China was looked upon by the P.K.I. leadership. *After the decisive meeting of the party's Central Committee at the end of 1963, it seems that the interest in the ins and outs of the quarrel between communist superpowers waned considerably.*

The main point still to elicit some attention was the question of a meeting of communist parties in the tradition of the ones held in Moscow in 1957 and 1960. This was closely linked with the 'organizational issue' and had of course an immediate bearing upon the position of communist parties as independently operating agents. Through 1963 preliminary bilateral Sino-Soviet talks had been advanced by the P.K.I. as the best way to prepare such a grand conference, but after the failure in the middle of that year of the Moscow-meeting between high level Chinese and Soviet delegations the whole idea became rather academic also to Aidit and his followers. Even a watered-down preparatory meeting the Soviet Communist Party had planned for – and convened in March 1965 – had to make do without the Indonesian communists who, by staying away, ranged themselves in the eyes of

Moscow completely on the side of the Chinese.

Indirectly, however, the Sino-Soviet rivalry kept spilling over into Indonesian affairs. When in the spring of 1964 Peking decided to step up its confrontation with Moscow and direct its attention particularly to the Afro-Asian world and its various international organizations, Indonesia looked like an ideal partner. Skillfully using Sukarno's new obsession, the Malaysia-question, China succeeded in stimulating a boycott of the Soviet Union as a potential participant of the second 'Bandung' conference of Afro-Asian nations. In exchange, China was willing to support Indonesia to the hilt in its superfluous 'confrontation' policy so long as it did not interfere with its commercial interests. The other side of the picture was that the Soviet Union found reason to complain to Djakarta that it was towing the Chinese anti-Soviet line and was insensitive to past services rendered in the field of military and 'economic aid. Under Aidit the P.K.I. played an active role in this, equating the Soviet Union more and more with western, equally 'white' powers – *vide* the row between the P.K.I. leader and the Soviet ambassador – and probably found, with reason, grounds to complain that Moscow was trying to 'split' their forces either through a build-up of the left-nationalist Murba Party or by helping an internal anti-Aidit opposition. *A temporary truce was found in the wake of the Mikoyan visit in July 1964, both between the P.K.I. and the Soviet comrades and between the governments in Djakarta and in Moscow.*

But a new danger for Aidit and his policy of cautious, persistent maneuvering towards a take-over began to loom. This was what could be called the Sukarno-Njoto-Peking configuration which in the second half of 1964 in its combined effect threatened to overtake the P.K.I. chairman 'on the left'. The role of Sukarno especially in this three-pronged force was crucial because the Indonesian President needed to reinforce his image both at home and abroad and would normally tend to look for the easiest way out, that is, chalking up a few 'successes' abroad. Inspired no doubt by Njoto, whose inclinations were similarly directed towards a radical foreign posture and who had begun to occupy an influential position as Sukarno's counsellor, the Malaysia confrontation was escalated in August 1964. The Cairo conference of non-aligned countries to be held in October of that year was further to provide a good occasion to project Sukarno's ideas before a world audience. Judged by his increasingly extremist pronouncements and behavior Moscow had concluded that the Indonesian President might swing his weight further behind Chinese positions in the Afro-Asian world, and thought it useful to try to pin him down to a more moderate, pro-Soviet line. This Kruschov attempted to do on the eve of the Cairo meeting, but although Sukarno signed 'on the dotted line' and seemed to endorse fully Moscow's current tenets – particularly on the need for peaceful co-existence – the Soviet leaders soon found themselves completely fooled by the wily Indonesian President. Though unsuccessful in trying to enlist the non-aligned nations assembled in Cairo in his anti-Malaysia crusade, Sukarno at least earned himself with his radical stand at the conference a hero's welcome in China soon afterwards.

The Sukarno-Chou-En-Lai meeting in Shanghai in the autumn of 1964 set the stage for the conspiracy that within a year would start bringing doom to both the Indonesian President and the P.K.I. The prospect of finding in China a mighty and useful ally was alluring enough for the Indonesian President to be taken in by rather 'cheap' promises of small arms and a dubious share in the atomic glory of a fellow Asian nation. At home it would, in the event, reinforce the radical P.K.I.-Sukarno configuration to which increasingly Subandrio also began to belong. Before that consolidation in the course of December 1964 had taken place, however, the anti-P.K.I. forces in Indonesia had tried to use the long absence of Sukarno to turn the tide and cut the communists down to size. *This attempt, mounted by the 'Body for the Promotion of Sukarnoism' though without lasting effect, showed how vulnerable the P.K.I. was without the protecting hand of Sukarno, a fact apparently not taken into account when the Untung coup was prepared.* The compromise that ended the B.P.S.-interlude, the so-called Bogor Declaration of December 1964, put a temporary restraint upon the P.K.I. as to its violent actions in the countryside in exchange for a more permanent elimination of the few remaining civilian opponents of the Indonesian communists, such as the Murba Party. Another result was to push the P.K.I. and Sukarno further down the path of interdependence, altough the advantage was still on the side of the Indonesian President.

In the early months of 1965 the de-facto alliance between Indonesia and China, sealed by the official and unofficial arrangements between Chou En-Lai and Subandrio, also set the course for Aidit and the

P.K.I. Ideological considerations more than ever receded into the background and were supplanted by factors of power politics. China could and would provide arms for the 'fifth force', help in subversion – as shown in the case of the 'Gilchrist letter' – and had a most powerful influence upon Sukarno. The Soviet Union on the contrary was of almost no practical use, could be considered to favor Nasution and the general staff of the army more than the Indonesian comrades and – after the celebration of the 45th anniversary of the party in May 1965 – went all out to break the preponderant position of the Sino-Indonesian alliance in Afro-Asian circles, also driving the Indonesian government further into the arms of Peking.

Within the context of this growing reorientation towards concrete, radical 'Chinese' foreign options, both by Sukarno and his inner-cabinet and by Aidit and the leading communists around him, a dual conspiracy developed at home. Sukarno on the one hand allowed himself the growing conviction that the foremost stumbling block for his grand designs was located in a few obstinate, 'disloyal' members of the army general staff who should be taken care off. The P.K.I. leadership on the other hand was on the alert to use any opening that presented itself to increase their grip on Sukarno and his entourage and to detract from the strength of the one remaining adversary to reckon with, the army. Though the P.K.I. leaders may have entertained vague plans for promoting 'reshuffles' around or even against Sukarno, this was still in line with Aidit's previous 'salami-tactics', maybe somewhat intensified, i.e. further piecemeal elimination of various opponents by intrigue, subversion, cajolery and intimidation. *The action decided upon and leading to the '30 September movement' and its murders was not a long-term P.K.I. initiative, for otherwise f.i. its foremost leaders Aidit and Njoto would not have embarked upon an extended foreign trip in June 1965.*

It was the Indonesian President who, losing patience with General Yani's opposition and uncooperative attitude, took the first decisive steps to redress a situation which ran counter to his wishes. There is no doubt that in this crucial move that led to the Untung coup – the 'Sukarno part' of the conspiracy – the Indonesian leader was suffering from the effects of high living and old age that had already made him, by all accounts of the preceding period, an increasingly irrascible, explosive, uncontrollable, and suspicious man. *It also fits the picture from a medical point of view that Sukarno as an immediate consequence of his instruction to Lieutenant-Colonel Untung suffered a slight stroke.* This sequence, however, outlined above in detail, eliminates the much talked-about 'illness' of the Indonesian President that befell him in August 1965 as a cause of the train of events culminating in the purge of the generals on October 1, 1965. *On the contrary, it formed part of the results, and not even an important one at that.*

The 'Aidit part' of the conspiracy was set in motion after it had become clear to the inner core of leaders of the P.K.I. that Sukarno meant business and that he found himself, by needing the organizational skill and political acumen of the party, in a position that should and could be taken advantage of. *The real planning of the '30 September movement' started for the P.K.I. only after its leaders had learned that Sukarno's intention – a purge of the army general staff, with or without bloodshed – had begun to be translated into action, i.e., after the return of Aidit and Njoto from China and after the Politburo had met on August 7.* The part the P.K.I. intended to play from then on was in a most vital sense contingent on the basic aim the Indonesian President had set himself, and the communist plans proceeded on the assumption of his continuing commitment. The targets set were limited – relatively speaking – and the 'reshuffle', aimed at by both partners in the plot, should have been endorsed after the event as a *fait accompli* with the help of a massive popular turnout of the type that used to accompany major Sukarno-style escalations, like the Trikora or Dwikora rallies, and therefore would be of a possibly violent, but basically unmilitary, nature. *To conclude from the lack of preparation for armed resistance and from the 'clumsy' way the '30 September movement' fell apart that the P.K.I. could never have been involved can only be the result of ignorance or of wishful thinking.* It was because of the combined effect of unwise reliance upon the role Sukarno was supposed, willy-nilly, to play on D-day and of accidental reverses such as General Suharto's unexpected action that Aidit saw his calculations misfire.

There was nothing wrong with his gradualist 'revisionist' approach as such. Maybe even the true Marx was with him, but luck was not. It is significant in this respect that both left and right communist opinion, both Peking and Moscow, have described the policy of the

P.K.I. that led to the events of October 1, 1965, and its aftermath, in similar terms as 'left adventurism' or a 'suicidal left policy' while in fact Aidit and his P.K.I. had followed to the last essentially a 'right', be it conspirational, line. But ideologies in general are not known for their respect for facts, and communist opinion is no exception apparently, otherwise Aidit and the P.K.I. could have been remembered simply as the mighty communist party that just failed to take over Indonesia.

Appendix: On sources

In this book the primary source material used consisted chiefly of public records like newspapers, news agency bulletins, radio broadcasts, and trial proceedings. The only novel feature here may have been the fact that these sources, scattered over three continents and mainly of Indonesian, Chinese or Russian origin, were introduced to provide the raw material from which the study has been built up.

In addition to these sources a number of documents also came to the knowledge of the author which had not – or had not yet – been made use of before in a published or quoted form. Broadly speaking, four categories can be distinguished: In chronological order there is the P.K.I. report on the Central Committee Plenum of December 1963, the record of the Subandrio-Chou En-Lai conversations of January 1965 in Peking, a set of official Indonesian papers relating to the period August-September 1965 and, finally, the testimony by Sukarno-aide Colonel Bambang Widjanarko and others on events related to the Untung coup of September 30, 1965. The first three were acquired from official sources in Indonesia, the last from people who undoubtedly had access to the military investigation records but could not be closely identified with the top leadership surrounding Suharto. As this material, all of which is in the Indonesian language and in the possession of the author, was pertinent to some of the conclusions in the book, it seems appropriate to discuss its authenticity, or at least give the author's evaluation of it.

The internal report of the proceedings of the December 1963 plenum of the P.K.I. Central Committee is a document that appears genuine, both as to content and form. It is in accordance with what has been published about that party meeting and also displays inherent consistency. What might have been of particular interest at the time – e.g. the prediction that only two forces would remain, Nasution and the P.K.I., and the rather unflattering assessment of Sukarno – had lost most of its novelty by the time the author secured the report (spring 1968) and it lacked, therefore, value as a 'plant'. No acceptable reason is discernible for assuming the text has been tampered with, and its tenor has tended to confirm what was then known or could be known from other sources. The use made of it in the book has accordingly been to illustrate and confirm to only a limited extent.

The 'conversation' between the Indonesian and Chinese foreign ministers in January 1965 consists of photostats of a report of 26 pages (four chapters). It is on stationery of the Indonesian Foreign Ministry. Although not verbatim it represents, or purports to represent, an elaborate reflection of what went on between the two leaders. As in the case of the P.K.I. report, this documentation bears the stamp of authenticity if judged by what went on during these talks and the manner in which they were recorded. The main purpose of it being made available to the author (spring 1968) must have been semblance of credibility to the charge made during the Subandrio trial of collusion between the ex-foreign minister and the Chinese government. However, in this respect it did not add anything to what had already emerged from the trials against Subandrio two years earlier.

It is not completely impossible of course that more of the talks were recorded and kept in the files of the Indonesian foreign ministry than were put at the disposal of the author. This might, for example, have been the case where matters were mentioned which were detrimental to Sukarno's image. Certainly, if one accepts the main conclusions of the study, this sort of tactful consideration for certain aspects of the role of the Indonesian President has – at least in the opinion of the author – led to trials which clearly gave a less than truthful account of events surrounding the Untung coup. The trials of Subandrio, Omar Ohani and Supardjo come to mind. Accordingly the document in question could have been 'bowdlerised' before being passed to the author. There is no marked indication, one way or the other, but the impression prevails that the record of the talks was not edited selectively. Important, however, in this context is what the document relates and not what it omits. As already indicated, it gives the impression of genuine minutes. Given the detailed manner in which the conversations are handled the likelihood that it was, even partially, contrived seems remote. Here, too, one can wonder what purpose this could have had, granted the sophistication to dream up part of the talks.

The third category of documents contains a series of cablegrams exchanged in the summer of 1965 between the foreign ministry and the presidential office in Djakarta on the one hand, and the Indonesian embassies in Moscow and especially in Peking on the other. They number 26 in all and are photostats of typewritten or handwritten messages under the appropriate letterheadings. They show that on July 31, 1965, Subandrio sent urgent calls for both Njoto and Aidit, in the name of the Indonesian President, to return to Djakarta. One may also conclude from a telegram signed 'The President' and sent by his secretariat, that Sukarno wanted Njoto (then thought to be in Moscow) to return as soon as possible. This, of course, is not an indication – let alone proof – that Sukarno himself did in fact recall only Njoto (as he maintained in a written statement submitted during the Subandrio trial) and not Aidit (who was in Peking) as well as the ex-Foreign Minister asserted. But again, as in the case of the Subandrio-Chou conversations, the documents had to bolster the theses developed or 'facts' proven against Subandrio and were probably given to the author (spring 1968) with that very purpose in mind. The issue of who was lying, Subandrio or Sukarno? turned out to be inconsequential, except perhaps as an indication of the unreliability of Sukarno as a witness. Whatever may have been the purpose of putting these cablegrams at the disposal of the author, it was possible on the basis of them to trace almost to the minute the whereabouts of Aidit (and partly also of Njoto) and establish the fact that the P.K.I. chairman decided only in the course of August 4, 1965, to heed Sukarno's urgent summons of July 31 and return to Djakarta directly, changing his previous plans and dropping the idea of making a stopover in Hanoi. This was a not-uninteresting side effect but was clearly accidental and not intended. Without proper motive (apart from reinforcing the findings of the Subandrio trial) the chances of the cablegrams being 'planted' are negligible. To the author they are trustworthy evidence, certainly in the limited way they were used in the study.

Apart from the cablegrams, the most important other document in this category (August-September 1965) is the police report (in three parts) on the movements of the team of Chinese doctors who treated the Indonesian President from July 22, 1965, until they left on September 1. It is a detailed account, almost from minute to minute, of what the eight (after August 7 ten) doctors did during their stay in Indonesia. There is little reason to doubt its authenticity. One can only speculate why the Indonesian authorities at the time (spring 1968) thought it useful to impart it to the author. It was only later that – again incidently – the document established that the arrival of two more doctors was decided upon not earlier than August 4, 1965, and that they were neurologists and not kidney specialists.

The last and most consequential document to be mentioned here is the testimony of Colonel Widjanarko (and others) before a military investigation team of Kopkamtib at the end of 1970. It consists of four parts, numbering 105 pages of typewritten text. The interrogation is said to have been conducted by two officers, Lieutenant Colonel S. Sugiarjo and the Assistant Police Commissioner, Azwir Nawie, on October 3, 21-28, 30-31, and on November 2-4 and 6-9. In this period Widjanarko was detained, a fact that could reflect upon the validity of his statements. The documents provide a mass of information, not all of equal interest and repeating here and there what is also known from other sources such as the trials before the military tribunals. The tone throughout is matter-of-fact. Apart from an occasional lapse (as when Widjanarko gave the wrong date of the Sukarno visit to Shanghai) it was possible to check his statements against other sources, and they show consistency. Furthermore, the new light Widjanarko sheds upon the role of Sukarno and upon the related complicity of many of his followers fits other known facts and supplies in a logical fashion (if true) parts of the jigsaw puzzle still missing.

But is this enough to make it a reliable piece of evidence? The author, after ample consideration and consultation with experts, tends to conclude that Widjanarko's testimony is genuine and represents a fair degree of accuracy. Nevertheless, use is made of those statements of Widjanarko that were relevant to the study only when they were corroborated by others, or when they were reinforced by circumstantial evidence, for example, where ex-Deputy Premier Leimena confirmed the discussions on the 'disloyal' generals between Sukarno and his entourage held in the summer of 1965 at various places. This is also the case with the order issued to Lieutenant Colonel

Untung on August 4, 1965, which has been confirmed by other witnesses and, moreover, is only plausible against the background of all the other facts established independently from Widjanarko's contribution. Thus guarantees have been sought to use what Sukarno's aide had to say with the necessary precaution and reserve.

Nevertheless it is quite legitimate to remain doubtful as to the authenticity of Widjanarko's testimony, even though it is used in the guarded way as described here. Logic and consistency are in themselves not sufficient proof that his story is not a fabrication. Even the argument that it would require considerable sophistication on the part of whoever concocted this 'plant' to bring in the various details unknown until then is not strong enough to dispel these doubts.

Perhaps it would be better to approach this key question from another angle: Who is blamed and what motive can be behind it? The importance of the testimony is, of course, to be found in what is said about Sukarno and the role he is supposed to have played as instigator of the Untung coup. If we assume the document is a fake, dissemination of its anti-Sukarno tenor could possible have been in the interests of the ruling circle of the time, i.e. Suharto and his followers. The motive behind it could then have been to provide a further legalising of its power, or better, an ex-post facto justification of it. The Suharto régime might have wished to discredit Sukarno in order to strengthen its own position and to make it appear more acceptable in the eyes both of the Indonesian and the outside world. On the other hand, it could be argued that to undermine the prestige of the first President of Indonesia, even posthumously, could easily prove to be detrimental to the existing leadership and disturb the delicate political balance achieved. It should be recalled here that at a more crucial period – in early 1967 – evidence against Sukarno had been used behind the scenes to force him to transfer actual power to General Suharto but that pressure for a public trial was resisted then by the post-1965 leaders.

As to the question of whether the Widjanarko reports were 'official' forgeries originating with the Suharto circle, there are several points which militate against this assumption. First of all the document is dated October-November 1970 – that is, four months after the death of Sukarno – at a moment, therefore, when there was less political need than ever for anti-Sukarno action, as had been typical of the period between the end of 1965 and middle of 1970. In this respect it would not make any difference whether the purported date – late 1970 – was in itself a falsification or not. More pertinent is that it came to the knowledge of the author only in the course of 1971, while ample opportunity had existed in the previous period for 'planting' a report. Another element here is the fact that during his visit to Indonesia in March 1972, the author was able to establish that the immediate entourage of President Suharto up to the closest of his advisors and confidants still maintained – even in the face of other evidence than Widjanarko's – that Sukarno hat *not* been involved in any way in the preparation of the Untung coup. This would reinforce the suggestion that the testimony of Widjanarko and his followers was at least not a 'plant' set up by the present leadership (nor even a deliberate leak on their parts, but that would assume that the reports themselves were genuine and is here beside the point).

This leaves the possibility that the Widjanarko statements were, possibly only in part, a forgery, by someone or ones other that those who now form the inner circle of powerful officials in Indonesia. Notwithstanding all the arguments that, to this author, can be adduced convincingly in favor of accepting the authenticity of Widjanarko's testimony – arguments reinforced by the elimination of the Suharto-group as possible instigators – one should never exclude the possibility, however small, that some other Indonesian group with stronger anti-Sukarno sentiments than Suharto's tried to take revenge by means of a forged document. The question which immediately arises is then: Why so belatedly? Moreover, this would assume a conspiratorial activity which could never have been the work of one person or even of a few only. In the total context of the recent Indonesian scene this must seem to any but the most suspicious observer very unlikely.

To the author then the Widjanarko reports are to be seen as genuine documents leaked by those in the lower echelon or in more peripheral circles which, contrary to the wishes of the central leadership around Suharto, thought it would be useful to have this contribution to contemporary history finally emerge into the open. It is for that reason that the author felt justified in making use of it in the manner described above.

Selected bibliography

Allen, Richard, 1968, *Malaysia, Prospect and Retrospect.* Oxford University Press, New York – Kuala Lumpur.

Barnett, A. Doak, Ed., 1963, *Communist Strategies in Asia*, Frederick A. Praeger, New York.

Brackman, Arnold C., 1963, *Indonesian Communism.* Frederick A. Praeger, New York.

–, 1966, *Southeast Asia's Second Front: The Power Struggle in the Malay Archipelago.* Frederick A. Praeger, New York.

–, 1969, *The Communist Collapse in Indonesia.* W. W. Norton & Company Inc., New York.

Conte, Arthur, 1965, *Bandoung, tournant de l'histoire.* Robert Laffont, Paris.

Dallin, Alexander, Ed., 1963, *Diversity in International Communism, A Documentary Record 1961-1963.* Columbia University Press, New York.

Dahm, Bernhard, 1971, *History of Indonesia in the Twentieth Century.* Praeger Publishers, New York.

Eudin, Xenia, and North, Robert C., 1957, *Soviet Russia and the East, 1930-1927.* Stanford University Press, Stanford.

Griffith, William E., 1963, *Albania and the Sino-Soviet Rift.* The M.I.T. Press, Cambridge, Massachusetts.

–, 1964, *The Sino-Soviet Rift.* George Allen and Unwin Ltd., London.

–, 1967, *Sino-Soviet Relations 1964-1965.* M.I.T. Press, Cambridge, Massachusetts.

Gunawan, Basuki, 1968, *Kudéta, Staatsgreep in Djakarta.* J. A. Room en Zonen, Meppel.

Halperin, Morton H., 1967, *Sino-Soviet Relations and Arms Control.* M.I.T. Press, Cambridge, Massachusetts.

Hindley, Donald, 1964, *The Communist Party of Indonesia 1951-1963.* University of California Press, Berkeley.

Hinton, Harold C., 1966, *Communist China in World Politics.* Houghton Mifflin Company, Boston.

Hudson, G. F., Ed., 1961, The Sine-Soviet Dispute, *The China Quarterly.* London.

Hughes, John, 1967, *Indonesian Upheaval.* David McKay Company, New York.

Jones, Howard P., 1971, *Indonesia, the Possible Dream*. Harcourt, Brace, Jovanovich, New York.

Kardelj, Edvard, 1960, *Socialism and War*. Publishing House Yugoslavia, Belgrade.

Karni, R. S., 1966, P.K.I. Brochures, unpublished manuscript.

Kroef, Justus M. Van der, 1956, *Indonesia in the Modern World*. Masa Baru Ltd., Bandung.

–, 1965, *The Communist Party of Indonesia, Its History, Program and Tactics*. University of British Columbia, Vancouver.

Kux, E., and Kun, J. C., 1964, *Die Satelliten Pekings: Nordvietnam-Nordkorea*. W. Kohlhammer Verlag, Stuttgart.

McVey, Ruth T., Ed., 1963, *Indonesia*. Yale University, New Haven.

–, 1965, *The Rise of Indonesian Communism*. Cornell University Press, New York.

Mehnert, Klaus, 1966, *Maos Zweite Revolution*. Deutsche Verlag-Anstalt, Stuttgart.

Mozingo, D. P., 1965, *Sino-Indonesian Relations: An Overview, 1955-1965*. Rand Corporation. Santa Monica, California.

Muntz, Jeanne S., *Indonesia*. D. van Nostrand Company Inc., Princeton, New Jersey.

Pauker, Guy J., 1969, *The Rise and Fall of the Communist Party of Indonesia*. Rand Corporation. Santa Monica, California.

Ra'anan, Uri, 1969, *The U.S.S.R. Arms the Third World: Case Studies in Soviet Foreign Policy*. M.I.T. Press, Cambridge, Massachusetts.

Röder, O. W., 1969, *The Smiling General*. Gunung Agung Ltd., Djakarta.

Röling, B. V. A., 1958, *Nieuw Guinea als Wereldprobleem*. Van Gorcum Comp. N.V., Assen.

Rubinstein, Alvin Z., 1970, *Yugoslavia and the Non-aligned World*. Princeton University Press, Princeton.

Rupen, Robert A., and Farrell, Robert, 1967, *Vietnam and the Sino-Soviet Dispute*. Frederick A. Praeger, New York.

Schwartz, Benjamin I., 1964, *Chinese Communism and the Rise of Mao*. Harvard University Press, Cambridge, Mass.

Simon, Sheldon W., 1969, *The Broken Triangle: Peking, Djakarta and the P.K.I.* Johns Hopkins Press, Baltimore.

Tang Tsou, Ed., 1968, *China in Crisis*. University of Chicago Press, Chicago.

Wolfe, Bertram D., 1957, *Khruschev and Stalin's Ghost*. Atlantic Press, London.

Zagoria, Donald S., 1962, *The Sino-Soviet Conflict 1956-1961*. Princeton University Press, Princeton.

Index of names

Withdrawn